Stages of the Buddha's Teachings

The Library of Tibetan Classics is a special series being developed by the Institute of Tibetan Classics aimed at making key classical Tibetan texts part of the global literary and intellectual heritage. Eventually comprising thirty-two large volumes, the collection will contain over two hundred distinct texts by more than a hundred of the best-known authors. These texts have been selected in consultation with the preeminent lineage holders of all the schools and other senior Tibetan scholars to represent the Tibetan literary tradition as a whole. The works included in the series span more than a millennium and cover the vast expanse of classical Tibetan knowledge—from the core teachings of the specific schools to such diverse fields as ethics, philosophy, linguistics, medicine, astronomy and astrology, folklore, and historiography.

Stages of the Buddha's Teachings: Three Key Texts

The "Stages of the Teachings" or *tenrim* (*bstan rim*) refers to a genre of Tibetan spiritual writing that expounds the Mahayana teachings of the bodhisattva path within the framework of a graded series of topics, from the practices required at the start of the bodhisattva's career to the final perfect awakening of buddhahood. This approach, inspired by Atiśa's seminal *Lamp for the Path to Awakening,* evolved within the Kadam school, and its associated texts came to be known as the *stages of the path* (*lam rim*) and the *stages of the doctrine.* The present volume contains three key texts of the stages genre, all of which exerted seminal influence in the Tibetan Buddhist tradition. The first text, the *Blue Compendium,* is a masterly work in verse conveying the teachings of the Kadam teacher Potowa (1027/31–1105), who is accredited with founding the Kadam lineage of the great treatises. This root work attracted comments from great Tibetan spiritual masters and became one of the key sources for Tsongkhapa's *Great Treatise on the Stages of the Path to Enlightenment.* This text is followed by Gampopa's (1079–1153) revered *Ornament of Precious Liberation,* which remains the most authoritative text on the path to enlightenment within the Kagyü school. The final text, *Clarifying the Sage's Intent,* by Sakya Paṇḍita (1182–1251), was chosen for inclusion in *The Library of Tibetan Classics* by His Holiness the Dalai Lama. This masterly exposition of the bodhisattva's path is crucial for understanding the general development of Buddhist thought and practice in Tibet during the critical period of the twelfth and thirteenth centuries.

THE LIBRARY OF TIBETAN CLASSICS • VOLUME 10

Thupten Jinpa, General Editor

STAGES OF THE BUDDHA'S TEACHINGS

Three Key Texts

Dölpa, Gampopa, and Sakya Paṇḍita

Translated by
Ulrike Roesler, Ken Holmes, and David P. Jackson

Wisdom

in association with the Institute of Tibetan Classics

Wisdom Publications
199 Elm Street
Somerville, MA 02144 USA
wisdompubs.org

Library of Congress Cataloging-in-Publication Data
Names: Roesler, Ulrike, translator. | Holmes, Ken, translator. | Jackson, David Paul, translator. | Shes-rab-rgya-mtsho, Dol-pa, 1059–1131. Be'u bum sṅon po. English. | Sgam-po-pa, 1079–1153. Dam chos yid bzhin gyi nor bu Thar pa rin po che'i rgyan. English. | Sa-skya Paṇḍi-ta Kun-dga'-rgyal-mtshan, 1182–1251. Thub pa'i dgoṅs pa rab tu gsal ba. English.
Title: Stages of the Buddha's teachings : three key texts / Translated by Ulrike Roesler, Ken Holmes, and David P. Jackson.
Description: Boston : Wisdom Publications, 2015. | Series: The library of Tibetan classics ; v. 10 | Includes bibliographical references and index.
Identifiers: LCCN 2015010198| ISBN 0861714490 (hardcover : alk. paper) | ISBN 9780861717989 (Ebook)
Subjects: LCSH: Lam-rim—Early works to 1800. | Bka'-gdams-pa (Sect)—Doctrines—Early works to 1800.
Classification: LCC BQ7645.L35 S83 2015 | DDC 294.3/85—dc23
LC record available at http://lccn.loc.gov/2015010198

ISBN 978-0-86171-449-0 ebook ISBN 978-0-86171-798-9

19 18 17 16 15
5 4 3 2 1

Cover and interior design by Gopa&Ted2, Inc.
Set in Adobe Garamond Premier Pro 10.5/13.5.

Wisdom Publications' books are printed on acid-free paper and meet the guidelines for permanence and durability of the Production Guidelines for Book Longevity of the Council on Library Resources.

This book was produced with environmental mindfulness. We have elected to print this title on 30% PCW recycled paper. As a result, we have saved the following resources: 100 trees, 13 million BTUs of energy, 2,575 lbs. of greenhouse gases, 13,967 gallons of water, and 934 lbs. of solid waste. For more information, please visit our website, wisdompubs.org.

Printed in the United States of America.

Message from the Dalai Lama

THE LAST TWO MILLENNIA witnessed a tremendous proliferation of cultural and literary development in Tibet, the "Land of Snows." Moreover, due to the inestimable contributions made by Tibet's early spiritual kings, numerous Tibetan translators, and many great Indian *paṇḍitas* over a period of so many centuries, the teachings of the Buddha and the scholastic tradition of ancient India's Nālandā monastic university became firmly rooted in Tibet. As evidenced from the historical writings, this flowering of Buddhist tradition in the country brought about the fulfillment of the deep spiritual aspirations of countless sentient beings. In particular, it contributed to the inner peace and tranquility of the peoples of Tibet, Outer Mongolia—a country historically suffused with Tibetan Buddhism and its culture—the Tuva and Kalmuk regions in present-day Russia, the outer regions of mainland China, and the entire trans-Himalayan areas on the southern side, including Bhutan, Sikkim, Ladakh, Kinnaur, and Spiti. Today this tradition of Buddhism has the potential to make significant contributions to the welfare of the entire human family. I have no doubt that, when combined with the methods and insights of modern science, the Tibetan Buddhist cultural heritage and knowledge will help foster a more enlightened and compassionate human society, a humanity that is at peace with itself, with fellow sentient beings, and with the natural world at large.

It is for this reason I am delighted that the Institute of Tibetan Classics in Montreal, Canada, is compiling a thirty-two-volume series containing the works of many great Tibetan teachers, philosophers, scholars, and practitioners representing all major Tibetan schools and traditions. These important writings will be critically edited and annotated and will then be published in modern book format in a reference collection called *The Library of Tibetan Classics,* with their translations into other major languages to follow later. While expressing my heartfelt commendation for this noble project, I pray and hope that *The Library of Tibetan Classics* will not only make these important Tibetan treatises accessible to scholars of Tibetan studies, but will create a new opportunity for younger Tibetans to study and take interest in their own rich and profound culture. Through translations into other languages, it is my sincere hope that millions of fellow citizens of the wider human family will also be able to share in the joy of engaging with Tibet's classical literary heritage, textual riches that have been such a great source of joy and inspiration to me personally for so long.

The Dalai Lama
The Buddhist monk Tenzin Gyatso

Special Acknowledgments

THE INSTITUTE OF TIBETAN CLASSICS expresses its deep gratitude to the Tsadra Foundation for most generously providing the entire funding for the direct costs of this translation project. This is the second of nine volumes being sponsored by Tsadra Foundation from *The Library of Tibetan Classics.*

We also acknowledge the Hershey Family Foundation and the Ing Foundation for their multi-year support of the Institute and its project of compiling, editing, translating, and disseminating key classical Tibetan texts through the creation of *The Library of Tibetan Classics.*

Publisher's Acknowledgment

THE PUBLISHER wishes to extend a heartfelt thanks to the following people who have contributed substantially to the publication of *The Library of Tibetan Classics*:

Pat Gruber and the Patricia and Peter Gruber Foundation
Nita Ing and the Ing Family Foundation

We also extend deep appreciation to our other subscribing benefactors:

Anonymous, dedicated to Buddhas within
Anonymous, in honor of Elizabeth Mettling and Ginger Gregory
Anonymous, in honor of Dzongsar Khyentse Rinpoche
Dr. Patrick Bangert
Nilda Venegas Bernal
Serje Samlo Khentul Lhundub Choden and his Dharma friends
Eric Colombel
Kushok Lobsang Dhamchöe
Tenzin Dorjee
Richard Farris
Gaden Samten Ling, Canada
Rick Meeker Hayman
Steven D. Hearst
Heidi Kaiter
Paul, Trisha, Rachel, and Daniel Kane
Land of Medicine Buddha
the Nalanda Institute, Olympia, WA
Kristin A. Ohlson
Arnold Possick
Randall-Gonzales Family Foundation
Andrew Rittenour
Jonathan and Diana Rose
the Sharchitsang family
Nirbhay N. Singh
Tibetisches Zentrum e.V. Hamburg
Richard Toft
Timoth Trompeter
the Vahagn Setian Charitable Foundation
Ellyse Adele Vitiello
Nicholas Weeks
Claudia Wellnitz
Robert White
Kevin Michael White, MD
Eve and Jeff Wild
and the other donors who wish to remain anonymous.

Contents

Part III: Clarifying the Sage's Intent

Sakya Paṇḍita Kunga Gyaltsen (1182–1251)

Translated by David P. Jackson

General Editor's Preface

THIS VOLUME in *The Library of Tibetan Classics* contains three seminal texts, all with a long and rich history in the world of Tibetan Buddhism. Inscribing the instructions of the master Potowa (eleventh century), *The Blue Compendium*, our first text, is one of the earliest systematic Tibetan formulations of the stages of the path to enlightenment. The great Tsongkhapa, whose own *Great Treatise on the Stages on the Path to Enlightenment* later became the most well known of this "stages of the path" genre, famously remarked that any spiritual teacher worth his salt should be familiar with *The Blue Compendium*. The second text in our volume, Gampopa's (1079–1153) *Ornament of Precious Liberation*, remains to this day the quintessential understanding of the Buddhist path to enlightenment in the Kagyü school of Tibetan Buddhism. Trained in the Kadam teachings stemming from the Bengali master Atiśa as well in the *mahāmudrā* instructions of Marpa Lotsāwa and his famed disciple Milarepa, Gampopa presents in his work a unique blending of two important streams of Tibetan spiritual instructions. Our third and final text is the famed *Clarifying the Sage's Intent* by Sakya Paṇḍita (1182–1251). An enduring classic in Tibetan literature, this work masterfully weaves together key elements of the Mahayana path as detailed in the Indian Buddhist sources. Sakya Paṇḍita's classic has been selected for this volume at the express wish of His Holiness the Dalai Lama.

Two primary objectives have driven the creation and development of *The Library of Tibetan Classics*. The first aim is to help revitalize the appreciation and the study of the Tibetan classical heritage within Tibetan-speaking communities worldwide. The younger generation in particular struggle with the tension between traditional Tibetan culture and the realities of modern consumerism. To this end, efforts have been made to develop a comprehensive yet manageable body of texts, one that features the works of Tibet's best-known authors and covers the gamut of classical Tibetan knowledge. The second objective of *The Library of Tibetan Classics* is to help make these texts part of global literary and intellectual heritage. In this regard, we have tried to make the English translation reader-friendly and, as much as possible, keep the body of the text free of unnecessary scholarly apparatus, which can intimidate general readers. For specialists who wish to compare the translation with the Tibetan original, page references of the critical edition of the Tibetan text are provided in brackets.

The texts in this thirty-two-volume series span more than a millennium—from the development of the Tibetan script in the seventh century to the first part of the twentieth century, when Tibetan society and culture first encountered industrial modernity. The volumes are thematically organized and cover many of the categories of classical Tibetan knowledge—from the teachings specific to each Tibetan school to the classical works on philosophy, psychology, and phenomenology. The first category includes teachings of the Kadam, Nyingma, Sakya, Kagyü, Geluk, and Jonang schools, of miscellaneous Buddhist lineages, and of the Bön school. Texts in these volumes have been largely selected by senior lineage holders of the individual schools. Texts in the other categories have been selected primarily in recognition of the historical reality of the individual disciplines. For example, in the field of epistemology, works from the Sakya and Geluk schools have been selected, while the volume on buddha nature features the writings of Butön Rinchen Drup and various Kagyü masters. Where fields are of more common interest, such as the three codes or the bodhisattva ideal, efforts have been made to represent the perspectives of all four major Tibetan Buddhist schools. *The Library of Tibetan Classics* can function as a comprehensive library of the Tibetan literary heritage for libraries, educational and cultural institutions, and interested individuals.

It has been a profound honor for me to be part of this important translation project. I wish first of all to express my deep personal gratitude to H. H. the Dalai Lama for always being such a profound source of inspiration. I thank Ulrike Roesler, Ken Holmes, and David Jackson for their work in translating into English the three Tibetan texts featured in this volume with such care and diligence. I thank the three translators especially for their patience and understanding, as our editor at Wisdom, David Kittelstrom, and I strove to integrate the work of the diverse translators into a single volume in accordance with the standard readers of our series have come to expect. The following individuals and organizations I owe my sincere thanks: to Victoria Scott and Lea Groth-Wilson for their intensive copyediting; to the Tibetan Buddhist Resource Center for providing full access to its amazing collection of digitized Tibetan texts; and to my wife Sophie Boyer-Langri for taking on the numerous administrative chores that are part of a collaborative project such as this.

Finally, I would like to express my heartfelt thanks to Tsadra Foundation, who most generously provided the entire funding for the direct costs of this translation project. Without this support, no amount of dedication on the part of the Institute or the depth of talent and skill on the part of the translators would have resulted in such a successful conclusion to the project. In particular, I would like to express my personal admiration of Eric Colombel for the profound vision and the deep dedication to the Tibetan Vajrayana tradition that underlie the mission of Tsadra Foundation. I would also like to thank the Hershey Family Foundation for its longstanding support of the Institute of Tibetan Classics, without which the task of creating *The Library of Tibetan Classics* simply would not have gotten off the ground. I would also like to acknowledge the Ing Foundation for its generous patronage of the Institute since 2008, which has enabled it to continue to oversee and support ongoing work of this multi-volume translation project. It is my sincere hope that the translations offered in this volume will be of benefit to many people. Through the efforts of all those who have been involved in this noble venture, may all beings enjoy peace and happiness.

Thupten Jinpa

Translators' Introduction[1]

Expositions of the Stages of Buddhist Practice in Tibet

THIS VOLUME PRESENTS expositions of the stages of Buddhist practice by three Tibetan luminaries of the twelfth and thirteenth centuries—Geshé Dölpa, Gampopa, and Sakya Paṇḍita. Each text explains how to ascend the bodhisattva's path of practice in a graduated progression, from the level of a beginner up to the final awakening of supreme buddhahood. While Geshé Dölpa was an early master of the Kadam school and Gampopa and Sakya Paṇḍita were founding masters of the Kagyü and Sakya traditions, respectively, the later two authors owed a significant debt to the Kadam school's spiritual and literary legacy. All three manuals belong, in fact, to Kadam genres of literature: the first can be classified as an exposition of the "stages of the path," or *lamrim* (*lam rim*), while the second and third are manuals of the "stages of the doctrine," or *tenrim* (*bstan rim*), in the tradition of the Kadam monastery of Sangphu Neuthok. The lamrim tradition in Tibet flourished most famously in the Geluk school, and volume 6 in the *Library of Tibetan Classics* series features texts from that tradition. The present volume highlights texts on the stages of spiritual development that were influential in other Tibetan lineages.

THE BASIC CONTENT OF THE STAGES TREATISES

Both the lamrim and tenrim genres aim at leading students to transform their outlook and lives by internalizing a series of ascending spiritual truths. Both kinds of manuals typically lead students through a series of preparatory reflections, beginning with the preciousness of their human birth and then moving on to its precariousness—the contemplation of mortality turning students' minds away from the things of this life. Reflecting on the consequences of harmful deeds that will be experienced at the time of death and in the life to come inspires a strong desire to ensure that one's future birth is in a pleasant realm. Then, reflecting on the drawbacks of life in all realms in the wheel of existence (*samsara*), even human and divine ones, inspires students to desire liberation (*nirvana*). Yet personal liberation for oneself alone is also not a perfectly satisfactory solution. All three manuals accordingly aim to motivate students to strive compassionately for the highest spiritual goal—the perfect awakening of a buddha in order to benefit all living creatures. Such altruistic aspirations and practices are characteristic of the bodhisattva, and the bodhisattva practices leading to buddhahood are the main subject of all three texts, practices for developing such qualities as universal compassion and the highest insight into the nature of reality. Tenrim treatises in particular typically end with a chapter extolling the virtues of a buddha's awakening, the highest destination on the path.

Most stages texts follow this basic framework, but to these basic elements have been added other emphases and topics over the years. Sakya Paṇḍita's text in this volume, for instance, addresses the preparatory themes listed above more indirectly because he begins addressing the path of the bodhisattva right from the outset. According to the abilities of both teacher and intended students, the explanations in a given lamrim or tenrim treatise can be simple or complex, with more or fewer quotations and dialectical discussions. Throughout this introduction, we will be looking at some of the variations in structure among texts in these genres.

Readers of Tibetan Buddhist manuals on beginning practice will be familiar with the preliminary contemplations described above, which parallel the so-called *four thoughts that turn the mind*, four contemplations that inspire a person to reject worldly life and pursue spiritual practice: the reflections on (1) the difficulty of finding a well-endowed human existence and on (2) the impermanence of life (which together turn the mind away from this life and toward future lives); and the reflections on (3) the defects of cyclic existence and on (4) the workings of karmic causality (which together induce the mind to reject samsara and desire liberation). Many beginner's manuals in Tibetan Buddhist literature draw on these contemplations and proceed in a graduated manner through the specific practices.

Should all such manuals, then—including the preparatory manuals of the Lamdré (Path with Its Fruit) and Dzokchen (Great Perfection) instructions—be classified as lamrim or tenrim texts? Although such introductory manuals (*sngon 'gro khrid yig*) contain similar step-by-step expositions of general Buddhist and Mahayana practice, they are primarily appendages to other teaching cycles. Against this view, some might argue that lamrim treatises typically also include at the end a brief introductory mention of the superiority of tantra. Still, there is probably sufficient reason to follow well-established Tibetan literary usage and continue classifying the introductory manuals to the tantric practices as a distinct genre. In a similar way we distinguish the commentarial literature on Mahayana "mind training" instructions as a genre in its own right, though topically it covers much of the same ground as the lamrim and tenrim treatises.[2]

The distinction between lamrim and tenrim

The term *lamrim* is sometimes used loosely to refer to any graded exposition of the path, and in such cases it encompasses tenrim texts as well.[3] When the term *lamrim* is understood as a genre more restrictively, however—as it is with Geshé Dölpa's *Blue Compendium*, the first work translated in this volume—it refers to a work that presents the key "stages" (*rim pa*) of the spiritual "path" (*lam*) through the special pedagogic device of the three spiritual capacities (*skyes bu gsum*), ending with a brief mention of the superior efficacy of tantric methods. The three spiritual capacities are determined by the practitioner's motivation. Practitioners of the lowest capacity pursue spiritual activities out of a desire for rebirth in the higher, happier realms in the next lifetime—as a god (*deva*) or at the very least in a good human family. Medium-capacity beings are driven by the wish to escape cyclic existence altogether and achieve nirvana's cessation of suffering. Finally, beings with the highest capacity strive not for their own welfare but for the happiness of all sentient beings—that is, they have the motivation of a bodhisattva. We can see how these three levels of motivation are built into the progressive levels introduced earlier. The motivation of greater pleasure or reputation in the present life is not considered a spiritual motivation but a worldly one, even if the action pursued is a religious one.

This particular tradition traces its origin back to an instruction called *Lamp for the Path to Awakening* (*Bodhipathapradīpa*) written by the Indian master Atiśa Dīpaṃkaraśrījñāna (ca. 982–1054), who spent the last twelve years of his life in Tibet. The teaching tradition inspired by this text was transmitted primarily through Dromtön Gyalwai Jungné (1005–64), the founder of the Kadam school, to Geshé Dölpa's teacher Potowa Rinchen Sal (1027/31–1105), and it is today most prominent within the Geluk school of Tibetan Buddhism, where it was expounded in several renowned texts by the Geluk founder Tsongkhapa Losang Drakpa (1357–1419) and by Dalai Lama and Paṇchen Lama incarnations.[4]

Tenrim works also largely descend from Atiśa, and he even composed a short treatise of this type himself, the *Sādhana for Practicing the Mahayana Path*.[5] Unlike most lamrim works, tenrim texts do not frame their presentation around the three spiritual capacities, although they may certainly mention these three types of beings. Tenrim texts are Buddhist manuals that expound, through a series of doctrinal and practical topics, the "stages" (*rim pa*) of the Mahayana "doctrine" (*bstan pa*). The known works of this genre were not transmitted by Dromtön and his main disciples but via another of Atiśa's Tibetan disciples, Ngok Lekpai Sherap (1018–1115). According to Thupten Jinpa, in his introduction to the 2009 Tibetan edition of the present volume,[6] the term *tenrim* may well have been used by Lekpai Sherap, who founded Sangphu Neuthok Monastery south of Lhasa (see the discussion on tenrims in the Kadam school below). The Sangphu, or Ngok, tradition was a scholastic subschool of the Kadam tradition, and it had a great effect on the lineages of the so-called New schools—the Sakya, Kagyü, and Geluk.

Lamrim and Tenrim in the Kadam School

The Lamp for the Path to Awakening of Atiśa

The Kadam was a restorative movement, the first seeds of which were planted by Tibetan monarchs in the far west of Tibet who invited the great Indian master Atiśa to teach there in the hope that he might help return Buddhism to its fundamentals and thus redress what they saw as doctrinal imbalances. Although Atiśa was himself a disciple of Tilopa and an accomplished tantric practitioner, he chose to promulgate almost exclusively the Mahayana dimension of Buddhism during his years in Tibet. He actually accomplished very little during his life by way of formally founding monasteries or an order, but he did tremendously inspire a few promising disciples.[7]

As we have seen, both the lamrim and tenrim genres stem from Atiśa, particularly from his *Lamp for the Path to Awakening*. Atiśa's *Lamp* is a lucid and succinct work of sixty-eight verses, a masterwork among the treatises that he composed in the course of his missionary activities in Tibet. He composed it at the beginning of his stay in Tibet, in Gugé (where he arrived in 1042), to fulfill the request of the western Tibetan ruler Jangchup Ö.[8]

Through this work, Atiśa showed the Tibetans how to integrate the three main but ostensibly contradictory systems of Indian Buddhist practice—*prātimokṣa* discipline (including monasticism) to curb the hedonic impulses, the bodhisattva's vast altruistic endeavors to save all beings, and transgressive tantric practice to transform conventional appearances—demonstrating that all three cooperate and contribute essentially to attaining the ultimate spiritual goal, buddhahood. Though this way of harmonizing the three systems did not originate with Atiśa—many Indian monastics before him followed such an approach—he was among the first to set it forth so explicitly to Tibetans in a general treatise; traditionally, each system of practice had been taught separately in its own context or on its own level. In the *Lamp* in particular, Atiśa was motivated by a desire to clarify for the Tibetans just how a single person could embody all three strands of practice, demonstrating that accepting the supreme efficacy of the tantric path by no means entailed a rejection of the fundamental ethical principles and practices of the prātimokṣa and bodhisattva paths.

Since the work was so brief, Atiśa also wrote a *Commentary on the Difficult Points in the Lamp for the Path to Awakening*.[9] Atiśa conceived the main structure of his root text as teaching five main subjects that together constitute the path of a person of superior spiritual capacity—the bodhisattva. As he lists them in his commentary on verse 6, they are:

1. Taking refuge in the Three Jewels
2. Generating the thought of awakening (*bodhicitta*) in its two aspects
3. Producing the superknowledges (such as clairvoyance, etc.)
4. Completing the two accumulations through conjoined method and wisdom
5. Completing the two accumulations through the extraordinary mantra method

Judging by the basic text and commentary, Atiśa did not consider the teachings appropriate for the lower two spiritual capacities to be worthy of detailed exposition here. He uses the threefold division of spiritual capacities mainly as a way to clarify who was suited for the highest spiritual teachings, those of the Mahayana. In other words, unlike for later lamrim authors, for Atiśa the description of the three capacities was merely an introductory device and not a description of the main content of the work. It remained for the later Kadampa teachers to flesh out these parts of the teaching so that these lower stages of the path could also be taught systematically and in greater detail.[10]

Geshé Dölpa and the Blue Compendium

Many lamrim treatises were composed and taught by followers of the Kadam tradition.[11] One of the earliest extant Tibetan lamrim works—if not the earliest—is the *Blue Compendium* (*Be'u bum sngon po*) of Geshé Dölpa (1059–1131).[12] Its author, a prominent transmitter of the Kadam teachings, is known by several names, including Dölpa Marshurwa, Sherap Gyatso, and simply "Spiritual mentor of Döl" (Geshé Dölpa), after his home region. After studying with a number of teachers, he met the highly influential Kadampa master Potowa Rinchen Sal (1027/31–1105) and stayed with him for twenty-two years. In later years Geshé Dölpa founded his own monastery of Yangang in Döl. The chronicles mention that he had more than a thousand disciples, including the famous Kagyü hierarch Phakmodrupa Dorjé Gyalpo (1110–70).[13]

The title of the work has been rendered in various ways. Literally, it could mean the "Blue Udder," perhaps alluding to spiritual nourishment for the reader.[14] Tibetan commentaries, however, take the word *be'u bum* as designating a little book of instructions,[15] and therefore the translation *Blue Compendium* seems more appropriate. Designation by a color is frequently found in Tibetan literature, where a genre designation is often qualified by a color term, such as *Blue Compendium, Red Compendium,* and *Variegated Compendium* in the Kadam tradition; the *Yellow Volume, Black Volume,* and the like in the Path with Its Fruit tradition;[16] and the *Red Annals, Blue Annals,* and the like for historical works.

The *Blue Compendium* contains lamrim instructions from the lineage of Dromtönpa and Potowa. These early teachers did not commit their instructions to writing. However, a tradition of written lamrim and tenrim as well as *lojong* ("mind training") works emerged within the next two generations of Kadampa teachers. This development went hand in hand with a transition from individual instructions for selected disciples (*lkog chos*) to public teachings for a wider audience (*tshogs chos*). It can therefore be viewed as an attempt to preserve the teaching in an authentic form while at the same time making it accessible to a larger public. It is in this context that the *Blue Compendium* was composed, not long after its sister text, the *Dharma Exemplified: A Heap of Jewels* (*Dpe chos rin chen spungs pa*), which stems from the same generation and teaching lineage. Tradition regards these two works as the seminal treatises of their genre,[17] and they have been described as complementing each other, containing the meaning and the examples, respectively, of the lamrim teachings.[18] Both were composed in the early twelfth century by disciples of Potowa following his death in order to preserve his teachings.

Potowa, as we have noted, had been a student of Dromtönpa, the founder of the Kadam school. About a decade after Atiśa's death, Dromtönpa founded Radreng Monastery in the region of Jang, some 130 kilometers north of Lhasa, in 1056–57. Of Dromtönpa's disciples, Potowa is one of three who are known as the "three spiritual brothers," the other two being Chengawa Tsultrim Bar (1038–1103) and Phuchungwa Shönu Gyaltsen (1042–1106). Three distinct teaching lineages originate with them: Potowa's lineage is called *those who teach the "core texts"*;[19] Chengawa's lineage is called *those who transmit the [oral] instructions*; and Phuchungwa is said to have transmitted the diverse esoteric and biographical traditions that were later collected in the compendium entitled the *Book of Kadam*.[20]

Among Potowa's disciples are the "eight great spiritual sons who received transmissions." The Kadam geshé Dölpa Rinpoché, the author of the *Blue Compendium*, is one of them; another is Drapa Phodrang Dingpa, who compiled the first version of *Dharma Exemplified*. The *Dharma Exemplified* was written down for the first time by Drapa in 1111 and later revised by Drakarwa and then by Chegom Sherap Dorjé (1124/25–1204/05),[21] who created the only version of the *Dharma Exemplified* commentary that has been preserved to the present day. According to Dölpa Rinpoché's biographies, he wrote the *Blue Compendium* after he had heard about the composition of *Dharma Exemplified*. The *Blue Compendium* was initially intended as an aide-memoire for Dölpa's personal use, but he then thought that it might be beneficial for others, too, and decided to "publish" it. Allusions to this significant step are found in the first and in the final stanzas of his work.

These two works, taken together, bear witness to the lamrim as it was taught by Potowa, and they became the prototypes of later lamrim literature. Their common origin is mirrored in their close similarities. Both works subdivide the graded path into training methods for the three types of individuals, or spiritual capacities, as defined in the commentary on Atiśa's *Lamp*. Contrary to the *Lamp*, which skips the sections for the first two types of individuals and focuses on the Mahayana path alone, both works from Potowa's tradition contain full instructions for all three levels. They begin with an introductory section about the right way to study the Buddhist doctrine and about taking refuge in the Three Jewels. They then give the instructions for individuals at the initial level by explaining the four thoughts that turn the mind. Thus the practitioner becomes an individual at the middle level and is instructed about the shortcomings of samsara and about the life of a monk. After this, he or she is instructed how to develop the attitude of a bodhisattva and embark on the practice of the six perfections. Both works contain a brief section on Tantra, but not without warning the reader about the risks of the tantric path if it is not applied correctly. They close with a dedication of merit and an epilogue.

As this brief outline shows, the sequence of steps is parallel for the most part, though not in every detail. For example, the *Blue Compendium* places the explanation of the "four wheels" (the conditions for a fruitful spiritual practice) toward the end of the work, after the sections on the six perfections, whereas *Dharma Exemplified* gives these explanations at the beginning of the section for the excellent individuals, as a precondition for embarking on the bodhisattva path. These differences, however, can be considered to be minor in comparison to the overwhelming parallels.

The *Blue Compendium* and *Dharma Exemplified* share a number of stories and examples, which is remarkable because most of these are not drawn from canonical sources and do not belong to the stock material of "graded path" teachings. These may well have been teaching stories devised by their teacher Potowa. The stories nicely illustrate how the early Kadampa teachers tried to explain the Buddhist doctrine in a way that was easy for a Tibetan audience to understand. At the same time, the authors underpin their instructions with quotations from the Buddhist scriptures, proving that what they taught was authentic Indian Buddhism.

The language, too, seems suited to making the instructions accessible to a local audience. The style is concise, colloquial, and sometimes exhibits a charming and wry sense of humor. The commentators describe the idiomatic expressions as "local dialect" (*yul skad*), and the language may reflect the dialect of the region of Phenyul (just north of Lhasa), where Potowa lived and taught during the last period of his life. Because of the idiomatic expressions, the language is not always easy to understand, as the Tibetan commentators of subsequent centuries have remarked.[22]

The *Blue Compendium* is composed in trochaic tetrameter (/ x / x / x / x). Such even-syllable meters are found in popular songs and folk poetry (though more often with six syllables per line) and are atypical of doctrinal works.[23] Perhaps the meter was intended to give the work a colloquial feel. In addition the work is not divided into four-line stanzas but flows in a continuous series of eight-syllable lines, giving the whole work a narrative tone. The work also has no chapters per se but only semantic units, which are often introduced by references to Indian Buddhist sources (or to what would later become canonical sources).

Dölpa Rinpoché's stanzas are rather concise and would be hard to interpret correctly without the *Commentary on the Blue Compendium* written by his disciple Lha Drigangpa (fl. twelfth century).[24] A number of illustrative stories and explanations from this commentary have been included in the notes to the translation of the *Blue Compendium* in this volume. Readers familiar with the Tibetan language can also consult the explanations of difficult words and expressions given by Akya Yongzin Yangchen Gawai Lodrö (1740–1827) in his *Explanation of Some Difficult Words in the Blue Compendium: The Dispeller of Darkness*. There is also a recent and extremely helpful commentary by the late Geluk scholar Jé Shardong Rinpoché (Losang Shedrup Gyatso, 1922–2001) that covers most of the work except the last portion.

So far, neither *Dharma Exemplified* nor the *Blue Compendium* has received the attention in Western secondary literature that they deserve. The translation of the *Blue Compendium* here is the first to appear in a Western language. Lha Drigangpa's commentary has yet to be translated, though Helmut Eimer has written three articles on legends and historical information found in that commentary. Ulrike Roesler has translated the *Dharma Exemplified* into German[25] and hopes to produce an English rendering at some point.

Tenrims in the Kadam school

The best-known early examples of the tenrim genre were written by teachers from the school of Ngok Lekpai Sherap, also known as Sangphuwa, and his followers at Sangphu Neuthok Monastery. According to Thoyön Yeshé Döndrup (1792–1855) in his *Selected Kadam Writings*, Lekpai Sherap composed a so-called *Tenrim in Six Stanzas*. As a commentary on that, Lekpai Sherap's nephew, the famous translator and scholiast Ngok Lotsāwa Loden Sherap (1059–1109),[26] composed the basic text of a tenrim in just twenty stanzas. As commentaries on that, Ngok Loden Sherap's student Drolungpa Lodrö Jungné (fl. late eleventh to early twelfth century) then composed a brief tenrim and also the earliest major text of this genre we have today, his very extensive *Great Treatise on the Stages of the Doctrine*, or simply *Great Tenrim* (*Bstan rim chen mo*).[27] Thuken Chökyi Nyima (1737–1802), in his survey of tenets, writes that:

> The *Great Treatise on the Stages of the Doctrine* is an incomparable commentary on the meaning of Atiśa's *Lamp for the Path to Awakening*, so when the conqueror Tsongkhapa saw this book,

> he received it with various offerings and composed his *Great Treatise on the Stages of the Path* mostly to accord with it.[28]

Thuken was stretching things to say that Drolungpa explained in his tenrim the purport of Atiśa's *Lamp*, unless he meant it in a most general way. Be that as it may, the work of Drolungpa has survived down to the present time no doubt in large part because Tsongkhapa obviously valued it so highly.[29]

The full title of Drolungpa's work is *A Detailed Exposition of the Stages of the Path for Entering the Jewel of the Sugata's Doctrine*—and note that "stages of the path" (*lam rim*) occurs in that full title. The treatise is extensive in length and scope; it is a compendium of Buddhist teachings in the early later-propagation (*phyi dar*) period, on a scale possibly never before attempted by a Tibetan. It illustrates what a high level of learning had been attained within the Sangphu tradition by the early twelfth century, and it no doubt also embodies, directly or indirectly, other Kadam traditions.

The work has a pleasantly clear and direct style of exposition, though it is more loosely structured than most later Tibetan scholastic treatises since it lacks the detailed subject outline typical of later treatises. Its chapters present ten main topics in a practical sequence:

1. How to study under a religious teacher (folios 8a–37a)
2. How to cultivate an awareness of the value of a human life that is free from the conditions that obstruct the practice of religion (37a–47a)
3. How to cultivate an awareness of death and impermanence (47a–55a)
4. How to cultivate an understanding of the working of moral causation (55a–152a)
5. How to cultivate an awareness of the drawbacks of cyclic existence (152a–183a)[30]
6. How to cultivate the thought of awakening (183a–213a)
7. How to engage in the conduct of the bodhisattva (213a–345a)
8. How to cultivate through meditation a realization of ultimate reality (345a–447a)
9. How to ascend the levels (*bhūmi*) of the bodhisattva (447a–507a)
10. The attainment of the fruit, the level of buddhahood (507a–546a)

Part of Drolungpa's tenth chapter—a series of verses praising the qualities of buddhahood that are themselves drawn from the *Ornament of Mahayana Sutras* (21:43–59) with commentary—is silently quoted at great length by Sakya Paṇḍita in his *Clarifying the Sage's Intent*,[31] perhaps an indication that the *Great Tenrim* had within a century or so become an esteemed standard work or classic. Drolungpa's *Great Tenrim* also contains a wealth of scriptural quotations, which is another reason it should one day be thoroughly translated, studied, and indexed. It is impossible to do justice to this remarkable work here.[32]

Stages of the Doctrine in the Kagyü School

Gampopa Sönam Rinchen

The second work translated in this volume is the well-known *Ornament of Precious Liberation* (*Dam chos yid bzhin gyi nor bu thar pa rin po che'i rgyan*) by Gampopa Sönam Rinchen (1079–1153). It has been known among Western readers for fifty years as *The Jewel Ornament of Liberation*, thanks to the translation by Herbert Guenther, which was excellent for its time.[33] It is honored again by this new English rendering.

Gampopa, who was also known as Dakpo Rinpoché, was born in 1079 in Dakpo district of central Tibet.[34] He originally trained to be a physician; hence the other common title he is known by, Dakpo Lhajé ("Doctor of Dakpo"). He began his adult life as a married layman and only began intensive religious practice after experiencing the shock of his beloved wife's sudden death when he was still in his early twenties (ca. 1100). He eventually became one of the foremost disciples of the venerable Milarepa (1040–1123),[35] but only after extensive studies in other traditions. Before meeting Milarepa, he had received full monastic ordination at the age of twenty-five (1104) and had sought out tantric initiations in Lower Dakpo from the master Maryul Loden. He had also studied intensively in Phenyul under masters of the Kadam tradition such as Jayulpa, Nyukrumpa, and Chakri Gongkhawa. Jayulpa (or Jayulwa) Shönu Ö (1075–1138) was a student of Chengawa (one of the above-mentioned "three spiritual brothers," along with Potowa, who were Dromtönpa's principal students), and Nyukrumpa was in the lineage of Geshé Naljorpa Chenpo (1015–78). Gampopa sought out Milarepa only later, finally receiving the key instructions from him (especially on "inner heat," *gtum mo*) for thirteen months in 1110–11. After meditating for an additional three years, he attained awakening. He tried to return to see his master Milarepa twelve years later (1123), but the master had already passed away. He continued a primarily contemplative life for some years but then began his career as spiritual teacher, which became more and more illustrious with each passing year.

Gampopa established the first Kagyü monastery, Daklha Gampo, which attracted a multitude of disciples during his lifetime. It is not for nothing that virtually the entire Kagyü lineage in Tibet calls itself the Dakpo Kagyü (literally, "teaching lineage of Dakpo") in his honor. Through him, a discrete lineage composed of a series of secret tantric traditions from India, and limited to a handful of advanced followers, became integrated with the main elements of basic and Mahayana Buddhism, forming the broad and accessible basis of the Kagyü teaching tradition as it is today. This broad-spectrum Buddhism was then nurtured by his four main disciples, and in particular by the Karmapa lineage of reincarnations.[36]

The chapter on Gampopa in the *Hundred Thousand Songs of Milarepa* by Tsangnyön Heruka (1452–1507) tells more about his life story and indicates his spiritual standing as a tenth-level bodhisattva who had "served thousands of buddhas" before his birth in Tibet. It also identifies him as the person predicted by the Buddha in the *King of Meditation Sutra* to perpetuate the teachings of that sutra at a later age, appearing as a doctor in the "dark land to the north" (Tibet). Those teachings, on the absolute nature of reality, and particularly of one's own mind, are known in the Kagyü tradition as *mahāmudrā* and constitute its greatest treasure. Gampopa is seen as being the reincarnation of Candraprabhakumāra, the main interlocutor of the Buddha in that sutra.

Besides being the perfect heir to the tantric lineages of the father, mother, and nondual tantras gathered by the Indian great tantric adept (*mahāsiddha*) Tilopa, and to the *mahāmudrā* lineage springing from great adept Saraha, Gampopa was an accomplished scholar within the early Kadam tradition.

In Gampopa we find a fusion of three elements. First, he was a true holder of the Vinaya and an exemplary monk. Dakla Gampo Monastery was the start of monasticism within the Kagyü lineage. Second, through his mastery of the Kadam tradition, he was a great exponent of Indian Mahayana Buddhism, presenting both of its major streams—those from Nāgārjuna and Asaṅga. Third, he was a main tantric disciple of the famous yogi Milarepa and became the principal holder of the tantras and mahāmudrā teachings, mentioned above, that Milarepa's guru, Marpa, had so meticulously sought in three major journeys to India.

Ornament of Precious Liberation

Ornament of Precious Liberation is the main textbook for the study of Mahayana Buddhism in the Kagyü monastic schools and colleges. It is seen as a meditator's textbook, inasmuch as it is not a scholarly masterpiece of eloquent prose or elaborate discussion but a need-to-know manual of essentials for a meditator. The language is down-to-earth and direct. The eminent twentieth-century Tibetan scholar Kyapjé Kalu Rinpoché, who was recognized as an authority by lamas of all Tibetan schools, presented this text as an enlightened being's (i.e., Gampopa's) overview of the vast scriptures of nontantric Buddhism, and commented, "Even if you want to spend the rest of your life meditating in a cave, you must know Gampopa's *Ornament of Precious Liberation* by heart, and you must understand Maitreya's buddha-nature teachings." In this work, Gampopa carefully picks out the most salient points on each topic and, more importantly, provides students with an overall Dharma framework of topics into which subsequent studies can easily be integrated. Gampopa is always careful to back up his statements or summaries with quotations from the two main Indian Mahayana lineages. Although this is a graduated stages textbook for Vajrayana meditators, the entire work remains exclusively a Mahayana treatise, except for one or two minor references to his guru Milarepa and to *mahāmudrā*.

Gampopa's *Ornament of Precious Liberation* does not, strictly speaking, belong to the lamrim genre; rather, it is a tenrim. Like the *Great Tenrim* of Drolungpa, which probably preceded it by a few decades, *Ornament of Precious Liberation* is a systematic exposition of the bodhisattva's path. In its overall structure, it is both more penetratingly and more broadly conceived than Drolungpa's work, though it omits none of Drolungpa's main topics. Its structure thus may represent an original plan conceived or adapted by Gampopa. He confirms his connection with Atiśa's tradition by quoting the *Lamp* prominently numerous times, and he cites the relevant verses from that work on the three spiritual capacities in chapter 2 and several times later, whenever relevant. But since Gampopa does not use those three types as rubrics to organize his main topics, his work should not be classified as a lamrim but as a tenrim. Thus, when Gö Lotsāwa Shönu Pal (1392–1481) mentions in his *Blue Annals* that Gampopa composed a "tenrim treatise of the Kadam tradition," he is probably referring to this work.[37]

Gampopa divides his treatise into six main topics:

1. The motivating cause for attaining highest awakening: the buddha nature (*tathāgatagarbha*)
2. The corporeal basis for achieving awakening: the precious human existence
3. The contributing condition that impels one to achieve it: the religious teacher
4. The means for achieving it: the instructions of the religious teacher

5. The fruit that is so achieved: the bodies (*kāya*) of buddhahood
6. The enlightened activities that follow the attainment of buddhahood, i.e., the spontaneous benefitting of living beings through buddha activities free from conceptual thought

To expound these topics in more detail, Gampopa divides his treatise into twenty-one chapters, one for each of those six main sections except for section 4, to which he devotes sixteen chapters. This is justified by the fact that section 4 contains the instructions on the general preparations—the bodhisattva's perfections, and so forth. Thus sections 3 through 9 of Drolungpa's *Great Tenrim*, as outlined above, would fit into section 4 of *Ornament of Precious Liberation*, each comprising one or more chapters.

We should note that Gampopa expounds the motivating cause—buddha nature—as his first chapter. That subject was not made the topic of a separate chapter by Drolungpa. Drolungpa classifies spiritual lineage (*gotra*, Tib. *rigs*) near the beginning of his second chapter, and he treats buddha nature and lineage again in his eighth chapter, on how to cultivate in meditation a realization of ultimate reality.[38] Gampopa also includes at the end of his treatise a section that is lacking in Drolungpa's work as a separate section. It expounds the enlightened activities that a buddha manifests spontaneously and without conceptual thought. Drolungpa, for his part, treats this topic within his tenth chapter, on the fruit of buddhahood.[39]

The Tenrim of Phakmodrupa

Another Kagyü treatise that we can classify as a tenrim can be found among the writings of one of Gampopa's most influential disciples, the master Phakmodrupa Dorjé Gyalpo (1110–70): *How to Enter into the Buddha's Doctrine by Stages* (*Sangs rgyas kyi bstan pa la rim gyis 'jug pa'i tshul*). Among Phakmodrupa's countless disciples, eight of the most eminent founded subschools within the Dakpo Kagyü tradition, including the Drigung, Taklung, and Drukpa Kagyü. Phakmodrupa had studied under numerous teachers before meeting Gampopa, including most notably here the Sakyapa founding master Sachen Kunga Nyingpo (1092–1158), the Kadampa geshé Dölpa Rinpoché (author of the *Blue Compendium*), and at least one prominent representative of Sangphu Monastery. Thuken Chökyi Nyima, in his survey of philosophical systems, records that Phakmodrupa wrote a treatise of the tenrim type, presumably referring to this one.[40]

Like Drolungpa's *Great Tenrim*, Phakmodrupa's treatise is divided into ten main sections. Yet by including a section on which spiritual type can act as a suitable recipient and on the necessary personal qualities such as faith, Phakmodrupa shifts the emphasis somewhat, perhaps reflecting the teachings of Gampopa, who similarly devoted a chapter to these topics.[41]

Phakmodrupa treats these stages as the essential preparation for meditation practice. The bodhisattva's discipline is included within chapter 9, which explains the production of the thought of awakening, and his tenth chapter is remarkably inclusive, in that it contains not only an exposition of the final meditation on ultimate reality through integrated wisdom and compassion but a discussion of the attainment of the fruit of buddhahood. The wording of the treatise's title, *How to Enter into the Buddha's Doctrine by Stages*, is also worth noting. Does Phakmodrupa's choice of the phrase "by stages" reflect a "gradual" versus "simultaneous" distinction that he may have wanted to emphasize? Also noteworthy is the appearance in the final chapter of decisive quotations from songs of realization (*dohā*)—for example, by Saraha (fols. 46 and 47b)—many of which Gampopa had cited. The work thus presumably dates to sometime after Phakmodrupa's meeting with Gampopa (i.e., ca. 1150–70).

The ten chapters of Phakmodrupa's work are:

1. The person who practices this path, and faith (fols. 1b–2b)
2. The defining characteristics of the teacher (3b–8a)
3. The difficulty of obtaining a human life that is free from the conditions that obstruct the practice of religion (8a–11b)
4. The awareness of death (11b–14a)
5. The cultivation of an awareness of the drawbacks of cyclic existence (14a–17b)
6. The taking of refuge (17b–21a)
7. Moral causation and the prātimokṣa vows (21a–25b)
8. The cultivation of loving kindness and compassion (25b–30b)
9. Producing the thought of awakening (30b–45b)
10. The fruit, i.e., the three bodies of buddhahood (45b–52a)

Phakmodrupa devotes eleven subsections to chapter 9, in which the six perfections (39b) and the four means of attraction (42b) occur as subsidiary topics. He divides chapter 10 into two main sections: the cultivation of emptiness and compassion as inseparable, and the teaching of the fruit as being the attainment of the three bodies of buddhahood (47a). The first section he establishes in three ways: through reasoning, through the instructions of the guru, and through scriptural quotation. The first two of these are not to be taught here, he says, only the last. Still, he utilizes concepts from the Tibetan Buddhist epistemological tradition to reject the first (namely, reasoning) and establish the necessity of the second (namely, the guru's instructions):

> Since a theory derived from learning and reflection is [mere conceptual] understanding of a universal (*don spyi*), for directly understanding the cognitive object as a particular (*rang mtshan*), one needs to cultivate in meditation the orally transmitted practical instructions of the noble guru.[42]

Phakmodrupa concludes with a discussion of the opposing views on whether gnosis exists for a buddha (50b) or not (51b), an almost compulsory subject in such Tibetan treatises of the twelfth and thirteenth centuries.[43] In sum, this work is certainly a tenrim of the early Kagyü tradition, and it represents in places the sort of adaptation one might expect of the basic tenrim structure to the demands of a more strictly practice- and meditation-oriented tradition—namely, Gampopa's lineage, with its emphasis on *mahāmudrā*.

Clarifying the Sage's Intent by Sakya Paṇḍita

Sakya Paṇḍita Kunga Gyaltsen

The third and final work translated in this volume is *Clarifying the Sage's Intent* (*Thub pa'i dgongs pa rab tu gsal ba*), one of the major doctrinal treatises of Sakya Paṇḍita Kunga Gyaltsen (1182–1251).[44] Among all the writings of Sakya Paṇḍita (or Sapaṇ, for short), it formulates most completely the theory and practice of the Mahayana. It was meant to gradually lead and inspire the student to practice the bodhisattva's path, and its perennial importance within the Sakya tradition is underlined by the fact that it is the required text for the first teaching of each new Sakya Trizin after his enthronement.

As its title indicates, Sapaṇ used his *Clarifying the Sage's Intent* to elucidate the key points that he believed the Great Sage—Buddha Śākyamuni—had in mind when teaching his Dharma. In particular, he recounts and summarizes the crucial teachings that were transmitted by the greatest masters of both the Madhyamaka and the Yogācāra strands of the Indian

Mahayana. On some points, he attempted to correct what he took to be misinterpretations, and a few of his controversial remarks were responded to critically in later generations by masters of other schools in their own writings.

Sapaṇ wrote this book in his maturity, in about his fifties (ca. the 1230s). Parts of the work clearly reflect the tenuous historical situation in which he found himself as a Buddhist teacher. The late twelfth and early thirteenth century witnessed many losses of temples and shrines in northern India, culminating in 1201 with the sacking of the great vihāras, or monastic universities, of the Buddhist heartland, Bihar and Bengal.[45] Another setback was the destruction by the Mongols in 1227 of the Central Asian Buddhist kingdom of Xixia, whose rulers had close ties with Tibetan lamas. Since the early thirteenth century, Mongol cavalries had streamed out of Central Asia to the east and west, causing untold destruction wherever they went. By the 1220s and 1230s—the era of unhindered Mongol military expansion across the Asian landmass, from Korea to the gates of Western Europe—the situation had become so bleak that some prominent Buddhists in the few surviving islands of Buddhist culture to the south, in the Himalayas and on the Tibetan plateau (i.e., Nepal, Kashmir, and Tibet), were convinced that their own days could well be numbered.

These great disasters to Buddhism left a deep imprint on Sapaṇ, convincing him that the final days of the Dharma had arrived, and of the importance of transmitting it as correctly as possible. This is reflected in his words near the end of this work, "Nowadays, the doctrine of the Śākya Sage has become weak, like a fire whose fuel is exhausted," and in many similar statements elsewhere. That he followed a chronology of Buddhism that held that more than 4,500 years had already elapsed since the enlightenment of the Buddha also contributed to his pessimistic view of his own historical period, since he thought he was even closer to the time of predicted decline.

Ironically, Sapaṇ benefitted personally from the destruction of the great Indian vihāras in 1201. Four years later, when he was twenty-three, a group of outstanding Indian Buddhist refugees who had fled India arrived nearby in his home province of Tsang. Thus he gained as his teachers some of the finest scholar-monks from the last generation of Indian Buddhism, and studied intensively under several of them for the next decade. Thereafter, through his writing and teaching, he introduced the methods and principles of Indian Buddhist scholarship, such as the full logic and epistemology (*pramāṇa*) tradition of Dharmakīrti and the basics of Indian poetics. The careful, critical approach to scholarship that he championed sought to integrate all levels of Indian Buddhist practice, and continues to inspire important strands within the spiritual and intellectual life of Tibet.

Sapaṇ was born in 1182 in western Tsang Province. As the first son of his generation in the Sakya Khön noble lineage, he was the likely heir to the religious traditions of his family at the monastery of Sakya, then led by his accomplished uncle Drakpa Gyaltsen (1147–1216), his first and most influential spiritual teacher. Like his other uncle, Sönam Tsemo (1142–82), and his grandfather Sachen Kunga Nyingpo (1092–1158), Sapaṇ left home as a young man to learn advanced Buddhist doctrine and dialectics under some of the greatest exponents of the main Tibetan Buddhist school of scholastics, the Ngok tradition of Sangphu Neuthok Monastery and its branches. After several years he forged ahead, studying under several of the Indian refugee teachers through the medium of Sanskrit. When he had concluded his formal studies, he spent many further years reflecting, teaching, writing, debating, and meditating. He lived almost to the age of seventy, and when he came to write his main doctrinal works in the last two decades of his life, they were the fruits of a great tree with widely spread roots and branches.

Sapaṇ inherited a religious and intellectual birthright that was then practically unrivaled in Tibet. The monastery of Sakya, which his great-grandfather had founded in 1073, in the Dromchu Valley of western Tsang, was already an established center for tantric ritual practice, meditation, and realization. It possessed a rich library accumulated by his ancestors, and its temples and senior masters (which in Sapaṇ's youth meant mainly his uncle Drakpa Gyaltsen) attracted not only ordinary pilgrims but outstanding masters as disciples.

Most of the Indian tantric traditions that Sapaṇ inherited as an almost patrilineal birthright had been gathered and taught by his grandfather Sachen Kunga Nyingpo and then systematized and expounded in more detail by his two uncles. These included teachings that Sachen had received from his father, Khön Könchok Gyalpo (1034–1102), such as the Nyingma teachings of the Vajrakīla introduced in Tibet in the eighth century, and also New Translation cycles from masters such as Shangtön Chöbar, Malgyo Lotsāwa, and the Namkhaupa brothers. Although Sachen and the Sakya lineage he founded were later best known as specialists in the traditions of Hevajra Tantra studies established by Drokmi Lotsāwa (992–1072?), and in the practical instructions of the Hevajra cycle known as the Path with Its Fruit, or Lamdré, which Drokmi had received from the Indian pandit

Gayadhara, Sachen received and taught numerous other traditions of tantric practice in the early twelfth century at Sakya. This multifarious wealth of Indian Buddhist doctrines and instructions called out to be systematized. To encourage a better understanding and practice of these traditions, Sapaṇ's grandfather and two uncles each wrote synthetic and classificatory treatises on tantra and other subjects, in addition to manuals for ritual practice.

Sapaṇ's illustrious ancestors—especially his uncle Sönam Tsemo—were also qualified in nontantric studies. By the mid-twelfth century, the study of all branches of Buddhist learning had begun to establish itself as an ideal in some Tibetan religious circles, and Sönam Tsemo was one of the first to try to achieve it at Sakya.[46] His generation witnessed the start, among certain Tibetan ecclesiastics, of nondoctrinal literary education that embraced even subjects that were not purely religious. This included the beginnings of the study of language and literature in their own right, extending not only to Sanskrit (which might have been expected, since the work of translating from Sanskrit was still continuing) but also to the systematic study of Tibetan language or grammar. Sönam Tsemo composed manuals on music, language, and history, and by studying them carefully, Sapaṇ absorbed their influence as a youth.

As a child, Sapaṇ was introduced to the essentials of tantric *sādhana* ritual practice, and in his teens he was taught tantric theory, so that by the age of nineteen he had already composed a few commentatorial works on tantric subjects. At the same time he had begun to follow in his late uncle Sönam Tsemo's footsteps, writing works on language and even on music and prosody. Then, no doubt with his family's support, he left Sakya to pursue advanced nontantric scholastic studies, which later won him great renown. Among the first five founding masters of Sakya—and among all Tibetans up to his generation—Sakya Paṇḍita pursued nontantric scholastic studies to an unprecedented degree.

After mastering the basics of Tibetan Buddhist scholastics, Sapaṇ continued studying under the Kashmiri pandit Śākyaśrībhadra (1140s–1225) and several of the lesser refugee pandits during the next decade.[47] Eventually he became the first Tibetan of his period to be honored with the Indian title of *paṇḍita*, or "all-around scholar," a title that indicated mastery of all major branches of traditional knowledge—not just Buddhist doctrine but also logic-epistemology, Sanskrit grammar, medicine, and even the techniques of art and building.

The genre of Clarifying the Sage's Intent

In his resolution to compose *Clarifying the Sage's Intent*, Sakya Paṇḍita declares that he "will briefly explain here the *stages* for embarking upon the excellent *path* of the Conqueror's sons." Despite this declaration about the stages of the path, the work in its general structure was not directly or primarily an outgrowth of the Kadam lamrim traditions stemming from Atiśa as transmitted through Dromtön and Potowa, even though Sapaṇ (like Gampopa and Phakmodrupa) had studied these as subjects in their own right. To which genre, then, does Sapaṇ's text belong? Some indications are given by its overall topical arrangement, which continues a tenrim tradition of the Ngok school that Sapaṇ's uncle Sönam Tsemo had received at Sangphu from Chapa Chökyi Sengé (1109–69). This tradition expounded the stages of the bodhisattva path in accord with two key verses from Maitreya's *Ornament of Mahayana Sutras*:[48] verses 61–62 of chapter 20.[49]

Sönam Tsemo drew on the same two verses when he earlier taught the general Mahayana path in his exposition of tantric doctrine, the *General System of Tantras*. He taught that work to his younger brother Drakpa Gyaltsen, who in due course became the main teacher of this presentation of the bodhisattva path—as of so much else—to his nephew Sapaṇ. In the *General System of Tantras*, the two verses are explained as teaching eight stages:

1. At the very first is "spiritual lineage," which is the motivating cause of possessing the spiritual endowments or capacities.
2. Then, being motivated by the cause, compassion, and having gone for refuge in the Three Jewels, there is "devoted adherence to religion."
3. Then there is the generation of the "thought of awakening," which is the basis for entering the [bodhisattva's] conduct.
4. Then there is the actual conduct practicing the six perfections. These four are called "the level of devoted application."
5. Then there is the bodhisattva's "entering the faultless [attainment]," which is the occurrence of the attainment of the first level (*bhūmi*).
6. Then, with "bringing sentient beings to maturity," there is [the attainment] up to the seventh level.
7. Then the two phrases "purified field" and "nonsituated nirvana" refer to the three irreversible levels. Those are the path.
8. Then comes awakening—that is, the "full awakening" and "great nirvana"—the working of benefits for sentient beings, which is the fruit.[50]

Near the start of *Clarifying the Sage's Intent*, however, Sapaṇ renders *Ornament of Mahayana Sutras* 20:61–62 this way:

(1) [Recognizing] spiritual potential, (2) appreciating Dharma,[51]
(3) generating the thought [of awakening],
(4) accomplishing the perfections of generosity and the rest,
(5) bringing sentient beings to maturity,
(6) entering into the faultless [levels of an ārya]
and the pure fields [and into]
(7) nonsituated nirvana,
highest awakening, and the displaying" [of a buddha's deeds].

Based on these two verses, Sapaṇ follows a special sequence of seven main topics:[52]

1. Spiritual potential or lineage (*gotra*)
2. Taking refuge
3. Generating the thought of awakening
4. The six perfections
5. The four means of attraction
6. The five paths and ten levels
7. The fruit, buddhahood

The six perfections take up the lion's share of the treatise.

The last phrases from the two key verses—namely, "(6) entering into the faultless [levels of an ārya] and the pure fields [and into] (7) nonsituated nirvana, highest awakening, and the displaying"—are thus said to refer to the two final main topics. The paths and levels are thus treated as one main section ("entering into the faultless and the pure fields"), as are the attainments and qualities of buddhahood, which are alluded to by the final three phrases ("nonsituated nirvana, highest awakening, and the displaying").[53] The English translation presented in this volume preserves all these topics.

It is difficult to demonstrate direct links between Sapaṇ's thematic structure, which is based on the *Ornament of Mahayana Sutras*, and that of the early Kadam treatises that are now accessible to us. But a similar approach had been used by some early Kadampa masters. Thupten Jinpa, in his introduction to the 2009 Tibetan edition of the present volume, documents the existence within the Kadam school of a similar-sounding tradition: "The early Kadam master Naljorpa Chenpo (1015–78), following Maitreya's

Ornament of Mahayana Sutras, taught a practice instruction starting with spiritual lineage (*rigs*), which was spread in the lamrims of Tölungpa and Jayulpa." He later adds: "According to Thoyön Yeshé Döndrup, a quite large tenrim previously existed in Tibet that was known as the 'tenrim of Naljorpa Chenpo.' Its author was [named in full] Naljorpa Amé Jangchup Rinchen. Neusurpa studied and set down a series of notes based on his text."[54]

Despite such suggestive parallels, there is still no proof that Sapaṇ's work was derived from the teachings of Naljorpa Chenpo. Rather, it seems more likely to have grown from the tenrim tradition originating at Sangphu. As we saw above, Sapaṇ admired Drolungpa's *Great Tenrim* enough to silently quote verbatim in his final chapter a long section from it praising the Buddha's qualities (on the seventeen verses of praise from *Ornament of Mahayana Sutras* 21:43–59).[55] Thus some of the contents of *Clarifying the Sage's Intent*—albeit a small part—can be shown to descend directly from the *Great Tenrim.*

The indebtedness of Sapaṇ and his uncles to Ngok Lotsāwa Loden Sherap's lineage (especially as passed down through Drolungpa and Chapa Chökyi Sengé) for this way of teaching the general Mahayana through these verses of the *Ornament of Mahayana Sutras* is confirmed by a later scholar of the Sakya school, Gorampa Sönam Sengé (1429–89). Gorampa notes that Sönam Tsemo was probably influenced both by his father, Sachen, and by receiving teachings on Drolungpa's *Entry for the Conqueror's Sons* (*Rgyal sras 'jug ngogs*) from Chapa.[56] This *Entry for the Conqueror's Sons*, then, may well be the source for the tradition of arranging the topics according to *Ornament of Mahayana Sutras* 19:61–62. We cannot say much more about this crucial work of the Sangphu tradition until it becomes available. However, we do know that Drolungpa wrote two tenrims, one longer and one shorter, and *Entry for the Conqueror's Sons* may possibly refer to the shorter one.[57] The tradition may even go back as far as Ngok Loden Sherap, if not his uncle Ngok Lekpai Sherap. Though the existence of such a work is not recorded in Drolungpa's biography of Ngok Loden Sherap or in other lists of Ngok Loden Sherap's writings, both Thuken Chökyi Nyima and the Amdowa bibliophile Akhu Chin Sherap Gyatso (1803–75) mention that Ngok Loden Sherap wrote his own tenrim.[58] Could this have been the *Entry for the Conqueror's Sons*?[59] Until that work turns up, this question, too, will remain unanswered.

Also clear from Gorampa is the fact that Sönam Tsemo, a devoted disciple of Chapa who had received extensive scholastic training in the Sangphu school, did not consider this lineage to be the sole source of his general Perfection Vehicle teachings. The same should be said even more strongly for Sapaṇ, who opposed Chapa and some of his successors on many doctrinal points (though mainly in the fields of epistemology and dialectics). In other words, the outer structure of *Clarifying the Sage's Intent* and most of its detailed contents probably reflect the Sakyapas'—and in particular Sapaṇ's—own special integration of this Kadam formulation into a larger body of doctrine received from other traditions.

Among Sapaṇ's five major works, *Clarifying the Sage's Intent* inspired relatively few ancillary works by later Sakyapa scholars. No true commentary, for instance, exists for it. Much of the work was probably considered easy enough for an educated teacher to expound. While most of the doctrines set forth in the treatise are not exceptionally difficult, the work does contain some difficult passages (such as its exposition of the levels and paths) that would have benefitted here and there from learned commentatorial glosses or discussions of the sort that such great exegetes as Gorampa and Shākya Chokden (1428–1507) often give in their commentaries on Sapaṇ's other major texts. Of the four main secondary works by Sakya lamas that do explain *Clarifying the Sage's Intent*, three were by Lowo Khenchen Sönam Lhundrup (1456–1532), the most prolific commentator on Sapaṇ's writings, and one by Shang Dodé Pal (fl. thirteenth century), one of Sapaṇ's students. These are largely aids for teachers, supplemental works providing scriptural quotations, or elaborations of the teaching stories. Lowo Khenchen adopts the seven-topic structure in his works, whereas Dodé Pal in his topical outline divides Sapaṇ's work into only six topics.

Other Important Texts on the Stages

The lamrims of Tsongkhapa

The series of smaller and larger lamrims by Tsongkhapa Losang Drakpa (1357–1419) are now the best-known examples of the genre. They range from the very concise *Summary of the Lamrim* (*Lam rim bsdus don*) in just twenty-five verses to his very extensive summa, the *Great Lamrim* (*Lam rim chen mo*), whose complete title is *The Stages of the Path of Awakening: A Treatise that Expounds Exhaustively All Stages of Practice of the Three Spiritual Types.* Information about Tsongkhapa's opus is already widely disseminated in English, including a complete translation and a contemporary five-volume commentary by a leading Gelukpa scholar,[60] but a few comments about its origins are germane to our discussion here.

Tsongkhapa wrote his longest lamrim when reaching his prime as a religious scholar and teacher. When concluding his text at the Kadam monastery of Radreng in late 1402, Tsongkhapa specifies in his colophon that he composed the work at the request of Könchok Tsultrim, a great scholar of the Ngok tradition, and of Khenchen Sulphuwa Könchok Palsangpo, a great upholder of the Kadam tradition of Ja Dulzin, as well as in response to the later requests of Sempa Chenpo Kyapchok Palsangpo. He also records that he expounded the import of the instructions on the stages of the path that he had received from Lhodrak Drupchen Namkha Gyaltsen—the lineages from Neusurpa and from Chengawa—and the teachings he personally received from Chökyap Sangpo—the transmission from Potowa passing through Sharawa and Geshé Dölpa. As part of the prologue to mentioning his own name, Tsongkhapa records his extraordinary respect for his main guru, Rendawa Shönu Lodrö, acknowledging prominently, even in this ostensibly Kadampa context, the crucial support and inspiration that Rendawa, a Sakyapa teacher, had given him in his scholarly and spiritual development.[61]

In the same colophon, Tsongkhapa says that he did not adhere closely to the words of the fundamental work of the tradition (i.e., Atiśa's *Lamp for the Path to Awakening*), except for the general definitions of the three spiritual orientations, thinking that the wording of that text was easy. Instead, he states that he based himself on the contents of the lamrim works of Lotsāwa Chenpo (i.e., Ngok Loden Sherap) and his main disciple Drolungpa, and gathered essential points from many lamrim treatises. Tsongkhapa thus acknowledged that much of his *Great Lamrim* was not entirely (or even mainly) based on Atiśa's *Lamp*. Instead, he had combined within it various traditions, including the Sangphu tenrim traditions from Lotsāwa Chenpo and Drolungpa. Still, in its overall structure, his work belongs to the lamrim genre proper, and its ultimate inspiration in that respect was clearly Atiśa's *Lamp*. Tsongkhapa also quotes the *Blue Compendium* of Geshé Dölpa many times in his *Great Lamrim*, and though he does not name it explicitly as a major source, it belongs among the "many other lamrim treatises" that he mentions.

Tsongkhapa seems, from one point of view, to have used the lamrim genre and Kadam tradition as traditional frameworks within which he could present some of his latest doctrinal findings and philosophical conclusions. In the early parts, he shows more direct dependence on Atiśa and his *Lamp*. But later, especially in his long and masterful discourse on insight, Tsongkhapa's *Great Lamrim* becomes a truly independent treatise.[62] By writing it formally as a lamrim, he evidently wished to stress the legitimate and exalted origins of his teachings, which became more independent the further he went. Writing the work at the Kadam seat of Radreng—and appealing to Atiśa at the beginning as its main inspiration—would have made for a sympathetic hearing from the monks in Central Tibetan monasteries who were then still linked to the Kadam tradition. Tsongkhapa seems to have written the work at the request of some Kadampa masters of his day (evidently offering it to serve as a vehicle for reviving the then much-declined Kadam order). But the most important doctrinal and philosophical insights that he formulated there first occurred to him in a different scholarly environment.

Tsongkhapa received his original scholastic grounding as a young monk in Central Tibet, at a branch of Sangphu Neuthok Monastery, and his decisive advanced training from Rendawa, the leading Sakya expert on Madhyamaka philosophy. Tsongkhapa emulated Rendawa's strict adherence to the Vinaya rule, extraordinary mastery of all religious subjects, and deep practice of tantric meditation. He did not differ radically from the key Madhyamaka interpretations of his guru, though within two or three decades after Tsongkhapa's death, one of his early successors as abbot of Ganden would accentuate what doctrinal differences did exist through sharp and uncompromising polemics.

Written in a very thorough and circumspect way, the *Great Lamrim* embodies scholastic subtlety even as a bare outline, though Tsongkhapa's more purely philosophical writings are far subtler. Tsongkhapa's sophisticated trains of thought do not lend themselves to being reduced to a short list of chapter headings. The full outline of the text is included in the back matter of the English translation.[63]

In his record of teachings received, Tsongkhapa confirms the origins of some of these lamrim teaching lines. There he records the lineage for the lamrim teachings in the tradition of the Kadam master Gönpawa, which he received from Khenchen Namkha Gyaltsen—a lineage beginning with Atiśa rather than with the Indian lineage leading up to him.[64] Tsongkhapa asserted that this was also his lineage for vows of refuge and the bodhisattva vows. He records a little later a different lineage for his study of Atiśa's *Lamp* that he calls the essence of the later Kadam stages-of-the-path teachings. This lineage passes through Potowa and Sharawa.[65] He records a longer lineage for the Kadam stages-of-the-path teachings, also received from Khenchen Chökyap Sangpo.[66]

The lamrim of Bodong Paṇchen

A second important example of the lamrim genre is a work from the pen of an eminent master of the Bodong school, Bodong Paṇchen Choklé Namgyal (1375–1451). He was the leading scholar of his generation at the seminary of Bodong É Monastery of Tsang Province, which prior to him had been the seat of a succession of luminaries from the Pang lineage and also of the illustrious Kadampa master Gyalsé Thokmé Sangpo (1295–1369). Though Bodong Paṇchen is often considered retrospectively as the founder or main systematizer of a distinct Bodong school, he evidently considered himself to be as rightful an heir to the Kadam lamrim teachings as his senior contemporary Tsongkhapa or anyone else.

Bodong Paṇchen's work was entitled in full *A Detailed Exposition of the Stages of the Path of the Three Personality Types Arranged as Practical Instructions*. It was fairly rare outside Kyirong and western Tsang. A reprint was published in New Delhi in 1977, a reproduction of prints from an elegant blockprint edition from Mangyul Gungthang blocks dated 1546.[67] The work is noteworthy for presenting the practices of the people of the three spiritual capacities as preparation, main practice, and conclusion, or as the work of a farmer in spring, summer, and autumn. Bodong Paṇchen teaches tranquility and insight near the end, precisely as Atiśa and Tsongkhapa had done. The section on insight includes some of the most interesting doctrinal discussions, such as the main lines of reasoning of the Madhyamaka and the four delaying pitfalls (*gol sa*) of meditation. This section, like the treatise as a whole, deserves to be studied among the major lamrim treatises of its time.

Other works

Though not strictly belonging to the stages genre, two important works in the Nyingma tradition are closely related to it. Longchen Rabjampa's *Mind at Ease* and its commentary the *Great Chariot* (vol. 3 in *The Library of Tibetan Classics*) and Dza Paltrul's *Words of My Perfect Teacher*. In both of these texts, the practices associated with the stages approach are presented explicitly as preliminaries to the instructions and practices of Dzokchen, the Great Perfection. For the Jonang school, Taranatha's *Essence of Nectar: A Guide to the Instructions for the Persons of Three Capacities* is a standard work on that tradition's understanding of the teachings stemming from the stages literature.

In conclusion, we can only marvel at how skillfully the Tibetan works of the stages genre have synthesized the teachings of the Buddha, as well as those of the great Indian Mahayana teachers, and presented them within a coherent framework that can be practiced by a single spiritual aspirant seeking to travel from the beginner's stage to the final awakening of the buddha. Inspired by Atiśa's seminal text *Lamp for the Path to Awakening*, the step-by-step instructions developed in these Tibetan texts continue to guide and elevate the attentive reader and practictioner of Tibetan Buddhism even today. Imbued by their authors with so much insight and helpful instruction, it is not surprising that all three manuals featured in this volume were considered classics of Buddhist literature in Tibet.

With translations of three well-known works of the stages genre, we hope that students and teachers of Tibetan Buddhism will have direct access to these seminal works and have a chance to directly engage with the insights and instructions of three great spiritual masters. For the general reader, we hope that translations presented in this volume, as well as the accompanying explanatory notes and this general introduction, will offer an opportunity to appreciate the richness of the Tibetan tradition and its creative synthesis of the vast corpus of classical Indian Buddhist teachings.

Acknowledgments

I am grateful to Dr. Helmut Eimer for his valuable comments on an earlier draft of this translation of Geshé Dölpa's work and Dr. Amelia Hall for checking the English. I would also like to express my sincere thanks and appreciation for Thupten Jinpa's unfailing guidance throughout the editing process, and for the meticulous work of the editorial team at Wisdom Publications in bringing this volume together.

Ulrike Roesler

I shall be ever indebted to Khenpo Tsultrim Gyamtso Rinpoché for taking me carefully through Gampopa's text, term by term, on three occasions, and to Khenchen the Ninth Thrangu Rinpoché for his subsequent clarifications.

Ken Holmes

I am indebted to the Venerable Khenpo Appey for first suggesting in 1982 that I translate this work of Sapaṇ's and for setting aside time to explain the text, line by line, at the Sakya College, near Dehra Dun. I couldn't yet fully appreciate his excellent explanations, and the resulting translation was just a rough draft. In subsequent years I was able to slowly improve it thanks to comments from translators (chiefly Cyrus Stearns) who used it when interpreting for teaching lamas. The translation has also benefitted from the remarks of students with whom I read individual chapters over the years in Hamburg. I was also helped more recently by recordings of Khenpo Appey explaining the chapter on the ten levels and five paths at the International Buddhist Academy in Kathmandu.

I am grateful to Thupten Jinpa for forcing me to finish this translation by including it in this series, under the able editorship of David Kittelstrom. Victoria R. M. Scott, through her careful editorial work, has patiently improved many inconsistencies and unclear passages. Whatever weaknesses may remain, I hope that this translation will live up to the hopes of those who encouraged it over the years, and that it will convey to future readers the sense and spirit of this great treatise of Sakya Paṇḍita.

David P. Jackson

Technical Note

The Tibetan title of the volume translated here is *Bstan pa la'jug pa'i rim pa ston pa'i gzhung gces btus*, which means *Entering the Stages of the Doctrine: Selected Key Texts*. This edition was prepared specifically for *The Library of Tibetan Classics* and its Tibetan equivalent, *Bod kyi gtsug lag gces btus*. Bracketed numbers embedded in the text refer to page numbers in the critical and annotated Tibetan edition published in New Delhi in modern book format by the Institute of Tibetan Classics (2009, ISBN 81-89165-10-0) as volume 10 of the *Bod kyi gtsug lag gces btus* series.

The conventions for phonetic transcription of Tibetan words are those developed by the Institute of Tibetan Classics and Wisdom Publications. Transliterations of the phoneticized Tibetan terms and names used in the text can be found in the table in the appendix. Sanskrit diacritics are used throughout except for Sanskrit terms that have been naturalized into English, such as samsara, nirvana, sutra, stupa, Mahayana, and mandala.

The chapter headings in Geshé Dölpa's *Blue Compendium* are taken from the Beijing edition of 1991 and are identical to those in the new Tibetan edition prepared by the Institute of Tibetan Classics. They do not form part of either the root verses or the commentary; it seems that the modern editors have extracted them from the prose explanations of the commentary. Additional chapter breaks have been added for the benefit of the English-language reader by the translator.

Several translations of Gampopa's text have appeared under the title *Jewel Ornament of Liberation*, no doubt because the first English translation by Dr. Herbert Guenther bore this title. However, the Twelfth Tai Situpa has made it very clear to the present translator that the adjective *rin po che* ("precious") in the main title modifies the noun "liberation" not "ornament."

As was the case for the new edition of the text published by the Institute of Tibetan Classics, three xylographic editions have been consulted for this translation, the main reference being (1) the version from the former Tsipri

(Rtsib ri) printing house in southwestern Tibet (abbreviated "Tsipri"), the woodblocks of which have been preserved in Solukhumbu Monastery of northern Nepal. Also consulted were (2) the Dergé edition from Palpung Monastery (abbreviated "Palpung") and (3) the modern edition found as volume 20 in the *Gangs can rig brgya'i sgo 'byed lde mig* series (Beijing: Mi rigs dpe skrun khang, 1987–97; abbreviated "Beijing").

The translation of Sakya Paṇḍita's *Clarifying the Sage's Intent* follows the Dergé edition of 1736 except as specified otherwise in the notes. The translator regrets that he could not check every doubtful passage for variants in the Sakya edition of 1439 or with the readings of the manuscripts preserved at Shalu and Luphu monasteries that are recorded in a new comparative edition recently published in Tibet (described in Thupten Jinpa's introduction to the new ITC edition, p. xliv).

The ITC edition provides a useful basis for more detailed textual work in the future. Its policy was to take the Dergé edition as the authority, except when dealing with obvious errors. Its editors document numerous variants from the Shalu and Luphu manuscripts, but they did not have access to—and hence could not take into account—the Sakya xylographic edition or the several manuscripts photographed in northern Nepal by the NGMPP (Nepal German Manuscript Preservation Project), except for a few cases that the translator provided to them. (One drawback of the ITC edition is that it does not indicate the page breaks in its source, the Dergé edition.) In some cases where the existence of missing passages of text is supported by two independent manuscripts (Shalu and Luphu), it would be acceptable to restore those missing passages, showing them between brackets if the editors prefer to do so. Two examples are found on p. 470, footnotes 395 and 396 of the ITC edition. The first is, the translator believes, a lost introductory passage to the subject of the final chapter, so the translator has added it to the present translation.

All the references to the vast number of works cited in the three texts have been reproduced here from the new Tibetan edition of the Institute of Tibetan Classics. When refering to works from the Tibetan canons, the Dergé edition has been used as the primary source with all details such as category, volume, and page numbers provided accordingly. "Toh" stands for the Tohoku catalogue entry of the Dergé editions of the Kangyur and Tengyur. In the translation of Sapaṇ's text, the translator has also provided the equivalent volume and page numbers of the canonical works from the Peking edition.

Pronunciation of Tibetan phonetics

ph and *th* are aspirated *p* and *t*, as in *pet* and *tip*.
ö is similar to the *eu* in the French *seul*.
ü is similar to the ü in the German *füllen*.
ai is similar to the *e* in *bet*.
é is similar to the *e* in *prey*.

Pronunciation of Sanskrit

Palatal ś and retroflex ṣ are similar to the English unvoiced *sh*.
c is an unaspirated *ch* similar to the *ch* in *chill*.
The vowel *ṛ* is similar to the American *r* in *pretty*.
ñ is somewhat similar to the nasalized *ny* in *canyon*.
ṅ is similar to the *ng* in *sing* or *anger*.

Abbreviations

Beijing	The modern edition of Gampopa's *Ornament of Precious Liberation,* found as volume 20 in the *Gangs can rig brgya'i sgo 'byed lde mig* series (Beijing: Mi rigs dpe skrun khang, 1987–97)
ITC	Institute of Tibetan Classics, *Bstan pa la 'jug pa'i rim pa ston pa'i gzhung gces btus,* by Dge bshes Dol pa, Sgam po pa Bsod nams rin chen, and Sa pan Kun dga' rgyal mtsan; introduction by Thupten Jinpa; Bod kyi gtsug lag gces btus 10 (New Delhi: Institute of Tibetan Classics, 2009)
Lha Drigangpa	Lha Drigangpa, *Be'u bum sngon po'i 'grel pa* (commentary on Potowa's *Blue Compendium*), the Drepung edition initiated by the Seventh Dalai Lama, reproduced in *Gangs can rig brgya'i sgo 'byed lde mig (deb bcu drug pa): Bka' gdams be'u bum sngon po'i rtsa 'grel* (Beijing: Mi rigs dpe skrun khang, 1991), pp. 47–463
MHTL	Akhu Chin Sherap Gyatso, *Dpe rgyun dkon pa 'ga' zhig gi tho yig, Materials for a History of Tibetan Literature, Part 3*. Lokesh Chandra, ed., Śata-Piṭaka Series, vol. 30 (New Delhi: International Academy of Indian Culture, 1963; reprint Kyoto: Rinsen, 1981), pp. 503–601
P	Peking edition of the Tibetan *Tripiṭaka,* reprinted under the supervision of Ōtani University, Kyoto, Daisetzu T. Suzuki et al., eds., vols. 1–168 (Tokyo–Kyoto: Tibetan Tripitaka Research Institute, 1955–61)

Palpung	Dergé edition of Gampopa's *Ornament of Precious Liberation* from Palpung (Dpal spungs) monastery
Shardong	Jé Shardong Rinpoché, *Rje Shar gdong Blo bzang bshad sgrub rgya mtsho'i gsung 'bum*, part 4: *Be'u bum sngon po'i rtsa 'grel gyi bshad pa dwangs shel me long* (commentary on Potowa's *Blue Compendium*), (Xining: Mtsho sngon mi rigs dpe skrun khang, 1999)
SKB	*Sa skya pa'i bka' 'bum* (collected works of the founding Sakya masters), reprint of the Dergé edition of the collected works of the Five Founding Masters of Sakya, together with the collected works of Ngorchen and Gorampa (Tokyo: Tōyō Bunko, 1968–69)
TG	Sa skya Paṇḍita Kun dga' rgyal mtshan, *Thub pa'i dgongs pa rab tu gsal ba* (*Clarifying the Sage's Intent*)
Toh	The Tibetan *Tripiṭaka,* Dergé edition, as described in H. Ui et al., eds., *A Complete Catalogue of the Tibetan Buddhist Canon* (Sendai, Japan: Tohoku University, 1934)
Tsipri	The version of Gampopa's *Ornament of Precious Liberation* from the former Tsipri (Rtsib ri) printing house in southwestern Tibet, the woodblocks of which have been preserved in Solukhumbu Monastery of northern Nepal

Part I

The Blue Compendium

Teachings on the Graded Path of Potowa Rinchen Sal (1027/31–1105)

Compiled in verse by
Dölpa Sherap Gyatso (1059–1131)

Translated by Ulrike Roesler

1. Preliminaries

1. Homage and need for composing the work[1]

Having bowed with reverence to the teachers,
the treasury of all good qualities,
I, a person of weak intellectual power, have made a compendium
by uniting what was scattered here and there.

In the section on not giving up the spiritual mentor from the
Compendium of Trainings,[2]
it is stated that the starting point of all advice is, in brief,
to never give up the noble spiritual mentor.
Deeds, faith, the thought of awakening, and the like
come from him, and he is a treasury of all good qualities.

2. How to find a religious teacher and rely on him

The right way to seek out a spiritual mentor and rely on him
is to emulate the way of our mentor.
We should not seek out many; we should invest our life for the one
we've sought.
It's not fit for a person who has not cultivated the mind to seek many.
These days we behave like an ox in autumn or summer
that sniffs at everything and becomes engaged with nothing;
our way has come to be
to listen to everyone without holding anyone as our teacher.
A lack of respect for his instruction and for all his explications
of the Dharma
is the main reason our insight declines.
Therefore, as long as we have not examined our relationship with
a teacher, there are not many [obligations].[3]

Once we have examined and adopted a teacher, we must respect him.
Then we will not be deprived of our teacher in the future.
That is the nature of things: karma does not vanish.

When someone from Tsang asked about the way to rely [on the teacher, he was told that][4]
we should devote ourselves to the teacher with the notion that he is a buddha.
This notion when it is not genuine leads nowhere.
It must be generated in this way whether he is a teacher of the secret mantra
or of the path of the perfections.
The story of the Nepalese Hangdu can be presented in this context,[5] and
Fifty Verses about the Guru also [prescribes] the same manner toward both [sutra and tantra teachers].[6]
In the teacher, the buddhas of the three times appear to us.
To a bodhisattva who has mastered the ten bodhisattva levels, they appear in the enjoyment body (*saṃbhogakāya*).
They appear here as is appropriate for the recipient.
When we honestly regard the teacher as a buddha
and follow him in this way, to enjoy our share of the teachings
is not just like enjoying our share of material things. [2]
The whole way of relying on the spiritual mentor is contained in this.

Since all good qualities depend on the teacher,
someone who is never separated from him
will achieve all purposes in no more than an instant.
To one who is endowed with great faith and wisdom
the teacher will give the whole instruction at one time.
Even if you have fully acquired knowledge and understanding,
if you practice and do not stay with him but live separately,
no good qualities will arise from this,
and even if some good qualities have arisen, they will vanish quickly.
Even if your wisdom is weak, as long as the root of faith is there
and you always stay with the teacher without separation,
all the teachings of the Buddha are fully contained in him.
Therefore you should always remain with him full of respect
and always consider the teacher's good qualities, not the faults.

With regard to the teacher's body and speech, whatever his deeds,
never think of it as something to either adopt or reject.
If you speak about him as you would about aged cheese and the like,[7]
and think accordingly, everything will become rotten.
If you harbor doubts about his instructions,
there will be no blessing at all; that's the way it is.
Trust, therefore, in his actions and teaching.
In this way the blessing will arise.

While ordinary beings act as spiritual mentors,
they will never be without flaws.
Therefore never ponder their flaws
but always think about their virtues.
In this way the blessing will reach you.
Turning away [from this attitude] will cause you to not meet
[a spiritual mentor in the future].
Moreover, you need to know the right time to approach him.
To follow him is something very precious.
In this way, all aims will be accomplished.
Not observing the appropriate time
is a serious transgression.

All good qualities depend on the teacher;
Even pratyekabuddhas up to the stage of the highest worldly
realization rely on a teacher.[8]
Therefore please the teacher in every possible way.
First become acquainted with him through material offerings and
respect.
When you have become acquainted, there are two obligations
with regard to the noble field of merit,
and the true way of fulfilling these obligations
is to practice according to his words.
To [attempt to] please him by honoring him without practicing
is not the way to behave toward the teacher.[9]

In the Hinayana, everyone who knows the Tripiṭaka,
even a householder who is not equipped with the thought
of awakening,

is worth listening to, he says,[10] though this can be difficult.
In the Mahayana, however, someone may know the Tripiṭaka,
but if he is not equipped with the thought of awakening, he is not suitable at all;
even if you listen to him, no good qualities will arise.
The Mahayana depends on the blessing [of the teacher].
If [a Mahayana teacher] possesses the four kinds of readiness in speech,[11]
you must listen with respect, no matter what he may do, says [Potowa].
The teachings will never be corrupted by the faults of the person [who teaches].
This does not contradict what was said above [about the need of choosing your teacher carefully]
but refers to the fact that those who have reached a certain level [3]
perceive [any teacher] as a buddha.
As long as you have not trained [your mind], it is as stated above; there is no contradiction.

This is as in the case of Buddhajvāla's question[12]
and the story of Ratnabhadra.[13]
It's the way in all the traditions of Mahayana
that everything comes from pleasing the teacher, so this is critical.
When the teacher has become greatly pleased,
any practice will lead to the great purpose [i.e., liberation] itself.
If you turn away from that,
no blessing at all will arise, even if the teaching is complete.
Therefore you should please him with all your energy.
If you persevere with unceasing respect
and please him with great effort,
then even if the teacher has given up his life and
the blessing has not arisen during this lifetime,
you will not be deprived of the teacher in the future; this is the truth,
because your karma does not vanish.

As it says in the section on gratitude at the beginning of the *Compendium of Trainings*,
the extent of the teacher's blessing
lies not in itself but rather in you.

If you are not grateful and have no faith in him,
it would be of no benefit at all
if even Mañjuśrī or Avalokiteśvara were to appear before you.
But as long as you have faith, respect, and gratitude toward him,
the blessing will arise accordingly,
even if the teacher is not fully endowed with all good qualities.
Therefore it is essential to have faith and gratitude.

In the passage on the fault of abandoning the Dharma from the
Compendium of Trainings,[14]
it is said, about being tamed or not being tamed by another,
that we are tamed by the one in whom we have faith.
Therefore, we should not hear the noble teaching from a person
in whom we have no faith.
If we have no respect for the teaching and the teacher,
this will cause our insight to decline.
Therefore we should listen to the teacher in whom we have
confidence;
then the blessing will reach us.

In the initial section of the *Letter to a Friend*,[15]
it is said that if we do not have respect for the teachers,
it would be of no benefit even if we were to rely directly on the
Buddha himself.
This is as in the case of Sunakṣatra:[16]
Even though he devoted himself [to the Buddha] for twenty years,
could recite the twelve sections of the sutras,
and had attained the first level of contemplation,
because he did not have any faith in the Buddha,
it was predicted that
the wholesome roots would be completely severed
and he would remain in the hells for many eons.
But if you respect a teacher who has the thought of awakening
and listen to him, then whether he is learned or not,
his blessing will reach you.
Therefore it has been said that respecting the teacher, without
arrogance,
is of the utmost importance.

When it is stated in the *Lamp for the Path* that "it has to be explained clearly,"[17]
what is clearly explained there is the mental capacity of a buddha.
If you wonder how our sole lord [Atiśa] was capable of making this clear,
he had mastered all the instructions of the most important systems on Jambudvīpa:[18] [4]
the transmission coming from Nāgārjuna, that coming from Buddha Maitreya,
the tradition of the Three-Necked One,[19] and so on.
Kusali possessed all these instructions,
then his disciple Kusali the Younger,
and also [Atiśa's teacher] Serlingpa; that's why our sole lord was capable of doing so.
Moreover, he had three teachers who possessed supernatural knowledge:
Avadhūtipa, whom he served for seven years,
and Yamāriyogin and the Lama of Blessing [Ḍombhipa].
First he learned from Yamāriyogin[20] the views of the Cittamātra school;
then he obtained the understanding of the Madhyamaka school.
The Lama of Blessing appeared in a dream,
and lord Atiśa obtained a special contemplation.[21]
Therefore Atiśa was truly blessed by him.
When someone asked to be instructed, Atiśa agreed.
[In one case Ḍombhipa said to a novice monk:] "You have no karmic connection with me. Ask him [i.e., Atiśa]."
When the novice had made offerings to Atiśa for four or five days
and offered a little [betel] at his feet, Atiśa's kindness embraced him,
and the mandala of Heruka became manifest.
In this way Atiśa was endowed with the personal instructions of the teachers
and had also seen the faces of the meditation deities;
he was learned in all five fields of knowledge[22]
and therefore was able to make the path to awakening clear.
Thus, when we seek the personal instructions coming from this lineage,
we have to enter the path to awakening,

but we should not pursue it in a random way;
for if we do, it would be extremely difficult for it to be the right path.

3. How to contemplate the teacher with faith and respect

In the passage "As taught by the teachers,"[23]
what has been taught is personal instruction. Whatever good qualities arise
in your mind, they are the blessing of the teacher.
Always remembering him in this way, the blessing will reach you completely.
If you reject him, you will know what you have heard from your teacher
but will think that it has arisen from the cleverness of your own insight.
If you reject him, no blessing will arise from him,
you will not meet the spiritual mentor in the future,
and even if you do meet him, his teaching will be useless.
When you have understood this, you should practice constantly, as stated above.

When teaching the passage on the teacher in the chapter on moral discipline,[24]
[Potowa] cited Atiśa himself as the source.
In the section on the spiritual mentor in the *Questions of Subāhu Tantra*[25]
and other sources, it has been written that
generating the thought of awakening and similar things can also be done with any teacher.
As long as he possesses one eighth or so of the [sixteen] qualities,
it is right to accept [any such teacher] in the age of discord.[26]
Otherwise the transmission would be interrupted.

People who wish for liberation
should rely on a single teacher they have examined,
not on all kinds of different ones.
Otherwise even the traces of the teachings received before will perish, [5]
and they will end up seeing the teacher's faults

but not his virtues within.
This is just like when a robe is dragged here and there:
The dust sticks to it because it is rough,
but a jewel hidden under the dust does not stick to it.

Take the words of Rinchen Lama as an example[27]
and sever all doubts about your own teacher;
even if the Buddha came in all his glory,
you should listen to no other teacher anywhere.
You should also cultivate great pride [in having such an excellent teacher].
When you behave like a stupid dog running around in the street,
you will never reach what you are longing for:

This is what this spiritual mentor has said. The one who is most kind
is the teacher for ordinary persons.
When our minds have been trained by him, we see him as an emanation body (*nirmāṇakāya*),
and still later, we also see him as an enjoyment body (*saṃbhogakāya*).
Therefore, out of these, the kindness of the first one—
the teacher for ordinary persons—is particularly great,
and so we should always remember his kindness.

According to the passage on the four reliances,
faith in the definite meaning and the interpretable meaning and the like[28]
must be gained from the explanation of the teacher.
It cannot be gained merely from written texts.
Our faith is in our sole lord [Atiśa].
Things like the thought of awakening and the path of the six perfections
lie in the lineage that comes from Ārya Maitreya,
the lineage of the philosophical system of Master Nāgārjuna
as interpreted by Master Candrakīrti,
and the Yogācāra-Madhyamaka of the tradition of Avadhūtipa,[29]
the teacher Atiśa himself followed for seven years;
having established these through the four reliances,
we must put them into practice.

4. How to really embark on Buddhist practice

When someone sets out to embark on the teaching of the Buddha,
is born human, and is fully capable[30]
—when there is a teacher who is endowed with all good qualities
and the disciple is able to be guided,
and when the disciple is also worthy of being guided on the path—
then the teacher should take care of the disciple
like a wise mother nurtures her little son.
He should be given as much as he can grasp and apply.
If he is given too much before he is big and well developed, he will die.
To make him grow up swiftly,
there is no other method than guarding him in this manner;
just as, the moment a poor farmer has sown the seeds,
he longs for the fruit but there is no choice [but to wait].

The way a teacher should instruct a disciple
is like the way a good mother feeds her inexperienced little son
or a wise nurse heals a sick person.
Even if we want something, [the teacher] does not give it, and he controls how much we can grasp. [6]
We will understand [his instructions] according to what we have experienced in our minds.
[Potowa said:] When Jolek was sick, three of us were his attendants.
There was a famine and we did not have enough provisions.
We wanted to go elsewhere as soon as possible,
and for this reason we wanted him to recover quickly.
Although the remedy against the illness worsening is to eat good food,
we gave him only a little bit, out of fear that otherwise [his illness] might increase.
The spiritual mentor [Dromtönpa] helped us understand the teaching [in the same careful manner].
In this way, teacher and student should be without too much fervor.

Provided someone is born human and is capable,
the teacher will prepare such a student in the following manner:
After the student has reflected on the nature of the teacher's virtues,

the teacher delivers him into refuge and thereby makes him a Buddhist.
Then he leads him from [contemplation of] the difficulty of obtaining a precious human body
to contemplation of death.
After that, he teaches him the ten wholesome and the ten unwholesome actions:
how to think about them, how to meditate on them, and how they must be studied.
Then, through constantly thinking about the four noble truths,
the student must be taught that samsara is full of defects.
When the student has understood that others are just like himself [in wanting to avoid suffering and find happiness],
the teacher should introduce him to love and compassion toward all.
When the student has thereby generated the thought of awakening and is endowed with it,
within is contained all the teachings in their entirety;
it is like sending one's last will by the wind.[31]

Therefore the student must be introduced in this way
and cannot advance all of a sudden, in one leap.
This can also be known from the scriptures.
When [Potowa] expounded Atiśa's *Lamp* in Ganggya
and explained how the successive steps are studied,
he told the story of the smith from Dokham as an example,
[in which the smith said,] "I do as I have been instructed by my father."
Jotsun asked for a teaching for the aged, [but Potowa answered:]
"In your youth, you always looked after your immediate needs.
Now you are old and have turned toward the Dharma,
and it has become a pressing need. However, my teaching is just as it is;
I do not have one teaching for the old and another for the young."[32]

5. How to reflect on the recollection of the Three Jewels

Therefore, first you must bring to mind the recollections.[33]
With respect to the cause and result [of becoming a buddha, the first recollection],
the cause is the practices of a bodhisattva:

Recollect how, when he has acted according to the six perfections,
he gathers the two accumulations.
As to the result, there is both a benefit for himself and a benefit for others:
The benefit for himself consists of the acts of abandonment and wisdom;
the benefit for others consists of the acts of compassion and blessing.
Having recollected in terms of a buddha's cause and result in this way again and again,
you gain faith in all the buddhas' good qualities.
Also, as it says in the *King of Meditation Sutra,*
"You must be instructed," and so on.[34]
When this [faith] is obtained, all teachings are obtained. [7]

In the passage on recollection from the *Letter to a Friend,*
it is said that the root of all teachings is faith,
and this in turn rests on the recollection of the Buddha.
If you genuinely recollect the virtues of the Buddha,
the recollection of the Dharma and Sangha will arise by themselves.
Therefore you should recollect the ten virtues and so on;
all good qualities of the Buddha are completely contained in them.
Thereby you subsequently recollect his words: the Dharma.
First, give up wrong deeds by contemplating actions and their results.
Then establish the wish for liberation by contemplating the cycle of rebirth.
Then establish the wish for the highest goal by contemplating sentient beings.
Having recollected the Dharma by contemplating these topics,
reflect in the same way on those who study it: the Sangha.
Through this contemplation, you recollect the Sangha, being pleased with it.
You recollect generosity and moral discipline, one being the cause for the other.
With regard to deities, you think of them as the noble masters.[35]

If someone has not comprehended the very existence of the Buddha,
it is like the gentleman from Lo:
By comprehending Teu Nagong,

he gained faith in the explanation about the lineage of the teachers
that stems from the Buddha, and so he gained [faith in the existence of the Buddha].[36]
When you have comprehended what his good qualities are like,
you have comprehended the whole teaching.
If you have not comprehended them, how can you have faith?

In the passage on the seven jewels from the *Letter to a Friend*, it is said that
of the two—practicing faith and practicing wisdom—
practicing wisdom is higher.[37]
Nevertheless, so long as we don't see the truth,
we must practice just this very faith.
Within all teachings—those of karmic actions and their results, and all the others—
the Buddha must be recollected as the witness.
We will not get anywhere through our own reasoning.
Therefore we should make following through faith most important.

When we take refuge in the Three Jewels,
we are protected by their blessing and by the scriptures.
If you have faith in your refuge, you also have faith in the scriptures,
and when you have faith in the scriptures, this bestows blessing;
they are the original source from which the blessing originates.
If you turn away from them, you are also not protected through the blessing.
As long as you see things as really existing,
do not think that refuge is like an illusion,
much less that it is [empty] like the sky!
Reflect on it as real with pure acceptance;
if you do not do this, you will be attached to yourself,
and because refuge is not taken as real, no respect for it will arise.
Therefore this is declared to be very important,
and you must reflect on it in this way. [8]

2. The Training for Individuals at the Initial Level

6. How to reflect on the difficulty of obtaining a precious human body

When you have thus developed faith in the refuge,
you will recollect [the Buddha] as the evidence of all teachings.
You will then recollect the difficulty of obtaining the leisures[38] and recollect death.
When you contemplate these together, all teachings will come forth from this.
If you think of it this way, the teachings will arise in your mind.

So reflect on the difficulty of obtaining the leisures
and the other topics again and again. Take care with the bottom of the pastry,
as in the case of the man from Dokham who could not get the pastry shell up to his mouth.[39]
Contemplate these topics again and again.

As in the passage, "O virtuous one, worthy of the good,"[40]
we become a suitable vessel for the teaching by possessing the right conditions from former lives.
Therefore [the teaching] has been designed for us, who are worthy of the good.
Having successfully passed many dangerous paths, we possess virtues.
Now that we are worthy of the good, there is no time to be idle.
To acquire a nature full of virtues is very difficult.

Recollecting the Three Jewels, we have taken refuge.
After this, we make death the most important point of focus.
By thinking of suffering, which is never ending

and consists of illness, old age, and so forth,
we are introduced to hearing, thinking about, and reflecting on
the remedy that can cure this long disease: the three trainings and so forth.[41]
Now is the time! [Potowa] gave the example about a song:
When someone from Gyaphu [in Loteng] arrived in Tsang, the people there sang these words,
"Those who are sons of Loteng
should dig from the mountain of gold!"
The man thought, "That applies to me! How could I stay here and not dig?!"
So he went back and dug from the mountain of gold.[42]
In the same way, we must admonish ourselves constantly
since we have been born as human beings, are young, and so on:
"I must fulfill my vow! How can I remain here?!"
Ārya Asaṅga can be cited here as a source.
Even if we are not yet capable, we can lay the foundations
and make a strong effort.

In the *Precious Garland* it is said, in the passage on instructing without hesitation,
that "I, a monk, tell you without hesitation."[43]
As it is said in the *Sutra on Moral Discipline*,[44]
we must think that, now that we have obtained the leisures and embarked on the Dharma,
if we act in a way that contradicts this,
it will lead to constant suffering.
There is a story how the good food
was suddenly snatched away by the dog.[45] I regard this [kind of behavior] as wrong.
It will get dark [and the Buddhist teachings will finally fade away],
but as long as there are one hundred or only ten or even a single person
who thinks about all this and does not waste [the precious human body],
this process will be delayed a little,[46] because people always cleave [to such good companions].[47]
Therefore these kinds of people [9]

should understand what they have been told in this way and in other ways.[48]
[In the *Precious Garland* it is said that] because it is going
to benefit you in this and future lives, you should act accordingly.[49]
The benefit for yourself is manifest [in the present]; benefitting others creates the [karmic] provisions [for your future lives].
Also those buddhas of former times [realized]:
"When we take care of ourselves, this is the provisions for ourselves.
But even when we seek provisions for ourselves, these depend on others.
We gather accumulations of merit by making others the object [of our virtuous deeds],
and these will cause us to experience benefit [in the future]."

The words from the *Guide to the Bodhisattva Way of Life* on the initial topic, the precious human body,
stating that the leisures are difficult to obtain
have been heard and learned by heart and taught frequently.
Try to find anybody who would not generate this idea in their mindstreams!
When the advice has been given, who would not adopt it?
However, in this northern region this is a little difficult.
An irrigation canal may look clear,
but this is only on the surface; at the bottom it is full of mud.
Therefore there can never be hope in general,
but if some individuals
gain the notion that this teaching is true,
they will realize that it must not be neglected.
Therefore each and every part of this instruction
must be considered earnestly in various ways;
it is not something to ponder just once or twice.
Until the meaning of this has been born in us,
we should think about it, and then all the other teachings will follow.
If it is taught merely to obtain food, that is not enough.
When we truly see it,[50] our minds will become determined.[51]

When [Potowa] was explaining the chapter on conscientiousness,[52]
he said, "To be a human being is like when Chakhar had been won:

Thinking, 'This isn't just a dream, is it?'[53] we must practice
[diligently].
What if we have ingested poison
and must experience the effects?
Like someone reaching a forked road,
depending on whether we set foot on the right or the left path,
we reach a high or low state; that's the nature of things.
We cannot reach a bad state of mind
when we set foot on the path to the right, even if we want to,
and we cannot reach heaven
when we set foot on the path to the left, even if we wish for it."
Having heard this, we must think that setting foot on the wrong path
is not the right way. Without being in control,
we will be tormented by our deeds and experience the ensuing fate.

In this life we have obtained the excellent leisures.
We have not been born here because the sins have ceased completely
in our minds;
the reason we have been born at this time is
because between the two, sins and merits, [10]
we have previously pursued meritorious deeds,
or because the merits we have are so strong,
or because at the moment of death our minds adopted [a beneficial
attitude].[54]
We have now obtained an excellent precious human body,
so we must do what will help us attain it [again]
and purify the sins that have been accumulated since beginningless
time.
All beneficial propensities must be cultivated;
then we will finally reach the light.
When it does not go well, there is a great risk
that the merits will be consumed, and we will end up in darkness.

As stated in the [*Verses Addressed to*] *Prasenajit* and by the teacher
Nāgārjuna,[55]
it is important to go from light to light.
This is not dismissed by any of the vehicles;

there is nothing greater to be attained than this vast light.
If we want to reach this light
that will never again lead to darkness,
we must accomplish the *Aspiration Prayer of Nāgārjuna*.[56]
Someone who wants this must act against teachers and students
[when necessary];
it is not appropriate to simply agree.[57]
We must gather the accumulations in various ways.
If we are intent on this in all of life's situations
and thereby gather the accumulations, purify the mind, and make
aspiration prayers,
we will reach the light; it cannot be otherwise.

7. How to reflect on death and impermanence

Now that we have a precious human body, so difficult to obtain,
if we only tend to this life, then we are like animals,
and in this respect animals are even more skillful than we humans.
Therefore, even if we cling to this lifetime with a fist [as stiff as that]
of a corpse,
we can transform this through reflecting on the "great [method for]
dispelling conceptions,"
and dispelling conceptions is what we must do by all means.
When we recall death as our great [method of] dispelling
conceptions,
we arrive at a state where all conceptions have been cleared away,
and therefore we must reflect on death from many different angles.
Furthermore, an indication of how genuinely we have generated this
notion is
if our inner attitude becomes like someone
who has lived in a foreign land for a long time
and then meets a companion who is about to
return home for good the day after tomorrow, and he thinks:
"I must go without delay, like him!"
We are still fettered to this life like a calf that is bound to a peg:
We may run far and engage in the Buddhist teachings,
but we just run around in circles and are again bound to this life.

Like [a calf that is] set loose from the peg,
we must move toward liberation without paying attention to this [lifetime].

[Nāgārjuna] said to the king: "[When death comes] you will have no choice but to leave your possessions behind,
wherever you may try and go."[58]
It is the same with us. It is said that we cannot return,
and that we have no livelihood for the future; thus we have nothing at all.
Our former possessions will fall into the hands of new owners.
When we are going to have neither the former teachings, nor welfare, nor fame,
how can we make a livelihood for future lives?
We must apply ourselves now, while we are at ease.
What it will be like in the future is not under our control. [11]
We must keep in mind that we are in the realm of the Lord of Death and of the causes of death,
like a candle that stands in a strong wind,
and so we must quickly apply ourselves.

8. How to gain a firm understanding of the law of cause and effect

Once we have recollected death in this manner,
we may wonder how happiness and sorrow originate in the next life.
The cause of happiness and sorrow is actions.
Even after a hundred eons, the [results of our] deeds will not be exhausted.
From a small deed can arise immeasurable consequences.
Furthermore, our own happiness and sorrow arise
only from our own deeds; therefore,
this, in brief, is how to reflect on deeds and their consequences.
Remember that the Buddha is the witness of all phenomena,
even the smallest deeds and results;
therefore do not commit any transgressions.
We cannot [fully] comprehend [the karmic chain of cause and effect] through reasoning.

Giving up the ten unwholesome actions is the path of all the vehicles.

Believing in [the karmic law of] action and result and forsaking the ten unwholesome actions
out of a wish for the happiness of gods and humans within the cycle of existence—
this is the vehicle of well-being for beings at the initial level.
Practicing these very same ten [actions] with the help of the four noble truths
is the vehicle of the śrāvakas. Practicing with the help of the chain of dependent origination
is the path of the pratyekabuddhas. This is for intermediate beings.
Practicing with both method and wisdom
is the path of the Mahayana, which is for excellent beings.
Giving up the ten unwholesome actions is always the same;
therefore we must give up the ten unwholesome actions in every way.
If we don't, we achieve nothing at all.

Some members of a philosophical school maintain, according to their school,
that in the three bad kinds of rebirth, and in the form realm and the formless realm, the deeds committed there
will not ripen and are without result—
or they maintain that they do ripen but that the result is small.[59]
In the realm of gods and human beings—the desire realm—where karma works,
there are three continents,[60] among them Jambudvīpa,
and on that continent there are men and women.
When these men and women make fervent vows,
their good and bad deeds have a very strong force.
Therefore, though an unwholesome deed may be small,
we must not disregard it and must give it up, and for even a small wholesome action, we must strive hard.
The results are fearful and pleasant, respectively,
and therefore we must be afraid [of evil deeds]. The spiritual mentor [Dromtönpa] has declared that this is a secret.[61]
Avadhūtipa, the teacher of our sole lord Atiśa, often explained
which deed caused a certain scholar to obtain a certain result
and descend into this present [bad state] here, and which bad deed
caused a certain yogi to end up here.

Therefore, as long as there is still clinging to the ego,
the karmic force of even a trifling deed is inexhaustible, [12]
and we must fear even a tiny little sin and avoid it.

On the other hand, the following can be cited from the Abhidharma:
When we have seen the truth, we are not cast [into samsara by former deeds].
And in the tantras it is said that when we see rebirth as [being empty like] the sky,
karma does not cast us into existence.[62]
Still, as long as it is not so, karma harms us.
Therefore, as long as we have not seen the truth
and have not seen [everything as empty like] the sky,
actions and their results must not be disregarded.

[Potowa] said to Saten Tönpa:
"Even if you have doubts as to whether karmic actions and their results exist in the hereafter,
and likewise if you have doubts as to whether [good behavior] will be useful,
there is good reason to adopt [good behavior] and avoid [bad behavior]."[63]
This is like when the people from Gyal and Tölung were at war
and they did not risk crossing the pass of Pö, even under the cover of darkness.
Similarly, the people at Tera took a loan and sowed [the seeds they bought with the money].[64]
But for us there is not even that much [wisdom], and we do not refrain [from harmful deeds]!
What do we gain when we try to be dominant or to be the fastest in the race?
In this respect animals are more capable [than humans],
as we can see in the stories about the crows and the owls from Drakgyap,
the snake and the lizard, and the nest of birds from Sho.[65]
Human beings cannot act like this.
We must give up sins out of fear of a bad rebirth in the next life.

When we have called to mind the faults of samsara and long for liberation,
we enter the three trainings with the method of the four noble truths.
Avoiding the Hinayana, we must cultivate the thought of awakening.
This is how a human being behaves.
If it were different, how would we be human?!

In the chapter on diligence [in the *Guide to the Bodhisattva Way of Life*], it is said that
the [causal connection of] actions and their results is extremely profound.[66]
Emptiness can be understood through reasoning.
Actions and their ripening have been declared to be beyond imagination;
they are even more inconceivable than the [five] fields of knowledge.
For our minds, [comprehending karma] is a hopeless task!
Having set their minds quickly on emptiness,
Tibetans are in no danger of giving it up again.
They learn the alphabet and the *Heart Sutra*.
However, karma and its results are more profound than this;
therefore we should constantly strive [to understand them].
Furthermore, when we have first of all mastered the recollection of the Buddha
and believe in him, [we will know that] his words are not wrong.
In this way we must become mentally accustomed to [the law of] actions and their results.

In the passage [in Śāntideva's *Guide*] on "the unbearable fires of repentance,"[67]
it is said about repentance
that when we are reborn in hell, at first we remember our birth,
and at that time we repent, but after that we cannot remember it any more.
The animals cannot repent because they are stupid.
The hungry ghosts are powerless,
and therefore it is very difficult for them to repent, although they know about their faults,

and even if they do repent, they are unable to refrain from [harmful deeds].
We can know how much they are unable to control themselves
by hearing the story of the elder from Vikramaśīla Monastery
who died and was reborn among the hungry ghosts [13]
and then seized a child from the village of Muken.[68]
Therefore obtaining a precious human body is a great opportunity
because when we have done a harmful deed, we can repent and turn away [from further harmful deeds].
Also, Ārya Asaṅga has advised us
to use what we lack as an aid
and strive to obtain it [by accumulating good karma]; this is how it is.
We must avoid even mixed deeds
and strive to do only good deeds—
and the bad deeds that we did previously must be put to an end.

Because good and bad deeds
ripen in a chain according to their respective causes
and thus increase considerably,
we get much closer to or much further from liberation as a result.
Therefore we must become thoroughly accustomed to good behavior,
and we must strictly avoid bad behavior.

First we must perceive ourselves correctly:
We must consider whether we are experiencing a result
originating from good deeds,
from bad deeds,
or from mixed deeds.
When we recognize that something is the result of good deeds,
we must take care that the good deeds, done with great care,
do not perish. When we recognize
that it is the result of mixed deeds,
we must remember our discontentment [with the world] and give up the mixed deeds.
When we have thus become firmly accustomed to [the law of] actions and their results
and do not act in harmful ways under any circumstances,
this is called "the great right view within this world."

Ārya Asaṅga has stated that [the right view is gained] at the stage of forbearance.
It is also possible that it occurs at a previous stage
when we have not yet completed the path of accumulation.[69]
When we have met a good teacher
and have considered actions and their results,
we will not transgress the rules out of desire or other emotions.
Therefore we must become thoroughly accustomed to actions and their results.

3. The Training for Individuals at the Middle Level

9. How to reflect on the four noble truths

As an instruction for the middle kind [of person], it has been explained
that even when someone has turned away from bad deeds out of fear of a bad rebirth
and attained the state of a god or a human, it does not mean that he has reached a definite state [of everlasting happiness].
Until we reach the end of our suffering within the cycle of rebirth,
there is no happy state to be found.
When we think of samsara as a burning house,
or like being locked in a horrible prison,[70]
like being thrust into the swirling waves of the ocean,
or like wandering in an unpleasant wilderness,
then we will hasten from samsara to liberation
as fast as one whose clothes have caught fire. [14]
Then the intermediate state of mind has been produced.
When we train the mind on this level,
we must apply ourselves to the methods of liberation from this [cycle of existence].

Toward the end of his stay in Nyenpo, [Potowa] said
that the fact that samsara is without beginning
has been established both by the scriptures and by reasoning.
Furthermore, it has been said in the scriptures that since beings are
as endless as the sky,
there is not a single being who has not been our mother.
It has been said that the number of those who have been our mothers
is greater than the infinite directions of the sky.
Hence we have been wandering in samsara for a long time.

The very cause for this is delusion,
and the chief element of delusion is ignorance.
When we have thus created the twelve links [of the chain of dependent origination],
we are in a constant and endless cycle of existences.
The time to reverse this process is right now;
the method is the three kinds of training.[71]
In short, if we train ourselves in faith and wisdom,
everything is contained in this;
therefore we must constantly practice these two.
This is the instruction, and thus we must act accordingly.

This big house of samsara has many doors,
and wherever we set out, there we may depart from it.[72]
The boundless path of the secret mantra and the path of the perfections
are the very same path, and both lead to liberation.
Whether the excellent scope or the middle scope has arisen,
they will lead to liberation from this [cycle of existence].
How could it be otherwise!?

[Potowa] explained to Changtön from Khartok:
"We have been wandering in samsara for a long time;
the time to reverse it is right now![73]
The method is not to conform to worldly aims;
rather, it is to embrace the doctrine of what does not conform to them,
and for this purpose we must not pursue them in any way.
It is not appropriate to act out of this or that necessity.
When we do not pursue [worldly aims] in any way,
[emancipation from them] will follow, and we will avert them in this way."

[Potowa also] explained to Shönu Öser in Drak
why living beings get sick and die—
namely, that disease is the cause for disease and dying is the cause for dying:

They do not occur by accident; they are inherent [in the cycle of
rebirth].
Someone who is weary of this must abandon
undesirable rebirths. The causes for these rebirths
are karma and delusion. If delusion is absent,
actions have no result. If, out of the three elements of delusion—
desire, grasping, and ignorance—
ignorance is absent, there is neither desire nor grasping. Ignorance
is the main element
and must be removed by all possible means.
The causes that remove it are the three trainings.
Through them, the mind is calmed.
Attaining thus in this way is the Hinayana.
Those who practice the three kinds of training
because they also want to teach others [how to obtain liberation]
are bodhisattvas. [15]

4. The Training for Excellent Individuals

10. How to train the mind in the single vehicle

Having trained the mind in the way of the middle kind of beings,
we should apply ourselves to the attitude of the excellent beings.
The awakening of the śrāvakas is not a permanent liberation;
only an all-knowing [buddha] is permanently liberated.
Therefore strive for the conditions to reach this [state].
The awakening of śrāvakas and pratyekabuddhas
have been explained as the vehicles for those with weaker mental abilities,
like an illusory city for those wandering in the wilderness,
or like an illusory island for those who are in the middle of the ocean.
We need to cross over in one go because there won't be a second [opportunity].
So right from the beginning we should enter the Mahayana path,
the cause of which is the thought of awakening.
The root of this, in turn, is great compassion;
that comes from loving kindness as its precursor,
and the cause that engenders this is repaying the kindness of others.
This again originates from recognizing all beings as mothers.
So from such a root and through gradual development,
all good qualities such as the thought of awakening emerge.

11. Reflecting on loving kindness and compassion

Taking your mothers as the object and reflecting on their kindness
is considered the cause of loving kindness that is unafflicted.
This is not the same when we take other loved ones as the object,
for if it goes wrong, it can lead to the affliction of desire.

Therefore our lord [Atiśa] declared [the method] outlined above to be the best.
The measure of having become accustomed to it is that we develop an attitude
like that of an old father who has only one son,
and who holds him dear and loves him as though he were adorned with all virtues,
and benefits him in every way.
If we extend this to all beings, that is [loving kindness].

The sole lord himself has said that
although elsewhere it is said that there are four immeasurables,[74]
when we cultivate loving kindness and compassion, the other two are encompassed.
To develop these in an impartial way is equanimity.
Joy is that [living beings] are happy and free from suffering.
Therefore what are taught as four are contained in the two.

When it is said that the mind has to be firm in awakening,[75] [this means that]
for those who train the mind in loving kindness and compassion
this practice turns into the method of the Mahayana,
even if they hold the views of the Vaibhāṣikas[76]
and enter [the teaching] through the four noble truths,
just as the teacher Aśvaghoṣa himself has said.
For in the treatise entitled *Ornament of Mahayana Sutras,*[77]
he presented the instructions on this in detail.
Therefore, as long as we train in the thought of awakening,
our path becomes that of the Mahayana, even if our views remain that of the Hinayana. [16]

Recalling that kindness has been declared the beginning of all teachings,
reflect on the two—the faults and benefits of gratitude and ingratitude.
Reflect on this as found in the *Verses about Bherī,* [*the Nāga King*].[78]
This is also implied by the proverb about giving water to a friend.[79]

So we should remember the faults and the virtues of this and the other [attitude],
and always recall others' kindness and avoid not doing so.

Moreover, the teacher Kamalaśīla has very aptly said that
before we can develop loving kindness, we must reflect on equanimity.[80]
Then [loving kindness can flow] as easily as water flowing over even ground.
Also, our lord [Atiśa] has given the advice that
when we have cultivated an attitude like the one we have toward our mother,
we will become like a horse storming ahead on a race course.

As much as we have extended loving kindness in this life,
to that same extent will we be masters in the future;
that's how it is, said the one who died at Sangphu.[81]
There is no fixed sequence of loving kindness and compassion.
[According to Kamalaśīla's second treatise on the *Stages of Meditation*,] compassion arises when we have become accustomed to loving kindness.
However, when the mind is powerful, compassion arises first,
and in that case, if loving kindness arises before it, it is the wrong order.[82]
When we have become accustomed to them both, any sequence is correct.

In the Mahayana, compassion is of the utmost importance
and must be [as inevitable] as [a bird] falling into the mouth of a snake;[83]
otherwise we are not suitable to be bodhisattvas.
Moreover, we must strengthen our affection for the real world;
then we can both reflect on emptiness and remain connected to the world.
Just as it is difficult to give up the clinging to an "I" completely
when we have contemplated emptiness, but are still accustomed to clinging to an "I,"
so it is difficult to adopt the stance of compassion

when we contemplate emptiness without being accustomed
to [affection toward sentient beings].
Therefore we must strengthen our affection for the real world.

12. Generating the thought of awakening

When we generate the thought of awakening for the first time,
and if we wonder whether the long or the short version [of the vow] is more suitable
for training constantly in the exercises of the thought of awakening,
it is as in the story of the servant who asked the master [whether he wanted his meal hot or cold].[84]
When practicing the thought of awakening, loving kindness, and compassion,
even without words we may train the mind.
Yet words devoid of thought do not achieve it.
To develop an earnest wish for the training, we must contemplate its benefits,
as has been explained [in the *Marvelous Array Sutra*].[85]
This can be understood [by considering the life story] of the lord [Atiśa] himself.
When he was circumambulating [the Mahābodhi Temple], in the west and the north
there were deities who instructed the master about it. When Kusali was asked
by his friends, he told them to do a mirror divination [to confirm the importance of the thought of awakening].[86]
So, in short, someone who has the thought of awakening
possesses all good qualities, and someone who does not has no good qualities at all.
Thinking of the good qualities in this way, constantly practice [the thought of awakening]
and endeavor to increase it through every kind of effort. [17]
The best kinds of effort are in loving kindness and compassion.
Moreover, we must train in the thought of awakening through gathering the accumulations.
The best way is through making offerings to the Three Jewels
and serving the monastic community in various ways.
We must purify bad deeds and abandon bad friends,

stick to the spiritual mentor, and become acquainted with emptiness.
Through these and other methods,
make it increase. This is the true training in the thought of awakening.

Those who constantly practice the thought of awakening rooted in faith
will soon develop understanding of the true nature of phenomena,
even if they hold the views of the Vaibhāṣikas.
This is like the teacher of our lord [Atiśa] who gave away his flesh.[87]
If we have the mental power to understand it,
we should study the great Madhyamaka view itself now.
It corresponds entirely to the true nature of phenomena.
Completely unite with the thought of awakening rooted in faith.[88]

If the thought of awakening rooted in faith is firm,
this will be the cause for obtaining omniscience, even if
we regard things as real and the three spheres are not completely purified.[89]
So long as we have not trained in wisdom, this is sufficient.
Once we have trained in [wisdom], it will assist us.

We practice the thought of awakening in many ways.
Whatever little favor we have done for the sake of sentient beings,
we must dedicate the merit for the purpose
that they and others may all obtain liberation.
This is the great method for quickly obtaining buddhahood.
[Thus we may think:] "I am sad because I have not seen [Atiśa];
however, I will practice according to his instruction, and
then I will eventually become like him, even though I have not seen him."

We practice the thought of awakening in this life from the moment we take the vow.
This is like throwing some seed on the ground;
and when we practice, constantly taking the vow,
we obtain a purpose as great as obtaining the great seal (*mahāmudrā*).[90]

5. The Practice of the Perfections

13. How to practice generosity

Having thus trained ourselves in the thought of awakening,
driven by the thought of awakening, we should gather the accumulations.
And with respect to whatever roots of virtue we engage in,
the spiritual mentor [Drom]tönpa stated this:
"As a preparation [the action] should be propelled by the thought of awakening;
the actual act should be endowed with the six perfections;
when completed, it should be dedicated toward awakening.
In this the practice of all the perfections is contained.

The thirty-six methods—sixfold armor into six—
and the four—discarding, guarding, purifying, and increasing—mean the same.[91]
The six roots are contained in the four, and we must apply ourselves to these four with energy.
By contemplating these four, the [thirty-six] methods become effective.

In the section on the perfections in the *Ornament of Mahayana Sutras*,
it is said of the six perfections of the bodhisattva that,
even taken separately, each is the cause of all six.[92] [18]
This is how it is understood correctly.
All that is contrary to this is not [the way] of a bodhisattva.

We should not stick to the literal meaning
when the scriptures say that everything is contained within contemplating wisdom.[93]

This has been said in the sutras that require interpretation,[94] which were expressed in an interpretative way for the sake of those
who rely on the five [other perfections,] cling to them,
and therefore do not engage in wisdom.
Even when we meditate on wisdom, there is no risk of ignoring [the other perfections if we have developed them first].
This is what the scriptures mean when they say this,
and seeing it in a different way would not correspond [to the scriptures' true meaning].
Having developed [the other perfections] first, you can later engage in [contemplating wisdom],
therefore this is what the scriptures mean with the above statement.

Recognizing that the opposing forces
of the six perfections are empty, we must not engage in them.
We must know that the relative truth of actions and their results is infallible
and constantly adhere to the antidotes [for wrong attitudes and actions];
then the relative truth and the ultimate truth
will both correctly turn into the great method of the path.
If we turn away from this, it will cause wrong views.

14. How to practice moral discipline

For a great bodhisattva, the seven unwholesome actions[95]
are permissible because he commits them only when his compassion does not leave him a choice.
Those who are not yet mentally capable [of this behavior]
should constantly practice the conventional thought of awakening with compassion.
For that purpose we must first make calming and taming ourselves the most important thing,
as it is taught in the four points contained in the *Sutra Encouraging Nobler Intention*,[96]
and we should also think of the example of preparing a heavy load.[97]
As long as we have not reached the bodhisattva level, the best benefit for sentient beings is
that we act according to the *Praise [of the Virtues] without End*.[98]

Although the things that are permitted or prohibited among the
practices of a bodhisattva have been declared to be innumerable,
there are, in short, not more than these two kinds.
If someone has the thought of awakening, endowed with love and compassion,
and his or her mind is free from delusion,
the things that are [usually] prohibited are allowed.
But as long as the mind is still deluded,
they are not permitted, even when the scriptures say they should be done.[99]
Therefore we must find out what is allowed and what is prohibited
through examining our own minds.
Once we have taken the monastic vows and the bodhisattva vow,
we should observe the mind and assess it.
If the mind is pure, we should make bodhisattvahood the foremost thing.
If it is not pure, or if it desires benefit for only ourselves, we should adhere to the former [i.e., the monastic vows].

When we are fully guided by compassion
there will be no fault, whatever kind of practice of the stages we have done,
even if we do not possess supernatural knowledge, as in the case of the teacher of our sole lord.[100] [19]
It is said in the scriptures that when we have taken the monastic vows and the bodhisattva vow,
a transgression against the monastic vows is best confessed in front of a person.
When a transgression has occurred against the bodhisattva vow, though,
it is best confessed in front of the Three Jewels.
To not follow this is inappropriate.

To know what the moral discipline of a bodhisattva is,
we should understand it as the set of the three kinds of morality:[101]
The morality of the vow means not doing what is not suitable,
and since through this we accumulate virtues, it is [at the same time the morality of] acquiring virtuous qualities,

and by doing so we act for the benefit of sentient beings, either in reality or in our minds.
Therefore all the three [kinds of moral discipline] are present in a single one.

15. How to practice patience

In the chapter on patience from the *Guide to the Bodhisattva Way of Life*, it is said that
anger is the opposing force to patience.
This anger grows strong when the mind feels displeased.[102]
The conditions for feeling displeased are the eight worldly concerns.
Therefore we must constantly strive
to conquer them with the various antidotes.
Considering them to be illusions is one antidote,
and to think about the shortcomings of samsara is another.
Moreover, if we calm them permanently
through the great method of removing them [i.e., through thinking about impermanence],
we will remain content amid the four undesirable states among the eight [worldly concerns].[103]
With this attitude it becomes easy to be patient,
and moreover it is the cause for all wholesome factors.
For this very reason, we must constantly
contemplate this, and understand the respective verses
from the first to the last line.[104]
[Atiśa] told the yogi [Gompa Rinchen Lama][105] to apply himself to this earnestly.
Therefore this is of the utmost importance,
and we must master it by all possible means.

We should seek freedom
from the four undesirable states among the worldly concerns
by choosing those very same states;
for when people have not noticed our treasure, there can be no harm,
whereas once they notice it and take it away, there is harm.[106]
The four [desirable states,] such as obtaining [things and so on] appeal to others, too,

but we must realize that things obtained will be lost again,
as in the case of the master from Domé who was carrying honey
mixed with butter.[107]
Therefore we must regard the four [desirable states, such as] obtaining
things and so on, as enemies.
From prosperity the whole ocean of misery breaks forth.
Know this also from the scriptures.

16. How to practice diligence

When we strive with diligence for the wholesome factors,
our minds are constantly accompanied by the thought that [20]
we are like someone who has arrived in a very dangerous place,
or like a mother whose son has been thrown into prison,
or like someone who is in a burning house together with his
mother;[108]
in this way we must constantly exert our minds in the wholesome
factors.

When we strive with diligence merely to hear the teachings,
our wisdom may remain weak, and we will not grasp [the doctrine]
properly.
Therefore it is not proper to make hearing the most important thing;
we must above all try to accomplish what the instructions say.
To love listening is of course very virtuous,
but there is more blessing in spending our time practicing.

When we strive to achieve liberation through diligence,
we should not act like the people from Semodru.[109]
Rather, like merchants from Kham setting out on their way,
we must proceed with constant ease and care.[110]
When we rush forward in haste, we will get nowhere.
When we go, we must proceed step by step—we cannot leap;
that's what the one who died at Sangphu[111] said.

While striving with diligence for accomplishment,
if we are not accustomed to [the right attitude],
[we will mix up] the happiness of entering the teaching

and the happiness of the desires, just as if we were
eating the bristles and husks [of raw barley] together with the tsampa.
When we are unpracticed, we eat the bristles and husks and get no proper food—
that's what a person is like who has not become accustomed.
Those who know how to enter the teachings step by step
experience [the effects] in their minds, like cattle that have been trained.
Therefore we must strive to experience [the teachings] in our minds.

If we strive in this lifetime as if it were a matter of life and death,
it is like rolling a copper boulder uphill.
When the copper boulder has been rolled to the top of the mountain pass,
we won't require much effort in the future [for making it roll down],
and we will naturally achieve great gain.

[When explaining] the passage on skillful actions [from the *Ornament of Mahayana Sutras*],[112]
[Potowa said that] when we wish for complete liberation with all our hearts,
we must take as an example the understanding of Ligom, [who said that]
when we generate a mind that is far sighted and broad minded,
live with a carefree attitude putting all commerce aside,
have pure moral discipline, gather the accumulations,
and clear the obscurations through various means, then final emancipation is not far away.[113]

[When explaining] the passage, "You are endowed with the four wheels,"[114]
[Potowa said that] those who want to apply diligence
need to be both coaxed and encouraged.
They must be urged to apply diligence without giving in.
[Potowa] gave the example of the woman from Dokham who sang the song,
"Adorned with an arrow quiver made of tigerskin on the right," and so on.[115]

When we look for a situation where all [four wheels]—
the appropriate place and so on—come together, we may become dejected.[116]
However, while we look for the four wheels elsewhere,
their causes are right here,
and right here we find the means for fulfilling the Mahayana. [21]
Where there is no king, there is more autonomy.[117]
We have encountered the teaching of our sole lord; we would be hard pressed to find a better
spiritual mentor anywhere in Jambudvīpa.[118]
We have encountered the [four wheels] because we have behaved appropriately, because we are endowed with the three trainings,
and through the merit we have accumulated before.
When we look at these and other virtues,
we should delight in them and enter the Dharma.
Coaxing and encouraging ourselves in this manner
is the great method of perpetual effort.

When [Potowa] was explaining the *Precious Garland*,[119]
he said that we must make all the three times and periods
something virtuous.
Everything—the early, late, and middle periods of life,
and the early, late, and middle periods
of the year, the month, and the day,
as well as everything we do with body, speech, and mind,
the foremost, the middle, and the last [of our actions]—
must be turned into Dharma and should not be mingled with behavior that is contrary to the Dharma.
If we act accordingly, our existence will be beneficial.
To establish this, we must apply diligence.

Referring to the passage on the five fields of knowledge from the *Ornament of Mahayana Sutras*,[120]
[Potowa said that] we must apply diligence in all the five fields of knowledge.
However, life is short, and there are many impediments.
Moreover, our intellects are weak, and therefore we are not able

to study all five fields of knowledge in this very lifetime,
and even the little that we are capable of may decline.
Therefore, it is said to be most beneficial
if in this lifetime we reflect on the personal instructions that summarize the Buddhist teachings
and make aspiration prayers to accomplish the five fields of knowledge [in the future].[121]

Through diligence, our wholesome factors will increase.
The spiritual mentor [Dromtönpa] has explained how we can do this:
When we are supported by the power of a spiritual helper in this lifetime,
the wholesome factors will increase greatly, but through this alone
we will not achieve buddhahood. In the future
these qualities will ripen and, increasing through favorable circumstances,
become a hundred or a thousand times stronger.
It may happen that even then we still will not achieve [buddhahood].
When there is a foundation in ourselves, then the buddhas can bless us.
If there is no foundation within us, then there is no chance.
Citing the source about "being obscured and without the causes,"[122]
[Dromtönpa said that] we will obtain the blessing when the foundation is there,
and through this we will quickly attain buddhahood.
This is the way to increase [our good inner qualities].[123]

17. How to practice meditative concentration

In the chapter on meditative concentration,
it is said that when we have meditative absorption, wisdom will increase.[124] [22]
Through wisdom, the afflictions will be destroyed.
To generate meditative absorption, we must abide in its conditions,
the most important of which is moral discipline.
And just as stated by conqueror Maitreya,
the five results [of morality] support meditative absorption.[125]
The [results of morality] are the ripening of the vessel, and so on.

Through the ripening we become a vessel for [meditative absorption];
due to this we become endowed with power;
by its concordant cause, aspiration, [meditative absorption] is enhanced;
for its cessation result, we become free from its opposing forces.
In this way, they [morality and its fruits] serve as conditions of meditative absorption.
A fellow practitioner should be similar to you in view and conduct.
In this context, "view" does not mean Madhyamaka, Cittamātra, or the like;
it means he shares your thoughts on how to conduct oneself.
This is important, for if you are not in accord,
then where one of you yearns for solitude, the other seeks diversions;
where one of you wishes to meditate, the other wants to study, and so on.
Thus one leaning upon the other, you will become obscured
and fail to develop; so to be in accord is vital.

When [Potowa] was teaching the *Stages of Meditation* in Shungkhen,
he said that genuine tranquil abiding (*śamatha*) and insight (*vipaśyanā*)[126]
are quite remote in this life, and even their conducive practices
are very difficult, so we must strive as much as we can
to plant their potent seeds. Of the two,
the seed of insight is more important.
Solely applying ourselves to thorough examination,
we must reflect on loving kindness toward all, and so on.
He had seen, heard about, and experienced [examples of the two types of meditation, Potowa said].[127]
For example, a man who was said to have a good mental abiding and was well admired
is now practicing sorcery and has returned to his previous state.[128]
When we frequently apply ourselves to thorough examination
it is extremely helpful. It is very important
to sow the potent seed of insight through experiencing [thorough examination] in our minds.
We must abide frequently by means of thorough examination.

The teacher [Dromtönpa] said that through practicing
just a little meditation now, we will generate
a continuous state of meditation in the future.
So know that it will multiply in the future.
This is the great method for fulfilling all purposes.

With regard to the passage on "giving away the roots of virtue,"[129]
[Potowa explained that] if we meditate now in various ways,
if our moral discipline is pure, and if we utter an aspiration prayer,
then the [respective good qualities] will arise in the future
and we will naturally become true yogis.
Even if someone does not become [a yogi] now, [it may be as in the case of] the son of a minister,
or [as in the case of Ḍombhipa], the Lama of Blessing of our sole lord,
or the novice who studied the teachings in the presence of his master
and, through the intervention of a teacher, became an accomplished yogi.[130]
Even if this does not happen, [the results] will arise
according to the guidance of our teacher; that's the nature of things.
Therefore you must constantly train the mind with moral discipline [23]
and guide it with aspiration prayers.
This is the great method for success.

As in the passage about "giving of women" from the *Precious Garland*,[131]
meditative absorption must be achieved through various means.
We must create the necessary conditions by training the mind
with moral discipline and wisdom as well.
Moreover, when creating these [conditions],
we must seek favorable conditions and discard the unfavorable ones.
Without [seeking] the causes, nothing can be achieved.
Now when we have meditated a little but have not attained any results,
we may think that this is due to an [imperfect] instruction and look elsewhere for instructions,
and if these do not work either, we may search somewhere else again.
Acting like this is like a dog that pursues a bird[132]—
this is how it goes in the end, and we have reached nothing.

The spiritual mentor [Dromtönpa] said that nowadays
we only want to abide in mental concentration.
As we were wandering in samsara,
what meditative absorptions
below the summit of existence[133]
are there that we haven't attained?
Nonetheless, we still haven't attained or experienced [awakening] in any way.
So far the thought of awakening has not arisen in us;
not even a genuine attitude of the middle scope has arisen,
for if it had, we would have embarked on the path of the Hinayana.
At present, for us, none of these has come to be,
so we must now strive as much as we can
to make the thought of awakening, which we have not yet experienced, arise in us,
and through all sorts of ways gather the accumulations.
Thus, to ensure that at some point in the future
we become endowed with the four wheels,
we must gather the causes for [fulfilling] our aspirations.
This will enable us to reach the very end in the future,
since becoming an ārya in this lifetime is very difficult.

6. Wisdom

18. How to learn wisdom

When explaining [Śāntideva's] chapter on wisdom,
[Potowa said that all the steps]—beginning with taking refuge and then
[continuing with reflecting on] death, the laws of karma, the four noble truths,
loving kindness, compassion, the thought of awakening,
the six perfections, and so on—will not turn into the right path if wisdom is missing.
Therefore we must rely on a qualified teacher
and first of all listen to his teachings; then we should reflect and meditate on them.
This kind of wisdom will support us in every [step of spiritual progress],
as all good qualities rest on being endowed with wisdom.

If we have not become really stable with respect to
karma, compassion, and the like
but embark on meditation on emptiness,
one of two errors will occur:
If we do not believe [in emptiness], we will discard it saying that it is not Dharma;
or if we do believe in it, we will arrive at a nihilistic view.
Therefore we must first become firm in the methods.[134]
When they have become stable and we meditate on emptiness,
then even when we determine phenomena to be empty,
we will believe in the ripening of karma,
and so we will naturally develop great compassion for

all the beings who have not understood [the true nature of phenomena].
Therefore the instruction is to meditate in this way.

Beginners will first become firm in the [practice of] method. [24]
When this has become stable, they can alternate between wisdom and method,
just as the right and the left foot of a person [alternate when walking].
When these have become very stable, [the two aspects are] like the wings of a bird.

When we begin to contemplate that all phenonema are empty,
we must begin step by step, not in one instant,
as in the cases of telling [the king] that the queen has died,
taming cattle, the [father reclaiming his] lost son,
and entering the ocean.[135] If we practice this way,
we can embark [on meditation on emptiness] easily, and there is no risk of turning back.
Someone who is scared [by emptiness] will either discard it or fall into a nihilistic view.

The *Compendium of Trainings* cites the *Meeting of Father and Son Sutra*,
[advising] that you should not put full reliance on others.[136]
That we should not solely rely on others means that
we must first reflect thoroughly on topics such as faith and the thought of awakening,
and after that study according to the explanations,
examining each topic in many ways,
just as it is said in the *Meeting of Father and Son Sutra*.[137]
If we treat the method aspect as the most important point
and apply the method practices in various ways,
every single hindrance will be removed through its respective method.
Knowing all these [hindrances and methods] to be like a mirage,
we must gain a clear understanding and enter this path.
We must not run around searching elsewhere.
Think, "I myself know where the path leads,
whatever else other people may say,"

like the three people from Kham who were not familiar with the way
but went where their staff pointed and arrived in Ü.[138]
"Not putting full reliance on others" means acting in this way.

When the aspect of method has become increasingly stable,
it is time to study wisdom. Thus, think like this:
When we look at actions and their results, we find that
actions, which are are illusory and correspond to nothing at all,
have results that are illusory and correspond to nothing at all, too.
There can be no doubt that they are of an illusory nature.
It has been taught that by understanding origination to be [empty]
  like the sky
we become free from birth through karmic causation;
so recognize all the suffering of entire cyclic-existence
as having sprung from an illusion,
just like the terror of being swept away by water in a dream.

Therefore we must strive to leave this illusion behind.
We must understand that all other sentient beings are like this, too.
To free all living beings, for whom we feel compassion,
from all illusion,
we must increase our efforts a hundredfold.
Moreover, we must also understand that
samsara, nirvana, [25] and the way of obtaining [nirvana] are
just like in the story of the magician who deceived the minister,
where the lake, the boat for crossing over it, and the ferryman[139]
are all without doubt nothing but an illusion;
in fact there is nothing that is not illusory.
With regard to this, both [sutra and tantra] have been cited as sources
  saying that
a knot made in the sky will be untied
by [recognizing] the true nature of the sky itself.[140]

Some, while on the stage of learning and reflection,
establish through reasoning that nothing has intrinsic existence,
yet when it is time to meditate, they claim to do so on "non-
  mentation" alone.
Done this way, [meditation] does not become the antidote,

for they are meditating on an emptiness that is not related [to their former reasoning].
Therefore, while meditating, we must examine everything thoroughly,
becoming accustomed to the idea that things are neither one nor many, or to the idea of dependent origination, or to similar things,
but we must also abide a little in a state free of discursiveness.
If we meditate in this way, it becomes a remedy against afflictions.
This is the correct way to meditate on wisdom
if we wish to follow our sole lord [Atiśa]
and practice the perfections.
When we have become used to the fact that the person is without a self,
then we embark on [meditation on the emptiness of all phenomena] in the same manner.

19. Why it is necessary to meditate on no-self

The main cause of samsara is ignorance,
and within that, seeing a self where there is no self is the primary factor.
If we wish the self to be happy in this lifetime, we will arrive in a bad rebirth.
If we wish the self to be happy in a future life, we will become a god or a human being.
If we wish the self to have the happiness of tranquility, we will reach the form realm or the formless realm.
[Only] when we reach [the understanding of] no-self will we reach nirvana.
Therefore we must try to subdue the view that we have a self.

Meditating on dependent origination
will remove wrong views like the eternalist and nihilist views.
[Wrong views are] not removed by merely enumerating [the links in the chain of dependent origination].
Rather think about this according to the three instructions—
Phenomena are neither eternal nor nonexistent but [arise] based on causes.
They are not eternal because they do not continue in the next life.

And they are not nonexistent because the next life is not free from them [since the results of karma persist].
They arise when the causes come together, and they are not created without an external cause.
If we constantly reflect like this,
wrong views like eternalism and nihilism will be removed,
and emptiness will be quickly grasped.

In the chapter on diverse topics from the *Precious Garland*,[141]
the meaning of the Madhyamaka system is expressed the following way:
Because it leaves the extremes of existence and nonexistence behind, it is a middle way.
Phenomena do not exist through a nature of their own.
Because there is no existence, there is also no nonexistence.
Therefore it is the middle way that leaves the extremes of existence and nonexistence behind. [26]
Alternatively, things do exist in a conditioned way so they are not nonexistent,
yet because they do not exist ultimately they are not existent [either].
Therefore it is the middle way that leaves the extremes of existence and nonexistence behind.
That is the meaning of "middle way."

Those who have become thoroughly purified
must understand the following:
The true nature of all phenomena
must be understood to be just one, not manifold.[142]
The Yogācāra-Madhyamaka school and others hold the view
that on the level of relative truth, there is also no manifoldness.
As for the self, all traditions from the Vaibhāṣika school on
likewise hold that it does exist even on the level of relative truth.

When we consider the self and the other and leave [the notion of a self] behind,
then the other cannot be ascertained either,
and therefore it cannot exist on the level of relative truth.

Our sole lord [Atiśa] himself was asked by someone
to explain how appearances are dispelled or not dispelled.
He did so by giving as examples the stories of
the magician who deceived the minister and
the vision of someone who is afflicted with an eye disease.
If relative truth and ultimate truth are like this,
how can we then say that [the wrong view] is dispelled or not dispelled?[143]
Because of this statement we must strive
to dispel the unclear view that is caused by [illusions that function like] a disease of the eyes.

Determining whether or not the appearances have truly been dispelled
cannot be accomplished just by becoming learned.
Only when we have gathered the accumulations and meditated in manifold ways
will we know for ourselves the truth as it really is.
Therefore we must apply ourselves earnestly to gathering the accumulations and to meditation.

Also, in the case of a beginner, it is necessary to help him see.
This is like the [story of the] water and the toxic vapor:[144]
Rely on the scriptures and on reasoning,
and by all means do not give in to the power of your [deluded] mind.
Always pursue that which leads beyond.
When we have gone beyond, then we can rest in our own [state of mind].[145]

20. How to meditate combining method and wisdom

The tradition of those who do not accept a gradual training
goes back to the tradition of Ārya Kāśyapa.[146]
Lord Setsun[147] said: "I know that this was said [by Kamalaśīla],
and I know myself that this tradition is good.
Meditating only briefly
or not meditating at all is no basis for the Mahayana.
Teachers like Kamalaśīla have said that
giving this [wrong] system up completely
and being endowed with method is the right path."

Through wisdom alone we are fettered to nirvana,
and then we will again be fettered to samsara.[148]
Without method, no true wisdom can arise, [27]
and therefore it is essential that [wisdom] be combined with method.
At the same time, method without wisdom will again lead to samsara as well.
Wisdom cuts through the fetters
and so it leads to liberation. Increasing it again [with the aid of method], it will become greater.
So [buddhahood] is not achieved through either alone,
or when the accumulations are incomplete, as in the painter's case.[149]
We reach buddhahood [only] when all the necessary causes come together.

Regarding the fact that [the qualities of a buddha] are caused by corresponding kinds of merit,
it is said that he does not abide in the two [samsara and nirvana]
because on the causal stage he contemplates the defects of samsara, and because of [his] compassion.
In other words, the way of the Mahayana is not to abide in [samsara or nirvana]
because one discerns the characteristics [of samsara][150] and one is endowed with compassion.
Then it is natural that one will not abide [in them] at the stage of result either.[151]
Therefore when we recollect the Buddha,
[we must understand that] he has performed limitless acts of merit.
In this manner, the cause and the result are commensurate.
The way of the bodhisattvas is
to abide neither in a state where they create the causes for becoming accustomed to emptiness
but are not compassionate,
nor in a state where they produce the causes of merit
within samsara but cannot find nirvana.

This is how bodhisattvas abide
neither in samsara nor nirvana:
they clearly see the faults of samsara
and are also compassionate and unable [to feel indifferent],

and therefore they abide in neither.
This is like reaching a city in the wilderness
and remembering your son when putting your foot on the threshold;
or like fleeing from a burning house
and going back when thinking of the children who are still inside;
or like acting like a mother whose son who has fallen into a cesspit.[152]
Acting in these ways
bodhisattvas remain in samsara
but understand the true nature [of phenomena] and are therefore not defiled by the faults [of samsara].
Out of compassion, they do not leave samsara behind.
Thus, bodhisattvas do not abide in either of the two [states, samsara or nirvana].

They are driven by uncontrollable compassion,
and therefore they combine [the two aspects of wisdom and method] even during absorption in emptiness.
Also when they practice method after their meditation sessions,
they know the true nature [of phenomena] and combine [the two aspects].
Whatever good deeds bodhisattvas do,
they accomplish it through combining the two.

During insight meditation, [they know] it is most important to meditate
without appearances, like the [empty] sky.
When they have investigated [both emptiness and appearances], they will quickly reach certainty.
After [the meditation session], while not experiencing this state,
they gather the accumulations through various means, driven by compassion.

When emptiness is filled with the essence of compassion
and attitudes such as loving kindness are free from the perception [of agent, object, and action],
they remain attached when they act because of their compassion,
even though they meditate on emptiness as the true basis.

Through this practice, [bodhisattvas] reach [the state that bears]
the [respective] names.[153]

When method and wisdom are not combined, [28]
the two kinds of no-self are not understood properly.
Even the śrāvakas recognize that phenomena have no self,
as the teacher Candrakīrti has said.[154]
The scriptural source says that from the seventh bodhisattva level on
it is no longer possible to be carried away by the attitude of the
śrāvakas.[155]
Thus, if there were nothing but the selflessness of the person,
what need is there to worry about those on the seventh level?
When the path of seeing has arisen, we must distinguish
and therefore understand the two kinds of no-self.
If we are then carried away by the attitude of the śrāvakas,
this is the result of not being connected to the method aspect.

Recalling that beings are tormented by things
that do not exist, we must
keep them in our minds,
and in this way always strive for our own and for their benefit.
The time for doing this is right now.

When explaining the short [treatise on] truth according to the
middle way,[156]
[Potowa said that] Lord Atiśa's teachers Serlingpa and Śāntipa
upheld the true-aspectarian and false-aspectarian Mind Only views
respectively.[157]
Our lord [adhered to] the middle way of complete nonabiding,
which is also referred to as Yogācāra-Madhyamaka.
Serlingpa was deeply astonished and
said again and again: "Someone like you is very wise indeed!
To comprehend a view like this is wondrous."
Thereupon [Atiśa] became further pleased with it.
When Lama Śāntipa explained wisdom,
he refuted what is found in [Haribhadra's] Madhyamaka one by one.[158]
Saying "My Madhyamaka was made even clearer,"

Lord Atiśa relied firmly on the Yogācāra-Madhyamaka
and believed the system of Master Candrakīrti to be the greatest,
and when he was asked why, he said:
"This is what Avadhūtipa stated, and I hold the same view."
Geshé [Drom]tönpa upheld the system of *Entering the Middle Way*.
There is no difference at all within the ultimate truth.
The others split it up into two kinds and so on—
into the nominal and the absolute ultimate[159]
and into that which is free from the two illusions and the view of complete nonabiding.
These views are not the truth.
Therefore examinations according to the inferior theories—
those that are different from the view of complete nonabiding—
and [the misconception of] the moon in the water and so on, regard things
from the perspective of a mistaken relative truth, and [in this respect] there is no difference among them.[160]
Correct relative truth is that which makes the mind happy as long as it has not been examined,
and where origination and destruction do appear.[161]
All the things like action and result, the thought of awakening, and so forth,
are no [misconceptions], so we must be sure not to reject them.
If [relative truth] did not exist, we would not reach the top of the house of right [understanding].[162]
Therefore we must strive for the thought of awakening and so forth
and try to put it into actual practice.
This is the instruction concerning [correct] view and practice. [29]

21. Explanation of the fruit of combining method and wisdom

"When conditions cease their continuity,
[the effects] do not arise even on the conventional level."[163]
When [Potowa] explained this stanza, he said the following:
The commentators explain this passage in a different manner,
for if this is the case, what is the difference [between this view]
and the view of the śrāvakas about nirvana?[164]
Therefore [the passage] must be explained like this:

If we want to know how sentient beings can be
the cause for a buddha to appear [in the world], it is like this:
When he first generates the thought of awakening, he promises
not to leave all sentient beings behind but to save them and so forth.
Therefore a buddha cannot pass into [final] nirvana
until every single sentient being has been rescued.
This is exactly what the tradition of our sole lord maintains.
An illusion-like continuity of wisdom does remain [for a buddha]
but not its subsequent stage of attainment;
nonetheless, because of his past [vow] he acts as if he does possess this.
This is in accordance with the earlier statement [that the buddhas will not enter into final nirvana until all beings have been liberated].
Understood thus, as the teacher Śāntideva maintains,
one could also uphold the view that the continuity of wisdom has ceased.[165]
First he is driven by compassion, the thought of awakening, and so forth,
then he sustains all sentient beings,
and, having achieved the power to benefit them in every respect,
if he actualizes the diamond-like [meditative state],
[the continuity of thoughts] will come to an end.
But even then [his activities for] the welfare of sentient beings will come about.
This is just like a Garuḍa charm [that remains potent] even after the death [of the healer].[166]
The beings themselves are the cause for this fact;
and on their part there is no end to those who need to be tamed.

Therefore, when we begin our practice,
we must support other beings with loving kindness and compassion
and gather immeasurable accumulations of merit and wisdom,
and when it comes to the [time when we attain] the fruit, the benefit for sentient beings will occur in any case,
whether [the continuum of wisdom] ceases or continues,
and whether or not we reach the subsequent stage of attainment.
Also when we pray for this, we will receive the respective blessing.

The Buddhist scriptures contain various views.
As has been predicted by the Buddha himself,
we must rely on the tradition of Master Nāgārjuna.
Our sole lord [Atiśa] too takes this to be most important.
When Atiśa saw all the small tools in Tibet,
such as a "mouse thorn," a "pig's head,"[167] or the fire lighter,
he would say: "How come the master [Nāgārjuna] did not invent these!"[168]
Thus he viewed Nāgārjuna to be the master of all knowledge.
He is the special regent for us here on Jambudvīpa,
so we must regard his word as paramount.

7. Enhancing the Conditions for Practice

The life of a renunciate[169]

[When Tsangpa Gyiltön was asked] how to live on alms, [30]
[he said:] Have modest wishes and your mind will not torment you with desires.
Like the sun and the moon, roam here and there,
not clinging to one spot and not staying in one place.
Do not have a single donor or a single companion,
and never present your neck to anyone.[170]
When you select a benefactor who provides your food for a while,
you should not choose one who is too powerful or a habitual liar,
an immoral person, a self-righteous one,
or a leper,[171] but someone with inner discipline,
and he who has [these qualities] in excess is excellent. Having examined his qualities
you may select him, but even then, do not stay long,
and if it is for a longer period, it should not be more than one year: one summer and one winter.
You must leave at the right time,[172] for when it lasts too long, the two of you will become too close, [so that]
you will become a prisoner, and [your minds] will be alike.[173] But even when you rely on [a good benefactor],
do not be oversensitive; if you do, anger will arise.
Remember the words about the difficulties of enduring suffering.
The benefactor should not be the manager of a small monastery,
although this may be alright in a bigger monastic community.
Otherwise you will be powerless against what happens,
and if it goes wrong, disrespect will not be far behind.
It is not meritorious to receive more and more material goods,
but turning the mind toward the topics [of Buddhism] is meritorious.

We know this, but we do not commit ourselves to the idea.
When we have the wrong wishes, it indicates a flaw in our attitude.
When someone is compassionate toward us,
we are pleased, and when he remains like that,
we think, "In him is the Dharma; it is not elsewhere."
Contemplating the pointless suffering of samsara
makes us practice the Dharma, and we are told: "We must endure suffering
and risk our lives [for this goal]!" However, we need not [necessarily] do this.
So we need not flee this minimal suffering [we endure as renunciates].[174]
Just as it is said that a hero [sometimes backs away], even if we take three steps backward
when we feel inclined to flee,
this does not mean that we will not achieve the merit of generosity.[175]
We need not suffer long, and if it is long, it is [still only, say,] three years.
It is very important to avoid the extremes in everything.
Someone who makes the Dharma the most important thing, who avoids doing things that are not beneficial,
and who remains sitting there [without doing business] will naturally become poor.
When you are [a little] hungry, you will not die from it.
Those with minimal desires are worshiped by gods and men.
We must be capable of entering the practice [of a renunciate]; [otherwise] we should not so vow.
We should estimate [our abilities] step by step[176] and enter [the path] gradually.
If we are very capable, then we do not heed popular opinion.
The spiritual mentor [Dromtönpa] said that we should stay neither too close to
nor too far from a teacher who is fully endowed with all good qualities.
Using the method of a donkey, we should not be too eager but should relax.
We must practice in all kinds of ways: that is very important.

When we meet difficulties, we should talk with old people and ask
them for advice.
There is also a story about the two sons where one of them received
wealth as his share.[177] Old people are experienced,
and it is said: "When there is great need, ask someone who can give
advice!"
Furthermore, if you confide in someone, the matter will become clear
to you.
There is also a story about the king who had an eye disease.[178] [31]
Those with little knowledge talk; those with great knowledge ask
others.
The latter [i.e., asking others] is greater than the former.

Those who wish for liberation with all their hearts
leave their birthplaces and those who are close to them.
They must stay in an appropriate place and constantly rely on the
spiritual mentor,
avoid all turmoil, and make their minds accord with moral discipline;
then liberation is not far away for them.
Those who practice like this must take a low position,
wear ragged garments, and eat poor food,
endure harsh words, drink water, and take all kinds of hardship upon
themselves.
Those who live like this will achieve all [that has been described]
above.
But if they want to turn away from this way of life, they are far from
[liberation].

22. How to create favorable conditions for practicing the Mahayana in future lives

If we wish to become liberated for the sake of all sentient beings,
we won't be able to do so unless we are endowed with the four
wheels.[179]
If we have not striven to create their causes in the past,
they will not be complete in our present life.
We will not be able [to complete the Buddhist path] in our future life
if they are not there,

so we must now try to create the causes for obtaining them.
The basis is that we strive in this life
for a suitable environment [in which to practice] and so on,
always accompany our practice with aspiration prayers,
and accumulate merit. Then we will obtain all [the four wheels in the future].
The most important element of a favorable environment is the good spiritual mentor.
In this respect, relying on a good friend now
and gaining good qualities through a beneficial practice
creates the cause for meeting a noble person [again in the future].
That we take our present masters as masters
is mainly caused by such behavior [in previous lives].
When Gomön asked, this is what the spiritual mentor [Dromtönpa] said:
"If you have not paid respect to your former teacher from whom you heard the teaching and so on
and have not pleased him,
and he is currently not present so that you cannot please him now,
there is a very good method:
Because all teachers are the same with respect to their dharmakāya,
you must please the teachers who are
currently present with great effort.
Then the defilement through your former actions will be removed.
If you also try to create the causes
by making a prayer for meeting him again [in the future]
and have practiced this prayer,
this will be the most essential cause [for meeting your teacher]."
Saying that [achieving the four wheels] depends on the aspiration prayer means that
if we adhere to the four wheels carefully in our present life,
this will create the accumulations for truly attaining the four in the future,
and then all good qualities and factors [for liberation] will be ours.

When Sherap Kyap had offered some tea
and asked [Potowa] for a very profound teaching, [32]
[Potowa said that] it is not right to remain in samsara forever,

but as long as we have not turned away from it, we are also unable
to leave it behind without aid.
The condition for turning away from it is that we are endowed with
the four wheels.
Out of these, the place should not be merely partially suitable
but should be a place fit to achieve
what accords with the vast Buddhist teachings. In such a place, there
are no unfavorable conditions at all
and all the favorable conditions are present.
The noble person is one who possesses six or seven qualities—
being learned and so on.[180]
Our present teacher must be treasured like our own eyeballs,
that's the cause for finding [a noble teacher in the future].
Our aspiration prayer is first to establish a firm basis
such as faith and the thought of awakening; then to be able to listen
and to understand [the meaning],
and finally to be able to really embark on meditation.
The cause for reaching such a state [in the future] is our efforts
to train the mind in this present life.
This is the great method that helps us fulfill [our prayer].
The accumulation of merit is the cause for everything.
With this, samsara will quickly be left behind.
Recognizing that it is not enough that we ourselves leave it behind
but
that this is also necessary for others, we avert it for the sake of all.
When we do this, we take them with us along the way,
and gathering [beings] through the four means of attraction,[181]
we guide them all—
for this we must dedicate [our merit].

The most important aspect of a suitable place that possesses the five
qualities
is the company of good people who are virtuous and who live in
accord with the right view.
We may have up to two or three companions;
but when we stay with a whole crowd, this is an unstable
environment.

We should settle down with the sutras, without trying to get additional personal instructions,
and constantly train the mind in the practices already begun.
If we act like this, we may acquire some competence [in the Buddhist teachings].

Staying in a suitable place means
a place where the three trainings, driven by the thought of awakening,
will grow when we stay there;
and a companion means someone with whom these qualities will increase.
Whatever makes us turn back from them is not a proper place or companion.

Nowadays we are on the threshold between light and darkness;
therefore everything depends on what we do now.
We must not pin our hopes on the conventional reality of this life
but must apply ourselves to the achievements of the future.
Moreover, whatever of the four wheels is achieved
will contain all the future achievements [because it creates the causes for these].
We must pursue a life that is not contingent on
[other] teachers, students, and the like—
and how much less on other [circumstances]!
Moreover, if we wish to achieve the great seal (*mahāmudrā*) in this lifetime,
we must practice accordingly.

When [Phodrang Dingpa] was teaching, Jayajñāna asked
why his mind and the Dharma had not become one even though he had devoted himself [to his teacher] for a long time,
and what he could do to make them one.
[The teacher said:] "The best method for making them one is
to reflect [on what you have been told] and to reflect with respect
for a long time without interruption. [33]
Furthermore, if you reflect while the favorable conditions are there—
the companion, the spiritual mentor, and the [appropriate] place—
[your mind and the Dharma will become one], that is certain.

Moreover, gather the accumulations in all possible ways;
this is how you make them one."
The sign that they have become one is that [the Dharma] is born in our minds.
At first this is a state that can change [for better or for worse], but then it will grow stronger,
and finally we will have reached buddhahood.
We should know that these are
the causes and the characteristics of making them one.

23. How to avert unfavorable conditions that would create an obstacle

If there is a great flood of negativity in our minds,
this will prevent the wholesome factors from arising.
In particular, if we have done a [harmful] deed, the result of which we cannot avoid,
we must quickly extinguish these [negativities] through the four powers.[182]
We must apply a special antidote
and imagine that it will extinguish the negativities.
The object of purification can have the very form [of a monk]
or he can also be dressed in white [like a layperson].
When he has the form [of a monk], we must renew our vows in his presence
and confess the deed before nightfall.
If the night has already begun,
we must restore [our vows or moral integrity] in front of ourselves.
How could it be in front of another person?
If there is a root of faith, like the thought of awakening,
then even if one of the four root transgressions[183] has occurred,
it can easily be removed with the aid of the four powers.
But if [such a root of faith] is not there, the method for removing it is destroyed.
When we purify [our negative deeds] we should not make it contingent on other factors.

The right order of applying the four powers is the following:
First we must develop remorse, then we remain resolute,
then we rely on the basis, and then we apply the antidote [of good deeds].
The right order of explaining [the four powers] is different from this.

When the Buddha's teachings decline,
the pleasure in harmful deeds grows stronger
and the pleasure in beneficial deeds gets weaker.
Therefore those who undertake things that are contrary to the Dharma
gain great profit, live long, and live without harm,
while for those who engage in the Dharma, it is just the opposite.
This is the nature of things, and therefore those entering the Dharma should not be discouraged;
this is what spiritual mentor [Drom]tönpa told us.
Because this is how it is, we should set our minds on the antidotes.

When [Yagepa] was staying at the hermitage of Entsa Trawo,
[he explained that] the extent of our merit
does not depend on whether we have donated many or few material gifts;
it depends on whether or not a correct view
has arisen in our minds.
If our minds are capable of what the teacher teaches us,
this will generate immeasurable merit.
Moreover, if we live an ascetic life, the merit will be even greater. [34]
We must know that if the material goods increase
but [our minds and way of life] are not appropriate, the merit will diminish.
If we aspire after the wrong option among these two,
we must realize that this indicates our own incompetence.

The proof that the Dharma is true is
to see that tantra, sorcery, and the like
cause all factors to multiply,
and therefore we must consider it most important to practice without any doubt.
We will immediately see the proof that [the Dharma] is not false.

For those with lion-like confidence[184]
who can eat or drink anything,
there are no restrictions with respect to where they stay and so on.
Those who do not have this mental strength
must be advised where to stay:
They must not stay in places that are
inhabited by noxious nonhuman spirits and the like.
They should not stay in one region nor dwell [permanently] in one place,
and they should not promise their companion or benefactor to remain with them for a long time
but only for a short while.
When seeking a place to sleep, it may be on rocky ground in a remote place,
and when we rest we may be squatting on a flat boulder.

The doors to liberation are inconceivable,
and a single person cannot enter them all.
Therefore other ways have been taught,
but we should not abandon the way that we ourselves have entered,
and we should not abuse or despise it.

When [Potowa] was staying at Nyenpo, he gave Gomchö
the example of the words of the benefactor from Rimo:
"Although some may be learned or virtuous or good at contemplating,
they may not be wise. Those who do not plunge into the stream [of worldly activities]
but remain secluded [from the world]—they possess [the Dharma], that's what I think."

The proper view of sentient beings[185]

Whether we follow the Mahayana or the secret mantra,
we must never despise sentient beings,
humans in particular,
and never treat them with disrespect
or denigrate them and talk about their faults,

because this would cause great harm.
As an antidote within Mahayana practice,
we regard sentient beings as our fathers and mothers on the level of relative truth,
and as being identical with emptiness on the level of ultimate truth,
and therefore we treat them with respect.
As an antidote within tantric practice,
we regard ourselves [and others] as deities, and therefore as objects of respect.

Because it is normal for sentient beings to have flaws,
we should never think badly of them.
When we see even the slightest virtue in others,
we should be full of admiration and respect for them,
because this is very rare among living beings.

We must look at our own minds first
if we wish to speak about our own virtues and about other people's faults.
If it is out of a higher motivation [to help others], [35]
we should speak; if it is not out of a pure motivation, we should remain [silent] like a log,[186]
particularly when we are afflicted by disturbing emotions.

In the *Question of Candraprabha the Youth*
within the passage on the method for giving up harm [from the *Compendium of Trainings*],[187] it is stated
that we must keep in mind that even though beings commit harmful deeds such as transgressing moral discipline,
they have the essence of awakening
and follow the teachings of the Buddha in many ways.
We should also remember that [these good qualities] make their way [toward buddhahood] shorter.
If they are old, we should honor them through respect and material gifts.
We should neither imitate them nor despise them.
We must keep in mind that if we imitate them, both will get hurt,

and therefore we should neither cling to them with our minds nor
scrutinize their faults.

With respect to the passage on people being like mangos,[188]
the same point has been stressed
both by sutras and by doctrinal works.
If we do not examine the faults in others, no damage will arise;
if we do, the damage can be manifold. Therefore we should not
examine them.
If we are not impartial and talk about [other people's] faults and the
like,
[it is as in the example where someone said:] "Even if I will be born a
hundred times as a camel—isn't it [possible to escape this]?"[189]
We should examine ourselves and not obsess about others;
otherwise we will go to hell,
and would we deserve anything different?

When we avoid harming others
we must take particular care to control our bodies.
[This is necessary] when keeping the benefit of others in mind,
and especially in the case of bodhisattvas.
In this respect it is vital
that we always regard everyone as a teacher.[190]
Persons who wish to avoid harming others
must discern their own faults
but must be impartial towards others and not examine what their
faults are like.
When our intentions are not mingled [with selfish thoughts], then
we may make them turn away [from their faults].
Otherwise, it is as in the case of the Thargyal.[191]

The appropriate view of the Dharma[192]

In the passage on the harm caused by the taint of rejecting the Dharma,[193]
it is said that all doctrines are contained in the Mahayana,
so we should not revile them but pay respect to them equally.
The scriptures speak about a difference between the Hinayana and
the Mahayana.

They declare the transgressions of moral discipline to be either seven or ten.[194]
The purpose [of the different vehicles] is benefit for oneself and for others.
There are differences between the schools
both in terms of the view, for instance regarding impermanence or emptiness,
and in terms of the fruit, for instance whether nirvana means extinction [of suffering] or whether [suffering] has been calmed from the very beginning,
but although there are great and small ways of understanding,
there is no difference in the Dharma itself.
Therefore we must pay equal respect to all schools
because rejecting the Dharma is a serious taint.

All vehicles are a supporting basis for the Mahayana,
and there is nothing that does not belong to the path of the bodhisattvas.[195]
Because sentient beings have different minds, the Dharma has been taught as three [vehicles].
Like an island that is created magically for the weary,
they have been taught as resting-places [for those getting weary on the long path to liberation].
Because they lead to permanent liberation and the stage of an all-knowing buddha [36]
we must never revile the doctrines and those teaching them
but treat them with the greatest respect,
since there is no greater fault than abandoning the Dharma.

In the passage on having harmed a bodhisattva,[196]
it is said that when we have done harm to a certain object or person,
we must pay respect to and ask for forgiveness from that very same object or person.
When we act like this, it is easy to purify the trespass.
It is the same even when we have [committed a transgression] concerning the Three Jewels.

24. How to proceed in the preservation of benefit after having averted the obstacles

Thus beginners [on the path of a bodhisattva] must primarily
enable their own minds to mature
and not make benefitting others the most important thing just yet.
They must live as it is said in the *Sutra Encouraging Nobler Intention*.
In their minds there is nothing but the benefit of sentient beings,
but with their body and speech they do not yet embark [on the full bodhisattva practice].
When they have not achieved the supernatural kinds of knowledge and try to work for the benefit of sentient beings,
they are like a blind man who shoots an arrow when he is told that there is a deer.
Therefore we should never act too hastily.

We are all like people who live praising sandalwood [without possessing it].
If we don't want to live praising the sandalwood
but want to obtain the sandalwood ourselves,
then we must give up just praising the sandalwood
and must constantly strive and search for it.
Those who don't have the supernatural kinds of knowledge
cannot achieve the benefit of sentient beings, like the blind man shooting at the deer.
As long as we just act out of enthusiasm, our work for the benefit of beings
will mostly be fruitless, as the scriptures say.
Also our sole lord has said that
once we have acquired the supernatural knowledges, we will [be able to help others],
but as long as we haven't, we will be of no use to them.
Nowadays we are not truly able
to accomplish the benefit of living beings, just as in the example given above.
If we want to accomplish it, we must try to
ensure that the teachings of the Buddha remain in the world for a long time.

And because this depends on the monastic community,
we must make the monastic community last if we can.[197]
If we cannot do this, we must guard our own minds
in accord with our vows for the sake of sentient beings.
If we live according to the four instructions from the *Sutra Encouraging Nobler Intention*,[198]
then, as beginner bodhisattvas, we will work for the benefit of beings [by making our own minds more mature];
acting otherwise is simply to deceive ourselves.
This is what the passage on the four means of attraction says.

In the passage from the *Compendium of Trainings* on seeking what accumulates the right conditions,[199]
it is said that there are three [duties]: maintaining the Dharma, protecting it, and preserving it.
The first is that we maintain the Dharma in our minds
through the three trainings and by listening, reflecting, and meditating on it.
The second is that we protect from harm the persons who maintain the Dharma. [37]
To assist them by all possible means is the third.
Everyone is able to protect and preserve it,
no matter whether their abilities are great or small.
This is like the begging children
who were able to protect the hut.[200]
In former times it was persons such as kings who protected and preserved [the Dharma];
now this task has become ours,
and we must try to fulfill the three duties in various ways.
If, however, we are not able to do so, this is no fault.
We are not allowed to preserve or protect [the Dharma] by methods that are contrary to the Dharma.
Leaving others to ruin and destruction although we have the power [to help them]
is not even allowed for the śrāvakas.
All this has been said about those who are not able [to fully act like a bodhisattva].

The passage on harm done by the evil spirits[201]
is a secret instruction, but we now proclaim it in the marketplace:
There are two kinds of evil spirits: nonhuman spirits and imagined spirits.
We must give up hope and fear and become as unshakable as a mountain;
then these two kinds will not appear.
If we need to drive them back, we must first summon them.
Then, there are three remedies against the first kind: the recollection [of the Three Jewels],
loving kindness and compassion, and [seeing them] as an illusion or [as empty] like the sky.
Against the second kind, the remedy is to recognize
that they are fabrications of our minds; we need nothing but this.

The passage on seeing them as an illusion[202]
is also a secret instruction, but we now proclaim it in the marketplace:
When persons who meditate have
wonderful or really good
or excellent meditation experiences,
they must not become proud. If they do, the demons will carry them away.
If this has happened, they must first invite [the demons]
and then understand that the appearances are illusory.
By this antidote the hostile side will be conquered;
we must understand this to be like
an illusory king who conquers another [illusory] king. That's the instruction.

The statement that nothing is to be feared except mind[203]
means that our own imagination is an obstacle.[204]
If it were not there, what could others do to us?!
The teacher Sheyung was afraid of a broom
and cried out in fear.[205]
When someone from Thugar was digging out a boulder,
another person put a fish [underneath it], and both were stupefied.
The servant of a meditation master made a mask of wheat dough to scare him;

and there are many more similar cases.
Therefore our own imagination is an obstacle.
If imagination is absent and we have become courageous,
nothing will be able to harm us.
Whatever appears for us, be it pleasant or unpleasant,
we should think that it is similar to the appearance of a human being.
Thus our sole lord was not even afraid of a being with a horse's head.
We should not cling to the fabrications of our own minds.
Whatever appears [when we meditate],
we must first of all give up hope and fear,
because harm is near when we are possessed by hope or fear.[206]
It is as [in the saying that] the wind enters wherever there is a hole.[207] [38]
Like the old monk from Shangshung,[208] we will be ridiculed by everyone
if it is easy to find an opportunity to do so. If there is no opportunity, who would do that?!
Therefore we must first give up all hopes and fears.
When we have left all weak and unstable states of mind behind,
we must next regard all appearances as being the mind itself,
train ourselves in the thought of awakening endowed with love and compassion,
keep a pure discipline with respect to our vows,
and gather the accumulations in many ways.
Then no hindrances will appear,
and even if they do, they will quickly be appeased.

If our own minds are free from defects,
the evil spirits cannot cause obstacles by threatening us and the like.
Therefore they first make us gain some profit,
and then they can produce causes [for wrong attitudes] like desire or hatred.
From these [wrong attitudes] delusion grows, and then our minds will be scorched
and we will necessarily fall into bad states like hell.
This is how the evil spirits create obstacles.
It is like the way the sun burns a forest:
The sun itself does not really burn it,

but when its rays fall on a lens made of glass,
flames will blaze up
and eventually incinerate the entire forest. Similarly,
our wholesome factors can be burned up by the evil spirits,
and thus our minds must be free from defects
so that the evil spirits cannot afflict us; that's the instruction.

According to the passage on giving up fear when we are in the wilderness,[209]
no fear will arise when we meditate with the power of analytical discrimination
on the two kinds of selflessness [of the person and of phenomena].
Then we will not be afflicted by obstacles.
Although this has been explained to be the antidote,
we may find ourselves unable to produce [this attitude] in our minds.
Then what has been taught as an antidote
will not really help us.
This should not make us doubt the instructions.
We must know that it is a defect of our own minds.
Therefore we must gather the accumulations, remove the obscurations,
pray to the teacher, and so on in order to become more capable;
and when we have become capable through these methods, [the analytical method outlined above] will become an antidote without fail.

When we have removed the obstacles,
we need not seek for any other remedy than
the mental fruits of whatever wholesome practice we have done.
When [we experience obstructions in our meditation], we must apply the very same practices:
recollecting the Buddha, loving kindness and compassion,
and reflecting on the form of a meditation deity or on emptiness.
Whatever [deities or spirits] appear in our perception, we should not rejoice,
even if they preach the Dharma,
but be unwavering in [our meditation on] emptiness.
If we [apply methods] like these, nothing will afflict us.

The method of discerning whether [an apparition] is a deity or an evil spirit
is to meditate on emptiness; if it becomes more distinct, [it is a deity, whereas]
if it is the other kind of being and you meditate [on emptiness], it will quickly vanish.
This is how you can distinguish between the two.
Whether the afflictions fade or increase in your mind
when you see them, is another way to examine what they are.

The spiritual mentor [Dromtönpa] said to Yungchung: [39]
"You are the youngest in our group.
Some meditation masters say
when they have reached the age of eighty,
'I have seen the face of the Buddha in person,'
and their delusions increase instead of getting smaller.
You must know that when this happens, they are carried away by the demons.
We must dispel the face of the Buddha when we see it
and understand that it is just like a dream.
Some say, 'I have reached meditative absorption,'
and their delusions increase, just as in the former case.
[Others say,] 'I perceive the right view [of emptiness],' and thinking little of
the law of deeds and their results, commit bad deeds.
We must understand that in this case they have developed a wrong view.
The sign of a right view is
that we know phenomena to be [empty] like the sky.
Nevertheless, to perceive [this emptiness correctly],
we do not think little of the relative truth of cause and effect.
For people who have not seen the truth,
even a small deed will have results.
Therefore the old layperson [Dromtön] has told you this.
You should also tell this to someone in the future."
This is what he said, and this is what we must know.

25. The need to gather the accumulations through the ten religious actions[210] *and so forth*

If we wish to be fully endowed with all these good qualities
and become free from all faults,
we must gather the accumulations in various ways.
Whatever [meritorious deed] we do,
we must constantly strive to do nothing but this,
as if this meritorious deed were the only thing we do.
If we do not work to accumulate merit,
but just do this and that—whatever occurs to us—
this will not prepare us for anything,
and we will be unable to apply any of the methods that might help us.
Therefore it is very important to become firm in accumulating [merit].

According to the chapter on inclinations from the *Ornament of Mahayana Sutras*,[211]
we must gain merit by all possible means.
Someone who has gathered merit will achieve all good qualities,
just as the king of Brisha did,[212]
and the teacher Prajñākaragupta,
who adopted the view of the logical system of Dignāga
and attained the understanding of the truth according to the Yogācāra-Madhyamaka system.
There was also Avalokitavrata,[213] who through merely seeing
the middle way view of Nāgārjuna,
changed his non-Buddhist view and adopted the Great Madhyamaka;
these and other events have been described.
Therefore we must strive to remove the obscurations and to gain merit. [40]
We should also think about the stories of Cūḍapantha and Svāgata.[214]

Also, yogis must pay respect to the noble monastic community,
the field for gathering merit that will protect them from obstacles.
If they do not have the necessary means,[215] the Sangha can also appoint [a single monk to receive the gifts].

If they have honored a single monk, it is as if they have honored all of them,
as long as they have invited everyone and the Sangha has appointed someone [as their representative].

If the meditative concentrations and the formless meditative attainments
do not arise if we have not gathered immeasurable accumulations,
how much more do we need immeasurable accumulations
to gain a mind so contrary to the mundane.

The path of tantra[216]

You may wonder whether the path of secret mantra
is shorter than the path of the perfections.
If someone whose mind is free from ordinary conceptions
practices them [without looking back]
—the way a bird escapes from a net
or a man escapes from prison—
then the path of secret mantra and the path of the perfections
are equal in length: both of them are very fast.

The sole lord himself said that the path of secret mantra
and the path of the perfections are equal in length.
When it was stated that one of them is shorter, it was said with a certain intention,
and it was intended for certain personalities.[217]
In reality the path of the perfections can be shorter,
as we can see in the story of Sadāprarudita,
because in the beginning he heard a voice speaking about the path of accumulation
and understood it before he had attained the contemplation of a constant stream of Dharma.
In less than a year, he traveled 500 [leagues],[218]
and within this [brief period of] time reached the path of seeing.[219]
Therefore they are the same when the ordinary conceptions have been abandoned;
the two paths are equal in length.

If there is a master who has the necessary qualities
and a disciple who is a suitable recipient,
the disciple will please the master, and the master will give him tantric initiations and practice instructions,
and if he practices accordingly, he holds buddhahood in his hand.
But if he does it in a wrong way, it will bring him to the very bottom of hell.
Moreover, if we follow the words of our spiritual mentor, the sole lord,
we cannot give preference to the path of secret mantra [over the path of the perfections]
[because teachers] with the necessary qualities are extremely rare.

26. Brief epilogue and dedication of merit

This is a record of the instructions of my teacher,
compiled by me in chapters.
I wrote it down because I wished to remember it myself,
and because I was afraid to forget it. I intended to keep it hidden,
but then I did not want to be stingy with Buddhist teachings.
However, it should strictly be kept secret because if it falls into the hands
of people who are without blessing or who are not suitable recipients,
they might abuse it and accumulate the bad karma of rejecting the Dharma.
If I have made mistakes, I beg those who hold this book in their hands
to forgive me.
May the little merit that I have gained
by making this record of the instructions of my teacher [41]
help me and all other sentient beings
to travel the Mahayana path and reach buddhahood.

The virtuous deed of recording the instructions of my teacher—beginning, middle, and end—is completed.

Part II

Ornament of Precious Liberation

A Wish-Fulfilling Gem of Sublime Dharma

Gampopa (1079–1153)

Translated by Ken Holmes
and edited by Thupten Jinpa

Author's Preface

[45] I prostrate to Youthful Mañjuśrī.[1]

Having paid homage to the buddhas, their spiritual heirs, the sublime Dharma,
and also to the gurus who are the root of all these,
I will now write, through the gracious kindness of revered Milarepa,
this *Gem of Precious Dharma, a Wish-Fulfilling Jewel* for both my own and others' benefit.

Generally, phenomena can be subsumed into the two classes of samsara and nirvana. That which is known as *samsara* is, by nature, emptiness, taking the form of illusions and characterized by suffering. That which is known as *nirvana* is also, by nature, emptiness, taking the form of the exhaustion, then disappearance, of the illusions and characterized by liberation from all suffering.

Who is deluded by these illusions of samsara? All sentient beings of its three realms.

On what are the illusions based? The illusions are projected onto emptiness.

What causes the delusion? It occurs through great ignorance.

In what way do they come to be deluded? They come to be deluded with regard to the sphere of experiences of the six classes of beings.

What would be a suitable metaphor for such an illusion? This resembles the illusion experienced in one's sleep and dreams.

Since when have these illusions been happening? Since time without beginning.

What is wrong with them? One experiences nothing but suffering.

When will the delusion become pristine awareness? It does so when highest enlightenment is reached.[2] Those who think that illusion may dissolve on its own should be aware that samsara is renowned for being endless.

Having, in the above way, carefully considered samsara in terms of it being an illusion, the extent of its suffering, the length of its time, and that there is no self-release, strive in all earnestness and with great diligence, from this very moment onward, to attain unsurpassable enlightenment.

What exactly is needed to strive so? The synopsis[3] is:

> **Prime cause, basis, condition, means, results, and activity:**
> **by these six general key terms should the wise know peerless enlightenment.**

This means that one needs to know (1) the **prime cause** for highest enlightenment, (2) the beings whose existence forms a **basis** for achieving it, (3) the **condition** that incites [46] that attainment, (4) the **means** by which it is attained, (5) the **results** of it being attained, and (6) the enlightened **activity** once there has been such attainment. These will be explained, in the above order, as being the following:

> The prime cause is buddha nature
> The basis is a most precious human existence.
> The condition is the Dharma master.
> The means is the Dharma master's instruction.
> The results are the bodies of perfect buddhahood.
> The activity is to nonconceptually fulfill the welfare of beings.

This is merely an outline of the main structure of this text. What follows is a detailed explanation of each point.

1. Buddha Nature

I. The Prime Cause

THE LINE "The prime cause is buddha nature" states the following. As mentioned above, you need to gain freedom from the deluded nature of samsara and to attain highest enlightenment. However, you might well wonder, "Even if we or other ordinary people[4] like us were to try very hard, how could we ever possibly attain enlightenment?" In truth, anyone who practices with great effort cannot fail to reach enlightenment. Why? Because all forms of conscious life, including ourselves, possess its prime cause. Within us is buddha nature. The *King of Meditation Sutra* states:

> Buddha nature totally permeates all beings.[5]

The shorter *Great [Passing into] Nirvana Sutra* says:

> All sentient beings possess buddha nature.[6]

Further, the longer *Great [Passing into] Nirvana Sutra* says:

> Just as butter, for example, exists in milk as something totally permeating it, so does buddha nature permeate all sentient beings.[7]

The *Ornament of Mahayana Sutras* also states:

> Suchness is the same
> for all and everyone; it is that which is pure.
> Since this is the Tathāgata,
> all beings are endowed with this essence.[8]

If this is so, you may wonder why sentient beings are endowed with buddha nature. [47] It is because: (1) Dharmakāya, emptiness, pervades all beings.

(2) The universal essence (*dharmatā*), suchness (*tathatā*), is without differentiation. (3) Every sentient being has the potential to become a buddha. This is just what is stated in the *Uttaratantra*, where it says:

> Because the dharmakāya pervades all,
> because suchness is without differentiation,
> and because they possess the potential,
> every living being at all times has buddha nature.[9]

To explain the first reason, "dharmakāya, emptiness, pervades all beings," here the Buddha is the dharmakāya, and the dharmakāya is emptiness. Since emptiness is something pervading all sentient beings, it follows that all those beings have the essence of buddhahood. The second reason, "the universal essence, suchness, is without differentiation," means that whether it be in terms of good and bad, great and small, or higher and lower, there is no difference between the universal essence in buddhas and the universal essence in sentient beings. Thus sentient beings possess the buddha essence. That "every sentient being has the potential to become a buddha" is explained through the five ways in which they stand in respect to enlightenment potential. These are outlined in the following synopsis:

> **Those with enlightenment potential can be summed up as belonging to five groups: those with severed potential, undetermined potential, śrāvaka potential, pratyekabuddha potential, and those with the Mahayana potential.**

Those with **severed potential** are characterized by six traits, such as lacking a sense of shame in public, having no dignity in private, lacking compassion, and so forth. The great master Asaṅga has said of them:

> Though seeing what is wrong with samsara, they are not in the least put off by it.
> Though hearing about the qualities of enlightened beings, they feel not the slightest faith in them.
> Without conscience and shame, and devoid of even a little compassion, they feel not the slightest regret for the unwholesome acts in which they fully indulge.
> When those these six absences converge, they are far from ready for enlightenment.[10]

It also says, in the *Ornament of Mahayana Sutras*:

> It is certain that some are solely engaged in what is harmful.
> Some are constantly destroying whatever is good.
> Others lack those virtues conducive to liberation.
> They are devoid of anything that could in any way be
> wholesome.[11]

Although those who have the above traits are said to have severed potential, this refers to their having to pass an exceedingly long time in samsara and does not mean that they have definitively cut off any chance of achieving enlightenment. Provided that they make the effort, [48] they can attain enlightenment. It says of this, in the *White Lotus of Compassion Sutra*:

> Ānanda! Were someone lacking the fortunate circumstances for nirvana merely to cast a flower up in the sky, visualizing the Buddha, then that person thereby possesses the fruit of nirvana. I declare that person to be one who will reach nirvana and who will penetrate to its furthest end.[12]

The lot of those with **undetermined potential** depends on the circumstances. Those who train under śrāvaka spiritual teachers, become involved with śrāvakas, or come across śrāvaka scriptures will place their trust in the śrāvaka way and, having entered that way, will actually become śrāvakas themselves. Likewise, those who encounter pratyekabuddha or Mahayana circumstances will embrace the pratyekabuddha or Mahayana ways.

Those with **śrāvaka potential** fear samsara, believe in nirvana, and have limited compassion. The scriptures say:

> Seeing the sufferings of samsara, they are afraid;
> they manifestly aspire for nirvana;
> they are not interested in working for the welfare of sentient
> beings:
> Those who bear these three characteristics have the śrāvaka
> potential.[13]

In addition to the above three characteristics, those with **pratyekabuddha potential** have enormous self-confidence, keep quiet about their teachers, and are loners. It is said:

> Grieved by samsaric existence they are keen for nirvana;
> weak in compassion they are exceedingly confident;
> secretive about their teachers, and they love solitude:
> These the wise should recognize as having the pratyekabuddha potential.[14]

The above two groups—those with śrāvaka and those with pratyekabuddha potential—although they may enter these two vehicles and attain their respective results, what they achieve is not true nirvana. At the time of their achievement they will, on account of a latent ignorance, acquire and exist in a subtle mental body brought about by their former untainted karma. They will be convinced that the state of untainted profound absorption they enjoy *is* nirvana and that they *have* attained nirvana.

One might object, "If this is not real nirvana, [49] it would be inappropriate for the Buddha to teach these two paths." It is, in fact, entirely appropriate for the Buddha to teach them as he did. Let us consider the following example. Some merchants from Jambudvīpa[15] set out to the far-off oceans to obtain precious gems. At one point in their journey, they felt so tired and downhearted while crossing a great wilderness that they began to think they would never manage to get the jewels, and they contemplated turning back. However, through his magical powers, their leader created a great illusory citadel where they were able to rest and recuperate.

Like the merchants in this story, beings of weak resolve will feel overwhelmed when they learn of the tremendous wisdom of the buddhas, and they may feel that the task of achieving it is too daunting and far beyond the capacity of the likes of them. On account of the awe they feel, they will either never undertake the task of enlightenment or they will give up easily. By teaching the two paths of the śrāvaka and pratyekabuddha, the Buddha enables them to attain the refreshing, healing state of a śrāvaka or pratyekabuddha. In the *Lotus Sutra* it says:

> Likewise all the śrāvakas are
> under the impression that they have attained nirvana.
> The Buddha tells them that
> this is not nirvana but a respite.[16]

When they have rested and refreshed themselves in the state of a śrāvaka or pratyekabuddha, the Buddha knows it is time to encourage them to achieve full enlightenment. How is this done? The Buddha inspires them through perfect body, pure speech, and wisdom mind. Light rays stream from his mind. By these beams merely touching their mental bodies, śrāvakas and pratyekabuddhas are awakened from their untainted meditative concentration. Then the Buddha manifests his own perfect physical presence and declares the following with his pure speech: "O monks! By merely doing what you have done, the task is not accomplished and the work is not yet done. Your nirvana is not nirvana. Monks! Now approach the Tathāgata and pay heed to what he says; understand his instruction." That he motivates them thus is taught in the verses of the *Lotus Sutra*:

> O monks! I therefore tell you today
> that by this alone you will not attain nirvana,
> and that for you to gain the pristine awareness of the omniscient ones,
> you must give rise to a noble and mighty wave of effort.
> By so doing, you will achieve all-knowing pristine awareness.[17]

Through being exhorted in this way, śrāvakas and pratyekabuddhas will cultivate the great bodhicitta.[18] Having conducted themselves as bodhisattvas for countless ages, they will become buddhas. [50] Thus it is stated in the *Sutra on Going to Laṅka* as well. In the *Lotus Sutra* it states:

> Those śrāvakas have not attained nirvana;
> so through having practiced the bodhisattva way of life,
> all these śrāvakas will become buddhas.[19]

The synopsis for those with **Mahayana potential** is the following:

> **Mahayana potential is summed up through six topics: its categories, their essential characteristics, its synonyms, the reasons it is particularly outstanding, the forms it takes, and its signs.**

First, there are two main **categories**: the potential as it exists naturally and the potential as something attained.

Second is an analysis of the **essential characteristics** of each of these. The *potential as it exists naturally*, since time without beginning, is the innate capacity of suchness to give rise to enlightened qualities. The *potential as something attained* is the capacity of one's former cultivation of virtue to give rise to enlightened qualities. Both these aspects of Mahayana potential make a readiness for enlightenment.

The **synonyms** for this are *potential, seed, element*, and *essential nature*.[20]

The **reasons** it stands far above the other forms of potential are as follows. The śrāvaka and pratyekabuddha potentials are lesser ones, because to realize them, only the afflictions need be eliminated. The Mahayana potential is outstanding because its total realization involves eliminating both obscurations.[21] This makes the Mahayana potential peerless, better than all the others.

The different **forms** of Mahayana potential are its *activated* and *dormant* states. When the potential has been activated, its signs are manifest and "the results have been attained." While it is dormant, the signs are not manifest and "the results have not [yet] been attained."

What activates the potential? Freedom from adverse conditions and the support of favorable ones activate it. While their contraries prevail, it remains dormant.

There are four adverse conditions: (1) birth in an unfavorable existence, (2) a lack of good inclinations,[22] (3) involvement in aberrant ways, and (4) being flawed with obscurations.

There are two favorable conditions [51]: (1) Externally, there are Dharma teachers, and (2) within, there is a proper mental attitude, aspiring to what is wholesome and so forth.

The **signs** [or evidence] of this potential are found in the *Ten Dharmas Sutra*, where it describes the indications of its presence:

> The bodhisattvas endowed with intelligence,
> their potential is detected by means of its signs,
> just as one infers the presence, through smoke, of a fire
> and through the presence of waterfowl, water.[23]

What are these signs? Naturally and without contrivance, such beings are peaceful in what they do and say, their minds have little deceit or hypocrisy, and they are loving and joyful in their relations with others. As it says in the *Ten Dharmas Sutra*:

> Never rough or rude,
> beyond deceit and hypocrisy,

and full of love for all beings:
They are the bodhisattvas.[24]

Further, they engender compassion toward all beings before entering into any activity. Genuinely aspiring to Mahayana Dharma, they undertake difficult tasks with forbearance that is never discouraged by the enormity of the undertaking, and they practice most properly and excellently that which generates virtue and has the nature of the perfections. It says in the *Ornament of Mahayana Sutras*:

Compassion prior to action,
aspiration as well as forbearance,
and engaging perfectly in virtues:
These should be recognized as signs of their potential.[25]

The above means that of the five types of potential, the Mahayana one is the most direct cause for buddhahood. The śrāvaka and pratyekabuddha potentials are also causes for attaining buddhahood but remoter ones. The undetermined potential is sometimes a direct cause, sometimes a remote cause. The disconnected potential is considered a very remote cause but not a total breach of the possibility of enlightenment: It is therefore an exceedingly far-removed cause for it.

Thus we have seen that, due to having one or another of these types of potential, sentient beings possess buddha nature, and this has also been demonstrated through the three reasons. The actual way they possess it can be exemplified by the way silver is present in silver ore, the way sesame oil is present in sesame, or the way butter is present in milk. Just as it is possible to obtain the silver that is in ore, the oil that is in sesame seeds, and the butter that is in milk, [52] so it is possible to attain the buddhahood that is in all sentient beings.

This concludes the first chapter, concerning the prime cause, of this *Ornament of Precious Liberation, a Wish-Fulfilling Gem of Sublime Dharma.*

2. A Precious Human Existence

II. The Basis

Given that all sentient beings have buddha nature, can the five types of nonhuman beings—hell beings, hungry spirits (*preta*), and so forth—achieve buddhahood? They cannot. The excellent type of existence that provides a working basis for achieving buddhahood is known as a *precious human existence*, meaning someone who materially has *freedoms* combined with *assets* and who mentally has the three kinds of *faith*. The synopsis of the explanation of this is the following:

> **The very best basis is summed up in five points: freedoms, assets, conviction, aspiration, and clarity. Two of these are physical and three are mental.**

They are **freedoms** inasmuch as the person is free from eight unfavorable conditions. According to [Prajñākaramati's *Commentary on the Guide to the Bodhisattva Way of Life*, in his summary of what is found in the] *Attention to Mindfulness Sutra*:

> The eight unfavorable states are to be
> a hell dweller, a hungry spirit, an animal,
> a barbarian, a long-living god,
> someone with fixed aberrant views, one born in a time without a Buddha,
> or a person with severe difficulty in understanding.[26]

Why are these states deemed unfavorable for the attainment of enlightenment? Hell is unsuitable because the very character of its experience is constant suffering. The hungry spirit state is unsuitable because of its mental anguish. The animal state is unsuitable because of its generalized benightedness. These three states are also devoid of a sense of dignity or regard for others.[27] Such beings do not really have any possibility of practicing Dharma because the above conditions render their general way of existing inappropriate for it.

The "long-living" gods are those without cognition. Because their stream of consciousness, along with its related mental activities, is in a state of suspension, they do not have the possibility of practicing Dharma: their mind is incapable of applying itself to it. Apart from these particular gods, all desire-realm gods live long compared to humans, and so could also be included in this category.

In fact, all the gods are in an unfavorable condition due to their attachment to the well-being of their situation. This makes them unsuited because they are unable to strive for virtue.[28] [53] In this respect, the relatively limited degree of manifest suffering present in human life is a [helpful] quality, inasmuch as it fosters rejection of samsara, quells pride, gives rise to compassion for other beings, and makes us shun unwholesome action and appreciate virtue. This is also mentioned in *Guide to the Bodhisattva Way of Life*:

> There are further virtues to suffering:
> World-weariness helps dispel your arrogance,
> you experience compassion for those in samsara,
> and you shun nonvirtue and delight in virtue.[29]

The above explains why those four [nonhuman] sorts of existence simply do not have the freedom to work toward enlightenment. But neither do some forms of human existence: barbarians, because of the improbability of their interacting with spiritual teachers; those with fixed aberrant views, because of the difficulty they have in understanding virtue to be the cause of rebirth into better states and of liberation; those born in a world without a Buddha, because of the absence of teachings on what is and what is not to be done; and those with severe impediments, because these make them unable to understand the Dharma teachings explaining which things are worthwhile and which things are harmful.

The "very best freedom" is to be free from the above eight.

There are **ten assets**: five are personal and five are other-related. The *five personal assets* are described as:

> To be human, born in a central land, with complete faculties, free from having committed the worst of actions, and having appropriate trust.[30]

"To be human" means to have been born the same as other humans, with male or female organs. To have been born in a "central land" means birth in a place with accessible holy beings. To have "complete faculties" means that you have the intellectual faculties needed for the actual practice of virtue, suffering from neither a severe learning difficulty nor a severe communication impediment. "Free from having committed the worst of actions" means you have not committed the actions of immediate consequence[31] in this life. "Appropriate trust" means confidence in all those wholesome things that truly merit trust—the noble teachings declared by the Buddha as a way of taming the mind.

The *five other-related assets* are: (6) a Buddha has manifested in the world, (7) the noble Dharma has been taught, (8) the teachings of noble Dharma are still extant, (9) there are those who follow them, and (10) loving kindness can be developed due to others.[32]

Someone possessing these ten personal and situational factors is called "a person with the very best assets." Where these two—the freedoms and the assets—are complete, that is the precious human existence. Why is it called "precious"? [54] It is so termed because, being rarely encountered and exceedingly beneficial and useful, its qualities are comparable to those of a wish-fulfilling gem.

It is *rarely encountered*: It says in the *Bodhisattva Collection*:

> It is difficult to be born human,
> and then difficult to stay alive.
> The noble Dharma is a rare thing to obtain,
> and it is also rare for a buddha to manifest.[33]

Furthermore, it says in the *White Lotus of Compassion Sutra*:

> It is not easy to come by a human existence. A person possessing the finest freedoms is also rarely encountered, and it is difficult, too, to find a world in which a Buddha has appeared. Further, it is not at all easy to aspire to what is virtuous, nor is it easy to find most perfect aspiration.[34]

It also says, in the *Marvelous Array Sutra*:

> It is rare to encounter that which is free from the eight unfavorable circumstances. It is rare, too, to be born human. It is also

> rare to obtain the very best form of freedom, in its plenitude. It is rare, too, for a Buddha to manifest. It is also rare not to have deficient faculties. It is rare, too, to be able to study the Buddhadharma. It is also rare to be in the company of holy beings. It is rare, too, to find truly qualified spiritual teachers. It is also rare to be able to practice properly that which has been taught so purely. It is rare, too, to maintain a truly right livelihood, and rare, in the human world, to earnestly do what is in accord with Dharma.[35]

Furthermore, it says in *Guide to the Bodhisattva Way of Life*:

> These freedoms and assets are exceedingly rare.[36]

What could exemplify this rarity, for whom is it so rare, and just why it is such a rare thing? *Guide to the Bodhisattva Way of Life* gives an analogy:

> On account of it being like that,
> the Buddha has said that to be human is as rare
> as a turtle putting its neck through the hole
> of a wooden yoke floating on a turbulent ocean.[37]

Where does this quotation come from? In the most excellent scripture it says, among other things:

> Were this vast land to be transformed into water, and were someone to set afloat a single one-holed wooden yoke to be driven in the four directions by the winds, a poor-sighted turtle might take thousands of years [to surface and put its head through it].[38] [55]

For those born in the lower states of existence, this [precious human existence] is very hard to obtain. The rarity is due to causality, since the principal cause for obtaining an existence with freedoms and assets is a prior accumulation of merit in the continuum of lives. Once born into the lower realms, a being constantly does nothing but wrong and does not know how to develop virtue. For this reason the only ones born in the three lower realms who can attain a human existence are those who have built up relatively little evil, or those who have created karma that will have to be experienced but in some later life.

It is *exceedingly beneficial and useful*. It says in *Guide to the Bodhisattva Way of Life*:

> Concerning the attainment of making an able human life meaningful....[39]

The "able human life" renders the Sanskrit term *puruṣa*,[40] a word [for a human life] connoting power or ability. A human existence endowed with the freedoms and assets is this "able human life," because it has the strength or ability to attain higher rebirth and ultimate good. Further, since there are three levels of this ability, there will be three corresponding categories of powerful human potential. Thus it says in *Lamp for the Path to Awakening*:

> One should know there to be three types
> of human ability: lesser, middling, and best.[41]

Those with the lesser type of powerful human potential have the ability to achieve human or divine rebirth by avoiding descent into the lower states. Thus it says:

> He who through whatever means
> strives for personal welfare
> and aspires merely worldly well-being,
> that person is described as someone with lesser ability.[42]

Those with the middling human ability are able to attain a state of peace and well-being by liberating themselves from samsara:

> Someone who turns away from worldly happiness,
> turns away from unwholesome action,
> and strives for their own peace alone,
> that person is refered to as the "middling" type.[43]

Those with the highest human ability are capable of attaining buddhahood for the benefit of sentient beings:

> Someone who, on the basis of his own suffering,
> aspires to totally eradicate

the entire suffering all beings,
that person is most excellent.[44]

Master Candragomin has also commented on the great benefit and use of a precious human existence, saying:

There are those who would reach the end of the ocean of rebirth
and, further, plant the virtuous seed of supreme enlightenment.
[56]
Such people, whose qualities far excel a wish-fulfilling gem,
how would they engage in fruitless tasks?
The path found by a human with such great strength of mind
cannot be attained by gods, nāgas, demigods, garuḍas, knowledge holders, kiṃnaras, and uragas.[45]

This human existence endowed with freedom and assets gives the ability to relinquish nonvirtue, cross samsara's ocean, tread the path of enlightenment, and attain perfect buddhahood. Therefore such an existence is far superior to those of gods, nāgas, and the like. It is something even better than a most precious wish-fulfilling gem. Because this human existence endowed with freedoms and assets is hard to obtain and of such great benefit, it is called "most precious."

Although it is so hard to obtain and of such tremendous benefit, it is *very easily destroyed*. This is because there is nothing that can perpetuate the life force, there are many causes of death, and the flow of moments never ceases. Thus it says in *Guide to the Bodhisattva Way of Life*:

It is not right to contentedly think,
"At least I won't die today."
It is without doubt that at one time or another
I will be annihilated.[46]

Thus, through its rarity, fragility, and real purpose, this physical existence should be considered a boat for doing whatever is needed to find a haven from the ocean of samsara. Thus it says:

Making use of this vessel of able human life,
get free from the mighty river of suffering.

> Since such a craft will be hard to come across in the future,
> don't fall into confusion: There is no time for sleep![47]

Considering this existence as a steed to be ridden, do whatever must be done to get free from the hazardous path of samsara and suffering. Thus it says:

> Having mounted the steed of a pure human existence,
> gallop away from the hazardous paths of samsara's suffering.[48]

Considering this physical existence as a servant, make it do wholesome tasks. Thus it says:

> This human existence should
> be employed in service [of others].[49]

The *three types of faith*: In order to act in such a way, faith is needed. It is said that without faith, noble qualities will not develop in a person. Thus the *Ten Dharmas Sutra* says:

> The noble qualities will not arise in someone without faith, [57]
> just as a green shoot will not emerge from a scorched seed.[50]

The *Flower Ornament Sutra* also says:

> Those of worldly disposition with little faith
> will be unable to know the buddhas' enlightenment.[51]

Therefore, you should cultivate faith. As the Buddha teaches in the *Vast Manifestation Sutra*:

> Ānanda, cultivate faith; this is what the Tathāgata asks of you.[52]

What exactly does *faith* mean? When analyzed, it has three aspects: faith as conviction, faith as aspiration, and faith as admiration.

Faith as conviction arises from contemplating actions and their consequences, the truth of suffering, and the truth of suffering's origin. *Conviction* means being convinced that the consequence of virtuous action is to experience well-being in the desire realm,[53] the consequence of nonvirtuous action is to experience misery in the desire realm, and the consequence of unwavering karma is to experience well-being in the form and formless realms. It means being convinced that through the power of karma and afflictions, explained as the *truth of all origination*, you will obtain the five contaminated aggregates, explained as the *truth of suffering*.

Faith as aspiration is to consider highest enlightenment as something very special indeed and to ardently study how it can be attained.

Faith as admiration [54] is something stable that emerges with respect to its object, the Three Jewels—being a joyful clear mind that has devotion and respect for the most precious Buddha as teacher of the path, for the most precious Dharma as that which is the path itself, and for the most precious Sangha as the companions who practice the path. Thus it says, in the *Treasury of Higher Knowledge*:

> What is faith? It is confidence in karma and its results, the [four] truths, and the most precious ones. It is aspiration and it is lucidity of mind.[55]

Further, it says in the *Precious Garland*:

> Whoever, despite temptation, anger, fear, or confusion,
> never strays from Dharma
> is said to possess faith.
> Such a person is a wonderful vessel for the highest good.[56]

"Not to stray from Dharma despite temptation" means not to abandon Dharma out of craving. [58] You would not renounce it despite temptations of food, wealth, consorts, kingdoms, or any enticement intended to persuade you to give up the Dharma.

"Not to stray from Dharma despite anger" means not to abandon Dharma out of aggression. For example, you would not relinquish a Dharma way of life for the sake of [fighting] someone who had not only harmed you greatly in the past but is also harming your greatly in the present.

"Not to stray from Dharma despite fear" means not to abandon Dharma out of fear. For instance, even faced with the threat that, were you not to abandon Dharma, three hundred fierce warriors would cut five ounces of flesh from your body every day, you would still not relinquish it.

"Not to stray from Dharma despite confusion" means not to abandon

Dharma out of ignorance. For instance, even though people might argue convincingly that cause and effect, the Three Jewels, and so forth are false, and thereby throw your Dharma into question, still you would not relinquish it.

Someone who can maintain conviction when faced with these four types of situations is a person with faith. Such faith makes you ideally suited to achieving liberation. Such faith will create countless benefits, including giving rise to the mentality of the best of beings, eliminating the unfavorable, sharpening and brightening the faculties, ensuring the nondegradation of moral discipline, removing afflictions, taking one beyond domains of experience marred by evil, enabling one to encounter the way of liberation, gathering a vast store of virtue, making one see many buddhas, and causing the buddhas' blessing to be received. As it says in the *Jewel Lamp Dhāraṇī Sutra*:

> If, through faith in the enlightened beings and their teachings
> and trust in the activity of the bodhisattvas,
> one comes to have faith in the peerless enlightenment,
> the mental attitude of a great being arises.[57]

This and more is said. Further, it is taught that all the buddhas, the blessed ones, will appear before a person of faith. The *Bodhisattva Collection* says:

> Thus the buddhas, the blessed ones, having recognized them as being worthy vessels of the Buddhadharma, will appear before them and will most properly teach them the way of the bodhisattva.[58]

Thus a "most precious human existence," [59] having two sets of qualities (the freedoms and assets) as well as three mental qualities (the aspects of faith), is the proper basis for achieving peerless enlightenment.

This concludes the second chapter, concerning the basis, of this *Ornament of Precious Liberation, a Wish-Fulfilling Gem of Sublime Dharma.*

3. Relying on the Spiritual Teacher

III. The Condition

Now to explain the line, "The special condition is the Dharma master." Even with the very best *basis*, it will be very difficult to progress along the path to enlightenment without the encouragement of a good Dharma master, who represents the *condition* [for enlightenment]. The difficulty is due to the strength of ingrained habits—unwholesome tendencies fashioned by former harmful actions. Therefore one needs to rely on Dharma teachers. The synopsis is:

> **Relying on Dharma masters is treated through five points: justification, the different kinds, the specific characteristics of each kind, how to rely, and its benefits.**

The necessity of relying on Dharma masters is **justified** in three ways: scripturally, logically, and through analogy.

For the *scriptural justification*, it says in the *Verse Summary of the Perfection of Wisdom*:

> Good disciples devoted to their teachers should
> always rely on wise and skillful Dharma masters.
> Why? Because from this will emerge the qualities of the wise.[59]

In the *Perfection of Wisdom in Eight Thousand Lines* it says:

> Thus realized bodhisattvas who wish to genuinely and totally awaken to peerless, utterly pure, and perfect enlightenment should from the very outset seek out, rely on, and serve Dharma masters.[60]

For the *logical justification*, the reasoning is: Given that you wish to attain omniscience [subject], you need to rely on Dharma masters [predicate], because by yourself you do not know how to accrue spiritual wealth or how to dispel your obscurations [reason]. The buddhas of the three times are an example substantiating this assertion. The pratyekabuddhas are an example of the contrary.

The above is explained as follows. For us to achieve perfect buddhahood, [60] all forms of spiritual wealth will need to be accrued, and that accrual depends on Dharma masters. Furthermore, we will need to rid ourselves of all the obscurations, summarized in terms of the afflictions obscuration and the knowledge obscuration. Their removal is also dependent on Dharma masters.

The *justification by analogy* is that a Dharma master is like a guide when traveling an unknown path, like an escort when in a dangerous land, and like a ferryman when crossing a mighty river.

The first example is that of a *guide*. Traveling in unfamiliar lands without a guide, you risk going in the wrong direction or making a longer or shorter detour. But if there is a companion guide, there are none of these risks, and the destination can be attained without a single wasted step. Like this, if there is no good Mahayana Dharma teacher when setting out on the path to peerless enlightenment and heading for that state, then there is the danger of mistakenly taking an aberrant path or, even without straying that gravely, of making the greater detour of the śrāvakas or the lesser detour of the pratyekabuddhas. When accompanied by good Dharma teachers, who are like guides, there is no longer this danger of taking a completely wrong path, or of a large or small detour, and the citadel of omniscience will be reached. Thus it says in the *Instructions for Liberation of Śrī Saṃbhava*:

> Leading you along the path that reaches the farther shore, a good master is like a guide.[61]

The second example is that of the *escort*. In dreaded places there are harmful things such as bandits, thieves, wild animals, and the like. Going to such places without an escort is dangerous for possessions, for physical safety, and even for life itself. When accompanied by a powerful escort, however, we pass through without mishap. Similarly, without a Dharma master to act as an escort on the path to enlightenment, accruing spiritual wealth, and heading for the citadel of omniscience, [61] we risk having our wealth of virtue plundered by that band of thieves [that consists of] ideas and mental afflictions within and harmful forces and misleading influences without. There is even the risk of our life in the happier realms being cut short. Therefore, it is said:

> As soon as that gang of robbers and thieves, the afflictions,
> find the opportunity,
> they will steal virtue
> and put an end to life in the higher states.[62]

Never straying from the Dharma master who is like an escort, the wealth of virtue will not be lost, existence as a being in the higher realms will not be cut short, and the citadel of omniscience will be attained. Therefore it says in the *Instructions for Liberation of Śrī Saṃbhava*:

> All the merit of a bodhisattva is protected by the Dharma master.[63]

One also reads, in the *Instructions for Liberation of Upāsikā Acalā*:

> Good Dharma masters are like an escort because they ensure our safe passage to the state of omniscience.[64]

The third example is that of a *ferryman*. Crossing a mighty river, you may be securely aboard the boat, but if there is no ferryman, you cannot reach the other shore, and the boat may sink or be swept away by the currents. With a ferryman and through his striving, however, the other shore will be reached. Likewise, when trying to traverse the ocean of samsara without Dharma masters who are like ferrymen, you may well be aboard the ship of Dharma yet drown in samsara or be carried off by its currents. Thus it is said:

> When there is no oarsman,
> the vessel will not reach the other shore.
> Even if one may be accomplished in all,
> yet without a master, existence will be endless.[65]

Staying on board with the ferryman-like Dharma master, nirvana—the dry land of the far shore of samsara—will be attained. Therefore it says in the *Marvelous Array Sutra*:

> Delivering us from the ocean of samsara, the Dharma master is like a ferryman.[66]

Thus one really needs to rely on Dharma masters, who are like guides, escorts, and ferrymen.

The second point examines the **different kinds** of Dharma master. There are four: (1) the Dharma master as a specific individual, (2) the Dharma master as a bodhisattva who has attained the levels (*bhūmi*), (3) the Dharma master [62] as an emanation body (*nirmāṇakāya*) of a buddha, (4) the Dharma master as an enjoyment body (*saṃbhogakāya*) of a buddha.

These correspond to the personal situation. Since one is totally unable to rely on buddhas or bodhisattvas while still a beginner in the Dharma, a Dharma master in the form of a specific individual is relied upon. When most of the action-related obscurations have been purified, one is able to rely on a Dharma master who is a bodhisattva on the levels. From the topmost stage of the path of accumulation onward, one can rely on a Dharma master in the nirmāṇakāya form of a buddha. Once the bodhisattva levels are attained, it is possible to rely on a Dharma master in the saṃbhogakāya form of a buddha.

Which of these four types is kindest to us? At the outset, when still in the dark pit of action and affliction, were we to try to rely on Dharma masters of the three latter types, we would not even be capable of seeing their faces; it is only due to our path being illuminated by the lamp held aloft by teachers who are specific individuals that we will eventually encounter them. Therefore, masters in the form of specific individuals are the kindest.

The third point concerns the **specific characteristics** of each of these four kinds of Dharma masters.

Buddhas embody the highest, most complete form of purification because they have eliminated both sorts of obscuration. They also embody the highest, most complete form of pristine awareness because they possess the two forms of knowledge.

Dharma masters as bodhisattvas on the levels will have whichever degree of purification and pristine awareness is appropriate to their particular level, from the first to the tenth. Of particular import are bodhisattvas of the eighth to tenth levels, for they have ten powers enabling them to nurture others: powers related to life, mind, requisites, karma, birth, aspiration, prayers, miracles, pristine awareness, and Dharma:

1. *Power over life* is the ability to stay in a world as long as wished.

2. *Power over mind* is the ability to enter stably into meditative absorption, just as is wished.
3. *Power over requisites* is the ability to shower an immeasurable rain of precious objects on beings. [63]
4. *Power over karma* is the ability to rearrange karmic results in terms of dimension, state, type of existence, and mode of birth that might otherwise be experienced in other states.
5. *Power over birth* is the ability to take birth in the desire realm yet to always maintain profound meditative concentration and not experience any sort of degeneration, remaining completely unsullied by the evils of that state.
6. *Power over aspiration* is the ability to transform the elements—earth, water, and so forth—into one another, as wished.
7. *Power of prayer* is the ability to pray or compose prayers in a way that will most properly accomplish the well-being of oneself and others; also the power to make prayers become realities.
8. *Power over miracles* is the ability to demonstrate countless miracles and supernatural feats in order to kindle aspiration in beings.
9. *Power of pristine awareness* is knowledge that encompasses, in the best possible way, the ultimate meaning of Dharma, of key points, of the true sense of words, and of bodhisattva prowess.
10. *Power of Dharma* is the ability to teach beings that which is suited to them, in just the right amount. This is achieved by presenting all the different nouns, terms, and characters of Dharma, in the various sutras and other teachings, in such a way that their sole speech is understood by each in his or her own language and in a totally satisfying way that makes sense.

Dharma masters as specific individuals have as their characteristics qualities described sometimes as eightfold, fourfold, or twofold. Of those with eight qualities, *Bodhisattva Levels* says:

> Concerning the above, if one has eight things, then one should be known as a bodhisattva who is completely qualified as a Dharma master. What are the eight? They are: (1) to have a bodhisattva's moral discipline, (2) to be learned in the bodhisattva scriptures, (3) to have realization, (4) to be kind and loving to one's followers, (5) to be fearless, (6) to be patient, (7) to be of untiring mind, and (8) to know how to use words.[67]

Of those with four qualities, the *Ornament of Mahayana Sutras* says:

> Broad based, eliminators of doubt,
> worthy of recollecting, and teaching the two natures:
> such are the very best
> of bodhisattva teachers.[68]

This means that: (1) Their teaching is very broad based because they have studied many things; (2) they can remove others' doubts because they themselves have superb discerning awareness; (3) their speech is worthy of recollection because their deeds are those of holy beings; [64] and (4) they teach the two natures: the characteristics of the completely defiled and of the utterly pure.

Of those with twofold qualities, *Guide to the Bodhisattva Way of Life* says:

> Even should it cost your life,
> never forsake a qualified Dharma master,
> who is skilled in the meaning of Mahayana
> and maintains the noble bodhisattva discipline.[69]

The fourth point is **how to rely on** the Dharma master skillfully. Once someone has connected with such Dharma masters, there are three ways of relying on them: (1) by showing respect and rendering service, (2) by cultivating the relevant reverence and devotion, and (3) by personal Dharma practice and earnestness.

The first of these [has two parts]. *Showing respect* is accomplished by prostrating to them, rising quickly [when they enter], bowing to them, circumambulating them, speaking at the appropriate time with a loving mind, looking at them again and again with an insatiable mind, and so forth. This was exemplified by the way that Maṇibhadra, a powerful merchant's son, related to his teacher. It says in the *Marvelous Array Sutra*:

> Gaze insatiably at your Dharma master. Why? Dharma masters are rarely seen, rarely manifest, and seldom met with.[70]

Relying on Dharma masters by *serving* them is accomplished by catering to their needs. This means providing them with food, clothing, bedding, seating, medicines when they are unwell, funds, and the like, in a way that accords with the Buddhist teaching. This is to be done without heed for one's own life or physical well-being, as exemplified by the realized being Sadāprarudita. In the *Instructions for Liberation of Śrī Saṃbhava* we read:

> A buddha's enlightenment is attained by serving Dharma masters.[71]

The second way is to rely on them by [cultivating] *reverence and devotion*. Having established the concept that the teacher is a buddha, whatever the teacher says is taken to be instruction, never to be transgressed, to be followed in constancy and with the cultivation of reverence, devotion, and joyous trust. [65] This was exemplified by the way master scholar Nāropa relied on his guru. It says, in the *Mother of the Conquerors*:

> Earnestly cultivate reverence for Dharma masters, follow them, and have joyous trust.[72]

Besides this, wrong ways of thinking about the personal conduct of masters should be abandoned, because their conduct is in fact their skillful technique at work. Instead, cultivate the noblest devotion for it. This was exemplified in the biography of King Anala.[73]

The third way to rely on masters is by *Dharma practice and earnestness*. There are three steps to Dharma practice in this respect: first to study Dharma under the masters' guidance, then to contemplate its significance, and finally to make it a reality in practice.

Do these earnestly; that is what will be most satisfying for the teacher. Thus the *Ornament of Mahayana Sutras* says:

> The firm one who practices just as instructed
> will surely make their minds most pleased.[74]

When someone's Dharma master is satisfied, that person will attain buddhahood. It says in the *Instructions for Liberation of Śrī Saṃbhava*:

> By satisfying the master, the enlightenment of all the buddhas will be attained.[75]

As far as requesting Dharma teachings from one's Dharma masters is concerned, there are three phases: the preparation, the actual instruction, and the conclusion. The preparation is to have the bodhisattva motivation when requesting the teachings. During the actual instruction, consider yourself to be like a patient, the Dharma to be like medicine, the teacher to be like the physician, and the earnest practice of Dharma to be the best and quickest way to recovery. The conclusion is to avoid the three mistakes of being like an upturned container, a leaky container, or a filthy container.[76]

The fifth point is about the **benefits** of relying on Dharma masters. In the *Instructions for Liberation of Śrī Saṃbhava* we read:

> Child of noble descent! A bodhisattva who is most properly nurtured by a good Dharma master will not fall into the lower states. A bodhisattva who is totally protected by a Dharma master will not be swayed by corrupting friends. A bodhisattva who is perfectly trained by a Dharma master will not abandon the bodhisattva way. A bodhisattva who is most excellently sustained will completely transcend the activities of ordinary people.[77] [66]

The *Perfection of Wisdom* [*in Eight Thousand Lines*] also says:

> A realized bodhisattva who is most properly nurtured will swiftly attain peerless, totally pure, and perfect enlightenment.[78]

This concludes the third chapter, concerning Dharma masters, of this *Ornament of Precious Liberation, a Wish-Fulfilling Gem of Sublime Dharma.*

4. The Impermanence of Conditioned Existence

IV. The Means: The Dharma Master's Instruction

We have the *cause*, buddha nature. Furthermore, because samsara has existed since time without beginning, at some point we must already have had the *basis*, a precious human existence, through which we met the *condition*, the Dharma master. What prevented us from becoming buddhas then? It was the harmful mistake of falling under the sway of four blockages that stopped us, and those like us, from attaining buddhahood.

The *four impediments that have prevented the attainment of buddhahood* are: (1) attachment to the experiences of this life, (2) attachment to worldly well-being in general, (3) attachment to the well-being of peace, and (4) ignorance of the means by which buddhahood is achieved. What can eliminate these four impediments? They are eliminated by heeding the instruction of Dharma masters and by putting those instructions into practice.

What does those masters' advice consist of? Here is the synopsis:

> **All the Dharma masters' instruction can be condensed into four topics: meditation on impermanence; meditation on samsara's faults and on actions and their consequences; meditation on love and compassion; and the teachings concerning the cultivation of bodhicitta.**[79]

This means that the Dharma masters' instruction comprises advice on (1) how to meditate on impermanence, (2) how to meditate on the defects of samsara and on actions and their consequences, (3) how to cultivate love and compassion, and (4) how to cultivate bodhicitta.

These act as remedies as follows.[80] Meditation on impermanence counteracts attachment to the experiences of this life. Meditation on the defects of samsara counteracts attachment to worldly well-being in general. [67] The meditations on love and compassion counteract attachment to the well-being of meditative peace. The teachings on cultivating highest enlightenment counteracts ignorance of how to attain buddhahood.

These cover all teachings—from taking refuge up to the meaning of the two types of absence of self, or from the five path phases and the ten bodhisattva levels down through all the teachings on bodhicitta. Some of these topics form the basis for bodhicitta, some are its objective, some are the rituals connected with bodhicitta development, some are advice pertinent to bodhicitta, some concern its qualities and benefits, and some present its results. There is no Mahayana topic that is not included in the bodhicitta teachings. Hence all those forms of instruction stem from the Dharma master: they depend on the Dharma master. Therefore the *Marvelous Array Sutra* says:

> The Dharma master is the very source of all the teachings of virtue.[81]

and

> Omniscience depends on the instruction given by Dharma masters.

Meditation on impermanence

Of these, I first present impermanence, which is the remedy that counteracts attachment to the experiences of this life.

In general, every composite thing is impermanent. Therefore the Buddha taught:

> O monks! All composites are impermanent.[82]

How exactly are they impermanent? What is accumulated will eventually dwindle, what is built up will eventually disintegrate, what comes together will eventually part, and what lives will eventually die. Quoting the *Collection of Aphorisms*:

> The end of all accumulation is dispersal,
> the end of construction is disintegration,
> the end of meeting is parting,
> and the end of life is death.[83]

How to meditate on this is explained through the synopsis:

> **Meditation on impermanence is well summarized in three topics: its categories, the meditation techniques, [68] and the benefits of having meditated on it.**

First, the **categories** are two: the impermanence of the world and the impermanence of sentient beings. The first of these, the impermanence of the world—the outer vessel—has two subcategories: gross impermanence and subtle impermanence. The second, the impermanence of sentient beings—the inner essence—also has two subcategories: the impermanence of others and the impermanence of oneself.

Second, the **techniques for meditating** on these will be discussed in two parts: that of the world and that of its beings. For the world, first we consider its *gross level of impermanence.*

There exists nothing, from the wind mandala below [at the base] up to the four levels of meditative concentration [of the form realm] above, that will not change, that is permanent by its very nature, or that has lasting materiality. At times, everything below the first level of concentration is destroyed by fire. At times, everything below the second level of concentration is destroyed by water. At times, everything below the third level of concentration is destroyed by wind. As these things occur, when there is destruction by fire not even ashes are left, just as when oil is consumed by flame. When there is destruction by water, there is not even sediment left, just as when salt is dissolved by water. When there is destruction by wind, nothing remains, just as when powder is blown away. Therefore the *Treasury of Higher Knowledge* says:

> There will be seven [destructions] by fire [followed] each by
> water;
> thus after seven by water,
> there will be seven by fire;
> finally there will be destruction by wind.[84]

The fourth level of concentration will not be destroyed by fire, water, or air. The beings in that state are subject to death and transmigration, and therefore it ends automatically [at their death]. Thus it says:

> The celestial abodes of the impermanent arise and disintegrate
> along with the conscious beings that inhabit them.[85]

Also, the destruction of this universe by fire, at a certain point, is foretold in the *Questions of the Layman Vīradatta Sutra*:

> After one eon, this world,
> the nature of which is space, will become space;
> even the mountains will be incinerated and destroyed.[86]

The *subtle impermanence* of the environment is that of the flux of the four seasons, the rising and setting of the sun and the moon, and moment-to-moment change.

Let us consider the first of these. Due to the powerful influence of the coming of spring, our environment, the world, changes as follows. The land becomes soft and ruddy in color, and the trees, grasses, and plants bud. [69] However, this is but the manifestation of a transitory period. Due to the powerful influence of the coming of summer, the land becomes predominantly deep green, and leaves and branches grow on the trees, grasses, and plants. This, too, is but the manifestation of a transitory period. Due to the powerful influence of the coming of autumn, the land then hardens and is predominantly golden. Its trees, grasses, and plants bear fruit. This, too, is but the manifestation of a transitory period. Due to the powerful influence of the coming of winter, the land becomes frozen and whitish, and the trees, grasses, and plants are dried up and brittle. This, too, is but the manifestation of a transitory period.

Now let us consider impermanence in terms of the rising and setting of the sun and moon. The power of day breaking makes our environment, the world, become light and bright. The power of night falling makes it disappear into darkness. These are also signs of impermanence.

Finally, let us consider impermanence in terms of moment-by-moment change. Our environment, the world of one small instant of time, does not persist into the next instant of time. It gives the impression of remaining the same, yet in fact something similar has taken its place. Cascading water is an example of this.

The second technique of meditation contemplates the *impermanence of* the inner essence, *sentient beings*, first considering the impermanence of others and then one's own impermanence.

The *impermanence of others*: All conscious beings in the three realms are impermanent. It says in the *Vast Manifestation Sutra*:

> The three realms are impermanent, like autumn clouds.[87]

One's own impermanence is based on understanding that "I also have no power to remain in this life and must go on to another." The way to understand this is twofold: (1) by examining your own existence and (2) by applying to yourself what is observed of others' existences. The way to meditate on the first of these is as follows: meditate on death, on the specific characteristics of death, on the exhaustion of life, and on separation.

Meditation on death is to contemplate "I will not stay long in this world and will soon be moving into the next."

Meditation on the specific characteristics of death involves contemplating the thought "This life force of mine will be used up, respiration will stop, and this body will take on the appearance of a corpse, while this mind will be obliged to wander off to another life."

Meditation on the exhaustion of life is to contemplate: "Since a year ago, a year has passed, and now my life is precisely that much shorter. Since a month ago, a month has passed, and now my life is precisely that much shorter. [70] From yesterday until today, a day has gone by, and now my life is precisely that much shorter. A moment has just gone by, and my life is precisely that much shorter." It says in *Guide to the Bodhisattva Way of Life*:

> Without ever stopping for even a day or a night,
> this life is constantly on the wane.
> Because what is left diminishes and disappears,
> how could the likes of me not die?[88]

Meditation on separation is to contemplate: "The friends and relatives, wealth and possessions, body, and so forth that I have at present and that I value so much will not always be able to accompany me. Soon will we be parted." As it says in *Guide to the Bodhisattva Way of Life*:

> By not knowing that I would have to leave
> everything behind and depart....[89]

Alternatively, one could engage in the ninefold way of meditating on death. The ninefold technique is centered on three main contemplations: "I will certainly die," "The time of death is indefinite," and "When I die, nothing whatsoever can accompany me."

There are three reasons *it is certain one will die*: (1) No one previously has escaped death. (2) The body is a composite phenomenon. (3) Life is consumed from moment to moment.

1. It is certain I will die because there was no one in the past who did not die. The great master Aśvaghoṣa said:

> Whether it is on earth or in the upper realms,
> have you ever seen or heard,
> or have wondered about someone,
> who has been born but has not died![90]

Therefore even "seers of truth"[91] cannot find a place to go to escape death and encounter immortality. They will all die, not to mention the likes of us! It is said:

> Even the great rishis endowed with
> five types of clear cognition who travel far through space,
> they would be unable to travel to that place
> where they can enjoy immortality.[92]

Besides this, even realized beings such as pratyekabuddha or śrāvaka arhats had to leave their bodies in the end. What, then, for the likes of us! Therefore it says, in the *Collection of Aphorisms*:

> When even the pratyekabuddhas
> and the śrāvakas [disciples] of the buddhas,
> if they too have to quit their bodies,
> what need is there to speak ordinary beings?[93] [71]

Besides this, if even the totally purified, utterly perfect emanation body (*nirmāṇakāya*), adorned with the marks and signs of a supreme being, whose very nature was like a vajra, had to leave behind his body, then so much the more is it true of ordinary folk like us. The great master Aśvaghoṣa said:

> If even the vajra bodies of the buddhas,
> adorned with the special marks and signs, are impermanent,
> then there is no point even mentioning
> other beings' bodies, which are like plantain trees.[94]

2. It is certain I will die because my body is something composite. Any composite whatsoever is impermanent, and every composite is destructible by nature. The *Collection of Aphorisms* says:

> Alas, all composites are impermanent,
> characterized by birth and decay![95]

Hence, since this body is not noncomposite but composite, it is impermanent, and so it is certain that it will die.

3. It is certain I will die because life is consumed from moment to moment. Life gets closer to death with the passing of each instant. If this is not obvious, let us examine examples that bear some similarity: an arrow shot by a strong archer, a torrent cascading over the edge of a steep cliff, and a prisoner being led to the place of execution and imminent death.

The first example is that of an arrow shot by a strong archer. Not halting even for an instant at any one place in space, it speeds swiftly to its target. Life, too, never stands still even for an instant and heads swiftly toward death. As is said:

> An arrow loosed from a bowstring
> by a mighty archer never hovers
> but speeds to its target;
> human life is like that, too.[96]

The second example is that of a torrent cascading over the edge of a steep cliff. Its waters tumble down without pausing even for an instant. Likewise, it is extremely clear that human life is unable to pause. This is found in the *Crown Jewel Dhāraṇī Sutra*, where it says:

> Friends, this life passes as swiftly
> as water gushing over a waterfall.
> Immature beings, unaware of this and living unskillfully,
> proudly intoxicate themselves with sense pleasures.[97]

Furthermore, the *Collection of Aphorisms* says:

> It flows on like the current
> of a mighty river, never turning back.[98]

The third example is that of a prisoner being led to the place of execution, whose every step brings death closer. We are just like that. In the *Noble Tree Sutra* it says:

> Just like a prisoner being led to the place of execution, [72]
> whose every step brings him closer to death.[99]

The *Collection of Aphorisms* also says:

> Just as those on their way to execution
> draw closer to their death
> with every step that is taken,
> so it is with the life force of humans.[100]

There are three reasons why *the time of death is not definite*: (4) The lifespan is uncertain. (5) The body has no single vital essence. (6) There are many possible causes of death.

4. The time of death is not definite because lifespan is uncertain. Although the lifespan is fixed for some other sentient beings and for human beings in other parts of the cosmos, the lifespan of ordinary people in this world is not definite. In the *Treasury of Higher Knowledge* it says:

> Here it is not definite: ten years at the end
> and inestimable at the beginning.[101]

Just how it is indefinite is explained in the *Collection of Aphorisms*:

> Some will die in the womb,
> some when they are born,
> some when they can only crawl,
> some when they can run,
> some when aged, some when young,
> and some in the prime of life.
> Eventually they all go.[102]

5. The time of death is indefinite because the body has no single vital essence. This body has no solid, enduring essence, only its thirty-six impure substances. Thus *Guide to the Bodhisattva Way of Life* says:

Using the scalpel of discerning awareness,
first dissect yourself mentally,
peeling away with the layer of skin
and going through the flesh to the skeleton.

Having even dissected the bones
and gotten to the marrow,
examining carefully, ask:
"What is there that could be its vital essence?"[103]

This is what we ourselves ought to investigate.

6. The time of death is not definite because there are many potential causes of death. There is nothing that could not become a cause of death, either for me or for someone else. It says, in the *Letter to a Friend*:

There are many things that damage life.
As life is more unstable than an air bubble in water,
it is a wonder that in-breaths give way to out-breaths
or that anyone awakens from sleep.[104]

There are three contemplations on how, once dead, *nothing can accompany you*: (7) Wealth and objects cannot accompany you, (8) friends and relatives cannot accompany you, and (9) your own body cannot accompany you.

7. Wealth and objects cannot accompany you after death. *Guide to the Bodhisattva Way of Life* says:

Although you may have obtained so many things, [73]
and have used and enjoyed them for a long time,
you depart naked and empty-handed,
as though robbed by thieves.[105]

Not only do wealth and possessions not accompany you at death, they also harm both this life and the next. They harm this life on account of the suffering caused through quarrels over them, having to protect them from theft, and enslavement to them. The ripening of karma planted in this way harms future lives, taking one to the lower states.

8. Friends and relatives cannot accompany you at death. As it says in *Guide to the Bodhisattva Way of Life*:

> When the time comes to die,
> children will not be a refuge,
> nor father and mother,
> nor friends and loved ones.
> None could be your refuge.[106]

Not only do relatives and friends not accompany you at death, they also harm both this life and the next. They harm this life through the anguish of worrying about their well-being and their lives. The full karmic ripening of these fears spoils your future lives by taking you to the lower realms.

9. Your own body cannot accompany you at death, nor can its physical qualities do so. No strong or courageous person can turn death away, no swift athlete can outrun it, and no eloquent speaker or negotiator can dissuade it. That would be like trying to prevent or delay the sun from setting behind a mountain: No one can.

The physical substance of the body cannot accompany you, either. *Guide to the Bodhisattva Way of Life* says:

> Your body, which you have clothed and fed
> at the expense of great hardship, will be unable to help you:
> It will be eaten by jackals or birds, be burned by fire,
> rot in water, or be buried in a grave.[107]

Not only can your body not accompany you, as just explained, it also harms both this life and the next. It injures this life through the great sufferings that occur when it cannot bear sickness, heat, cold, hunger, or thirst, or when there is fear of being killed, bound, or beaten. [Actions related to] these misfortunes will drag you into the lower states in future lives.

The second way [of contemplating your own impermanence] is by *observing what happens to others and applying it to yourself.* This means that when actually witnessing others die, hearing of their deaths, or recollecting people dying, you imagine this happening to you and then meditate accordingly. [74]

Applying to yourself the deaths of other people you have witnessed dying is done as follows. Think of those closely related to you who were strong at first, of healthy complexion, feeling happy, and never giving a moment's thought to death, yet who were then stricken by fatal illness. Their bodily strength waned, they could not even sit up, their complexion lost its luster, becoming pallid and dry, and they suffered distress. There was no way to cure the pain or lessen the emotional burden. Medicines and examinations were of no more help, and even religious ceremonies and special prayers could not make them better. They knew that they were going to die and that nothing that could be done to prevent it. Surrounded by their remaining friends, they ate their last meal and spoke their last words. Evoking these images, think: "I, too, am of the same nature. I will also be subject to this. I, too, have these characteristics and have not transcended this particular phenomenon."

Then, from the moment the breath stopped, that person's body was considered unfit to stay even a day in the very place that had been the beloved home from which the person could not bear to part. Once the corpse was laid on a bier, swathed, and bound, it was lifted up and carried out of the house. At that moment some embraced it and clung to it, some wept and wailed, some fainted and were overcome with grief. Yet others remarked, "This dead body is simply the likes of earth and rock, and you are small-minded to carry on as you do!" Contemplating such scenes as a corpse making its one-way journey over the threshold, think: "I, too, am of the same nature...."

Then, contemplating the corpse once it has been left in the charnel ground, where it is ripped apart by jackals and dogs, decomposed by insects, and where there are the disintegrated remains of skeletons, think: "I, too, will be like this...."

The way to apply to yourself the instances of other peoples' deaths that you have heard about is as follows. Whenever people say "Such and such a person died," or "There is a corpse in such and such a place," think, as above: "I, too, am like that...."

The way to apply to yourself the instances of other peoples' deaths that you recollect is as follows. Think about all the people—some elderly, some young, and some lifelong friends—who have died in your area, town, or in your own house. Bearing their deaths in mind, think, as above, "I, too, am like this...," and reflect on how, before too long, you will also go that way. In the sutras it says:

> Since no one knows which will come first— [75]
> tomorrow or the next life—
> it makes sense to strive for what has meaning in the next life
> and not put a lot of effort into what is just for tomorrow.[108]

The third point discusses the **benefits** of meditating on impermanence. By understanding that all composite things are impermanent, strong craving for this life will be countered. Further, the seed of trust will be planted, diligence will be reinforced, and this will be an important factor in realizing sameness, since it quickly frees the mind from attraction and rejection.

This concludes the fourth chapter, concerning the impermanence of composite phenomena, of this *Ornament of Precious Liberation, a Wish-Fulfilling Gem of Sublime Dharma.*

5. The Suffering of Samsara

ONE MIGHT FEEL, "What does it matter if there is impermanence and death, since I'll be reborn anyway? In that next life I could experience the very finest that being human or divine has to offer. That is fine by me!" To think thus is to be attached to the pleasures of cyclic existence (*samsara*). As the remedy for this I shall explain how to become familiar with the defects of samsara. The synopsis is:

> **The defects of samsara are covered by three topics: the suffering of conditioned existence, the suffering of change, and overt suffering.**

These three sufferings can be explained through metaphors: the suffering of conditioned existence is like uncooked rice, the suffering of change is like cooked rice mixed with poison, and overt suffering is like stomach pains due to eating the poisoned rice. The three sufferings can also be explained in terms of their character. The suffering of conditioned existence has a neutral feeling, the suffering of change has a feeling of pleasure about it, and overt suffering actually feels like suffering. The three sufferings can also be explained in terms of their essential characteristics, as follows.

First, the **suffering of conditioned existence**: We suffer merely through having taken on [a human life composed of] the aggregates, to which suffering is inherent. [76] Ordinary people do not feel this suffering of conditioned existence and can be compared to people stricken by raging fevers, who are insensitive to trivial physical ills like an itchy ear. Stream-enterers and the other three types of emancipated being [i.e., once-returners, non-returners, and arhats] can perceive this suffering of conditioned existence. They can be compared to someone virtually cured of the fever and hence now quite aware of minor aches and pains. A small hair put on the palm of the hand causes neither discomfort nor pain, but should that same hair get into the eye, it will cause great irritation and unpleasantness. Similarly, ordinary people are insensitive to the suffering of conditioned existence, whereas realized beings are greatly distressed by it. As it says in the *Commentary on the Treasury of Higher Knowledge*:

> When a single hair in our palm
> enters into our eyes,
> it engenders discomfort and pain.
> The childish, akin to the palm, do not recognize
> the suffering of conditioned existence.
> The noble ones, akin to the eyes, perceive
> conditioned existence as suffering.[109]

Second, **the suffering of change** is so called because all the pleasures of samsara, whatever they may be, will eventually change into suffering. As it says in the *White Lotus of Compassion Sutra*:

> The divine realms are a cause for suffering to arise. The human realms are also a cause for suffering.[110]

Hence even those who attain the human status of a universal monarch (*cakravartin*) will, in time, change and find themselves in a state of suffering. It says, in the *Letter to a Friend*:

> Even a universal monarch will,
> in the course of time, become a servant.[111]

Furthermore, even someone who achieves the physical form and the experiences of Indra, lord of the gods, will eventually fall from that state, first dying, then transmigrating. It says:

> Even having become Indra, worthy of offerings,
> you fall back to earth through the power of karma.[112]

Besides this, the likes of the king of the gods, Brahma, who has transcended sensual desire and attained the felicity of evenly resting in meditative concentration, will also eventually fall. It says:

> From the pleasures of being Brahma, free of desires,
> you'll have to put up with the unceasing suffering
> of being fuel in the Hell of Relentless Agony.[113]

[77] The third point is that of suffering as **overt suffering.** This is the significant and quite obvious sufferings experienced above and beyond that of having a life composed of aggregates to which suffering is inherent. They are to be known through two categories: those of the lower states of existence and those of the higher states.

The *sufferings of the lower states of existence* are those of the three lower states: hells, hungry spirits, and animals. Each is to be understood through four points: their respective subcategories, locations, sufferings experienced, and lifespan.

The hells. The subcategories are: the eight hot hells, the eight cold hells, the occasional hells, and the peripheral hells, making eighteen types in all.

The [eight] hot hells. Where are these hot hells? They are situated beneath Jambudvīpa, for there are many who go from here to there. In the very lowest live the sentient beings of Relentless Agony Hell. Above them, working upward, are the Exceedingly Hot, Hot, Great Wailing, Wailing, Gathering and Crushing, Black Line, and Reviving hells, respectively. Therefore the *Treasury of Higher Knowledge* says:

> Twenty thousand [leagues] beneath here
> is Relentless Agony,
> with seven other hells above it.[114]

The reason for their names will be given, as well as a general explanation for the sufferings endured in those places. The first is the Reviving Hell, where beings are bound, immolated, and hacked to death by each other. Subsequently, a cold wind blows to revive them, and the process resumes. This continues relentlessly throughout their stay there.

In the Black Line Hell, a black line is traced on the body, which is then sawed with blazing saws and chopped with flaming, red-hot axes. As it says:

> Some are cut up with saws,
> others chopped up by unbearably sharp axes.[115]

In the Gathering and Crushing Hell, beings are gathered between mountains and also crushed and squeezed in iron presses. In the first instance, mountains in the form of ram's heads come together, crushing the trapped beings. The hills then draw apart, and a cold wind arises to restore the people to their former condition. They are crushed and restored time after time. The *Letter to a Student* says: [78]

> Two terrifying mountains, like rams with long horns,
> crush all the bodies gathered between them and grind them to
> powder.[116]

Some are squeezed between iron presses, their blood squirting out like four rivers. It says:

> Some are ground like sesame seeds,
> others milled to dust like fine flour.[117]

Beings in the Wailing Hell scream with terror as they are burned. Beings in the Great Wailing Hell scream even louder. In the Hot Hell beings are tortured by fire and the like. Boiling metal poured into their mouths burns their viscera, and they are pierced through with one-pointed spears from the anus to the top of the head. In the Exceedingly Hot Hell they are tortured even more than this. Without skin, they are burned by molten metal poured down their throats so that fire comes out their orifices. Then they, too, are pierced—by tridents that puncture the soles of the feet and the anus and penetrate up through the top of the head and the shoulders. It says:

> Similarly, some are forced to drink
> a blazing liquid of molten metal
> while others are impaled
> on blazing iron stakes bearing many spikes.[118]

Relentless Agony (Avīci) Hell is a blazing iron building, twenty thousand leagues (*yojana*) in height and breadth, within which are copper and iron cauldrons several leagues wide, into which are poured molten bronze and iron that are kept boiling by unbearable fires coming from the four directions. It says:

> Some are cast head first into iron cauldrons
> and boiled up like rice soup.[119]

It is so named because the suffering there is unremitting.

The lifespans of hell beings are taught as:

> In the first six, starting with the Reviving Hell,
> a day and night is equivalent to the life of the sense-dimension
> gods,
> and hence their lifespans are calculable
> working from the lifespans of those gods.[120]

The lifespan of the class of the Four Great King gods is equivalent to a day and night in the Reviving Hell. Thirty days make a month, and twelve months make a year. Reviving Hell beings live for five hundred of their own years. This makes their lifespan 1,620 billion human years. [79]

In a similar way, lifespan in the Black Line Hell is calculated according to that of the gods of the Heaven of the Thirty-Three. Since beings can live for up to a thousand hell years, their lifespan is the equivalent of 12,990 billion human years.[121] Correlating the Gathering and Crushing Hell with the Aggression-Free god realm then, since beings can be there for two thousand hell years, their lifespan is the equivalent of 100,680 billion human years.[122] Correlating the Wailing Hell with the Joyful god realm then, since beings can stay there for four thousand hell years, their lifespan is the equivalent of 844,420 billion human years.[123] Correlating the Great Wailing Hell with the Delighting in Creation god realm then, since beings can stay there for eight thousand hell years, their lifespan is the equivalent of 6,635,520 billion human years. Correlating the Hot Hell with the Rulers of Others' Creations god realm then, since beings can stay there for sixteen thousand hell years, their lifespan is the equivalent of 51,084,010 billion human years.[124] Those in the Exceedingly Hot Hell can remain there for half an intermediate cosmic eon, and those in the Relentless Agony Hell for a whole intermediate cosmic eon. As it says:

> In the Exceedingly Hot, a half, and in the Relentless Agony,
> a whole intermediate cosmic eon.[125]

The neighboring hells. These are situated in the four cardinal directions around the eight hells mentioned above. The first of these is the Glowing Coals Hell, where there are knee-deep glowing coals. As beings there take a step, seeking escape, the flesh, skin, and blood are completely burned off their legs when they put their feet down, yet restored as they lift them up again. That is the first additional hell. Nearby is the Impure Swamp of Putrefied Corpses Hell, infested by white worms with black heads. With sharp, hard, pointed mouths, they enter the flesh, penetrating to the bone. This is the second additional hell. [80] Nearby is the Great Razor Highway Hell, where beings are molested by a forest of sword-like leaves, terrifying large black dogs, and iron trees with lacerating leaves and branches, on which perch ravens with iron beaks. This is the third additional hell. Nearby is the Most Extreme River, full of boiling lye in which beings are cooked. They are prevented from leaving the river by beings who stand along the banks brandishing weapons. This is the fourth additional hell. It says, about these:

> Besides the eight there are sixteen others,
> in the four cardinal directions from them:
> the Glowing Coals, a Swamp of Putrefaction,
> the Razor Highway, and so on, and the River.[126]

You may wonder whether the guardians of the hells—who appear to be humans or ravens with iron beaks—are actual sentient beings. The Vaibhāṣika schools hold them to be sentient beings, whereas the Sautrāntika schools say they are not. The Yogācāra schools and the lineage transmission of Marpa and Milarepa hold them to be manifestations of their perceiver's own mind, due to former evils enacted. *Guide to the Bodhisattva Way of Life* accords with this interpretation:

> Who could have created the beings there
> and their hellish weapons for such purposes?
> Who made the burning iron ground,
> and from what are the fires generated?
>
> The Great Sage has said that all these sorts of things
> are due to the existence of an unwholesome mind.[127]

The eight cold hells. These are: (1) the Cold Sore Hell, (2) the Burst Cold Sore Hell, (3) the Chattering Teeth Hell, (4) the Sneezing Hell, (5) the Alas! Hell, (6) the Hell Where Frostbitten Skin Cracks in the Shape of an Utpala, (7) the Hell with Cracks Like a Lotus, and (8) the Hell with Cracks Like Giant Lotuses. It is said:

There are eight cold hells: the Cold Sore Hell and the others.[128]

They are located beneath this Jambudvīpa, directly beneath the hot hells. Below is a general outline of the sufferings experienced in those states and an explanation of their names.

In the first two hells, the cold is so unbearable that the beings have cold sores or [in the second] festering cold sores. The next three are named after the sounds and cries that beings there are heard to make due to the unbearable cold. The last three derive their names from the bodily changes that take place: in the sixth the skin turns blue with cold and cracks open in fivefold or sixfold cracks, looking like an utpala flower; in the seventh it has turned from blue to red, and the cracks have ten or more lips, like a lotus; and in the last the skin is violently inflamed and split into a hundred or more flaps, like an open, giant lotus. [81]

How long does the lifespan of these beings last? Just as an example, the Bhagavan Buddha stated the following:

> O monks, here is an example. Say a storehouse able to hold eighty bushels of sesame seeds, like those of this land of Magadha, were to be filled with such seeds. If once every hundred years one grain were to be removed, then after a certain period all the eighty bushels of that Magadha sesame would eventually be emptied from that store. I could not tell you which of the two—that period of time or the lifespan of those in the Cold Sore Hell—would be the longer. O monks! The lifespan in the Open Cold Sore hell is twenty times that of the Cold Sore Hell. O monks! The lifespan in the Great Open Lotus Hell is twenty times that in the Open Lotus Hell.[129]

Master Vasubhandu taught this in a briefer form:

> The lifespan in the Cold Sore Hell
> [approximates] the time it would take to empty a store of
> sesame seeds
> by removing just one seed every hundred years.
> The lifespan in the others increases by a factor of twenty.[130]

Therefore the lifespan in the Cold Sore Hell is the time it would take to empty a full sesame store; that of the Open Cold Sore Hell is that multiplied by twenty; that of the Chattering Teeth Hell is that multiplied by four hundred; that of the Sneezing Hell is that multiplied by eight thousand; that of the Alas Hell is that multiplied by 160,000; that of the Utpala Wound Hell is that multiplied by 3,200,000; that of the Lotus-Like Wounds is that multiplied by 64,000,000; and that of the Great Lotus Wounds is that multiplied by 1,280,000,000.

The occasional hells. These are created by the karma of one or two people or many people, and depend on the specific action performed. They take many different forms and have no definite location. Some of their hell beings live in rivers, some in the hills, and some in desolate areas or yet other places. Some are in subterranean realms. Some are in the human realm, such as those seen by the realized Maudgalyāyana. Likewise some are in destitute places, like those seen by Saṅgharakṣita.[131] Their lifespan is not fixed.

This concludes the explanation of hell beings' sufferings.

Hungry spirits. There are two categories: the king of the hungry spirits—Yama, lord of the dead—and the scattered spirits.

As for their habitats, Yama, the ruler of the hungry spirits, lives some five hundred leagues beneath this Jambudvīpa world. [82] His scattered subjects have no set location, living in deserts and the like. There are three types of the latter: those that have an external eating or drinking impediment, those that have an internal impediment, and those with a general eating or drinking impediment.

The sufferings endured are as follows. Some anguished spirits have supernatural powers and experience almost god-like splendors. However, those with an external eating or drinking impediment see food and drink as pus and blood. They cannot eat or drink it because they perceive themselves as being prevented from so doing by other beings. Those with an internal impediment are not prevented by others from ingesting the food but are themselves unable to do so. It is said:

> Some have a mouth the size of a needle
> but a belly the size of a mountain.
> Anguished with hunger, those with the strength to look for
> food cannot find a morsel even among rubbish.[132]

Among those with an eating and drinking impediment there are two types: fire garlands and filth eaters. As soon as the first type ingests food or drink, they are burned by it, as if by fire. The second eat excrement, drink urine, and cut off their flesh to eat. This was seen in a wilderness by Koṭikarṇa.[133]

How long does the lifespan of a hungry spirit last? A month of human time is the equivalent of a day and night of hungry spirit time. This enables us to calculate how long, in human terms, they live, because their lives last five hundred of their years. It is said:

> ... hungry spirits live
> for five hundred [years]: a day being a month.[134]

Animals. There are four main categories: many-legged ones, quadrupeds, bipeds, and the legless.

Their habitat can be water, open land, or forest, but the majority live in the oceans.

The sufferings they experience are those of enslavement and being slaughtered and butchered when exploited by humans, or being eaten by each other in the wild. It says of domesticated animals:

> Powerless, they are exploited:
> beaten, kicked, chained, and goaded.[135]

And of wild animals, it is said:

> They are those slaughtered for their pearls, wool, [83]
> bones, blood, flesh, or hides.[136]

Concerning those living in the great oceans:

> They eat whatever is in front of the face.[137]

Animal lifespan is not fixed. The longest living continue for up to an intermediate cosmic eon. It says:

> The lifespan of animals is an eon, at most.[138]

This concludes the section on the sufferings of the lower states.

The *sufferings of the higher states of existence* are considered in three areas: humans, demigods, and gods.

Humans. Humans experience eight principal sufferings. It says in *Nanda's Abiding in the Womb*:

> Likewise birth is a suffering, aging is a suffering, sickness is a suffering, death is a suffering, to be separated from what one likes is a suffering, to encounter what one dislikes is a suffering, to strive after and obtain what one wants is a suffering, and also to undergo hardship in order to maintain what one has is a suffering.[139]

The first of these is the *suffering of birth*, which also serves as the source of all the others. Although four possible modes of birth[140] are taught, most humans are born from a womb. When that is the case, various sufferings occur in the period starting from the intermediate state (*bardo*) and continuing until a womb is entered. In general, bardo beings have certain supernatural abilities. They are able to move through space and to see remote birth states through a type of divine vision. This leads to the subjective experience of four types of hallucinations generated by the force of former actions, such as the stirring of a mighty wind, a heavy fall of rain, a darkening of the sky, and the presence of frightening sounds made by hordes of people.

Then, according to how good or bad the person's karma is, the following ten distorted perceptions will come to arise: "I'm entering a celestial palace," "I'm going on top of a multistory building," "I'm approaching a throne," "I'm entering a thatched hut," "I'm going into a house made of leaves," "I'm slipping in between blades of grass," "I'm entering a forest," "I'm going through a hole in a wall," or "I'm slipping in between straws." [84]

Furthermore, seeing from afar the future parents in sexual embrace, [the bardo being] heads toward them. Beings who have accumulated a great store of merit and who will have a high rebirth see a celestial palace, multistory building, or the like and head for it. Those with a middling store of merit who will have a middling rebirth see the grass-thatched hut and so forth and head toward that. Those who have gathered no merit and who will have a low rebirth see the hole in the wall and so forth and head toward that. Having reached there, one who is to be born a boy will feel attracted to the mother and averse to the father, whereas one who is to be born a girl will feel attraction for the father and aversion toward the mother. By these feelings of attraction and aversion, the bardo consciousness becomes fused with the impure substances of the parents.[141]

It is taught that from that moment on, thirty-eight weeks will be spent in the womb.[142] It is also taught that some spend eight months, some nine, and some ten. Some spend an indefinite period, and there are even some who spend up to sixty years in the womb.[143]

During the first week in the mother's womb, it is just like being cooked and fried in a hot cooking pot, due to the consciousness combined with the physical constituents causing experiences of unbearable suffering. This stage of the embryo, called the *ovoid*, is in form like rice jelly or yogurt.

In the second week in the mother's womb, the "all-touching" energy stirs. Its contact with the mother's womb makes the four elements become manifest. This is called the *oblong* and is like curds or churned butter in appearance.

In the third week in the mother's womb, the "activator" energy stirs the womb, making the four elements further consolidate. This is known as the *lump* and looks like a metal spoon or an ant.

Likewise, in the seventh week spent in the mother's womb, the "twister" energy arises. [85] Its effect on the child in the womb causes formation of the two arms and two legs. The suffering undergone during this period is as though one strong person were pulling out the limbs while another was using a rolling pin to spread out the body.

Likewise, in the eleventh week spent in the mother's womb, the "orifice-forming" energy occurs. Its effect on the child in the womb is to cause the nine bodily orifices to appear. The suffering at that time is like that of a fresh wound being probed by a finger.

Furthermore, when the mother eats irregularly or eats predominantly cold food, one suffers as if one had been thrown naked onto ice. Very hot, sour, or spicy foods will create pain in a similar way. If the mother overeats, the pain is like that of being crushed between rocks. If she does not eat enough, the child also suffers, feeling as if it has been sent spinning through space. When she moves quickly, jumps or turns around sharply, or suddenly bends her body, the child is pained as though it were falling over a precipice. At times of violent intercourse, it suffers as though being beaten by thorny sticks.

In the thirty-seventh week, the child becomes aware of being in a womb, preceiving it as a dirty, foul-smelling, pitch-black prison. Completely fed up with it, the thought of leaving occurs. In the thirty-eighth week, the "flower-gathering" energy stirs the mother's womb, turning the fetus around toward the gateway of birth. The suffering at that time is like that of being placed upon a [rapidly rotating] iron machine.

Thus, as one develops during the pregnancy from a week-old embryo into a fully developed fetus, one is boiled and stirred around in the womb, as in a hot or even scalding pot; one is affected and shoved about by the twenty-eight different vital energies; and one is nurtured and developed by nutrients coming from the mother's blood and so forth. Therefore it says, in *Nanda's Abiding in the Womb*:

> From the week-old embryo—the ovoid—
> a flesh bubble arises,
> and from this arises the oblong,
> the second-week embryo.
> This grows more solid,
> giving rise to the head and four limbs,
> and once the bones are well formed and connected,
> the body becomes complete.
> The cause of all this happening is karma.[144]

Then the "heading-downward" [86] energy stirs, turning the head downward. The body leaves the womb, arms outstretched, experiencing pains that feel as though it were being drawn through an iron press. Some die in the process. Sometimes both mother and child die in childbirth.

At birth itself, when the child first has contact with surfaces, it suffers as though it has been thrown onto a bed of thorns. A little later, when wiped, it feels as though its skin is being peeled off and its body rubbed against a wall.

One's entire stay [in the womb] is as uncomfortable, confined, dark, and impure as just described: even if a really tough person were offered three measures of gold in return for putting up with being in that kind of an impure, filthy hole for just three days, could such a person manage it? The suffering of being in the womb is even worse than that. As it says in *Letter to a Student*:

> Stifled by unbearable smells and impurities,
> totally confined in utter darkness, staying in a womb is like
> being in hell
> because one has to put up with great suffering,
> while the body remains totally constricted.[145]

Once convinced of this, think: "Who could possibly enter a womb even one more time?"

Although the *sufferings of aging* are also immeasurable, they can be summarized as tenfold: radical change in physique, hair, skin, complexion, abilities, prestige, quality of life, health, mental ability, and the life force itself.

1. There will be *marked physical change* as the body, previously strong and robust and holding itself erect, becomes bent, twisted, and needing to support itself with a stick.
2. There will be *marked change in hair.* Formerly jet black, it becomes white or is lost.
3. There will be *marked change in the skin*. Once as fine and smooth [87] as Benares fine cloth or Chinese silk, it becomes coarse, lined, and heavily wrinkled, looking like braided copper bangles.
4. There will be *marked changes of complexion*. Once filled with brightness and luster, like a freshly opened lotus, it now fades, becoming bluish or grayish, like an old, withered flower.
5. There will be *marked changes in ability and power*. The enthusiasm and ability that were previously enjoyed will change, as declining physical strength prevents the harder tasks from being undertaken and as mental decline takes away any enthusiasm for doing things. The sense faculties become blunt and lose their abilities, perceiving their objects in an unclear and confused way.
6. There will be *marked changes in prestige*. Although formerly praised and respected by others, the elderly wane in other people's esteem and become the object of inferiors' scorn. Even strangers find them unappealing, and they become the object of children's tricks and become a source of shame for their children and grandchildren.
7. There will be a *marked change in quality of life*. The pleasure given by possessions, food, and drink deteriorates. The body cannot feel properly warm, nor can the mouth find good taste in anything. There is a fancy for what is not available and difficulty getting others to get supplies or make food.
8. There will be *marked change in health*. Once stricken by old age, the greatest of ailments, there is suffering, for age brings on all the other diseases.
9. There will be a *marked change in mental ability*. Becoming senile and

confused, the elderly forget almost immediately what has just been said or done.

10. When time is up, *life's end is reached*. Short of breath and starting to wheeze since all the component elements of the body have worn out, death is now at hand.

The *Vast Manifestation Sutra* says of all this:

> Old age turns a pleasant physique into an unpleasant one.
> Old age steals prestige and damages abilities and strength.
> Old age steals happiness and increases suffering.
> Old age is the maker of death and the robber of beauty.[146]

Although the *sufferings of sickness* are also immeasurable, they can be summed up as sevenfold: (1) being struck down by a powerful disease, (2) undergoing painful physical examinations, (3) having to take strong medicine, (4) being prevented from eating and drinking what is enjoyable, [88] (5) having to follow the doctor's orders, (6) the diminution of wealth, and (7) fear of death. The *Vast Manifestation Sutra* says of this:

> Tormented by being prey to—and actually falling victim to—
> the sufferings of hundreds of maladies, they are like human
> ghosts.[147]

The *sufferings of death* are also countless. It says of them, in the *Advice to a King Sutra*:

> Great King! Someone tormented like this, on the torture spike of death, is no longer so arrogant. Protectors, allies, or friends help you no more. Stricken by disease, the mouth is thirsty, the face changes, the limbs give way, you are unable to work, and you soil your body with saliva, snot, urine, and disgusting vomit, and you also wheeze noisily. The doctors abandon hope, and you sleep on your bed for the last time, sinking into the stream of samsara and becoming frightened of the lord of death's emissaries. The breathing stops, the mouth and nostrils gape. You leave this world behind and head for the next. It is the great departure, the entrance into deepest darkness, the fall over the greatest

> precipice, and the mighty ocean sweeping you away. Borne away by the winds of karma, you go to the place of no settling, and this without being able to take one iota of your possessions. Though you cry out "O Mother! O Father! Oh, my children!" there is, at that time, Great King, no other protector, no other refuge, no other ally, than Dharma.[148]

Then there is the *suffering of being separated from loved ones*. When father, mother, children, or friends die, there is immeasurable suffering, in the form of misery, grief, weeping, wailing, and the like.

The *suffering of encountering the unwanted* is the distress of conflict that occurs when meeting hated enemies. There are many sufferings, such as arguments, physical conflict, and so forth.

The last two types of suffering—the *strife of obtaining* and the *difficulty of maintaining*—are self-evident.

Demigods. Besides having suffering akin to that of the gods, the demigods also suffer from pride, jealousy, fighting, and quarrelling. It says:

> Demigods endure great mental torment because they are,
> by their very nature, resentful of the gods' splendors and
> enjoyments.[149]

Gods. Gods of the desire realm suffer through having to fight off the demigods, through dissatisfaction due to their endless desires, [89] and through losing their self-confidence. They also suffer by their limbs being severed and parts of their bodies being amputated, by being killed or expelled, and at the end of their lives, they suffer through death, losing their divine status and going to another existence. It is said:

> When death comes, divine child, five signs will appear: Your clothes start to smell bad, flower garlands wither, your two armpits begin to sweat, foul smells arise from your body, and you begin to find seats uncomfortable.[150]

Gods of the form and formless dimensions do not have the abovementioned sufferings. However, since they die, transmigrate, and do not have the power to remain in their state, they suffer through having to take birth in a lower state.

Likewise, once the good karma of humans or gods of any level is exhausted, they have to fall into states of suffering. Therefore the whole condition of samsara, the very nature of which is suffering, is like that of a house ablaze. To quote *Nanda's Abiding in the Womb*:

> Woe and alas! Because this immensity of self-perpetuating existence is ablaze, completely flaming, really burning, totally blazing, not even a few remain undefeated by it. What is this raging inferno? It is the fire of aggression, passion, and stupidity; the fire of birth, aging, and death; the fire of sorrow, lamentation, mental unhappiness, and unrest. Because these fires are constantly raging and blazing, no one escapes them.[151]

Knowing the sufferings of samsara to be just like that will, in itself, turn the mind away from the pleasures of worldly existence. To quote the scriptures, the *Meeting of Father and Son Sutra* states:

> Recognizing the sufferings of samsara,
> true weariness with it will arise,
> and fear of its three realms will
> stimulate a diligent abandoning of it.[152]

The great teacher Nāgārjuna has also said, in a similar vein:

> Since samsara is like that, there is no good birth
> as a god, a human, a hell being, a hungry spirit,
> or as an animal. So know rebirth to be
> a vessel for many harms.[153]

This was the fifth chapter, explaining the sufferings of samsara, from this *Ornament of Precious Liberation, a Wish-Fulfilling Gem of Sublime Dharma*. [90]

6. Karma and Its Effects

IF YOU WONDER what causes the sufferings described above, understand them to arise from tainted *karma* (actions). The *One Hundred* [*Stories*] *about Karma* says of this:

> Actions are of various kinds;
> those actions have created beings in all their variety.[154]

The *White Lotus of Compassion Sutra* says:

> The worlds have been made by actions. Their manifestation is due to actions. Sentient beings have been created by actions and have sprung from actions. Through action arises all their different types.[155]

The *Treasury of Higher Knowledge* says:

> The various worlds were generated by actions.[156]

If you wonder what exactly karma is, know that it falls into two areas: mental activity and activity propelled by thought. The *Compendium of Higher Knowledge* says of this:

> What is karma? It is mental activity [itself] and mentally motivated action.[157]

The *Treasury of Higher Knowledge* says:

> *Karma* is intention and what is done because of that.[158]

Furthermore, in the *Fundamental Verses on the Middle Way*, it says:

> The Supreme Sage has taught that *karma* means
> mental activity and that which is done because of thought.[159]

You may wonder what these two actually are. "Mental activity" means the actions of mind. "That which is done" means whatever physical and verbal activity has been intended and provoked by mind. The *Treasury of Higher Knowledge* says:

> Intention is mental activity;
> what it generates is physical and verbal activity.[160]

The following synopsis outlines actions and the results they generate:

> **Actions and their consequences are summed up through six points: their categories, characteristics, ownership, apportionment, inflation, and ineluctability.**

First are its **categories**: (1) nonvirtuous actions and their effects,[161] (2) virtuous actions and their effects, (3) the action of unwavering karma and its effect.

The second point concerns the **characteristics** of these three.

Nonvirtuous actions and their effects. Although generally speaking there are very many sorts of nonvirtuous actions, they can be summarized as the *ten nonvirtues*. Three are physical: killing and so forth. Four are verbal: lying and so forth. Three are mental: greed and so forth. [91] Each of these is itself treated through three points: its categories, its results, and some particular instances.

Killing has three categories: killing through desire and attachment, killing through anger and aversion, and killing through confused ignorance. The first of these is to kill for the sake of meat, hides, and so forth; for sport or financial gain; or to safeguard yourself or loved ones. The second is to murder those you feel aversion for, on account of grudges or competition and the like. The third is done in order to make offerings.

The results of killing are also threefold: the ripened result, the result corresponding to the cause, and the dominant result. The ripened result is rebirth as a hell being. The result corresponding to the cause is that even if you are reborn human, you will have a short life and many sicknesses. The dominant result is to be reborn in an ill-fated and unattractive land.

The particular instance—the most heinous among all forms of killing—is to kill an arhat who is also your father.

Stealing has three categories: stealing by force, stealing by stealth, and stealing through cheating or fraudulence. The first of these is to steal with needless violence; the second is to steal unnoticed, by burglary and the like; and the third is to cheat through corrupt weights and measures.

Of the three types of result, the ripened result is rebirth as a hungry spirit. The result corresponding to the cause is that even if reborn human, you experience poverty. The dominant result is to be reborn in a place where there is much frost and hail.

The worst case of stealing, the most pernicious act, is to take wealth belonging to your guru or to the three precious refuges.

Sexual misconduct has three categories: sex proscribed by family ties, [92] sex proscribed by belonging to someone else, and sex proscribed due to religious factors. The first of these is intercourse with parents, siblings, and so forth [blood relations]. The second is intercourse with someone committed to another person or belonging to a monarch. The third includes five areas of improper intercourse because of organs involved, place, time, degree, or manner. *Inappropriate organs* refers to oral or anal intercourse. An *inappropriate place* is in the proximity of a guru, temple, stupa, or large gathering. *Inappropriate times* are those when lay precepts are being observed, during pregnancy, while the mother is breastfeeding, or during daylight hours. An *inappropriate degree* is five or more times consecutively. *Inappropriate forms* of intercourse are the likes of rape and anal or oral intercourse with a person of the same sex or with a hermaphrodite.

Of the three types of result, the ripened result is rebirth as a hungry spirit. The corresponding result is that even if reborn human, your partner will be like a hateful enemy. The dominant result is to be reborn in a very dusty land. The worst case is the pernicious act of having intercourse with your own mother who also happens to be an arhat.

Lying is of three types: lies that are your undoing, big lies, and trivial lies. The first of these are those of false gurus and involve pretense about spiritual accomplishment. The second are lies told with the intention of self-benefit or harm to others. The third are lies that are neither beneficial nor harmful.

Of the three types of result, the ripened result is rebirth as an animal.

The corresponding result is that, even if reborn human, you are denigrated by others. The dominant result is to have bad breath. The worst case is the pernicious act of lying to your guru when you have slandered the Tathāgata.

Divisive speech is of three types: vehement, insinuated, or via third parties. The first separates friends by direct slander; the second separates them through insinuations made in their presence; [93] and the third does so through rumors.

Of the three types of result, the ripened result is rebirth in hell. The corresponding result is that, even if reborn human, you will be separated from friends. The dominant result is birth in a place where the landscape is erratic and dangerous. The worst instance among such divisive speech acts is the pernicious act of causing a schism in the Sangha.

Wounding speech is of three types: direct, insinuated, or via third parties. The first is to tell someone openly of their faults and weaknesses. The second means to say hurtful things, in a half-disguised manner mingled with jest, relevant to someone present. The third is to gossip about someone's faults or weaknesses to their friends and third parties.

Of the three types of result, the ripened result is rebirth in hell. The corresponding result is that, even if reborn a human, the sounds and words you hear will be disturbing. The dominant result is rebirth in a hot and arid place where there is much evil. The worst instance, the most pernicious act of all wounding speech, is to speak harshly to your father or mother or to a realized being.

Useless speech is of three types: deluded useless speech, useless worldly chatter, and true but useless speech. The first concerns the formulas and recitations of deluded belief systems. The second concerns silly talk, jokes, and the like. The third concerns attempts to explain Dharma to those lacking respect or an appropriate frame of mind.

Of the three types of result, the ripened result is rebirth as an animal. The corresponding result is that, even if reborn a human, the person's words will carry no weight. The dominant result is rebirth in a place where the seasons are completely erratic. The worst instance, the most pernicious type of useless speech, is that which distracts those who are practicing Dharma.

Avarice is of three types: avarice concerning your own things, other people's things, and those things that belong to neither you nor others. The first is a grasping attachment to family status, physical appearance, [94] qualities, wealth, and possessions, thinking, "There is no one quite like me." The second is to covet the good things others possess, thinking, "If only this were mine." The third involves attachment to things that belong to no one, such as the precious substances buried in the earth, thinking, "If only I could own that."

Of the three types of result of avarice, the ripened result is to be reborn as a hungry spirit. The corresponding result is that even if reborn human, avarice will dominate the mind. The dominant result is rebirth in a place where the quality of food is poor. Of all the sorts of avarice, the most pernicious is the wish to steal the possessions of those who have truly renounced the world.

Malevolence is of three types: that due to hatred, jealousy, and resentment. The first is to contemplate killing another because of hatred, as happens in times of war. The second, due to competition and the like, is to think about killing or harming another through fear of being surpassed. The third, due to long-standing resentment, is to contemplate killing or hurting someone who has previously wronged one, or the like.

Of the three types of result of malevolence, the ripened result is rebirth in hell. The corresponding result is that even if reborn human, hatred dominates your mind. The dominant result is rebirth in a place where the food is bitter and coarse. Of all types of malevolence, the worst instance and most pernicious act is to plan to commit one of the five acts that have an immediate consequence.[162]

Aberrant belief is of three types: aberrant beliefs about actions and their consequences, about the truth(s), and about the precious refuges. The first of these means not believing that virtuous and nonvirtuous actions produce their respective consequences—happiness and suffering. The second is to consider that the truth of cessation will not be obtained through practice of the truth of the path.[163] The third is to deprecate the three precious refuges, believing them to be untrue.

Of the three types of result of aberrant belief, the ripened result is rebirth as an animal. [95] The corresponding result is that even if reborn human, stupidity and confusion dominate your mind. The dominant result is rebirth in a place without harvests. The worst instance and most pernicious act among aberrant beliefs is to become caught up in the "thorn-like" view.[164]

The above was a general explanation of the ripened results of such actions. Three kinds of ripened results of an action can be distinguished according to the affliction present, the frequency of action, or the person acted on:

1. If the actions were done through anger or hatred, rebirth in hell is more likely. If they were done through passion or attachment, rebirth as a hungry

spirit is more likely. If they were done through stupidity and confusion, rebirth as an animal is more likely. Thus the *Precious Garland* says:

> Through attachment, you will become a hungry spirit,
> through anger, you will be cast into hell,
> and through confusion, you become an animal.[165]

2. Innumerable nonvirtuous acts lead to rebirth in hell. A great deal of nonvirtuous acts lead to rebirth as a hungry spirit. A few such harmful actions lead to rebirth as an animal.

3. If the nonvirtuous act is committed against a very special person, there may be rebirth in hell. If committed against someone of medium importance, there may be rebirth as a hungry spirit. If committed against a lesser person, there may be rebirth as an animal.

The above was an explanation of nonmeritorious actions and their consequences. To quote the *Precious Garland*:

> Attachment, anger, ignorance, and the actions
> to which they give rise are nonvirtue.
> Nonvirtue brings all the sufferings
> and hence all the lower states of existence.[166]

Virtuous actions and their effects. First, we consider the actions. The ten virtuous actions consist of renouncing the nonvirtuous ones and, furthermore, engaging in their counterparts, the things that should be done: protecting the lives of others, giving lavishly, maintaining pure sexual conduct, speaking the truth straightforwardly, dispelling discord among people and bringing them into harmony, speaking peacefully and sincerely in a way that pleases others, speaking in a way that is meaningful, reducing desires and being content with what one has, cultivating loving kindness and the like, [96] and penetrating the highest meaning.

These actions have threefold consequences. The ripened result is rebirth in the human or divine planes of the desire realm. The corresponding result will be, for instance, that by abandoning harm to others and by protecting life, longevity is gained, and similarly for the other virtues. The dominant result is that by giving up killing you will be reborn in a very prosperous and powerful place, and so on and so forth, according to the virtue concerned.

The above was an explanation of beneficial actions and their consequences. The *Precious Garland* says:

> What is generated by non-attachment,
> non-anger, and non-delusion is virtue.
> Virtue brings all fortunate rebirths
> and happiness in all lifetimes.[167]

The action of unwavering karma and its effect. Cultivating the meditative attainment creates causes that give rise to rebirth in similar meditative states. These meditative attainments consist of the eight preparatory absorptions, the eight actual absorptions, and the special meditative attainment. Their consequences—birth in the absorption [realms]—consist of the seventeen types of form-realm gods and the four types of formless-realm gods. The general condition for these causes and effects to occur is the practice of the ten virtues.

The first of the meditative concentrations is propelled by meditatively cultivating its obstacle-removing stage. This is the preparatory attainment that removes inability. It leads into the first completing concentration proper, which is a meditative absorption accompanied by investigation, sustained analysis, joy, and bliss. Through cultivating this, there will be rebirth among the gods of the [first two] Brahma realms. By then cultivating the special aspect of this concentration, there will be rebirth in the Great Brahma heaven.

The second meditative concentration is propelled by meditatively cultivating its obstacle-removing stage, the preparatory attainment. This leads into the second completing concentration itself—a meditative absorption accompanied by joy and physical well-being but in which concept and analysis have been abandoned. By cultivating this, there will be rebirth among the gods of the second concentration, in the Small Light, [Limitless Light, and Radiant] heavens.

It is likewise for the propelling meditative attainment for the third and fourth meditative concentrations. By cultivating the actual meditative absorption of the third completing concentration, in which there is physical well-being but mental joy is abandoned, there will be rebirth among the third concentration gods of the Lesser Virtue, [Limitless Virtue, and Complete Virtue] heavens.

By cultivating the actual meditative absorption of the fourth completing concentration, in which investigation, sustained analysis, joy, and bliss have all been left aside, there will be rebirth among the fourth concentration gods of the Cloudless Heaven and so forth [up to Akaniṣṭha, eight heavens in all].

[97] That which has arisen out of the transcendence of these four meditative concentrations is the Sphere of Infinite Space, and cultivating this gives

rise to rebirth as a god of the Sphere of Infinite Space. That which has arisen out of the transcendence of this is the Sphere of Infinite Consciousness, and cultivating this gives rise to rebirth as a god of the Sphere of Infinite Consciousness. That which has arisen out of the transcendence of this is the Sphere of Nothing Whatsoever, and cultivating this gives rise to rebirth as a god of the Sphere of Nothing Whatsoever. That which has arisen out of the transcendence of this is the Sphere of Neither Cognition Nor Absence of Cognition, and cultivating this gives rise to rebirth as a god of the Sphere of Neither Cognition Nor Absence of Cognition.

What exactly is meant by the phrase "that which has arisen out of transcendence"? It means that the subsequent stage represents a transcendence of the previous mind condition and moves toward another condition that is freer from desire and attachment.

Are the spheres of Infinite Space and so forth so called because limitless space itself [and the others] are the actual object of meditation? No. The first three are called Infinite Space and so forth because the mind is anchored by evoking terms such as "infinite space" and so on during the meditative attainment. Later, when the preparatory stage is over, there is no such anchoring of the mind. The last of the four is so called because of its diminished cognition. Although there is barely any lucid cognition, it cannot be said that there is absolutely none at all.

All the eight actual absorptions consist of single-pointed, virtuous mind. With these the cause and effects of unwavering karma have been presented. The *Precious Garland* says:

> Through the absorptions, the immeasurables, and the formless
> [states],
> the happiness of Brahma [heaven] and so forth is experienced.[168]

Thus the three kinds of tainted action described above [i.e., nonvirtuous, virtuous, and unwavering] give rise to the substance of samsara.

The third point is [**ownership**—the fact] that actions determine your personal lot. The consequences of the actions that someone has done will be experienced by that person alone: They come to maturity in the aggregates of their doer and in no one else. In the *Compendium of Higher Knowledge* it says:

> What does it mean, "Actions determine your personal lot"? Because individuals experience the full maturation of actions

> they themselves have done, and because that [maturation] shares nothing in common with others, it is called "personal."[169]

Were this not the case, then karma could dwindle or become exhausted, or someone might receive evil consequences from acts committed by someone else. This is why the sutra says:

> The deeds committed by Devadatta [98] will not come to maturity in the earth or in water and so forth. They will come to maturity solely in his very own aggregates and sense spheres. In those of whom else could they possibly come to maturity?[170]

The fourth point is [**apportionment**—the fact] that experiences due to action are strictly apportioned. Happiness or suffering is infallibly experienced as the respective consequence of virtuous or harmful action. By accumulating virtuous action, happiness will be experienced as a result. By accumulating harmful action, suffering will be experienced as a result. The *Compendium of Higher Knowledge* says of this:

> How will experience be apportioned? Subject to the ripened result of actions, a person experiences his own share that corresponds specifically to the virtuous or nonvirtuous actions that have been done.[171]

The *Shorter Sutra on Mindfulness* says:

> Through virtue, one attains happiness.
> Through nonvirtue, suffering occurs.
> This is the reason for teaching clearly
> the virtuous and nonvirtuous actions and their consequences.[172]

And in the *Questions of Surata Sutra*:

> From the seeds of spicy plants,
> spicy fruits will grow;
> and from sweet seeds,
> sweet fruits will come to grow.

Wise and skillful people should know
through this example the full consequence of
evil to be like the spicy [fruit]
and bright action to be like the sweet.[173]

The fifth point is [**inflation**—the fact] that great results can be created by a small cause. It has been taught that it is possible even for a single moment of evil action to cause you to experience an eon in the hells. In *Guide to the Bodhisattva Way of Life*, it says:

The Sage has said that whoever generates an evil mind
against a benefactor such as the bodhisattva
will stay in hell for as many eons
as there were moments of evil mind.[174]

It is also said that a person will experience suffering for five hundred existences for each instance of bad speech uttered, and so forth. The *Collection of Aphorisms* says:

Even a small bad action
can generate much fear and considerable damage
in a future existence:
it is like poison that has entered the system.[175]

It is also the case that even a small virtuous act can induce great consequence. The *Collection of Aphorisms* says [99]:

Even doing a small wholesome act
can produce great happiness in future existences
and create great consequence,
like grains that produce the most abundant harvests.[176]

The sixth point is [**ineluctability**, the fact] that karma never just fades away. Except for the case of action that has been properly remedied, results will not be lost or become any weaker [with time], even though the karma may not ripen for endless eons. Although you may have been in a state of ease for a considerable period, the result will be induced whenever you encounter the requisite circumstances, whatever they may be.

Being convinced about actions and their consequences, as explained above, and fearing the sufferings of samsara, then, as it is said:

> Someone who turns away from worldly happiness,
> turns away from unwholesome action,
> and strives for their own peace alone,
> that person is refered to as "middling" type.[177]

A "middling" person who cultivates such an approach would be the likes of the seven daughters of King Kṛkin.[178] Thus it says in the *One Hundred* [*Stories*] *about Karma*:

> The karmas of physical beings are
> not lost or weakened even for a hundred eons.
> Once they are gathered and when the time comes,
> their results will ripen.[179]

In the *Shorter Sutra on Mindfulness*, it says:

> Fire may become cold,
> the wind may be caught by a lasso,
> and the sun and moon may fall down,
> but the consequences of karma are infallible.[180]

This concludes the sixth chapter, concerning actions and their effects, from this *Ornament of Precious Liberation, a Wish-Fulfilling Gem of Sublime Dharma.*

7. Loving Kindness and Compassion

Now I present, as the antidote to counteract attachment to solitary peace, the practice of compassion. "Attachment to solitary peace" means longing only for one's own nirvana and lacking altruistic activity due to absence of loving concern for sentient beings. This is the Hinayana. As it is said:

> When personal welfare takes priority, thinking,
> "To really benefit myself, I must ignore
> all the various things that need to be done to help others,"
> then self-interest has taken control.[181]

When loving kindness and compassion become part of you, you have so much care for other conscious beings that personal liberation alone would be unbearable. [100] Therefore you need to cultivate loving kindness and compassion. Master Mañjuśrīkīrti has said:

> A follower of the Mahayana should not be without loving kindness and compassion for even a single moment.[182]

and

> It is not anger and hatred but loving kindness and compassion that vouchsafe the welfare of others.[183]

The development of loving kindness

The first of these two topics is loving kindness. The synopsis for this sub-chapter is:

> **Limitless loving kindness is well summarized by six topics: its categories, its object of reference, the form it takes, the means of cultivating it, its measure, and its qualities.**

First, there are three **categories**: (1) loving kindness focused on sentient beings, (2) loving kindness focused on the nature of things, and (3) loving kindness with no objective reference. It says of these, in the *Akṣayamati Sutra*:

> Loving kindness focused on sentient beings is that of bodhisattvas first cultivating bodhicitta; loving kindness focused on the nature of things is that of the bodhisattva engaged in the deeds; and loving kindness without any objective reference is that of bodhisattvas who have attained the patience accepting unborn phenomena.[184]

Second, to explain the first category of loving kindness, its **object of reference** includes all sentient beings. Third, the **form it takes** is that of a mind longing for [all sentient beings] to find happiness. Fourth, the **way to cultivate loving kindness** is as follows. Since gratitude is the root of love, bring to mind the kindness of sentient beings. In this respect, the person who has been kindest to you in this life is your own mother. In what way? She has been kind by creating your body, kind through undergoing hardships [on your behalf], kind by nurturing your life, and kind by teaching you the ways of the world. The *Perfection of Wisdom in Eight Thousand Lines* says:

> Why is this? Mothers gave birth to us, underwent hardships, kept us alive, and taught us all about the world.[185]

First consider *the kindness of nourishing your body*. This body of yours did not start out fully grown, with its flesh fully developed and with a healthy complexion. It developed gradually inside your mother, through the different embryonic and fetal stages, being gradually created and nourished by vital fluids from her very own flesh and blood. [101] It grew thanks to nourishment from the food she ate. It came into being by her having to put up with all sorts of embarrassment, sickness, and suffering. Furthermore, generally speaking, it was she who helped make this body, which started out a tiny infant, into [its present] bulk as big as a yak.

Next, consider *the kindness of undergoing hardships*. You did not come into this world clothed, finely adorned, with money in your pocket and provisions for the journey. When you came into this unfamiliar place, where you knew no one and had nothing, the only wealth you had was your howling mouth and empty stomach. Your mother gave you food so that you would not go hungry, drink to keep you from thirst, clothes to fend off the cold, and wealth to keep you from poverty. It was not as though she just gave you things she no longer needed herself: she herself went without food, without drink, and without new clothes.

Furthermore, not only did she sacrifice her happiness as far as this existence is concerned, she also deprived herself of using her assets [as offerings] to provide for her own prosperity in future lives. In brief, without regard for her own happiness in both this life and the next, she devoted herself to rearing and caring for you, her child. Nor did she obtain what was needed easily and pleasurably. To provide for you she was obliged to sin, to suffer, and to toil. She sinned by having to resort to fishing, killing animals, and so on to provide for you. She suffered because what she gave you was the fruit of trading, laboring in the fields, and so forth, wearing the late evening or early morning frost for her boots, the stars as a hat, riding the horse of her calves, beaten by the whip of the long grass, her legs exposed to be bitten by dogs and her face exposed to the looks of men.

She also treated this undefined person who had become her child with more love than her own father, mother, or lama, even though she knew not who this being was or what you would become. She looked at you with loving eyes, gave you her gentle warmth, cradled you in her arms, and spoke to you with sweet words, saying, "My joy! Ah my sunshine, my treasure! Coochie coochie, aren't you Mummy's happiness?" and so forth.

Next, consider *the kindness of keeping you alive*. It is not as though you were born as you are now, knowing how to feed yourself and endowed with the necessary ability to accomplish difficult tasks. When you were helpless, useless—a little worm unable to think—your mother did not discard you but did an inconceivable number of things to nurture your existence. She took you on her lap, protected you from fire and water, held you away from dangerous precipices, [102] got rid of all sources of harm, and prayed for you. At those times when she feared for your life or health, she resorted to divinations, astrology, exorcisms, recitations of texts, special ceremonies, and so on.

Finally, consider *the kindness of teaching you the ways of the world*. At first you were not the clever, experienced, strong-minded person you are now. Apart from being able to bawl out to other members of your family and flap your limbs about, you were ignorant. When you did not know how to feed yourself, it was she who taught you how to eat. When you knew not how to dress yourself, it was she who taught you. When you did not know how to walk, it was she who taught you. When you could not even speak, it was she who taught you, repeating "Mama," "Dada," and so on. Having taught you various crafts and skills, she helped you become a balanced being, strengthening your weaker points and introducing you to the unfamiliar.

Moreover, apart from being your mother in this life, she has also been your mother in previous lives, an inestimable number of times, due to the unending round of existences that has been going on since time without beginning. The *Beginningless Time Sutra* says:

> Were one person to set down a little jujube kernel for every piece of earth, stone, plant, or forest that there is in the world and a second person to count them, eventually a time would come when the count would be completed. Yet were we to try to count the number of times that one being has been our mother, it would be impossible.[186]

The *Letter to a Friend* says:

> If you reduced the earth to little balls the size of jujube kernels,
> their number would be less than that of the number of times
> any one being has been your mother.[187]

Recalling the kindness shown by her in the ways described above every time she was your mother in the past and contemplating it all, you will recognize that her kindness has been absolutely immeasurable. Bearing this carefully in mind, cultivate as sincerely and as frequently as possible a loving, positive mind longing for her happiness.

Furthermore, every sentient being has been your mother, and they have all shown you the same kindnesses enumerated above. Just how many sentient beings are there? Sentient beings are as vast as space itself. The *Prayer of Excellent Conduct* says:

> Whatever the farthest end of space may be,
> that is the limit of sentient beings' existence.[188]

Therefore, a sincere mind that longs to benefit and bring happiness to all beings throughout space [103] is to be cultivated as much as possible. When that has arisen, it is true loving kindness. The *Ornament of Mahayana Sutras* says:

> A bodhisattva acts toward sentient beings
> as though they were an only child,
> with a love so great coming from the very marrow of their
> bones,
> and thereby wishes to benefit them continuously.[189]

Great loving kindness is benevolence so strong that it brings tears to your eyes and makes the hairs of your body stand on end. *Limitless loving kindness* occurs when you no longer discriminate between beings.

The fifth point is the [**measure** or] gauge of accomplishment. Loving kindness has been achieved when your sole wish is for others' happiness and your mind no longer yearns for personal happiness alone.

Sixth, the [**qualities** or] benefits of cultivating loving kindness are immeasurable. The *Candraprabha Sutra* says:

> The merit of limitless offerings made to the Supreme Being,
> even if they fill a hundred quadrillion buddhafields, does not
> equal the benefit
> derived from a benevolent mind.[190]

The good results generated by even an instant's practice of loving kindness are countless. The *Precious Garland* says:

> The merit of offering, three times a day, every day,
> three hundred pots of food
> cannot even begin to compare with that created
> by one tiny instant of loving kindness.[191]

Until buddhahood is attained, you will be benefitted in eight ways by this practice. These are described in the *Precious Garland*:

> Even before you achieve liberation, you will derive
> these eight[192] benefits from loving kindness:
> You will be loved by gods and humans,
> and they will also protect you;

your mind will be happy and full of joy;
you will not be harmed by either poison or weapons;
all your aims will be effortlessly accomplished;
and you will take rebirth in the Brahma realms.[193]

The practice of loving kindness also affords excellent protection. This is illustrated in the story of Mahādatta.[194] It also affords excellent protection for others, as illustrated by the example of King Bāla Maitreya.[195] Once loving kindness has been attained, it will not be difficult to cultivate compassion.

The training in compassion

The synopsis for this subchapter is:

> **Limitless compassion is well summarized by six topics: its categories, its object of reference, the form it takes, the means of cultivating it, its measure, and its qualities.**

First, there are three **categories** [104]: (1) compassion focused on sentient beings, (2) compassion focused on the nature of things, (3) compassion with no objective reference.

The first kind is compassion that arises through understanding the sufferings of beings in the lower states of existence. The second occurs when there is familiarity with the meaning of the four truths of the noble ones and hence understanding of both causes and consequences, thereby counteracting belief in permanent, concrete realities. Compassion arises through realizing how much other beings are unaware of karmic cause and effect and how they perceive things as concrete and lasting. The third kind of compassion occurs when meditative penetration has brought realization of the emptiness of all phenomena. Extraordinary compassion then arises toward sentient beings who grasp at essential existence. As it says:

When, through meditative equipoise,
a bodhisattva becomes perfected through practice,
compassion arises in particular toward
those gripped by the demon of grasping at essential existence.[196]

Of these three, only the development of the first will be discussed here.

Second, this first type of compassion has every sentient being as its **object of reference.**

Third, the **form** it takes is that of a mind longing for [each sentient being] to become free from suffering.

Fourth, the **way to cultivate compassion** is through reflections based on the mother. You imagine her right here, in front of you, being cut up by some people and being beaten, boiled, or burned by others. Or perhaps her body is completely frozen with cold, to a point where is it covered with cold sores, blistered, and cracked open. If this were really the case, would you not experience compassion for her? Since it is a definite fact that those beings suffering in hell have also been our mothers and that they are currently enduring such sufferings, how can compassion not arise toward them, too? Cultivate actual compassion by contemplating in this way and by wishing those beings to be free from suffering and its causes.

Equally, were your own mother to be right in front of you, tormented by hunger and thirst, afflicted by disease and pain, full of fear, utterly terrified and completely disheartened, would you not experience profound compassion for her? It is certain that those hungry spirits who suffer torments like these have all been your own mothers. How can you not feel compassion? Contemplate this and wish them to be freed from their sufferings.

Equally, were your own mother to be right in front of you, old and withered by age, [105] and yet other people nevertheless made her labor as a defenseless slave, beat her hard, killed or chopped her up alive, would you not experience great compassion? It is certain that those beings born as animals are subject to these sufferings and that they were formerly your very own mothers. How can you not feel compassion? Contemplate this and wish them to be free from suffering.

Equally, were your own mother to be right in front of you, blind and near the edge of a precipice a thousand miles deep, unaware of her danger and without anyone who could lead her away or cry out, "Hey, be careful of the abyss!" and then she started wandering toward the edge, would you not experience very great compassion? It is certain that gods, demigods, and humans are all three standing at the edge of the abyss that is the lower states of suffering. Unaware of cause and effect, they do not know that to avoid falling they must give up unwholesome action and practice virtue. Because they do not benefit from the support of a Dharma teacher, they fall into and experience the three lower realms. As it is then so hard to get out of those states, how can you not feel great compassion for them, since they, too, were formerly your own mothers? Contemplate compassion thus and wish them all to be free of suffering.

Fifth, the [**measure**, or] gauge of accomplishment, is that compassion has been achieved when the shackles of cherishing oneself more than others have been cast off and when there is a real, rather than merely verbal, desire that all beings may be liberated from suffering.

Sixth, the [**qualities** or] benefits of this practice are immeasurable. The *Section Discussing the Realization of the Lord of the World* [in the *Perfectly Gathering the Qualities of Avalokiteśvara Sutra*] says:

> Were one thing like all enlightened qualities in the palm of your hand, what would it be? Great compassion![197]

The *Perfectly Gathering the Qualities* [*of Avalokiteśvara*] *Sutra* says:

> O Blessed One! It is like this: wherever the precious wheel of the universal monarch goes, it is automatically accompanied by all his attendant hosts. O Buddha! Wherever the great compassion of the bodhisattva goes, all enlightened qualities accompany it.[198]

Also, it says in the *Sutra of the Tathāgata's Secrets*:

> O master of the secret teaching [Vajrapāṇi]! The root of pristine awareness that knows everything lies in compassion.[199]

As taught above, loving kindness is the wish for the happiness of all beings, and compassion is the wish for them all to be free from suffering. When these are present, a person can no longer find contentment in striving solely for the happiness of personal peace [106] and is joyful at the prospect of attaining buddhahood so as to benefit all beings. Therefore love and compassion constitute the remedy to clinging to the well-being of mere peace.

Once loving kindness and compassion have arisen, others will be cherished more than oneself. It is said:

> Someone who, on the basis of his own suffering,
> aspires to totally eradicate
> the entire suffering all beings,
> that person is most excellent.[200]

Among those who have become such "excellent beings" were the brahman Mahādatta and so forth.

This concludes the seventh chapter, concerning love and compassion, from this *Ornament of Precious Liberation, a Wish-Fulfilling Gem of Sublime Dharma.*

8. Taking Refuge

Now, as an antidote to counter ignorance pertaining to the means for attaining buddhahood, I present the factors associated with generating bodhicitta. For this, the synopsis is the following:

> **The development of supreme bodhicitta is covered through twelve topics: basis, nature, different types, aim, causes, source from which the vow is taken, ceremony, benefits, failings, causes for breakage, methods of restoration, and instructions.**

First topic: The basis for cultivation of bodhicitta

First, the sentient beings that constitute a suitable **basis** for the cultivation of bodhicitta are those who: (1) are endowed with lineage toward Mahayana, (2) have taken refuge in the three most precious refuges, (3) have taken one of the seven classes of prātimokṣa vows, and (4) have developed the aspiring aspect of bodhicitta.

Whereas to have taken refuge in the three precious refuges is the minimum requirement for a life becoming a suitable basis for aspiration bodhicitta, the above four conditions make that life also a proper basis for cultivating engaged bodhicitta. Why is this? It is explained in *Bodhisattva Levels* that aspiration must precede actual practice, and it is explained in *Lamp for the Path to Awakening* that one needs to have taken refuge in order to develop aspirational [mind]. Furthermore, the latter text also states that you need one of the prātimokṣa vows as a foundation for the bodhisattva vow, and in the *Treasury of Higher Knowledge* it says that refuge is the basis on which the prātimokṣa vows are taken. Lastly, *Bodhisattva Levels* says that bodhicitta development cannot even occur in those who are not of the Mahayana type. [107] Thus a combination of all these various factors must be present.

The first point is that there needs to be the Mahayana potential in general, and more particularly that this needs to have been awakened.[201] These points can be understood from the fuller explanation above.[202]

The second point concerns the need to have taken refuge. Should you seek refuge in powerful worldly deities, such as Brahma, Viṣṇu, Śiva, and so forth, or in powerful local forces such as gods or serpent spirits that inhabit mountains, rocks, lakes, ancient trees, and the like? These are not true refuges because none of them has the power to be a refuge. A sutra says of this:

> People of the world seek protection
> from the gods of the mountains and forests,
> from shrines and offering groves, and from sacred trees,
> but these refuges are not true refuges.[203]

Should you then perhaps seek refuge in your parents, friends, relatives, and so forth—those beings who care about you and are glad to help? In fact, these cannot be a refuge either. It says in the *Sutra of the Play of Mañjuśrī*:

> Parents are not your refuge;
> neither are loved ones or relatives.
> Subject to their own wishes,
> they abandon you and go where they please.[204]

Why are none of these able to provide refuge? Because to constitute a refuge, there must be no fear [of samsara] and there must be liberation from its sufferings. None of the above has transcended fear, and they are still subject to suffering. Other than buddhas, no one is definitively liberated from suffering. Other than Dharma, there is no way to achieve buddhahood. Other than the Sangha, there are none who can help us practice Dharma. Hence refuge should be sought in those three. It is said:

> Today, take your refuge in the Buddha,
> in the Dharma, and in the supreme community, the Sangha,
> for it is they who can dispel fear in the fearful
> and it is they who can protect the unprotected.[205]

Since they do possess the ability to protect, do not let yourself be devoured by doubt, wondering, "But can they really protect me once I have taken refuge in them?" [108] The *Great [Passing into] Nirvana Sutra* says:

> One who has taken refuge in the Three Jewels
> will attain fearlessness.[206]

The synopsis explaining refuge in those three is:

> **Taking refuge is summarized through nine topics: categories, basis, source, duration, motivation, ceremony, function, instruction, and benefits.**

First, there are two different **categories** of refuge: general and particular.

Second, there are two types of person who form a **basis** for taking refuge: (1) those who constitute the general basis: people who fear samsara's sufferings and who conceive of the three precious refuges as deities, and (2) those who constitute the particular basis: people of Mahayana potential who have a relatively pure human or divine existence.

Third, there are also two **sources** of refuge:

1. *The general source*: The most precious Buddha is the Blessed One, awakened and complete, who has the most excellent purity, pristine awareness, and greatness of nature. The most precious Dharma has two aspects: the Dharma of teachings, comprising the twelve branches of [the Buddha's] supreme speech, and the Dharma as realization, comprising the truths of cessation and the path. The most precious Sangha is also twofold: the Sangha composed of worldly people, as a gathering of four or more full monks (*bhikṣu*) who have properly maintained their vows; and the most excellent Sangha, as the eight types of beings belonging to the four stages of result.[207]

2. *The special source*: This is explained as the source actually present, the source that is direct realization, and the ultimate source. For the *source actually present*, the Buddha is an image of the Tathāgata, the Dharma is the Mahayana scriptures, and the Sangha is the bodhisattva sangha. For the *source in terms of direct realization*, the Buddha is the one possessing the nature of the three bodies, the Dharma is the sublime Dharma of peace and nirvana, and the Sangha is bodhisattvas who have attained the levels of sublime realization. The *ultimate source*, in terms of ultimate essence, is the Buddha alone. About this the *Uttaratantra* says: [109]

> In ultimate terms the refuge for beings is
> the Buddha and the Buddha alone.[208]

Why is the Buddha capable of providing the [only] totally dependable source of refuge?

> Because the Sage possesses the dharmakāya
> and in terms of the Sangha he is the ultimate sangha.[209]

Sages (*muni*), free from generation and cessation, totally pure, and without desire, are the highest refuge because they possess the dharmakāya and because they are the ultimate achievement of the Sangha of the three vehicles, having attained the dharmakāya, the ultimate conclusion of total purity. This being the case, are the Dharma and the Sangha lasting refuges or not? The *Uttaratantra* says:

> The two aspects of Dharma and the assembly of noble ones
> are not the supreme lasting refuge.[210]

Why is it that they are not a lasting source of refuge? Of the two types of Dharma, the Dharma as teachings, being a collection of terms and an assembly of letters, is something to be abandoned once it has served its purpose, like a vehicle once the journey is done. Hence it is not a lasting refuge. As for the two aspects of Dharma as realization, the truth of the path is not a refuge because it is by its very nature unreliable, being impermanent on account of being a composite creation. The truth of cessation is not a lasting refuge because, according to the śrāvakas, it is a nonexistence—the end of a continuum—like the extinction of a flame. As for the Sangha, they themselves take refuge in the Buddha through fear of samsara and cannot constitute a supreme and lasting refuge because of having that fear. The *Uttaratantra* says:

> Because it is to be abandoned, it's unreliable,
> it's nonexistent, and it's endowed with fear:
> the two aspects of Dharma and the assembly of noble ones
> are not the supreme lasting refuge.[211]

Therefore Master Asaṅga said:

> The inexhaustible refuge, the permanent refuge, the eternal refuge, the most elevated refuge is one and one only. What is it? It is

> the Tathāgata, the defeater of the enemy, the totally and utterly perfect Buddha.[212]

Well, then, does this not contradict what has been said above about the three refuges? The latter originated as a skillful means for guiding those training as Buddhists. The *Great Liberation Sutra* says:

> In brief, the refuge is one, but in terms of method [it] is three.[213] [110]

How are these three refuges presented as skillful means? The *Uttaratantra* says:

> The three refuges are presented
> as teacher, teaching, and those training,
> in terms of the three vehicles, three activities,
> and in accordance with [diverse] aspirations.[214]

Thus the refuges are presented in terms of three qualities, three capacities, three modes of action, and three types of aspiration: (1) Emphasizing the qualities of the teacher, those of bodhisattva capacity, as well as those who aspire to actions that principally elevate the Buddha, take refuge in the Buddha saying, "I take refuge in the Buddha, the most sublime human." (2) Emphasizing the qualities of the teachings, beings of pratyekabuddha capacity, and those aspiring to act in a way that principally elevates the Dharma, take their refuge in the Dharma saying, "I take refuge in the Dharma, the most sublime of all that transcends desire and attachment." (3) Emphasizing the qualities of the trainees, those of śrāvaka capacity, and those who aspire to act in a way principally focused on the Sangha, take refuge in the Sangha saying, "I take refuge in the Sangha, the most sublime of communities."

Thus the above three points present the three refuges in terms of six types of person. The noble Buddha has taught that these are mere conventional realities, designed to help beings progress gradually through their respective courses of training.

Fourth, there are two possible **durations**. The *general duration* is to take refuge from the time [of the ceremony] onward for as long as one lives. The *special duration* is to take refuge from that time onward until the essence, enlightenment, is attained.

Fifth, there are two possible **motivations**. The *general motivation* is to consider personal suffering unbearable. The *special motivation* is to consider others' sufferings unbearable.

Sixth, there are two forms of **ceremony**, general and special. For the *general ceremony*, the refuge seeker first requests refuge from the teacher. Then the teacher either makes offerings to the three precious refuges as a prelude to the ceremony or, when there are no representations present, visualizes them in space and makes mental homage and offerings. [111] Then the refuge seeker repeats the following three times, after the teacher, with utmost sincerity:

> All buddhas and bodhisattvas, please heed me, I pray. Master, please heed me, I pray. I, [so-and-so] by name, take refuge from now until I reach the essence—enlightenment—in the Buddha, the most sublime of all humans, in the Dharma, the most sublime of all that transcends desire, and in the Sangha, the most sublime of communities.

The *special ceremony* is in three parts: a preparation, the actual ceremony, and a conclusion.

The preparation involves first offering a mandala, together with flowers, to an appropriate preceptor, after which the preceptor is requested to confer refuge. Provided the supplicant is a suitable person and someone with Mahayana potential, the preceptor, having accepted the request, will, on the first evening, set up representations of the three precious refuges, arrange offerings, and explain both the benefits of taking refuge and the shortcomings of not doing so.

The actual ceremony takes place on the second evening. The supplicant first cultivates the notion that the [symbols of refuge] on the shrine are the real presence of the most precious refuges, and then pays homage and makes prostrations to them. The following words are then repeated three times, after the preceptor:

> All buddhas and bodhisattvas, please heed me, I pray. Master, please heed me, I pray. From this moment on, until the essence of enlightenment is reached, I, [so-and-so] by name, take my refuge in the buddhas, the blessed ones who are the most sublime

> humans. I take refuge in the Dharma that is peace and nirvana, the most sublime of all that is free from desire and attachment. I take refuge in the Sangha of realized bodhisattvas who are beyond turning back, the most sublime of communities.

Then, inviting the sources of refuge in terms of direct realization and imagining them to be really present, homage is paid to them and offerings made, thinking, "Whatever I do, you are aware of it." Following this, the refuge prayer, as above, is repeated.

Next, in terms of the one-and-only essence as a source of refuge, homage is expressed, offerings are made, and refuge is taken in a way in which the three spheres[215] are totally pure. [112] Since all phenomena have been, from the very beginning, without self and without any truly existing nature, the Buddha, Dharma, and Sangha must be envisioned as also being thus. This is the inexhaustible refuge, the permanent refuge, the eternal refuge. Thus the *Questions of Nāga King Anavatapta Sutra* says:

> What is it to have taken refuge with a mind free from pollution? By knowing all phenomena not to exist, by not envisioning them as being form, as possessing characteristics, or as being something, but by envisioning them as being totally pure awakened realities,[216] refuge has been taken in the Buddha. By envisioning all phenomena as following after dharmadhātu,[217] refuge has been taken in the Dharma. By envisioning them in a way that is nondual and without conceptual elaboration, refuge has been taken in the Sangha.[218]

On the third evening, there is the concluding ceremony, during which thanksgiving offerings are made to the most precious sources of refuge.

Seventh, concerning the **function** of refuge, the *Ornament of Mahayana Sutras* says:

> It is the highest refuge because
> it protects from all sorts of harm,
> from the lower states, from unskillful action,
> from the ego-view of the perishable composite,[219] and from
> lesser vehicles.[220]

The general refuge protects from all harms, from falling into the lower states, from ineffective courses of action, and from false beliefs about the self based on the perishable collection (the aggregates). The particular refuge protects from the lower paths as well.

Eighth, the **instructions** concerning refuge are ninefold: three common instructions, three particular instructions, and three specific instructions.

The three instructions *common* [to all three refuges] are: (1) to strive at all times to make offerings to the three precious refuges, at least dedicating the first mouthful of food when eating; (2) to never abandon the three precious refuges even should this cost life itself or involve personal loss; and (3) to develop the habit of repeatedly calling to mind the qualities of these three most precious things and taking refuge in them.

The three *particular* instructions are: (1) Having taken refuge in the buddhas, refuge need no longer be sought in any other divinity. In the *Great [Passing into] Nirvana Sutra* it says:

> The best of all those who love virtue are
> those who have taken refuge in the buddhas.
> They will never go soliciting
> refuge from other divinities.[221]

(2) Having taken refuge in the Dharma, harm should no longer be done to any sentient being. [113] The sutra says:

> Having taken refuge in the noble Dharma,
> a person is removed from a mentality of harm and violence.[222]

(3) Having taken refuge in the Sangha, trust should not be placed in the misguided (*tīrthika*).[223] The sutra says:

> Those who have taken refuge in the Sangha
> will not side with the tīrthikas.[224]

The three *specific* instructions are: (1) Respect should be shown for images of the Tathāgata, whatever they may be, from a small image molded in clay upward, because they represent the real, most precious Buddha. (2) Respect should be shown for the volumes and collected works of scripture, from a mere letter of scripture upward, because they represent the most precious

Dharma. (3) Respect should be shown for Buddhist garb, from a simple patch of yellow cloth upward, because it represents the most precious Sangha.

Ninth, eight [principal] **benefits** come from taking refuge: (1) A person becomes a Buddhist. (2) It is the basis for all the [other] precepts. (3) All evils formerly committed will be consumed. (4) Hindrances created by humans or nonhumans can no longer overwhelm [the person]. (5) All that is wished for will be achieved. (6) Great causal merit is accrued.[225] (7) The person will not fall into the lower states and (8) will soon become truly and perfectly enlightened.

The first point in this overall section on the persons whose lives constitute a basis for bodhicitta discussed the necessity of [having] Mahayana potential, [that is, belonging to the Mahayana fold]. The second concerned the need to have taken refuge, as explained above. The third point deals with the need to have taken one of the prātimokṣa commitments.

Prātimokṣa vows

There are four main types of prātimokṣa vows, which, when considered through the individuals [males and females] who take them, make eight categories. Of these, if you disregard the temporary precepts observed when fasting,[226] there are seven types. Whichever one of these seven is appropriate is adopted. The seven classes of prātimokṣa commitment are those of the monk, nun, novice monk, trainee nun, novice nun, ordained layman, and ordained laywoman.[227] *Bodhisattva Levels* says of these:

> The seven categories of those who have most properly adopted the precepts of prātimokṣa are these: those [observing] the moral discipline of the monk, nun, novice monk, trainee nun, novice nun, ordained layman, and ordained laywoman. According to their content, these precepts are those of laypersons or renunciates, as appropriate.[228]

Now, one might ask, "Why is it that one needs to have prātimokṣa vows as a prerequisite for generating the engaged bodhicitta?" They should understand this need for such vows as a basis [for engaged bodhicitta] in three ways: by simile, by scriptural authority, and by reason. [114]

The first way is by *simile*. A place to which a great universal monarch is invited to come and stay should not be filled with impurities such as dung and rubbish. It should be an excellent dwelling place, spotlessly clean and decorated with many fine adornments made of precious substances and the like. It should be a pleasing place. Likewise, when someone is cultivating the great monarch bodhicitta and hoping for it to remain, the "place" where it can abide is not in a person who is not committed to avoiding wrong physical, verbal, and mental actions. It is not in one who is tarnished by the stains of evil. It is to be invited to reside in someone without the stains of physical, verbal, and mental evil, someone whose physical existence is properly adorned with the moral discipline of commitment.

The second way is by *scriptural authority*. In the bodhicitta section of the *Ornament of Mahayana Sutras*, it says, "Its basis is extensive vows."[229] The temporary lay vow are of limited extent because they only last for a day and a night. Unlike this, the other seven classes are extensive commitments, and this is why those seven are taught as constituting the foundation for bodhicitta. Further, *Lamp for the Path to Awakening* states:

> Only those who have the lasting commitment
> in one of the seven classes of prātimokṣa vows
> are suitable for the bodhisattva vow;
> it is not so for others.[230]

This is explained as meaning that you should observe whichever one of those seven types is appropriate.

The third way is by *logical necessity*. Through the prātimokṣa vows, you abandon harm to others along with its basis. Through the bodhisattva vows, you benefit others. There is no way in which you can benefit others without first renouncing harming them. However, according to some people, the prātimokṣa vows are not necessarily a prerequisite for giving rise to the bodhisattva vow because hermaphrodites, eunuchs, gods, and so on who are unable to take the prātimokṣa vows *are* able to give rise to bodhicitta. Some also assert that the prātimokṣa precepts cannot be a prerequisite because they expire at death, whereas the bodhisattva commitment does not.

If you wonder about these points, understand that the prātimokṣa precepts fall into three categories, determined by the attitude with which they are taken: (1) When these vows are taken because of a motivation to reach happiness in the three dimensions of existence, they are called *the moral discipline of vested interest*. (2) When they are taken with the wish of being rid of suffering forever, they are known as *the moral discipline of* śrāvaka *renunciation.* [115] (3) When they are taken through a wish to achieve great enlightenment, they are called *the moral discipline of the bodhisattva vow.*

The first two of the above cannot be taken by hermaphrodites, eunuchs, gods, and the like. They finish at death and cannot be restored if damaged, and so are not the foundation for the bodhisattva vow. The moral discipline of the bodhisattva vow can be taken by hermaphrodites, eunuchs, gods, and so on, is not lost at death, and can be restored if damaged. For these reasons it is the prerequisite for both taking and keeping the bodhisattva vow. Thus it says in the commentary to the *Ornament of Mahayana Sutras*:

> What is the foundation of that mentality? The vow of bodhisattva moral discipline is its foundation.[231]

Therefore prātimokṣa precepts are needed as a basis for giving rise to bodhicitta but are not necessarily required as a continuous basis for maintaining bodhicitta.

> This is a similar case to the meditative concentration vow being a necessary basis for giving rise to the untainted vow but not necessarily required for the latter's continuance.[232]

There is no need to take the bodhisattva prātimokṣa precepts through a special ceremony. If they have already been taken as part of śrāvaka training, they will still be extant when the mind has the special inspiration [of bodhicitta] and will automatically become the bodhisattva's prātimokṣa commitment, since the lesser motivation will have been abandoned but not the spirit of renouncing harming others.

Thus we have seen that someone who has Mahayana potential, who has taken refuge in the three most precious refuges, and who has taken whichever is appropriate of the seven classes of prātimokṣa vow is a suitable person for giving rise to bodhicitta.

This concludes the eighth chapter, concerning refuge and taking precepts, from this *Ornament of Precious Liberation, a Wish-Fulfilling Gem of Sublime Dharm*a.

9. The Proper Adoption of Bodhicitta

Second topic: The essential nature of bodhicitta development

HAVING EXPLORED the first point, the basis for bodhicitta, at length, the second point defines the **essential nature** of bodhicitta development, which is a wish for utterly pure and perfect enlightenment so as to be able to benefit others. This is clearly defined in the *Ornament of Clear Realization*:

> Developing bodhicitta means wanting
> utterly perfect enlightenment for the sake of others.[233]

Third topic: Types of bodhicitta

The **different types** of supreme bodhicitta are described in three ways [116]: by simile, according to what demarcates levels, and according to their characteristics.

The *similes* typifying bodhicitta, from that of an individual person through to that of a buddha, were taught by Ārya Maitreya in the *Ornament of Clear Realization*:

> These are the twenty-two examples:
> earth, gold, the moon, fire,
> treasure, a jewel mine, an ocean,
> a vajra, a mountain, medicine, a virtuous friend,
> a wish-fulfilling gem, the sun, a song,
> a king, a treasury, a highway,
> a carriage, a reservoir,
> melodious sounds,[234] a river, and a cloud.[235]

These twenty-two similes cover bodhicitta from [initial] aspiration through to [final] dharmakāya. To relate these to the five phases of the path: (1) Bodhicitta endowed with aspiration is like the *earth*, for it serves as the foundation for all good qualities. (2) Bodhicitta endowed with commitment is like a *gold*, for it will not change until enlightenment is achieved. (3) Bodhicitta endowed with profound commitment is like the waxing *moon*, for [with this] every virtuous quality will increase. These three constitute the beginner's stage, that is, the lower, middle, and higher sections of the path of accumulation.

(4) Bodhicitta endowed with integration is like *fire*, for it burns away the fuel that is the obstacles to the threefold wisdom, such as omniscience. This is encompassed by the path of application.

(5) Bodhicitta endowed with the perfection of generosity is like a *great treasure*, for it brings satisfaction to all beings. (6) Bodhicitta endowed with the perfection of moral discipline is like a *jewel mine*, for it acts as the supporting ground for precious qualities. (7) Bodhicitta endowed with the perfection of patience is like an *ocean*, for [with this] one remains untroubled by whatever unwanted thing turns up. (8) Bodhicitta endowed with the perfection of diligence is like a *vajra*, for one remains indestructible. (9) Bodhicitta endowed with the perfection of meditative concentration is like a *mountain*, for one remains unshaken by distractions posed by the mind's objects of attention. (10) Bodhicitta endowed with the perfection of wisdom is like *medicine*, for it pacifies the sicknesses that are the affliction and knowledge obscurations. (11) Bodhicitta endowed with the perfection of skillful means is like a *virtuous friend*, for [with this] one never relents from bringing benefit to beings, no matter what the circumstances. (12) Bodhicitta endowed with the perfection of aspiration is like a *wish-fulfilling gem*, for [with it] one achieves whatever result is wished. (13) Bodhicitta endowed with the perfection of powers [117] is like the *sun*, for it helps bring disciples to full maturity. (14) Bodhicitta endowed with the perfection of pristine awareness is like the *melody of Dharma songs*, for [with it] one gives disciples Dharma teachings that inspire them. These ten, mentioned above, correspond in their respective order to the ten bodhisattva levels, from the Joyous [the first level] to the tenth. Thus they lie within the sphere the path of seeing and the path of cultivation.[236]

(15) Bodhicitta endowed with clear awareness is like a powerful *king*, for with it one benefits others with unimpeded power. (16) Bodhicitta endowed with the wealth of goodness and pristine awareness is like a *treasury*, for one becomes a storehouse of many accumulations. (17) Bodhicitta endowed with the factors conducive to enlightenment is like a great *highway*, for

with it one treads the way that all the noble ones have trod. (18) Bodhicitta endowed with great compassion and deeper insight is like a *carriage*, for with it one travels directly to one's goal, straying into neither samsara nor the mere peace of nirvana. (19) Bodhicitta endowed with *dhāraṇī*[237] and prowess is like a *reservoir*, for with it everything learned through study or otherwise is retained and not wasted. These five are encompassed by the special bodhisattva path.

(20) Bodhicitta endowed with the "beautiful garden of Dharma" is like listening to a *melodious sounds*, for it makes those disciples keen on liberation eager to listen. (21) Bodhicitta endowed with the one and only way [traveled by all the buddhas] is like the flow of a great *river*, for with it one never deviates from the purpose of benefitting others. (22) Bodhicitta endowed with the dharmakāya is like a rain *cloud*, for on it depends the bringing about of the welfare of sentient beings, such as through demonstrating the deed of residing in Tuṣita Paradise. These last three points are encompassed within the stage of buddhahood. Thus the twenty-two [aspects of bodhicitta presented by means of similes] cover the entire path from the beginner's level through to the buddhahood.

Classified in terms of *what demarcates levels,* bodhicitta is fourfold: (1) bodhictta endowed with aspiration, (2) bodhicitta endowed with extraordinary intention, (3) bodhicitta in its full maturity, and (4) bodhicitta with obscurations eliminated. The first of the above corresponds to the levels of practice motivated by aspiration; the second applies to the first seven great bodhisattva levels; the third, to the eighth through tenth levels; and the fourth, to the level of buddhahood. Thus the *Ornament of Mahayana Sutras* says:

> Bodhicitta on the various levels is held
> to be accompanied by aspiration, pure extraordinary intention,
> full maturity,
> and the elimination of all obscurations.[238] [118]

Classified in terms of *essential characteristics* bodhicitta is twofold: the ultimate bodhicitta and the relative bodhicitta. As the *Sutra Definitely Elucidating the Noble Intention* says:

> There are two aspects to bodhicitta: ultimate bodhicitta and relative bodhicitta.[239]

What, then, is ultimate bodhicitta? It is emptiness having compassion as its very essence, an unvacillating state that is lucidity, free of the extremes of conceptual elaboration. Therefore the sutra says:

> Of those, ultimate bodhicitta is that vivid clarity that transcends the world, without any extreme of conceptual elaboration, extremely clear, having the ultimate meaning as its object, unpolluted and unwavering, as still as a flame protected from the breeze.[240]

And what would relative bodhicitta be? Quoting the same sutra:

> Relative bodhicitta is the commitment, through compassion, to lead all sentient beings out of samsara.[241]

Of the two forms of bodhicitta mentioned above, it is stated in the *Ornament of Mahayana Sutras* that the ulimate bodhicitta is attained by means of realizing suchness, while the relative bodhicitta arises through language in the form of adopting it [in a valid ritual].[242] Furthermore the *Detailed Exposition of the Ornament of Mahayana Sutras* says:

> At what stage is there ultimate bodhicitta? From the first great bodhisattva level, the Joyous, onward.[243]

In terms of categories, relative bodhicitta has two aspects: *aspiration bodhicitta* and *engaged bodhicitta*. Thus *Guide to the Bodhisattva Way of Life* says:

> Bodhicitta can be summed up
> as being known through two aspects:
> the mind aspiring to enlightenment
> and the mind proceeding to enlightenment.[244]

There are many different explanations of the particularities of these two aspects of relative bodhicitta—aspiration and engagement. According to Master Śāntideva, of the tradition stemming from Ārya Mañjuśrī through Master Nāgārjuna, *aspiration* is like a wish to go and comprises in reality all intentions longing for perfect buddhahood, whereas *engagement* is like the actual going [119] and is in reality the practical application of all that will achieve buddhahood. Thus *Guide to the Bodhisattva Way of Life* says:

> Just as wanting to go and actually going
> are known to be different,
> so should these two be respectively
> distinguished by the wise.[245]

According to the great Serlingpa, of the lineage stemming from Ārya Maitreya through Master Asaṅga, aspiration is to make a promise committing oneself to the result, thinking, "For the benefit of all sentient beings I will attain perfect buddhahood," whereas engagement is to make a promise committing oneself to the cause, thinking, "I will train in the six perfections as the cause of buddhahood." In line with this interpretation, the *Compendium of Higher Knowledge* says:

> Those who develop bodhicitta are of two types: those who are not special and those who are particularly excellent. Of these, those who are not special think, "Oh, if only I could become totally enlightened in unsurpassable, totally pure, and perfect buddhahood." Those who are particularly excellent think, "May I totally accomplish the perfection of generosity... and so forth ... through to the perfection of wisdom."[246]

Fourth topic: The focus of bodhicitta

Fourth, the **focus** of bodhicitta encompasses both enlightenment and the welfare of sentient beings. It says of this, in *Bodhisattva Levels*:

> Hence bodhicitta is something focused on enlightenment and focused on sentient beings.[247]

Of these two, bodhicitta focused on enlightenment is that which is focused on striving for Mahayana pristine awareness. In the chapter in the *Ornament of Mahayana Sutras* concerning bodhicitta development, it says:

> ... likewise that which it is focused on is pristine awareness.[248]

That which is focused on sentient beings does not mean focused on just one, two, or several beings. Space is pervaded, for as far as it stretches, by conscious life forms, and they in turn are permeated by karma and affliction. Wherever the latter pervade, suffering pervades also. Bodhicitta is developed to remove those beings' sufferings. Thus the *Prayer of Excellent Conduct* says: [120]

> Whatever may be the limits of space,
> they are the limits of sentient beings.
> They are also the limits of karma and the afflictions,
> and they are the limits of my aspirations as well.[249]

Fifth topic: The causes of bodhicitta

Fifth, concerning the **causes for bodhicitta development**, the *Ten Dharmas Sutra* says:

> Such a mind will arise on account of four causes: insight into the benefits and qualities of such a mentality, faith in the Buddha, recognition of the sufferings of sentient beings, and proper encouragement from a Dharma teacher.[250]

Further, *Bodhisattva Levels* says:

> What are the four causes for that? (1) The first cause for the arising of the bodhisattva mind is that of possessing the very best potential. (2) The second cause for the arising of the bodhisattva mind is to be properly supported by the buddhas, bodhisattvas, and by spiritual teachers. (3) The third cause for the arising of the bodhisattva mind is to have compassion for sentient beings. (4) The fourth cause for the arising of the bodhisattva mind is fearlessness in the face of samsara's suffering and the sufferings of undergoing hardships, even though these may be long enduring, manifold, difficult to cope with, and without respite.[251]

In the *Ornament of Mahayana Sutras*, separate causes are mentioned for the generation of the two aspects of bodhicitta: (1) generation of a verbally arisen bodhicitta on the basis of having received it through a perfect ritual, and (2) generation of ultimate bodhicitta. With respect to the first, it says:

> Through the power of support, of the cause, and of the root,
> of learning, and of virtuous habits,
> it is taught that, respectively, stable and unstable bodhicitta,
> and bodhicitta taught by others will emerge.[252]

The generation of "bodhicitta taught by others" refers to that which has arisen on the basis of other's revelatory speech (*vijñapti*) and is also known as "that which is properly received and occurs by means of words." This is relative bodhicitta. Within this there are those that arise through the power of *support*—that is, through the presence of a spiritual teacher. Then there are those that arise through the power of *cause*, meaning by the force of our natural potential; those that arise through the power of the *root* of virtue, meaning the activation of that potential; those arising through the power of *learning*, when the varieties and meaning of the Dharma are explained; and those that arise through the power of *virtuous habits*, [121] through whatever has been routinely studied, directly understood, firmly adhered to, and so forth in this life.

Of the above, that which arose through the power of support is unstable, while those that arose through the power of the cause and the rest are stable.

As to the cause for the arising of ultimate bodhicitta, it is said that:

> Having pleased well the perfect buddhas,
> and having gathered perfectly merit and wisdom,
> nonconceptual pristine awareness of reality arises;
> this is held to be the ultimate bodhicitta.[253]

That is, ultimate bodhicitta is generated through study of scriptures, practice, and realization.

Sixth topic: The source from which the vow is taken

The sixth point concerns the **source** from which the bodhisattva vow is adopted. There are two ways [of taking the vow]: one involving a preceptor and one without a preceptor. If it poses no obstacle to life or practice of purity, the aspirant should go to a preceptor, if one is available, and take the commitment personally, even if the latter is far away. The characteristic qualities of such teachers are (1) skill in the ritual ceremony for administering the vow, (2) having received the vow themselves and kept it unimpaired, (3) the ability to convey the meaning of the ritual's physical gestures and words, (4) a loving care for their disciples that is undefiled by the pursuit of material gain. Thus it says, in *Lamp for the Path to Awakening*:

> Take the vow from a good master,
> possessing the very best characteristics.
>
> A good master should be known as someone
> skilled in the ceremony for taking the vow
> who has personally kept whatever the vow entails
> and gives the vow patiently and compassionately.[254]

Bodhisattva Levels says:

> To be able to give the bodhisattva wish, the preceptor should be in accord with Dharma, have taken the vow, be skilled, know how to communicate the meaning of the ritual words, and know how to make the disciple understand.[255]

However, if such a lama resides close by but there is a possibility of some threat to life or to purity in going to him, then there is the "lama-less" method. For this, stand before an image of the Buddha and sincerely recite three times the words of the aspiration bodhicitta or the engaged bodhicitta vow, whichever is appropriate. Thereby you receive the aspiration or practice vow. Thus, *Bodhisattva Levels* says:

> Should it happen that there is no such person with the requisite qualities, bodhisattvas properly go before an image of the Buddha and take the vow of bodhisattva moral discipline by themselves.[256]

If neither a preceptor [122] nor a Buddha image is available, the words of the aspiration or engaged bodhicitta vow are recited three times in front of buddhas and bodhisattvas visualized as truly present, assembled in space before the aspirant. The *Compendium of Trainings* says:

> Further, should there be no such spiritual mentor, meditate that the buddhas and bodhisattvas dwelling in the ten directions are really present and take the vow through the strength of your own mind.[257]

Seventh topic: The ceremony

The seventh point explains the **ceremony** for adopting bodhicitta. Many ways and traditions of taking the bodhisattva vow have emerged, evolving from the specific styles of instruction of lineages originating from the great learned masters. Though there are many, the subject matter here concerns the two [main] traditions: Master Śāntideva's tradition, of the lineages passed down from Ārya Mañjuśrī to Master Nāgārjuna; and Master Serlingpa's tradition, of the lineages passed down from Ārya Maitreya to Master Asaṅga.

Master Śāntideva's tradition. This is the lineage passed down from Ārya Mañjuśrī to Master Nāgārjuna; it has a ceremony in three stages: (1) a preparation, (2) the actual ceremony [generating bodhicitta], and (3) a conclusion.

[Preparation]

The *preparation* is in six parts: (1) making offerings, (2) confessing past wrongs, (3) rejoicing in virtue, (4) requesting the buddhas to teach the Dharma, (5) supplicating the buddhas not to abandon the world, and (6) dedicating the roots of virtue.

The first, *making offerings*, needs to be understood in terms of both recipients and the offerings themselves. The offerings are made to the most precious refuges. Since it is explained that making offerings to them creates the same merit whether or not you are actually in their presence, offerings are made both to those present and to those not actually present. Thus the *Ornament of Mahayana Sutras* says:

> With a mind filled with faith,
> offer robes and so forth to the buddhas,
> both in reality and with your imagination,
> in order to complete the two accumulations.[258]

As for the offerings, there are two types: surpassable and unsurpassable offerings. The *surpassable offerings* are also twofold: material offerings and the offering of realization.

Material offerings comprise prostrations, praises, [123] material goods neatly and properly set out in the right order, and also the offering of things that belong to no one in particular. These can be actual things of good quality as well as creations of the imagination and the offering of your own body. Such offerings can be studied in detail in other works.

Realization as an offering entails offering Mahāmudrā[259] meditation of the deities' forms as well as the various arrays [of offerings] emerging from the profound meditative absorptions of the bodhisattvas.

Unsurpassable offerings are twofold: those that take place within what appears to be objective reality and those beyond objective reality. The first of these is bodhicitta meditation. As it is said:

> When a wise person cultivates bodhicitta,
> this is the highest offering he can make
> to the buddhas and their heirs.[260]

The second, offering that is beyond objective reality, refers to meditation on the absence of self-entity, which is the supreme offering. Therefore it says in the *Questions of the Devaputra Susthitamati Sutra*:

> Were a bodhisattva, desirous of enlightenment,
> to make offerings to the Buddha, the best of all humans,
> offering quantities of flowers, incense, food, and drink
> equal in number to the grains of sand on the banks of the river
> Ganges,
> so doing for ten million cosmic ages,
> and were another such bodhisattva to offer his training
> in the teachings on no-self, absence of life force, and absence of
> personality,
> along with the resulting achievement of being able to sustain
> clear lucidity,
> it would be the latter bodhisattva who made the better
> offering.[261]

It also says, in the *Lion's Roar Sutra*:

> Not to create ideas or descriptions is to make offerings to the Tathāgata. To be without adopting or rejecting and to penetrate that which is nondual is to make offerings to the Tathāgata. Friends, since the very character of the body of the Tathāgata is insubstantial, do not make offerings while conceiving it to be substantial.[262]

This concludes the section on making offerings.

The second [of the six parts of the preparation] is *confessing past wrongs.* Generally speaking, good and evil depend on the mind's motivation: mind is the master, and body and speech are its servants. The *Precious Garland* says:

> Since mind precedes all things,
> it is often said, "Mind is master."[263]

Hence when the mind is motivated by a defiled state—desire, anger, and the like—people may commit the five acts with an immediate consequence, the five like them, or the ten negative actions. They may break vows or profound commitments [124] or perhaps incite others to do such things. Even if they do not do these things personally, they may delight in the fact that others are perpetrating such evils. All the preceding are what is meant by the terms "wrong" and "nonvirtue." Not only those [manifestly wrong actions] but even Dharma activities such as study, contemplation, or practice that are motivated by a mind under the sway of passion, anger, and the afflictions also become nonvirtue. Thus the *Precious Garland* says:

> Attachment, anger, ignorance, and the actions
> to which they give rise are nonvirtue.
> Nonvirtue brings all the sufferings
> and hence all the lower states of existence.[264]

Further, in *Guide to the Bodhisattva Way of Life,* it says:

> From nonvirtue will arise suffering.
> The correct thing to do, day or night and in every circumstance,
> is to contemplate one thing and one thing alone:
> How can I attain definitive release from this?[265]

This is the reason every wrong needs to be confessed. Will calling wrongs to mind actually purify them though? Most definitely! The *Great [Passing into] Nirvana Sutra* says:

> Although a wrong may have been committed, subsequent remorse will put things right, in much the same way as cetain

> precious substances restore water's clarity or as the moon retrieves her brilliance when emerging from clouds.[266]

and

> Hence it is by unburdening yourself of wrongdoings, with remorse and without dissimulation, that there will be purity.[267]

In what way exactly should you rid yourself of wrongdoings? By applying the four powers. Thus it says, in the *Sutra Teaching the Four Qualities*:

> Maitreya! If bodhisattva mahāsattvas have these four things they will overcome evils that have been committed and established. What are these four? They are (1) the power of the thorough application of total remorse, (2) the power of thoroughly applying the remedy, (3) the power of renouncing harmful acts, and (4) the power of the support.[268]

First is the *power of the thorough application of total remorse*. This is to disclose sincerely and with ardent regret, in the presence of the refuges, wrongs done in the past. How to stimulate remorse? There are three ways: (1) by considering the pointlessness of those wrongs, (2) by considering fear, and (3) by considering the urgent need for purification.

[First,] *remorse by considering their pointlessness* is engendered by reflecting, "I have committed wrongs sometimes to subdue my enemies, sometimes to protect my friends, [125] sometimes for the sustenance of my own body, and sometimes to accumulate material wealth. However, when I die and the time comes to move on to another life, my enemies and friends, my country and my body, and my wealth and possessions will not accompany me. Yet I shall be shadowed by the wrongs and obscurations created by my harmful actions; no matter where I am reborn these will rise up as my executioners." This is why the *Questions of the Layman Vīradatta Sutra* says:

> Father, mother, brothers, sisters, spouse,
> servants, wealth, and acquaintances
> cannot accompany those who die,
> but their actions do follow and trail after them.[269]

It also says:

When great suffering comes,
children and spouse offer no refuge.
You experience the agony alone,
and they cannot share your lot.[270]

Guide to the Bodhisattva Way of Life says:

I must go, leaving everything behind.
Unconscious of this,
I commit various wrongs
for the sake of the loved ones and those I dislike.

However, those I love will cease to exist,
those I dislike will cease to exist,
and even I myself will cease to exist.
In such a way, everything comes to the end of its existence.[271]

Thus we have committed wrongs for the sake of those four: friends, enemies, our body, and possessions. Those four will not accompany us for very long, yet on their account we have committed wrongs that bring much trouble and little benefit. Contemplating the reality of this, great remorse will arise.

There are those who think that even if wrong actions are of little benefit, they will not really bring harm to their doer. They should contemplate the second point: *remorse by considering fear*. Reflecting, "The consequence of wrong is fear," remorse will arise. Wrong actions result in three main times of fear: fear prior to death, fear when actually dying, and fear after death.

Prior to death, those who have committed wrongs will experience unbearable sufferings, feeling struck to their very marrow and so forth. It is said:

As I lie on my bed,
I may be surrounded by my friends and relatives,
but it is I and I alone who will experience
the feelings of life coming to its end.[272]

At the time of actual death, the result of wrongdoing is fear. The wrongdoer experiences the henchmen of the Lord of Death, black and horrible beings [126] brandishing lassos, coming to place their lassos around his neck so as to lead him off to hell. Later others, bearing sticks, swords, and all sorts of weapons, torture and torment in many differing ways:

> When grabbed by Yama's henchmen,
> what use are relatives, what use are friends?
> At that time merit alone provides shelter,
> and merit have I not pursued![273]

The *Letter to a Student* says:

> Having locked time's noose around our necks,
> Yama's ferocious henchmen prod us with sticks and drag us along.[274]

A person who thinks "I shan't be afraid of Yama's henchmen" should reflect as follows:

> Even those taken to a place
> where their limbs are to be hacked off
> become terror-stricken and dry-mouthed,
> their eyes bulging and bloodshot and the like.
>
> What need to mention my unspeakable horror
> when gripped by the fear that comes at the time of death
> and I am seized by the terrifying emissaries
> of the Lord of Death, vivid as if in flesh and blood?[275]

There will also be fear beyond death as a consequence of wrongdoing. Having descended into the great hells, the unbearable sufferings of being boiled, burned, and so on are experienced, and this is quite terrifying:

> Seeing hells depicted, hearing about them,
> thinking about them, reading about them, and seeing models—
> if these make people shudder with fear, what need is there to speak of
> those who actually experience the unbearable fruition of their acts [in the hells].[276]

Thus wrongdoing will come to be regretted by understanding the terrible fears that result from it.

Third is remorse *by realizing the urgent need for purification.* If you think that it will probably be all right to rectify wrongdoings at some later time, realize that it will not be all right at all and that atonement is needed urgently. Why? Because there is a distinct possibility that death will come before wrongs have been purified. It says:

> Before my wrongs are purified
> I may well come to die.
> Pray save me swiftly
> so that I am definitely released from my wrongdoings.[277]

If you think that somehow you will not die before misdeeds have been purified, then consider this: the Lord of Death will not bother in the least about how many misdeeds have or have not been purified. He will steal life away whenever the opportunity presents itself; the time of death is uncertain. Thus it says:

> It is wrong to feel so confident.
> My death will not wait for me to finish the things I have to do.
> As far as this ephemeral life is concerned, [127]
> it matters not whether I am sick or healthy.[278]

Since those who do not realize the uncertainty of their lifespan are quite likely to die without having cleared up their misdeeds, all wrongs should be purified as quickly as possible. The risk is very real, so give rise to great remorse. When sincere remorse has been stimulated by the three contemplations described above, misdeeds should be admitted and purification requested in front of either the general or special sources of refuge.

Thus, it has been taught, that the power of total repentance will purify misdeeds, just as a plea from someone who cannot afford to repay a debt to a rich man may persuade him to wipe out that debt.[279]

There was once an evil person known as Aṅgulimāla. Even though he had committed grave misdeeds, killing 999 people, he managed to purify his evils and achieve the state of an arhat by practicing this power of the thorough application of total and utter remorse.[280] Thus, it is said:

> Once someone who previously did not care
> later comes to learn to be heedful,
> he becomes beautified, like the moon breaking free from clouds,

> as was the case with Nanda, Aṅgulimāla, Ajātaśatru, and Udayana.[281]

Second [of the four powers] is the *power of thoroughly applying the remedy.* Virtuous actions are the remedy for misdeeds. They will consume impurities. Thus the *Compendium of Higher Knowledge* says:

> Actions with remedial power will prevent corresponding misdeeds from coming to unwholesome fruition by transforming the consequence into something else.[282]

In the *Treasury of the Tathāgatas,* it says that cultivating awareness of emptiness purifies misdeeds.[283] In the *Diamond Cutter Sutra,* it says that misdeeds will be purified by reciting the profound scriptures.[284] In the *King for Establishing the Three Commitments Tantra* and in *Questions of Subāhu Tantra,* it says that misdeeds will be purified by reciting mantras.[285] In the *Heap of Flowers Dhāraṇī,* it says that faults are purified by making offerings to the stupas of the Buddha.[286] It also says, in the section on buddha images,[287] that making images of the Buddha will purify misdeeds. Elsewhere it says that listening to teachings, reading or writing out the scriptures, and so forth—[128] whichever one feels for the most—will also purify wrong actions. The *Basis of Vinaya* says:

> Whosoever has committed evil action
> but then annihilates it through virtue
> shines in this world
> like the sun or moon emerging from clouds.[288]

You may wonder, "If engaging in virtue is the antidote for evil, then do you have to do a quantity of good that is equivalent to the amount of bad previously done?" Not so. The *Great [Passing into] Nirvana Sutra* tells us:

> Even a single virtuous act overcomes many evils.[289]

And:

> Just as a small vajra can destroy a mountain, a little fire can burn down a forest, or a minute amount of poison can kill beings, like-

> wise a small beneficial action can overcome a great wrong. It is most efficacious![290]

The *Sutra of Golden Light* explains:

> Someone may have committed unbearable evils
> for a thousand ages,
> yet performing just one perfect purification
> will cleanse all their wrongs.[291]

Thus it has been taught that misdeeds will be purified by the power of thoroughly applying remedies. It is like someone who has fallen into a putrid swamp and, once out of the swamp, bathes and is anointed with perfumed oils.[292]

[For example] there was once a nobleman's son called Udayana. Even though he had killed his own mother, he managed, through this power of thoroughly applying the remedy, to purify himself of his misdeeds. He was reborn as a god and obtained the Dharma result of a stream-enterer.[293] [Thus, as already quoted:]

> Once someone who previously did not care
> later comes to learn to be heedful,
> he becomes beautified, like the moon breaking free from clouds,
> as was the case with Nanda, Aṅgulimāla, Ajātaśatru, and Udayana.[294]

Third [of the four powers] is the *power of renouncing harmful acts.* In awe of the full consequences of karma, you desist from wrong henceforth, thinking,

> Guides of humanity, please [help me]
> remove these evils I have committed.
> These misdeeds are indeed bad.
> Never will I do them again.[295]

Thus, it has been taught, that the power of renouncing evil will purify misdeeds, just as diverting a dangerous river removes the threat from a town.[296] [For example] once there was a person called Nanda who harbored much desire for women. Even though he had committed wrongs, through practicing this power of renouncing evil, his faults were purified [129] and he attained the state of an arhat.[297] [As already quoted:]

> Once someone who previously did not care
> later comes to learn to be heedful,
> he becomes beautified, like the moon breaking free from clouds,
> as was the case with Nanda, Aṅgulimāla, Ajātaśatru, and
> Udayana.[298]

Fourth [of the four powers] is the *power of the support.* This comes from taking refuge and developing bodhicitta. Seeking shelter in the three most precious refuges will purify misdeeds, as it says in the *Story of the Sow*:

> Those who have taken refuge in the buddhas
> will not take birth in states of suffering.
> Having left their human bodies,
> they obtain celestial ones.[299]

The *Great [Passing into] Nirvana Sutra* says:

> One who has sought refuge in the Three Jewels
> will attain fearlessness.[300]

The development of bodhicitta will purify misdeeds. The *Marvelous Array Sutra* says:

> It will put an end to all nonvirtuous actions, like burying them for good.... It will burn up all evil, like the fire at the end of the eon.[301]

Guide to the Bodhisattva Way of Life also tells us:

> The support of someone strong and fearless can free us from fear.
> Likewise, if supported in this way we will be quickly liberated,
> even though we may have committed unbearable wrongs.
> How then could those who care not rely on such support?[302]

Thus the power of the support purifies faults. For example, the support of refuge could be compared, it has been stated, to that of a strong person helping weak followers. The support of bodhicitta development could be compared to the neutralization of a powerful poison by reciting the appropriate mantra.

There was once a prince called Ajātaśatru who had committed the great evil of patricide.[303] Nevertheless he was purified through the power of support and became a bodhisattva. [Thus, as quoted above:]

> Once someone who previously did not care
> later comes to learn to be heedful,
> he becomes beautified, like the moon breaking free from clouds,
> as was the case with Nanda, Aṅgulimāla, Ajātaśatru, and
> Udayana.[304]

Since each of the above four powers is capable of purifying misdeeds, there is no need even to mention how effective all four combined will be. In actual practice, those who do admit and repair their wrongs, in the ways explained above, experience signs of their purification in dreams. The *Dhāraṇī of Encouragement* explains:

> Dreams of the following are signs of breaking free from fault: vomiting bad food, or drinking milk or yogurt or the like; [130] seeing the sun and the moon; flying in the sky; seeing a blazing fire; seeing buffalo; seeing a dark, powerful person, or an assembly of monks or nuns; seeing a milk-producing tree; seeing elephants or mighty bulls; sitting on a mountain, a lion throne, or a mansion; listening to Dharma teachings; and so forth.[305]

This concludes the explanation on confessing past wrongs.

The third [of the six parts of the preparation] is *rejoicing in virtue*. This is about the need to cultivate a joyous appreciation of all the virtuous actions of sentient beings throughout the three times, thinking:

> I delight in all the roots of virtue established by every one of the limitless, inconceivable enlightened beings who have appeared in the past, throughout the universe, from their first generating bodhicitta all the way through to their perfect awakening due to their amassing the two accumulations and purifying the two obscurations. I further delight in whatever roots of virtue have been produced subsequent to their enlightenment, from

> the time they turned the wheel of Dharma to bring to maturity those ready for instruction, until they manifested leaving the world of suffering. I also delight in the roots of virtue generated by their teachings between their parinirvāṇa and the eventual disappearance of their teaching, as well as in the virtue produced by whatever bodhisattvas have appeared in the interim before the manifestation of the following Buddha. I further delight in whatever roots of virtue have been produced by accomplished pratyekabuddhas and likewise in those of any śrāvakas who have appeared. Further, I delight in the roots of virtue generated by ordinary people.

By contemplating joyfully in the above way, cultivate appreciation. Likewise, nurture similar thoughts about virtuous actions being performed in the present moment and those that will be performed in the future. In each instance, the training is to cultivate joyous appreciation. As it is said:

> I delight in the enlightenment of all the saviors,
> and in the levels of the conqueror's heirs as well.[306]

The fourth [of the six parts of the preparation] is *requesting that the wheel of Dharma be turned*. Even at this moment in all the worlds of the ten directions, [131] there are many buddhas not teaching Dharma. Addressing them mentally, offer requests to them to teach the Dharma. Thus one reads:

> With hands joined, I beseech the buddhas
> throughout the directions:
> Please light the torch of Dharma
> for all beings obscured in the darkness of suffering![307]

The fifth [of the six parts of the preparation] is *supplicating the buddhas not to pass away from the suffering worlds*. At present there are buddhas in the worlds of the ten directions who are at the point of entering into ultimate nirvana in order to stimulate those who believe in permanence to abandon their misconceptions and to inspire to diligence those who are wasting their time. With these buddhas in mind, supplication is made to them not to pass beyond the suffering worlds:

I pray with joined hands to those victors
who are considering passing beyond to nirvana
to remain for countless ages,
so as not to leave all their beings in obscurity.[308]

The sixth [and last part of the preparation] is *dedicating the roots of virtue.* All these previous roots of virtue are dedicated to removing the sufferings of all beings, and as a cause for their achieving happiness:

Having thus engaged in all such deeds,
whatever virtues I may have gathered,
May this help clear away the sufferings of all beings.[309]

This and what precedes it conclude the explanation of the preparatory stage of the bodhisattva vow ceremony.

[The actual ceremony for generating bodhicitta]

The *actual ceremony* consists of uttering the pledge in words. As stated in in the *Compendium of Trainings*, just as when Ārya Mañjuśrī was King Amba he took the prātimokṣa and bodhisattva vows together from Buddha Megharava, likewise we too should receive [the two] simultaneously. Then recite such as the following three times:

For as long as this samsara
without beginning endures,
so long I will engage in limitless deeds
to benefit all other beings. [132]

Before the Buddha, protector of the world,
I generate the mind for supreme enlightenment.[310]

Alternatively, one could receive on the basis of a more consdensed formula, such as the following from the *Guide to the Bodhisattva Way of Life*:

Just as the sugatas of the past
cultivated their minds toward supreme enlightenment

and worked stage by stage
through the bodhisattva training,
so also will I, in order to benefit sentient beings,
cultivate my mind toward enlightenment,
and train stage by stage
in the relevant disciplines.[311]

This is repeated three times. Should someone wish to receive the bodhicitta and bodhisattva vows separately, the words relevant to whichever aspect is to be adopted should be recited. This concludes the actual ceremony.

[Conclusion of the ceremony]

As a **conclusion of the ceremony**, make offerings of thanksgiving to the most precious refuges and cultivate great joy and delight on the basis of contemplating the great purpose [of bringing about other's welfare]. So one reads:

The wise, having seized with a clear confidence,
the mind for enlightenment
to be victorious at the conclusion as well,
should uplift their minds in the following manner.[312]

This and more is said. This concludes the explanations on the preparation, actual ceremony, and conclusion for taking the bodhisattva commitment according to the tradition of Dharma Master Śāntideva.

Master Serlingpa's Tradition

According to this system of lineage, passed down from Ārya Maitreya to Dharma Master Asaṅga, there are two parts: generating the aspiring bodhicitta, and upholding to the engaged bodhicitta vow. The first has three parts: the preparation, the actual ceremony, and its conclusion.

First, the *preparation* also has three parts: supplication, establishing the accumulations, and taking the special form of refuge.

For the first, *supplication*, the person wishing to dedicate him or herself to enlightenment should go to a properly qualified spiritual mentor and pay homage. That spiritual mentor too, having given some instruction, helps engender revulsion for samsara in the supplicant, compassion for sentient beings, aspiration for enlightenment, faith in the Three Jewels, and respect for one's gurus. [133] Next, repeating after the preceptor, the student recites:

> Preceptor, pray attend to me. Just as the tathāgatas, defeaters of the enemy, the utterly pure and perfectly enlightened ones, the blessed ones of the past first raised an essential longing for the highest, utterly pure and perfect highest enlightenment—as did the bodhisattvas who are now actually established in the bodhisattva levels—so also I, [such-and-such] by name, pray to you, the teacher, to awaken in me the essential force for unsurpassable, utterly pure and perfect, highest enlightenment.

Recite this three times.

For [the second,] *establishing the accumulations*, the supplicant first prostrates to the rare and precious refuges and to the preceptor. Then material offerings prepared for the occasion are offered, along with any amount of visualized and other offerings. It is taught that the novice vow is received from an abbot (*upādhyāya*) together with a preceptor (*ācārya*), that the full vow is received from the Sangha, and that the two types of bodhicitta are attained through the accumulation of merit.

It would be inappropriate for wealthy people to make meager offerings; they should offer on a grand scale. Extremely wealthy bodhisattvas of the past made such vast offerings. Some even, when they gave rise to bodhicitta, took their vow making offerings as extensive as ten million monastic residences (*vihāra*). The *Good Eon Sutra*[313] tells us:

> Sugata Yaśodatta first gave rise to bodhicitta
> when, as king of Jambudvīpa,
> he offered of ten million monastic residences
> to Tathāgata Śaśiketu.[314]

However, it suffices for someone who is not rich to make only modest offerings. In the past, poor bodhisattvas made very simple gifts; some even gave rise to bodhicitta offering the light of a burning twist of straw.

> Sugata Arciṣmant first gave rise to bodhicitta
> when, as a poor city dweller,

> he offered grass "candles"
> to Tathāgata Anantaprabha.[315]

For one who possesses nothing at all, it suffices to make three prostrations. In the past there were certain bodhisattvas who had nothing and who awakened their bodhicitta joining their hands in homage three times: [134]

> Tathāgata Guṇamālin first gave rise to bodhicitta
> when he joined his hands in homage
> and three times said "Praise to the Awakened One"
> to Tathāgata Vijṛmbhitagāmī.[316]

The third, *taking the special form of refuge*, is to be done as explained in the previous chapter.

For the *actual ceremony*, the preceptor should instruct the student as follows and help him contemplate thus:

> Wherever there is space, there are sentient beings. Wherever there are beings, there are afflictions. Wherever there are afflictions, there is harmful karma, and whenever there is harmful karma, there will be suffering. All those beings beset by suffering are actually our parents; all our parents have been exceedingly kind to us. All those former parents who were so kind in the past are presently plunged into this powerful ocean of samsara, enduring immeasurable sufferings. With no one to protect them and be their refuge, they undergo terrible hardships and great pain. Thinking, "Oh, if only they could find happiness; if only they could get free from suffering," rest your mind in loving kindness and compassion for a while.
>
> Now think, "At present, I have no power to help these beings. Therefore, to be able to come to their aid, I will achieve what is known as pure and perfect enlightenment—the ending of all that is wrong, the perfection of every quality, the power to accomplish the benefit of all beings, however many they may be." Rest your mind in these thoughts for a while.

Then, repeating after the preceptor, the supplicant should recite the following formula three times:

> All buddhas and bodhisattvas throughout the ten directions, pray heed me. I, [such-and-such] by name, do now—by the power of the roots of virtue that I gathered in former lives through the practice of generosity, moral discipline, and meditation, through the roots of virtue that I have encouraged others to establish, and through those that I have joyously appreciated—take the commitment to reach unsurpassable, pure, and perfect enlightenment, in the same way as in the past the tathāgatas, the victorious ones, the pure and perfect buddhas, the perfectly gifted and liberated victors first took the commitment to reach pure and perfect great enlightenment, [135] and as did those bodhisattvas of the bodhisattva levels. Like them, I, [such-and-such] by name, will, from this moment until I reach the essence of enlightenment, awaken the force of unsurpassable, pure, and perfect highest enlightenment in order to rescue beings who are to be carried over, liberate those who are not free, let release their breath those who have not let out their breath, and take completely beyond suffering those who have not yet completely gone beyond it.

Through repeating these words after the teacher, the vow is taken.

The meaning of these words is as follows: Those "who are to be carried over" are hell beings, hungry spirits, and animals, since they have yet to cross the ocean-like sufferings of samsara. "To rescue" them means to free them from the sufferings of the three lower states and establish them in the higher states so that they can continue in human or divine existences. "Those who are not free" are the humans and gods, since they are not yet free from the bondage of the afflictions, which are like shackles. "To liberate" means to help free them from the bondage of the afflictions by setting them on the path of liberation so that they can attain liberation. "Those who have not yet let out their breath" are the śrāvakas and the pratyekabuddhas, because they have not yet relaxed into the Mahayana path. "Those who have not yet gone completely beyond suffering" are the bodhisattvas, because they have yet to achieve the nirvana that is rooted in neither samsara nor peace. "In order to" is the commitment to achieve buddhahood in order to be able to accomplish all the above aims.

As for the *conclusion*, make the students generate great joy and delight on the basis of thinking that a tremendous and useful thing has just been achieved. The preceptor should also pronounce the precepts as well.

Someone who has thus developed the initial commitment of bodhicitta is called a *bodhisattva*, [136] because they have the wish to achieve enlightenment for the sake of other sentient beings, because they focus on enlightenment as well as the sentient beings, and because they remain heroic for the sake [of beings] and are endowed with courageous determination.

This concludes the traditional ceremony for giving rise to the aspiration for supreme enlightenment.

[Taking the vow of engaged bodhicitta]

Taking the vow of engaged bodhicitta too has three three parts: preparation, actual ceremony, and conclusion.

First is the *preparation*. It is in ten parts, in which the preceptor: (1) [leads with the formal] supplication, (2) enquires about any general obstacles there may be to taking it, (3) explains the gravity of breaking the commitment, (4) [outlines] the harmful consequences of letting it degrade, (5) [outlines] the benefits of adopting it, (6) [helps the supplicant] establish the accumulations, (7) inquires about any specific obstacles, (8) encourages the supplicant, (9) inspires a special motivation in the supplicant, and (10) gives some summarized instruction.

Second, with respect to the *actual ceremony*, the student should generate the intention to take the vow. Then, the preceptor says:

> Child of good family, known as [such-and-such], do you wish to receive from me, bodhisattva [such-and-such], the following commitments to follow whatever was the basis of training and moral discipline of all the bodhisattvas of the past, to follow whatever will be the basis of training and moral discipline of all the bodhisattvas of the future, and to follow whatever is the basis of training and moral discipline of all the bodhisattvas presently throughout the universe in the ten directions? Such moral discipline was what the bodhisattvas of the past trained, is what the bodhisattvas of the future will train, and remains what the bodhisattvas in throughout the universe in the ten directions at present are training. That basis of training and way of right action are all founded in the moral discipline of restraint, the moral discipline of accumulating virtue, and the moral discipline of working for the welfare of sentient beings. Do you wish to receive these from me?[317]

This is asked three times of the supplicant, who assents "Yes, I do" each time.

Third, the *conclusion* [of the ceremony] has six parts. (1) The supplicant requests the preceptor's kind attention, (2) the preceptor gives an explanation of the benefits of gaining insight into pristine awareness, [137] (3) he explains the importance of not speaking about the vows to others casually for no reason, (4) he gives a summary instruction to help understand the precepts, (5) the supplicant makes offerings in recognition of the [preceptor's] kindness, and (6) he dedicates the roots of virtue.

This concludes the explanation of the tradition of the illustrious Serlingpa.

Eighth topic: The benefits of bodhicitta

The eighth point concerns the **benefits** of developing bodhicitta. These are of two types: enumerated and unenumerated.

First, the *enumerated benefits* are themselves of two types: those arising from aspiration bodhicitta, and those arising from engaged bodhicitta. The first [*those arising from aspiration bodhicitta*] are eightfold: (1) You enter the Mahayana, (2) it serves as the basis for all the other aspects of bodhisattva training, (3) it helps you eradicate all evils, (4) it helps you plant the root of unsurpassable enlightenment, (5) it helps you gain unsurpassable merit, (6) all the buddhas are pleased, (7) all beings are benefitted, and (8) perfect buddhahood is swiftly attained.

The first of these points is explained as follows. People's conduct may be the very best possible, but if they have not given birth to bodhicitta, then they have not yet entered the Mahayana. Without entering the Mahayana, buddhahood cannot be attained. A person who has awakened the bodhisattva mind becomes a Mahayanist. Thus it says in *Bodhisattva Levels*:

> As soon as one has generated this mind, one has entered the Great Vehicle to unsurpassable enlightenment.[318]

The second point is explained as follows. If you do not have aspiration bodhicitta—the longing to achieve enlightenment—you cannot generate and sustain the bodhisattva's training consisting of the threefold moral discipline. However, if you do so aspire, you lay the very foundation for what is achieved by first adopting the threefold moral discipline and then training in it. *Bodhisattva Levels* says:

> Giving rise to this attitude is the basis for all the bodhisattvas' training.[319]

The third point is that virtue is the remedy for former wrongs. The best of all virtues is the bodhisattva mind. By bringing this remedy into play, all adverse factors will be annihilated. Thus one reads: [138]

> Blazing like the fire at the age's end, instantly
> it will definitely burn away the great wrongs.[320]

The fourth point is that when the moisture of loving kindness and compassion saturates the ground that is the mind of a being, into which the root—the mind set on enlightenment—has been well and firmly planted, then the branches full of leaves—the thirty-seven factors conducive to awakening—are developed. Once the fruit—perfect buddhahood—has ripened, great benefit and happiness will arise from it for all beings. Thus when the bodhisattva mind has arisen, the root of buddhahood is firmly planted. *Bodhisattva Levels* says:

> The awakening of the bodhisattva mind is the root of unsurpassable, pure, and perfect enlightenment.[321]

The fifth point is that immeasurable merit is obtained. The *Questions of the Layman Vīradatta Sutra* says:

> Whatever merit there is of bodhicitta,
> if it were to posssess a form,
> it would fill up the whole expanse of space
> and extend well beyond its bounds.[322]

The sixth point is that it pleases all the buddhas. The same sutra says:

> Were one person to fill as many buddhafields
> as there are grains of sand on the banks of the Ganges
> with gems and most precious substances
> and offer them to all the buddhas,
> and were another person, through compassion,
> to join his hands and incline the mind to enlightenment,

then it would be the latter who made the superior offering.
For this has no limits.[323]

The seventh point is that it will benefit all beings. The *Marvelous Array Sutra* says:

It is like a foundation because it brings benefit to all beings.[324]

The last of the eight points is that one will quickly become a genuinely perfect buddha. It says, in *Bodhisattva Levels*:

Once this mentality has arisen, one will dwell in neither of the two extremes but quickly achieve really perfect buddhahood.[325]

The enumerated benefits *arising through the engaged bodhisattva* are tenfold. These are the eight mentioned above along with (9) you derive constant benefit and (10) it accomplishes the welfare of others, in all kinds of ways.

The ninth point is that once this commitment to bodhisattva practice has been undertaken, unlike previously, the flow of merit will be uninterrupted in all circumstances, even when asleep, unconscious, not being especially conscientious, and so forth. [139] *Guide to the Bodhisattva Way of Life* says:

The moment this mind is adopted then on,
whether the person is asleep or remains idle,
a multitude of merits equal to the expanse of space
will befall him with their force uninterrupted.[326]

The tenth benefit is that it will dispel the sufferings of beings, bring them happiness, and sever their afflictions. *Guide to the Bodhisattva Way of Life* says:

To those who are deprived of happiness
and who experience many sufferings,
it brings the satisfaction of many forms of happiness,
it eradicates sufferings,
and, moreover, it dispels ignorance.
Is there any virtue that can match this?

> Is there anywhere such a friend
> or merit in such measure?[327]

The *unenumerated benefits* consist of all the qualities that emerge between its [initial] adoption and [the attainment of final] enlightenment. They remain beyond calculation.

Ninth topic: The consequences of abandoning bodhicitta

The ninth point describes the **harmful consequences of abandoning bodhicitta.** This is a damaging thing, because those who abandon it will (1) be reborn in states of suffering, (2) impair their capacity to help others, and (3) delay considerably any achievement of the bodhisattva levels.

The first of these is that by not fulfilling the bodhisattva promise and abandoning the commitment to enlightenment, a person is effectively cheating all beings. Rebirth in states of suffering is the consequence of such deception. *Guide to the Bodhisattva Way of Life* says of this:

> Should it happen that, having made the pledge,
> I do not do the work that needs to be accomplished,
> what sort of a being will I become,
> after having thus deceived all those beings?[328]

The second point is that the capacity to help others is impaired:

> If such a thing should happen,
> the welfare of all beings is diminished.[329]

The third point is the delay in achieving the [sublime bodhisattva] levels. It says:

> Those who alternate between strong lapses
> and strong bodhicitta
> will continue cycling in samsara
> and experience serious delay in attaining the bodhisattva
> levels.[330]

Tenth topic: The causes for losing the cultivated bodhicitta

The tenth point concerns the **causes of losing the cultivated bodhicitta.** These are considered in two areas: the causes for losing the aspiration, and the causes for losing the practice.

The aspiring vow will be lost by abandoning any sentient being from your intention, by adhering to the four dark actions, or by adopting an attitude incompatible with the aspiration. The engaging vow will be lost according to *Bodhisattva Levels*, as follows:

> If you have committed the four great offences analogous to the grounds of defeat with great involvement—this is described as losing [the generated mind]. [140] It is further stated that the commitment with a medium or a lesser involvement will injure [the generated mind].[331]

In *the Twenty Verses on the Vows* it states that the loss of aspiration bodhicitta also brings the loss of engaged bodhicitta. In *Establishing Summaries of the Levels of Yogic Practice*, it is stated that there are four causes for relinquishing the bodhisattva vow.[332] These are the two mentioned above [abandoning any sentient being from one's intention and indulging in the four dark actions] and third, renouncing the bodhisattva training, and fourth, giving rise to aberrant views. Master Śāntideva, too, says that engendering an incompatible mental attitude will break the vow.[333]

Eleventh topic: How, if lost, to restore the bodhisattva vow

As for **how, if lost, to restore the vow**, if it is the aspiration vow that has been broken, it can be restored by taking it again. In the loss of the engaging vow by virtue of having lost the aspiration vow, then rectifying the aspiration bodhicitta brings about automatic restoration of the engaged bodhicitta vow. If the engaging vow has been broken due to some other cause, it will have to be taken again. If it is lost due to commiting the four offenses analogous to the grounds of defeat with a medium or lesser involvement, this can be rectified through declaration and purification.[334] *Twenty Verses on the Bodhisattva Vows* says:

> One needs to retake the vow.
> [If commited] with middling pollutant, confess it to three [or more],
> and in the presence of one for the rest.
> For those with [lesser] afflictions or none, purify them in your own mind.[335]

This then concludes the ninth chapter, discussing the proper adoption of bodhicitta, from this *Ornament of Precious Liberation, a Wish-Fulfilling Gem of Sublime Dharma.*

10. Precepts for Generating Aspiring Bodhicitta

Twelfth topic: Precepts related to generating bodhicitta

THE PRECEPTS related to the generation of bodhicitta is twofold: (1) the precepts related to the aspiring bodhicitta and (2) the precepts related to the engaging bodhicitta. To present the first, the synopsis is the following:

> **The precepts of aspiration are summed up in five points: to never mentally abandon sentient beings, to remain mindful of the benefits of that mind, to gather the two accumulations, to repeatedly train in bodhicitta, and to nurture the four bright modes of action while abandoning the four dark ones.**

Of these five points, the first consists of the means for not abandoning bodhicitta; [141] the second the means for preventing bodhicitta from degrading; the third the means for strengthening bodhicitta; the fourth the means to increase bodhicitta; and the fifth consists of the means for not forgetting bodhicitta.

To explain the first, namely to **never abandon any sentient being from your intention**, which constitutes the means of ensuring that your bodhicitta does not get lost, the *Questions of* [*Nāga King*] *Anavatapta Sutra says*:

> What one thing could bodhisattvas possess that would embrace fully every quality of the Enlightened One, endowed with the best of everything? It is the aspiration to never abandon any being from their intentions.[336]

To abandon beings from your intentions means, for example, no longer feeling any sympathy for a person who has treated you unfairly, thinking, "Even if I could help you, I wouldn't; were I able to save you from harm, I wouldn't." If you think like this, you have excluded someone from your compassionate intentions.

Does "abandon beings from your intentions" mean all beings or even just one being? Except for śrāvakas and pratyekabuddhas,[337] no one abandons all beings from the mind—not even birds of prey or wolves [do this]. Thus, someone who has mentally abandoned just one being and not rectified that within one watch of the day [i.e., four hours] has lost bodhicitta. This means that those who exclude beings from their intentions while engaging in bodhisattva conduct yet still think of themselves as bodhisattvas are completely mistaken. That would be like clinging to your only child's belongings after having killed him.

Since it is quite possible to drop the bodhisattva attitude even toward those who have been helpful, the risk of losing it toward those who are harmful is indeed high. Therefore, paying special attention to practicing compassion toward the latter, you should try to help them and make them happy. This is the way of the sublime beings, for it is said:

> Even if your kindness is repaid with harm,
> cultivate compassion in return.
> The most excellent beings of the world
> respond to even the negative with goodness.[338]

To explain the second point, to train in **remaining mindful of the benefits of bodhicitta**, which constitutes the means of guarding against its degradation, there are statements such as the following from the *Lamp for the Path to Awakening*: [142]

> Whatever benefits there be
> in developing the aspiration for enlightenment
> have been explained by Maitreya,
> through the *Marvelous Array* [*Sutra*], and in similar texts.[339]

In that sutra, the benefits of bodhicitta are presented through two hundred and thirty similes, and it states that that all of these benefits can be subsumed into four main categories.

The sutra states, "Child of good family! This bodhicitta is like the seed of all the buddhas' qualities. Because it dispels spiritual poverty, it is like the god of wealth."[340] This and other similes concern the *benefits for oneself*. Then it says, "Because it provides excellent protection for all beings, it is like a refuge," and "Because it sustains all beings, it is like the supporting earth."[341] This statement and others illustrate the *benefit for others*. Next, it says, "Because it defeats the enemy, the afflictions, it is like a spear... Because it fells the mighty tree of suffering, it is like an axe."[342] These statements and others illustrate the *benefit it brings in cutting away wrong views*. Then it says, "Because it completely fulfills all intentions, it is like the enchanted vase... Because it makes all wishes come true, it is like a wish-fulfilling gem."[343] These statements illustrate its *benefit in causing the accomplishment of everything that goes in the right direction*.

Through being mindful of the above benefits, you will come to greatly value the bodhisattva mind and appreciate its excellence. When this has been first achieved and then maintained through practice, it protects bodhicitta from degradation. Therefore always be mindful of bodhicitta's benefits, even should it be just for a short while in every watch of the day.

To explain third point, training in **gathering the two accumulations**, which constitutes the means of strengthening bodhicitta, the *Lamp for the Path to Awakening*, for instance, states the following:

> The accumulations, consisting of virtue and pristine awareness,
> are the cause for perfect [enlightenment].[344]

Of these, the *accumulation of merit* consists of the skillful means aspect, comprising the ten activities pertaining to Dharma practice and the four means of gathering beings[345] and so on. The *accumulation of pristine awareness* consists of the profound wisdom aspect, such as the awareness of the total purity of the three spheres.

Thus, it is through gathering the two accumulations that the force of bodhicitta arises within your mental continuum. [143] Therefore always gather the two accumulations. Since even a simple recition of a brief mantra once during each watch of the day can lead to completion of the two accumulations, even if it is only for a brief moment, you should gather the accumulations. *A Discussion of Accumulation* says of this:

> "What will I do today to gather
> the accumulations of merit or of wisdom?"
> "What will I do today to help sentient beings?"
> So a bodhisattva constantly contemplates.[346]

To explain the fourth point, **training repeatedly in bodhicitta**, which constitutes the means to increase bodhicitta, *Lamp for the Path to Awakening* says:

> Having given rise to bodhicitta as an aspiration,
> strive to increase it in every way.[347]

This striving should be understood as applying to three areas of activity: (1) training in the attitude that gives rise to bodhicitta, (2) training in bodhicitta itself, and (3) training in the attitude related to bodhisattva conduct.

The attitude that gives rise to bodhicitta is to always be disposed to loving kindness and compassion toward sentient beings, or at least to engender such a thought once every watch of the day.

Training in bodhicitta itself is to nurture an intention longing to attain enlightenment so as to be able to benefit beings. This should be the subject of contemplation during the three periods of the day and the three periods of the night. Alternatively, the longer bodhisattva ritual can be performed; or else, at a minimum, the following prayer, [recommended by] the great Atiśa, can be recited once every watch of the day:

> To the buddhas, the Dharma, and the supreme community,
> I go for refuge until attainment of enlightenment.
> Through my engagement in generosity and so forth,
> may I achieve buddhahood for the benefit of all sentient beings.[348]

Training in the *attitude related to bodhisattva conduct* is twofold: developing the willingness to work for the benefit of others and developing the intention to purify the mind. The first of these means dedicating body, possessions, and whatever virtues have been established in the three times to the service of others and their happiness; it implies cultivating a willingness to give. Developing the intention to purify the mind involves constant examination of personal conduct as well as the elimination of afflictions and harmful actions.

To explain the fifth point, **abandoning the four dark actions and nurturing the four bright ones**, which constitutes the means for not forgetting bodhicitta, *Lamp for the Path to Awakening* says:

> To remember this in other lives as well,
> carefully observe the precepts thus explained.[349]

Where are these precepts explained? The *Kāśyapa Chapter Sutra* states the following, with respect to the four dark actions, for instance:

> Kāśyapa! A bodhisattva possessing these four things will forget his bodhicitta. What are these four? They are....[350]

To summarize them, the four dark actions are: (1) to deceive a guru or person worthy of receiving offerings, (2) to cause others to regret actions that should not be regretted, (3) to speak improperly to a bodhisattva who has generated the mind, and (4) to engage with sentient being through pretense and deceit. With respect to the four bright actions as well, that same sutra states:

> Kāśyapa! Should a bodhisattva possess these four, then in all future lives bodhicitta will definitely manifest from birth onward. Without any interruption, that bodhicitta will never be forgotten until enlightenment is attained. What are these four? They are....[351]

To summarize the four, they are: (1) never knowingly to tell lies,[352] even should it cost your life; (2) to establish all beings in virtue and, further, to establish them in Mahayana virtue; (3) to consider a bodhisattva, meaning one who has taken the vow, as being the Teacher, the Enlightened One, and to proclaim that person's qualities in every quarter; and (4) to constantly abide within a noble disposition of mind, free of pretense and deceipt toward any sentient being.

I will now explain the *first dark action* [and its opposite, bright action]. If, with an intention to deceive, you have actually been deceitful toward anyone "worthy of offerings"—meaning a guru, an abbot, a preceptor, or a person who is an object of your giving—the bodhisattva vow is broken, unless you do something to remedy the fault within a single watch of the day. It does not matter whether or not the person knew he [or she] was being deceived, whether or not the deception caused displeasure, whether it was a major or minor deception, or whether or not the deceit actually worked. Whatever the case, the vow is broken. The remedy to this is the *first bright action*, which is, in all circumstances, to avoid the intentional telling of untruths, even should that put your life at risk.

The *second dark action* occurs in relation to the virtuous actions of others.[353] [145] It involves trying to make them feel remorseful by stirring up notions of regret [for the good they have done]. In the case of generosity, we could take the giver as an example. Although that person did a good deed, someone else may try to stir up regret by saying that in days to come the loss of resources caused by the generosity will leave the giver hungry and a beggar—and then what will he do? If this dark action is not remedied within a watch of the day, the bodhisattva vow has been broken, whether or not the person actually does regret the deed. The remedy for this is the *second bright action*: to establish all beings in virtue, and in particular in Mahayana virtue.

The *third dark action* occurs through anger or hatred and involves talking about the faults of someone who has taken the bodhisattva vow. They may be ordinary faults or Dharma failings, addressed directly to that person or indirectly, and it could be done in a pleasant or unpleasant way. Whether or not the bodhisattva concerned is disturbed by what has been said, the bodhisattva vow is broken unless this is remedied within a watch of the day. The remedy is the *third bright action*: to conceive of anyone who has taken the bodhisattva vow just as you would conceive of a buddha and to let their qualities be known everywhere.

The *fourth dark action* entails intentionally trying to deceive anyone at all. Unless remedied within a watch of the day, this will break the bodhisattva vow, whether or not the person is aware of the deception and whether or not any actual harm is done. The remedy is the *fourth bright action*: to act always with the noblest intentions toward beings. This means intending to benefit them without self-interest.

This then concludes the tenth chapter, on how to develop aspiration bodhicitta, of this *Ornament of Precious Liberation, a Wish-Fulfilling Gem of Sublime Dharma.*

11. Presentation of the Six Perfections

THE PRECEPTS related to engaged bodhicitta is threefold: (1) higher training in moral discipline, (2) higher training in [applying] the mind [i.e., meditation], and (3) higher training in wisdom. In this respect, *Lamp for the Path to Awakening* says:

> Those who abide within the vow of engaged bodhicitta,
> having correctly trained in the three aspects of moral discipline,
> will greatly deepen their appreciation of those three trainings.[354]

The higher training in *moral discipline* consists of three: generosity, discipline, and patience; the higher training in *mind* consists of meditative concentration; and the higher training in *wisdom* consists of profound wisdom. As for diligence it serves as a complementary factor to all three [trainings]. The *Ornament of Mahayana Sutras* says:

> The Victorious One has most perfectly explained
> the six perfections in terms of the three trainings:
> the first three are the first training, the last two are the last two,
> while one [diligence] applies to all three.[355]

Thus the synopsis for this chapter is the following:

> **Training in engaged bodhicitta can be summarized as sixfold: generosity, moral discipline, patience, diligence, meditative concentration, and wisdom.**

In the *Questions of Subāhu Sutra*, too, it says:

> Subāhu! For a great bodhisattva to quickly achieve real and perfect enlightenment, the six perfections must be applied

> constantly and in all circumstances until their utter completion. What are those six? They are the perfection of generosity, the perfection of moral discipline, the perfection of patience, the perfection of diligence, the perfection of meditative concentration, and sixth, the perfection of wisdom.[356]

One should understand these six perfections in two ways: (1) through a summarized explanation or an overview, treating them as a group, [147] and (2) through a detailed explanation of the individual perfections. First to present the summary, the synopsis is this:

> **The six perfections are summarized through six topics: their definite number, definite order, essential characteristics, etymology, subdivisions, and groupings.**

First, their **definite number** is six. In terms of higher states of rebirth and liberation, there are three conducive to higher rebirth and three conducive to liberation. Of the three that lead to higher states, the perfection of generosity nurtures material prosperity, the perfection of moral discipline nurtures a good physical existence, and the perfection of patience nurtures a favorable environment.[357] Of the three that lead to liberation, the perfection of diligence nurtures increase of qualities, the perfection of meditative concentration nurtures tranquility (*śamatha*), and the perfection of wisdom—the *prajñāpāramitā*—nurtures deep insight (*vipaśyanā*). The *Ornament of Mahayana Sutras* says:

> Higher states—the best possible prosperity, body, and retinue....[358]

Second, the perfections occur in a **definite order**. First, there is the *order in which they develop within the mental continuum of a person*. Generosity enables proper conduct without concern for material well-being. Possessing moral discipline, patience can be cultivated. Through patience, diligence is enabled. Through diligence, meditative concentration can be developed. The mind that rests skillfully in meditative concentration will know properly the true nature of phenomena, just as it is. Alternatively, the order of sequence could be considered in terms of the *gradual progression from lesser to higher*. The lesser are those explained first, and those founded in what is nobler are explained subsequently. Or the order of sequence relates to the *gradual progression from the grosser to the subtler.* That which is grosser is easier to engage in and is thus presented earlier, while those that are subtler, because of their being more difficult to engage in, are presented later. In this regard, the *Ornament of Mahayana Sutras* says:

> The latter arises on the basis of what comes before;
> and since some are inferior and others superior,
> some grosser and others subtler,
> they abide in their respective sequence.[359]

The third point concerns the four **essential characteristics** of bodhisattva generosity and the other perfections: (1) They diminish the strength of the unfavorable forces; (2) they enable the arising of pristine awareness, utterly free of concepts; (3) they bring perfect accomplishment of aspirations; [148] and (4) they bring sentient beings to their full maturity in three ways [of the vehicles]. The *Ornament of Mahayana Sutras* says of this:

> Generosity curtails unfavorable forces,
> brings nonconceptual pristine awareness,
> perfectly fulfils all wishes,
> and brings beings to maturity in three ways.[360]

The fourth point relates to the **etymology** of the perfections. Since it clears away suffering, it is *generosity*;[361] since it is the attainment of coolness, it is *moral discipline* since it copes with [what would cause] anger, it is *patience*; since it is application to that which is sublime, it is *diligence*; since it keeps the mind turned inward, it is *meditative concentration*; and since it causes awareness of that which is ultimate and meaningful, it is *wisdom.* Since all of them transport one to the far shore of samsara—namely, to nirvana—they are referred to as "what lead to the other shore" (*pāramitā*). In this regard the *Ornament of Mahayana Sutras* states:

> Since through them one eliminates poverty,
> obtains coolness, forbears wrath,
> connects with supreme goal, retains the mind,
> and knows the ultimate, they're thus termed.[362]

The fifth point concerns the six **subdivisions** within each of the perfections—the generosity of generosity, the moral discipline of generosity, and so forth, thus giving rise to thirty-six subdivisions. The *Ornament of Clear Realization* says:

> With respect to the six perfections, generosity and so forth,
> each encompassing a sixfold division,
> this armor-like complete means of attainment
> is explained exactly in terms of six sets of six.[363]

The sixth point examines their **groupings**. They fall into two groups based on the two accumulations. Generosity and moral discipline belong to the accumulation of merit. Wisdom belongs to the accumulation of pristine awareness. Patience, diligence, and meditative concentration belong to both. Thus the *Ornament of Mahayana Sutras* says:

> Generosity and moral discipline belong
> to the accumulation of merit, while wisdom belongs
> to the accumulation of pristine awareness,
> and the remaining three belong to both.[364]

This then concludes the presentation of the six perfections, the eleventh chapter of the *Ornament of Precious Liberation, a Wish-Fulfilling Gem of Sublime Dharma.* [149]

12. The Perfection of Generosity

Of the detailed explanation of the individual perfections, first, to explain the perfection of generosity, the synopsis is the following:

> **The perfection of generosity is summarized as sevenfold: reflections on the drawbacks of its absence and the benefits of its practice; its nature; its various aspects; the defining characteristics of each aspect; how it can be increased; how it can be made pure; and its fruits.**

The first point is reflections on **the drawbacks of its absence and the benefits of its practice**. A person lacking generosity will constantly suffer from poverty. Rebirth among hungry spirits is most likely, but should there be human rebirth, the person will be poverty-stricken. The *Verse Summary of the Perfection of Wisdom* says of this:

> The miserly will be reborn among hungry spirits.
> Even if reborn human, they will be poor.[365]

Also in the *Basis of Vinaya*, we also find the following where a hungry spirit responds to the questions of Śroṇa:

> "We who are ridden with miserliness
> never practiced giving even the slightest.
> Thus we are condemned to this hungry spirit state."[366]

Furthermore, without generosity, a person can neither help others nor achieve budddhahood. So it is said:

> Those unaccustomed to giving are without wealth
> and have no power at all to gather beings to them,

so what need is there even to consider
their chances of reaching enlightenment?[367]

The opposite of this is that generous people will be happy due to having plentiful possessions throughout all their existences. The *Verse Summary of the Perfection of Wisdom* says:

Bodhisattva generosity severs the possibilities of rebirth as a hungry spirit.
It will abolish poverty and destroy all afflictions.
Giving will bring limitless and tremendous wealth.[368]

The *Letter to a Friend* tells us:

Practice generosity correctly;
there is no better friend for the next life.[369]

Further, in *Entering the Middle Way* it says:

Everyone manifestly wishes for happiness;
human happiness cannot be attained without resources;
and because the Enlightened One knew that wealth comes through generosity, [150]
the Sage taught the practice of generosity first.[370]

Generosity also brings the ability to help others. Those drawn to someone through generosity can then be established in sublime Dharma. So it is said:

It is through generosity that suffering beings are brought to full maturity.[371]

Furthermore, being generous makes it easier to achieve enlightenment. The *Bodhisattva Collection* says:

Enlightenment is not hard to find for those who have been generous.[372]

Also the *Clouds of Jewels Sutra* says:

> Generosity brings about the enlightenment of a bodhisattva.[373]

Further, we find a presentation of the drawbacks of a lack of generosity and the advantages of its practice interspersed in the *Questions of the Layman Ugra Sutra*:

> What I have given is mine; what I have hoarded is not mine. What has been given has purpose; what is hoarded is pointless. That which has been given does not require protection; what is hoarded does. What has been given brings no anxiety; whatever is hoarded is accompanied by worries. What has been given shows the way to buddhahood; what is hoarded shows the quick way to evil. Giving will bring great wealth, and hoarding will not. Giving will never know the end of wealth; hoarding will exhaust it.[374]

The second point is **its nature**. Generosity means to give completely, with an unattached mind. *Bodhisattva Levels* says:

> What is the essence of generosity? It is to give what is appropriate to be given on the basis of being motivated by mental states that arise together with nonattachment.[375]

The third point concerns **its different aspects**. There are three: giving material necessities, giving freedom from fear, and giving the Dharma. Of these, giving material necessities strengthens others' physical existence, giving freedom from fear strengthens the quality of other's lives, and giving the Dharma strengthens their minds. Furthermore, the first two kinds of generosity bring well-being to others in this life, [151] whereas the gift of Dharma brings well-being for [both this and] future lives.

The fourth point develops **the essential characteristics of each aspect.** *Giving material necessities* is itself of two kinds, proper and improper, the former to be cultivated and the latter abandoned.

Improper material giving is discussed in terms of four aspects: improper motivation, inappropriate gifts, inappropriate receiver, and an improper way of giving.

An improper motivation can be either a distorted motivation or an inferior one. Giving out of distorted motivation is giving in order to harm others, to gain fame, or because of competition. A bodhisattva should renounce all three. *Bodhisattva Levels* says:

> Bodhisattvas should not give in order that others be killed, tied up, punished, imprisoned, or banished.[376]

and

> Bodhisattvas should not give in order to acquire fame or be praised.[377]

and

> Bodhisattvas should not give in order to compete with others.[378]

Giving through inferior motivation means practicing generosity through fear of poverty in future lives or through hoping for it to be the cause of future human or divine rebirth and future wealth. Bodhisattvas should not have these two types of motivation. It says:

> Bodhisattvas should not give through fear of poverty. Bodhisattvas should not give in order to gain the backing of Indra, a universal monarch, or Īśvara.[379]

Bodhisattva Levels discusses other kinds of improper giving as well. To summarize, inappropriate giving that needs to be abandoned involves giving of fire, poison, weapons, and the like, which can harm either their receiver or someone else.[380] [152] Bodhisattvas should not respond to requests for snares, hunting devices, and so forth—in brief, for whatever may harm others. They should not give away their parents or use them as collateral. They should not give away a nonconsenting spouse or offspring. A person of much wealth should not give little. Communal wealth should not be misused as charity.

Abandoning inappropriate recipients refers to the following. Even though demons with harmful intentions may beg you for your body, you should give neither it nor parts of it to them. Neither should you give your body to those who are under the sway of demons or to those who are mad or temporarily deranged. Their need is not real: they are irresponsible, and their words are for the most part nonsense. It is not generosity to give food and drink to those who are well sated.

Abandoning an improper manner of giving means that it is not a correct generosity to give reluctantly, to be angry about the giving, or to give with a disturbed mind. A person should not give to the deprived in a state of contempt or disrespect for them; neither should he dishearten, threaten, or deride the person begging.

As for the practice of *proper [material] giving*, [first] there are three points—the objects, the recipient, and the manner of giving. The first, in turn, is explained in terms of "inner" and "outer" objects. The inner ones are body-related. For example, the *Questions of Nārāyaṇa Sutra* says:

> If it is beneficial to give and if a person's attitude is pure, a hand can be given if a hand is required, a leg if a leg is required, an eye if an eye is required, flesh if that is what is needed, and blood if that is required.[381]

Those bodhisattvas on the beginner's stage who have not yet realized the mental state of equalizing and exchanging of self and others may give their body in its entirety, not through separating it into bits and pieces. The *Guide to the Bodhisattva Way of Life* says of this:

> Without a pure mind of compassion
> do not give away your body;
> that would be to give up the basis for achieving
> very great goals in this life and the next.[382] [153]

The outer objects are food, drink, or whatever else nourishes steeds, children, spouse, and so forth that have been acquired in a way that accords with Dharma. The *Questions of Nārāyanā Sutra* says:

> What is "outer objects"? It is the likes of wealth, grain, silver, gold, jewelry, ornaments, horses, elephants, sons, daughters.[383]

Lay bodhisattvas are permitted to give away whatever inner or outer gifts they possess. The *Ornament of Mahayana Sutras* says:

> There is nothing that a bodhisattva would not give to others,
> be it his body, wealth and so on[384]

Ordained bodhisattvas are allowed to give everything except their three Dharma robes. In *Guide to the Bodhisattva Way of Life*, we read:

> One should give everything except the three Dharma robes.[385]

This is because giving away these three robes could undermine your work for the benefit of beings.

As for the recepient, there are four types: (1) those particularly designated by their qualities—gurus, the Three Jewels, and so forth; (2) those particularly designated by the benefit they have brought—father, mother, and so forth; (3) those particularly designated by their sufferings—the sick, the unprotected, and so forth; and (4) those particularly designated by the harm they have done—enemies and so forth. The *Guide to the Bodhisattva Way of Life* says,

> If one strives in the arenas of qualities, benefits, and suffering,
> great good will ensue.[386]

Concerning the way in which the gift is given, (1) there is the giving with the very best of intentions and (2) through the best act of giving. The first consists of giving with a compassionate motivation to attain enlightenment and to benefit beings. As for the second, giving through the best possible action, it is said in *Bodhisattva Levels*:

> A bodhisattva should give joyfully, with respect, by one's own hand, at the right time, and without harming others.[387]

The first of these means to be joyful about giving during all three periods of the act—that is, to be glad about it before giving, to give with clear-minded joy, and to have no regrets once the giving has been done. "With respect" means with respect for the receiver. "By one's own hand" means not delegating the task to someone else. [154] "At the right time" means when what is pledged has already been acquired. "Without harming others" means giving in a way that does not cause harm to your immediate circles or to their guardians. In this respect, even though the thing you are giving may be yours, if by doing so brings tears [of sadness] to the eyes of those within your immediate circles who helped acquire the article, you should not give it. Generosity should not be practiced by giving goods that have been embezzled, burgled, or misappropriated. The *Compendium of Higher Knowledge* says:

> Give again and again, give without bias, and give in order to fulfill wishes most perfectly.[388]

In this quotation, "give again and again" is the particular quality of the donor, who should practice generosity repeatedly. "Give without bias" is the particular quality related to the receiver and means giving impartially. "Give in order to perfectly fulfill wishes" is related to the gift itself. It means giving what corresponds most closely to the expectations of the receiver.

This concludes the section on giving material necessities.

Giving freedom from fear refers to giving protection to those who are afraid of robbers, thieves, beasts of prey, illness, water, and so forth. *Bodhisattva Levels* says:

> The gift of fearlessness should be known as the provision of complete protection from lions, tigers, crocodiles, kings, robbers, water, and so forth.[389]

This concludes the teachings on supportive generosity.

Giving the Dharma is explained through four points: (1) the person being taught, (2) the motivation, (3) giving authentic Dharma, and (4) the actual presentation. The first of these means explaining the Buddhist teaching to those who wish to hear it and who have respect both for it and for the person expounding it.

As for motivation, wrong motivations are to be abandoned and only correct ones should be present. To give up wrong motivations means to teach Dharma without concern for honors, praise, or fame and to not have materialistic incentives. The *Verse Summary of the Perfection of Wisdom* says:

> Without material gain one teaches the Dharma to beings.[390]

In the *Kāśyapa Chapter Sutra* it says:

> The Buddha speaks highly of the gift of Dharma
> being given with a pure mind unconcerned with material
> gain.[391] [155]

Having correct motivation means that you should teach the Dharma motivated by compassion. The *Verse Summary of the Perfection of Wisdom* says:

> One gives the Dharma to the world in order to extinguish suffering.[392]

Giving authentic Dharma means teaching unerringly the unmistaken meaning of the sutras and other texts. *Bodhisattva Levels* says:

> Giving the Dharma means to teach the unerring Dharma, to teach the appropriate Dharma, and to make sure that the fundamental points of training are well understood.[393]

As for the actual manner in which the Dharma is taught, when someone requests Dharma instruction, it is not fitting to explain things there and then. The *Candraprabha Sutra* says:

> Should someone request you
> for a gift of the Dharma,
> you should first utter the words
> "I have not studied it extensively."

And:

> Do not teach straightaway;
> having examined the suitability, however,
> if you know the person to be a worthy vessel,
> then teach the Dharma even without being requested.[394]

When teaching the Dharma, it should be in a clean and pleasant place. The *Lotus Sutra* says:

> In a clean and pleasant place,
> arrange well a wide seat [for teaching]...[395]

In such a place, you should sit on a teaching throne and then expound [the Dharma]. It says:

> Well seated on an elevated Dharma seat
> that is beautifully arranged with various pieces of cloth.[396]

The teacher should bathe, be properly dressed and tidy, and explain the Dharma in an appropriate demeanor. The *Questions of Sāgaramati Sutra* says:

> One who teaches Dharma should be tidy and behave in a proper fashion. He should have bathed and be nicely attired.[397]

When everyone has assembled and taken their seats and the person teaching is on the Dharma seat, the latter should recite the following mantra that overcomes the power of harmful influences (*māra*), so that their hindering power cannot obstruct the teaching. The *Questions of Sāgaramati Sutra* says:

> It is this: *Tatyathā śame śamevati śametaśatruṁ aṁkure maṁkure mārajite karoṭe keyūre tejovati oloyani viśuddha nirmale malāpanaye khukhure khakha grasane omukhi paraṁukhi amukhi śamitvani sarvagraha bhandhanāne nigrihitva sarvapārapravādina vimukta mārapāśa sthāpitva buddhamudra anuṅgarirva* [156] *sarva mare pucari tapari śuddhe vigacchantu sarvamāra karmaṇi*
>
> Sāgaramati! If someone recites the words of this mantra beforehand, no demons or negative forces within a radius of a hundred leagues will be able to come and harm the teaching. Even were they to manage to come, they would be unable to create an obstacle. Thereafter, the Dharma words should be explained clearly, articulately, and in just the right amount.[398]

This concludes the explanation of Dharma generosity.

The fifth point is **how generosity can be increased**. There are ways of transforming even a small amount of the above three types of generosity into something much greater. In the *Bodhisattva Collection* it says:

> Śāriputra! Skillful bodhisattvas transform a little generosity into a lot. Through the power of pristine awareness it is elevated, through the power of wisdom it is expanded, and through the power of dedication it is made immeasurable.[399]

"The power of pristine awareness elevates it" signifies awareness of the utter purity of the three spheres [of the act of giving]. "The power of wisdom expands it" means that deep understanding is applied in order to give rise to a vast amount of merit, as follows. At the outset, whatever is given is done so in order to establish all beings in the state of buddhahood. During the giving there is no attachment to the gift itself. At the conclusion there is no expectation of good future-life consequences from giving. The *Verse Summary of the Perfection of Wisdom* says:

> Not making their giving something substantially existent
> and never practicing generosity in anticipation of its full
> karmic rewards—such is the way the wise and skillful practice
> generosity;
> so a little gift becomes much, to an inestimable extent.[400]

"The power of dedication makes it immeasurable" means dedicating such generosity to the ultimate enlightenment of every sentient being. *Bodhisattva Levels* says:

> Do not be generous with a view to the specific results of that act of generosity. Dedicate all generosity to the ultimate, perfectly pure, and complete enlightenment of each and every sentient being.[401]

Dedication not only increases [the results] but makes them inexhaustible. [157] The *Akṣayamati Sutra* says:

> Noble son Śāradvati! Should a drop of water be put in the ocean, it will not be consumed until the end of the eon. Likewise the roots of virtue dedicated to enlightenment will never become exhausted or in the least diminished until the very heart of enlightenment is reached.[402]

The sixth point concerns **how generosity can be made pure.** To quote the *Compendium of Trainings*:

> Applying emptiness with compassion as its essence,
> virtue will be made pure.[403]

When the above-mentioned forms of generosity are supported by realization of emptiness, they will not become a cause for samsara. When they are supported by compassion, they will not become a cause for [attaining] the Hinayana. In such a way, generosity is made pure because it becomes a cause solely for attaining the nonabiding nirvana. In the *Questions of Ratnacūḍa Sutra*, it is taught that generosity is marked with four seals of emptiness. It says:

> Practice generosity by applying four seals to it. What are these four? To apply the seal of emptiness of the inner, one's body; to apply the seal of emptiness of the outer, the gift; to apply the seal of emptiness to the mind, the subject; and to apply the seal of the emptiness to the reality, enlightenment. Having applied those four seals, one engages in the act of giving.[404]

"Being supported by compassion" means to engage in giving because one is unable to tolerate the suffering of other beings in general or more specific kinds.

The seventh point concerns the **fruits of generosity**, which should be understood in both immediate and ultimate terms. Ultimately, generosity brings total enlightenment. *Bodhisattva Levels* says:

> When bodhisattvas totally complete the perfection of generosity, they truly become perfect buddhas who have reached peerless, manifest, and perfect enlightenment.[405]

The immediate results are that material giving brings the most perfect wealth even if one does not desire it. Furthermore, having attracted others through giving one can connect them with the supreme attainment as well. The *Verse Summary of the Perfection of Wisdom* says:

> Bodhisattva generosity destroys the route to rebirth as a hungry spirit.
> It suppresses poverty and also cuts through affliction.
> While practicing, they will enjoy vast and limitless wealth. [158]
> Through giving they will bring suffering beings to greater maturity.[406]

Bodhisattva Levels says:

> Gifts of food will bring strength,
> gifts of clothes will bring a good complexion,

> gifts of steeds will provide the basis for happiness,
> and offering oil lamps will bring good eyesight.[407]

Giving freedom from fear brings immunity from harm by negative forces and obstacles. The *Precious Garland* says:

> By giving giving freedom from fear to the fearful,
> you will not be harmed by any negative force
> and will become supreme among the mighty.[408]

By giving the gift of Dharma, someone will soon meet the buddhas, be close to them, and attain everything wished for. The *Precious Garland* says:

> Through giving the Dharma to those who listen,
> you eliminiate their obscurations,
> and by being a companion of the buddhas,
> you will swiftly attain what is longed for.[409]

This then concludes the twelfth chapter, presenting the perfection of generosity, in this *Ornament of Precious Liberation, a Wish-Fulfilling Gem of Sublime Dharma.*

13. The Perfection of Moral Discipline

To present the perfection of moral discipline, the synopsis is:

> **The perfection of moral discipline is summarized as sevenfold: reflections on the drawbacks of its absence and the benefits of its practice; its nature; its different aspects; the essential characteristics of each aspect; how it can be increased; how it can be made pure; and its fruits.**

To explain the first point, reflections on **the drawbacks of its absence and the benefits of its practice**, if someone possesses the quality of generosity but lacks moral discipline, he will be unable to obtain the very best physical human or divine existence. In *Entering the Middle Way*, it says:

> If a person has broken his limbs of moral discipline,
> he may obtain wealth through generosity but will fall into lower realms.[410]

Further, if one who lacks moral discipline he will not encounter the Buddhadharma. The *Sutra on Moral Discipline* says:

> Just as the blind cannot see form,
> so those without moral discipline will not see the Dharma.[411]

Nor will those without moral discipline become free from existence within the three realms of samsara. That same sutra says:

> How can the legless walk along a path? [159]
> Likewise those without moral discipline cannot become liberated.[412]

Those lacking moral discipline also cannot attain enlightenment because their path to buddhahood is incomplete. In contrast, if someone has the qualities of moral discipline, he will attain the very best physical existence. The *Verse Summary of the Perfection of Wisdom* says:

> Moral discipline eliminates the very nature of [what causes
> rebirth in] various animal forms and the eight unfavorable
> rebirths.
> Through it, a rebirth with freedoms is always encountered.[413]

Further, if you possess moral discipline, you lay the very foundation of all that is excellent and joyous. The *Letter to a Friend* says:

> Moral discipline is taught as being the very foundation and basis
> for every quality,
> just as the earth is the basis for all animate and inanimate life.[414]

Also, possessing moral discipline is like owning a fertile field from which crop after crop of good qualities can be harvested. Therefore it says in *Entering the Middle Way*:

> Because good qualities develop specifically on the field of moral
> discipline, the fruition draws nearer, inevitably.[415]

Further, if someone has moral discipline, he will find that it opens many doors of meditative absorption. Thus the *Candraprabha Sutra* says:

> The rapid attainment of meditative absorption free of
> afflictions;
> this is a benefit arising from very pure moral discipline.[416]

Also, if you have moral discipline, whatever prayers are made will be come to be fulfilled. Thus the *Meeting of Father and Son Sutra* says:

> It is through properly maintained moral discipline
> that every prayer made comes true.[417]

Moreover, if you possess moral discipline, you will attain enlightenment more easily. The same sutra says:

> Since purity of discipline brings so many benefits,
> it will not be difficult to achieve enlightenment.[418]

Thus there are the above and other benefits. The *Sutra on Moral Discipline* says, among other things:

> Those with moral discipline encounter the coming of the
> buddhas;
> those with moral discipline are the finest of all ornaments;
> those with moral discipline are the source of every joy;
> those with moral discipline are praised by all.[419]

The second, **the nature** of moral discipline is that it is characterized by four qualities. For example, *Bodhisattva Levels* states:

> That which is endowed with the four qualities should be understood to be the essential nature of moral discipline. What are these four? [160] (1) It has been adopted from another, most properly and purely; (2) the intention is extremely pure in every respect; (3) it is rectified if it deteriorates, and (4) to prevent its deterioration, it is respected and ever borne in mind.[420]

The four qualities mentioned above can be summed up as covering two main areas: the correct adoption of moral discipline, which relates to the first, and its proper maintenance—the latter three.

The third, in terms of **its different aspects**, moral discipline is threefold: (1) the moral discipline of restraint, (2) the moral discipline of amassing virtues, and (3) the moral discipline of working for the welfare of others. The first pertains to stabilizing the mind, the second brings the elements within the person's mental continuum to maturity, and the third causes other beings to achieve full maturity.

The fourth, to explain the **essential characteristics of each aspect**, first, the *moral discipline of restraint* consists of both what is common and what is uncommon. The *common vows* refer to the seven classes of prātimokṣa vows. *Bodhisattva Levels* says:

> Right bodhisattva conduct related to restraint refers to the seven categories of prātimokṣa of those who have most properly adopted the precepts: those with the moral discipline of a monk,

> nun, novice monk, trainee nun, novice nun, ordained layman, and ordained laywoman. These should be understood as applying to those who have fully renounced and to laypersons, as appropriate.[421]

All of these represent turning away from harming others as well as from the bases of such harm. Within this, the prātimokṣa vows on their own turn away [harm] for one's own sake, while bodhisattvas refrain from harm out of concern for the welfare of others. The *Questions of Nārāyaṇa Sutra* says that:

> Moral discipline is not to be observed in order to gain royal status, nor for the sake of higher rebirth, nor to become like Indra or Brahma, nor for the sake of possessions, nor for the sake of physical well-being, and so on. Likewise moral discipline is not to be observed through fear of the horrors of rebirth in hell, fear of rebirth in animal states, or fear of the terrifying worlds of the Lord of Death. Not for those sorts of things but through considering it as the way to enlightenment is moral discipline observed—and so that every being can be drawn closer to what is beneficial and joyous.[422]

As for the *uncommon vows*, in the tradition coming through Master Śāntideva, they follow the *Ākāśagarbha Sutra*. On this view, there are five root downfalls specific to monarchs, five specific to ministers, and eight specific to Dharma novices. Altogether these make eighteen in number, but in substance there are fourteen root infractions that need to be relinquished. So it is understood. Thus it says: [161]

1. To steal what belongs to the Three Jewels—this is held to be a downfall and a state of defeat.
2. To make others abandon the Dharma; this and the above were declared by the Sage.
3. To take away the robes of a fully ordained monk, to have him beaten or imprisoned, or to oblige him to give up his commitments, even if he has broken vows.
4. To commit one of the five heinous acts.
5. To adhere to aberrant philosophy.
6. To destroy towns and the like.

These were taught by the Buddha as root downfalls.[423]

1. To speak about emptiness to those inadequately prepared.
2. To turn those who have entered the way to buddhahood away from perfect enlightenment.
3. To practice Mahayana yet totally abandon prātimokṣa ethics.
4. To believe that vehicle of the disciples cannot eliminate desire and so forth and to cause others to so believe.
5. To extol one's own qualities in pursuit of wealth, respect, or praise, and to denigrate others.
6. To speak falsely, such as, "I've attained forbearance toward profound emptiness."
7. To have promised to do something virtuous and then go back on the promise, or to make offerings to the Three Jewels and then take them back.
8. To abandon tranquility and immersion in the highest reality in favor of ritual recitations.

These then are the root downfalls
and a prime cause of the great hells.[424]

Lord Serlingpa [Dharmakīrti], following [Asaṅga's] *Bodhisattva Levels*, states that one needs to train in relinquishing four offenses that are analogous to the grounds of defeat and forty secondary faults.

The four actions that are analogous to the grounds of defeat are described as the following in *Twenty Verses on the Bodhisattva Vow*, which is an abridgement of *Bodhisattva Levels*:

> Praising oneself and denigrating others, seeking honor and respect;
> out of avarice not giving wealth or Dharma to those who are
> suffering and helpless;
> inflicting vengeance, even though someone may have apologized;
> abandoning authentic Mahayana and teaching a [mere] semblance
> of Dharma.[425]

As for the forty-six faults, the same text says the following, for example: [162]

> Not making offerings to the Three Jewels three times daily,
> being carried away by desires....[426]

The second, *moral discipline of amassing virtues*, is as follows. Following a correct adoption of the bodhisattva's moral discipline of restraint, whatever virtues one might gather through body and speech aimed at great enlightenment, all of these, in brief, constitute the moral discipline of amassing virtue. What are they? In *Bodhisattva Levels*, it says:

> The following is to be understood as being the bodhisattva's moral discipline of amassing what is virtuous. Relying on and abiding within the bodhisattva's moral discipline, it is to enthusiastically apply yourself to study, contemplation, and meditation and to maintain solitude. It is to respect gurus and to serve them, and to serve and care for the sick. It is to give properly and proclaim good qualities, to appreciate the attributes of others and to be patient with those who are scornful. It is to dedicate virtue to enlightenment and make earnest prayers to that end; to make offerings to the Three Jewels and strive to be diligent; to be ever caring and careful, to be mindful of the training and through awareness to keep to it; to guard the doors of the senses and to know how much to consume; to not sleep in the first and last parts of the night but to persevere in joining the mind with what is wholesome; to rely on holy individuals and Dharma masters and to examine delusions, admit them, and get rid of them. These sorts of qualities need to be practiced, nurtured, and thoroughly increased.[427]

The third, *the moral discipline of working for the welfare of others*, can be known in brief in terms of eleven. What are they? *Bodhisattva Levels* states:

> To support those doing worthwhile activities; to remove the suffering of beings in torment; to teach those without skill how to deal with things intelligently; to recognize other's kindness and to render benefit in return; to protect beings from dangers;to alleviate the distress of those who are suffering; to provide those deprived of resources with provisions; to skillfully assemble a Dharma following; to engage them in accordance with their mentalities; to make them happy through the very finest of qualities; [161] to tame [the wrathful] with firmness, by inspiring awe through extraordinary abilities, and making them long for [the good and wholesome].[428]

Furthermore, both to instill confidence in others and to prevent their own conduct from degrading, bodhisattvas should get rid of impure physical, verbal, and mental behavior and only resort to what is pure. Concerning *impure physical behavior*, you should avoid unnecessary wild behavior—running, jumping, and so forth. Purity means you remain relaxed and smooth, with a kind expression on your face. It says:

> Having become self-controlled like that,
> always have a smiling face.
> Completely rid yourself of that constant frown and those dark
> looks,
> and become a friend to beings and treat them sincerely.[429]

How should you look at others? It says:

> When looking at others,
> look at them in a pleasant, kind way,
> knowing that it is through them
> that you will become a buddha.[430]

As to how to sit, it says:

> Do not sit with legs outstretched
> or fidget with the hands.[431]

On how should one eat, it says:

> When eating, do not overfill your mouth
> or chew noisily, with the mouth agape.[432]

As to how to move around:

> Do not be noisy and hasty
> when getting up from a seat, for example,
> and do not slam doors.
> Take pleasure in being unobtrusive.[433]

And on how to sleep, it says:

Just like the savior lied down for nirvana,
orient whichever direction you prefer.[434]

With regard to *impure speech*, you should give up excessive or harsh speech. The shorcomings of excessive speech are explained below in the *Clouds of Jewels Sutra*:

The childish completely undermine the sublime Dharma.
Taking away the mind's flexibility and making it rough,
taking one far from tranquility and profound insight—
such are the flaws of delighting in excessive speech.

One will have little respect for Dharma masters.
People come to enjoy corrupt speech, becoming absorbed
in what is of meager value, and wisdom deteriorates—
such are the flaws of delighting in excessive speech.[435]

About the faults of *harsh speech*, [164] it says in the *Candraprabha Sutra*:

Even if you may see another's error,
do not broadcast it;
for whatever kinds of acts you engage in,
you yourself will obtain the commensurate results.[436]

In the *Sutra Teaching the Nonorigination of All Things*, it says of this, among other things:

If you describe the lapses of a bodhisattva, enlightenment recedes into the distance. If you talk through jealousy, enlightenment recedes far into the distance.[437]

Therefore excessive and harsh speech are to be given up. How then should you speak? As stated in the following:

When speaking, say something that is purposeful,
clear in meaning and appealing,
free from greed and aversion,
smooth, and in just the right amount.[438]

The *impurity of mental engagement* refers to faults such as clinging to material gifts and honors as well as being attached to sleep and mental dullness. The fault of craving for material gain and honor is explained in the *Sutra Encouraging Nobler Intention*:

> Maitreya! A bodhisattva should examine how gaining material gifts and being honored in such a way gives rise to desire and attachment. He should know how gaining material gifts and being honored give rise to anger and aversion. He should know how material gifts and honors give rise to confused ignorance. He should know how material gifts and honors give rise to underhandedness. He should consider how none of the buddhas ever encouraged material gifts or receiving honors, and he should examine how material gifts and honors steal the roots of virtue. He should consider how material gifts and honors are like a prostitute trying to seduce a potential client.[439]

This and more is said. Even if material things are gained, the thirst for them is never sated. The *Meeting of Father and Son Sutra* says:

> Just as water imagined in a dream
> does not quench thirst even when drunk,
> likewise the objects of sensory pleasures
> even when sought do not satisfy.[440]

Having considered in this manner, reduce your desires and be content with what you have.

Of the fault of enjoying sleep, it is said:

> Those who are addicted to sleep and indolence
> will suffer considerable degradation in their understanding.
> Their mental capacity will deteriorate, too.
> Whatever arises from pristine awareness will be constantly
> impaired.[441]

and

> Those who are addicted to sleep and indolence
> will disintegrate through ignorance, lassitude, and laziness.

> Such people become prey to nonhuman forces
> and may be harmed [165] by them when meditating alone in the forests.[442]

Therefore the above forms of impure mental conduct should be abandoned.

Pure mental engagement is abiding with faith and the other qualities mentioned above.

The fifth, **how the power of moral discipline can be increased**, refers to enhancing [moral discipline] by means of the three factors already referred to earlier—these being (1) pristine awareness, (2) wisdom, and (3) dedication.[443]

The sixth, **making one's moral discipline pure**, refers to it being sustained by emptiness and compassion, as mentioned earlier.

Seventh, the **fruits of moral discipline**, should be understood in terms of two—its temporary and ultimate results. As for its ultimate fruit, you attain the unsurpassed enlightenment. *Bodhisattva Levels* says:

> A bodhisattva who has completely perfected moral discipline genuinely becomes a perfect buddha, with peerless, true, and perfect enlightenment.[444]

As for temporary results, whether sought or not, you will obtain greatest happiness and well-being within the samsaric world. The *Bodhisattva Collection* says:

> Śāriputra! There will not be even a single one of the most wonderful splendors known to gods and humans that a bodhisattva who keeps such completely immaculate conduct will not be able to experience.[445]

There may be these worldly delights and joys, yet the bodhisattva will not be dazzled by them and will enter the path to enlightenment. In the *Questions of Nārāyaṇa Sutra*, it says:

> A bodhisattva endowed with such amassed moral discipline will not become corrupted in any way, even by the possessions of a universal monarch. That bodhisattva will still exercise mindful care and will still long for enlightenment. That bodhisattva

> will not take a detour even though he becomes Indra. Then, too, the bodhisattva will exercise mindful care and long for enlightenment.[446]

Furthermore, those who are endowed with moral discipline will receive offerings from and be cared for by humans and nonhumans alike. It says, in the same sutra:

> The gods always respect those who keep the amassed virtues of moral discipline; the nāgas will constantly express their appreciation of them; the yakṣas will ever praise them; the gandharvas will constantly make offerings to them; brahmans, princes, merchants, and landowners will supplicate them; the buddhas will constantly embrace them with their compassion; and they will gain power over worlds and the divine forces present therein.[447] [166]

This then concludes the thirteenth chapter, discussing the perfection of moral discipline, in this *Ornament of Precious Liberation, a Wish-Fulfilling Gem of Sublime Dharma.*

14. The Perfection of Patience

FOR THE PERFECTION of patience, the synopsis is the following:

> **The perfection of patience is summarized as sevenfold: reflections on the drawbacks of its absence and the benefits of its practice; its nature; its different aspects; the essential characteristics of each aspect; how it can be increased; how it can be made pure; and its fruits.**

To present the first, reflections on **the drawbacks of its absence and the benefits of practicing it**, if someone possesses generosity and moral discipline yet lacks patience, anger can still arise. Once anger has arisen, all the virtue created up to that time—through generosity, moral discipline, and so on—can be consumed right there and then. Thus it says in the *Bodhisattva Collection*:

> This thing we call anger can overpower the roots of virtue established over a hundred thousand eons.[448]

Guide to the Bodhisattva Way of Life also says:

> Whatever excellent deeds
> one may have gathered over a thousand eons—
> generosity, making offerings to the buddhas, and so forth—
> they will be destroyed by one burst of anger.[449]

Furthermore, anger that has found a niche inside someone lacking patience is like the festering wound of a poisoned arrow. The mind thus afflicted knows no joy, no peace, and in the end the person cannot even find rest in sleep. Thus it is said:

> In the grip of anger's affliction
> the mind cannot experience peace;
> it cannot find joy or well-being,
> and thus a person cannot sleep and becomes unstable.[450]

and

> In brief, through their anger,
> those in good circumstances find no joy.[451]

The anger dwelling within someone lacking patience will also show on the outside as a violent demeanor. Through this, friends, relatives, and employees all become fed up with the angry person; even gifts of money or valuables cannot persuade them to put up with his or her presence any longer. Thus it says:

> Friends and loved ones grow wary;
> even if lured through giving, they are not loyal.[452]

Furthermore, those lacking patience lay themselves open to harmful forces (*māra*), which then create obstacles for them. [167] Therefore the *Bodhisattva Collection* says:

> A mind under the influence of anger is prey to harmful forces and encounters obstacles.[453]

Moreover, if you lack patience, you will not get the benefit of having all six perfections, the combination of which forms the path to buddhahood. Thus you will not attain enlightenment. Therefore the *Verse Summary of the Perfection of Wisdom* says:

> Where there is anger and no patience, how can there be enlightenment?[454]

In contrast, if you possess patience, it stands supreme among all the roots of virtue. Therefore it is said:

> There is no evil comparable to anger
> and there is no fortitude like patience.

> Therefore cultivate patience most earnestly
> by every means available.[455]

Besides this, if you are endowed with patience, all sorts of happiness and well-being are found in everyday circumstances. Therefore it is said:

> Whoever, through self-control, overcomes anger,
> he will be happy in this and other lives.[456]

Furthermore, if you possess patience, you will attain the unsurpassed enlightenment. Thus it says in the *Meeting of Father and Son Sutra*:

> Saying "Anger is not the way of the buddhas"
> while constantly cultivating loving kindness,
> from this enlightenment will arise.[457]

The second, **the nature of patience**, consists of being unperturbed by anything.[458] *Bodhisattva Levels* says:

> To have no regard for material gains and to remain unperturbed strictly through compassion. Understand this, in brief, to consitute the essence of the bodhisattva's patience.[459]

The third, to classify **its different aspects**, patience is threefold: (1) patience when confronted with harmful beings, (2) patience as voluntary acceptance of suffering, and (3) patience as confidence born of definite contemplation of the Dharma. Of these, the first is to be patient through analyzing the nature of the beings who cause harm, the second is to be patient through analyzing the essential nature of suffering itself, and the third is to be patient through a discerning analysis of the correct nature of phenomena. The first two aspects cultivate patience in terms of [contemplating] the relative, the third in terms of the ultimate.

Fourth is to explain **the essential characteristics of each aspect**. Of these, the first refers to being patient on your part when confronted with situations where someone does something undesirable—such as strike, insult, show hostility, or defame you or your loved ones—[168] or obstruct you from obtaining what you want. What does it mean to be patient in such circumstances? Patience means remaining unperturbed, not retaliating in kind, or not holding on to the event in one's mind.

According to Master Śāntideva's teachings, we are taught to cultivate patience on the basis of considering: (1) the fact that the other person, the aggressor, has no control, (2) the fault due to your own karma, (3) the fault of your physical existence, (4) the fault of your mind, (5) how there is no difference of fault, (6) the practical utility, (7) the enormous kindness, (8) that the buddhas will be delighted, and (9) the tremendous benefits.

For the first, *the fact that the aggressor has no control*, reflect, "Those who do me harm have lost control of themselves through anger, as did Devadatta toward the Buddha. Anger is such that people lose all restraint when something they do not like occurs. Since they are not in control of their acts, it is inappropriate to retaliate." Therefore it says:

> All beings are thus under some influence, and they are,
> by that very fact, not in control of themselves.
> Knowing this, someone will not become angry
> toward concrete realities that are but mental projections.[460]

Considering *the fault of your own karma* means to reflect, "The harm that I am experiencing now is a hurt arising through something quite similar that I did in a previous existence. Therefore it is not fitting to retaliate against someone else for the mistakes of my own bad karma." Hence it is said,

> Since I harmed sentient beings
> in former times in just this sort of way,
> it is fitting that this harm should come
> to me now for my aggression.[461]

Considering *the fault of your physical existence* means reflecting, "If I did not have this body, then the others' weapons and so forth would have nothing to harm. The actual hurt occurs through the presence of this body, and from that point of view it is not right to retaliate." Thus,

> His weapon and my body
> are both causes for this suffering.
> He brought the weapon and I my body,
> so who should I be angry at?[462]

Considering *the fault of mind* involves reflecting, "This mind of mine did not take on a really good body—one that could not be harmed by others. By having taken a lesser and vulnerable body, it is afflicted by harms. Therefore, since it is my own mind that caused such a body to be mine, it is not right to retaliate against someone else." [169] Thus it says:

> A human body is like a sore:
> it cannot bear to be touched.
> As it was I, craving blindly, who took it on,
> with whom should I get angry for the harms it encounters?[463]

Considering *how there is no difference of fault* means to reflect,

> Some, through ignorance, make harm;
> others, through ignorance, get angry at them.
> Who among them is faultless?
> Who is at fault?[464]

As this is the case, you should avoid the faults and practice patience instead.

Considering the *practical utility* means that to develop patience you need to have a source of harm. Through cultivating patience, wrongdoings are purified and the accumulations are perfected. Through perfecting the accumulations, there will be enlightenment. Therefore, having harm is incredibly useful, and so you should practice patience:

> In dependence on them, many wrongs
> are purified because of my patience.[465]

Considering the *enormous kindness* means to recognize that without the perfection of patience, enlightenment will not be achieved, and to cultivate patience, the presence of perpetrators of harm is indispensable. Therefore this person, the agent of harm, is a most kind Dharma support. Hence I shall be patient toward him. It says

> I should be joyful about my enemy
> because he supports my bodhicitta practice.
>
> By achieving patience through him,
> both of us will receive its results;
> since he is my patience's cause,
> he deserves its results first.[466]

Considering that *the buddhas will be delighted*:

> Furthermore, the buddhas are the most steadfast of friends
> and benefit us immeasurably.
> What way is there to repay their kindness
> other than by respecting beings?[467]

Considering the *tremendous benefit*:

> These who show respect in many ways
> thereby cross excellently to the other shore.[468]

In *Bodhisattva Levels*, it teaches us to cultivate patience on the basis of developing five recognitions. It says

> Recognize the perpetrator of the harm as someone dear to your heart, recognize him as a mere phenomenal reality, recognize him as impermanent, recognize him as suffering, and recognize him as someone to be utterly cared for.[469]

Recognizing the harmer as someone dear to your heart means that these beings who are at present causing harm were not like this in former lives. Then they were parents, relatives, or teachers, and there is not one of them who was not at one time your mother. In that sense they have been helpful and beneficial to a degree that no one could ever calculate, [170] and hence it is not right to retaliate against the sort of trouble they are making at present. Patience can be found through relating to the situation in these terms.

Recognizing the harmer as a mere phenomenal reality means that the harm that is taking place is dependent on conditions. As such, it is no more than mere notions, mere phenomena. There is not even the slightest trace of an instigator, a life, or a sentient being who is being abusive, strike you, defame you, or obstuct your activities. Practice patience through notions like these.

Recognizing him as impermanent means to contemplate thus. Sentient beings are impermanent; they are mortal, and the greatest harm that can befall them is to lose their lives. Thus you can practice patience by contemplating that there is no need to kill them since they will die anyway, due to the very nature of their existence.

Recognizing him as suffering: Every sentient being is afflicted by the three types of suffering. Think that you should be removing sufferings and not creating further ones. This is practicing patience by seeing suffering.

Recognizing him as someone to be utterly cared for means thinking, "Since I have taken the bodhisattva vow, I should be working for the welfare of all sentient beings." Bearing this in mind, hold every sentient being very dear to your heart, with a fondness like you have for your own spouse. Give rise to patience by seeing that it is not fitting to retaliate for trivial harms done by someone treasured so dearly.

The second [aspect of patience], *patience as voluntary acceptance of suffering*, means accepting joyfully and without regret all the sufferings involved in achieving highest enlightenment. It says in *Bodhisattva Levels*:

> It is to accept the eight sorts of suffering, such as those due to one's dwelling and so forth.[470]

The main points here are to accept the sufferings encountered in one's efforts to acquire Dharma robes, alms, and so forth following becoming a renunciate, the sufferings faced in one's efforts in making offerings to and respectfully serving the most precious refuges and gurus, in studying the Dharma, in explaining it, in reciting texts, in meditating, in striving in yoga during the first and last parts of the night instead of sleeping, in working for the welfare of others in the eleven ways mentioned above, and so forth, and to do so without being discouraged by such factors as physical hardship, exhaustion, heat, cold, hunger, thirst, or mental anxiety. An analogy of such voluntary acceptance is to be found in the way someone is glad to receive a painful treatment—such as blood-letting or moxibustion—in order to be cured of a serious illness. *Guide to the Bodhisattva Way of Life* says of this:

> The suffering of my achieving
> enlightenment is confined.
> It is like the suffering inflicted on the body by surgery
> to rid it of an unbearably painful internal ailment.[471]

Someone who accepts the suffering involved in Dharma development and who manages to swing the battle with samsara and defeat the enemy—the afflictions—is a truly great hero. There are some people renowned in the world as heroes, but there is really no comparison, because they only defeat ordinary enemies, who by their very mortal nature will be slaughtered by death anyway. What they achieve is like striking a corpse with a weapon.

The *Guide to the Bodhisattva Way of Life* says:

> By slaughtering reservations about any sort of suffering,
> you defeat the enemies—anger, hatred, and so on.
> Someone who achieves that victory is a real hero;
> the rest is akin to slaying a corpse.[472]

The third [aspect], *patience as confidence born of definite contemplation of the Dharma*, is explained in *Bodhisattva Levels* in terms of "confidence with respect to eight factors, such as the qualities of the Three Jewels."[473] It also relates to the patience born [of contemplating] the meaning of suchness—that is, the emptiness of the two types of selfhood.

The fifth, **how patience can be increased**, refers to it being enhanced by means of pristine awareness, wisdom, and dedication. This is as already explained earlier [in the context of the perfection of generosity].

The sixth, **how it can be made pure**, refers to patience being supported by emptiness and compassion, as explained earlier.

The seventh, **the fruits of patience**, should be understood in terms of two—temporary and ultimate fruits. As for the ultimate result, you attain the unsurpassed enlightenment. *Bodhisattva Levels* says:

> Vast and immeasurable patience will result in great enlightenment. Relying on this, bodhisattvas will become purely, most excellently, and perfectly enlightened.[474]

In the meantime the temporary consequences, even though you may not intentionally seek them, you will attain, in every future existence, a beautiful form, no illness, fame and acclaim, a long life, and the attributes of a universal monarch. Thus *Guide to the Bodhisattva Way of Life* says:

> While in samsara, through patience
> one obtains beauty and so forth and will live long,
> with absence of illness and with fame;
> one will attain the delights of a universal monarch.[475]

This then concludes the fourteenth chapter, on the perfection of patience, in this *Ornament of Precious Liberation, a Wish-Fulfilling Gem of Sublime Dharma*.

15. The Perfection of Diligence

FOR [the presentation of] the perfection of diligence, the synopsis is:

> **The perfection of diligence is summarized as sevenfold: reflections on the drawbacks of its absence and the benefits of its practice; its nature; its different aspects; the essential characteristics of each aspect; how it can be increased; how it can be made pure; and its fruits.**

To explain the first, reflection on **the drawbacks of its absence and the benefits of its practice.** Even if a person possesses the qualities of generosity and so forth, if he is devoid of diligence, then he will remain indolent. When there is indolence, virtue is not accomplished, there is no ability to benefit others, and enlightenment is not attained. Therefore the *Questions of Sāgaramati Sutra* says:

> A person who is indolent is without generosity, moral discipline, patience, meditative concentration, and wisdom. A person is indolent performs no actions to benefit others. For a person who is indolent, enlightenment is far, exceedingly far.[476]

Possession of diligence—the opposite of indolence—prevents all the bright qualities from becoming tainted and fosters their increase. The *Verse Summary of the Perfection of Wisdom* says:

> Through diligence the bright qualities will not become tainted,
> and the buddhas' treasure of infinite pristine awareness will be
> found.[477]

Furthermore, if someone is endowed with diligence, he will be able to get across the mountain that is [the ego view of the] perishable composite.[478] Thus the *Ornament of Mahayana Sutras* says:

> Through diligence, someone goes beyond perishable composite
> and is liberated.[479]

Moreover, if someone possesses diligence, the attainment of enlightenment will be rapid. Therefore the *Ornament of Mahayana Sutras* says:

> Through diligence one will become supremely enlightened as a buddha.[480]

The *Questions of Sāgaramati Sutra* also says:

> Ultimate, totally pure, and perfect enlightenment is not difficult for those who practice diligence. Why is this? Sāgaramati! Whoever has diligence has enlightenment.[481] [173]

The *Questions of Pūrṇa Sutra* says in a similar vein,

> It will not be difficult for enlightenment to come
> to one who constantly exerts diligence.[482]

The second, the **nature** of diligence is to delight in virtue. Thus the *Compendium of Higher Knowledge* says:

> What is diligence? It is the antidote against indolence, for it makes one's mind to take genuine delight in virtue.[483]

The *Commentary on the Ornament of Mahayana Sutras* also says, "[The line] 'To take utter delight in virtue' presents its essential nature."[484] With respect to the phrase "the antidote against indolence," which is its opposing force, indolence is threefold: (1) indolence as idleness, (2) indolence as underestimating potential, and (3) indolence in the form of lowly pursuits.

Indolence as idleness means being attached to the pleasures of letting the mind drift: through sleep, idling in bed, and lounging around. These are to be given up. Why give them up? Because there is no time for such things in this life. It is said:

> Monks! If your cognition will come to dim, your life will be cut off, your will to live will be lost, and if even the Teacher's doctrine will disappear for certain, why would you not practice with diligence and unflinching discipline?[485]

Guide to the Bodhisattva Way of Life says too:

> While death is swiftly encroaching,
> I must gather the accumulations.[486]

Someone may think that it will be all right to establish the accumulations [of virtue and wisdom] at the time of death, but when that time comes, there will be no freedom to establish anything. As it says:

> At death, even if you were to relinquish indolence,
> what is the point, for it is too late![487]

You may feel falsely confident, thinking that somehow death will not happen before you have completed your [accumulation of] virtue. That is an unreliable notion. As is said:

> It is wrong to feel so confident.
> My death will not wait for me to finish the things I have to do.
> As far as this ephemeral life is concerned,
> it matters not whether I am sick or healthy.[488]

This being the case, you might ask, "How then do I eliminate the indolence of idleness?" You should relinquish it as you would react to a snake that had slithered onto your lap or if your hair were on fire. Thus *Guide to the Bodhisattva Way of Life* says:

> Just as you would hurriedly jump up
> if a snake came onto your lap,
> so when sleep and idleness come along,
> swiftly counteract them![489]

And *Letter to a Friend* says:

> Even if your hair or clothes suddenly catch fire,
> instead of doing everything possible to put out the blaze, [174]
> strive instead to extinguish future uncontrolled rebirth.
> Nothing else is as important as that.[490]

Indolence as underestimating potential refers to a defeatist attitude whereby you feel, "How could a lowly person like me ever achieve enlightenment, even were I to make great efforts?" Such discouragement is unnecessary. In fact, the waste of potential caused by such an attitude needs to annihilated. Those who wonder why such discouragement is unnecessary [should take heart from the scripture] that says:

> If they develop the power of diligence,
> even bees, flies, mosquitoes,
> or any insect whatsoever
> will achieve enlightenment, so hard to attain!
>
> That being the case, how could one like me—
> born human and knowing what is beneficial and what is harmful—
> not achieve enlightenment,
> provided I do not abandon the bodhisattva conduct?[491]

Indolence as lowly pursuits means involvement in nonvirtuous activities such as overcoming enemies, amassing possessions, and the like. As those are very real causes of suffering, they are to be abandoned.

Third, the **different aspects** of diligence. Diligence is threefold: armor-like diligence, applied diligence, and insatiable diligence. The first is the most excellent attitude. The second is the most excellent activity. The third is what carries the first two through to their conclusion.

The fourth point develops the **essential characteristics of each aspect**. [First,] you wear the *armor*[*-like diligence*] of the attitude, "From this moment onward and until every sentient being has been established in highest enlightenment, I will never lay aside diligence in virtue." It is said in the *Bodhisattva Collection*:

> Śāriputra! Wear this as inconceivable armor: until the furthermost end of samsara, whatever it may be, and never relax your diligence dedicated to enlightenment.[492]

The *Sutra Teaching the Wearing of Armor* also says:

> Bodhisattvas should wear such armor
> in order to gather beings to them.
> Since the number of beings is incalculable,
> the time for wearing of the armor should likewise be limitless.[493]

The *Akṣayamati Sutra* also says:

> The bodhisattva does not seek enlightenment on the basis of calculating the eons in terms of "I shall wear armor for this many eons and not for this many eons." He puts on armor for an inconceivable length of time.[494]

Bodhisattva Levels says:

> "If, to liberate one single being from suffering, [175] I must abide in hell for a thousand eons, this fills me with joy. It does not matter how much or how little time it takes or how much or how little suffering it involves." Such an attitude is the bodhisattva's armor-like diligence.[495]

[Second,] *applied diligence* has three aspects: (1) diligence in getting rid of affliction, (2) diligence in accomplishing virtue, and (3) diligence in working for the welfare of others.

[1] For the first, [*diligence in getting rid of affliction*,] it is the afflictions—desire and so forth, as well as the actions they motivate—that are the root of suffering. Therefore, to put a stop to its arising, a correspondingly prolonged action that is both specific and global is needed. *Guide to the Bodhisattva Way of Life*:

> Amid the hordes of the amassed afflictions,
> keep your stance firm in a thousand ways;
> like a lion among foxes,
> do not let the hosts of the afflictions injure you.[496]

Is there in fact some example of the vigilance and discipline that are needed? It is said:

> One observing the discipline should be as vigilant
> as a terrified person carrying a pot full of mustard oil
> while being held at sword-point,
> threatened with death should a drop be spilled.[497]

[2] *Diligence in accomplishing virtue* involves striving hard in the practice of the six perfections, without any regard for your life or physical well-being. How to strive? By means of five aspects of diligence: continuous diligence, enthusiastic diligence, unshakeable diligence, diligence as remaining undeterred, and humble diligence.

Continuous diligence means working uninterruptedly. Of this the *Clouds of Jewels Sutra* says:

> Since bodhisattvas apply diligence to every aspect of their daily lives, nothing can cause them regret about their acts of body or mind. Such application is known as "a bodhisattva's continuous diligence."[498]

Enthusiastic diligence means acting joyfully, appreciatively, and rapidly. As it is said:

> Since this task must be completed,
> plunge into it
> like an elephant scorched by the midday sun
> plunges into a pool.[499]

Unshakeable diligence means [176] not being distracted from the task by impediments due to thoughts, afflictions, or sufferings.

Diligence as remaining undeterred means not being deterred by witnessing others' violence, brutishness, aggressiveness, degenerate views, or the like, as is mentioned in the *Vajra Victory Banner Sutra*.[500]

Humble diligence means practicing the above forms of diligence without a haughty mind.

[3] *Diligence in accomplishing the welfare of others* is to make effort in the eleven fields, such as supporting activities that are unsupported and so forth.

[Third,] *Insatiable diligence* is striving after virtue in a way that knows no satisfaction until enlightenment is reached. As it is said:

> If you cannot get enough of sense pleasures,
> which are like honey on a razor's edge,
> how could you ever be satisfied by whatever peaceful,
> happy results ripen from virtue?[501]

The fifth point concerns **how diligence can be increased.** It is increased by the three powers taught above: pristine awareness, deep understanding, and dedication, as explained before.

The sixth point is **how it can be made pure.** This is accomplished through the two supports—emptiness and compassion—mentioned above.

The seventh point, the **fruits of diligence** is to be understood in terms of two: the immediate and ultimate fruits of diligence. As for its the ultimate result, you attain the unsurpassed enlightenment. *Bodhisattva Levels* says:

> Through perfectly completing the perfection of diligence, bodhisattvas truly became perfect buddhas, are truly becoming perfect buddhas, and will truly become perfect buddhas with highest, utterly pure, and perfect enlightenment.[502]

The temporary result consists of achieving the highest happiness even while remaining in cyclic existence. Thus the *Ornament of Mahayana Sutras* says:

> Through diligence, the pleasures of existence are achieved.[503]

This then concludes the fifteenth chapter, on the perfection of diligence, in this *Ornament of Precious Liberation, a Wish-Fulfilling Gem of Sublime Dharma.* [177]

16. The Perfection of Meditative Concentration

FOR THE PRESENTATION of the perfection of meditative concentration, the following is the synopsis:

> **The perfection of meditative concentration is summarized as sevenfold: reflections on the drawbacks of its absence and the benefits of its practice; its nature; its different aspects; the essential characteristics of each aspect; how it can be increased; how it can be made pure; and its fruits.**

The first of these, [namely, the **drawbacks of its absence and the benefits of its practice,**] is as follows. Whoever has the qualities of generosity and so forth, if he lacks meditative concentration he can be overpowered by distractions and so will be wounded by the sharp fangs of the afflictions. Thus *Guide to the Bodhisattva Way of Life* says:

> Humans whose minds are very distracted
> live between the fangs of the afflictions.[504]

Furthermore, if you lack meditative concentration, clairvoyance will not arise, and if clairvoyance has not arisen in you, you will not be fully equipped to benefit others. *Lamp for the Path to Awakening* says:

> Without the achievement of tranquility,
> clairvoyance will not emerge.[505]
> And without the force of clairvoyance,
> other's welfare will not be achieved.[506]

Moreover, if you lacks meditative concentration, wisdom will not arise, and if wisdom has not arisen, enlightenment will not be attained. Thus the *Letter to a Friend* says:

> There is no wisdom where there is no meditative concentration.[507]

In contrast, if you are endowed with meditative concentration, you will abandon craving for lesser things, clairvoyance will emerge, and many doors of meditative absorption (*samādhi*) will be opened within you. Thus the *Verse Summary of the Perfection of Wisdom* says:

> Through meditative concentration, craving for lowly sensual pleasures are rejected,
> and one truly attains intelligence, clairvoyance, and meditative absorption.[508]

Furthermore, if you are endowed with meditative concentration, wisdom will develop, and this will cause every affliction to be overcome. Thus *Guide to the Bodhisattva Way of Life* says:

> Understanding that the afflictions are totally vanquished
> by profound insight (*vipaśyanā*) conjoined with tranquility....[509]

Moreover, if you are endowed with meditative concentration, you will have insight into the perfect truth and therefore generate compassion for sentient beings. Thus *Perfectly Gathering the Qualities [of Avalokiteśvara]* says:

> Through settling the mind in meditative equipoise, there will be insight into the ultimate just as it is. Through insight into the ultimate just as it is, bodhisattvas will enter into a state of great compassion for sentient beings.[510] [178]

Further, if you are endowed with meditative concentration, through it you will establish disciples in enlightenment. Thus the *Ornament of Mahayana Sutras* says:

> Through meditative concentration itself, all individuals will become established in the three types of enlightenment.[511]

The second, the **nature** of meditative concentration, is this: It is characterized by tranquility wherein the mind rests within, focused on virtue. Therefore, in the section dealing with the nature of meditative concentration of the *Bodhisattva Levels*, it says:

> It is a one-pointed mind, abiding in virtue...[512]

This kind of meditative concentration is attained through eliminating its opposing force, namely, powerful distractions. Hence the first priority is to overcome distraction. This involves seclusion, inasmuch as the body needs to be secluded from worldly pursuits and the mind needs to be secluded from its habitual thought processes. Thus *Guide to the Bodhisattva Way of Life* says:

> With body and mind secluded,
> distracted thoughts will not arise.[513]

Of these two, *secluding the body from worldly pursuits* will be explained on the basis of six points: (1) the nature of distractive activities, (2) the cause of distractive activities, and (3) harmfulness of distractive activities, (4) the nature of seclusion, (5) the cause of seclusion, and (6) the benefits of seclusion.

(1) The *nature of distractive activities* is this: it is to be in a state of distraction due to involvement with children, spouse, acquaintances, or possessions.

(2) The *cause of distractive activities* is attachment, meaning attachment to people, such as spouse, household, and the like; attachment to material things, such as food, clothing, and the like; and attachment to reputation and respect, such as others' praise and so on. Being attached to such things, it becomes impossible to shake free from worldly busyness. Thus it is said:

> Because of attachment and craving for material possessions,
> the world is not relinquished.[514]

(3) The *harmfulness of distractive activities* should be known in terms of both the general and the specific. The general harm caused by distractive activities is explained in the *Sutra Encouraging Nobler Intention*:

> Maitreya! The twenty shortcomings of distractive activities are these. What are they? There is no restraint of body, there is no restraint of speech, there is no restaint of the mind, the afflictions are strong, one is polluted by mundane talk, one will be vulnerable to negative influences, [179] one will be given over to heedlessness, one will fail to attain tranquility and insight ....[515]

With respect to the specific harms of distractive activities, through attachment to people you will not attain enlightenment. The *Candraprabha Sutra* says:

> Indulging in desires thoroughly,
> you become attached to children and spouse
> and rely on the pitiable home [life],
> thereby never attaining the unsurpassed enlightenment.[516]

Guide to the Bodhisattva Way of Life also says of this:

> Through attachment to those beings,
> the highest purpose is completely blotted out.[517]

[The meditator] should therefore get rid of attachment to those people. As it is said:

> Neither do they benefit you
> nor do you benefit them,
> so steer well clear of the immature![518]

On the benefits of casting off these attachments, the *Candraprabha Sutra* says:

> Perfect enlightenment is not hard to find
> for those who, having rid themselves of clinging
> to spouse and offspring and fearing domestic life,
> have genuinely shaken free from it.[519]

The harm caused by attachment to material possessions and to reputation is twofold: One cannot sustain them permanently, and they give rise to suffering. It says of the first, in *Guide to the Bodhisattva Way of Life*:

> What has become of those who have amassed
> wealth and fame is quite unknown.[520]

Of the second it says:

Whatever you are attached to
will come back a thousandfold as suffering.[521]

(4) The *nature of seclusion* consists in being free from ditracting pursuits.

(5) The *cause of seclusion* is to abide in solitude in an isolated place. An isolated place would be the likes of charnal grounds, forests, caves, meadows, and so forth. To qualify as an isolated place, it should be out of earshot of worldly habitations, meaning a distance of some five hundred bow-spans. It says in the *Treasury of Higher Knowledge*:

A place is considered secluded when it is out of earshot,
which means five hundred bow-spans away [from dwellings].[522]

(6) The *benefits of seclusion* is as follows. When someone has abandoned distractive activities and gone to stay in seclusion, for the sake of both enlightenment and other sentient beings, the *benefits* are manifold: It is the best way to serve and respect enlightened beings; the mind will emerge from its samsara, [180] there will be freedom from the eight worldly concerns, and afflictions will not increase; and meditative absorption swiftly develops. These will be explained point by point.

As for the first point, [seclusion being the best way to serve the buddhas:] When, through bodhicitta, just seven paces are taken toward a hermitage with the intention of staying in retreat to benefit beings, it is far more pleasing to the totally pure and perfect buddhas than offering them food, drink, flowers, and so on. Thus the *Candraprabha Sutra* says:

Food, drink, and robes,
flowers, incense, and garlands are
not what best serve and honor the Victor, the finest being of all.
Whoever, longing for enlightenment and saddened with
the evils of conditioned life, takes seven paces toward a place of retreat
with the intention of staying there to benefit beings
his merit is far greater than those who make such offerings.[523]

The same sutra explains how the mind will shake free from samsara and from the eight worldly concerns and how afflictions will not be fostered:

> Likewise you will definitively transcend [life's] artifices,
> you will be without the slightest longing for worldly things,
> and things that are tainted will not be fostered.[524]

It also tells how what is needed more than all else—meditative absorption—will swiftly develop. The same sutra states:

> Leave enjoyment of towns and village
> and ever resort to solitude and the forests.
> Like a rhinoceros, always remain single-pointed,
> and before long the best meditative absorptions will be attained.[525]

This concludes the explanation of the need for physical seclusion, away from distractive activities.

To *seclude your mind from habitual thought processes*, you should abide in a quiet retreats. While staying in retreat, contemplate, "Why exactly did I come to this hermitage? I came to this secluded place in fear and in terror of the places of distraction, such as towns and cities. Fleeing them, I came to retreat." What was so frightening there? The *Questions of the Layman Ugra Sutra* says:

> I am afraid and terrified of the distractive activities; I am afraid and terrified of material possessions and honors; I afraid and terrified of corrupting friends; I am afraid and terrified of those who teach bad ways; I afraid and terrified of the dangers of desire, anger, and delusion; [181] I afraid and terrified of the māra of the aggregates, the māra of afflictions, the māra of death, and the māra of seductive pleasure; I afraid and terrified of the three rebirths—animals, hungry spirits, and hell beings. Through such fear and terror I have I come to the wilderness.[526]

Being afraid and terrified in the manner described above, think, "Here, in this place of solitude, what are my body, speech, and mind doing right now?"

Contemplate, "If while in retreat my body is killing, stealing, or the like, then there is no difference between myself and beasts of prey, hunters, thieves, and robbers. Is this really accomplishing my initial purpose in coming here?" In this way counter these behaviors.

Examining your speech, contemplate, "If while in retreat I chatter, slander, misuse speech, and so forth, then there is no difference between myself and peacocks, parrots, songbirds, larks, and the like. Is this really accomplishing my initial purpose in coming here?" In this way, counteract these [inappropriate speech activities].

Examine your mind and contemplate, "If while here in retreat I have unwholesome thoughts of desire, anger, and jealousy, then I am no different from wild animals, baboons, monkeys, wild bears, northern bears, and the like.[527] Is this really accomplishing my initial purpose in coming here?" In this way, counteract these [inappropriate mental activities].

This concludes the explanation of secluding the mind from unwholesome thoughts.

When body and mind are both secluded, distractions will no longer arise, and once free of distraction, one can enter into meditative concentration. For that, the mind needs to be cultivated. First there should be some reflection with a view to establishing which affliction is the greatest, and then follow this by cultivating its counterforce. As the remedy for desire, meditate on what is unpleasant; as the remedy for anger, meditate on loving kindness; as the remedy for ignorance, meditate on dependent origination; as the remedy for jealousy, meditate on the equality of self and others; as the remedy for pride, meditate on exchanging of self and others; and if all the afflictions are equal in their coarseness, or in the case of excessive thought processes, as the remedy, meditate on your breathing.

(1) If, for you, *desire is the predominant affliction*, and for its remedy you were to meditate on the unpleasant, this is as follows. First contemplate your body as being composed of thirty-six impure substances—flesh, blood, skin, bones, marrow, serum, bile, phlegm, mucus, saliva, urine, and so forth. [182] Then go to a charnel ground and observe the corpses that were placed there—fresh ones, two-day-old ones, three-day-old ones, four-day-old ones, and five-day-old ones. Observe their decay, their complete transformation, and how they become black and eaten by small worms. Then reflect, "My own body is also of that nature, a similar phenomenon, and I have not yet transcended such a condition." When observing corpses brought to the charnel ground, skeletons with little flesh left, those where there is just the muscle structure as interwoven fibers, those broken down into many pieces, or skeletons of those dead for many years, of which the bones are shell- or pigeon-colored, meditate as above, thinking, "My own body is also of that nature, a similar phenomenon, and I have not yet transcended such a condition."

(2) If, for you, *anger is predominant*, and for its remedy you were to meditate on loving kindness, this is as follows. In general there are three aspects of loving kindness, as mentioned in an earlier chapter.[528] The aspect developed in this context is loving kindness focused on sentient beings. First consider someone naturally dear to you and start thinking about making that person happy and well cared for. This should generate corresponding feelings of loving kindness [in you for that person]. That feeling of love is then extended toward others who you are familiar with It is next expanded to embrace ordinary people, then to people within your vicinity, then to those living in your town, and finally to include everyone living in all ten directions.

(3) If, for you, *delusion is predominant*, and for its remedy you were to meditate on dependent origination, this is as follows. It says, in the *Rice Shoot Sutra*:

> Monks! Whoever understands this rice shoot understands dependent origination. Whoever understands dependent origination understands the nature of phenomena. Whoever understands phenomena understands buddhahood.[529]

There are two ways of presenting dependent origination: dependent origination of the forward order pertaining to origination of samsara, and the dependent origination of the reverse order pertaining to nirvana.

The first, in turn, is twofold: the dependent origination of inner phenomena and dependent origination of outer phenomena.[530] This latter is discussed in terms of two aspects—the dependent origination of inner phenomena in terms of their causes [183] and the dependent origination of inner phenomena in terms of their conditions. With respect to the first, [the Buddha stated]:

> "Monks! Because this exists, this will come to be. This having arisen, this arises. That is how it is. Conditioned by ignorance, there will be formations[531]..." and so forth, "...birth, and through that condition there will be aging and death, sorrow and lamentations, pain, mental stress, and disturbances. That is how this great cluster of nothing but misery is produced."[532]

This [quotation] relates to the desire realm in terms of dimension of existence, and to a womb birth in terms of mode of birth.[533]

Here, first what is referred to as *ignorance*, which is confused about the nature of what is to be known, arises. Stirred by this, one comes to form the contaminated actions, such as those that are virtuous and nonvirtuous. This is what is referred to as "Conditioned by ignorance, *formations* come to be." The mind that is imbued by the seed of that karma is what is being referred to in the phrase "Conditioned by karma, *consciousness* comes to be." Due to the power of karma, one's mind becomes distorted and joins up with the procreative elements in the mother's womb to become the various stages of embryo and then fetus. This is what is referred to as "Conditioned by consciousness, *name and form* come to be." Through the development of this name and form, the various sense faculties—of sight, smell, and so forth—become complete. This is what is known as the "Conditioned by name and form, the *six sense bases* come to be." When these various sense faculties, such as sight and so on, meet up with their corresponding objective fields through the appropriate consciousness, the meeting of the three causes an actual experience of the object. This is known as "Conditioned by the six sense bases, *contact* comes to be." Just as the contact arises, feeling, in the sense of a pleasant, unpleasant, or indifferent experience arises. This is known as "Conditioned by contact, *feeling* comes to be." Taking pleasure in that feeling, craving and intensely craving for it, is known as "Conditioned by feeling, *craving* comes to be." On the basis of such clinging, and with the thought "May I never be separated from this," attachment in the form of not wanting to let go and of longing for it arise. This is known as "Conditioned by craving, *grasping* comes to be." Due to this striving, actions are performed—physically, verbally, or mentally—that give rise to rebirth. This is known as "Conditioned by grasping, *becoming* comes to be." Whatever existence composed of the five aggregates is generated by those actions is known as "Conditioned by becoming, *birth* comes to be." Through having been born, the development and maturity of the aggregates is aging and their destruction is death. [184] Thus, "Conditioned by birth, there will be *aging and death*."

At death, when you manifestly grasp on to things due to ignorance and are thoroughly assailed within by forces such as attachment, this is *sorrow*. *Lamentations* are the verbal outcry emerging from such sorrow. *Pain* means the unpleasant sensations experienced by the five groups of consciousness. *Mental distress* is the pain in the mind resulting from various sorts of mental activity. The various other forms of distress are the *disturbances*—a term relating to the secondary afflictions.

The above factors of dependent origination should be understood as falling into three distinct groups: Ignorance, craving, and grasping are *afflictions*; formations and becoming are *karma*; and the other seven factors—consciousness and so forth—are *suffering*. The *Verses on the Essence of Dependent Origination* says:

> The twelve specific links
> should be understood in terms of three groups.
> These links of dependent origination taught by the Sage
> are encompassed by three categories:
> affliction, karma, and suffering.
> The first, eighth, and ninth are afflictions,
> the second and tenth are karma,
> while the remaining seven are suffering.[534]

Furthermore, to illustrate them by means of analogy, ignorance is like the one who sows a seed, karma is like the field, consciousness like the seed itself, craving is like moisture, name and form like a shoot, and the remaining links are like the branches and leaves [of the plant].

Now if ignorance did not occur, formations too would not manifest. Likewise, if birth did not happen, then aging and death could not occur. However, it is because of the presence of ignorance that formations and so forth do actually come into being. Therefore because of the existence of birth, aging and death will actually happen. In these processes, however, it is not the case that ignorance consciously thinks, "I will make formations truly manifest," nor do the formations have the thought, "We were made to be manifested by, and created by, ignorance." Likewise birth does not think, "I will make aging and death truly happen," nor do aging and death consider themselves actually brought into being by birth.

Nevertheless, it is through the existence of ignorance that formations and so forth do become manifest realities and will occur, and it is likewise through the existence of birth that aging and death are [185] made manifest and will happen. This is how to view inner dependent origination in terms of its causes.

The dependent origination of inner phenomena is connected also with *conditions*. This is because they are comprised of the six elements—earth, water, fire, wind, space, and consciousness. Here, the "earth element" is the body's firmness and its actual material existence; the "water element" is what holds the body together; the "fire element" transmutes food, drink, and so forth; the "wind element" moves the breath in and out; the "space element" refers to the inner cavities of the body; the "consciousness element" is comprised of the five sense consciousnesses and the tainted[535] mental consciousness. Without these conditions, a body cannot come into being; furthermore, the presence of all six inner elements is universal and hence comprises everything. It is due to them that the body will have its actual manifest existence.

In these [processes], the six elements do not think, "I will establish the body's firmness," and so on, and neither does the body think, "I am generated by these specific conditions." Nevertheless, it is through these specific conditions that the body occurs in all the ways it does.

In how many lives do these twelve links of dependent origination complete their cycle? In this respect, the *Ten Levels Sutra* says:

> Formations due to the condition of ignorance applies to what happened in past lives. The [links] from consciousness up to feelings apply to the present life. Craving through to becoming apply to the next life. Everything else emerges inexorably from that.[536]

Dependent origination of the reverse order that pertains to nirvana refers to the following. Through realizing the true nature (*dharmatā*) of all phenomena to be emptiness, ignorance ceases, and through its cessation, [all the other links] through to aging and death will come to cease in their due order. As is said:

> By stopping ignorance, karmic formation is stopped... [up to] by stopping birth, aging and death, and sorrow and lamentations, pain, mental stress, and disturbances are stopped. That is how this great cluster of nothing but misery will cease.[537] [186]

(4) If, for you, *jealousy is predominant*, and you were to meditate on the equality of yourself and others as a remedy, this is as follows. Just as you wish for happiness for yourself, so do other beings wish for happiness for themselves. Just as you do not want suffering yourself, neither do other beings want to suffer. Thinking in such a way, cultivate the same care for others as you have for yourself. *Guide to the Bodhisattva Way of Life* says:

From the very outset make efforts
to meditate on the equality of self and others.
Protect all beings as you protect yourself,
since all are equal in wanting happiness and not suffering.[538]

(5) If, for you, *pride is predominant*, the remedy is to meditate on substituting self for others, which is as follows. Immature beings suffer in a samsara that they themselves have created through a motivation of caring for self alone. Buddhas, motivated by their care for others and acting solely for the welfare of others, have attained enlightenment. Thus it says:

Immature beings act out of self-interest.
The Sages act for the good of others.
Consider the difference between these two![539]

Therefore cast off self-grasping by understanding self-cherishing to be a fault. Treat others as yourself by understanding cherishing others to be a positive quality. The *Guide to the Bodhisattva Way of Life* says:

Through understanding ego to be faulty
and others to be an ocean of qualities,
cultivate a rejection of self-grasping
and a commitment toward others.[540]

(6) If, for you, *all the afflictions are equally present*, or if there is excessive discursive thought, the remedy is to train in breathing, which is as follows. These are the six [main] aspects of practice, such as counting the breaths, following after them, and so on, presented in the *Treasury of Higher Knowledge*:

There are held to be six:
counting, following, resting,
thinking, transformation,
and utterly purifying them.[541]

As for the practice whereby these afflictions are neither eliminated, indulged in, or transmuted, such as according to the way of secret mantra or of the tradition and instructions of Marpa and his spiritual heirs, this is to be learned orally [from a qualified guru]. You should understand the Innate Union [of Mahāmudrā][542] and the Six Dharmas of Nāropa.[543] [187]

All the above represent the various stages of mental training that lead to entering [the practice of] meditative concentration.

The third point concerns the **different aspects of meditative concentration itself.** There are three: (1) meditative concentration that procures tangible well-being, (2) meditative concentration that gives rise to good qualities, and (3) meditative concentration that accomplishes the welfare of others. The first of these makes one's mind a suitable vessel, the second produces enlightened qualities in someone who is already a fit vessel, and the third works for the benefit of beings.

The fourth point concerns the **essential characteristics of each aspect.** *Meditative concentration that procures tangible well-being* is described in *Bodhisattva Levels*:

> This is the meditative concentration of bodhisattvas. It is free of all discursive thought. It gives rise to excellent pliancy of mind and body. It is supremely peaceful in the very best way. It is without arrogance, it does not get involved with experiencing the taste of meditation, and it is free from any [clinging to] signs. Such is what should be understood by "well-being during this life."[544]

In the above: "Free of all discursive thought" means that it remains fully concentrated without any interference due to the discursive intellect producing ideas of existence, nonexistence, and so on. "It gives rise to excellent pliancy of mind and body" means the destruction of every bad condition that body or mind might adopt. "Supremely peaceful in the very best way" means that it enters such a condition naturally. "Without arrogance" refers to an absence of the affliction of [false] views. "Does not get involved with experiencing the taste of meditation" refers to an absence of the affliction of craving. "Free from any [clinging to] signs" means free from experiencing sense objects such as form and so on [as though they were independent entities].

In terms of the gateway to all [higher qualities], there are four meditative concentrations (*dhyāna*): the first dhyāna, the second dhyāna, the third dhyāna, and the fourth dhyāna. Of these, the first dhyāna is accompanied by investigation and sustained analysis, the second dhyāna is accompanied by bliss, the third dhyāna is accompanied by joy, and the fourth dhyāna is accompanied by equanimity.

Meditative concentration that produces good qualities is of two kinds: the exceptional and the common. The first refers to to the various meditative absorptions encompassed within the ten powers, which are immeasurable and inconceivable. Since śrāvakas and pratyekabuddhas are not even aware of the names of such meditative attainments, [188] what need is there to speak of their ever actually engaging in them.

The common ones refer to the likes of the "complete liberations," "surpassings," "gateways of exhaustion," "excellent specific intelligences," and so forth, which are common to both the Mahayana and the śrāvakayāna. It is on the level of their names they share commonality; in actual fact, however, they are not identical at all.

As for *meditative concentration that accomplishes the welfare of others*, whichever meditative concentration is resorted to, there can be countless physical emanations. These meditative concentrations operate for the benefit of beings in eleven ways, such as supporting beings according to their needs and so forth.

You might ask, "Since there are tranquility and insight, which are well known, what is tranquility and what is insight?" *Tranquility* refers to placing one's mind within the mind on the basis of perfect meditative absorption. *Insight* refers to what follows on from this, an excellent discerning awareness of phenomena that understands what is and what is not to be done. The *Ornament of Mahayana Sutras* says:

> Through abiding in the most excellent,
> mind is made to rest within mind,
> and there is supreme discernment of things.
> These are tranquility and insight.[545]

Tranquility is the meditative concentration itself, and insight is the wisdom aspect.

The fifth point is **how the power of meditative concentration can be increased.** It is increased by the three powers described above: pristine awareness, wisdom, and dedication. This is as explained before.

The sixth point, **how it can be made pure,** refers to meditative concentration being supported by emptiness and compassion, just as described above.

The seventh point, the **fruits of meditative concentration**, should be understood in terms of two—the temporary and ultimate results of meditative concentration. As for its ultimate result, one attains the unsurpassed enlightenment. *Bodhisattva Levels* says:

> Through taking the perfection of meditative concentration to its utter completion, bodhisattvas truly became perfect buddhas, are truly becoming perfect buddhas, and will truly become perfect buddhas—with highest, utterly pure, and perfect enlightenment.[546]

In the immediate term, one will obtain the existence of birth as a god free of dersire. Master Nāgārjuna says:

> Due to the four meditative concentrations,
> through which sensory experience, physical bliss, mental joy,
> and suffering are completely shed, [189]
> you attain a state similar to that of the gods
> in the Brahma, Luminous, Complete Virtue, and Great Result
> heavens.[547]

This then concludes the sixteenth chapter, on the perfection of meditative concentration, in this *Ornament of Precious Liberation, a Wish-Fulfilling Gem of Sublime Dharma.*

17. The Perfection of Wisdom

FOR THE PERFECTION of wisdom, the following is the synopsis:

> **The perfection of wisdom is summarized as sevenfold: reflections on the drawbacks of its absence and the benefits of its practice; its nature; its various aspects; the essential characteristics of each aspect; that which is to be understood; how to cultivate it; and its fruits.**

The first point is to reflect on **the drawbacks of its absence and the benefits of its practice.** A bodhisattva may abide within the perfections from generosity through to meditative concentration, yet if he lacks the perfection of wisdom, he will never attain the state of omniscience. Why is this so? The [first five perfections] are like a group of blind people without a guide and hence unable to journey to the city they wish to visit. Thus the *Verse Summary of the Perfection of Wisdom* says:

> How could even a trillion blind people
> know the road or ever reach the city without a guide?
> Without wisdom, the five sightless perfections,
> since they are without an eye, cannot reach enlightenment.[548]

In contrast, when they possess wisdom, all the wholesome aspects of virtue—generosity and so on—are transformed into the path to buddhahood, and the state of omniscience will be attained, like a throng of blind people being led by their guide to the city. Thus *Entering the Middle Way* says:

> Just as a whole group of blind people is easily led
> to the place of their choice by one sighted person,
> so are the sightless qualities
> led to the Conqueror's state by wisdom.[549]

The *Verse Summary of the Perfection of Wisdom* says:

> Every aspect of the three realms will be completely transcended by thoroughly understanding the nature of phenomena through wisdom.[550]

This being so, some may wonder, "Wisdom alone might suffice, and what need is there for the skillful means—generosity and so forth?" [188] This is not the case. *Lamp for the Path to Awakening* says:

> Wisdom lacking skillful means
> and skillful means lacking wisdom
> are both bondage, it has been taught.
> Therefore do not abandon this combination.[551]

Exactly what bondage occurs if either wisdom or skillful means are practiced on their own? A bodhisattva who resorts to wisdom without skillful means will fall into the partial nirvana considered to be peace by the śrāvakas and become utterly bound, never reaching nonabiding nirvana. According to the viewpoint that upholds the ultimacy of the three vehicles, it is maintained that one remains stuck in that [nirvana] state permanently. According to the theory of a single vehicle, too, it is maintained that one will remain in that state for eighty thousand major eons.

Now, if a bodhisattva resorts to skillful means without wisdom, he or she will never get beyond the state of childish ordinary being and will be bound to samsara and samsara alone. In the *Akṣayamati Sutra*, it says:

> With wisdom lacking skillful means, one is tied to nirvana. With skillful means lacking wisdom, one is tied to samsara. Therefore the two must be combined.[552]

It also says, in the *Teachings of Vimalakīrti Sutra*:

> What is bondage for bodhisattvas and what is their liberation? Their bondage is wisdom not supported by skillful means whereas their liberation is wisdom supported by skillful means.[553]

Hence, to practice either skillful means or wisdom on its own is to engage in the work of Māra. The *Questions of Nāga King Anavatapta Sutra* says:

> The works of Māra are two: skillful means without wisdom and wisdom without skillful means. Those should be recognized as the work of Māra and rejected.[554]

Further, to give an analogy, just as someone wishing to reach the town of his choice needs a combination of eyes to survey the way and legs to cover the distance, so those going to the city of nonabiding nirvana need the union of the eyes of wisdom and the legs of skillful means. The *Gayāśīrṣa Hill Sutra* says:

> In brief, Mahayana is twofold: means and wisdom.[555] [191]

Wisdom will not arise of its own accord. For example, while a small amount of wood may be ignited but never becomes a powerful, enduring blaze, a great quantity of extremely dry branches stacked together can be ignited to make a mighty, long-lasting blaze that is inextinguishable. Similarly, if only a small amount of wholesome action has been established, great wisdom will not arise, but when vast amounts of the great merits of generosity, moral discipline, and so forth have been established, a great wisdom will emerge, and this will burn away all the obscurations.

Therefore it is for the sake of wisdom alone that one must resort to generosity and so forth. The *Guide to the Bodhisattva Way of Life* says:

> The Victor has taught that all these factors
> are for the sake of wisdom.[556]

The second point, the **nature** of wisdom consists of an accurate, discerning appreciation of phenomena. Thus the *Compendium of Higher Knowledge* says:

> What is wisdom? It is an accurate, discerning appreciation of phenomena.[557]

The third point concerns **its various aspects**. The commentary to the *Ornament of Mahayana Sutras* speaks of three types of wisdom: mundane wisdom, lesser supramundane wisdom, and greater supramundane wisdom.

The fourth point explains the **essential characteristics of each aspect**. *Mundane wisdom* is the wisdom emerging from the four domains of knowledge: the sciences of healing, logic and epistemology, linguistics, and creative skill.[558] *Lesser supramundane wisdom* is the wisdom that arises through the study, contemplation, and meditation of the śrāvakas and pratyekabuddhas. It is to realize the self-perpetuating aggregates to be impure, ridden with suffering, impermanent, and devoid of any entity. *Greater supramundane wisdom* is the wisdom that arises from Mahayana study, contemplation, and meditation. It is the awareness that each and every phenomenon is, by its very nature, empty, unborn, without foundation, and without root. [192] Thus it says in the *Perfection of Wisdom in Seven Hundred Lines*:

> To understand that every phenomenon has no existence as something arisen—that is the perfection of wisdom.[559]

The *Verse Summary of the Perfection of Wisdom* also says:

> To understand every phenomenon to be without own-nature
> is to engage in the practice of excellent perfection of wisdom.[560]

Lamp for the Path to Awakening says:

> To understand emptiness, the essential nature,
> in terms of perceiving the aggregates,
> the sense bases, and elements as devoid of arising,
> this is clearly stated to be wisdom.[561]

The fifth point concerns **that which is to be understood**. Of the three types of wisdom mentioned above, it is the third type—greater supramundane wisdom—that one needs to understand. I shall present this by means of six topics:

A. Refutation of belief in substantial reality
B. Refutation of belief in unreality
C. The mistake of believing in nonexistence
D. The mistake of both beliefs
E. The path to liberation
F. The nature of liberation—nirvana

A. Refutation of belief in substantial reality

In his *Lamp for the Path to Awakening*, Atiśa presents this on the basis of analysis through the major reasoning. He says:

> It is illogical for something existing to arise;
> for nonexistents also, they are like sky flowers....[562]

As he explains in the teachings on the gradual path, all substantial realities, or beliefs in substantiality, are included within the two kinds of self, and that both those entities are by their very nature emptiness. What, then, are the two kinds of self? They are known as the *self of persons* and the *self of phenomena*. What is the self of persons?[563] There are many views on this. In fact, what is referred to as a "person" is the continuum of aggregates accompanied by awareness; it is that which does all sorts of things, always thinking this and that, moving and hopping about. About this the *Sutra of Fragments* says:

> The continuum is termed "person";
> it is this that constantly moves about and scatters.

Believing such a person to be eternal and unitary entity, and grasping onto it and being attached to it, this is called the "selfhood of person" or of mind. Through the notion of self, afflictions will be generated; [193] through the afflictions, karma will be generated; and through karma, suffering will be generated. Thus the root of all sufferings and faults is the self or mind. Therefore the *Thorough Exposition of Valid Cognition* says:

> When "I" exists, "other" is known.
> Through the I-and-other pair comes
> clinging and aversion.
> Through the complex interaction of these arises
> all harm.[564]

What is self of phenomena? Here, *phenomena* refers to the outer perceived world and the inner perceiving mind. Why are those two aspects called *phenomena* (*dharma*)? Because they possess their own defining characteristics.[565] Thus the *Sutra of Fragments* says,

> That which holds defining characteristics is called *dharma*.

Thus holding the two—the objective perceived world and the subjective perceiving world—to possess substantial reality and clinging to them is called *self of phenomena*.

(1) To present how these two types of self are empty by nature, first there is the *refutation of the self of persons*. Master Nāgārjuna says, in his *Precious Garland*:

> The notions "I" and "mine"
> deviate from what is ultimately true.[566]

This means that, from the point of view of ultimate reality, those aspects of self do not exist. If such a self existed as an ultimate reality, it should equally be there when ultimate truth is "seen"; yet when a mind with insight into the truth sees the essential nature, there is no such self. Therefore it does not have any true existence. The *Precious Garland* says:

> For when the ultimately pure is fully recognized
> just as it is, these two will not arise.[567]

In that text, "the ultimately pure is fully recognized just as it is" refers to insight into the truth. "These two will not arise" means that there will be not grasping at "I" or "mine."

[a] Were a mind or self to truly exist, it could be examined as originating from itself, from something else, or through the three phases of time.

It does not arise from itself because [as far as the process of origination is concerned] its production must have either already happened or have not yet happened. If it does not yet exist, it cannot possibly serve as a cause [for its own production,] and if it does already exist, it cannot possibly become [its own] result. Thus something producing itself is a contradiction.

It does not arise from others because they are substances [other than itself]. Why can they not be causes? A "cause" only exists with respect to a result, and as long as there is no result, there is no cause. As long as there is no cause, no result can manifest either. [194] This is similar to the previous argument.[568]

It does not arise from both [*self and others*] of the above since both concepts are faulty, as explained above.

It does not arise from the three phases of time: It is not a product of the past because the past, like a seed gone rotten, no longer has any power. It is not produced by the future—that would be like the child of a barren woman. It is not a product of the present because it is illogical that it could be both creation and creator [in the same instant]. Thus the *Precious Garland* says:

> As it is not being obtained from itself,
> something other, a combination, or the three times,
> belief in a self will be consumed.[569]

"Not being obtained from" means not generated by.

[b] Alternatively, one should understand it in the following manner. Examine whether or not this "self" exists in the body, in the mind, or in a name.

The nature of *the body* is that of the four elements: the body's solidity is the earth element, its fluids are the water element, its warmth is the fire element, and its breathing and movement constitute the wind element. The four elements possess neither self nor mind, just as the four outer elements—earth, water, and so on—are without mind or self.

Does the self exist in *the mind*, then? Mind has no existence whatsoever, for neither you nor anyone else has ever seen it. If mind has no actual existence, then self as mind can have no actual existence either.

Does self or own mind exist in *the name*? A name is merely something given arbitrarily; it has no substantial existence and bears no relation to a self.

Thus the three reasons presented above demonstrate that the self or mind of persons has no true existence.

(2) Second there is] the *refutation of the self of phenomena*. This is in two parts, demonstrating the nonexistence of the objective perceived world and the nonexistence of the subjective perceiving mind.

[a] As for the first, [the *nonexistence of the objective perceived world*,] some believe in the substantial existence of the objective perceived world. Vaibhāṣikas, for example, hold there to be minute particles of matter that exist substantially; they are round and partless. The aggregation of these particles constitutes objects such as material form and so forth. As the particles agglomerate, there are interstices between them. They presently appear as something homogeneous, just as a yak's tail or a pasture of grass does. [195] The minute particles do not drift apart because the karma of beings causes

them to bond as they do. Sautrāntikas hold that when such partless particles conglomerate, they are without interstices yet do not actually touch. These are the views of those [two main Hinayana traditions,] but neither is really the case.

Were such a particle to be unitary, then would it not have sides? If so, would it not have relative east, west, north, south, top and, bottom areas? This makes six sides and destroys the contention of it being unitary. If it had no spatial dimension, all matter would be, by nature, a sole atom. This is obviously not the case either. The *Twenty Stanzas* says:

> If the six are applied to what is one,
> the ultimate particle has six different parts.
> If those six are one,
> then substance is only one particle.[570]

Are particles multiple? If one partless particle could be proved to exist, it would be reasonable to propose that many of them could conglomerate to make multiple entities, but since the existence of a partless unit cannot be proved, multiples of them cannot be proved to exist either. As a consequence, since particles have no substantial existence, an outer substantial reality composed of particles of such a nature cannot exist either.

You may wonder, "What is actually manifesting right now?" It is an image in the mind that appears to the mind as being an outer world. This occurs through delusion. If you ask, "How can we know that is so?" the answer is that it can be known through scriptural authority, reason, and examples:

The *scriptural authority* can be found in the *Flower Ornament Sutra*, where it says,

> Children of good family! This world of the three realms is mind only.[571]

Also in the *Sutra on Going to Laṅka*, where it says:

> Mind agitated by its imprints
> will manifest thoroughly as objective realities.[572]
> There are no objective realities but mind alone;
> the perception of external reality is erroneous.[573]

[Refutation of external reality through] *reason* can be presented in the form of the syllogism: "Those things that appear as external" is the logical subject; "they are illusory manifestations of mind" is the proposition; "because that which has no true existence is being perceived" is the reason. (For instance, human horns or a visualized tree.)[574]

Such manifestations (the subject) are also simply illusory projections of the mind (the proposition) because they do not appear as what they really are—changing appearances brought about by certain causes and conditions, or appearances that can transmute and disappear through the power of imagination and familiarization, the way things manifest being different according to the projections of each of the six types of sentient being (the reason). *Examples* of such a process would be dreams, magical illusions, and the like.

Thus these above presents how the external perceived world is devoid of [substantial] existence. [196]

[b] The second point [is the *nonexistence of a perceiving mind*]. Some—pratyekabuddhas and Cittamātrins—consider the subjective, perceiving mind really to exist, as something apperceptive and self-illuminating. They hold such a view, but it is inaccurate for three reasons:

1. Mind does not exist when examined in terms of moments of time.
2. Mind does not exist because no one has ever witnessed it.
3. Mind does not exist because there is no objective reality.

(1) Concerning the first of these, [nonexistence *in terms of moments of time*]: "Is the apperceptive, self-illuminating mind that you postulate present in one instant or several? Were it truly to exist in each instant, would that instant have past, present, and future?[575] If it were so, this would refute its existence as a unique existing unit of mind. If it were not so, [the idea of sequences of] many instants becomes absurd." Thus the *Precious Garland* says:

> One must examine the instant: just as it has an end,
> it must also have a middle and a beginning.
> Since an instant is thus threefold,
> the world cannot exist as an instant.[576]

Without the existence of the threefold division of time, the [true existence of the] instant is refuted by its being insubstantial. Through the instant being unproven, the existence of mind [composed of such instants] is also unproven.

Does mind exist as multiple instants? Were one instant to be proven, it would be reasonable to postulate an accumulation of many instants, but since the existence of one instant is not proven, the idea of mind as multiple instants is not demonstrated either.

(2) Now for the second point, the nonexistence of the perceiving mind *because it has never been witnessed.* Seek out the location of "mind"—in the body, outside it, or between the two; seek it high and low. Examine most thoroughly to determine whether it has any form or color whatsoever. Seek until there is a sense of conviction, whatever it may be. Search for it according to the master's instructions—such as how to vary the object of inspection. When, no matter how you seek, mind is never seen, never encountered, and no substantial characteristic such as color or something visible is to be found, it is not the case that mind exists but you have not yet been able to find it or witness it. If it cannot be seen, no matter where it is sought, it is because the investigator is the investigated and the seeker is beyond the scope of his or her own intellect—beyond the scope of words, thoughts, ideas, or expression. That is why in the *Kāśyapa Chapter Sutra* it says:

> Kāśyapa! Mind is found neither within, without, nor in between. Kāśyapa! Mind cannot be investigated, cannot be shown, cannot be used as a basis, cannot appear, cannot be known, and has no abiding. [197] Kāśyapa! Mind has never, is never, and will never be seen, even by any of the buddhas.[577]

In the *Sutra That Perfectly Seizes Sublime Dharma* it says:

> Therefore, by coming to understand perfectly
> the various degrees to which
> mind is a contrivance, a fake,
> one will no longer perceive it as an essence.
> Devoid of any essence,
> phenomena are without any real existence.
> All phenomena are imputed [by the mind];
> I have taught their nature to be such.
> Outshining the two extremes,

> the wise practice the middle way;
> this emptiness of essential reality,
> this is the path to enlightenment;
> I too have taught this path.[578]

The *Unwavering Suchness Sutra* says:

> Every phenomenon is, by its very nature, unborn, essentially nonabiding, free from the extremes of acting and action, and beyond the scope of thought and nonthought.[579]

Since no one has ever witnessed mind, it is pointless to speak of it in terms of apperception and self-illumination. As *Guide to the Bodhisattva Way of Life* states:

> Since none has ever seen it at any time,
> to ask whether it is self-illuminating
> is as meaningless as discussing
> the elegance of a barren woman's child.[580]

Tilopa said:

> Marvel! This is the self-cognizing pristine awareness;
> it is beyond speech and is not the domain of the intellect.[581]

(3) The third point—the nonexistence of the perceiving mind *because no objective reality exists*—is explained as follows. Since, as was demonstrated above, visual forms and so forth—the outer objective reality—have no substantial existence, the inner mind that perceives them cannot have substantial existence either. In the *Sutra on the Indivisibility of the Dharmadhātu*, it says:

> Investigate whether this thing you call "mind" is blue, yellow, red, white, maroon, or transparent; whether it is pure or impure, "permanent" or "impermanent," and whether or not it is endowed with form. Mind has no physical form; it cannot be shown. It does not manifest, it is intangible, it does not cognize, it resides neither inside, outside, nor anywhere in between. Thus

> it is utterly pure, totally nonexistent. There is nothing of it to liberate; it is the very nature of the dharmadhātu.[582]

Furthermore, *Guide to the Bodhisattva Way of Life* says: [198]

> When there is nothing to be known,
> what is the point of speaking of knowing?[583]

and

> It is certain, therefore, that without the presence
> of something knowable, there can be no knowledge.[584]

Through the above points, it has been demonstrated that the perceiving mind, a subjective mind, has no ultimate existence. This concludes the section discussing the belief in substantial reality.

B. Refutation of belief in unreality

If the two types of self have no authentic existence as real things, could they be nonexistent, unreal? In fact, they do not even exist as unrealities. Why? Were one or the other to have had true existence in the first place, as something real, and then to have ceased existing, a "nonexistence" would be feasible. However, since neither the two kinds of self or mind ever had substantial existence in the first place, they cannot be classed in either of these extreme definitions of existing or nonexisting. Saraha said:

> To believe in reality is to be like cattle.
> But to believe in unreality is even more stupid![585]

The *Sutra on Going to Laṅka* says:

> Externals are neither existent nor nonexistent.
> Mind cannot be truly apprehended either.
> The characteristic of the unborn is
> to be utterly other than all these views.[586]

The *Precious Garland* says,

> When no substantial reality can be found,
> how can there be unrealities?[587]

C. The mistake of belief in nonexistence

If belief in existence is the root of samsara, will those who hold a view of nonexistence become liberated from samsara? In fact, this mistake is even worse than the one explained above. As [already mentioned,] Saraha said:

> To believe in reality is to be like cattle.
> But to believe in unreality is even more stupid![588]

It also says in the Heap of Jewels [in the *Kāśyapa Chapter Sutra*]:

> Kāśyapa, the view of personality—even if it is as big as Mount Meru—is relatively easy [to abandon], but not so for a decidedly arrogant view of emptiness.

And, furthermore it is stated:

> Flawed views concerning emptiness will be
> the downfall of those of little wisdom.[589]

In the *Fundamental Verses on the Middle Way*, it says:

> Those who believe in emptiness
> are said to be incurable.[590]

Why are they incurable? Take the example of a strong purgative: if both the constipation and the medicine are eliminated, the patient will recover. [199] If the blockage is removed but the patient fails to cleanse the purgative itself from his system, he may not recover and may even die. Likewise, belief in substantial reality is eliminated by cultivating the notion of emptiness, but if the person clings to emptiness and makes it a "view," the "master of emptiness" will annihilate himself and be on his way to the lower states. The *Precious Garland* says:

A realist goes to the higher states;
a nihilist to the lower ones.[591]

Thus the latter mistake is worse than the former.

D. The mistake of both beliefs

In fact, belief in existence and belief in nonexistence are both mistakes because they are beliefs that have fallen into the two extremes of eternalism and nihilism. The *Fundamental Verses on the Middle Way* says:

"Exists" is the view of eternalism,
and "does not exist" is the view of nihilism.[592]

To fall into the extremes of eternalism or nihilism is confused ignorance, and while there is such confused ignorance there will be no liberation from samsara. The *Precious Garland* says:

To believe that this mirage-like world
either "exists" or "does not exist"
is confused ignorance.
With [such] confusion, there is no liberation.[593]

E. The path to liberation

"Well, then, what does bring liberation?" It is a middle way that does not abide in extremes and that leads to liberation. As the *Precious Garland* says:

Those who fully understand the truth just as it is (that each and
every phenomenon is and always has been nonproduced)
and do not depend on the two (eternalism and nihilism) will
become liberated (from samsara).[594]

Thus someone who does not resort to them (the extremes of eternalism and nihilism) is liberated, so it is taught. The *Fundamental Verses on the Middle Way*, too, says:

Therefore the wise should not dwell
on existence or nonexistence.[595]

What is the "Middle Way" that abolishes the two extremes? The Heap of Jewels [in the *Three Vows Chapter*] answers:

> Kāśyapa! What is the correct way for bodhisattvas to approach phenomena? It is this. It is the middle way; the correct, discerning appreciation of phenomena. Kāśyapa! What is this middle way that is a proper, discerning appreciation of phenomena? Kāśyapa! "Permanence" makes one extreme. [200] "Impermanence" makes a second extreme. Whatever lies between these two extremes cannot be analyzed, cannot be shown, is not apparent, and is totally unknowable. Kāśyapa! This is the "middle way that is a correct, discerning appreciation of phenomena." Kāśyapa! "Self" is one extreme. "Selfless" is a second extreme... [etc.]. Kāśyapa! "Samsara" is one extreme. This nirvana is a second extreme. Whatever lies between these two extremes cannot be analyzed, cannot be shown, is not apparent, and is totally unknowable. This is the "middle way that is a correct, discerning appreciation of phenomena."[596]

Also, Master Śāntideva has taught:

Neither inside nor outside,
nor elsewhere can the mind be found.

It is not a combination [with the body],
and neither is it something other.
It is not the slightest thing.
The very nature of sentient beings is nirvana.[597]

Therefore, even though someone may practice this middle way that does not consider things in terms of the two extremes, the middle itself is never something that can be examined. It abides beyond the intellect, free from understanding that believes sense data to be this or that. Atiśa has said:

> Likewise, the past mind has ceased and is destroyed. The future mind is not born and has not yet occurred. The present mind is

> exceedingly hard to investigate, is colorless, without form, and, like space, without concrete existence.[598]

The *Ornament of Clear Realization* also says:

> Not in the extremes of this shore or that
> nor abiding between the two.
> And since it perceives all times to be the same,
> it is held to be the perfection of wisdom.[599]

F. The nature of liberation—nirvana

If all the phenomena of samsara have no true existence, either as things substantial or insubstantial, then is "nirvana" something that has substantial or insubstantial reality? Some philosophers do consider nirvana actually to have some concrete existence. However, this is not correct, as the *Precious Garland* explains:

> Since nirvana is not even unreal,
> how could it be substantially real?[600] [201]

Were nirvana something substantial, it would have to be a composite thing, and whetever is composite will eventually disintegrate. Hence the *Fundamental Verses on the Middle Way* states, among other things:

> Were nirvana to be substantially real,
> it would be a composite thing.[601]

It is also not the case that it is something unreal. The same work says:

> There is no unreality in it.[602]

Well then, what is it? Nirvana is "the exhaustion of all of the grasping at substantial reality and unreality. It is beyond the scope of the intellect and is beyond words."

The *Precious Garland*:

> The cessation of all notions of substantial reality
> or unreality: that is "nirvana."[603]

It also says, in *Guide to the Bodhisattva Way of Life*:

> Whenever substantial reality or unreality
> no longer dwell before the mind,
> since there will be no other alternative way,
> free of objectification, one will be utterly at peace.[604]

The *Questions of Brahma Viśesacinti Sutra* says:

> *Total nirvana* is the complete pacification of every distinctive characteristic and freedom from any sort of fluctuation.[605]

The *Lotus Sutra* says:

> Kāśyapa! To comprehend the utter equality of all phenomena, this is nirvana.

Therefore, other than being the pacification of all mental activity, nirvana does not exist in terms of any phenomena, something that arises or ceases, something to be eliminated or to be attained. The *Fundamental Verses on the Middle Way* states:

> No abandoning, no acquiring,
> no nihilism, no eternalism,
> no cessation, no arising:
> this is nirvana.[606]

Since nirvana is without any arising, cessation, relinquishment, or attainment whatsoever, there is nothing in relation to nirvana that is, on your part, constructed, fabricated, or modified. Therefore the *Precious Space Sutra* says:

> Nothing to remove from this;
> not the slightest thing thereon to add.
> One views perfectly the perfect truth;
> when seen thus, one is utterly freed.[607]

Therefore, although the terms "what is to be known is one's own mind" or "what is to be known is wisdom (*prajñā*)" and so forth are employed in the context of analytical investigation, in actual fact, wisdom or mind remain beyond cognition or verbal expression. [202] As the *Sutra Requested by Suvikrāntavikrami* says:

> As the perfection of wisdom cannot be expressed through anything phenomenal, it transcends all words.[608]

Furthermore, in *Rāhula's Praises to the Mother* it says:

> I prostrate to the mother of all the Victors of the three times:
> the perfection of wisdom inexpressible in word or thought;
> unborn, unceasing, the very essence of space;
> the field of experience of discerning, self-knowing pristine
> awareness.[609]

With this, the explanation of what is known as wisdom is completed.

Now, I will explain the sixth point, **how to cultivate deep wisdom**.

"If all phenomena are emptiness," someone may wonder, "is it really necessary to cultivate this awareness?" Indeed it is necessary. For instance, even though silver ore has the very nature of silver, the silver itself will not be apparent until the ore has been smelted and worked on. Likewise all things have always been by their very nature emptiness, beyond every form of conceptual elaboration, and nevertheless there is a need to develop awareness of it because beings experience it in various material ways and undergo various sufferings. Therefore, having become aware of what was explained above, cultivating this awareness has four elements:

A. The preliminary practices
B. The meditation session [practice]
C. The post-meditation [practices]
D. The signs of having cultivated

(A) The first, the *preliminary practices*, involves bringing your mind to a natural settled state.[610] How does one achieve this? By following what it says in the *Perfection of Wisdom in Seven Hundred Lines*:

> Sons and daughters of this noble line should seek the path of solitude! They should delight in the absence of distractive activities. They should sit cross-legged, not bringing to their attention any extraneous signs....[611]

You should do these as found in the Mahāmudrā preparatory practices.[612]

(B) Next, as for the method of the *actual meditation session* [*practice*], following the Mahāmudrā system of instruction, place your mind free from effort or exertion, without any thought pertaining to existence or nonexistence, affirmation or rejection. Tilopa says:

> Not dwelling on, not intending, not analyzing,
> not meditating, not contemplating,
> leave mind to itself.[613]

Also, about letting the mind rest:

> Listen, child! Whatever mental activity occurs,
> within this there is no one bound, no one free.
> Therefore, O joy, shedding your fatigue,
> rest naturally, without contrivance or distraction.[614] [203]

Nāgārjuna has also said:

> A mind that has stably relaxed within itself,
> like an elephant that has been trained,
> has stopped running to and fro, and remains naturally at ease.
> Thus have I realized, and hence what need have I of teachings?[615]

And the same said:

> Don't adopt an attitude or think in any way whatsoever.
> Don't interfere or contrive but leave mind loose in its natural
> state.
> The uncontrived is the unborn, true nature.
> This is of the trail set by all the victors of the three times.[616]

The Lord of Hermits [i.e., the Indian mahasiddha Śavaripa] has also said:

> Do not see fault anywhere.
> Practice that which is nothing whatsoever.
> Do not foster longing for signs of progress and the like.
> Although it is taught that there is nothing whatsoever to meditate on,
> do not fall under the sway of inactivity and indifference.
> In all circumstances, practice with mindfulness.[617]

In the *Achievement of the Very Point of Meditation* it says:

> When meditating, do not meditate on anything whatsoever.
> To call it "meditation" is simply use a convention.[618]

As Saraha said:

> If there is involvement with anything, let it go;
> once realization has occurred, everything is that;
> apart from this, no one will ever know anything else.[619]

In the words of Atiśa:

> This is suchness, profound and free of elaboration.
> Luminous and unconditioned,
> unborn and unceasing,
> it is primordially pure.
>
> It is the natural nirvana,
> the ultimate, without middle or end;
> behold it with the fine eye of mind free of concept
> and without the bluriness of laxity or excitation.[620]

And:

> In the ultimate expanse free of conceptual elaboration,
> place your mind free of conceptual elaboration.[621]

Placing the mind in the way described above is to employ an unerring method for cultivating the perfection of profound wisdom. The *Perfection of Wisdom in Seven Hundred Lines* says:

> Not to engage in, hold onto, or reject anything—that is to meditate on the perfection of wisdom. Not dwelling on anything is to meditate on the perfection of wisdom. Not to think about anything and not to focus on anything whatsoever is to meditate on the perfection of wisdom.[622]

The *Perfection of Wisdom in Eight Thousand Lines* says:

> To meditate on the perfection of wisdom is to meditate on no phenomena whatsoever.

And:

> To meditate on the perfection of wisdom is to meditate on space.[623] [204]

How can one "meditate on space"? The same sutra tells us:

> In that space is devoid of conceptualization, the perfection of wisdom, too, is devoid of conceptualization.[624]

The *Verse Summary of the Perfection of Wisdom* also says:

> Not to be both in *absence of arising* as well as *arising*,
> this is to practice the perfection of wisdom."[625]

In the words of the great master Vāgīśvarakīrti:

> Do not think about the thinkable.
> Do not think about the unthinkable either.
> By thinking neither about the thinkable nor the unthinkable,
> emptiness will be seen.[626]

How does someone "see emptiness"? As it says in the *Perfectly Gathering the Qualities [of Avalokiteśvara] Sutra*:

> To see emptiness is not to see [anything] at all.

And:

> Blessed One! Not to see any thing is to see excellently.

And:

> Without seeing any thing whatsoever, the one and only nature is seen.[627]

The *Shorter Text on Middle Way Truths* also says:

> It says in some exceedingly profound discourses
> that not-seeing is to see that [truth].[628]

The *Verse Summary of the Perfection of Wisdom* also remarks:

> People commonly use the term "seeing space."
> Consider carefully just how someone can *see* space.
> The Tathāgata taught the way to see phenomena as being like that.[629]

(C) The third point concerns the [*post-meditation* or] *between-sessions phase*. While viewing everything that occurs in between meditation sessions as illusory, every wholesome merit possible should be established, through the practice of generosity and so forth. As the *Verse Summary of the Perfection of Wisdom* says:

> Whoever understands the five aggregates to be like an illusion
> but does not make the aggregates and the illusion as separate things
> and is free of the notion of multiplicity but experiences peace,
> that is to practice the excellent perfection of wisdom.[630]

The *King of Meditation Sutra* says:

> Although magicians conjure up forms—
> making horses, elephants, carts, and all sorts of things—
> they know that nothing of what appears is actually there.
> Recognize all phenomena to be likewise.[631]

It is said in the *Suchness of Conduct*:

> The mind is attentive to not conceptualizing,
> yet the amassing of merit never ceases.[632]

Through such familiarity, the meditation and post-meditation phases will become indistinguishable and one will become free of conceitedness. Thus it says: [205]

> He will have no conceitedness in terms of "I am in meditative equipoise" or "I am arising from the equipoise."
> Why? Because there is awareness of the very nature of things.[633]

To be immersed, even for a short moment, in the perfection of wisdom—the ultimate, emptiness—constitutes an incomparably greater virtue than to spend eons receiving Dharma teachings, reciting scriptures, or planting roots of virtue in the form of generosity and similar wholesome actions. The *Sutra Teaching Suchness* states:

> Śāriputra! Compared to someone listening [to the Dharma] for up to an eon, if another person were to practice meditative absorption on suchness even for the duration of a finger snap, his merits would increase far more greatly. Śāriputra! For this reason you should earnestly instruct others to practice meditative absorption on suchness. Śāriputra! All the bodhisattvas who have been predicted as being future buddhas also abide solely in that meditative absorption.[634]

It is also stated, in the *Sutra on the Full Development of Great Realization*:

> It is more meaningful to practice meditative concentration for a session
> than to give life to beings of the three dimensions.[635]

In the *Great Uṣṇīṣa Sutra* it states:

> It is of greater merit to cultivate the true meaning of things for a day than to study and reflect for many cosmic eons. Why is

> this so? Because it takes one far away from the road of births and deaths.[636]

In the *Sutra on Excellently Nurturing Faith* [*in the Mahayana*], it says:

> There is greater merit in a yogi's session of emptiness meditation than there would be if all beings in the three dimensions spent their whole lives using their possessions to accumulate virtue.[637]

It is taught that if your mind is not dwelling on the key points of emptiness, then other virtues cannot deliver you to liberation. The *Sutra Teaching the Nonorigination of All Things*:

> Someone may observe moral discipline for a long time and practice meditative concentration for millions of eons, but without realization of this highest truth, those things cannot bring liberation, according to this teaching. Whoever understands this "nothing whatsoever" will never cling to anything whatsoever.[638]

In the *Ten Wheels of Kṣitigarbha Sutra* it states:

> It is through cultivating absorption doubts will be cut.
> Other than that, nothing can. [206]
> Hence the cultivation of absorption is supreme,
> and the wise practice it diligently.[639]

Furthermore:

> The positive result of meditating for a day far exceeds that of writing out, reading, studying, reciting, or explaining the teachings for eons.[640]

Once you become endowed with the key point of emptiness, as described above, there is nothing at all that is not encompassed within it.

This constitutes *to take refuge* as well. For example, the *Questions of Nāga King Anavatapta Sutra* states:

> Bodhisattvas recognize all phenomena to be without a self, with-

> out a sentient nature, without life, and without personhood. To see quite correctly in the way the tathāgatas see—not as forms, not as names, and not as specific phenomena—is to have taken refuge in the Buddha with a mind unpolluted by material consideration.
>
> The essence of the tathāgatas is the ultimate expanse; that which is ultimate expanse is referred to as that which pervades every thing. Thus, seeing it as the domain of all phenomena is to take refuge in the Dharma with a mind unpolluted by material consideration.
>
> Whoever is familiar with the ultimate expanse as being unconditioned and with the fact that the śrāvakayāna is founded in what is unconditioned, and who also understands the nonduality of the conditioned and the unconditioned, takes refuge in the Sangha with a mind unpolluted by material consideration.[641]

This constitutes the *generation of bodhicitta* as well. For example, the *Sutra of Great Bodhicitta*[642] says:

> Kāśyapa! Every phenomenon is, like space, without specific characteristics and is primordial lucid clarity and utter purity. That is "to give rise to bodhicitta."

The *deity meditation* and *mantra recitation* are all complete within this as well. In the *Hevajra Tantra* it says:

> No meditation, no meditator as well;
> no deities and no mantra either;
> within the nature free of conceptual elaboration,
> the deities and mantras are truly present:
> Vairocana, Akṣobhya, Amoghasiddhi,
> Ratnasambhava, Amitābha, and Vajrasattva.[643]

The *Union with All the Buddhas Tantra* says:

> From a cast image and the like
> a true union (*yoga*) will not emerge,
> whereas the yogi who strives excellently
> in bodhicitta will actually become the deity.[644] [207]

The *Vajra Peak Tantra* says:

> The intrinsic characteristic of every mantra
> is said to be the mind of all the buddhas;
> it is a means to cultivate the essence of Dharma.
> To be perfectly endowed with the ultimate expanse
> is said to be the intrinsic characteristic of mantras.[645]

It also comprises *fire offerings*. As the *King of Secret Nectar Tantra* says:

> What are fire offerings for?
> They are made to bestow the highest accomplishments
> and to overcome conceptualization.
> Burning wood and so forth is not a fire offering.[646]

The path in terms of *the six perfections* is also complete in it. The *Diamond Meditative Absorption Scripture* says:

> If unwavered from emptiness, the six perfections are embodied.[647]

According to the *Questions of Brahma Viśesacinti Sutra*:

> To be without intention is generosity. Not to dwell on the separatedness of things is moral discipline. Not to make differentiations is patience. Absence of adoption and rejection is diligence. Nonattachment is meditative concentration. Nonthought is wisdom.[648]

The *Ten Wheels of Kṣitigarbha Sutra* also states:

> The meditation of the wise and skillful on the teaching of
> emptiness
> does not resort to or dwell on anything of the world.
> It abides nowhere in any existence,
> and as such is the observance of pure moral discipline.[649]

It is said in the same sutra:

All phenomena are of one taste,
being equally empty and without any characteristics.
The mind that does not dwell on or become attached to anything
is [practicing] patience, and through this, benefit will increase
greatly.[650]
The wise who practice diligence
have cast far away every attachment.
The mind that neither dwells on nor clings to anything
whatsoever
should be known as a "field of finest virtue."[651]
To practice meditative concentration
in order to bring happiness and well-being to all sentient beings
is something that removes a great burden.
To thus clear away every polluting affliction
is the defining characteristic of the truly wise.[652]

It also constitutes making *prostrations*. The *Precious Space Sutra*:

Like water poured into water
and like butter poured into butter,
he who sees this pristine self-cognizing awareness
is also making prostration to it.[653]

It also represents the *making of offerings*. The *Meeting of Father and Son Sutra* says: [208]

To resort to the Dharma of emptiness
and aspire to that which is the domain of experience of the
buddhas—
such is to make offerings to the enlightened teacher,
and such offerings are unsurpassable.[654]

Also, in the *King of Secret Nectar Tantra* it says:

Meaningful offerings are pleasing,
but not so offerings of incense and the like.
By making the mind perfectly workable,
the great and pleasing offering is made.[655]

Furthermore, if you possess this perfection of wisdom, this constitutes the purification of past errors as well. In the *Sutra on Totally Purifying Karma* it says:

> You who are desirous of atonement!
> Sit straight and behold the perfect truth.
> Perfectly beholding the perfect truth
> is the most excellent form of repentence.[656]

It also comprises the *observance of moral commitments*. As is said in the *Questions of the Devaputra Susthitamati Sutra*:

> When there is no longer the conceitedness of *vow* or *no-vow*, there is the moral discipline of nirvana; that is the purest moral discipline.[657]

The *Ten Wheels [of Kṣitigarbha] Sutra* also says:

> Someone may be considered to be a layperson, living at home with head and beard unshaven. He may not wear monk's robes and may not even have taken [the precepts] of moral discipline. But if he is endowed with the suchness of the noble ones, that person is a true monk in the ultimate sense.[658]

Furthermore, it also comprises *all three stages of wisdom*—of study, of contemplation, and of meditation. As is said in the *Tantra of Supreme Nonabiding*:

> If one has eaten the food of the uncontrived naturalness,
> it fulfills all the philosophical tenets, whatever they may be.
> The immature, lacking realization, rely on terminology.
> Everything is but a characteristic of one's own mind.[659]

Saraha said, moreover:

> It is to read, it is to seize the meaning, and it is to meditate.
> It is also to assimilate the meaning of the treatises.
> There is no view capable of demonstrating it.[660]

It also comprises making *torma offerings and similar Dharma activities.* The *King of Secret Nectar Tantra* says:

> When someone has encountered the nature of mind,
> all different types of activity
> and deed are contained therein:
> offerings, *torma*, and so forth.[661]

Well, if meditation on this essence or the nature of mind comprises all those things, what was the reason for teaching so many graduated techniques? These evolved to guide those less-gifted beings who are still confused about the nature of things. The *Sutra That Adorns the Radiance of Pristine Awareness* says: [209]

> Explanations of causes, conditions, and interdependence,
> as well as the teaching of the graduated path,
> were given as skillful means for the confused.
> As for this spontaneous Dharma,
> what graduated training could there be?[662]

In the *Tantra of the Arising of the Supremely Blissful*, it says:

> Thus is attained an eternally liberated status—
> a status comparable to the vastness of space.[663]

In the *Precious Space Sutra*, it is said:

> Before dwelling in the ocean of the ultimate expanse, the stages and levels are held to be different. Once the ocean of the ultimate expanse has been entered, there is not even the slightest traversing of stages and levels.[664]

Illustrious Atiśa has said:

> When a mind is firmly settled in the one,
> do not strive in physical and verbal virtues.[665]

(D) The *six signs of having cultivated wisdom* are you become more heedful with respect to virtue, your afflictions decrease, compassion arises for sentient beings, you apply yourself earnestly to practice, you reject all forms of distraction, and you are no longer attached to and are free of clinging to the things of this life. Therefore it is said, in the *Precious Garland*:

> Through familiarity with emptiness,
> heedfulness with regard to virtue is attained.[666]

The seventh point explains the **fruits of the perfection of wisdom.** These should be understood as being twofold: the ultimate result and the temporary consequences. The ultimate result is to attain enlightenment. Thus the *Perfection of Wisdom in Seven Hundred Lines* teaches:

> Mañjuśrī! Through practicing the perfection of wisdom, bodhisattva mahāsattvas will rapidly and genuinely become perfectly enlightened in peerless, unsurpassable perfect buddhahood.[667]

In the short term, every good and excellent thing will occur. As it is said, in the *Verse Summary of the Perfection of Wisdom*:

> Whatever delightful, happy things are encountered
> by bodhisattvas, śrāvakas, pratyekabuddhas, gods, or any being,
> all derive from the supreme perfection of wisdom.[668]

This concludes the seventeenth chapter, concerning the perfection of wisdom, in this *Ornament of Precious Liberation, a Wish-Fulfilling Gem of Sublime Dharma.*

18. The Presentation of the [Five] Paths

[210] HAVING FIRST GIVEN rise to the intention to achieve supreme enlightenment and having earnestly engaged in the training presented earlier, a person will traverse the paths and levels of the bodhisattva in their respective sequence. To present the path, the following:

> **The paths are totally encompassed within these five: the path of accumulation, the path of application, the path of seeing, the path of cultivation, and the path of complete accomplishment.**

According to the treatise *Lamp for the Path to Awakening,* these five paths are taught as follows. The first, the path of *accumulation*, lays the foundation through cultivating the Dharma instructions suited to a persons of initial and middling capacities. These are followed by development of the two aspects of bodhicitta—aspiration and engagement—and the amassing of the two accumulations. The text then teaches how the path of *application* occurs, "through an understanding acquired progressively through the subphases of heat and so forth."[669] The paths of seeing, cultivation, and complete accomplishment are taught through "the Joyous and so on are attained."[670]

First is the **path of accumulation.** It represents all the efforts that those endowed with the Mahayana potential will have to make in the practice of virtue, from the moment they first set their mind on supreme enlightenment and receive some advice and instruction from a teacher until such time as the attainment of the pristine awareness of the heat subphase [of the path of application]. This phase of the path is itself subdivided into four, according to whether it is informed by understanding, aspiration, longing for the sublime, or actual attainment.

Why is it called the *path of accumulation*? It is so called because of its activities, which serve to gather and establish the accumulations of virtue and so forth in order to make a person a vessel suitable for realizations such as those of heat and so forth to arise. They are also referred to as "roots of virtue conducive to liberation." During that particular period, one cultivates twelve—that is, three sets of four—[of the thirty-seven] factors conducive to awakening. They are: (1–4) the four foundations of mindfulness, (5–8) the four perfect endeavors, and (9–12) the four bases of magical powers.

Of these, the *four foundations of mindfulness*, which constitute the lower stage of the path of accumulation, involve developing: (1) mindfulness of body, (2) mindfulness of feelings, [211] (3) mindfulness of mind, and (4) mindfulness of phenomena.

The *four perfect endeavors*, which constitute the middle stage of the path of accumulation, are: (1) relinquishing the existing evils and nonvirtues, (2) not giving rise to evils and nonvirtues currently absent, (3) giving rise to virtuous remedies not yet present, and (4) increasing virtues already developed.

The *four bases of magical powers*, which constitute the upper stage of the path of accumulation, are: (1) meditative absorption through aspiration, (2) meditative absorption through diligence, (3) meditative absorption through intention, and (4) meditative absorption through analysis. These above are emcompassed within the path of accumulation.

The second is the **path of application**. This follows on from the proper completion of the path of accumulation. It is the birth of "the four subphases of definite breakthrough in understanding" conducive to realization of the four noble truths. The four subphases are called: heat, the peak, fearless acceptance, and the highest worldly realization.

Why is it called the *path of application*? Here "application" refers to connecting with a direct realization of truth. During the subphases of heat and the peak, *five faculties* are employed: faith, diligence, mindfulness, concentration, and wisdom. In the subphases of fearless acceptance and highest worldly realization, these become *five powers*: faith, diligence, mindfulness, meditative absorption, and wisdom.

The third is the **path of seeing**. This follows on from the highest wordly realization subphase. It is the combination of tranquility and insight focused on the four truths of the noble ones. In relation to [the first truth, that of] suffering, there are [aspects of insight known as]: (1) receptivity to knowledge of the nature of suffering, (2) knowledge of the nature of suffering, (3) receptivity to subsequent knowledge of the nature of suffering, (4) subsequent knowledge of the nature of suffering. There are four such aspects for each of the four noble truths. The insight embodies these sixteen instants of receptivity and knowledge.

Why are those referred to as the *path of seeing*? Because at that stage authentic insight into the [four] truths of the noble ones is gained for the first time. During that stage, a person is endowed with the *seven aspects of enlightenment* [212]: (1) right mindfulness, an aspect of enlightenment (2) right discernment, (3) right diligence, (4) right joy, (5) right pliancy, (6) right meditation, and (7) right equanimity, an aspect of enlightenment.

The fourth is the **path of cultivation**. It is what follows the path of seeing. It has two aspects: the mundane path and the supramundane path.

The mundane path of cultivation comprises the first, second, third, and fourth worldly meditative concentrations (*dhyāna*) and the [four formless meditative attainments in the form of] the spheres of (1) limitless space, (2) limitless consciousness, (3) nothing whatsoever, and (4) neither awareness nor absence of awareness. There are three purposes in cultivating these: (a) to overwhelm the afflictions that are to be removed at the level of the path of cultivation, (b) to enable achievement of exceptional qualities such as the four immeasurables (c) to provide a basis for the supramundane path of cultivation.

The supramundane path of cultivation consists of tranquility and insight—along with their accompanying qualities—focused on the two aspects of pristine awareness. Now, of the sixteen facets of insight—the two facets of receptivity and two facets of knowledge corresponding to each of the four noble truths—gained during the path of seeing, the eight receptivities are proper to the path of seeing, and the insight gained is all that is needed to complete them. The eight facets of knowledge, however, require ongoing familiarization, and this is what is being developed through the path of cultivation. It is achieved through continued familiarity with tranquility and insight on the basis of the four meditative concentrations and the first three of the four formless meditative attainments. Cultivating the realization of suchness belongs to the aspect [of the path] known as *knowledge of phenomena*, whereas cultivating the realization of pristine awareness belongs to the aspect known as *subsequent knowledge*.

As [for the final formless meditative attainment], the sphere of neither awareness nor absence of awareness, given that the activity of awareness lacks clarity within this sphere, it remains entirely as a mundane sphere.

Why are the above called the *path of cultivation*? Because in it, the person cultivates familiarity with the realizations gained on the path of seeing. During this stage the meditator is endowed with the eightfold path of the noble ones: right view, right thought, right speech, right action, right livelihood, right effort, [213] right mindfulness, and right meditation.

The fifth is the **path of complete accomplishment**. This occurs subsequent to the diamond-like meditative absorption, and it consists of the knowledge of cessation and that of nonarising. *Diamond-like meditative absorption* refers to the final stage of elimination on the path of cultivation and thus is encompassed within the preparatory and uninterrupted stages of the path of cultivation. Since this particular meditative absorption is unimpeded, durable, stable, of a single taste, and pervasive, it is called "diamond-like." It is *unimpeded* because no worldly activity can be a cause which might unsettle it. It is *durable* because none of the obscurations can damage it. It is *stable* because no thought can trouble it. It is of a *single taste* because has one flavor. It is *pervasive* because it is focused on the ultimate nature common to each and every thing that is knowable.

Subsequent to the diamond-like meditative absorption, there is the *knowledge of cessation* of generation. This is pristine awareness focused on the four noble truths in terms of the exhaustion of all causes [of suffering]. There is also *knowledge of nonarising*. This pristine awareness is also focused on the four noble truths, but here in terms of the resultant sufferings themselves having been eliminated. In other words, pristine awareness related to the exhaustion of causes and the nonarising of results is the knowledge of cessation and nonarising.

Why are those referred to as the path of complete accomplishment? Because training has been completed, and it is the stage where the journey to the citadel of enlightenment has reached its end. At that stage there are *ten qualities of no-more training*.[671] They are [the eight qualities of the eightfold path—namely,] right view through to right meditation of no-more training, plus total liberation and perfect pristine awareness of no-more training. These ten factors, in which there is no more training to be performed form five uncontaminated aggregates. Right speech, right action, and right livelihood of no-more training constitute the *moral discipline aggregate*; right mindfulness and right meditation of no-more training constitute the *meditative absorption aggregate*; right view, right thinking, and right effort of no-more training constitute the *wisdom aggregate*; total, utter liberation of no-more training constitutes the *total liberation aggregate*; and right pristine awareness of no-more training constitutes the *aggregate of seeing the pristine awareness of total liberation*.

This concludes the eighteenth chapter, concerning the presentation of the paths in this *Ornament of Precious Liberation, a Wish-Fulfilling Gem of Sublime Dharma*.

19. The Presentation of the Levels

[214] WITH RESPECT to those five paths, if one asks, how many levels are there? For this, there is the following synopsis:

> **The [presentation of] levels has thirteen points: the beginner's level, the level of practice by means of aspiration, the ten bodhisattva levels, and the level of buddhahood.**

With respect to these levels *Lamp for the Path to Awakening* states:

> ... the Joyous and so forth are attained.[672]

Here, "the Joyous" is the name of the first bodhisattva level, and the words "and so forth" include the two levels below it and the ten above it.

The first point concerns the **beginner's level.** This applies to the stage when the person is on the path of accumulation. It is so called because it brings that which is immature to maturity.

The second point concerns the **level of practice by means of aspiration.** This corresponds to the period of the path of application. It is so called because its activity aspires singly to the meaning of emptiness. During this phase the following are crushed so as never to reoccur: (1) factors incompatible with the perfections—avarice and so forth, (2) afflictions that will be eliminated through the path of seeing, and (3) the acquired levels of cognitive obscuration.

The third point concerns the **ten bodhisattva levels.** These are the levels from the Joyous through to the Cloud of Dharma. The *Ten Levels Sutra* says:

> O child of good family! These ten are the bodhisattva levels: the bodhisattva level of the Joyous....[673]

The Joyous—the first of the ten levels—corresponds to the path of seeing, in which emptiness is directly realized. The second through tenth levels are the path of cultivation. During these, insight into the suchness realized during the first level is cultivated.

These ten bodhisattva levels should be understood both in general and specifically. First, the *general points* concerning the ten bodhisattva levels are three: (1) their nature, (2) the etymology of *level*, (3) the reason for a tenfold division. [215]

As for the *nature* of the levels, they consist of the wisdom directly realizing the selflessness of phenomena accompanied by the meditative absorption that exists within the mental continuum on the trainer's stage.

Concerning their *etymology*: they are called *levels*, or *grounds*, because they each serve as bases for all the qualities associated with them as well as with the states they represent. Furthermore, each one serves as the foundation that gives rise to the subsequent level. The following are analogies for the etymology of the term *level*. It is called *level* (or *ground*) because all [higher qualities] reside within that pristine awareness and partake in it just as, for example, [all the cattle] reside within and use the cattle yard. Also, it is called the *level* (or *ground*) because [all higher qualities] traverse that pristine awareness just as [horses run on] the running tracks. Lastly, they are like fields, since they are the foundations on which grow all the qualities proper to pristine awareness.

The *reason for a tenfold division* is their specific particularities of complete nurturing.

Second, the *specific points* about each bodhisattva level will be presented through nine particularities for each level: (1) name, (2) etymology, (3) thorough preparation, (4) practice, (5) purity, (6) realization, (7) things abandoned, (8) state of birth, and (9) ability.

The First Bodhisattva Level

Its **specific name** is the Joyous.

Its **specific etymology**: Those who have achieved this level feel immense joy because enlightenment is close at hand and benefit for sentient beings is now really being accomplished: hence its name, the Joyous. Thus it says, in the *Ornament of Mahayana Sutras*:

> On seeing that enlightenment is close

> and that the good of beings is accomplished,
> the most supreme joy will arise.
> For that reason it is called the Joyous.[674]

The **specific thorough preparation**: This level is achieved through mastery of ten qualities, such as having intentions that are never deceitful, no matter what domain of action or thought [the bodhisattva] is engaged in. Thus the *Ornament of Clear Realization* says:

> Through ten aspects of thorough preparations,[675]
> the first level will be attained.[676]

The **specific practice**: Although bodhisattvas at this level practice all ten perfections, it is said that they place particular emphasis on practicing the perfection of generosity because of their wish to bring contentment to all beings. Thus the *Ten Levels Sutra* says:

> From the outset of the first level, among all ten perfections, the perfection of generosity is emphasized, [216] although this does not mean that the others are neglected.[677]

The **specific purity**: As is said in the *Ten Levels Sutra*:

> On the first level, the Joyous, there is vast vision. Through the power of prayers, many buddhas are seen, many hundreds of buddhas, many thousands of buddhas... [etc.;] many hundreds of millions of buddhas manifest. On seeing them, you make offerings with a great and noble intention and express great respect... [etc.;] you also make offerings to their Sangha. You dedicate all those roots of virtue to unsurpassable enlightenment. You receive teachings from these buddhas, take them to heart, and remember them. These teachings are practiced earnestly, and beings are brought to maturity through the four means of attraction.[678]

In such a way, and for many eons, (1) they make offerings to the buddhas, Dharma, and Sangha and are cared for by them; (2) they bring beings to spiritual maturity; and (3) they dedicate virtue to highest enlightenment.[679] Thus, through these three causes, all their roots of virtue are made very great and very pure. It says:

> For instance, the degree of refinement and purity of gold, and its ability to lend itself to any desired use, will depend on the amount of work the goldsmith has put into its smelting. Like this, the roots of virtue of bodhisattvas on the first level are perfectly refined, completely pure, and fit for any use.[680]

The **specific realization**: In general, realization is one and the same during meditative equipoise throughout the ten levels. The differences are in respect to the phases subsequent to the equipoise periods, and it is this aspect that will be considered relevant to each level. On this first level, the expanse of suchness is [realized as being] all-pervading, and this provides full realization of the sameness of self and others. Therefore the *Clear Differentiation of the Middle and Extremes* speaks of the "all-pervading truth."[681]

The **specific things abandoned**: In terms of the afflictions obscuration, all the eighty-two afflictions[682] to be overcome through the path of seeing have been eliminated. Of the three types of knowledge obscurations, [217] the ones comparable to a rough outer skin are eliminated. Five types of fear or anxiety are absent. These are described in the *Ten Levels Sutra*:

> What are the five fears present until the level of the Joyous is attained? They are fear of not gaining a livelihood, fear of not having a good reputation, fear of death, fear of the lower states of existence, and anxiety about being stuck among many worldly people. At that level these are all annihilated.[683]

The **specific state of birth**: Bodhisattvas on this level are mostly reborn as universal monarchs in Jambudvīpa. There they remove the pollution of beings' avarice. The *Precious Garland* says:

> As a full consequence of this,
> they become a mighty ruler of Jambudvīpa.[684]

Although this is the special particularity of birth mentioned, through their pure intention to benefit others, they can manifest themselves anywhere and in any way needed to train beings, as was well taught in the Jātaka stories.

Their **specific ability**. On this point, it says:

> Bodhisattvas at this level of the Joyous exert themselves diligently through aspiration. The most advanced can, within an

> instant, a short moment, just a fraction of time: (1) enter into to a hundredfold meditative absorptions and experience their stable fruition, (2) see a hundred buddhas, (3) most properly be aware of those buddhas' blessings, (4) make a hundred world systems tremble, (5) visit a hundred buddhafields, (6) illuminate a hundred world systems, (7) bring a hundred sentient beings to full maturity, (8) live for a hundred eons, (9) be excellently aware of the past and future up to a hundred eons past or future, (10) open a hundred doors of Dharma, (11) manifest a hundred emanations anywhere, and (12) constantly manifest each of these physical forms as being accompanied by a hundred other bodhisattvas.[685]

The Second Bodhisattva Level

Its **specific name** is the Stainless.

Its **specific etymology**: This level is known as the Stainless because it is unstained by violations of moral discipline:

> Being free from stains due to violations of proper conduct,
> it is known as the Stainless.[686] [218]

Its **specific thorough preparation**: This level is attained through eight kinds of mastery, such as those of moral discipline, actions, and so forth:

> Moral discipline, the accomplishment of action, patience, supreme joy, great compassionate love, and so forth.[687]

Its **specific practice**: Although bodhisattvas at this level practice all ten perfections, they are said to place particular emphasis on practicing the perfection of moral discipline.

Its **specific purity**: As previously explained, three causes make the roots of virtue created by these bodhisattvas very powerful and very pure:

> To give an example, fine gold re-treated and re-smelted by a goldsmith will be rid of all impurities, even more so than before. Likewise, the roots of virtue of the bodhisattvas on the second level are also purer, more refined, and more workable than before.[688]

The **specific realization**: On this level, the ultimate expanse is understood as being the highest and most significant thing. They think, "I will strive at all times and in all ways in the training through which it is really and totally achieved." Thus it is said:

> Highest thing....[689]

The **specific things abandoned** for this second level, and on through to the tenth level: As far as the afflictions are concerned, only the seeds of the sixteen afflictions that need to be eliminated by the path of cultivation have not been removed and remain present. However, their manifest levels have been overcome. As for the knowledge obscurations, the inner layer, like the flesh of a fruit, is eliminated.

The **specific state of birth**: Many of the bodhisattvas on this level become universal monarchs holding sway over the four-world system. There they turn beings away from the ten vices and establish them in the ten virtues. Thus:

> Through the full maturation of this,
> they become universal monarchs
> who benefit beings through possessing
> the seven precious and illustrious attributes.[690]

The **specific ability** is that, in one instant, a short moment, a fraction of time, they can enter into a thousand meditative absorptions and so forth.[691]

The Third Bodhisattva Level

Its **specific name** is the Shining.

The **specific etymology**: [219] It is known as the Shining because in that state the light of Dharma and of meditative absorption is very clear. Furthermore, it illuminates others with the great light of Dharma. Thus it is said:

> It is the Shining
> because it makes the great radiance of Dharma.[692]

The **specific thorough preparation**: This level is achieved through having developed five things, such as an insatiable appetite for studying [Dharma]. As is taught:

> Insatiable with respect to Dharma study,
> they impart teachings without material concern.[693]

The **specific practice**: Although bodhisattvas at this level practice all ten perfections, they are said to place particular emphasis on practicing the perfection of patience.

The **specific purity**: As explained above, three causes make the roots of virtue of these bodhisattvas very great and very pure:

> To give an example, if very fine gold is hand-polished by a skilled goldsmith, the defects and impurities are removed, yet this does not reduce the original weight of the gold itself. Likewise, the roots of virtue, established in the three periods of time by these bodhisattvas, remain undiminished and become very pure, very refined, and fit for any use.[694]

The **specific realization**: Bodhisattvas on this level understand the teachings of Dharma to be supreme among the favorable conditions conducive to [realizing] the ultimate expanse. To study just one verse of teaching, they would pass through a fire pit as large as a billionfold world system. Therefore,

> the supreme of meanings, which is conducive....[695]

The **specific things abandoned**: See the second level, above.

The **specific state of birth**: Most bodhisattvas on this level take rebirth as Indra, king of the gods. They are skilled in counteracting desires and attachments related to the desire realm:

> They become skillful great masters of the gods,
> who counteract attachment of the desire realm.[696]

The **specific ability**: In an instant, a short moment of time, a small fraction of time, they can enter a hundred thousand meditative absorptions and so forth.

The Fourth Bodhisattva Level

Its **specific name** is the Blazing.

The **specific etymology**: It is called the Blazing because the brilliance of pristine awareness, endowed with the qualities favorable to enlightenment, blazes everywhere, having consumed the two obscurations. [220] Thus:

> It is like a light since it thoroughly consumes
> the factors incompatible with enlightenment.
> Thus endowed, this level is Blazing,
> because the two have been consumed.[697]

The **specific thorough preparation**: This level is achieved through ten factors, such as remaining in solitude and so forth. Therefore:

> Remaining in forests, with little desire, easily contented,
> pure in behavior, observing vows. . . .[698]

The **specific practice**: Although bodhisattvas on this level practice all the ten perfections in general, it is said that they place particular emphasis on that of diligence.

The **specific purity**: As explained above, three causes make the roots of virtue of these bodhisattvas extremely great and pure:

> To give an example, fine gold fashioned into a piece of jewelry by a skilled goldsmith cannot be surpassed by pieces of gold as yet unworked. In a similar way, the roots of virtue of bodhisattvas on this level are not outshone by those of bodhisattvas on lower levels.[699]

The **specific realization**: Bodhisattvas on this level have truly realized that there is nothing whatsoever to really cling to. Thus all craving, even for Dharma, is quenched:

> The fact that there is nothing to really cling to and. . . .[700]

The **specific things abandoned**: See the second level, above.

The **specific state of birth**: Most bodhisattvas on this level take birth as a king of gods in the Free from Conflict Heaven. They are skilled in dispelling mistaken philosophies based on the view that the perishable composite is permanent. Thus:

> They become divine monarchs in the Free from Conflict Heaven
> and are skilled in totally defeating views of the perishable composite where these are predominant.[701]

The **specific ability**: In one moment, a short instant, a fraction of time, they can enter a billion meditative absorptions and so forth.

The Fifth Bodhisattva Level

Its **specific name** is Difficult to Master.

The **specific etymology**: On this level the bodhisattva strives to help beings to greater maturity, and in doing so they remain unassailed by the afflictions despite the repeated negative behavior of sentient beings. It is known as Difficult to Master because both [helping and not reacting] are hard to master. [221] Thus:

> Since they accomplish the good of beings
> and guard their own minds,
> it is a difficult training for the bodhisattvas;
> therefore it is known as Difficult to Master.[702]

The **specific thorough preparation**: This level is achieved through the elimination of ten factors, such as association with worldly people for purposes of gain and so forth. For instance:

> To hanker after acquaintances, a dwelling,
> places brimming with distraction, and so forth....[703]

The **specific practice**: Although bodhisattvas on this level practice all ten perfections in general, it is said that they place particular emphasis on that of meditative absorption.

The **specific purity**: As previously explained, three causes make the roots of virtue of these bodhisattvas particularly great and pure:

> To give an example, fine gold, first polished by a skilled goldsmith and then set with amber stones, will be incomparably beautiful; it cannot be outshone by other pieces made of [worked] gold alone. It is likewise for the roots of virtue of bodhisattvas on this fifth level. They are tested by the combination of wisdom and skillful means. They could never be outshone by the roots of virtue of bodhisattvas on lower levels.[704]

The **specific realization** is that bodhisattvas on this level realize the non-differentiation of [mind] streams. They are aware of ten sorts of sameness. Thus, "Undifferentiated streams and. . . ."[705]

The **specific things abandoned**: See the second level.

The **specific state of birth**: Most bodhisattvas on this level take birth as divine monarchs in Tuṣita Heaven. They are skilled in refuting the views of those holding distorted religious beliefs. Therefore:

> As a full consequence of that
> they become monarchs of the Tuṣita gods
> and are skilled in refuting the foundations
> of the afflictions and distorted beliefs of all tīrthikas.[706]

The **specific ability**: In one instant, a short moment, a small fraction of time, they can enter ten billion meditative absorptions and so forth.

The Sixth Bodhisattva Level

Its **specific name** is the Manifested.

The **specific etymology**: On account of the perfection of wisdom, there is no dwelling in [notions of] nirvana or samsara. [222] Thus samsara and nirvana manifest as purity.[707] Hence the name of this level, the Manifested:

> Through the perfection of wisdom,
> since both samsara and nirvana
> have become manifest,
> it is called the Manifested.[708]

The **specific thorough preparation**: This level is achieved through twelve factors of training. These are learning how to accomplish totally and perfectly six things, such as generosity and so forth, and learning how to eliminate six things, such as longing for the śrāvaka or pratyekabuddha [states] and the like. Therefore:

> Through the utter perfection of generosity, moral discipline, patience, diligence, meditative concentration, and wisdom, there is awareness and so forth.[709]

The **specific practice**: Although bodhisattvas on this level practice all ten perfections in general, it is said that they place particular emphasis on that of the perfection of deep wisdom.

The **specific purity**: As explained previously, three causes make the roots of virtue of bodhisattvas on this level extremely pure and powerful:

> To give an example, when a skilled goldsmith decorates fine gold with lapis lazuli, it becomes peerless and cannot be surpassed by other works of gold. Likewise, the roots of virtue of sixth-level bodhisattvas, assured by wisdom and skillful means, are both total purity and lucid clarity; they cannot be outshone by those of bodhisattvas dwelling on lower levels.[710]

The **specific realization**: On this level the bodhisattva realizes the nonexistence of both the afflictions and their purification. These bodhisattvas are aware that there are really no such things as affliction or purity, even though those things may arise through the play of dependent origination. Thus it is said: "... the meaning of no affliction and no purity."[711]

The **specific things abandoned**: See the second level.

The **specific state of birth**: Most bodhisattvas on this level take birth as a divine monarch among the Delighting in Manifesting gods. They are skilled in overcoming beings' vanity:

> Through this full consequence,
> they become kings of the Delighting in Manifesting gods.
> Unsurpassed by the śrāvakas,
> they eliminate vainglory.[712]

The **specific ability** is that in one instant, a short moment, [223] a small fraction of time, they can enter a trillion meditative absorptions and so forth.

The Seventh Bodhisattva Level

Its **specific name** is the Far-Reaching.

The **specific etymology**: This level is known as the Far-Reaching because it connects with the "one and only path" and one has come to the far end of activity:

> It is known as the Far-Reaching level because it connects with the sole path.[713]

The **specific thorough preparation**: This level is achieved through eliminating twenty factors, such as grasping at self, and through cultivating the opposite qualities, such as the three gates of total liberation and so forth. Therefore: "Grasping at self and persons...."[714] and "Awareness of the three gates of total liberation...."[715]

The **specific practice**: Although bodhisattvas on this level practice all ten perfections in general, it is said that they place particular emphasis on that of skillful means.

The **specific purity**: As explained previously, three causes make the roots of virtue of bodhisattvas on this level extremely pure and powerful:

> To give an example, when a skilled goldsmith decorates finest gold with all sorts of precious gems, it becomes most beautiful and cannot be excelled by other pieces of jewelry in this world. Likewise the roots of virtue of seventh-level bodhisattvas are extraordinarily great and pure; they cannot be excelled by those of śrāvakas, pratyekabuddha, or bodhisattvas established on lower levels.[716]

The **specific realization**: On this level the truth of the absence of differentiation is realized. All the various characteristics of Dharma, the sutras, and so forth do not appear as separate. Thus it is said: "The truth of no-differentiation...."[717]

The **specific things abandoned**: See the second level.

The **specific state of birth**: Most bodhisattvas on this level take rebirth as a divine monarch among the Delighting in Others' Manifestations[718] gods. They are skilled in bringing about realizations of the śrāvakas and pratyekabuddhas:

Through this full consequence,
they become kings of the Delighting in Others' Manifestations gods.
They become great, outstanding Dharma masters
with a genuine understanding of the [four] noble truths.[719] [224]

The **specific ability**: In one instant, a short moment, a small fraction of time, they can enter a hundred quadrillion meditative absorptions and so forth.

The Eighth Bodhisattva Level

Its **specific name** is the Unshakable.

The **specific etymology**: It is so called because it is unmoved by notions that either strive after characteristics or the absence of characteristics. Therefore:

It is known as the Unshakable
since it is unmoved by the two notions.[720]

The **specific thorough prepration**: This level is achieved through eight kinds of mastery, such as understanding the behavior of sentient beings and so forth. Therefore:

Awareness of the mind of every being,
love due to clear cognition....[721]

The **specific practice**: Although bodhisattvas on this level practice all ten perfections in general, it is said that they place particular emphasis on that of aspirational prayers.

The **specific purity**: As explained previously, three causes make the roots of virtue of bodhisattvas on this level extremely pure and powerful:

> To give an example, were a fine piece of golden jewelry, made by a master goldsmith, to be worn on the head or the throat of a ruler of Jambudvīpa, it could not be surpassed by gold ornaments worn by other people. Likewise, the roots of virtue of eighth-level bodhisattvas are so utterly and perfectly pure that they cannot be excelled by those of śrāvakas, pratyekabuddhas, or bodhisattvas established on lower levels.[722]

The **specific realization**: On this level the space-like and concept-free nature of every phenomenon is realized. Therefore its bodhisattvas are not shocked and frightened by emptiness—the unborn. This is known as the achievement of forbearance concerning the unborn. Through this forbearance of the unborn nature of everything, they realize the nonexistence of increase and decrease and do not consider the really afflicted or the totally pure as either decreasing or increasing, respectively. Hence: "No increase, no decrease...."[723] [225] It is also said that:

> This is also [the first of] the states with the four powers.[724]

The four powers are: (1) power over nonconceptuality, (2) power over very pure realms, (3) power over pristine awareness, and (4) power over actions. Of these four, bodhisattvas on the eighth level have realized the first two powers, those of nonconceptuality and of very pure realms. Furthermore, it is said [in other scriptural sources] that those on the eighth level have achieved the ten powers, the powers over lifespan, mind, commodities, action, birth state, prayer, intentions, miracles, pristine awareness, and Buddhadharma.

The **specific things abandoned**: See the second level.

The **specific state of birth**: Most bodhisattvas on this level take rebirth as a divine monarch among the Brahma gods with power over an entire thousandfold world system. They are skilled in expounding the meaning of the śrāvaka and pratyekabuddha paths:

> The full consequence is to take birth
> as a Brahma god, lord of a thousandfold world systems.
> They are unsurpassed by śrāvakas and pratyekabuddhas
> in the exposition of the doctrines.[725]

The **specific ability**: In one instant, a short moment, a small fraction of time, they can enter as many meditative absorptions as the number of particles in a quadrillion world systems and so forth.

The Ninth Bodhisattva Level

Its **specific name** is the Excellent Intelligence.

The **specific etymology**: It is so called because it is endowed with extremely fine intelligence, namely, clear and exact discernment. Therefore:

> That level is the Excellent Intelligence
> because of its good intelligence, clearly discerning.[726]

The **specific thorough preparation**: This level is achieved through twelve factors, such as infinite prayers and so forth. Therefore:

> The infinite number of prayers...
> and the knowledge of divine languages.[727]

The **specific practice**: Although bodhisattvas on this level practice all ten perfections in general, it is said that they place particular emphasis on that of the powers.

The **specific purity**: As explained previously, three causes make the roots of virtue of bodhisattvas on this level extremely pure and powerful:

> To give an example, were a fine piece of golden jewelry, made by a master goldsmith, to be worn on the head or throat of a universal monarch, [226] it could be excelled neither by the pieces of jewelry worn by the kings of the various regions nor by those worn by any of the inhabitants of the four continents [of that world system]. Likewise, the roots of virtue of ninth-level bodhisattvas are so adorned with great pristine awareness that they cannot be excelled by those of śrāvakas, pratyekabuddhas, or bodhisattvas established on lower levels.[728]

The **specific realization**: Of the four powers [mentioned in the previous section], bodhisattvas at this ninth level realize the state of the *power of pristine awareness*, since they have achieved the four modes of perfectly clear, discerning knowledge. What are the four modes of perfectly clear, discerning knowledge? The *Ten Levels Sutra* explains:

> What are the four modes of clear discerning knowledge? They are constant possession of: perfectly clear discerning knowledge of Dharma, perfectly clear discerning knowledge of meanings, perfectly clear discerning knowledge of definitions, and perfectly clear discerning knowledge of teaching skill.[729]

The **specific things abandoned**: See the second level.

The **specific state of birth**: Most bodhisattvas on this level take birth as a divine monarch among the Brahma gods with power over a millionfold world system. They are able to answer all questions:

> The full consequence is to take birth
> as Brahma, lord of a millionfold world systems.
> In dispelling qualms from the minds of sentient beings,
> they are unsurpassed by arhats and the like.[730]

The **specific ability**: In one instant, a short moment, a small fraction of time, they can enter as many meditative absorptions as there are pure particles in a million countless[731] buddhafields and so forth.

The Tenth Bodhisattva Level

Its **specific name** is the Cloud of Dharma.

The **specific etymology**: It is called the Cloud of Dharma because the bodhisattvas on that level are like a cloud that causes a rain of Dharma teachings to fall on beings, thereby washing away the fine dust of their afflictions. Alternatively, like clouds filling space, their meditative absorptions and the retention dhāraṇī they have attained pervade the entire space-like reality. Therefore:

> It is the Cloud of Dharma because like clouds,
> the two [meditative absorptions and dhāraṇis] pervade the
> space-like reality.[732]

The **specific thorough preparation**: [Unlike for the previous levels,] there is no presentation of this level in the *Ornament of Clear Realization*, but in the *Ten Levels Sutra* it says: [227]

> O children of the victors! Up to the ninth level, bodhisattvas have thoroughly analyzed and do thoroughly analyze immeasurable aspects of knowledge with an investigatory intelligence.[733]

Through such statements, we see the teaching that this level is achieved through an empowerment of pristine awareness of omniscience due to ten thorough preparations. This tenth level is the "level empowered by omniscient pristine awareness." Why is it so called? Because, as the *Ten Levels Sutra* explains, the bodhisattvas on the tenth level are empowered with light by the buddhas of the ten directions. Further details can be found in that sutra. The *Precious Garland* also says:

> ... because the bodhisattva is empowered
> by rays of light from the buddhas.[734]

(This is the interpretation of Maitreya and that found in the commentaries of his tradition. It is said in the tantras that at the end of the tenth level, bodhisattvas receive empowerment from the buddhas of the ten directions and themselves become buddhas. These two views are in fact the same. Different questions attract different answers, but there is no contradiction between the two.)[735]

The **specific practice**: Although bodhisattvas on this level practice all ten perfections in general, it is said that they place particular emphasis on that of pristine awareness.[736]

The **specific purity**: As explained previously, three causes make the roots of virtue of bodhisattvas on this level extremely pure and powerful:

> To give an example, were a fine piece of golden jewelry to be made by a god skilled in crafts, who set it with finest precious gems, and then worn on the head or throat of an empowered king of the gods, it could not be surpassed by any other jewelry of gods or humans. Likewise, the roots of virtue of tenth-level bodhisattvas are so adorned with great pristine awareness that they cannot be excelled by those of any ordinary beings, śrāvakas, pratyekabuddhas, or bodhisattvas on the ninth level and below.[737]

The **specific realization**: Of the four powers [mentioned above], bodhisattvas at this tenth level realize the state of the *power over actions*, since they accomplish the welfare of beings just as they wish, through every type of emanation.

The **specific things abandoned**: See the second level.

The **specific state of birth**: Most bodhisattvas on this level take birth as the king of the gods, Īśvara, with power over a billionfold world system. They are skilled in teaching the perfections to all sentient beings, śrāvakas, pratyekabuddhas, [228] and bodhisattvas:

The full consequence of this
is to take birth as lord of the pure-realm[738] gods
and as a mighty lord over domains
of inconceivable pristine awareness.[739]

The **specific ability**: In one instant, a short moment, a small fraction of time, they can enter as many meditative absorptions as there are pure particles in a thousand million million "countless" buddhafields and so forth. Furthermore, in one instant they can manifest from just one pore of their skin countless buddhas in the company of incalculable numbers of bodhisattvas. They can manifest as all sorts of beings—as gods, humans, and so forth. According to whatever is necessary for the training of those to be trained, they can teach Dharma by adopting the physical form of Indra, Brahma, Īśvara, universal guardians, monarchs, śrāvakas, pratyekabuddhas, or buddhas. In *Entering the Middle Way*, it says:

In one instant they can manifest,
from a pore, perfect buddhas
in the company of countless bodhisattvas
and also gods, humans, and demigods.[740]

This completes the explanation of the ten bodhisattva levels.

The fifth point describes the **level of buddhahood**, the final stage of the path. When the diamond-like meditative absorption arises, it eliminates simultaneously the obscurations to be removed by the path of cultivation, that is, any afflictions or knowledge obscurations that remain, comparable to the core.[741] The achievement of this level is described in *Bodhisattva Levels*:

These levels are accomplished over the span of three countless cosmic eons. During the first great countless eon, [the bodhisattva] traverses the level of practice motivated by aspiration and achieves the state of the Joyous. Further, this is all achieved through constant effort, without which the achievement will not take place.

In the second great cosmic eon, [the bodhisattva] transcends the Joyous and works through to the seventh level, the Far-Reaching, to achieve the eighth level, the Unshakable. This is precisely the way it happens because bodhisattvas of pure intention will definitely make these efforts. [229]

In the third great cosmic eon, [the bodhisattva] traverses the eighth and ninth levels and attains the tenth, Cloud of Dharma. Some apply themselves to this most diligently and thereby reduce many sub-eons of progress into one. Some even reduce many eons' work into one. But there are none who reduce the countless eons into one. It should be known in this way.[742]

This concludes the nineteenth chapter, explaining the spiritual levels, of this *Ornament of Precious Liberation, a Wish-Fulfilling Gem of Sublime Dharma.*

20. The Bodies of Perfect Buddhahood

V. The Result

To expound the line, "The results are the bodies of perfect buddhahood."[743] When the paths and the levels have been completely traversed as described above, [the bodhisattva] becomes a perfect buddha within the three bodies (*kāya*), or "embodiments of enlightenment." Therefore it says, in *Lamp for the Path to Awakening*:

> Buddhahood and enlightenment no longer remain distant.[744]

Buddhahood is described in terms of the following synopsis:

> **The bodies of a perfect buddha are described through seven points: their nature, etymology, aspects, presentation, definite number, characteristic properties, and particularities.**

The first point concerns the **nature of a truly perfect buddha**. It is described through the perfect purity[745] and the perfect pristine awareness.

The *perfect purity* means that all the affliction and knowledge obscurations, which were being eliminated during the paths and the levels, are completely eliminated subsequent to the diamond-like meditative absorption. Other obscurations, such as those impeding various meditative attainments, are subcategories of the two main obscurations and hence disappear with the elimination of those two.

As for the *perfect pristine awareness*, there are different views. Some say that buddhas have concepts as well as pristine awareness. Some say that buddhas do not have concepts yet do have pristine awareness, which knows everything clearly. Some say that the continuum of pristine awareness is broken. [230] Some say that the Buddha has never possessed any such thing as pristine awareness. However, the authoritative texts of the sutras and treatises speak of the pristine awareness of the buddhas. Of the sutras, we find in the *Verse Summary of the Perfection of Wisdom*:

> Therefore, if you want to penetrate the supreme pristine
> awareness
> of the buddhas, trust in this, the mother of the conquerors.[746]

The *Perfection of Wisdom in a Hundred Thousand Lines* says:

> A totally pure and perfect buddha has secured pristine awareness that knows everything without any obscuration.[747]

It also says, in the twenty-first chapter of the same work:

> There is the pristine awareness of a perfect buddha. There is the turning of the wheel of Dharma. There is the bringing of beings to maturity.[748]

Many statements on pristine awareness are also to be found in other sutras. Of the treatises, we find, in the *Ornament of Mahayana Sutras*:

> You should know that just as when
> one sun ray shines all the others are shining too,
> so it is the case also
> with the pristine awareness of the buddhas.[749]...

And:

> The mirror-like pristine awareness
> is immovable and is the basis for
> the other three pristine awarenesses
> of equanimity, discernment, and activity.[750]

Buddha pristine awareness is also mentioned in other treatises. The opinion of those who say that buddhas possess pristine awareness is based on these authoritative texts. The following explains the way in which the buddhas possess pristine awareness. In brief, pristine awareness is twofold: (1) pristine awareness of the ways things are, and (2) pristine awareness of things in their manifoldnesss.

Of these, the *pristine awareness of the way things are* is the perception of the ultimate truth. For, as mentioned above, when through complete familiarity with suchness in the culimination of the diamond-like meditative absorption, every single conceptual elaboration pertaining to objectification has been severed, every form of mental activity has come to cease. As such the ultimate expanse free of conceptual elaboration and pristine awareness free of conceptual elaboration have merged into a single taste, indivisible like water poured into water or butter mixed into butter. So, like referring to seeing no form as "seeing empty space," the great wisdom devoid of any appearance had become the ground of all precious qualities. Therefore it is said:

> Like water poured into water,
> like butter mixed into butter, [231]
> the knowable free of elaboration
> and pristine awareness free of elaboration
> are totally fused.
> It is this that is called *dharmakāya*
> and that is the essential nature of all the buddhas.[751]

And:

> People talk of seeing space.
> Think about it and consider how they see space.
> The Tathāgatha taught that this is how to see phenomena.
> Such seeing cannot be expressed by any other example.[752]

The *pristine awareness of things in their manifoldness* is omniscience with respect to conventional, relative reality. All potential for obscuration has been destroyed by the diamond-like meditative absorption, and so there is great wisdom. Through its power, every aspect of the knowable throughout the three periods of time is seen and known, as clearly as if it were a fresh purple plum in the palm of the hand. The sutras speak of the buddhas' sublime awareness of what is relative in these terms:

> All the various causes of a single eye
> in a peacock's tail are unknowable
> by someone not omniscient, yet such knowledge
> is within the power of the Omniscient One.[753]

Furthermore, the *Uttaratantra* says:

> With great compassion he knows the world.
> Having seen everything in the world....[754]

When buddhas know and see as described above, it is not as though they perceive things as real. They see and know things as illusions. Thus it says, in *Perfectly Gathering the Qualities* [*of Avalokiteśvara*] *Sutra*:

> An illusionist is not himself duped
> by his conjurations and thus,
> through his clear knowledge of what is happening,
> does not become attached to his illusory creations.
> Similarly, those skilled in perfect enlightenment
> know the three worlds to be like an illusion.[755]

In the *Meeting of Father and Son Sutra*, it says:

> By remaining conscious of the fact
> that conjurations are but illusions,
> a magician will not fall under their spell.
> I pay homage and praise you, the omniscient ones,
> who regard all beings like this.[756]

Now, some hold the view that perfectly enlightened buddhas do possess the pristine awareness of the way things are—the awareness of the ultimate truth—but do not possess the pristine awareness of things in their manifoldness—the awareness of the relative. Their point is not that there is something there to be known and that the buddhas are not aware of it but rather that, since there is nothing relative to be aware of in the first place, there could be no pristine awareness that is aware of it.

"Relative" or "conventional" reality is something that appears to immature beings conditioned by afflicted ignorance. as well to [232] the three types of realized beings who are conditioned by ignorance that does not belong to the class of affliction. This is analogous to the appearance of falling hair and blurs to someone with impaired sight. As for a buddha, given that following the diamond-like meditative absorption he has totally eliminated ignorance and thus "sees" suchness in the way someone "sees" nothing whatsoever, for a buddha this illusion of the relative is not present. This is analogous to the fact that, to those with unimpaired sight, there is no perception of falling hair or the blurs.

Therefore this appearance of the relative occurs due to the power of ignorance and is posited only in relation to [the perspectives of] the worldly. In relation to buddhahood, they have no existence, and so there can be no buddha's pristine awareness that perceives it. Were the buddhas to posses a mind that contained relative appearances, then by definition, buddhas would themselves have to be deluded due to the manifestation of such deluded fields of experience. This is in contradiction to the scriptures, which state that the great victors are constantly in a state of meditative equipoise and so forth. (As it says, for instance, in the *Vast Manifestation Sutra*: "Totally pure and perfect buddhas are at all times in meditative equipoise."[757] So they say.

Of these the proponent of the former viewpoint asserts this. It is not the case that just by virtue of being a subsequent-meditation state that it involves distraction and so forth. Therefore there is no contradiction with the scriptures such as the ones that state [that the buddhas] always remains in meditative equipoise. It is also incorrect to state a perception to be deluded simply because illusory objects appear to it. For although all the illusory phenomena that are the objects of other's illusions do appear [to the buddhas], the mind perceiving them recognizes all of it to be illusions. Furthermore, they dispel them, using them as a cause for the higher rebirth, purity, and liberation of beings. So how could there be delusion? Thus:

> When they are recognized as mere illusions,
> that which is not an illusion is perceived with certainty.[758]

Yet others say that there is no great logical harm in holding the relative as a valid object, provided one does not cling to it as real. And if anything is free of logical harm, even if the buddhas were to perceive it, there would be no delusion.

Those who hold the first view maintain that buddhas *do* possess *subsequent* pristine awareness, what is referred to as [pristine awareness of] things in their manifoldness. Thus they say:

> The first, awareness of the way things are, is:
> undeluded, equipoised, and without mental activity. [233]
> The next, awareness of multiplicity, is:

> with deluded appearance, subsequent knowledge, and with
> mental activity.[759]

Those who hold the second view that buddhas *do not* possess the pristine awareness of things in their manifoldness quote as their authority the *Infinite Means of Purification Sutra*:

> Having reached true and perfect buddhahood, the Tathāgata neither knows nor has in mind any phenomenon whatever. Why is this? Because there exists no objective reality whatsoever to be known.[760]

Furthermore, it is said:

> Some non-Buddhists say
> that you speak of going to liberation,
> yet when you have arrived at peace
> nothing remains, like something burned away.[761]

This concludes my review of the divergent standpoints around this particular issue.

A geshé's position on buddha pristine awareness is as follows.[762] The actual pure and perfect buddha is the dharmakāya. The very term *dharmakāya*—"embodiment of Dharma"—is applied to the exhaustion of all errors, and thus its nature is that of the opposite of errors. It is expressed in this way merely in terms of conventional reality. In actual fact, dharmakāya itself is unborn and free of conceptual elaboration.

Jetsun Milarepa's position is as follows. "What we call pristine awareness is this very uncontrived awareness, beyond all such terms and intellections as 'is' or 'is not,' 'eternal' or 'nothing.' Therefore, no matter which terms are used to express it, there is no contradiction. Even if someone, with an ambition to become learned, were to ask the Buddha himself [about this topic], I do not think there is something definite that he can say about it. Dharmakāya is beyond the intellect; it is unborn and free of conceptual elaboration. So do not ask me; observe your own mind. That is the way it is."[763] Thus he does not uphold a standpoint in [dichotomous] terms characterized above.

It says, in the *Ornament of Mahayana Sutras*:

> Liberation is simply the exhaustion of error.[764]

Thus a buddha is the dharmakāya, and since the dharmakāya is unborn and free of conceptual elaboration, it does not possess pristine awareness.

One might say that this [standpoint] contradicts the sutras that speak of twofold pristine awareness. In fact, it does not, for just as visual consciousness arises with the perception of the color blue and one says, "I see blue," so the pristine awareness that is the ultimate expanse is pristine awareness of is the way things are, whereas the pristine awareness of manifoldness is the relative aspect [of that same pristine awareness] when it is triggered by whatever manifests to [the deluded minds of] beings. This position is taught to be the most convenient approach to the topic.

Thus the very essence or the very nature of a buddha [can be viewed as] the most perfect purity and the most perfect pristine awareness. As is said in the *Uttaratantra*:

> Buddhahood is indivisible yet can be categorized [234]
> according to its qualities of purity:
> Like the sun and space the purity of
> the two pristine awarenesses are characterized.[765]

Also, it says in the *Ornament of Mahayana Sutras*:

> Those who, through vast purification, have absolutely triumphed over the obscurations that have been consistently present for such a long time—
> the afflictions and knowledge obscurations, along with their latent potentials—
> and who possess the supreme good qualities through perfect transmutation: those are buddhas![766]

The second point is the **etymology** of *buddha*. Why *buddha*? The term *buddha* (Tib. *sangs rgyas*) is applied because they have awakened (*sangs*) from sleep-like ignorance and because the mind has fully expanded (*rgyas*) with respect to the two aspects of the knowable. As it says:

> He has woken up from the slumber of ignorance,
> and his mind has fully expanded, so he is the buddha.[767]

The third point concerns **its aspects.** Buddhahood can be divided into three aspects, namely, its three bodies: dharmakāya, saṃbhogakāya, and nirmāṇakāya. It says, in the *Sutra of Golden Light*:

> All tathāgatas possess three bodies: the dharmakāya, the saṃbhogakāya, and the nirmāṇakāya.[768]

Someone might remark that some scriptures speak of two bodies, others of four bodies, and some of even five bodies. Although they are discussed as such, the bodies are all covered by this categorization in terms of three bodies. Thus the *Ornament of Mahayana Sutras* says:

> Be aware that all the buddha bodies are included within the three bodies.[769]

The fourth point is a **presentation** [of the bodies]. The dharmakāya is what buddha really is. The *Perfection of Wisdom in Eight Thousand Lines* says:

> Do not view the Buddha as the form body. The Buddha is the dharmakāya.[770]

The *King of Meditation Sutra* says:

> Do not view the King of Conquerors as the form body.[771]

The two form bodies are a consequence of the convergence of the following three factors: (1) the power of transmission of the dharmakāya (2) the subjective experience of the spiritual trainees, and (3) one's past aspiration prayers. Were the form bodies due solely to the power of transmission of the ultimate expanse (*dharmadhātu*), [235] the logical consequence would be that everyone would be effortlessly liberated, since the ultimate expanse pervades all beings. Were that the case, it would follow that all beings would come face to face with the buddhas. However, since this is not so, they do not come solely from the power of transmission of the ultimate expanse.

Were the form bodies to be solely due to the subjective experience of beings training on the path, buddhahood would be dependent on error, since to perceive something that is not there is an error. Also, since beings have been perceiving erroneously since time without beginning, all of them should already be buddhas. But this not the case either, so the form bodies are not just the subjective projections of beings still training.

Were the form bodies to be solely due to former prayers, then has a true and perfect buddha achieved power over prayer? If not, then that buddha has not reached omniscience. If a buddha has, then since his prayers are unbiased and for the benefit of all beings, the logical consequence would be for each and every being to be liberated. But this is not the case, so the form bodies do not come solely from former prayers.

Therefore the form bodies are a consequence of the combination of these three factors.

The fifth point explains the reasons for **a definite number**. There are three bodies, and this number is determined by necessity, inasmuch as there is dharmakāya as benefit for yourself and the two form bodies as benefit for others.

How does the dharmakāya represent *benefit for yourself*? Once the dharmakāya has been achieved, it is the basis for all other qualities, such as the [four] fearlessnesses, the [ten] powers, and so forth, which gather as though they had been summoned. Furthermore, even if someone has not achieved dharmakāya itself, those who aspire to dharmakāya, have a little realization of it, a partial realization, or nearly complete realization of it will have just a few qualities, many qualities, a great number of qualities, or an immeasurable amount of qualities, respectively:

The qualities arising from *aspiration* to dharmakāya are those of the meditative absorptions, clear cognitions, and all the superb qualities up to and including the highest worldly realization.[772]

The qualities emerging from a *little realization* of dharmakāya are all the qualities of purification, clear cognition, supernatural ability, and so forth of realized śrāvaka arhats. [236]

The qualities emerging from a *partial realization* of dharmakāya are all the qualities of purification, meditative absorption, clear cognition, and so forth of realized pratyekabuddha arhats.

The qualities emerging from *nearly complete realization* of dharmakāya are the qualities of purification, meditative absorption, clear cognition, and so forth of bodhisattvas of the bodhisattva levels.

The two form bodies are presented in this way as *benefit for others*, inasmuch as there is the enjoyment body (*saṃbhogakāya*) that appears to pure disciples and the emanation body (*nirmāṇakāya*) that appears to impure disciples.

Thus there are definitely three bodies.

The sixth point describes the **characteristic properties of the three bodies.**

First, *dharmakāya* simply refers to the exhaustion of all error—the turning away from what is by nature delusory—once the meaning of emptiness (namely, the ultimate expanse) has been realized. However, as such, *dharmakāya* is simply a term representing a conceptual convention. In real essence, there is no dharmakāya whatsoever possessing true existence, either as dharmakāya, as characteristic properties of dharmakāya, or as anything that could serve as a basis for properties of dharmakāya. Since it is like that, this is how my guru Milarepa explained it.

Dividing it into its various aspects, dharmakāya has eight characteristic qualities—namely, being identical, profound, permanent, unitary, right, pure, lumionous, and linked to the enjoyment body. It is *identical* inasmuch as there are no differences among the dharmakāyas of the various buddhas. It is *profound* because it is difficult to realize, having nothing to do with conceptual elaboration. It is *permanent* because it is not composite; it is without coming into being or cessation; and it is without beginning, middle, or end. It is *unitary* because it is indivisible, the ultimate expanse [i.e., emptiness] and its pristine awareness being inseparable. It is *right* because it is without error, since it transcends the two extremes of underestimation and exaggeration. It is *pure* because it is free from the pollution of the three obscurations (namely, the afflictions and knowledge obscurations and the impediments to meditative attainment). It is *luminous clarity*. Free of conceptuality, it is focused on nonconceptual suchness. It is *linked to the enjoyment body*. It is the basis for the enjoyment body (*saṃbhogakāya*), which is the very expression of its vast qualities.

The *Uttaratantra* says:

> Beginningless, devoid of center and periphery, it is indivisible,
> without the two, free from the three, stainless, and
> nonconceptual—
> such is realized to be the nature of the ultimate expanse [237]
> when seen by the yogi resting in meditative equipoise.[773]

The *Ornament of Mahayana Sutras* also says:

> Identical, the nature body (*svabhāvakāya*),
> subtle and linked with the enjoyment body (*saṃbhogakāya*).[774]

Second, the *enjoyment body* (*saṃbhogakāya*) also has eight characteristics—those of entourage, domain, form, marks, teaching, deeds, spontaneity, and absence of an own-being. The *entourage* with which it is spontaneously experienced is composed solely of bodhisattvas abiding in the ten bodhisattva levels. The *domain* in which it is experienced is that of the utterly pure buddhafields. The *form* or way in which it is experienced is in the form of illustrious Vairocana and so forth. The *marks* with which it is endowed physically are the thirty-two marks of excellence and the eighty adornments. The Dharma *teachings* through which it is perfectly experienced are solely that of the Mahayana. The enlightened activity that forms its *deeds* is to predict the future enlightenment of the bodhisattvas and so forth. Its *spontaneity* is that those deeds and so forth are all accomplished without any effort, occurring spontaneously as in the example of the supreme [wish-fulfilling] gems. Its *absence of own-being* is that even though it manifests various sorts of form, they are not its true nature. They are like the colors picked up in a crystal.

Thus the *Ornament of Mahayana Sutras* says:

> Perfect experience: in every domain a complete entourage,
> the place, the marks, the form,
> the perfect use of Dharma teaching, and its deeds.
> These are the various characteristics.[775]

Also, in the *Ornament of Clear Realization*, it says:

> That endowed with the thirty-two marks
> and eighty adornments and
> partakes of the Mahayana is known as
> the enjoyment body of the Buddha."[776]

Third, the *emanation body* (*nirmāṇakāya*) also has eight principal characteristics—those of its basis, its cause, its domain, its duration, its character, its role of encouraging, its maturing function, and its liberating function. Its *basis* is the dharmakāya, [from which it emanates] without there being any movement. Its *cause* is tremendous compassion aspiring to benefit every single being. Its *domain* embraces both the very pure lands and quite impure ones. Its *duration* is that it endures, without interruption, for as long as the world endures. Its *character* is [238] to manifest forms as the three types of emanation:

- *Creative emanations* endowed with outstanding skill in and mastery of a given art or craft, such as playing lute and so forth
- *Birth emanations* that take birth in various inferior bodies as specific types of existence, for example, as a hare
- *Supreme emanations* that manifest [the twelve deeds]—descent from Tuṣita Heaven, entering the mother's womb, and so forth, and eventually entering great peace.

As it says in the *Ornament of Mahayana Sutras*:

> Constantly manifesting as an artist,
> a human birth, great enlightenment, and nirvana,
> the Buddha's emanation body is
> a great expression of liberation.[777]

As is said in the *Uttaratantra*:

> Through emanations of various kinds,
> he manifestly takes birth—(1) descends from Tuṣitā,
> (2) enters the womb, and (3) is born.
> (4) Skilled in all arts and crafts,
> he (5) enjoys the company of his consorts,
> (6) [renounces], (7) undergoes hardships,
> (8) goes to the seat of enlightenment,
> (9) vanquishes the armies of harmful forces,
> (10) attains perfect enlightenment,
> (11) turns the wheel of Dharma, and (12) passes away.
> In all those realms, quite impure,
> he shows these deeds for as long as worlds endure.[778]

The *role of encouraging* is that the emanation body makes ordinary, worldly beings long for and work toward whichever of the three types of nirvana corresponds to their mentality. The *maturing function* is that the emanation body brings to full spiritual maturity those already engaged in the path. The *liberating function* is that the emanation body frees from the fetters of existence those who have reached full maturity in virtue.

Thus it says, in the *Uttaratantra*:

> It causes worldly beings to enter the path of peace,
> brings them to full maturity, and is that which gives rise to
>   predictions.[779]

These are the eight characteristics of the emanation body. The *Ornament of Clear Realization* says:

> The body that acts simultaneously
> and in all sorts of ways to help beings
> for as long as existence continues
> is the unceasing emanation body of the Sage.[780]

The seventh point concerns the **three particularities** of the buddha bodies: those of identity, permanence, and manifestation.

The *particularity of identity* is that the dharmakāya of all buddhas is identical, being inseparable from its support, the ultimate expanse. The enjoyment body of all buddhas is identical since its noble disposition is the same. The emanation body of all buddhas is identical [239] because their activity is common. Therefore the *Ornament of Mahayana Sutras* says:

> These are identical because of
> their support, intention, and activity.[781]

The *particularity of permanence*: The dharmakāya is permanent by its very nature because, being the ultimate, its very identity is that which is without coming into being or ceasing. The enjoyment body is permanent through being continuous, inasmuch as the experience of Dharma that it manifests is uninterrupted. The emanation body is permanent insofar as its deeds are permanent. Although its manifestations disappear, it shows itself over and over again. Although that which manifests in correspondence to a certain need will cease, there is a functional permanence since it arises appropriately, without delay. The *Ornament of Mahayana Sutras* says:

> Permanence of nature,
> of uninterruptedness, and of continuity....[782]

The *particularity of manifestation*: The dharmakāya manifests through the purification of the knowledge obscuration that clouds the ultimate expanse. The enjoyment body manifests through the purification of the afflictions obscuration. The emanation body manifests through the purification of karmic obscurations.

This concludes the twentieth chapter, on the result—perfect buddhahood—of this *Ornament of Precious Liberation, a Wish-Fulfilling Gem of Sublime Dharma.*

21. Enlightened Activities of the Buddhas

VI. Enlightened Activities

HERE IS EXPLAINED the line, "The activity is to nonconceptually fulfill the welfare of beings."[783] At first bodhicitta is developed, then the path is practiced, and finally the fruition, buddhahood, is achieved. Because all these goals have been pursued solely to eliminate beings' sufferings and ensure their happiness, you may wonder how in fact there can be any benefitting of beings when buddhahood is attained, since buddhas are without either conceptual activity or effort. There does nevertheless occur spontaneous and uninterrupted benefitting of beings, even though buddhas do not think or make effort. To explain this point, is the following is the synopsis:

> **Enlightened activity is summed up in three points: the noble bodies of the buddhas, without deliberate thought, accomplish benefit for beings, and likewise do the magnificent speech and the noble mind.**

[240] Examples of this nonconceptual performance of the welfare of beings—physically, verbally, and mentally—are given in the *Uttaratantra*:

> Like Indra, the [divine] drum, a cloud, and Brahma,
> like the sun and a precious [wish-fulfilling] jewel
> is the Tathāgata;
> also like an echo, like space, and like the earth.[784]

First, we have examples of how the **noble forms** [or bodies] of the buddhas nonconceptually accomplish benefit for beings. The quotation "like the manifestation of Indra" gives the example of how the nonconceptualizing bodies can bring benefit to sentient beings. In this example, Indra, lord of the gods, dwells in his palace called the House of Victory in the company of a host of young goddesses. The palace is made of vaidūrya jewel[785] so pure and lustrous that Indra's reflected image appears on the walls and can be seen from the outside. Were humans living on Earth able to behold this image of Indra and his divine enjoyments in the heavens above them, they would long and pray to live like that. With such a goal in mind, they would make sincere efforts to be virtuous, and through such virtue they might be reborn in such a state after death. The vision that inspires them takes place without any effort of intention on the part of Indra.

In a similar way, those who have entered the path of highest good and who cultivate faith and similar virtues will see the forms of the perfect buddhas adorned with their special marks and signs; they will see them walking, standing, sitting, sleeping, teaching the Dharma, meditating, and accomplishing all sorts of miracles. As a result they will experience faith and yearn to attain such a state. To become like that, they will practice the virtues that are its cause: bodhicitta and all the other requisite practices. As a result, they will eventually become buddhas. The manifestation of the buddhas' form bodies takes place without any deliberate thought and without any movement [on the buddhas' part]. Thus it is stated:

> Just as, on the clear surface of vaidūrya jewel,
> there appears the reflected form of the lord of gods,
> so on the clear surface of beings' minds
> here appears the reflected form of the King of Conquerors.[786]

The line "like the divine drum" gives the example of how the buddhas' speech can accomplish the welfare of beings without forethought. In the example, a drumbeat sounds in the realm of the gods. It resounds as a result of the gods' former beneficial actions. The drumbeat does not have thought or intention, [241] yet its sound conveys messages such as "All conditioned things are impermanent!" that stimulate the gods, who are inclined to neglect virtue in the present. Thus it is stated:

> Just as through the power of the gods' former virtue,
> the Dharma drum in the divine realms—
> without any thought, effort, location, mind, or form—
> stimulates all the carefree gods over and over
> again with the words "impermanence," "suffering," "no self,"
> and "peace."[787]

As in the example, it is without any effort or deliberation that the speech of the buddhas transmits suitable teachings to those who are ready. So it is stated:

> Likewise, without effort and so forth,
> the omnipresent embraces all beings, without exception,
> with the speech of the enlightened ones,
> teaching the Dharma to those who are ready.[788]

In the above way, the speech of the buddhas accomplishes the welfare of beings without any [need for] conscious deliberate thought.

The line "Like a cloud..." presents the analogy of how the **perfect mind** of the buddhas nonconceptually accomplishes the good of beings.

During the monsoon, clouds gather effortlessly in the sky, and their rain, falling on the earth without any deliberation on the clouds' part, causes the growth of perfect crops and many other things to happen. It is stated:

> Just as from monsoon clouds
> falls down to earth
> effortlessly a mass of water,
> the condition for plentiful crops...[789]

In a similar way, the activity of the buddha mind, without requiring any deliberation, pours down the rain of Dharma onto beings training in virtue and ripens their crop of wholesomeness. Thus it is stated:

> Similarly, the clouds of great compassion cause,
> without any need of deliberation,
> a rainfall of the sublime teachings
> of the victorious ones.[790]

Thus the buddha mind accomplishes the welfare of beings without any need for conscious thought.

Regarding the line, "like Brahma...," Brahma, lord of the gods, manifests his presence in all the heavens yet never leaves his own Brahma heaven. In a similar way, without ever moving from the dharmakāya, the buddhas manifest the twelve deeds and other similar emanations to those training in virtue, thereby bringing them benefit. [242] So it is stated:

> Just as Brahma, without ever moving
> from the Brahma heaven,
> effortlessly shows his manifestations
> in all the other heavens,
> so also does a victorious one,
> without ever moving from the dharmakāya,
> effortlessly show his emanations everywhere
> to those whose karma makes them ready.[791]

In the example of the sun, the sun's rays, without any need for deliberation, cause lotuses and innumerable other kinds of flowers to blossom simultaneously. Similarly, without any thought or effort, the rays of the buddhas' teachings cause the lotuses that are the minds of infinitely varied disciples, with their different aspirations, to open toward that which is wholesome. Thus it is stated:

> Just as the sun, without any deliberation,
> through the simultaneous radiation of its sunbeams,
> brings the lotuses to full bloom
> and ripens other plants,
> so do the sunrays of the buddhas' sublime teachings,
> without any need for deliberation,
> pour into the lotus-like beings
> training in virtue.[792]

Taking this example of the sun another way, just as the reflection of the sun appears simultaneously on all surfaces that are sufficiently clear and smooth, so does the Buddha appear simultaneously to all disciples of sufficiently pure inner disposition:

> In all the water vessels
> that are those pure disciples,
> countless reflections of the buddha sun
> appear simultaneously.[793]

In the example of the wish-fulfilling gem, just as a wish-fulfilling gem does not think yet effortlessly produces whatever is requested by the person who calls on it, so the goals corresponding to the various motivations of the śrāvakas and other disciples are accomplished because of the buddhas. Thus it is stated:

> Just as a wish-fulfilling gem,
> without thought and spontaneously,
> completely fulfills the wishes
> of those within its sphere of influence,
> so also, on account of the wish-fulfilling buddha,
> those of various motivations hear
> different kinds of teachings,
> without any deliberation on [the Buddha's part].[794]

Similar to the above, there are three more examples—those of an echo, of space, and of the earth—showing how beings can be benefitted by the buddhas without requiring any conscious thought on their part.

This was the twenty-first chapter, on nonconceptual enlightened activity, of this *Ornament of Precious Liberation, a Wish-Fulfilling Gem of Sublime Dharma.*

* * *

This concludes this *Ornament of Precious Liberation, a Wish-Fulfilling Gem of Sublime Dharma*, progressively explaining the Mahayana path, composed by the physician Sönam Rinchen at the instigation of Darma Kyap and transcribed by the latter.

> May whatever merit there be in your transcription
> in terms of nonconceptual benefit for beings
> through the wish-fulfilling sacred Dharma
> help all beings attain supreme enlightenment. Virtue!

Part III
Clarifying the Sage's Intent
An Exposition of the Stages for Embarking upon the Excellent Path of the Bodhisattva

Sakya Paṇḍita Kunga Gyaltsen
(1182–1251)

Translated by David P. Jackson

The title in Sanskrit: Munimataprakāśanāmaśāstra
The title in Tibetan: Thub pa'i dgongs pa rab tu gsal ba

1. Spiritual Potential

Reverent homage to the guru and Mañjuśrī!

[247] THE COMPLETELY AWAKENED Buddha, the source of benefit and lasting happiness, arose from a Conqueror's son (a bodhisattva).[1] The Conqueror's son arose from the thought of awakening (*bodhicitta*), which is in nature emptiness and compassion.[2] Therefore, to benefit living beings, I pay homage to the thought of awakening and briefly explain here the stages for embarking upon the excellent path of the Conqueror's sons.

If an intelligent person has produced the thought of highest awakening and aspires to unsurpassable, perfect, and complete awakening, the folllowing are the stages of the religious path as taught in [Maitreya's] *Ornament of Mahayana Sutras*:

> (1) [Recognizing] spiritual potential, (2) appreciating Dharma,[3]
> (3) generating the thought [of awakening],
> (4) accomplishing the perfections of generosity and the rest,
> (5) bringing sentient beings to maturity,
> (6) entering into the faultless [levels of an ārya]
> and the pure fields [and into]
> (7) nonsituated nirvana,
> highest awakening, and the displaying" [of a buddha's deeds].[4]

If one wishes to practice as taught here, then such a person should first determine his or her spiritual potential (*gotra*), which is the basis for being suitably endowed to practice Dharma.

Concerning "spiritual potential," the *Ornament of Mahayana Sutras* teaches:

> The natural and developed
> are the support and the supported.

> As existence and nonexistence, know spiritual potential
> in the sense of liberating excellent quality.[5]

Accordingly, natural spiritual potential is present in all sentient beings. Developed spiritual potential is present in those who have produced the thought of gaining awakening.[6] It is absent in those who have not produced this thought. Natural spiritual potential is "the support"; developed spiritual potential is that which is supported. [The words "liberating excellent quality" are explained by the following Sanskrit tradtitional explanatory] etymology:[7] "Spiritual potential" in Sanskrit is *gotra*. By changing the *o* of *go* to *u*, and by adding the element *na*, you arrive at *guṇa* ("excellent quality"). If you divide the syllable *tra*, the result is *tāra* ("liberating"). Thus, because it liberates you to the far shore of the ocean of cyclic existence (*samsara*) on the basis of excellent qualities, it is a "liberating excellent quality."

The marks of possessing the spiritual potential of the Mahayana

These are stated in the *Ornament of Mahayana Sutras* to be:

> Before you have set out, to have compassion,
> to have appreciation and patience,
> and to practice virtue—these are specified[8]
> as signs of spiritual potential.[9] [248]

Thus there are four signs [needed] from the beginning, before commencing the practice of Dharma: great compassion, appreciation of the Three Jewels, great forbearance when others harm you, and pleasure in planting the roots of virtue. Whoever has these displays the buddha potential.

The impediments to that spiritual potential

These are stated in the *Ornament of Mahayana Sutras* to be:

> Habituation to the afflictions, having harmful friends,
> living in poverty, and being dominated by others—
> in brief, know the impediments
> to the spiritual potential as fourfold.[10]

The first impediment is irresistible craving for or aversion to food, wealth, and sentient beings, born of excessive *habituation to the afflictions*.

[The second impediment,] *having harmful friends*, means being unable to begin the practice of Dharma because of family bonds or a bad religious teacher. Even if you can begin, you cannot take up correct doctrines and practices but only erroneous ones. In particular, if you have previous contact with a bad teacher and request instruction, you receive only erroneous religious teachings. If you later request instruction from a religious teacher who teaches without error, your first teacher is displeased. Having to keep him happy prevents you from meeting the correct teaching, thus impeding your spiritual potential.

The third impediment is trepidation about practicing the Dharma because of *lacking adequate food and clothing*.

The fourth impediment is being prevented from embarking upon religious practice because of *being under the control of others*, such as relatives or a ruler. As Cāṇakya teaches [in his *Treatise on Political Morals*]:

> During childhood he is dominated by his parents.
> When early adulthood arrives he is dominated by his spouse.
> In his old age he is dominated by his children.
> Because of this, the fool never has independence.[11]

Severed spiritual potential[12]

The *Ornament of Mahayana Sutras* says:

> Some lack virtue that is conducive to good.[13]
> Some pursue only misconduct.
> Some have destroyed all morally positive factors.
> Some have inferior positive factors, and some are devoid of
> the cause.[14]

There are two types of people whose spiritual potential is severed:[15] those for whom it has been temporarily severed and those for whom it is permanently cut. The temporarily severed includes four types: (1) those who lack virtue of the sort that is conducive to good [that is, that leads to liberation], (2) those who engage only in misconduct, (3) those who have destroyed the seeds of good factors, and (4) those whose seeds of good factors have not been germinated and ripened by the moisture of virtue. The existence of people whose spiritual potential has been completely severed is maintained by the Yogācāra school but not by the Madhyamaka. Nevertheless you should view those whom the Madhyamaka say wander in cyclic existence without end as being, in fact, permanently severed from spiritual potential. [249] It is just as in the story of the bird hunters[16] of King Prasenajit,[17] or the parable of the Chinese child.[18]

2. Taking Refuge

THE SECOND KEY phrase quoted from the *Ornament of Mahayana Sutras*, "appreciating Dharma,"[19] refers to taking refuge to gain appreciation for this teaching. To explain this there are four main topics: identifying the essence of taking refuge, determining its nature, the rules to be observed for taking refuge, and the benefits of following such rules.

Identifying the essence of taking refuge

This has two parts. The *definition* of taking refuge is "the affirmation of your adherence to the highest object." The *Sanskrit etymology* is as follows. The Sanskrit words *śaraṇaṃ gacchāmi* mean "I go for refuge." It is called "refuge" because it protects. You speak of "going" because you approach in order to resort to it. As is also said in the *Ornament of Mahayana Sutras*:

> It is the supreme refuge because
> it protects from all harms,
> [the view of] a substantial personality, the Hinayana,
> ineffective methods, and the miserable destinies.[20]

Determining in detail the nature of taking refuge

There are two main approaches, mundane and supramundane. The mundane taking of refuge has two subtypes: worldly in mentality and worldly in terms of the objects in which refuge is taken. The supramundane taking of refuge [also] has two main types: the common and the ones not held in common. The common type has two subtypes: that of the śrāvaka and that of the pratyekabuddha. The uncommon type also has two subtypes: that of the Perfection Vehicle and that of the Vajra Vehicle. Thus six subtypes exist in all.

Differences between the two ways of taking refuge can be explained in terms of four types: differences in motivating cause, differences of object in which refuge is taken, differences of time, and differences of aim.

Differences in motivating cause. The chief causes for the worldly person taking refuge are fear and desire, whereas for the śrāvaka and pratyekabuddha, though fear and desire are present, faith is the main cause. The bodhisattva has those three causes, too, yet for him compassion predominates.

Differences of object. People belonging to the worldly and supramundane spheres take refuge in different objects. [250] *The worldly person* takes refuge in either an inferior or superior object. To take refuge in the first is to go for refuge to the great mundane gods such as Īśvara or Brahma, or to whatever other objects you prefer, such as trees or hills. As it is taught in a sutra:

> Some who are hard pressed by fears
> commonly seek refuge in hills,
> forests, or a large tree.
> But that is not the superior refuge,
> for by resorting to those refuges
> you will not escape the greatest dangers.[21]

The worldly taking of refuge in superior objects is taking refuge in the Three Jewels but with a worldly mentality—to gain protection from the fearsome aspects of this life or the next or to reap some advantage—so that even though you take refuge in the Three Jewels, that worldly motivation prevents your being liberated from cyclic existence.

People of a supramundane approach have different objects of refuge depending on whether they belong to the traditions held in common or those not held in common. The śrāvakas, who make up the first of *the two common traditions*, take refuge in the Three Jewels, and for them the Sangha is the primary refuge from among the three. The pratyekabuddhas, the second "common" tradition, take refuge in the Three Jewels, but for them the Dharma is primary. Among *the two traditions not held in common*, in the Perfection Vehicle refuge is taken in the Three Jewels with the Buddha as the main refuge. As [Maitreya's] *Uttaratantra* explains:

> Because they are to be abandoned, possess a deceptive quality,
> are nonexistent, and possess fear,

the two aspects of Dharma and the assembly of āryas
are not permanent places of refuge.

The refuge of living beings is,
in ultimate truth, the Buddha alone.
The Sage possesses a dharmakāya,
and the Sangha is his ultimate manifestation.[22]

As for the second, the Vajra Vehicle way of taking refuge, I won't explain this here because that belongs to the mantra tradition of teachings.

The traditional ways of identifying the Three Jewels also vary. The śrāvakas and pratyekabuddhas do not hold that the Buddha possesses three bodies (*kāya*). They hold that only buddhas such as Śākyamuni, who attained awakening at the vajra seat in Bodhgayā, are real buddhas in the strict sense of the word. As for the Dharma, they do not take the Mahayana sutras to be genuine; they merely affirm the śrāvaka scriptures. In their Sangha, too, they do not include the bodhisattvas but only the eight types of śrāvaka āryas.[23] [251] Among the followers of the Mahayana, the Perfection Vehicle maintains as places of refuge only a Buddha who possesses the three bodies of buddhahood (*trikāya*), the Dharma of the Mahayana teachings, and the Sangha made up of bodhisattvas. I will not explain the Three Jewels of the mantra tradition here.

Differences of time. Worldly people take refuge merely until they attain some minor personal goal pertaining to the present life or to the next. Apart from that, they are ignorant of the usages "as long as I live" and "until I reach the stage of awakening." Śrāvakas and pratyekabuddhas state "for as long as I live" but do not take refuge until the stage of awakening is reached. Bodhisattvas take refuge until reaching the stage of awakening and not for other periods.

Concerning this, some say that the words "as long as I live" do not refer to as long as this life continues but mean "as long as the mind continues to exist," and that to say those words is precisely to take refuge until attaining buddhahood. This is the so-called furtive production of the thought of awakening.[24] But if this were so, there would be no difference between the common and uncommon taking of refuge, and the vows of individual liberation (*prātimokṣa*) and of the bodhisattva would become a single system. This would contradict the explanation in the *Ornament of Mahayana Sutras* of Mahayana refuge-taking as having four special characteristics,[25] and such a principle is not taught in any sutra or tantra. For these reasons, those who maintain this possess the fault of having little religious knowledge and are taking presumptuous liberties with the doctrine.

Differences of aim. Worldly people take refuge merely for the purposes of this life or future lives, as you might use an escorting guard. Śrāvakas take refuge with the desire to obtain arhatship for their own sakes. Pratyekabuddhas take refuge for their own sakes through a desire to attain gnosis (*jñāna*) by themselves; this they do in a realm where no buddha dwells and through understanding dependent origination. The bodhisattva takes refuge for the benefit of others through the desire to attain perfectly omniscient buddhahood. As is stated in the *Uttaratantra*:

> The three refuges are established
> through [the excellent qualities of] the Teacher, the doctrine,
> and his disciples,
> taking into consideration the three vehicles
> and those who like to perform services to the Three [Jewels].[26]

The rules to be observed as part of taking refuge

These are of two types: points to be practiced with respect to all Three Jewels in common, and points to be practiced with respect to each refuge individually.

The general training includes both activities to be accomplished and things to be avoided. Three activities are to be accomplished: associating with noble people, studying the noble teaching, and accomplishing your activities in accord with the teaching. [252]

Associating with noble people means studying Dharma with a spiritual preceptor who possesses the defining marks of a genuine religious teacher.[27] You should also place your trust in friends who practice in accord with the Dharma and lead all your relatives, associates, and servants to the Dharma.

Studying the noble teaching consists of studying the three divisions of scriptures (Tripiṭaka) that were definitely taught by the Buddha or, if you have received the initiations, the four classes of tantra. Or you can study treatises that explain the intended sense of the Buddha's word—religious teachings you can trust as authentic, composed by such āryas and masters as Maitreyanātha, Asaṅga and his brother Vasubandhu, Nāgārjuna and his spiritual son Āryadeva, Dignāga, Dharmakīrti, Śāntideva, and Guṇaprabha. Also, when learning the mantra teachings, you should study treatises of authentic origin such as the three commentaries composed by the bodhisattvas,[28] the Seven Works on Accomplishment composed by adepts (*siddha*),[29] and the treatises composed by such realized teachers as the lord of yoga Master Virūpa, King Indrabhūti, and Vajraghaṇṭa.

In brief, the doctrine that the Buddha proclaimed, that the compilers gathered together, that the perfected adepts realized through meditative practice, that the great scholars expounded, that the translators translated, and that is well known among scholars is the doctrine of the Buddha. So you should study, teach, cultivate through meditation, and practically achieve this. If you come upon a religious teaching that is different from this—even if it seems very profound—it is not suitable to be learned, taught, meditatively cultivated, or accomplished, for it is not the doctrine of the Buddha. Seemingly very excellent teachings are also possessed by the non-Buddhist Indian sectarians (*tīrthika*) and by other erroneous religious traditions, but since these are not the Buddha's doctrine, cast them aside and abandon them.

Accomplishing your activities in accord with the teaching has two aspects: (1) in general, to act in conformity with the three divisions of scripture, and (2) in particular, the way of accomplishing immediate activities.

In general, your deportment should accord with the Vinaya, your meditation should accord with the sutras, your expositions should accord with the Abhidharma, and your practice of the mantra tradition should accord with the tantras. Nowadays here in Tibet, there are many Buddhists who do not accord with the three divisions of scripture and who go against the four classes of tantra, and yet they are marveled at by the credulous. I cannot make out what is so marvelous about them.

[*In particular,*] the way to accomplish immediate activities is as follows. When sitting, think that you are relying on the Three Jewels. [253] When going somewhere, think that you are going for refuge in the Three Jewels, particularly the Three Jewels who dwell in the direction in which you are traveling. By praying as you travel to Vairocana in the center, Akṣobhya in the east, Ratnasambhava in the south, Amitābha in the west, or Amoghasiddhi in the north, your immediate obstacles will be pacified, you will achieve your plan, and ultimately you will meet with the buddhas.

You should also make worshipful offerings with the first portion of whatever you eat or drink. Saying *Oṃ mahāguru vajra naividye āḥ hūṃ*, give a food offering to the spiritual preceptor in the manner taught in such works as *Ritual for Invoking the Tutelary Deity, Removing Bad Views* by Ācārya Maitripāda,[30] and *Practice for Beginners* by the Dharma lord, the great master of Sakya (Sönam Tsemo).[31]

Though it is good to propitiate the buddhas, bodhisattvas, and tutelary deities individually, you should offer one food offering to them en masse, saying *Oṃ sarvabuddhabodhisattvānāṃ vajra naividya āḥ hūṃ*. Then you should give sacrificial cakes to the spirits that eat these. The mantra of the sacrificial cake for spirits in general was authoritatively taught to be *Oṃ akāromukhaṃ sarvadharmāṇāṃ adyanutpannatvata oṃ āḥ hūṃ phaṭ svāhā*. To the hungry spirits give a Jvālamukhī sacrificial cake. For that you should first recite the mantra *Nāmaḥ sarvatathāgata avalokite oṃ sambhara sambhara hūṃ*, and afterward you should recite the names of the four tathāgatas, for this is what was taught in the dhāraṇī.[32] The ritual practice of some people is to recite first the names of the four tathāgatas and afterward to recite the mantra. But since this was not taught by the Buddha, it is incorrect. Water offerings [to hungry spirits] require the giving of water alone, unmixed with food. The Buddha taught that if you mix food in the water, those hungry spirits who cannot digest solid food will not be able to receive any offering. Hence the putting of food in water offerings is also something not taught by the Buddha.[33]

Then offer a lump of dough squeezed in the palms of the hands to the yakṣiṇī Hārītī, saying *Oṃ hārīte svāhā*. And saying *Oṃ hārīte vajrayakṣiṇī svāhā*, offer a squeezed lump to the five hundred sons of Hārītī. Then give one squeezed lump in general to the spirits who control the first portion of offered food, saying *Oṃ agrapiṇḍa asibhyaḥ svāhā*. In the *Sutra of Hārītī*, the Buddha said, "May those who accept me as a teacher bestow squeezed lumps of food on the yakṣiṇī Hārītī."[34] [254] The *Vajra Peak Tantra* teaches, "Offer a squeezed lump as the offering of the first portion of food."[35] And this is similarly taught in many sutras and tantras, such as in the *Kālacakra Tantra*.[36]

Nowadays here in Tibet, I see people making swollen-chested or three-sided cakes similar to the *yetak* Bönpo offerings made to indigenous Tibetan *tsentsen* deities rather than squeezed lumps and sacrificial cakes as taught by the Buddha.[37] I doubt that these [three-sided] offerings were taught by the Buddha.

Then, after those preliminary offerings, eat the food while practicing the eating meditation in accord with the particular scripture [you are following].

As for the meditation to be practiced when going to sleep, first lie on your right side, with your head pointing either east or north, just as it is taught in *Guide to the Bodhisattva Way of Life*:

> Lie down in the desired direction,
> in the position of the Lord when he passed into nirvana.[38]

Then, composing yourself in the meditative absorption of Amitābha, lie down to rest in the Dharma body of the Buddha, the condition of emptiness.[39] When waking up, arise with the pride of being the form body (*rūpakāya*) of the Buddha, and perform all activities as explained in the *Completely Pure Conduct Sutra.*[40]

Furthermore, whatever pleasures and happiness you experience should be offered to the religious preceptor and the Three Jewels. Whatever pain and unhappiness occur, put your reliance in the Three Jewels. And [to alleviate sickness and suffering,] apply yourself to the recitation of mantras, meditative visualization, medical treatments, and the reading of scriptures. Do not disparage these means, for they all are branches of the Jewel of the Dharma.

[Objection:] Some people say that to resort to medical treatment and the recitation of scriptures is not to trust in the Dharma Jewel, and that it is better to take refuge in the Three Jewels than to take medicine. They even say that it harms your going for refuge to take medicines.

[Reply:] Yet the Buddha taught in the medicine section of the Vinaya scriptures that monks should have recourse to doctors and medicines.[41] Even food and drink would then be detrimental to the taking of refuge, since the Buddha taught that food and drink belong to one of the four main classes of medicines. Hence as long as you continue to eat and drink, how could it be right to say that ingesting medicine injures the taking of refuge? If real scholars witnessed this, they would view it with disapproval.

Furthermore, do not renounce the Three Jewels for anything, even to save your life or for some reward. Train in making each and every act a service to the Three Jewels.

The rules of training with respect to each object of refuge individually

It was taught in a sutra:

> One who takes refuge in the Buddha
> is a correct lay adherent.

He or she should never take refuge
in other deities. [255]

One who takes refuge in the good Dharma
should be devoid of any thought of harming and killing.
And one who takes refuge in the Sangha
should not turn to the non-Buddhist tīrthikas.[42]

Therefore, if you have taken refuge in the Buddha, do not take some other god as the Great Teacher. If you have taken refuge in the good Dharma, do not harm sentient beings. If you have taken refuge in the Sangha, do not take a non-Buddhist *tīrthika* as your spiritual preceptor.

Moreover, if you have taken refuge in the Buddha, do not take another god as the Great Teacher. If you have taken refuge in the Dharma, do not take something besides that as your spiritual path, and if you have taken refuge in the Sangha, do not take those outside the Sangha as your spiritual friends or preceptor.

Merely to pay homage, to worship, and to offer sacrificial cakes to deities who belong to the mundane sphere, such as the mundane Dharma protectors and the ten guardians of the directions, does not destroy your taking of refuge in the Three Jewels.[43] But to actually take refuge in such deities does destroy your vow of refuge. To explain by way of example, if a retainer pays homage and makes worshipful offerings to someone who is not his lord, he still remains within the sphere of his lord's authority. But if a retainer entrusts himself to the protection of someone besides his lord, he has exceeded the limits of his lord's domain because the lord can no longer offer him any protection.

Nowadays here in Tibet, I have seen some people who say that to call [worldly] deities, such as Thanglha, "Lord" injures your refuge in the Three Jewels, yet at the same time they take refuge in the guardians of the directions, the great leaders of the yakṣa spirits, local deities, and even lesser deities. If you do this, you indeed injure your vow of taking refuge. If such people reply that those deities are members of the noble assembly of bodhisattvas, then in that case this practice can be included within taking refuge in the Three Jewels. But if you take refuge in them as being distinct from the Three Jewels, you will mix up your practice with that of the tīrthikas, because those non-Buddhist sectarians take refuge in just such world-protecting deities as Śakra (Indra), Brahma, and Maheśvara (Śiva).

Some also say that to commit disrespectful acts toward the scriptures—such as to walk over them, buy and sell them, or use them as a pledge for loans—is to abandon the Dharma and therefore amounts to losing your refuge in the Dharma. Yet the same people also say, "Do not engage in studying and teaching," thinking that to obstruct the study and teaching of the Dharma does not damage the taking of refuge. [256] In general, it is indeed a great fault to engage in the business of buying and selling a sacred book. Yet because the book will continue to be used for recitation and so forth when it is in the hands of the new owner, this cannot cause a decline in the doctrine in general, though the seller himself will be worse off. But if you put an end to studying and teaching, the lineage of wise ones will be broken. Even if many volumes of scriptures remain, if there is no one who can understand the teachings, the doctrine of the Buddha will have been destroyed. Therefore those who are afraid of lesser faults, such as trafficking in religious books, but commit the major fault of obstructing religious study and teaching do not understand the root of taking refuge in the Dharma.

I have also seen some who, while saying that to walk over some yellow cloth destroys your refuge in the Sangha, commit acts of harm and irreverence to noble, energetic upholders of the monastic vows and to great adherents of the basic Buddhist scriptures. To walk over yellow cloth is the subsidiary fault of irreverence, but it does not cause the actual refuge itself to be lost. However, disrespecting or injuring the noble and energetic upholders of the monastic vows and great adherents of the scriptures does impair your refuge in the Sangha. All distinctions of these sorts should be carefully differentiated and understood. Here I have not written about the other rules of training because I fear that this account may grow too long. To learn about these, read the sutras and the religious treatises.[44]

The benefits of following such rules

Two types of benefits accrue from taking refuge: temporary benefits and ultimate benefits. Immediate, *temporary benefits* actually include benefits of two sorts. The first is that *taking refuge frees you from undesirable things.* It purifies the obscurations created by past acts of misdirected faith. Thus you will avoid harm from humans and demons and be able to minimize physical pain and mental suffering; in brief, refuge removes all unfavorable factors. Moreover, great masters have taught that even without a deeply felt mental taking of refuge, benefits derive from merely reciting aloud the formula of refuge-taking. I have heard the following story:

> Once there was a monk who had taken ordination late in life and was very ignorant, but a certain lay patroness had faith in him. One day she offered him a roll of cloth and requested religious instruction. Unable to come up with anything to teach her, the monk became downcast and repeated over and over, "Not knowing, I am miserable." From that the patroness realized that the result, misery, arises from the cause, ignorance, and thus she beheld the truth. She then praised him, saying, "The master has freed me from the ocean of misery."
>
> A thief happened to witness this, and thinking that he would steal the cloth from this simpleton, he followed the monk. When the old monk entered his house, the thief called to him from outside, "Give me the cloth!" [257] The old monk called back, "I am too terrified to come out. Take it through the window!" When the thief reached in an arm to take the cloth, the old monk said, "My patroness bestowed this upon me with both hands. You, too, must take it with both hands." When the thief extended both hands, the old monk bound them with a rope and then fastened the rope to a pillar inside. Then he came outside, and shouting, "Let us recite the taking of refuge!" he repeated the words of the refuge formula, giving the thief a blow with his staff for each of the Three Jewels. Then he let the thief go.
>
> The thief limped away, and coming to a riverbank he met a traveler, who asked why he was limping. The thief replied: "I am a thief. But there is a monk—an even bigger thief than I am—who thrashed me, reciting the prayer of taking refuge and combining a blow of his staff with each of the Three Jewels. Through his possession of superknowledge (*abhijñā*), the Buddha limited the taking of refuge to only three. Had there been a fourth refuge, I would undoubtedly now be dead." So saying, and with faith in the Buddha, the thief went into the water under a bridge.
>
> At that time a horde of demons started to cross the bridge but were unable to do so. They thought, "Previously, we could easily cross. What is to blame for this?" They asked the man in the water below what special skills he had. He answered, "I know

the prayer for taking refuge in the Three Jewels. Other than that, I don't know anything." When he said that, the demons, too, attained a firm knowledge of the value of taking refuge. It is said that when they died, they were reborn as gods. The thief, too, feeling faith in the Buddha, took monastic ordination.

The second main type of immediate benefit of taking refuge consists of the *excellent qualities you gain thereby.* These excellent qualities are of two sorts: those involving a change of name and those involving a substantial change. The *change of name* is that you attain the name "Buddhist" through taking refuge, and you are included within the rank of those who are called "very noble." The *substantial change* is that by taking refuge you become an object worthy of worship by the whole world, including the gods. In general, you gain great protection, and in particular, you gain the protection of the gods who love the doctrine. Like a traveling merchant who has found an escorting guard, you gain peace of mind and the confidence that you will never be parted from the Three Jewels in all future lives.

Ultimate benefits. Some of the ultimate benefits of taking refuge accrue to yourself and some to others. You *yourself* ultimately benefit from taking refuge in the Buddha because the correct conditions are thereby established for your attainment of buddhahood. [258] By taking refuge in the Dharma, the conditions are set ultimately for you to teach the Dharma continually. And taking refuge in the Sangha establishes the correct conditions for you ultimately to gather together an immeasurably vast retinue consisting of the order of fully ordained monastics and the order of bodhisattvas. The benefits that accrue to *others* are that—purely by virtue of your own accomplishment of those things—your disciples will gradually be introduced into the doctrine of the Buddha and will ultimately achieve direct realization of the Three Jewels.

3. Generating the Resolve to Attain Awakening

Different traditions of generating the thought of awakening

For "generating the thought of awakening,"[45] there are two main traditions: that of the śrāvaka schools and that of the Mahayana schools.

In the śrāvaka schools, you produce the thought of attaining one of three goals: arhatship, pratyekabuddhahood, and perfect, complete buddhahood. But since that is the Hinayana, I will not explain it here.

The Mahayana has two schools: the Vijñānavāda (or Yogācāra) and the Madhyamaka.[46] The Vijñānavāda tradition of generating the thought of awakening is the teaching tradition originating from Maitreya, followed by the master Asaṅga, and taught in Asaṅga's *Bodhisattva Levels*; that is to say, it is the system of Candragomin's *Twenty Verses*. The tradition of the Madhyamaka is the teaching tradition originating from Ārya Mañjuśrī, followed by the master Nāgārjuna, and taught in the *Flower Ornament Sutra*. It is the tradition of Śāntideva's *Guide to the Bodhisattva Way of Life*, [for which manuals were] composed by such masters as Jetāri.

In my *Ritual for Generating the Thought of Awakening*, I have clarified the differences between these two systems about such things as the characteristics of a qualified teacher, the ritual for imparting the vows, and the rules of training, and I have explained in particular the Madhyamaka system of vow-imparting ritual, rules of training, and so forth. Therefore you should refer to it [to learn more].

The ways the thought of awakening can arise

Generating with and without ritual. Generally speaking, it was authoritatively taught that the vows of the *prātimokṣa* system, generating the thought of awakening of the bodhisattva, and the initiations of the mantra tradition are produced through ritual, whereas the vow of meditative concentration (*dhyāna*), the vow "free from outflows," and ultimate generation of the thought of awakening are not produced through rituals.[47] [259]

[Objection:] This contradicts the section on the seven branches of worship in the *Enlightenment of Vairocana*, where it says that the words of generating the ultimate thought of awakening should be repeated thrice.[48]

[Reply:] I can answer this objection in two ways: indirectly, by answering "in kind" [that is, through analogy or parallel reasoning], and directly, by giving the actual answer.[49]

[*The indirect answer, by analogy*:[50] Just as I maintain that the ultimate thought of awakening is not produced through ritual,] so you maintain that mahāmudrā cannot be consciously cultivated through meditation. But what you maintain is contradicted by the *Compendium of Principles* tantra, which explains that mahāmudrā is cultivated in meditation. You may object that the *Compendium of Principles* belongs to the yoga tantras, and that in it the meditative visualization of the form of the deity has merely been designated "mahāmudrā," which is not the real mahāmudrā of the unsurpassed (*anuttara*) yoga tantra system. In that case, I must reply similarly that the *Enlightenment of Vairocana Tantra* is an elaboration (*caryā*) tantra, and that in it a mantra for gathering the accumulation of gnosis has been designated by the name "generation of the ultimate thought of awakening." This, however, does not constitute an exposition of a ritual generation of the ultimate thought of awakening in the perfections tradition.

If you reply, "Even though the *Enlightenment of Vairocana* belongs to the mantra tradition, what is the incompatibility in applying its system to the perfections tradition?" then I reply similarly, "Even though the *Compendium of Principles* tantra is a yoga tantra, what is the incompatibility if you practice its system of mahāmudrā in an unsurpassed yoga tantra meditation?" You may reply that it is unacceptable to mix the ritual practices of the yoga and unsurpassed yoga tantras because they are different classes of tantras. If so, then how could it be acceptable for you to mix up the *Enlightenment of Vairocana*, which is a tantra of the mantra teachings, with the generation of the ultimate thought of awakening belonging to the perfections tradition?

If you object, "Even though it mixes up the rituals of different vehicles, what is the incompatibility if, through pious imagination, you practice a ritual for generating the ultimate thought of awakening?" then I might similarly ask, "Even though it mixes up the practices of different classes of the tantras, what is the incompatibility in practicing the mahāmudrā of the yoga tantras as an unsurpassed yoga tantra meditation?" You may say, "That would be a defective mahāmudrā that has lapsed into being [an object of conscious meditative cultivation]." To this I may reply, "Generation of the ultimate thought of awakening that has lapsed into being a ritual would also be defective." You ask, "What is the defect of lapsing into being a ritual?" I similarly ask, "What is the defect of lapsing into being consciously cultivated meditation?" You say, "Meditative cultivation is a discursive, conceptual activity, whereas mahāmudrā is nondiscursive." But I may also observe that since ritual belongs to the conventional, surface level and the generation of the ultimate thought of awakening is the absolutely real, these are equally incompatible. Therefore ignorant people who do not know the levels of the philosophical schools and classes of tantra find here an occasion for error in a mere similarity of terms and are simply unaware of the key points of the matter.

The actual, direct answer. Generally, for all religious teachings, the ordering of the systems of established philosophical tenets and the stages of the different vehicles are very important. You must understand the difference between a thing that actually is what it is called and a thing that is merely designated so. [260] In the established philosophical tenets, not only do you find that what for the śrāvakas is ultimate truth becomes relative truth for the Mahayana, but you also find that the mantra tradition explains generation of the ultimate thought of awakening as the visualization of colors and forms in meditation. In that tradition, you also find that the meditational realization of all things as emptiness by reciting such words as "emptiness" and "free from all existent entities" is designated by the name "generation of the ultimate thought of awakening." Countless such examples exist, such as the designation of a moon as the "conventional" and a vajra as the "ultimate" thought of awakening, so you must properly understand the reasons for this. Rituals of the mantra tradition and generation of the thought of awakening should not be confused through admixture.

The rituals for generating the aspiring and engaging phases of the thought of awakening are taught in all sutras and treatises. But the exposition of a ritual for generation of the ultimate thought of awakening does not occur in any sutra or treatise. In particular, such a ritual was not taught in the Madhyamaka system, such as in the writings of the master Nāgārjuna or in Śāntideva's *Guide to the Bodhisattva Way of Life*. Nor was it taught in the Yogācāra writings, such as those of the master Asaṅga, the *Twenty Verses* of Candragomin, or the manual on generation of the thought of awakening by the great lord Atiśa.

[Question:] Even though this was not taught by earlier masters, what is the incompatibility of conducting such a ritual through imagining [that you thus produce the ultimate thought of awakening]?

[Reply:] If a thought of awakening is born from a ritual, it must be the generation of the conventional thought of awakening. How could it be the ultimate? Though all the sutras teach attainment of the fearless acceptance of the "unborn factors of existence" [that is, of ultimate reality], I have never heard of the attainment of the fearless acceptance of "born factors." Therefore what greater confusion could there be than to ritualize something that can have no ritual, to degrade the ultimate to the level of the conventional, to make that which is not born into something that is born, to force the inexpressible into expressions, and to make what cannot be objectified into an object?

A statement in the *Ornament of Mahayana Sutras* also refers to confusions of this kind:

> What is this sort of darkness, such that
> someone does not see the existent but sees the nonexistent?[51]

A person who has certain faults of vision does not see the existent visual object but instead sees such things as nonexistent hairs or perceives a white conch as yellow. Just so, the ignorant disregard the doctrinal systems of the scriptures explained in the religious teachings and the profound rituals, such as those of tantric initiations, and yet they generate the aspiring and engaging phases of the thought of awakening by visualizing meditation deities in the manner of the mantra tradition, a practice not prescribed in the scriptures. By doing things that the Buddha never taught, such as turning generation of the ultimate thought of awakening into a ritual involving the repetition of words, those people harm the doctrine. They are the ones who are mentioned here as being like people with poor vision who have entered into darkness. [261]

Under what conditions can generating the conventional and ultimate thoughts of awakening occur? [First, concerning the conventional thought of awakening,] the *Ornament of Mahayana Sutras* states:

> The power of a friend, the power of the cause, and the power of
> a root...[52]

And continuing to:

> This is held to be the generation of the thought of awakening
> that is shown by another.[53]

Thus it teaches the causes for the arising of generation of the conventional thought of awakening, which is correctly received by repeating after the master and comes forth from language.

Second, the causes for the arising of generation of the ultimate thought of awakening are also described in the *Ornament of Mahayana Sutras*:

> When the Perfectly Awakened One has been gladdened,
> when the accumulations of merit and gnosis have been intensively gathered,
> and when the gnosis arises that does not conceptualize phenomena,
> that is held to be ultimate.[54]

Thus generation of the ultimate thought of awakening is not dependent on what the master orally recites. By virtue of your gratifying the Buddha and gathering on a large scale the accumulations of merit and gnosis, after the highest worldly realization[55] you will experience the path of seeing, the gnosis that has no conceptualizing with respect to phenomena. This is called "generation of the ultimate thought of awakening." Unlike generation of the conventional thought of awakening, this does not depend on ritual acts for its generation, and so it is called "ultimate." Therefore, though generation of the conventional thought of awakening is shown by another, generation of the ultimate thought of awakening is realized by yourself.

The points to be practiced for generating the conventional thought of awakening in its two aspects—aspiration and engagement

There are two traditions of training: that upheld by the Yogācāra school and that upheld by the Madhyamaka. You should learn the points to be practiced of the Yogācāra school from treatises such as [Candragomin's] *Twenty Verses*, and therefore I will not discuss them here. The points to be practiced in the Madhyamaka system have two divisions: the points to be practiced for the aspiring thought of awakening and those for the engaging thought of awakening.

Training in the aspiring thought of awakening can be explained briefly, in medium detail, and in great detail. The point to be practiced in *briefest form* is simply to think: "I must attain buddhahood for the benefit of sentient beings." The points to be practiced in *medium detail* consist of understanding the causes of abandoning the aspiration and cultivating the antidotes to those causes. Three such causes need to be counteracted, of which the first is faintheartedness.

Abandoning the thought of awakening through faintheartedness

Some will think, "It is difficult for a person such as myself to achieve buddhahood in which the two preparatory accumulations are perfectly complete," and so will not apply themselves to the training in aspiration. The antidote to this is to take courage. For this you should reflect on these words of the *Ornament of Mahayana Sutras*:

> At every moment unlimited numbers
> of beings who are humans
> are attaining perfect awakening.
> Therefore do not indulge in faintheartedness.[56] [262]

Also ponder what is said in *Guide to the Bodhisattva Way of Life*:

> Even houseflies, horseflies, bees, and worms,
> should they develop a diligent attitude,
> will attain the unsurpassable awakening
> so hard to achieve.
>
> If I do not abandon the way of life of a bodhisattva,
> why shouldn't a person of my sort,
> who can distinguish benefit from harm,
> attain awakening?[57]

Moreover, consider the following examples. Once, long ago, there were seven worms on a leaf floating in the ocean. Driven by the wind, the leaf thrice circled a great image of Vairocana resting on the bottom of the ocean.

Owing to this, the worms were reborn as seven girls of low caste. Oppressed by their poverty and low station, they devoted themselves to accumulating merit by gathering grass and wood, working as servants [and then using their income for virtuous purposes]. Consequently they became in their next lifetimes the seven daughters of King Kṛkin, at which time they gratified Buddha Kāśyapa through their service and received from him the prophecy that they would attain buddhahood. Likewise, there was once a pig who, when chased by a dog, circumambulated a stūpa three times and as a result later attained arhatship.

There is also the story of the young brahman woman who offered a full begging bowl of cooked rice to the Buddha.[58] The Buddha foretold that by that merit she would in all future lives be reborn in fortunate realms and would in the end attain the awakening of a pratyekabuddha. Her husband, a young brahman, said to the Buddha, "O Gautama, having renounced your kingdom, you now face hard times, telling greedy lies for the sake of each bowl of rice."[59]

The Sage responded [by asking], "How big is a seed from the big nyagrodha tree in front of your gate?"

The man replied: "It is tinier than a mustard seed."

The Buddha said, "You should not lie." Thereupon the young brahman understood, and he beheld the truth.

Likewise, in the *Good Eon Sutra* the Buddha taught that by offering as little as an *arura* fruit, a torch made of grass, or a cake of dung, and then formally generating the thought of awakening, you will attain perfect buddhahood.[60] As the Buddha also said in the same sutra:

> Thus these are the fruitions of giving
> a small offering to the buddhas.
> If such are the fruits for a person in cyclic existence,
> what wise person would not generate the thought of
> awakening?[61]

Abandoning the thought of awakening through discouragement

Some foolish people become depressed and do not continue to practice virtuous deeds because, though they had previously acted virtuously, the results did not appear in the present visible world of this life. [263] For example, though practicing generosity, their wealth decreased; though adhering to strict moral discipline, unpleasant things such as a weakened body occurred; and though they exerted themselves in virtuous practices, they received no sustaining spiritual favor. Or, for the recovery of a sick person, they performed with others propitiative religious ceremonies such as the recitation of the scriptures, the offering of sacrificial cakes, *thun* ceremonies,[62] the reciting of mantras and so on, and Uṣṇīṣavijayā rituals. If they did so and the outcome of the illness was death, they say that those methods are not expedient and, becoming discouraged, they give up those things.

The antidote for this is to generate enthusiastic joy [for practicing], for as said in *Guide to the Bodhisattva Way of Life*:

> Mounted on the horse of the thought of awakening
> [that dispels all discouragement and fatigue]
> and going to greater and greater happiness,
> what wise person would become discouraged?[63]

Moreover, in general, seven circumstances exist in which death will occur: (1) when the life force is exhausted, (2) when the force of previous deeds is exhausted, (3) when the force of merit is exhausted, (4) the exhaustion of both 1 and 2, (5) the exhaustion of both 1 and 3, (6) the exhaustion of both 2 and 3, and (7) the exhaustion of all three.

For the exhaustion of life force, such things as the Uṣṇīṣavijayā ritual for prolonging longevity and the *Purification of All Evil Destinies Tantra*[64] will help. For the exhaustion of the power of past deeds, it is helpful to ransom the lives of animals that otherwise would surely be killed, to save and sustain those who would otherwise surely die, and so on.[65] When merit has been exhausted, there is the restoration of merit—namely, the repelling of unfavorable circumstances through such means as making worshipful offerings to the religious preceptor; practicing the propitiative rites to the Three Jewels—worshipful offerings to the Buddha, reciting the sacred scriptures, and acquiring merit [through offerings and service] to the Sangha; offering sacrificial cakes to the spirits; renouncing all material possessions as an antidote to attachment; taking medicines as an antidote to disease; practicing meditative concentration as an antidote to mental instability; and reciting the universally beneficial invocations of the sustaining power [of the Three Jewels] and of the auspicious coming together of circumstances.

For the three instances where two elements coincide, if it is the life force and past deeds whose force is exhausted, you should revive those two. If it is the life force and merit, then revive those. And if it is the force of deeds and merit that are becoming exhausted, those should be restored.

By doing as described above, you can restore life in the three cases where only one element is exhausted. If two are exhausted in combination, through great effort they can be revived. But if someone is dying as a result of the exhaustion of all three forces, there is no means to restore that person to further life. Like the smoke of an extinguished fire or the pool of a stream whose headwaters have dried up, even the Lord Buddha himself cannot avert it. Therefore, death that occurs despite the performance of all the propitiative methods is a sign that all three causes sustaining life have become exhausted.

Thus it is wrong to say that propitiative religious practices do not work and thereby give up your faith in them. How could you rightly discard such things as beds, saying they do not work because the patient died on a bed? Or give up houses, food, drink, and medicines, saying that these are not effective because the patient died in a house, or after eating, drinking, or taking medicine? [264] Similarly, [when death occurs,] it is that the forces that propel life have become exhausted and not that propitiative religious practices and roots of virtue are ineffective.

Furthermore, three kinds of former actions exist: those whose results are experienced in the present visible world, those whose results will be experienced after the next birth, and those whose results are experienced at another, even later time. Whether an action is virtuous or nonvirtuous, for its result to be experienced in the present life, an exceptional recipient, motivating thought, and object must be involved. As it is taught:

> Because of a particularly [special] recipient and motivating thought,
> there are acts whose fruit is experienced in the [present] visible world.[66]

If you commit an exceptional act of virtue or nonvirtue involving an especially excellent object, through an extremely good or evil motivation, and toward an exceptional recipient, then that action will give rise to a result in this life, which is called "the present visible world." People who commit such acts of virtue or nonvirtue are extremely rare. If a person commits a slightly weaker deed, that act will give rise to a result in the next life, a result "to be experienced after the next birth." An act of still smaller strength is a "deed whose result will be experienced at another, even later time."

Therefore, if a person who only commits evil deeds seems to experience inappropriate happiness, or if a person who only commits virtuous acts seems to experience inappropriate suffering, that is a sign of their reaping the results of acts that ripen in the next life or even later, and for this reason you should be very careful about moral cause and effect.

Abandoning the thought of awakening through dread of the faults of cyclic existence

Here you see the sufferings of birth, old age, sickness, and death and are vexed by the ingratitude of evil people you have treated well. You therefore abandon the thought of attaining awakening for the sake of all sentient beings because you despair of remaining in cyclic existence for many eons, just as, long ago, King Bhīmasena gave up his thought to attain awakening.[67]

There are antidotes to this dread. You can dispel it by understanding that these defiling personal aggregates (*skandha*) are like an illusion; by cultivating the attitude of love toward sentient beings that a parent has toward an only son; and by the discerning wisdom that perceives no difference between an eon and an instant and realizes that the three times—past, present, and future—are without time.[68]

Also, you will be able to avoid abandoning the thought of awakening by meditating on the religious preceptor and the tutelary deities and by means of prayers dedicating the roots of virtue. An example of this occurred in the life of the master Dignāga. When he was about to abandon the thought of awakening, he was prevented from doing so by his tutelary deity Ārya Mañjuśrī.[69] [265] [The teacher here] should appropriately elaborate about those things in more detail.

The explanation of the training in great detail

This has three main topics: the causes for the thought of awakening to arise, the conditions that cause its increase, and the methods for keeping it from declining.

The causes for the aspiring thought of awakening to arise. The thought of awakening arises from compassion, which desires that you and others be free of suffering, and from loving kindness, which desires that you and others attain happiness. Therefore you must exert yourself in the cultivation of those two. As is said in the *Ornament of Mahayana Sutras*:

Compassion's moisture is loving kindness,
and it perfectly arises from suffering.[70]

The conditions that increase the aspiring thought of awakening. Seven conditions cause the aspiring thought of awakening to grow stronger: (1) serving a true spiritual friend as your teacher, (2) producing longing and trusting faith in the Three Jewels, (3) knowing and avoiding deeds of the evil one (Māra), as mentioned in the sutras, (4) supplicating all the buddhas and bodhisattvas of the ten directions that the deeds of the evil one will not occur, (5) recognizing the benefits of the thought of awakening and the faults of cyclic existence and nirvana, (6) recalling the excellent qualities of the Buddha and bodhisattvas, such as their magical powers and their superknowledges, and (7) delighting in accomplishing the welfare of yourself and others.

Once you have thus cultivated these, you will see the faults of existence in the round of births and will wish to renounce your evil deeds. By seeing the faults of nirvana, a mental attitude that thirsts excessively for emptiness will be averted. By seeing the great benefits [of the thought of awakening] for yourself and others, you will not despair of cyclic existence, and by seeing the excellent qualities of the buddhas and bodhisattvas, you will delight in the immediate and ultimate fruits of spiritual practice. By devotedly supplicating the religious preceptor and the Three Jewels, the obstructing deeds of Māra, the Evil One, will not occur, while the sustaining spiritual power of the buddhas and bodhisattvas will quickly emerge in your life. In this way, through removing hindering conditions and achieving conducive ones, the thought of awakening will increase.

The methods for keeping the aspiring thought of awakening from declining. The Mahayana thought of awakening will decline if, lacking devotion to the teacher and the Three Jewels, you cannot bear—through anger and jealousy—to see the excellent attainments of others. [266] If you do not hold the welfare of others to be important and exert yourself only for your own happiness, it will decline. If, unable to make efforts at accomplishing the skillful means on a large scale, you are content merely with "recognition of and acquaintance with [the nature of] mind," it will decline.[71] And if you do not know the excellent qualities of the buddhas and bodhisattvas and are not energetic in seeking such qualities for yourself, it will decline. Therefore, as the antidote to the above, cultivate devotion, enthusiastic joy, and so forth in various suitable ways. This concludes the training in the aspiration to awakening.

The points to be practiced in the engaging thought of awakening

These can also be explained in three degrees of detail: briefly, in medium detail, and in great detail.

In *briefest* form, the discipline to be followed is to avoid evil and accomplish virtue to the full extent that you are able. If you commit evil deeds that you are powerless to avoid, those committed in the day should be renounced and confessed by that night, and those done in the night should be confessed by the next day. Every root of virtue that you make, even slight ones, should be dedicated to buddhahood for the benefit of sentient beings.

Moreover, as the Buddha said in the *Advice to a King* [*Sutra*]:

> O great king, you have so many duties and so many activities that you are not able to train day and night in all the perfections, from generosity to wisdom. Therefore, great king, you should constantly call to mind, hold in mind, and mentally cultivate faith, striving, and aspiration toward the perfect, complete awakening. You should delight in the virtuous deeds of others. Having delighted, you should offer [that merit] to all the buddhas, bodhisattvas, śrāvakas, and pratyekabuddhas. After offering it, you should share it with all sentient beings in general. Then, every day, you should dedicate the merit to unsurpassable awakening so that every sentient being will perfectly realize the qualities of the Buddha.
>
> O great king, if you act in this way, you can rule your domain, your royal duties will not suffer, and you will also bring to perfect completeness the preparatory accumulation for attaining awakening.[72]

The explanation in *medium detail* is to train yourself in avoiding the four negative factors and adopting the four positive factors. These are explained in the Heap of Jewels [collection of] sutras:

> If you possess four factors, you will forget the thought of awakening. What are these four? They are: to deceive the Teacher and those worthy of worship, [267] to cause others to regret deeds that are not really occasions for regret, to disparage and criticize sentient beings who have entered the Mahayana path, and to

> not have an altruistic motivation but conduct yourself wrongly toward others through deceit and pretense.[73]

The four positive factors:

> If you possess four qualities, you will acquire the thought of awakening in all lifetimes as soon as you are born and will not forget it. What are these four? Never deliberately telling a falsehood. Maintaining an altruistic attitude toward sentient beings without any deceit or pretense. Perceiving all bodhisattvas as being the Great Teacher and singing their correct praises everywhere. And in order to help bring sentient beings to spiritual maturity, encouraging others not to uphold a limited vehicle but to adhere correctly to unsurpassable awakening.[74]

You should train thereby in avoiding and in employing.

The explanation in great detail of these points to be practiced has three main parts. The first is a description of *the cause for the engaging thought of awakening to arise.* This consists of your practicing the aspiring thought of awakening and then seeking the means to increase this thought and avoid the causes of its decline. Cultivating an awareness of the sufferings of cyclic existence and the disadvantages of nirvana, this cause also consists of quickly liberating all sentient beings from cyclic existence and turning away from nirvana as you would from poisoned food.

The second main part is *the conditions that increase* [*the engaging thought of awakening*]. For this, you should three times daily and three times nightly call to mind the buddhas and bodhisattvas, together with your teacher, and then recite the seven branches of worship. You can practice this at greater length following such texts as the *Prayer of Excellent Conduct*,[75] the *Confession of Infractions for the Bodhisattva*,[76] the *Prayer of Maitreya*,[77] or the twenty verses of Ārya Nāgārjuna[78] or as in Śāntideva's *Guide to the Bodhisattva Way of Life*. If you are not able to do that much, then apply yourself energetically to the *Seven Branches of Worship* composed by Śākyaśrībhadra,[79] my master of monastic ordination, or my own *Liturgy of Ten Verses*.[80] Otherwise you should train as much as you can in the bodhisattva's way of life as described in various Jātaka stories.[81]

The third main part of the detailed explanation involves *the methods for keeping the engaging thought of awakening from declining.* [268] For this you should prevent from arising—and generate the opposite of—the root infractions mentioned in the *Sky Essence Sutra*[82] and the root and branch infractions mentioned in such sutras as those in the Heap of Jewels collection.[83] Also train yourself in various methods of purifying evil deeds and infractions, such as reciting the hundred-syllable mantra of the tathāgata.[84]

4. The Perfection of Generosity

THE FOURTH KEY PHRASE from the *Ornament of Mahayana Sutras*, "accomplishing [the perfections of] generosity and the rest,"[85] refers to two main topics: practicing the six perfections, which brings about your own perfect attainment of the qualities of buddhahood, and practicing the four means of attraction, which brings about the spiritual maturation of other sentient beings.

The six perfections. To explain the practice of the six perfections, three topics are treated: the general definition of the perfections, their analysis,[86] and the Sanskrit etymology of the name of each perfection.

The *general definition* of the perfections is "the means that liberates you to the far shore of cyclic existence and nirvana."

The analysis of the perfections involves three topics: the common characteristic possessed by the things under analysis, how they are divided, and establishing that division as fixed.

Their common characteristic [as "perfections"] from which the division [into six] can be made is "a special method for achieving perfect buddhahood."

How they are divided. The perfections are divided into six, of which the first is the perfection of generosity.[87]

* * *

To understand the *perfection of generosity*, three topics require discussion: the definition of generosity, ascertaining the nature of generosity, and the benefits of practicing generosity.

The definition of generosity is "to give away an object that you possess because it will benefit another." If such an act is complete in terms of correct preparation, actual accomplishment, and conclusion, it will be the perfection of having practiced generosity.

Ascertaining the nature of generosity involves three points: identifying the antithesis of generosity, discerning the individual antidotes, and correctly accomplishing that generosity.

Identifying the antithesis of generosity

To begin with, three things oppose the correct act of generosity: (1) you are unable to give to others because of stinginess, (2) though you can give, you give in a way that is impure generosity, and (3) though your giving is not mixed with impure generosity, your giving is not a cause of attaining perfect buddhahood.

Second, reflect on the two types of harm that those bring about. First of all, they cause harm *in this life*. The whole world will scorn you. [269] As the Ārya [Nāgārjuna] said:

> By partaking of wealth you obtain happiness in this life.
> By giving wealth you obtain happiness in another life.
> From wasting it, without either enjoying it or giving it,
> there is only suffering. How could it be happiness?[88]

Also, reflect on the sense of the verses that I composed on this topic:

> The fool experiences only the suffering of gathering [wealth],
> but he never experiences the happiness of its enjoyment.
> The wealth that he greedily keeps, constantly scurrying about
> and watching,
> is like that of a rat.[89]

And:

> Wealth that can be taken and used at the time of need
> was taught by the Buddha to be true generosity.
> Wealth that is stored will, like honey,
> someday be enjoyed by others.[90]

The second kind of harm that these factors bring about is to destroy happiness *in all future lives*. On this, the *Verse Summary of the Perfection of Wisdom* teaches:

> Stingy people will be born in the realm of hungry spirits.
> And even if they are born as humans, they will be poor.[91]

Hence it is impossible for stingy people to attain a full measure of any attainment or happiness. Even though they perform some imperfect act of generosity, like a seed planted in a salty field, that act will not yield a fruit.[92] Even if a small result is obtained, like a spoonbill water fowl who finds a dead fish, partaking of it will not be conducive to happiness. And even if it leads to slight happiness, like the ripening of the fruit of the plantain tree, it will exhaust itself in either the extreme of cyclic existence or the extreme of nirvana.

Discerning the individual antidotes

The antidote to the cause of stinginess. The cause of stinginess is attachment to material things. Therefore you should mentally cultivate and realize its opposite. For this, reflect on the words of the *Guide to the Bodhisattva Way of Life*:

> Because of the torments of collecting, guarding, and losing it,
> you should know that wealth is an endless cause of harm.
> For those who are attached to wealth and distracted [by gaining
> and keeping it],
> there is no way to become free from the sufferings of existence.[93]

Also consider the following intermediary verse on this topic:[94]

> When you have no wealth, you are poor because of needing to
> seek it.
> If you get a little bit, you are poor because it is too little.
> If you get a lot, you are poor because you are not satisfied.
> To partake of wealth without satisfaction is a cause for
> suffering.

Here [the teacher] should tell the story of how the kings Amitayaśas and Māndhātā were not satisfied even though they ruled as emperor the four great continents, the sun and the moon, and even the heavens, up to and including the divine realm of the Thirty-Three (Trāyastriṃśa). The moment they conceived the intention, "Still, I must seize the entire wealth of Śakra [the king of gods, Indra]," their merit was exhausted and they fell to earth.[95] [270]

The antidote to the result. Owing to the cause, attachment to material things, the result of stinginess arises. The antidote that can dispel this is generosity. There are three classes of generous acts. As explained in the *Questions of Upāli Sutra*, these are the generosity practiced by a bodhisattva who has taken monastic ordination, the generosity of a lay bodhisattva, and the generosity of the advanced bodhisattva who has attained fearless patience toward the birthless factors of existence (*dharmas*).[96]

The generosity to be practiced by an ordained bodhisattva mainly entails the giving of fearlessness, love, and religious teaching. On the giving of material things, the Buddha taught that ordained people could give ink, pens, and paper. But he did not teach that they should nurture others through the giving of wealth in a big way.

Yet the Lord Buddha, too, in previous lives, when he was a layman with such positions as king, minister, householder, or merchant, did practice the generous giving of material things. And when he was a bodhisattva in his final existence, during his childhood [as Prince Siddhārtha], when playing he used to give others the things he possessed. Later, when he ordained himself by the bank of the Nairañjanā River, he sent his horse and jewelry back to his very wealthy father, Śuddhodana. Also, when the farmer's daughter Sujātā offered him food in a golden vessel, he returned the golden vessel to the girl. When she offered it again, requesting that he accept it out of compassion for her, he took it and then cast it into the waters of the Nairañjanā. Because of this, some tīrthikas even considered that Gautama was bad with wealth, saying, "It would have been more suitable to give the horse and jewelry to the poor than to the king, since the king did not lack for wealth. And to not give the golden vessel to the poor but to throw it into the river was a waste."

What the Lord Buddha had in mind when doing so was that if you give the highest kind of wealth to a recipient who is not of the highest sort, though that inferior recipient may benefit slightly in his physical circumstances in this life, ultimately he will go to the lower realms because he is unable to make good use of that wealth. Hence it is not right for a bodhisattva to create a cause that will send a poor person to the lower realms.

Indeed, if an ordained person fosters others by great acts of generosity, this will be an obstacle to his or her own learning, reflection, and realization through meditation. Hence the Buddha taught that an ordained person should not be attached to material things, and that it is the ordained person who fosters others not through generosity but through moral discipline, meditative absorption, and wisdom who accords with the doctrine of the Buddha.

Therefore in the sutras the Buddha taught that monks can give only the food remaining in their begging bowls and did not teach the giving of other things. Though ordained people are suitable recipients of offerings and worship from the entire world, including the gods, they are not donors. [271] Consequently, if you reverse the positions of donor and religious teacher, this will be the cause of famines and other deteriorations of conditions in the world.

The generosity to be practiced by a lay bodhisattva has two topics: how to perform acts of generosity and the method for training in those acts.

How to perform acts of generosity

There are three stages for learning generosity: at first, to free yourself from the inability to give, train in giving just a little; next, for those who are able to give, avoid impure acts of generosity and train in pure acts of giving; and lastly, to prevent even pure acts of generosity from failing to become causes of buddhahood, train in turning them into causes of buddhahood.

To free yourself from the inability to give, first *train in small acts of giving*:

> The Great Guide at the start encourages
> the giving of [small things] such as cooked vegetables.
> Later, after you have become accustomed to giving those,
> you will gradually [become able to] give even your own flesh.
>
> When you are able to produce a perception
> of your own body as being something like cooked vegetables,
> then what will be the difficulty of offering
> your flesh and so forth?[97]

So it was stated in the *Guide to the Bodhisattva Way of Life*. It is also said in the *Skill in Means Sutra*, "Beginners should first train in giving merely small cups of water."[98]

For those who can give, *avoid impure acts of generosity and train in pure generosity.* Many acts of generosity become causes for rebirth in cyclic existence and in lower realms because some people, though they give, do not know how to recognize what is a pure and what is an impure act of generosity. Therefore avoid those impure gifts and practice pure generosity. Here I summarize in verse the teachings of the *Questions of Ṛṣi Vyāsa Sutra* about the thirty-two kinds of impure generosity:[99]

> Giving (1) through wrong views and no faith, (2) in reply for help, (3) to water, (4) to fire, (5) to a king, (6) to free yourself from fear, (7) poison, (8) weapons, (9) meat from slaughter or (10) intoxicating beverages, (11) for the sake of gathering followers or (12) being praised, (13) to musicians or (14) to astrologers, (15) the wealth of others to loved ones, (16) the grain of another person to feed [wild animals], (17) to artisans, (18) to doctors for [curing you from] disease, (19) after [angering someone by] scolding,[100] (20) [while doubting that] a positive result will be experienced, (21) followed by regret, (22) hoping the recipient will afterward return it to you, (23) hoping the positive result will be experienced by yourself alone; making offerings at another's urging when you are (24) old, (25) sick, or (26) dying; giving (27) for the sake of attaining fame in other lands, (28) to demonstrate that you dare to give, (29) to obtain a woman or (30) [merely] because you have no sons, (31) to receive wealth in a future life, or (32) to the wealthy while excluding the poor—these thirty-two kinds of impure generosity were explained in the *Questions of Ṛṣi Vyāsa Sutra* and therefore should be avoided.

Having thus distinguished pure from impure acts of generosity, avoid the impure and train in the pure. [272]

Turn all pure acts of generosity into causes of awakening. Some acts of pure generosity do not become causes for attaining buddhahood. For example, some roots of virtue result in a full measure of excellent attainments for gods or humans—the beings in the higher realms of existence—while others become the cause for attaining the nirvana of the śrāvaka or the pratyekabuddha. To prevent this, train in making all acts of giving, no matter how trifling, into causes for quickly attaining perfect buddhahood. Do this by suppressing the extreme of nirvana through skillful means; by suppressing the extreme of cyclic existence through discerning wisdom; and by quickly bringing to perfect completion both means and discerning wisdom through the power of energetic application. As said in a sutra:

> Whoever is doing or has done acts of service
> for the Conqueror, the Great Guide,
> will pass through various lives in the higher realms
> and [ultimately] attain the place of immortality.[101]

Training in acts of generosity

To train in acts of generosity, lay bodhisattvas should practice both mental aspiration and how to do the deed.

First, to *practice mental aspiration*, whenever you see someone who begs, generate an expanded perception of the situation, thinking with happiness, "I will bring to completeness the perfection of generosity," "I will plant a seed from which to reap in future lives wealth that knows no exhaustion," "These [beggars] are emanations of the buddhas and bodhisattvas," "I will make them happy with me," "I will attain great fame in the whole human and divine world," and "To achieve the welfare of sentient beings, I must attract others through such means of attraction as this." For as it is taught in the *Ornament of Mahayana Sutras*,

> The sight of a beggar and fulfilling [his wishes] bring
> gladness...[102]

and as the Buddha proclaimed in sutras:

> When you see beggars,
> perceive them as being the Buddha.[103]

Second, the lay bodhisattva should *train in actual acts* of generosity with respect to three things: the recipient, the time, and the thing given.

Training with respect to the recipient. Some people, because of individual differences in mentality, are able to give only to certain recipients and not to others. For instance, some can bring themselves to make an offering to their religious teacher but not to others. Some can bring themselves to make offerings only to the Buddha, some are able to sponsor recitation of the scriptures, some can offer respectful service to the Sangha, and some can bring themselves to give only to the poor. Therefore, first fully develop your generosity toward those to whom you feel able to give, and then gradually train in also giving to those to whom you feel unable to give. [273]

Training with respect to time. Some cannot bring themselves to give continually but can practice acts of generosity only on special occasions. Those people, too, should first concentrate on giving at special times and then train in giving on other occasions. How should they train? First they should practice giving whatever they receive during just half the daylight hours of a single day. When they are accustomed to that, they should practice giving whatever they receive during the full daylight period of a single day. When they are used to that, then for a full day and night. When they are accustomed to that, they should practice giving whatever they receive for a single month, and after becoming used to that, for a full year, and so on, thus gradually extending the period of time in which generosity is practiced.

Training with respect to the thing given. Begin by giving a small cup of drink, a bowl of cooked vegetables, a piece of bread, a single strand of thread, or a patch of cloth. Even for each small thing, you should think that this is a great act of generosity. You should think, "Through this act of giving, may I attain buddhahood for the benefit of all sentient beings!" And you should formally aspire: "May I come to possess in the future the ability to give all beings whatever they desire!"

Compared with giving nothing, even to give a single cup of water is quite gracious. Compared with quarreling, even giving nothing is quite gracious. Compared with robbing, even to quarrel is quite gracious. Compared with killing, even fighting and beating are quite gracious.[104] In brief, if you abandon self-righteous pride, you will feel aversion toward no one and will accordingly feel joy in these deeds, [however small,] and they will become causes for your thought of awakening to not decline.

Therefore your mind will become adept at giving food to those who desire food, clothing to those who desire clothing, medicine to those who desire medicine, flower garlands to those who desire garlands, and so on, up to giving wealth to those who desire wealth, as explained in the sutras.[105] But until you have attained fearless acceptance of the birthless factors of existence, you should not give away your head, feet, arms, and so forth, even if you dare to do so. For as the *Guide to the Bodhisattva Way of Life* explains:

> You should not give away for a trifling purpose
> this body that practices the noble Dharma.
> By acting so [by not giving it], the hopes of sentient beings
> will be quickly fulfilled.[106]
>
> As long as your compassion is impure,
> you should not give away this body.
> By all means, you should use it
> to accomplish a great purpose in this and future lives.[107]

Some say that after producing the thought of applying yourself to attaining awakening, you must give away whatever is requested of you. These people say that as long as you are not able to give whatever is asked, you must maintain secrecy [about your vow], because it will damage your generating the thought of awakening if you do not give something. Such people are ignorant of the divisions of the scriptures. It is a poor method to put your hope in secrecy as a means of protecting the thought of awakening. [274]

The generosity to be practiced by an advanced bodhisattva who has attained fearless acceptance of the birthless factors of existence is of three special kinds: renunciation, renunciation to a high degree, and great renunciation.[108] The first is to give up rulership of your domain. The second is to give away those dear to you, such as your son or wife. The third is to give away part or all of your body, such as a gift of your head, legs, or arms. With this in mind, the Buddha taught at great length in the *Perfection of Wisdom* the passage beginning:

> When through skillful means you have completely perfected the perfection of generosity, you will attain the body of a great person, such as a universal emperor, and will say, "Take all my possessions from me and give them away in acts of generosity. Observe moral discipline...."[109]

And later in that passage it reads:

> If [after giving away my body] I have no attachment even toward this physical body, it goes without saying I will have none toward external objects of wealth.[110]

Some apply this scriptural passage to the generosity to be practiced by ordained bodhisattvas. Those people have simply not understood the intended sense of the sutras.

Now you should think about—and [the teacher] should also teach to others—the import of the accounts in the Jātakas about Viśvāntara's bestowing his son and daughter on a brahman as his servants,[111] the Śivi king's giving his eye to a blind man,[112] the hare's gift of his body to a wandering brahman,[113] and so forth, and also what is related in the sutras about King Candraprabha's gift of his head to a brahman,[114] King Kanakavarṇa,[115]

[King Śrīsena's] cutting his body in half at the waist and giving it away,[116] and so forth.

Correctly accomplishing generosity

This has two parts: achieving the four excellent qualities and eliminating the seven attachments.

Achieving the four excellent qualities is mentioned in the *Ornament of Mahayana Sutras*: [275]

> Generosity is the annulment of its antithesis,
> the possession of nondiscursive gnosis,
> the fulfilling of all the desires of others,
> and the maturing of sentient beings in three ways.[117]

Hence, as previously explained,[118] these four qualities are: (1) freeing yourself of stinginess, (2) realizing the nondiscursive, the absence of a substantial self in either a person or in phenomena, (3) fulfilling all the wishes of others by granting whatever others desire that accords with the Dharma, and (4) maturing sentient beings in three ways—attracting others through generosity and establishing them according to their capacities in one of the three vehicles: Śrāvaka, Pratyekabuddha, or the Mahayana.

Eliminating the seven attachments is also taught:

> The generosity of a bodhisattva should be unattached,
> not attached, without attachment,
> not attached at all, unattached,
> not attached, and without attachment.[119]

Thus this entails eliminating the attachments to: (1) wealth, (2) procrastination, putting things off until later, (3) feeling satisfied after only achieving a little, (4) the hope of getting something in return, (5) the future result of a deed in a later life, (6) the antitheses of generosity, such as not wishing to rid of oneself of stinginess and the like, and (7) distractions. The last includes two types of distractions: *the distraction of attention*, which is to take pleasure in the Hinayana, and *the distraction of conceptual thinking*, which is to be conceptually attached to the three spheres in the act of giving [that is, the giver, recipient, and the thing given]. I might summarize the above with this concluding verse:

Attachment to wealth, postponement, and satisfaction,
to hopes of something in return, and to future results,
to the opposed factors, and to the distractions—
these a wise person should be rid of.

The benefits of generosity

The benefits of generosity are of two types: those that are temporary and those that are ultimate. The *temporary benefits* [are felt both in this life and in later lives].

In this life, by making sentient beings happy by your generosity, you will attain wealth, a good name, fame, glorious attainments, and happiness in full measure. As the *Guide to the Bodhisattva Way of Life* teaches:

> Why do I not see that—
> regardless of the future attainment of buddhahood—
> in this very life gaining glorious wealth, fame, and happiness
> come from pleasing sentient beings?[120]

And as the *Ornament of Mahayana Sutras* teaches:

> Even though a donor does not desire wealth, he will meet with exceedingly bountiful and excellent wealth.[121] [276]

The benefits of generosity to be realized *in all future lives* include such inestimable benefits as attaining whatever you desire, this being the type of result in which what you experience agrees with the causing deed; becoming daring enough to give others whatever they desire, this being the type of result in which your future actions agree with the causing deed; and never being born in lands with barren and rough landscapes, in times of famine, or in similar bad circumstances.

And as the *Verse Summary of the Perfection of Wisdom* teaches:

> Through generosity, the bodhisattva cuts off going to a future
> life as a hungry spirit.
> He cuts off poverty and likewise all emotional afflictions.
> When he practices this generosity, he will attain infinite and
> vast wealth.[122]

As for the *ultimate benefits,* when you become a buddha, an ocean-like assembly of followers will gather from both the mundane and supramundane spheres. You will receive worshipful offerings arising from the virtuous roots of both these spheres and will attain immeasurably vast excellent qualities, such as mastery of the meditative absorption of the "sky treasury."[123]

5. The Perfection of Moral Discipline

THE EXPLANATION OF the perfection of moral discipline has three topics: the definition of moral discipline, ascertaining its nature, and the benefits of observing moral discipline.

The definition of moral discipline is abstaining from moral misdeeds in order to benefit others. If that moral discipline is endowed with correct preparation, actual action, and conclusion, it becomes the perfection of moral discipline.

Ascertaining the nature of moral discipline has three parts: identifying the antithesis of moral discipline, discerning the individual antidotes, and correctly accomplishing moral discipline.

Identifying the antithesis of moral discipline

There are three possible types of faulty moral discipline: (1) you are unable to keep any vows; (2) even though you can keep vows, your efforts at moral discipline are misdirected, like the tīrthikas; and (3) though not misdirected, your moral discipline, like that of the śrāvakas, is not a cause for attaining perfect buddhahood.

Next, *reflect on the harm that deficient moral discipline causes*: the harm it causes in the present life and its destruction of excellent attainments in all lifetimes.

In this life, a person of deficient moral discipline will be despised by the whole world of humans and gods. Moreover, people of corrupt moral discipline will themselves feel shame when in the presence of the religious preceptor and the Three Jewels. They will feel anxious about joining in the ranks of the Sangha, they will feel reluctant about accepting the faithful offerings of patrons, all humans will scorn them, all nonhuman demons will create obstacles, all gods will not offer protection, and all buddhas and bodhisattvas will view them with disfavor.

Deficient moral discipline destroys the possibility of excellent attainments *in all future lives*. As the *King of Meditation Sutra* teaches:

> He who has corrupt moral discipline will go to the lower realms,
> and much learning will not be able to save him.[124] [277]

Therefore, in general it is impossible for a person of corrupt moral discipline to attain a happy existence in the future. The Buddha taught that by breaking even a subordinate part of the moral discipline, you will be reborn in the realm of nāgas. Even if you escape from the miserable lower realms and are born in a higher existence, everything undesirable—such as a short lifespan—will befall you as a human. As it is taught:

> Because of killing others, your life will be short.
> Because you stole, you will lack wealth.
> Because of sexual misconduct, you will have many enemies.
> Because of lying, you will be slandered.
> Because of covetous thoughts, your hopes will be crushed.
> Because of harmful thoughts, suffering will arise.
> The primary result of all this for humans is to go to the miserable lower realms of existence.[125]

At this point [the teacher] should tell stories about people who were born in hells after committing the ten nonvirtuous deeds[126] and about the birth of Elapatra, king of the nāgas, after breaking a subsidiary part of the moral discipline.[127]

Discerning the individual antidotes

This involves two steps, the first of which is ascertaining *the antidote to the cause of deficient moral discipline*. The cause of breaking moral discipline is predominantly the afflictions (*kleśa*), so we must discuss the two types of antidotes effective against them, [partial suppresssion and eradication].

Partial suppression is the first antidote to the afflictions. On this the *Questions of Subāhu Tantra* teaches, for instance:

> Those in whom desire predominates should remove it by viewing

> [the object of desire] as excrement, fat, skin, or a skeleton.
> For anger, there is the [cooling] water of love.
> Bewilderment by [understanding] the path of interdependence.
> For pride, there is the differentiations of the elements.[128]

Eradication. The antidote that completely eradicates the afflictions is as taught in the *Thorough Exposition of Valid Cognition*:

> The view of emptiness will free you.
> The remaining meditations are for that purpose.[129]

And as the Ārya Nāgārjuna said:

> Ignorance ceases through knowledge
> of just this [ultimate reality] through meditation.
> Though the cessation of this and that [link],
> this and that [remaining link] will not arise.[130]

Therefore familiarize yourself with the meditative absorption on emptiness.

The antidote to the result. Based on the afflictions, incorrect apperceptions [such as seeing something impure as pure] occur, and mental and verbal offenses against moral discipline arise from these. The countermeasures to the arising of deficient moral discipline are three: the moral discipline of the vows, the moral discipline of gathering virtuous factors, and the moral discipline of benefitting other sentient beings.

The *moral discipline of the vows* has two parts: the vows of individual liberation (*prātimokṣa*) and the vows of the bodhisattva. [278]

The prātimokṣa vows

This also has two divisions: those to be trained in by bodhisattvas with vows of lay ordination and those to be trained in by ordained bodhisattvas.

Lay ordinations in the prātimokṣa system. The levels of ordination for lay followers in the individual liberation system of vows begin with "lay followers (*upāsaka* or *upāsikā*) who adhere to the Three Refuges," namely, those who have taken refuge in the Three Jewels and who observe other precepts merely as vows of limited duration (*upavāsa*). Next are the "lay followers who observe a single precept," namely, those who have taken the vow against killing. Those who also renounce stealing become "lay followers who observe some precepts." Those who also renounce lying and thus observe three vows are "lay followers who observe the majority [of precepts]." Those who in addition renounce sexual misconduct and drinking alcoholic beverages are "those who have taken the complete lay ordination." The latter are also those referred to in a sutra as "lay followers who rely on no other teacher [than the Buddha] and who practice the ten virtuous deeds."[131]

[Objection:] Here there is a contradiction, because lay followers who possess the complete ordination have to avoid the ten nonvirtuous deeds and accomplish the ten virtuous deeds, but they only take upon themselves five vows [rather than ten].

[Reply]: By observing the five vows, they implicitly observe all ten. When you give up killing, by implication you also give up harmful thoughts. In abstaining from stealing, you implicitly abstain from covetous thoughts. In giving up lying, you also implicitly give up slander, prattle, and harsh speech. And taking the lay follower's ordination indicates trust in the working of moral causation (*karma*), which is by implication the avoidance of wrong views.

In actual fact, the ordained lay follower accepts ten basic precepts (*śikṣāpada*). But the Buddha taught only five basic precepts of lay ordination to avoid scaring disciples off with that large number. For as the *Eight Verses on the Vows of Lay Ordination* teaches:

> The [ordination] ritual with five branches is held [to have been established]
> for the sake of introducing [disciples into the ten precepts].[132]

I have heard that some people say that the vows of the lay adherent entail the formal acceptance of a vow to avoid wrong views, but these people are simply ignorant of the scriptures.

The Vaibhāṣika school of the śrāvakas does not mention any additional classes of lay ordination. But the Sautrāntikas hold that there is also another class of lay ordination: the celibate lay adherent. For that they base themselves on this scriptural passage:

> Though ornamented with jewelry, he practices Dharma,
> he is controlled, is perfectly restrained, and is of celibate conduct.
> He avoids harmful acts toward all beings.
> That one is a [true] monk, ascetic, and brahman.[133]

Also, followers of the Ārya Sthavira school say that they have received orally transmitted instructions of the Ārya Sthavira lineage that state: "You become a cleric layman (*go mi'i dge bsnyen*) by accepting the eight-branched precepts of limited duration (*upavāsa*) for as long as you live," and thus maintain the existence of lay clerics.[134] [279] The Mahayana schools also accept this point. The Heap of Jewels collection of sutras explains that the prince Mahākaruṇācintin took the eight-branched precepts of limited duration for as long as he lived, but this was not termed a "lay cleric ordination."[135] The word *gomin* ("cleric layman") is Sanskrit. About [the etymololgy of the root *go* in] this word, scholars of Sanskrit say:

> Learned scholars should ascertain
> the word *go* in nine senses:
> voice, sky, earth, light ray, ox,
> eye, vajra, heaven, and water.[136]

The word would become too limited in its reference were it translated into Tibetan, which is the reason for leaving the word *gomin* in Sanskrit, just as the name Gautama was.[137]

The *Vinaya Sutra* [of Guṇaprabha] is a scripture belonging to the Sarvāstivādins, so it does not teach either the "celibate" (*brahmacarya*) or *gomin* levels of lay ordination. This is the reason the upholders of the Vinaya ordinations in Tibet did not receive the rituals for these two ordinations. Because those two have renounced the taking of a spouse, they are included within the category "ordained." But because they have not performed the "intermediate" (*bar ma*) ritual of ordination, some basic texts refer to them as "half-ordained."

Here I will not describe the results that ensue from the merit [of keeping the vows] and from the demerit [of breaking them] because I fear that such a discussion would make this book too long.

The points to be practiced by ordained bodhisattvas. You should understand the rules of the novice and of the fully ordained monk from their explanations in the Vinaya. If those monastic rules are not endowed with the thought of awakening and the pure perception of the three elements involved in the act [that is, yourself the doer, the other person affected by your moral discipline, and the thing involved in the act], they will belong to the śrāvaka school. But if those things are present and you practice [moral discipline] for the benefit of others, it becomes the individual liberation system of the bodhisattva.

The vows of the bodhisattva

After formally generating the thought of awakening in either the Madhyamaka or Yogācāra tradition, train yourself in that tradition's own rules of discipline. As general rules for both traditions, train in avoiding the four negative factors and in cultivating the four positive factors, as explained above [in the chapter on generating the resolve to attain awakening].

The practice [of moral discipline] can also be explained in both brief and expanded forms. To explain briefly, there are the trainings with respect to three things: the object of the action, the time of the action, the nature of the nonvirtuous deed.

Let me explain the *practice with respect to the object of the action* by taking the ten nonvirtuous deeds as examples. For the objects of the first of the ten nonvirtues, killing—namely, a person, an animal, or some other animate being—first practice not killing those with whom you live. Then, when you are accustomed to that, expand your practice and train in not killing any humans or animals at all. [280] Likewise for stealing: first train in not taking the wealth of those with whom you have close connections (such as relatives), the wealth of your neighbors, and so on. Then expand the practice to include all others. Likewise for lying and the rest; you should understand how to practice by applying the same method to the other nonvirtuous deeds as well.

The practice with respect to time. Train in abstaining from the ten nonvirtuous deeds by gradually accustoming yourself to longer and longer periods of practice. First practice observing moral discipline for a period lasting half the daylight hours, then for the full period of daylight, then for periods lasting a full day and night. Then you should practice for a half month at a time, for a full month, and so on, until you are observing the training for a year at a time.

For *the practice with respect to the nature of the nonvirtuous deed* itself, begin by abstaining singly from whichever of the ten nonvirtues you can. Then practice abstaining from two at a time, three at a time, and so forth, until you can abstain from all ten. Furthermore, practice first avoiding severe evil deeds and infractions, then avoid those of medium severity, until finally you train in abstention from very subtle deeds.

As to how to rectify a moral fault if one occurs: for infractions that are to be confessed within the period of a single watch [of four hours], confess them before that period has passed. As my spiritual master, the Dharma lord, the great master of Sakya [Drakpa Gyaltsen] said, "Just as the great ocean will not retain a corpse, so the practitioner of religion must not retain a moral infraction." Therefore, when you are about to go to sleep, check whether an infraction did or did not occur during the day. If it did not, delight in that and dedicate the merit to the attainment of buddhahood. If an infraction did occur, instill in yourself feelings of shame and remorse, and without delay confess them. Do not sleep without purifying the fault. Do likewise when you get up the next morning, and train in not breaking your fast without confessing your faults. As the *Excellent Accomplishment Tantra* teaches:

> Heedless deeds committed by day
> should be individually confessed at night,
> those commited in the evening confessed the next morning.
> Take great pleasure in good deeds.[138]

If a religious person becomes habituated to practicing in this way, he or she will become like the great ocean [which is said not to retain anything impure, such as a corpse, for longer than a day]. Also, the statement in a sutra that a noble person (*satpuruṣa*) has two main activites—to prevent committing moral infractions and to rectify those that he has committed—was taught with this in mind.[139]

When teaching or practicing this, call to mind such stories as the one about Devaputra, who broke the subsidiary precepts, as related in the Upavāsa section of the Vinaya scriptures.[140] On the subject of killing, also employ Jātaka stories such as the one about Supāraga.[141] Likewise, understand the benefits of observing the rest of the ten virtuous deeds and the harmful results of not observing them by introducing here appropriate accounts related in the Jātakas or in the sutras.[142]

The moral discipline of gathering virtuous factors consists of persistent attention (*sems pa*) to abstaining from the nonvirtuous factors together with their bases in order to accomplish the virtuous factors. [281] To analyze the training: it is to practice, in whatever ways are suitable, the gathering of virtuous factors, beginning with taking refuge and going all the way to the excellent qualities of buddhahood. As it is said in my *Jewel Treasure of Aphorisms*,

> Every day you should memorize
> a single phrase from a requisite treatise.

> Like [the forming of] an ant hill or like honey,
> before long you will become learned.[143]

Likewise, you should avoid—as much as someone on your own spiritual level can—those factors that are opposed to virtue. Whatever individual faults occur, confess those evil deeds and moral infractions in accordance with their own system [of discipline].

The moral discipline of benefitting other sentient beings consists of persistent attention to avoiding things opposed to achieving the welfare of others along with the conditions that lead to such acts. If it brings about the welfare of others, you may commit even the four defeats,[144] even though this may go against the moral discipline of the vows. Examples are such cases as the brahman Jyotis[145] and the greatly compassionate sea captain.[146] Also, if it brings about the welfare of others, you may even abandon your moral discipline of gathering virtuous factors, as was done, for instance, by the bodhisattva Supuṣpacandra[147] and by Indra.[148]

Correctly accomplishing moral discipline

This has two parts: achieving the four excellent qualities and eliminating the seven attachments.

Achieving the four excellent qualities. These have been taught in the lines beginning: "Moral discipline causes the destruction of the thing opposed to it...."[149] Accordingly, these excellent qualities are: (1) discarding deficient moral discipline, the antithesis, (2) realizing the nondiscursive, the absence of a substantial self, (3) perfectly fulfilling all the wishes of others by being tamed physically, verbally, and mentally among them through moral discipline, and (4) maturing sentient beings by establishing them in the three vehicles, having gladdened them through your moral discipline.

Eliminating the seven attachments is also explained in the lines beginning: "The moral discipline of the bodhisattva is unattached...."[150] These seven are to be abandoned: attachment to (1) deficient moral discipline, the antithesis of correct moral discipline, (2) procrastination, (3) premature satisfaction [with your moral discipline], (4) the hope of getting something in return, (5) the future result of a deed, (6) the latent propensities antithetical to moral discipline that have not yet been destroyed, and (7) the two distractions, which should be understood as explained above.[151] [282] Abandon these seven attachments together with the propensities toward them.

The benefits of observing moral discipline

There are two types of benefits, temporary and ultimate. The *temporary benefits* of moral discipline are twofold: those occurring in the present life and those occurring in future lives. The benefits of moral discipline realized *in this life* encompass inestimable excellent qualities, such as, by dwelling in moral discipline, you come to have no regrets in the present life. By virtue of that, your mind is happy and composed, and this becomes the cause for the three kinds of discerning wisdom. For as the *King of Meditation Sutra* teaches:

> The king of meditative absorptions, this meditation on emptiness,
> rests on the head of those of pure moral discipline,
> those who always meditate on the [empty] nature of phenomena;
> the childish who exert improperly do not understand this.[152]

Furthermore, the sutras proclaim the inestimable virtues of moral discipline, such as that the fame of your beautiful scent of pure moral discipline will pervade every direction, that the alms round in a city will be made meaningful, that you will receive worshipful offerings of the whole world of humans and gods, and that you will be beautiful and glorious amid an assembly.[153]

Regarding the benefits realized *in all future lives*, it is taught:

> Through faith you will not be born in circumstances lacking in
> freedom [to practice Dharma].
> Through moral discipline you will be born in an excellent
> existence.[154]

Accordingly, you will be born in higher realms of existence that possess seven excellent qualities. These I may express in the following verse, which summarizes the content of the *Discourse Explaining Seven Qualities*:

> Possessing good family, beautiful body, great wealth, fully endowed with intelligence, possessing power, free from illness, and having very great longevity—these are explained as the "seven excellent qualities of the higher existences."[155]

By correctly observing moral discipline, you will attain such excellent qualities wherever you are born in future lifetimes. As the *Verse Summary of the Perfection of Wisdom* teaches:

> Through moral discipline, one avoids rebirth as many of the animals
> and the eight human circumstances without freedom; one
> attain [all ten] favorable endowments.[156]

Ultimate benefits. When you attain perfect buddhahood, you will become famed as "the great teacher of all human and divine worlds" throughout all worlds exceeding the bounds of space. Because of your pure activities of awakened body, speech, and mind, you will attain the three freedoms from having to guard [your physical, verbal, and mental acts], that is, freedom from having to think about concealing anything because others will find out about it. You will also achieve inestimable excellent qualities, such as those explained in the *Ornament of Mahayana Sutras*: [283]

> Homage to you who,
> without the need for guardedness and because of your
> unforgetfulness,
> speak in a relaxed way in an assembly,
> and because you have eliminated the twin afflictions, attract
> a cricle of followers![157]

6. The Perfection of Patience

THE EXPLANATION OF the perfection of patience has three main parts: the definition of patience, ascertaining its nature of patience, and the benefits of cultivating patience.

The definition of patience is that the mind remains untroubled in the face of harm done by others. If that practice of patience is complete with the proper preparation, actual practice, and conclusion, it becomes the perfection of patience.

Ascertaining the nature of patience involves three things: identifying the antithesis of patience, discerning the individual antidotes to that, and correctly accomplishing those.

Identifying the antithesis of patience

This involves two steps: identifying anger and considering its harmful consequences. What is anger? *Anger* is the agitation within your mind that is caused by injuries done by others. When reflecting on the harmful consequences of anger, two things should be considered: its harmful consequences in the present life and its destruction of happiness in all future births.

The harmful consequences of anger *in this life* are explained in the *Guide to the Bodhisattva Way of Life*:

> If my mind holds tight to thoughts troubled by hatred,
> it will not experience peace.
> I will not find happiness and pleasure,
> and being unable to sleep, I will become unsteady.[158]

Hence in minds filled with hatred, happy thoughts will not continually arise. The body, too, will not find pleasure or comfort. At night, sleep will be interrupted. Through the power of anger and agitation, such people will not find the stability of physical and mental relaxation. They are unable to remain steady in themselves, and they elicit the censure of others.[159] As is said in the same work:

> Even those he has favored with
> wealth and respect and who have relied upon him
> may overthrow and kill
> an angry lord.[160]

There are examples of a ruler being killed even by followers or servants who depend upon him and who have been sustained by his food and wealth—if his disposition was exceedingly bad. As is also said:

> Close associates will despair of him;
> even lured with gifts, they will not approach him.[161]

Hence all relatives and friends of a short-tempered person will despair of him or her. [284] Even though such a person bestows food or wealth on others, this can only result in a loss of food and wealth and in the dissatisfation of others. For as it is said, "Though he gives with his hand, he burns with his mouth." Hence if you have an evil temperament, you will be miserable in both the present life and in future lives. And as is taught:

> In brief, nowhere is there
> an angry person who dwells happily.[162]

Even though you practice Dharma, if you do not know how to get along with any of your teachers, Dharma friends, patrons, or preceptors, only unhappiness can arise for you and an opinion among others that you are not a religious person. Those who are not concerned with Dharma and who are bad tempered will also afflict their spouse as long as they live with their miserable fighting, reaching a point where they are no longer on speaking terms with them and have to entrust a son or nephew with the job of intermediary. Having fought while they lived, even their sorrow after death is of no use for anything except their own suffering. Therefore you must rid yourself of hatred.

On the destruction of all happiness by anger *in all future lives*, the Heap of Jewels collection of sutras teach:

> What is anger? It is that which consumes the root of merit gathered over a thousand eons.[163]

And in the *Guide to the Bodhisattva Way of Life*:

> Whatever virtuous deeds
> you have amassed over a thousand eons,
> such as acts of generosity and venerating the Sugata,
> they will all be destroyed by a single moment of anger.[164]

And the *Precious Garland* teaches that hatred propels you into the hells.[165] Thus, through hatred, the merit accumulated over many eons is destroyed, and you will not escape from the miserable realms.

Discerning the individual antidotes to anger

This involves two topics: the antidote to the cause and the antidote to the result.

The antidote to the cause of anger. To get rid of anger, you must remove its cause. Hence, as the *Guide to the Bodhisattva Way of Life* teaches:

> Having found nourishment in an unhappy mind,
> hatred becomes full grown and destroys me.[166]

The same work teaches the method for eliminating that mental unhappiness:

> If it can be remedied,
> why be unhappy about it?
> And if there is no way to remedy it,
> what is the use of being unhappy?[167]

It does no good to feel unhappy about something that you cannot remedy, such as a dead person or a broken vessel. Therefore remind yourself that this the nature of things, and cheer yourself up. Nor is it necessary to feel unhappy about things that you can still remedy, such as a wounded body or destroyed house, because it is enough to set them right. If you do not possess an unhappy mind in that way, then even though slight harm may be done to you, you will not become enraged. Therefore apply yourself energetically to getting rid of hatred in both its causal and resultant aspects. [285] For as the *Guide to the Bodhisattva Way of Life* teaches:

> Whoever persistently destroys anger
> will be happy in the present life and hereafter.[168]

The antidote to hatred as the result. This has three types: patience in which you voluntarily undergo suffering, patience realized through ascertaining the factors of existence, and patience in which you disregard any harm done to you.[169]

Patience in which you voluntarily undergo suffering. This is a meditative realization of patience in which—for the sake of avoiding all wrong verbal and mental acts of yourself and others, and to achieve all virtuous things—you count as insignificant all ascetic austerities of body, speech, and mind and all sufferings such as heat and cold, hunger and thirst, sicknesses, and mental afflictions [such as spirit possession]. Viewing all those miseries as unimportant, you voluntarily take them upon yourself and cultivate patience, thinking, "All the previous buddhas and bodhisattvas also attained buddhahood by practicing difficult deeds such as this. Since for the sake of attaining buddhahood I must endure even the suffering of the hells, of course I must patiently endure suffering such as this."

A sutra teaches:

> Train yourself [for the attainment of awakening in] a pure realm and for the maturing of sentient beings in the following way: If you are a religious practitioner who dwells in a remote region and is eaten by fierce wild animals or injured by robbers, you should aspire: "May this purify all my obscurations caused by past misdeeds! May such harms not arise in the buddha realm in which I attain buddhahood!"[170]

Patience realized through ascertaining the factors of existence entails the meditative realization of patience through reflection on the surface level of reality and ultimate reality. To realize patience *through reflection on the surface level of reality*, reflect deeply as follows whenever someone harms you: "The nature of cyclic existence is suffering. The nature of fire is heat. And similarly, the nature of water is dampness (or cohesion), the nature of earth, solidity; the nature of air, mobility; and the nature of space is emptiness. Since the nature of sentient beings is to be unruly, it is unjustified to become angry with them." As the *Guide to the Bodhisattva Way of Life* teaches:

> This would be like resenting fire
> because its nature is to burn.[171]

And as it is also taught there:

> Unruly sentient beings are [endless] like the sky;
> how could you ever be equal to the task of defeating them all?
> If you can defeat this single enemy, anger,
> it will be the same as defeating all those enemies.[172] [286]

Someone might object, "The nature of sentient beings is good; their faults are merely adventitious." In that case it is still improper to be angry with them, for as it is taught:

> This would be like feeling spiteful toward the sky because smoke spreads through it.[173]

Moreover, dispel anger by examining your own former misdeeds. Think: "Why should I be angry with others when the result of harm that I myself formerly did to other sentient beings comes to pass?" As the *Treasury of Higher Knowledge* teaches,

> Karma is like a rice grain with its husk;
> likewise it is like a medicine and like a flower.[174]

The *Guide to the Bodhisattva Way of Life* also teaches:

> Previously I have caused harm such as this
> to sentient beings.
> Therefore it is fitting that I, who was harmful
> to sentient beings, am harmed in this way.[175]

And further:

> Since he [the enemy] has brought forth the weapon and I have
> brought forth this body,
> toward whom should I be angry?[176]

And further:

> Why did I previously commit that deed
> due to which others now cause me harm?
> Since all experiences depend on my former actions,
> why be spiteful about that?[177]

And further:

> Those who harm me come into being
> compelled by my own previous deeds.
> If they will go to hell through [my past actions],
> have I not caused their destruction?[178]

With these and similar verses, call to mind how anger-causing phenomena function on the surface level and thus dispel your anger.

To cultivate patience *through reflection on ultimate reality*, make yourself realize that, in ultimate reality, no self is established that is harmed, there is no enemy who harms, and there is no doing of harm. Thus you should purify anger through ultimate reality free from all conceptual elaborations (*niṣprapañca*). As the *Guide to the Bodhisattva Way of Life* teaches:

> What can be gained and what lost
> with regard to entities that are thus empty?
> And what is someone's respectful service
> or scorn?
>
> What is pleasure or pain?
> What is there to be unhappy about, and what to be happy about?
> When you search in reality,
> what is craving and what is there to crave for?
>
> Upon examination, who is there in this world of animate beings
> who will die? What is there that will come into being,

and what that has come into being?
And what are relatives and friends?

You should hold, as I do,
that all [things are empty] like space.[179]

Patience in which you disregard any harm done to you is realized meditatively through gradually training in three aspects: with respect to object, time, and the nature of harmful people. [287]

When training *with respect to different objects*, first train in cultivating patience toward your relations, then toward friends, then toward ordinary people, then finally toward enemies.

When training *with respect to time*, first cultivate patience for the duration of half the daylight hours of a day. If you are a layman, practice this after having taken the oath, "No matter who harms me during this time, I swear that I will patiently endure it!" But because the Vinaya teaches that monks should not take oaths, ordained people should cultivate patience after having made a formal commitment before the Three Jewels.[180] Then, after practicing successfully for that period, lengthen your period of training, practicing for a whole day at a time, then for a day and night at a time, then for half a month at a time, a full month, a year, and so on.

Training *with respect to different natures of harmful people* also has three parts. The first is to cultivate patience because *all sentient beings are your relatives* including harmful people. As the ārya master taught:

If you reduced the earth to little balls the size of jujube kernels,
their number would be less than that of the number of times
any one being has been your mother.[181]

As the *Vajra Peak Tantra* teaches:

Those śrāvakas who have no attachment
even for their own sons are unfortunate.
The fortunate one is illustrious Vajrapāṇi
who makes all beings happy.[182]

Accordingly, train in not hating others who harm you, because all beings are your own mother or son from past lives.

Also cultivate patience because *harmful people are the cause of achieving patience*. As the *Guide to the Bodhisattva Way of Life* teaches:

> If in its absence something does not arise
> and in its presence does,
> that is a cause.
> So how can one call it an obstacle?[183]

As it further teaches:

> Therefore, since patience is produced
> in dependence on someone with a mind filled with hatred,
> that very person, being the cause of patience,
> is worthy of veneration, just like the noble teaching.[184]

And still further:

> Therefore, just as I would welcome a treasure
> found in my house without having made any effort,
> so I should feel liking for my enemy,
> for he is an aid my practice aimed at awakening.[185]

Without an enemy, patience cannot arise. Therefore, when you see an enemy, make yourself feel happy, thinking, "My perfection of patience will be completed!"

Finally, cultivate patience because *harmful people are conditions for exhausting the force of your bad deeds*. As the *Guide to the Bodhisattva Way of Life* teaches:

> Wouldn't it be good if a person who was to be executed
> were set free after only having a hand cut off?
> Likewise, wouldn't it be good if I were freed from hell
> through experiencing human sufferings?[186] [288]

Hence, just as a person sentenced to death would be happy to merely be beaten or have a hand cut off but have his life be spared, be happy about your sufferings, thinking, "By this harm, the force of past deeds that would have resulted in birth in lower miserable realms has become exhausted, and now I will not have to be born there."

Correctly accomplishing patience

This has two parts: achieving the four excellent qualities and eliminating the seven attachments.

Achieving the four excellent qualities is explained in the lines beginning: "The destruction of the antithesis to patience...."[187] Thus the qualities to be attained are: (1) destroying the antithesis of patience, namely anger, (2) realizing the nondiscursive, the absence of a substantial self, (3) perfectly fulfilling all the wishes of others, accomplishing their welfare based on your practice of patience, and (4) maturing sentient beings by establishing sentient beings in the three vehicles based on your practice of patience.

Eliminating the seven attachments is explained in the lines beginning: "The patience of a bodhisattva is unattached...."[188] Accordingly, the seven attachments are to: (1) anger, (2) procrastination, (3) premature satisfaction, (4) the hope of getting something in return, (5) the future result of a deed, (6) the antithesis of patience, namely the undestroyed disposition toward anger, and (7) the two aspects of distraction, which was explained before [in the chapter on generosity]. Abandon these seven attachments together with the propensities toward them.

The benefits of cultivating patience

There are two main types of benefits, temporary and ultimate. The *temporary benefits* of patience are also of two types: those that occur in this life and those occurring in future lives.

The benefits of patience that accrue *in this life* include the following: By being able to disregard the harm others cause you, you will not act harmfully in return. By virtue of that, the harmful thoughts and efforts of others will be pacified of their own accord. When that occurs, your body and mind become comfortable. In the short term, troubles cease. In the long term, all enemies will become pacified of their own accord. You will experience inestimable other benefits, such as fearlessness even when dying and passing on to the next life.

As to the benefits arising *in all future lives*, wherever you are born in the future, you will have an excellent body, your life will be long and free from illness, and you will have neither human nor demonic enemies. Also, all the full and excellent attainments of gods and humans will automatically arise for you, such as being a universal emperor. As the *Guide to the Bodhisattva Way of Life* teaches: [289]

> While [wandering] in cyclic existence,
> a patient person will live for a very long time,
> have bodily excellences such as beauty, the enjoyment of freedom from illness, and good repute,
> and attain the extensive pleasures of a universal emperor.[189]

In the *Verse Summary of the Perfection of Wisdom* it is also taught:

> Through patience, you will attain an extremely beautiful and exalted body,
> golden in color, attractive and dear to the world of animate beings.[190]

As taught in the *Letter to a Friend*:

> One who has relinquished anger attains irreversibility [on the path to liberation].
> Thus did the Buddha promise.[191]

The *ultimate benefits* of patience are that you will attain the [thirty-two] marks and [eighty] physical characteristics of a buddha and will possess a body and voice that will captivate the minds of everyone. For as the *Ornament of Mahayana Sutras* teaches:

> When all embodied beings see you,
> they know you to be a great being.
> Homage to you who inspire
> intense faith merely by being seen![192]

7. The Perfection of Diligence

THE EXPLANATION OF diligence has three main parts: the definition of diligence, ascertaining its nature, and the benefits of undertaking diligence.

The definition of diligence is enthusiasm for what is virtuous in order to benefit others. For as the *Guide to the Bodhisattva Way of Life* teaches: "What is diligence? It is enthusiasm for the virtuous."[193] If that diligence is complete with proper preparation, actual practice, and conclusion, it becomes the perfection of diligence.

Ascertaining its nature entails discussion of three subsidiary topics: identifying the antithesis of diligence, discerning the individual antidotes, and correctly accomplishing those.

Identifying the antithesis of diligence

This has two parts: identifying laziness and considering its harmful consequences. What is laziness? *Laziness*, the opposite of diligence, is the failure of body, speech, and mind to engage in the virtuous. Or even if you do engage in that, it is to diligently cultivate what is not wholesome, taking it to be wholesome, as the tīrthikas do. Or, even if you do apply yourself to what is wholesome, it is to strive diligently at things that will result in either the extreme of cyclic existence or the extreme of nirvana. Reflecting on the harmful consequences of laziness has two aspects: reflection on the harmful consequences in this life and reflection on how it destroys the happiness of all future lives. [290]

Regarding harm caused by laziness *in this life*, the *Guide to the Bodhisattva Way of Life* teaches:

> Can the fainthearted and those who abandon endeavor
> find an escape from this impoverishment?

> Someone who is assertive and energetic
> will be difficult to overcome, even by great adversity.[194]

Thus if people who procrastinate because of timidity and laziness cannot even obtain food and clothing or accomplish farming and trading in the present life, it goes without saying that they will not be able to accomplish such virtuous things as learning, reflection, and meditation. [The teacher] should tell stories illustrating how, in brief, a lazy person cannot meet a buddha and does not receive religious teachings from a religious preceptor, and how laziness itself becomes an obstacle to achieving the wholesome Dharma. Through laziness kings lose their kingdoms, and even ordinary people fail in agriculture, trading, and so forth. [Here the teacher] should also suitably explain how lazy people become despised by the whole world of humans and gods.[195]

On the destruction of happinesses *in all future lives*, the Mother of the Conquerors [the Perfection of Wisdom sutras] teaches, for instance:

> Through laziness you cannot even accomplish your own welfare,
> let alone the welfare of others.[196]

As it is also said in the *Guide to the Bodhisattva Way of Life*:

> If, like a fish flopping about [on dry land],
> you remain tormented in this life [on your deathbed],
> what need is there to mention the unbearable agonies
> that your evil deeds [will cause you] in hell?[197]

You should ponder at great length the point of these and similar passages.

Discerning the individual antidotes to laziness

This includes two topics: the antidote to the causes of laziness and the antidote to the result.

The antidote to the causes of laziness. The *Guide to the Bodhisattva Way of Life* explains the causes of laziness as follows:

> Laziness, attachment to base [activities],
> discouragement, belittling yourself,

> indolence, enjoying pleasurable tastes,
> craving sleep, and not feeling disillusioned
> with the sufferings of cyclic existence—
> [by those things] laziness is produced.[198]

The "laziness" mentioned in this passage refers to procrastination about all activities. "Attachment to base [activities]" refers to being attached to inferior worldly activities such as trading and farming. "Discouragement" means aversion to applying yourself to religious activities because you formerly engaged in religious practice but all did not go according to your wishes. "Belittling yourself" means to think, "Someone like me could never accomplish virtuous practices." "Indolence" refers to not engaging in virtuous practices because you are always lying down or resting. "Enjoying pleasurable tastes" means being attached to eating, drinking, humorous chatter, and so forth. "Craving sleep" means not engaging in the virtuous because you spend so much time—both night and day—in sleep. [291] "Not disillusioned by cyclic existence " refers to someone who has no realization at all of the sufferings of birth, sickness, old age, and death and who therefore does not apply himself to the virtuous. This and the others give rise to laziness.

Concerning the antidotes to these, reflect on what is taught in the *Guide to the Bodhisattva Way of Life*:

> After being caught by the fisherman of the afflictions,
> and after entering the net of births,
> why do I still not realize
> that I have gone into the mouth of the Lord of Death?
>
> Have you not seen
> the gradual slaughtering of your kind?
> Someone who still resorts to sleep
> is like a water buffalo [sleeping] with a butcher.
>
> Blocking all routes of escape,
> the Lord of Death is staring at you.
> How can you enjoy eating?
> How can you enjoy going to sleep?

Death approaches quickly,
and so I must accumulate merit for as much time as remains.
What use will it be to abandon laziness at the time [of death
itself]?
By then, the proper time will have passed.

With this remaining undone, with that just started,
and with this other remaining half finished,
the Lord of Death suddenly will appear
and you will think, "Oh no! I am done for!"[199]

Through these and other verses, ponder again and again all the disadvantages of cyclic existence, and you will thereby turn away from laziness.

The antidote to the result. The antidotes to laziness take two forms: purifying the objects of experience and perfectly complete achievement.

Purifying the objects of experience. This practice should be understood according to the discourse on purifying of objects of experience that Ārya Mañjuśrī delivered to the bodhisattva Jñānaśrī, as found in the *Flower Ornament Sutra*.[200] If you are unable to practice in exact accordance with the words and sense expressed there, follow the summary of the *Bodhisattva's Completely Pure Conduct Sutra* composed by the great master Jñānagarbha.[201]

As it is taught there, when sitting at home a bodhisattva should formulate the resolution: "May I reach the city of liberation!"

And likewise, when going to sleep, he or she should resolve: "May I attain the Dharma body of buddhahood!"

If dreams occur: "May I realize that every phenomenon is like a dream!"

When waking up: "May I awaken from ignorance!"

When arising: "May I attain the form body of buddhahood!"

When dressing: "May I put on the robe of self-respect and shame!"

When tying your belt: "May [my mind] become connected with roots of virtue!"

When sitting on a mat: "May I attain the vajra seat at the stage of awakening!" [292]

When resting your back against something: "May I arrive at the tree alongside which awakening is attained!"

When lighting a fire: "May the afflictions be burned!"

When the fire is burning: "May the fire of gnosis blaze forth!"

When food has been cooked: "May I acquire the ambrosia of gnosis!"

When eating: "May I acquire the food of meditative concentration!"

When going outside: "May I escape from the city of cyclic existence!"

When descending stairs: "May I enter into cyclic existence for the benefit of sentient beings!"

When opening the door: "May the gate to the city of liberation be opened!"

When closing a door: "May the door to the three lower realms be closed!"

When entering upon a path: "May I enter upon the noble path!"

When going uphill: "May I and sentient beings be established in the pleasures of the higher realms of rebirth!"

When going downhill: "May the continuation of existences in the three lower realms be permanently broken!"

When you meet another sentient being: "May I meet with the completely awakened Buddha!"

When stepping down with your foot: "May I place my trust in accomplishing the welfare of all sentient beings!"

When lifting your foot: "May all sentient beings be brought forth from cyclic existence!"

When seeing someone wearing ornaments: "May I gain the marks and auspicious characteristics [of a buddha]!"

When seeing someone without ornaments: "May I come to possess the [twelve] excellent qualities of the purified person!"

When seeing a full vessel: "May I become filled with excellent qualities!"

When seeing an empty vessel: "May I become devoid of faults!"

When seeing many happy beings: "May I delight in the religious teachings!"

When seeing those who are unhappy: "May I not delight in any compounded thing!"

When seeing a sentient being experiencing pleasure: "May I become equipped for the bliss of buddhahood!"

When seeing a suffering being: "May the sufferings of all beings be pacified!"

When seeing a sick person: "May all sentient beings become free from every disease!"

When seeing an attractive person or animal: "May all beings become attractive to the eyes of all buddhas and bodhisattvas!"

When seeing an ugly body: "May all beings not feel devotion toward evil teachers!"

When seeing someone feeling grateful for another's kindness: "May I repay the kindnesses of the buddhas and bodhisattvas!"

When seeing an ungrateful person: "May none feel indebted to erroneous views!"

When seeing an ordained person: "May I enter into the noble Dharma!"

When seeing someone undergoing hardship: "May I be able to endure hardship for the good teaching!"

When seeing someone wearing armor: "May I gird myself for the quest for the noble teaching!" [293]

When seeing someone not wearing armor: "May I not gird myself for unwholesome deeds!"

When seeing an aggressive person: "May all attackers be defeated!"

When seeing a sentient being praised: "May all the buddhas and bodhisattvas be praised!"

When seeing a city: "May I see the city of liberation!"

When seeing a forest: "May I become a sanctuary for the whole world including the gods!"

When the Dharma is being taught: "May I attain inexhaustible confidence in [being able to teach] the doctrine of the Buddha!"

When crossing water: "May I cross over the ocean of cyclic existence!"

When washing: "May my body and mind become without stain!"

In times of hot weather: "May the torments of the afflictions be soothed!"

In cold weather: "May I attain the cool of nirvana!"

When a religious discourse is being given: "May I receive all the teachings of a buddha!"

Whenever you see a figure of the Buddha: "May I acquire unobscured eyes for the viewing of all buddhas!"

When you see a stūpa: "May I become a shrine of worship for all beings!"

When you are looking: "May I become worthy of being looked upon by the whole world of humans and gods!"

When physically paying homage: "May I obtain the head protuberance [of a buddha, the dimensions of which] the whole world of gods and men cannot perceive by looking!"

When circumambulating: "May I attain that which conduces to omniscience!"

When some are proclaiming the excellent qualities of the Buddha: "May I bring to perfection inexhaustible excellent qualities!"

Likewise, figure out other suitable and harmonious [ways of purifying how you view the objects of experience]; for example, when you see people engaging in trade, you should resolve: "May I attain the seven riches of an ārya!"[202]

When the fields are being watered and spread with fertilizer, you should resolve: "May the crop of the thought of awakening be vast!"

At the time of planting seeds: "May all sentient beings be implanted with the seed of the thought of awakening!"

When oxen are being paired up: "May method and discerning wisdom be conjoined!"

At the time of ploughing: "May the hard clumps of the afflictions be broken up!"

At weeding time: "May the weeds of the afflictions be uprooted!"

At harvest time: "May the crop of gnosis be gathered!"

When grain is being threshed: "May the obscurations, together with all propensities for them, be removed!"

When grain is being washed [or possibly stored]: "May I obtain the fruit of complete buddhahood!"

When climbing a ladder: "May I by stages complete the ten bodhisattva levels!"

When arriving at a house: "May I arrive at the stage of a perfectly awakened buddha!"

And so on and so forth. You should understand how to view whatever activities you do in accord with the above examples. I have set forth these examples for the easy retention of people of lesser capacity. For a more detailed account, consult the *Bodhisattva's Completely Pure Conduct Sutra* itself.[203] [294]

These are the bodhisattva's mental deeds that are referred to as "activities of attention," which constitute the instructions of the following line:

> Totally be with awareness whether traveling, strolling, lying, or sitting.[204]

Perfectly complete achievement. On this the *Guide to the Bodhisattva Way of Life* states:

> I should not engage in anything besides
> benefitting sentient beings either directly or indirectly.
> I should dedicate all [merit]
> solely for the benefit of sentient beings.[205]

Thus, in general, actions have two purposes: one's own benefit and the benefit of others. For the śrāvaka, one's own benefit predominates while the benefit of others is a secondary result. For the bodhisattva, the benefit to others predominates while one's own benefit is a byproduct. Here you are following the bodhisattva's way of life, so you must either eradicate nonvirtuous and neutral deeds through their antidotes or convert them into roots of virtue through skillful means. As Āryadeva said:

> By his intention, all acts,
> whether virtuous or nonvirtuous,
> become virtuous for the bodhisattva.
> Why? Because mind is predominant.[206]

And as Ārya Asaṅga said:

> For those who possess great skillful means,
> even the afflictions become an aid to awakening,
> and cyclic existence is peaceful by nature.
> These bodhisattvas are inconceivable.[207]

To illustrate [the arising of direct and indirect benefits], let me take first the giving of a material object. Not to waste wealth by guarding it will only indirectly benefit others. To help others by giving it away is of direct benefit to them. Through thus making the benefit of others your principle objective, you will indirectly benefit yourself: you will attain pleasure and fame and attract an excellent circle of followers in the present life, and in future lives you will obtain excellent wealth and bring to completion the perfection of generosity.

To illustrate [how the gift of Dharma teachings can bring about both kinds of benefits], if you study for the purpose of benefitting others, it will indirectly benefit others. But to teach for the sake of removing others' darkness of ignorance after having yourself understood the teachings is to benefit others directly. By thus beneficially using the Dharma teachings to help others, you will indirectly achieve your own benefit. In other words, by mastering the objects of knowledge, you will be happy in the present life and will enter the ranks of those acclaimed as "a learned wise one."[208] You will overwhelm all opposing disputants through your glory. And you will become a place of trust for the whole world, including the gods. In future lives you will achieve discerning wisdom that is enlightened about each and every knowable thing. [295] And through skillful means, your perfection of wisdom will be brought to completion.

Correctly accomplishing diligence

This includes two things: achieving the four excellent qualities and eliminating the seven attachments.

Achieving the four excellent qualities. The four excellent qualities are explained in the lines beginning, "[For] diligence, the destruction of the antithesis...."[209] Thus these four qualities are: (1) freeing yourself of laziness, the antithesis of diligence, (2) realizing the nondiscursive, the absence of a substantial self, (3) perfectly fulfilling all the wishes of others by benefitting them with your diligence, and (4) maturing sentient beings by establishing them in the three vehicles through your diligence.

Eliminating the seven attachments is taught in the lines beginning, "The diligence of the bodhisattva is unattached...."[210] Accordingly, the seven attachments are to: (1) laziness, (2) procrastination, namely putting off making a diligent effort, (3) premature satisfaction [with your own diligence], (4) the hope of getting something in return, (5) the future result of a deed, (6) the propensities antithetical to diligence, the laziness that has not yet been destroyed, and (7) the two types of distractions previously explained [in the chapter on generosity]. Rid yourself of these seven attachments together with the dispositions toward them.

The benefits of undertaking diligence

The benefits are twofold, temporary and ultimate. The *temporary benefits* of diligence are of two types: those realized in this life and those realized in future lives.

Among the benefits realized *in this life,* through diligence you will accomplish all worldly and religious activities. By virtue of that, you will become replete with a circle of followers, wealth, and excellent qualities. By obtaining wealth and acquisitions that are in harmony with the Dharma, you will be happy in the present life. At the time of death you will be without regrets. Men and demons who would cause obstacles will find no opening for attack. And you will attain inestimable excellent qualities, such as becoming the object toward which the whole world of humans and gods will offer their prayers. [296]

As far as benefits arising *in all future lives*, the *Verse Summary of the Perfection of Wisdom* teaches:

> Through diligence beneficial qualities will not be clouded,
> and one obtains the storehouse of limitless gnosis of a conqueror.[211]

Thus, through diligence, moment by moment all unwholesome factors are overpowered and all wholesome roots increase more and more. Whatever projects you have begun are quickly accomplished. And through this all excellent qualities of perfect buddhahood are achieved.

The *ultimate benefits* of diligence include: when you awaken to perfect buddhahood, all enlightened qualities, such as the strengths and fearlessnesses, will spontaneously be achieved, and you will accomplish without impediment activities that benefit all sentient beings. As the *Ornament of Mahayana Sutras* teaches:

> For attaining the characteristics of buddhahood, such as the strengths,
> this excellent quality is like a mine of jewels.
> It is also held to be like a great rain cloud
> for the crop of sentient beings' virtue.[212]

And further:

> In your activities for all beings in the world,
> you are never untimely,
> so your deeds are always meaningful.
> Homage to you who are unforgetful![213]

8. The Perfection of Meditative Concentration

The explanation of the perfection of meditative concentration has three main sections: the definition of meditative concentration, ascertaining its nature, and the benefits of realizing meditative concentration.

The definition of meditative concentration is placing the mind in calmed focus (*samāpatti*) for the sake of attaining complete buddhahood. If that meditative concentration is endowed with proper preparation, actual practice, and completion, it will become the perfection of meditative concentration.

Ascertaining the nature of meditative concentration has three main parts: identifying the antithesis of meditative concentration, discerning the individual antidotes, and correctly accomplishing those.

Identifying the antithesis of meditative concentration

For an understanding of the factors opposed to meditative concentration, you should do two things: identify distraction and reflect on its harmful consequences.

What is distraction? *Distraction*, the opposite of concentration, is the inability to place the mind one-pointedly on an object of focus. Or, even if you can focus the mind, that focus is erroneous, like that practiced by the tīrthikas. Or, even if it is not erroneous, it is to practice meditation that will become the cause of attaining [merely] nirvana or an existence in one of the higher realms.

The *harmful consequences* of distraction are of two sorts: harm that it causes in this life and its destruction of happiness in all future lives.

The harmful consequences *in this life* are explained in the *Guide to the Bodhisattva Way of Life*:

> A person whose mind is distracted
> dwells between the fangs of the afflictions.[214]

Thus people whose minds are distracted create sufferings and problems for themselves and sufferings and problems for others, like a stream flowing outside its banks or the riding of a wild, unbroken horse. [297] Because of distraction, your mind wants to engage in various incorrect things, and after experiencing various catastrophes, at the moment of death you die filled with remorse.

Regarding its destruction of happiness *in all future lives*, the *Guide to the Bodhisattva Way of Life* teaches:

> There, [in other lives] too, because of your habitual distraction,
> what means could there be to prevent it?[215]

Thus the distracted mind is difficult to turn back, like a torrent of water falling from a precipice or an amorous lover who has put on adornments. And after you have committed various unwholesome deeds under its impulsion, distraction becomes the cause for further births in cyclic existence and the lower miserable destinies. Even if you engage in concentrating the mind, by incorrect meditation your practice will be erroneous, like the spiritual path of the tīrthikas. As the *King of Meditation Sutra* teaches:

> Even if worldly people meditate on emptiness,
> that will not turn back the positing of entities.
> They will once again become endowed with their afflictions,
> as when Udraka cultivated this meditative absorption.[216]

Thus it is like the case of Udraka, who though he meditated for twelve years on emptiness, was afterward born as a cat. Furthermore, even when your meditative concentration cultivates loving kindness and compassion in a correct manner, this will not sever the root of cyclic existence. As the *Thorough Exposition of Valid Cognition* explains:

> Because loving kindness and so forth do not counteract
> ignorance,
> they do not completely defeat the faults.[217]

Thus such concentration can merely propel you into one of the two higher cosmic realms but cannot free you from cyclic existence. And even if you know how to cultivate insight into emptiness correctly, if you do not possess skillful means you will merely attain the cessation (*nirodha*) of the śrāvaka but will not be able to awaken to buddhahood. For as the *Enlightenment of Vairocana Tantra* teaches:

> The Great Hero [the Buddha]
> taught a gnosis and a discipline
> unequipped with skillful means
> so that the śrāvakas would enter it.[218]

Discerning the individual antidotes

This also has two parts: the antidote to the causes of distraction and the antidote to the result.

The antidote to the causes of distraction. The causes of distraction are attachment to other sentient beings and attachment to possessions. The antidotes to these are two: ridding yourself of the attachments and calling to mind the virtues of solitude.

Ridding yourself of the attachments has two parts: ridding yourself of attachment to sentient beings and ridding yourself of attachment to possessions.

First is ridding yourself of *attachment to sentient beings.* As the *Guide to the Bodhisattva Way of Life* teaches:

> If you are attached to living beings,
> reality becomes obscured.
> It will also undermine disillusionment [with cyclic existence],
> and ultimately you will be tormented by sorrow. [298]
>
> By thinking only of them,
> this life passes meaninglessly.
> Friends and relatives, who possess no permanence,
> will destroy [for you] the permanent Dharma.[219]

And:

> In just an instant they can become friends;
> in just an instant they can become enemies.
> Ordinary people are difficult to please
> because they become angry even with those worthy of
> affection.[220]

And:

> They feel envious of their superiors, competitive with their
> equals,
> arrogant toward inferiors, and conceited if praised.
> They become angry if you say anything unpleasant.
> When could childish people ever benefit you?
>
> Thus by my associating with others,
> only ruin can ensue. Because they will not benefit me
> and I cannot accomplish benefits for them,
> I should distance myself from childish people.[221]

And:

> Like a bee extracting honey from a flower,
> I should take just enough for my spiritual purposes
> and then remain without intimacy,
> as if I had never seen any of them before.
>
> "I have many acquisitions. I am respected,
> and I am popular among many people."
> If you take pride in such things,
> you will experience terror after death.
>
> Therefore, O confused mind,
> the sum of each and everything you are attached to
> will later arise as sufferings,
> multiplied a thousandfold.
>
> Therefore a wise person should not become attached.
> From attachment perils arise.[222]

And:

> If even the Conqueror cannot please
> sentient beings with all their various inclinations,
> it goes without saying that an evil person like myself cannot.
> Therefore I should abandon all thoughts of this world.

They belittle those without acquisitions,
and they grumble about those who have them.
How will those beings, whose company is by nature unpleasant,
ever produce joy?

The tathāgatas have taught that
you should never become close friends with childish people
because they are not happy
unless their self-interest is served.[223]

Call to mind the sense of these and similar verses and rid yourself of attachment to sentient beings. Moreover you should reflect: "If even the Buddha cannot please sentient beings, who are by nature faulty, it goes without saying that an inferior person such as I cannot do so." For example, Devadatta, when dying of indigestion, was cured by the Lord Buddha through the sustaining force of the truth yet remarked disrespectfully: "The ascetic Gautama is a skillful physician. Through healing he will have no trouble making a living when he is old."[224]

Another example is the case of Sunakṣatra,[225] who once said to the Lord Buddha: "In the world there is no omniscient person besides the naked ascetic Korakkhattiya."[226] [299] The Buddha replied: "Your 'omniscient one' will die in seven days of acute indigestion." Sunakṣatra then went to the Jaina naked ascetic and told him: "The ascetic Gautama says that in seven days you will die of indigestion, so for that period you should fast." That naked ascetic then fasted for six days. But on the seventh day he mistakenly thought that it was the eighth, and when he ate some molasses crust, he died of indigestion. He was then born as a hungry spirit who could eat only vomit.

Afterward, that hungry spirit met with Sunakṣatra and told him: "The Lord Buddha is all knowing and all seeing. Even I feel remorse because I did not have devotion toward the Buddha. Henceforth you should have devoted faith in him!"

"The ascetic Gautama has no such qualities," replied Sunakṣatra, "so don't talk like that!" And so saying, he sent him away. Later Sunakṣatra went to the Buddha and said: "You told me that Korakkhattiya would die after seven days. Well, it appears he has not!" The Buddha replied: "Don't you know that you met him after his death?" He answered, "Yes, I know. Nevertheless, he was born as a god." The Buddha replied: "Don't you remember the conversation you had with him after he was reborn as a vomit-eating hungry spirit?" At that Sunakṣatra was ashamed and fell silent.

If Sunakṣatra could have no devoted appreciation for the Buddha even after he knew that the Buddha was omniscient, it goes without saying that others will not feel devoted appreciation for people like us. Thus reflecting, you should rid yourself of attachment to them.

Second is ridding yourself of *attachment to possessions.* Achieving and maintaining wealth is unwholesome at three different times. First, at the time of accumulating wealth, you must gather possessions, forgetting to care about evils, sufferings, and ill repute, and with spite toward enemies, relatives, and ordinary people alike. By contrast, you cannot amass wealth that is in harmony with the Dharma. Consequently, the accumulation of wealth is unwholesome to begin with.

In the meantime, when you protect your wealth, you experience sufferings day and night, tormented by worries of its not increasing or of losing it even if it does increase. And you are kept completely occupied day and night because your body, speech, and mind have become a slave to greed. Not only are you completely tied up, but all your relatives and associates are preoccupied by the trouble of taking out and putting away the wealth. In this life you feel enmity toward everyone. [300] And because in future lives this yields no benefit at all but only becomes a cause for births in lower destinies, it is unwholesome in the meantime.

Ultimately, like an autumn cloud or like ice in spring, wealth dissolves, whether through the exhaustion of your merit, your own faulty plans, the fault of your relatives, or the force of a powerful enemy. Consequently, you experience the sufferings of its exhaustion, and thereby it is unwholesome in the end. As Ācārya Maitripāda taught:

> Because of material things, disputes arise.
> The absence of material things is the highest bliss.
> See how the crane attains bliss
> by completely renouncing material things.[227]

Here [the teacher] should also explain the harmful consequences of attachment to things, as taught above in the section on generosity, with such verses as the one from the *Guide to the Bodhisattva Way of Life* beginning, "Because of the torments of collecting, guarding, and losing it..."[228] and such verses as:

> Just like beasts of burden pulling a chariot
> who get only a mouthful of grass to eat,
> desirous people have this
> and many other disadvantages but little profit.[229]

And thus you should abandon attachment.

Calling to mind the virtues of solitude. As the verses of the *Guide to the Bodhisattva Way of Life* teach:

> When will I be able to dwell in the forest
> together with deer, birds, and trees,
> who do not speak unpleasantly
> and who are so agreeable to associate with?
>
> Someday, dwelling in a cave,
> empty temple, or at the foot of a tree,
> may I not look back
> and may I become free from attachments!
>
> When will I dwell,
> without attachment and autonomously,
> in a place naturally expansive,
> without possessiveness toward place?
>
> When will I dwell fearlessly,
> with a few humble possessions such as a begging bowl,
> wearing clothes unwanted by others,
> and not even needing to hide this body?
>
> When will I go to a cemetery
> and treat those bones and my body
> as all alike in being objects
> subject to destruction?[230]

And in such verses as:

> Before my body has been carried out
> by four pall-bearers

amid the sore distress of the community,
let me yet go to the forest!

Having done with both friendship and enmity,
and dwelling in solitude with only this body,
if I die there will be no mourning
because I am already counted as though dead.

Because of this,
others will not disturb
my mindfulness of the Buddha
and the other [five mindfulnesses to be cultivated at death].

Therefore I shall dwell with myself alone,
quelling all distractions in a very pleasant forest
where there are pleasures and joys
and few problems.[231] [301]

Also call to mind the words of disillusionment found in the Jātakas:

Alas! Worldly people with emotional afflictions
become unhappy because the present state of things is unstable!
Even the splendor of *kumuda*[232] water-lilies
will soon be just a memory![233]

The sense expressed here is that the entire present spectacle—such as a festival of *kumuda* lilies—and all pleasures, happinesses, and good things are impermanent and will thus abruptly come to an end. Afterward, when you recall "Ah! That was how it used to be!" those memories will afflict you. You should reflect on these words and on other expressions of these points and go to dwell in solitude.

The antidote to the resultant distraction

The antidote to distraction is meditative concentration. Three types require description: (1) the practices of meditative concentration held in common with practitioners of the mundane sphere, [that is, the tīrthikas,] (2) those held in common with the śrāvakas, and (3) those belonging exclusively to the Mahayana path.

The practices of *meditative concentration shared by the mundane and supramundane spheres* consist of the seven connected preparations (*sāmantaka*) for meditative concentration and the actual practice in which the first concentration (*dhyāna*) and the rest are cultivated. Train in these practices to the best of your abilities and learn about them from the explanation below in the section on the path of cultivation.[234]

The practices of *meditative concentration shared by the śrāvakas and the Mahayana.* When you reflect on the faults of cyclic existence, such as impermanence, and thereby enter the path, two methods of meditation are involved: preliminary meditations and the practice of meditative concentration itself.

Preliminary meditations. As a preparation to the main meditation, those in whom sensual desire predominates should first meditate on repulsiveness [of the objects of desire]. Those in whom discursive thinking predominates should meditate on their breath, counting or following each breath. As the *Treasury of Higher Knowledge* teaches:

> The initial practices are repulsiveness
> and awareness of inhalation of breath
> for those excessively lustful and discursive.[235]

The meditative practice itself is the cultivation of the five paths according to the thirty-seven factors conducive to awakening. This entails the cultivation of: (1) the path of accumulation through the four foundations of mindfulness, (2) [the path of application through] the level of "heat" through the four perfect endeavors, (3) the level of "the peak" through the four bases of magical powers, (4) "fearless acceptance" through the five moral faculties, (5) "the highest worldly realization" through the five moral powers, (6) the path of seeing through the limbs of the eightfold path of the āryas, and (7) the path of cultivation through the seven limbs of awakening. These do not accord with Mahayana practice with respect to their objects, ordering, and so forth. And since this is the tradition of the Hinayana, I will leave this topic for the present. [302]

The practices of *meditative concentration belonging exclusively to the Mahayana* has two parts, [Yogācāra and Madhyamaka].

The Yogācāra tradition consists of the stages of the path according to the tradition originating from Ācārya Asaṅga and his brother [Vasubandhu]. This should be learned from [Asaṅga's] *Compendium of the Mahayana* and therefore will not be discussed here.

The Madhyamaka tradition. What I will explain here is the Madhyamaka tradition, as expressed in the meditative concentration chapter of the *Guide to the Bodhisattva Way of Life*, which represents the thought of Ācārya Nāgārjuna and his spiritual son [Āryadeva]. Ācārya Śāntideva taught that the practice of meditative concentration should begin with cultivating the thought of awakening. But here I will first teach cultivating the four immeasurables, because cultivating the thought of awakening can be easily mastered if these four are cultivated first.

Cultivating the four immeasurables. On these, the *Ornament of Mahayana Sutras* teaches:

> You're compassionate toward sentient beings;
> you wish that they meet [with happiness] and part [from
> suffering]
> and that they be never separated [from happiness].
> I pay homage to you whose wish is to help and benefit.[236]

[Of the four immeasurables alluded to in the above verse,] the first three [are included within] the intention [that all beings be] happy, and the last is the intention [that all be benefitted]. Those two [categories of loving kindness and compassion], moreover, [include the four immeasurables as follows]: Out of kindness, to desire that sentient beings meet with happiness is *loving kindness*. To desire that they be parted from suffering is *compassion*. To desire that they never be separated from those two [i.e., from happiness and freedom from suffering] is *sympathetic joy*. The wish that they be impartial toward the eight worldly concerns—such as friends and enemies, desire and hatred—is *equanimity*. When you practice those four immeasurable things, you should practice them by including them within the pair: loving kindness and compassion. As the *Ornament of Mahayana Sutras* teaches:

> Compassion's moisture is loving kindness,
> and it perfectly arises from suffering.[237]

Cultivating loving kindness

This comes first and entails explaining three topics: the objects toward which loving kindness is cultivated, the method for cultivating loving kindness, and the benefits of having thus cultivated loving kindness.

The objects of loving kindness. Cultivate loving kindness toward those living beings who are feeling neutral, lacking both pleasure and suffering; toward those who have not met with the good teaching, the cause of happiness; and toward those who, though they may have come into contact with the good teaching, have not acquired the excellent qualities of the buddhas and bodhisattvas.

How to cultivate loving kindness. It is easiest to cultivate loving kindness toward all sentient beings after you have recognized that they are your relatives. Hence some sutras teach that you should cultivate [loving kindness toward all living beings] as if they were your mother. Some tantras, such as the *Vajra Peak Tantra*, teach the cultivation [of loving kindness toward sentient beings] as if they were your son.[238] [303] But since there is not a single sentient being who has not also been in other lifetimes your father, brother, sister, or other relative, train in loving kindness by imagining that all sentient beings are whatever relative is the closest and dearest to you.

Moreover, happiness alone is not enough to truly benefit a sentient being. Hence cultivate the wish, from the bottom of your heart and the core of your being, "May all sentient beings possess happiness and the cause of happiness!" Here "happiness" means physical and mental felicity that accords with the Dharma. "The cause of happiness" is held to consist of sentient beings coming into contact with the Dharma, because the result—permanent happiness—arises from the cause, which is to practice the Buddhist teachings.

By accustoming yourself again and again to cultivating loving kindness as described above, you will experience loving kindness toward all sentient beings like that of a mother for her only child.

The benefits of cultivating loving kindness in this way. As a sutra teaches:

> To offer every day as many sorts of offerings
> as there would be in ten million trillions of worlds filled with
> offerings
> would not measure up in number, or even equal in part,
> the merit of a single thought of loving kindness.[239]

And the *Precious Garland* teaches, for instance:

> Offering each day, in a timely fashion,
> three hundred cooking pots of food

cannot match a portion of the merit from
just one instant of loving kindness.[240]

Accordingly, by generating loving kindness in the short term, you will be born in the world of Brahma. Even if you are not born there, you will acquire eight excellent qualities, such as being loved by gods and men. Ultimately, loving kindness will become a cause for buddhahood. Examples of the wonderful benefits of loving kindness are found in the Jātaka story of Matrībala,[241] and in the story of the mother and daughter who drowned at the confluence of the Ganges and Yamunā rivers while trying to save each other and were reborn in the realm of Brahma.[242]

Cultivating compassion

This involves four topics: the objects toward which compassion is cultivated, the conditions that enable compassion to arise, the method for cultivating compassion, and the benefits of having cultivated compassion.

The objects of compassion can be explained in two ways, [objects that are separate and those that are combined.]

Cultivating compassion toward separate objects. The *Ornament of Mahayana Sutras* mentions [ten worthy objects for compassion]:

> There is compassion for sentient beings
> who are inflamed, dominated by an enemy,
> who are oppressed by suffering, obscured by darkness,
> who have embarked on a path difficult to travel,
> who possess great fetters,
> who are attached to food adulterated with poison,
> who destroy the path,
> who have taken a wrong road, and who are weak.[243]

Here "inflamed" refers to those who, through avid lust, are attached to the pleasures of desire. "Dominated by an enemy" refers to those who are prevented by the Evil One (Māra) from engaging in the wholesome. "Oppressed by suffering" means those who are overwhelmed by the sufferings of the three miserable destinies. [304] "Obscured by darkness" refers to those who engage exclusively in evil activities, such as butchers. These people are completely ignorant of the future results of deeds. "Who have embarked on a path difficult to travel" refers to those who will never be liberated from cyclic existence. "Who possess great fetters" means those who have entirely committed themselves to the spiritual paths of the tīrthikas, for they are bound by the fetters of various evil views. "Who are attached to food adulterated with poison" refers to those who covet the pleasures of meditative attainments (*samāpatti*) that nevertheless contain the afflictions, for such attainments will lead to destruction, just as food adulterated by poison does. "Who destroy the path" refers to those who are arrogant [about their supposed attainments], for they miss the path to liberation. "Who have taken a wrong road" refers to those of uncertain spiritual lineage who have committed themselves to the Hinayana. "Those who are weak" refers to bodhisattvas who have not completed the accumulative preparations. Thus these ten kinds of sentient beings are the objects of the bodhisattva's compassion.

Those who possess the six antitheses of the six perfections are also objects for compassion. As it is taught [in the, you should cultivate]:

> One is kind toward the miserly, kind toward the wicked;
> one is kind toward the agitated, kind toward the careless;
> one is compassionate toward those dominated by sense objects
> and is compassionate toward those attached to falsehood.[244]

Here "the miserly" refers to stingy people. "The wicked" means those of deficient moral discipline, who harm others. "The agitated" means angry people. "The careless" means lazy people. "Those dominated by sense objects" refers to those whose minds are distracted by desire. "Those attached to falsehood" refers to those of imperfect understanding, such as the tīrthikas.

Cultivating compassion toward combined objects. As the *Ornament of Mahayana Sutras* teaches:

> When the Tathāgata had entered into that [expanse],
> seated atop the lofty peak, he gazed down upon beings.
> If he felt compassion for minds that delight in quiescence,
> what need is there to mention minds that delight in existence.[245]

Thus beings in both nirvana and cyclic existence are objects of compassion.

Nirvana as an object of compassion. Śrāvaka and pratyekabuddha [arhats] do not completely achieve their own benefit, and they do not accomplish the benefit of others. Even if they do eventually attain buddhahood, they are worthy objects for compassion because they have taken a protracted, circuitous route; they are, for instance, forty great eons further from buddhahood than ordinary people.

Cyclic existence as an object of compassion includes both beings who contribute to the causes of suffering and those who experience the result, suffering itself.

The first group, *beings who contribute to the causes of suffering*, is made up of those with unwholesome intentions though born as gods or as humans with retinues and consummate wealth. [305] They harm spiritual teachers, the Three Jewels, and sentient beings and support erroneous religious doctrines. These beings are particularly worthy objects for compassion because [as soon as they die,] they go straight to lower miserable destinies like an arrow shot from a bow.

Beings who experience resultant sufferings include those born in the lower miserable destinies and also those in the higher destinies who suffer from indigence and want, physical ailments, mental miseries, separation from dear ones, meeting with hateful people, physical aging, failure of confidence, falling from high position, and not getting what they desire. Anyone who experiences these is an object for compassion. When explaining these topics, one should also expound other suitable teachings about the faults of nirvana and the sufferings of cyclic existence.[246]

The conditions that enable compassion to arise. [As the *Ornament of Mahayana Sutras* teaches:]

> With happiness and suffering as its causes,
> bodhisattvas' compassion arises;
> from its cause, the spiritual friend, and from its nature
> the compassion of the bodhisattvas arises.[247]

The sense of the first half of this verse is that there are three objective conditions [for compassion]: *the suffering of change* from loss of pleasant feelings, *overt suffering* from pain, and *the suffering of conditioned existence* that arises from the neutral causal basis of both pleasant and unpleasant feelings. A sutra teaches:

> Whatever feelings may occur, all are suffering.[248]

This was said with the above in mind. Thus the three kinds of suffering are the objective conditions for the arising of suffering.

The sense of the second half of the verse is: The condition of the motivating cause (*hetu pratyāya*) is the seed of latent compassion. The dominant condition (*adhipati pratyāya*) is the spiritual friend. The immediately preceding condition (*samanantara pratyāya*) is the nature [of mind and mental events]. In that way, compassion arises from four conditions.

How to cultivate compassion entails a description of three methods. The first is *the tīrthika's method* of cultivating compassion, which takes a person as its object with the wish, "May these sentient beings, who are permanent, single, and independent, become free from suffering, which is permanent, single, and independent!"

The second is *the śrāvaka's method* of cultivating compassion, which takes the factors of existence (*dharmas*) as its object with the wish, "Wouldn't it be wonderful if these sentient beings, who are merely an assemblage of factors—namely, personality aggregates, sensory bases, and elements—became free of suffering, which is merely an assemblage of factors!"

These first two ways of cultivating compassion are not cultivated by practitioners of the Mahayana because they conflict with discerning wisdom and emptiness. The third way of cultivating compassion is *the bodhisattva's method—nonobjectified great compassion*. [306] This is generated through the wish, "Wouldn't it be wonderful if these sentient beings, who are like an illusion, were freed of both the causes of suffering and suffering itself, which are like illusions!"

The benefits of cultivating compassion in this way. The *Ornament of Mahayana Sutras* teaches:

> The bodhisatta who undergoes suffering
> in order to help remove the woes of others
> may initially experience terror.
> But when he touches [the ārya level], he experiences intense bliss.[249]

The sense of the above is that the bodhisattva is initially frightened of the sufferings that, through his compassion for others, he will experience when he tries to relieve sentient beings of their pain. This is so because, when he is still on the "level of conviction" (*abhimukticaryā bhūmi*) [of the ordinary person], he has not yet attained[250] [the ability to undergo] the sufferings of self and others equally. But once he has reached the "level of pure altruism" (**adhyāśayaviśuddhi bhūmi*) of the ārya, he experiences intense bliss. Furthermore, as *Perfectly Gathering the Qualities [of Avalokiteśvara]* teaches:

> Avalokiteśvara said: "O Blessed One, a bodhisattva should not train in a great many factors. If a bodhisattva just realizes and adheres to one factor, he will have all the qualities of buddhahood in the palm of his hand. What is that one? It is great compassion. Blessed One, through great compassion you have all the qualities of buddhahood in the palm of your hand.[251]

Thus all immediate and ultimate benefits arise from compassion.

Cultivating the thought of awakening

If you have thus habituated yourself to loving kindness and compassion, the thought of awakening will easily arise. There are three stages in cultivating the thought of awakening: cultivating the view of self and others as equal, cultivating the exchange of self and others, and the method for perfecting those two.

Cultivating the view of self and others as equal

The *Guide to the Bodhisattva Way of Life* teaches:

> At first I should energetically cultivate
> viewing self and others as equals.
> Since happiness and suffering are the same for all,
> I should protect everyone as I would myself.[252]

Thus at the beginning you should cultivate the thought of awakening that views self and others equally. That should be done in this way: Consider that, among all sentient beings equal to the limits of the sky, not a single one has not been your father, mother, or relative in past lives. And you should systematically prove to yourself that all sentient beings are your family members, using reasoning and scriptures such as the words of Ācārya Nāgārjuna:

> If you reduced the earth to little balls the size of jujube kernels,
> their number would be less than that of the number of times
> any one being has been your mother.[253]

[307] Then, when you experience happiness, from this point on with all your heart you should cultivate the wish, "May all sentient beings come to possess happiness and the causes of happiness such as I possess!" And even if you experience suffering, wish from the bottom of your heart and from the core of your being, "May I and all living beings be freed from such sufferings and causes of suffering!"

At this time obstacles to that thought may arise, such as these thoughts of the śrāvaka mentality: "I should hope for others to remove my suffering. I shall never accomplish the removal of the sufferings of others." If so, call to mind the words of the *Guide to the Bodhisattva Way of Life*:

> In what way should I protect myself
> from future sufferings that now cause no harm?[254]

Thus you should reflect, "Why should I struggle to acquire for myself such things as good health, food, and clothing for tomorrow and the future, when my 'self' ceases to exist from one moment to the next, so that each moment it becomes someone different?" In this connection you should think, "Through my habitual tendencies of ignorance, I have erroneously thought that from tomorrow morning onward I will exist." For as the *Guide to the Bodhisattva Way of Life* teaches:

> "I will experience that":
> such a thought is deluded.
> The person who is born
> and the person who will die are different.[255]

For example, some simple-minded people may think, "This river carried off my robe last year" and "Tomorrow morning I will cross this river." But of course both the river that carried off the robe last year and the river that will be crossed tomorrow are different. Accordingly, neither my past mind nor my future mind is "I"; they are other people.

In this regard, some may say "I will accomplish my own purposes" because they think, "Though my future mind is not identical with my present self, it is *my* mental continuum." In that case you should engage in working for the benefit of others with the thought, "Although other sentient beings are not 'I,' they are *my* sentient beings." Some may think that even though this may be the case, if you carefully examine things, you can still achieve your own purposes with a thought that perceives things as "my continuum" from the viewpoint of an uncritical mind. In that case you should engage in accomplishing the welfare of others with a mind that perceives those other sentient beings, too, as belonging to you.

Someone else may think, "I will exert myself for my own benefit, in the manner of 'shaking the snow from my own head,' but I will not be able to cooperate with others, helping each to achieve his or her purpose." But why shouldn't the hand also remove a thorn stuck in the foot? For as the *Guide to the Bodhisattva Way of Life* teaches:

> The sufferings of your foot are not those of your hand.[256]

[308] Were each person or thing to look after only its own individual interests, this would entail absurd consequences—the hand would not aid the eye by removing a speck of dust that has fallen into it, parents would not assist their children, the hand would not help by putting food in the mouth, and so on. In brief, if anyone or anything had to accomplish things only for its own individual benefit without cooperatively helping each other, it would be extremely difficult to achieve anything. Therefore make yourself understand this and engage in accomplishing the welfare of others.

Cultivating the exchange of self and others

As the *Guide to the Bodhisattva Way of Life* teaches:

> If I do not exchange my happiness for the sufferings of others,
> I will not achieve buddhahood,
> and even in cyclic existence
> I will have no happiness.[257]

Accordingly, I should give sentient beings my own happiness and take their sufferings upon myself. The visualizations for cultivating this in meditation are mentioned in the *Guide to the Bodhisattva Way of Life*:

> Considering those below me and so on as myself
> and considering myself as the other,
> I should cultivate envy, competitiveness, and pride
> with a mind free from wandering thoughts.[258]

The meaning here is to imagine in meditation that your enemy is [firstly] in a position lower than you and that you yourself are in the high position of an enemy or another person of high standing. Then imagine that enemy feels begrudging jealousy toward you in your high position. When you have finished that meditation, a thought of this sort will occur to you: "How can it be acceptable to be jealous of others when suffering such as this arises merely from visualizing myself as high and others as low and imagining that those others are jealous of me?" By thinking in this way, jealousy will go away by itself.

Likewise cultivate competitiveness toward others who are your equals. For this, visualize that you change places with an enemy who is of equal standing with you. Then imagine that this enemy is competing with and striving against you in every possible way. Later, when you conclude that meditation, a thought such as this will occur to you: "How can it be right to injure others and strive against them when suffering such as this occurs just from imagining that I am an enemy and that others injure and mentally strive against me?" By thus reflecting, competitive thoughts will disappear of their own accord.

Cultivate pride in the same way. For this, imagine yourself in a position below your real status and elevate to your own position someone inferior to you. Then make that person who is now above you feel proud about his superior family, excellent mental qualities, and so forth in relation to you, his inferior. When you finish that meditation you will think, "If I experience such suffering when imagining that others are acting arrogantly toward me, how can it be right for me to be arrogant toward others?" In this way pride will be pacified naturally, of its own accord.

Practice these points in detail according to their explanation in the *Guide to the Bodhisattva Way of Life*. If you are unable to meditate as extensively as that and want to cultivate these things in a brief form, meditate on the sense of the following passages and recite them out loud. The *Precious Garland* teaches:

> May [the results of] others' evil deeds be experienced by me,
> and may [the results of] all my wholesome deeds be experienced
> by them!
>
> As long as even a few sentient beings
> remain unliberated anywhere,

> may I remain [in cyclic existence] for their benefit,
> even after attaining awakening!
>
> If the merit of saying this
> had physical form,
> it would not fit into worlds
> as numerous as the grains of sand in the River Ganges.
>
> The Blessed One taught this,
> and the reason is seen to be sound.[259]

And the *Guide to the Bodhisattva Way of Life* reiterates:

> May whatever sufferings living beings possess
> all be experienced by me instead!
> By the merit of the bodhisattva,
> may all living beings partake of happiness![260]

Regarding the above practice, some people may object, doubting they would be able to bear the sufferings of all sentient beings if those sufferings all came to them.[261] This is not a substantial objection. Meditating as above is like one dog chasing another or like dirt cleaning another impurity. In other words, it is as if, just after drawing close to wild birds and animals, you were to shout, "Everyone assemble in front of me!" They would all scatter. Similarly, by uttering the words "May the suffering of all sentient beings come to me!" the sufferings of yourself and others will be destroyed but they will not actually be experienced. It is just as is shown in the story of the captain Maitrakanyakā[262] and in the episode of the Jātakas when the Buddha-to-be was the puller of a cart of fire in hell.[263]

[Objection:] I have also witnessed others saying that it is unsuitable to cultivate the thought of awakening in which you vicariously exchange places with others. The reason they give is that the sufferings of others will definitely come to you because the ultimate realization of prayers is assured.[264] And since you will not be able to bear the burden of their suffering, it is not a skillful means to cultivate in these ways the thought of awakening in which you change places with others. [310]

[Reply:] This is unacceptable. Such people do not know the difference between possible (*sthāna*) resolves that are assured of yielding their result and impossible (*asthāna*) resolves that have no assured result. They are simply talking, without having understood the reasons explained above through such lines in the *Guide to the Bodhisattva Way of Life* as:

> If I do not exchange my own happiness for the suffering of others,
> I will not obtain buddhahood,
> and even in cyclic existence
> I will have no happiness.[265]

Therefore, if you understand this important principle of cultivating the thought of awakening through exchanging self and others, you will quickly attain buddhahood.

The method for perfecting those two meditations

For this, call to mind and recite aloud verses about the harmful consequences of working for selfish benefits, the beneficial consequences of working to benefit others, and the consequent rightness of having to exert yourself for others' benefit. As the *Guide to the Bodhisattva Way of Life* teaches:

> If in spite of those instructions,
> you, O mind, will still not do so,
> then since all faults are dependent on you,
> you simply must be defeated.[266]

The point of this verse is that if it will not engage in accomplishing the welfare of other sentient beings, then the mind itself should be defeated.

> That former time when you ruined me
> is gone.
> I now see where you are going,
> and I will subdue all your arrogance.
>
> Abandon the thought,
> "There is still some purpose of my own"![267]

These lines indicate that you should understand and abandon selfish interests because all the sufferings you have previously experienced, from beginningless time in cyclic existence down to the present day, have originated from selfish motives.

> Since I have sold you, [O mind,] to others,
> I will not grieve but will increase my power.
>
> If, having become careless,
> I do not give you to sentient beings,
> it is sure that you will hand me over
> to the guardians of hell.[268]

From the above I must reflect: "At the time of generating the resolve to attain awakening, I sold you [my selfish mind] to others, whereas if you had not been sold, you would definitely have handed me over to the guardians of the hells."

> Thus I have suffered long
> from your handing me over countless times.
> Now I will recall my grudges against you
> and will destroy your thoughts of selfish benefit.[269]

Thus if these convictions are not implanted in my mind and successfully practiced, then despite my cultivating a view of self and others as equal and of changing places with others, I will have to get directly to the point with my mind and forcibly make it practice, just as you would impel a wild horse with a whip. [311]

> O mind, though countless eons have passed
> with you wanting to achieve selfish purposes,
> through all those great pains,
> you have only achieved suffering.[270]

Thus I must reflect: "Though you have tried to accomplish your own benefit for countless eons, [O selfish mind,] it was not achieved, and on top of that you have achieved only suffering and have not created causes for happiness even for an instant." Thinking in this way, make yourself ashamed.

> Acting as the spy of others,

I will even rob whatever I find on my body
and I will make you
do what is beneficial for others.[271]

The sense of these lines is that you should act so that others become free of suffering. Thus when you see a suffering person, forcibly rob your own stinginess and use what you obtain in whatever way will benefit that suffering person.

"I am happy and others unhappy.
I am superior and others inferior.
I am benefitted and others are not."
Thinking that, why am I not jealous of myself?[272]

You should thus think that you are too happy and highly placed while others are too unhappy and low and in this way cultivate a feeling of jealousy toward yourself.

May I be parted from happiness,
and may the sufferings of others be put upon me![273]

Thus you should think that whatever happiness you have is immediately given to all sentient beings and that you take upon yourself whatever burden of suffering sentient beings possess.

Thinking, "What am I doing at this time?"
I should scrutinize my own faults.

Though others may do something wrong,
I should make it my own fault.
And though I do even a small wrong,
I should announce and confess it to many people.[274]

Scrutinize your physical, verbal, and mental activity, and if you find yourself engaging in wrong behavior, shame your mind by telling it, "Not frightened by as much wandering as you have already done, are you going to wander still more in cyclic existence and miserable destinies?" Even though others may harm you, think, "This person did not bring it about. It is my own evil deeds that have caused this." If you do even a small wrong to others, announce and confess it in front of many people, saying, "I have done a bad thing such as this." The *Guide to the Bodhisattva Way of Life* also teaches:

> By mentioning how others are even more renowned,
> cause your own repute to be eclipsed.
> Like the least of slaves,
> submit yourself to doing all sorts of work.[275]

If some people praise you, then mention the fame of others, saying, "This person is greater than I in terms of his family, excellent qualities, and so forth." In that way you yourself will be outshone. [312] And devoid of pride, submit yourself to doing work for the spiritual teacher, the Three Jewels, and other sentient beings. As the *Guide to the Bodhisattva Way of Life* also teaches:

> Do not praise yourself for incidental good qualities,
> for you are faulty by nature.[276]

If you see in yourself a few slight good qualities, think, "Such qualities are adventitious; by nature I am faulty," and thus humble your pride. Also:

> I should act so that no one at all
> knows about my good qualities.
>
> In brief, for the benefit of sentient beings
> may whatever harmful things you, O mind,
> have done to others for selfish motives
> all befall me!
>
> I should not become forceful
> in the manner of an obstinate person
> but modest, timid, and restrained,
> like a newly wedded bride.[277]

Reflect on the sense of these and similar verses and, strenuously cultivating feelings of jealousy toward yourself, apply yourself to benefitting others.

By abandoning self-interest and accomplishing the welfare of others in this way, a great interconnection is established with the final complete achievement of your personal benefit. It is also taught:

> Let me thus energetically engage
> in working for the benefit of others.
> Since the word of the Sage is infallible,
> I shall afterward witness the advantages of this.[278]

Thus, since the fully awakened Buddha possesses no falsehood, your personal benefit will be achieved through benefitting others. And furthermore:

> If you had previously done
> this work [of trading self for others],
> there could be no such circumstances as these,
> which lack the consummate bliss of buddhahood.[279]

You should think: "I am late in cultivating this thought of awakening in which self and others change places. If I had cultivated it from the beginning, I would already be a buddha, and how could there have occurred such present unhappiness and suffering as this?!" Thus reflecting, energetically apply yourself to changing places with others.

Some ask whether, after cultivating the thought of awakening, you should meditate on emptiness. At this stage you should not meditate on emptiness, for simple emptiness that has not been freed from false imputations through discerning wisdom is a great delaying diversion. As the Ārya master taught:

> Those of small discrimination are ruined
> if they view emptiness wrongly.[280]

And further:

> That emptiness that is known as "without birth,"
> "empty," and "without self," [313]
> when meditated upon by those of inferior natures,
> it becomes a meditation on a self.[281]

Therefore I will explain the method of meditating on emptiness later after cutting off all discursive notions about it by means of the perfection of wisdom.

Correctly accomplishing meditative concentration

This includes two things: accomplishing the four excellent qualities and eliminating the seven attachments.

Accomplishing the four excellent qualities. These are explained in the lines beginning: "Meditative concentration: the destruction of its opposite...."[282] Accordingly, these qualities are: (1) discarding its antithesis, distraction; (2) realizing the nondiscursive, the absence of a substantial self; (3) fulfilling others' wishes by accomplishing the benefits of self and others based on the meditative absorptions; and (4) maturing sentient beings by establishing them in the three vehicles of Buddhism.

Eliminating the seven attachments is explained in the lines beginning: "The meditative concentration of the bodhisattva is unattached...."[283] Accordingly, the seven attachments are attachment to: (1) the antithesis [of concentration, which is distraction], (2) procrastination, (3) premature satisfaction, (4) the hope of getting something in return, (5) the future result of a deed, (6) the antithesis that is the latent dispositions to distraction not yet destroyed, and (7) the two special distractions, as explained previously [in the chapter on generosity]. Rid yourself of those seven attachments together with all propensities toward them.

The benefits of realizing meditative concentration

These benefits are of two main sorts, temporary and ultimate. *Temporary benefits* themselves are of two sorts: those occurring in the present life and those that occur in future lives.

In this life, through the realization of meditative concentration, you will experience the benefit of tranquility (*śamatha*). That will dispel adventitious afflictions. The eight worldly concerns will be equalized. You will attain the joys and bliss of meditative concentrations, and to some extent there will arise excellent qualities such as supernatural powers and supranormal intuition. And those [meditators] who become known to others will become objects of delight for the world of humans and gods.

In future lives, you will benefit by acquiring a body, voice, and mind that are ready for use [in Dharma practice and meditation], the four concentrations (*dhyāna*), the four supranormal intuitions, and so forth. For as the *Verse Summary of the Perfection of Wisdom* teaches:

Through meditative concentration (*dhyāna*), you discard the
objects of sense enjoyment as blameworthy things
and achieve knowledge (*vidyā*), superknowledge (*abhijñā*), and
meditative absorption (*samādhi*).[284] [314]

Ultimate benefits. Because of meditative concentration, when you attain buddhahood you will attain such things as the four purities, by which activities for yourself and others are achieved. For as the *Ornament of Mahayana Sutras* teaches:

Homage to you who have achieved dominion over assuming [of
new existence],
its duration and its abandonment,
over emanations and transformation,
and over meditative absorptions and gnosis![285]

9. The Perfection of Wisdom

THE EXPLANATION of discerning wisdom has three parts: the definition of discerning wisdom, ascertaining the nature of discerning wisdom, and the benefits of producing discerning wisdom.

The *definition of discerning wisdom* is exact knowledge of the real nature of what is to be known.[286] If that knowledge is endowed with correct preparation, actual practice, and conclusion, it will become the perfection of wisdom.

Ascertaining the nature of discerning wisdom has three parts: identifying the antithesis of discerning wisdom, discerning the individual antidotes, and correctly accomplishing those.

Identifying the antithesis of discerning wisdom

This involves two things: identifying imperfect understanding, and reflecting on its harmful consequences.

Identifying imperfect understanding, the antithesis of discerning wisdom. Three types of imperfect understanding should be recognized. The first is the lack of understanding of someone who, like a simple person, has not pursued the virtue of discerning wisdom. The second type is the imperfect understanding of people who, like the tīrthikas, seek knowledge but exert themselves in incorrect ways. And the third is the imperfect understanding of people who, like the śrāvakas, are not erroneous in [the basic object of] their exertion but have cultivated a discerning wisdom that will not result in complete buddhahood.

Its harmful consequences. Reflecting on the harmful consequences of imperfect understanding has two parts: the harmful consequences in this life and the harmful consequences in all future lives.

As to the harm caused *in this life*, many disadvantages accrue in the present life from imperfect understanding. Because you are unwise, you do not feel confident. You do not know what you should do and what not. The whole world, including the gods, will scorn you. And you will not be able to join an assembly of scholars, just as a fox cannot go into the midst of lions. The words of the Vinaya, "Someone who is like a lion will not respectfully serve someone who is like a fox" are to the same effect.[287] And as Cāṇakya's *Treatise on Political Morals* teaches:

> Completely avoid fools,
> who though they have two legs are in fact cattle.[288]

And:

> "Without the wealth of learning, the earth will be blind."
> Think thus and act accordingly.[289]

Also reflect on this intermediary verse: [315]

> In the presence of the wise, he is timid and evasive.
> In a group of fools, he is gleeful and frolics.
> Though he has no hump or dewlap,
> he is an ox who possesses upper teeth.[290]

As to the harm caused *in all future lives*, the *Guide to the Bodhisattva Way of Life* teaches:

> People troubled by sickness
> lack the power to work.
> Likewise, a mind troubled by delusion
> lacks the power to work.[291]

And as the *Treasury of Higher Knowledge* explains:

> There is no way to pacify the afflictions
> without discriminating the factors of existence,
> and with afflictions beings wander in the ocean of existence.
> Therefore the Teacher taught abhidharma, so they say.[292]

Thus many disadvantages occur if you lack discerning wisdom, such as: Your work will have little impact, whatever you do, because you cannot differentiate what should be accepted and what rejected. Wherever you are born, you will be endowed with dull faculties. By virtue of that, even if you practice some religious teaching, you will only obtain erroneous teachings to practice. Even though you meditate, you will not be able to sever the root of self-postulation (*ahaṃkāra*). And even if you do, you will fall into the cessation of the śrāvaka [arhat] or of the pratyekabuddha, for you are not skilled in means.

Discerning the individual antidotes

This has two parts, of which the first is the antidote to the cause [and the second is the antidote to the result].

The antidote to the cause of imperfect understanding. The cause of imperfect understanding is ignorance, and its contributing condition is respect for bad spiritual teachers. And as the *Thorough Exposition of Valid Cognition* teaches:

> Ignorance is the root of all evils;
> it's the view of self on a transitory collection.[293]

About the bad religious teacher, who is a main contributing factor to imperfect understanding, the same text explains:

> And there are also those who repeat such [erroneous doctrines].
> Therefore evil people make darkness spread widely.[294]

And as a sutra teaches in great detail:

> [The Lord Buddha asked:] "Who made you experience those unbearable feelings of suffering in such great quantity?" [His respondent] answered: "Nonvirtuous teachers."[295]

Therefore exert yourself in learning and reflection, which are the means for avoiding that ignorance. As a sutra teaches:

> Through learning you will abandon the useless.
> Through learning you will turn back from evil.
> Through learning your discerning wisdom will grow.

> Through learning you will attain nirvana.[296]

And also:

> If you study, your insight increases.[297]

Accordingly, through learning, the habitual propensities of ignorance will diminish. [316] Moreover, you should acquire such learning from a genuine religious teacher whose instructions do not contradict the three divisions of scripture (Tripiṭaka) or the four tantric classes. But you should not take as your religious teacher someone who teaches a counterfeit imitation of Dharma that does not accord with those, even though at first glance his conduct appears to be excellent. In this context [the teacher] should relate such parables as those about "selling donkey flesh after showing a deer's tail,"[298] "like a hunter wearing the robes of an ascetic,"[299] and "one who, given food, puts it in a hole."[300]

The antidote to the resultant imperfect understanding has two parts: refuting mistaken understandings and achieving unmistaken understanding.

Refuting mistaken understandings has two sections: refuting the traditions of non-Buddhist schools, and refuting the erroneous opinions of Buddhist schools.

Refuting the false constructs of the non-Buddhist tīrthikas.[301] Although the Indian tīrthikas possess inconceivably many erroneous speculative views, they can all be included within the categories of eternalist and nihilist. There are four schools of eternalists: *Vaidika ("Followers of the Vedas," i.e., Mīmāṃsā-Vedānta), Sāṃkhya, Vaiśeṣika, and Kṣapanaka (Jaina). Nihilism is recognized within only one school, the Cārvāka. There are many alternate analyses of these schools by Tibetan religious scholars, but I see those to be erroneous.

These views, moreover, are produced by postulation of a self as the motivating cause. They are adhered to through the contributing condition of the nonvirtuous teacher. The nature of the view is to maintain that something is either permanent or annihilated. Moreover, the four schools of eternalists maintain that a self (*ātman*) is permanent. When that permanent self is fettered by karma and the afflictions, it exists in cyclic existence, and when that self becomes freed from those, it is liberated. The nihilists maintain an existent self, but they do not maintain that after it has died there is either a cyclic existence in which it is fettered or a liberation in which it is freed.[302]

To refute those, I may say this very briefly: It is clearly known that after removing [the false imputation of] a substantially existent self or entity in either a person or in phenomena, you become freed from both views of permanence (eternalism) and annihilation (nihilism) by just the realization that all phenomena are without own-natures (*svabhāva*).

Refuting erroneous constructs of Buddhists has three parts: refuting those who maintain the tenets of śrāvaka philosophical schools, refuting Mahayana followers who imagine the teachings of provisional meaning to be of definitive meaning, and refuting those who hold a doctrine that is neither Śrāvakayāna nor Mahayana to be the doctrine of the Buddha.

The *schools of śrāvaka tenets* are two: Vaibhāṣika and Sautrāntika.

The *schools of the Mahayana* include the Yogācāra and the Madhyamaka. The former is made up of "those maintaining the existence of a cognitive image" (Sākāra) and "those maintaining that the cognitive image does not exist" (Nirākāra). The Madhyamaka also includes two subschools: Svātantrika and Prāsaṅgika. If such Buddhist philosophical tenets fall into the extremes of existence or nonexistence, they too must be refuted, even if they claim to be the Middle Way, for they have not transcended the extremes of permanence and annihilation. [317] For the detailed refutation of these, consult my *Treasure of Reasoning*[303] and *Analysis of Established Tenets*.[304]

Refuting the *schools held to be the doctrine of the Buddha* that belong to neither the Śrāvakayāna nor the Mahayana has four parts: (1) refuting a Chinese tradition that formerly spread [in Tibet], (2) refuting a later tradition that follows [the earlier Chinese one], (3) refuting a current tradition that holds a cognitive-objectless Yogācāra meditation to be the mahāmudrā, and (4) refuting a tradition that maintains a specious perfection of wisdom to be mahāmudrā.

Refuting a Chinese tradition that formerly spread [in Tibet][305]

In the time of King Trisong Detsen, there was a Chinese monk who taught the following: "Words have no real pith. By means of a Dharma of conventional usage, you will not gain buddhahood. If you understand the mind, that is the white panacea."[306] Having composed treatises entitled *Reclining Wheel of Concentration*, *A Dam of Concentration*, *A Further Dam of Concentration*, *The Lining of the View*, and *Sources in Eighty Sutras*,[307] he spread throughout the realm of Tibet this doctrine of the white panacea.

Then, because that doctrine did not accord with the [Buddhist] tradition of India, the king invited Wa Yeshé Wangpo to court and asked him which religious tradition was true, that of India or that of China. Yeshé Wangpo told the king:

> Ācārya Śāntarakṣita stated this in the testament that he left behind: "The heterodox [non-Buddhist] religion will not arise [in Tibet] because Ācārya Padmasambhava has entrusted the Tibetan realm to the twelve guardian deities. But it is the 'greatness' of dependent origination that things appear in pairs—day and night, right and left, waxing and waning [of the moon], and even pure and impure Dharma. Consequently, after I have died a Chinese master will appear. And his doctrine will appear—a denigration of method and discerning wisdom called the white panacea that will teach that you gain buddhahood through merely understanding mind. Since the Lord Buddha taught in a sutra that one of the five impurities, the impurity of view, consists of delighting in emptiness, it is the nature of things that not only [some people] in Tibet but all people in whom the five impurities thrive delight in that. If this spreads, it will harm the doctrine of the Buddha in general. At that time you should therefore invite from India my disciple, the great scholar Kamalaśīla and have him debate the Chinese master. Then let the tradition of whoever wins be followed!" Since this was thus foretold, I beg you to act accordingly. [318]

The king then invited Ācārya Kamalaśīla and convened a meeting. At Samyé the king and the learned men acted as witnessing arbiters and collected all weapons. When garlands of flowers had been placed in their hands, the disputants vowed to bow to the victor and to discard the defeated tradition. They also agreed that whoever did otherwise would be punished by the king.

At that time in Kamalaśīla's row there were only a few adherents of the Indian religious tradition and a couple others, such as the minister Gö. In the Chinese master's there was a very large group that included the royal consort of the Dro clan, named Jangchup, and the chamberlain Cho Mama.

Ācārya Kamalaśīla elicited his opponent's position by asking: "What is the religious tradition of China like?" The Chinese master replied: "Your religious tradition, which begins with taking refuge and generating a resolve to attain awakening, climbs from the bottom up, like a monkey climbing to the top of a tree. Our religious tradition consists of attaining buddhahood through merely understanding the mind, having cultivated in meditation the absence of conceptual thinking, because you cannot attain buddhahood through a Dharma that consists of doing what is to be done [i.e., religious duties]. Our tradition is called the white panacea because it is a religious teaching that descends from above, like an eagle descending out of the sky to the top of a tree."

To that Kamalaśīla replied: "Both your analogy and your substance are unacceptable. To show first how your analogy is unacceptable, [let me ask you this]: Does that eagle descend from the sky to the top of a tree after having taken birth suddenly with completely developed wings? Or does he descend having first been born somewhere [on the ground,] such as on a crag, and then developing wings? The first alternative is impossible. And the second is suitable as an analogy for the gradual approach but not as an analogy for the simultaneous approach.

When the Chinese master had no reply to his analogy, Ācārya Kamalaśīla said: "Not only is your analogy wrong but your substance is mistaken. What is that meditative cultivation of nonconceptualization? Is it merely the stopping of one part of conceptual thought, or do you have to stop all conceptual thinking? If you say it is the stopping of one part, then such things as sleep and fainting would also be 'nonconceptualizing' because they involve stopping just one part of thought. If you say it is the stopping of all conceptual thinking, then [I must ask]: When you meditatively cultivate nonconceptualizing, do you or do you not need to formulate beforehand the thought, 'I will cultivate nonconceptualizing'? If you do not need to, then that meditative cultivation would arise in all sentient beings of the three realms of existence, for meditation would be born even though a thought of meditating had not been formulated beforehand. [319]

"If you do need to formulate beforehand the thought of cultivating nonconceptualization, since that is itself conceptual thinking, your assertion of meditatively cultivating nonconceptualization is ruined—just as, for example, your observance of silence is broken if you say 'Don't make any noise!'"[308]

With such words Kamalaśīla refuted that doctrine by means of scripture and reasoning so that the Chinese master lost his capacity to respond. At that, the king said: "If you have an answer, please give it." The master replied: "I am as if struck on the head by lightning; I know no answer." The king said: "In that case, offer your garland of flowers to the ācārya and beg his pardon. Abandon the religious tradition of the white panacea and practice according to the religious tradition of India, which does not conflict with either scripture or reasoning." The king promulgated throughout Tibet the edict: "Henceforth whoever follows the white panacea will be punished." And the Chinese texts were gathered together and hidden in a cache at Samyé.

Thereupon the Chinese master felt distraught and returned to his residence. It is said that he accidentally left behind at the religious school one of his shoes, and that on the basis of that sign he prophesied to his followers: "When the doctrine of the Buddha is about to perish, there will yet remain a little of my doctrine—as much as a shoe."[309] Afterward, learned religious teachers of Tibet said: "Though the Chinese master did not understand religious doctrine, he did know a bit about prognostication, for that is why people nowadays are discarding genuine religious traditions and going over to the white panacea, which holds that you attain buddhahood by the face-to-face meeting with and recognition of mind."

I have also seen it written in another testament (*bka' chems*) that a Chinese monk other than that master left his shoe behind when despondently leaving for China and that the above prediction was said about *his* shoe.

Then the Chinese master lit a fire atop his head and, facing Sukhāvatī in the west, passed away. The chamberlain Cho Mama committed suicide by beating his sexual organ, and so on and so forth. Here I have not set down the rest of the story because this book would become too long. But you should read about it in the *Testament of the King*, the *Testament of Wa*, and the *Testament of Ba* histories.[310]

Refuting a later tradition that follows the earlier Chinese one

[320] Nowadays some people teach the following instructions on mahāmudrā:

> Avoiding the three delaying diversions (*gol sa*) and the four occasions of lapsing (*shor sa*), cultivate the innate [mind], letting it be original, unaltered, and relaxed, like the spinning of a brahman's sacred thread.[311]

They say the sense of this is: Meditation on mahāmudrā can become delayingly diverted into bliss, luminosity, or nonconceptualization. If you become delayingly diverted into bliss, you will be reborn a god of the realm of desire; if into luminosity (*gsal ba*), you will be reborn as a god in the form realm; and if you are diverted into nonconceptualization, you will be born in the formless realm.

The four occasions of lapsing are (1) lapsing into [erroneous conceptions of] the original nature [of the ultimate] (*gshis la shor*), (2) lapsing into [erroneous] meditative cultivation (*bsgom du shor*), (3) lapsing into [erroneous conceptions of the] path (*lam du shor*), and (4) lapsing into [erroneous] "sealing" (*rgyas 'debs su shor*). Avoiding these, place the mind in the original (*so ma*), unaltered (*ma bcos*), relaxed (*lhugs pa*), softly at ease (*'bol le*), and loosened (*shig ge*) state, like the spinning of a brahman's sacred thread.

This teaching follows the white panacea of China; it is not the mahāmudrā taught by the Buddha. Moreover, mahāmudrā in general was not explained in the Sutra, Vinaya, or Abhidharma scriptures. In particular, I have never seen in those the teaching of a mahāmudrā such as this. In the four classes of the tantras, [the four mudrās] are explained as in the passage: "karma, dharma, samaya, and mahāmudrā." But the above is not the system of those four. In his *Establishing the Four Mudrās*, Ārya Nāgārjuna taught:

> If those who do not understand the karmamudrā will not understand the dharmamudrā, how will they understand even the name of the mahāmudrā?[312]

Likewise, that sort of mahāmudrā is refuted in the tantras and tantric treatises, though here I have not written down the relevant quotations from scripture because they belong to the mantra tradition.

[Question:] Even though this mahāmudrā may not be explained in the sutras, tantras, and treatises, is there any contradiction in practicing it?

[Answer:] The above teaching contradicts the sutras and tantras, and it is clearly unacceptable logically, precisely because it is a greater delaying diversion to be born as a god with no freedom to practice Dharma than as one of the gods of the three above-mentioned delaying diversions, since all sutras and tantras contain the prayer: "May I not be born in the eight circumstances that lack the freedom to practice Dharma!" Another reason is that some methods of meditation, through letting your mind remain in an unaltered state, are explained as "meditation on delusion" (*rmongs pa'i sgom pa*), being mentioned with the words:

> He who meditatively cultivates [unconscious, unaware] delusion
> will gain delusion through delusion.[313]

And another reason is that it has not even the slightest difference from the white panacea of the Chinese master.

Furthermore, for the attainment of buddhahood, even worse than the eight circumstances lacking the freedom to practice Dharma are the delaying diversions of the śrāvaka and pratyekabuddha. [321] For as it is taught:

> An existence in hell does not cause
> a permanent obstacle to awakening,
> but being a śrāvaka and pratyekabuddha are
> permanent obstacles to awakening.[314]

And as the *Recitation of Mañjuśrī's Names* teaches:

> You should never enter into the ascertained truths of a śrāvaka or pratyekabuddha.[315]

And in the *Perfection of Wisdom*:

> You should understand the motivating cause of the śrāvaka and the pratyekabuddha. You should understand their paths. You should understand their results. Having understood them, you should abandon them.[316]

And as the *Verse Summary of the Perfection of Wisdom* teaches:

> If, when practicing the ten paths of virtuous deeds for a great many eons,
> [a bodhisattva] generates the aspiration to attain the status of a śrāvaka [arhat] or of pratyekabuddhahood,
> that will make his moral discipline faulty and ruined,
> for to produce those aspirations is a graver fault than the defeating infractions.[317]

And as the noble Heap of Jewels collection of sutras teaches at great length:

> Realizing that five hundred monks would attain arhatship if Śāriputra taught them the doctrine, Ārya Mañjuśrī taught them the profound doctrine himself first. As a consequence the monks felt no faith in those teachings and fell flaming into hell.
>
> Śāriputra said to Mañjuśrī, "You have committed a terrible deed."
>
> Mañjuśrī replied, "Just so, Śāriputra. I have committed a terrible deed."
>
> Thereupon Śāriputra told the Lord Buddha, "Mañjuśrī has committed a terrible deed."
>
> The Buddha asked, "What has he done?"
>
> Śāriputra answered, "When five hundred monks would have become arhats had I taught them the doctrine, they fell flaming into hell because Mañjuśrī taught them."
>
> The Buddha replied, "Śāriputra, if you had taught them they would indeed have become arhats, but they would have become permanently incapable of attaining buddhahood. Though they have gone to hell because Mañjuśrī taught them the profound doctrine, they will later be freed and quickly attain buddhahood. Therefore only Mañjuśrī is skilled in means."[318]

Accordingly, all the sutras, tantras, and treatises reject the śrāvaka and pratyekabuddha attainments because these are great delaying diversions.

There are also occasions of lapsing greater than the four listed above. If [your meditation on emptiness] lapses into the cultivation of mindless delusion, or into tranquility (*śamatha*), that will obstruct your attaining all the common and uncommon qualities, from skillful means, the levels and paths, the resultant three bodies, the five gnoses, the ten powers, the four fearlessnesses, the four analytical knowledges, and so on, up to and including omniscience. [322]

Even if you did stop focusing the mind on reality and, impelled by such things as the sustaining spiritual power of the Buddha, exerted yourself in skillful means, your attainment of buddhahood would still be delayed a long time, like the repairing of something made wrongly to begin with. For as the *Ornament of Mahayana Sutras* teaches:

> Having been constantly occupied with renuncitation,
> Those two [śrāvaka āryas] delight in attaining nirvana;
> thus their realization is held to be slower.[319]

"Spinning the sacred thread of a brahman" is also unsuitable as an analogy. When spinning, it is impossible for a good thread to result without altering the fiber by lifting it, drawing it out, and twisting it, tightening it if loose, loosening it if tight, regulating its thickness, removing knotty bunches, and so forth. If you leave it in its unaltered state, it will never be anything but a pile of raw fiber, whereas if you take some fiber and start making a thread, that itself is an alteration. Accordingly, if you practice mahāmudrā by just leaving your mind as you like, without any alteration, what is the need of any instruction from a religious teacher? What more radical modification of mind could there be than that very cultivation of primordial mind, having excluded the three delaying diversions and the four occasions of lapsing? Thus this is an analogy that would gladden only the simple-minded because, like the analogy of the eagle used by the Chinese master, it cannot stand up to examination since the sense and exemplification are erroneous.

Refuting a current tradition that holds a cognitive-objectless Yogācāra meditation to be mahāmudrā

In his treatises *Ornament of Yogācāra*[320] and *Practical Instruction*[321] Ācārya Ratnākaraśānti taught four yogas called "one-pointed," "free from elaboration," "one taste," and "without meditative cultivation." These are meditations of the cognitive-objectless Yogācāra but are not recognized in the schools of the Madhyamaka. If you feel a devoted appreciation for this teaching, you should refer to Ratnākaraśānti's treatises themselves.

Nowadays I have seen some Tibetans who apply those four yogas to the five paths or ten levels and who consider it to be a meditative cultivation of mahāmudrā.[322] [323] But this is unacceptable because mahāmudrā is a special feature of the mantra consecrations and of the meditative absorption (*samādhi*) of the two stages [of generation and completion], whereas the above is not that. The wonderful stages and paths of inner interdependences are taught in the tantras, but the levels and paths in relation to the four yogas are taught nowhere. Hence that is just someone's invention. This is also unacceptable for the follower of mahāmudrā himself, for it contradicts the teachings that mahāmudrā alone is decisive and that the levels and paths need not be considered, as in the words:

> The deluded person errs who considers levels and paths
> within the singly and instantaneously decisive mahāmudrā.[323]

Refuting a tradition that maintains a specious perfection of wisdom to be mahāmudrā

Many varieties of so-called mahāmudrā are current, such as the "three introductions of mahāmudrā" maintained by some people based on the passage from the *Perfection of Wisdom in a Hundred Thousand Lines*:

> He set forth to sentient beings a teaching that stated, "All factors of existence have the natural mode of space."[324]

[According to this tradition, the three introductions are:] the introduction of all factors of existence as being mind, the introduction of the mind as being space, and the introduction of space as emptiness.

Some also hold that mahāmudrā is the absence of mindfulness and the lack of mental activities, basing themselves on the statement:

> Not recollecting and not thinking is recollecting the Buddha (*buddhānusmṛti*).[325]

And some also take as a meditation of mahāmudrā the passage:

> That which is mind is the nonexistence of mind, for mind is by nature luminosity.[326]

These will be mere semblances of the perfection of wisdom if their adherents are for the most part ignorant about how to cultivate them in meditation. And even if they know how to cultivate them, these are not the mahāmudrā practices of the mantra tradition but merely a meditation of the Perfection of Wisdom sutra class of teachings. If you feel attracted to these and wish to cultivate a realization of them through meditation, you should proceed as taught:

> Those who observe moral discipline and possess learning and
> reflection
> will apply themselves well to meditative practice.[327]

Accordingly, observe moral discipline as the basis and train your mind by means of an ocean-like understanding that arises from learning. After using your understanding that arises from reflection to consider carefully, through reasoning, whether the sense of what you have learned is erroneous, meditatively cultivate the nonerroneous sense, making your practice complete in terms of the preparation, actual meditation, and conclusion that are taught in the basic texts of the Perfection of Wisdom sutra tradition. But you should not cultivate it by erroneously making it into a mahāmudrā of the mantra tradition.

Therefore, for the realization of complete buddhahood, three factors must come together: compassion, which is like a bow; discerning wisdom, which is like an arrow; and skillful means, which is like an expert archer. [324] For as Ācārya Candragomin said:

> Oh! Though there was such a one as you, Blessed One, who by great merit possesses the bow of compassion....[328]

And in *Perfectly Gathering the Qualities [of Avalokiteśvara] Sutra*:

> Avalokiteśvara said: "Blessed One, a bodhisattva should not train in a great many factors. If a bodhisattva adheres to and realizes one factor, he will have all the qualities of a buddha in the palm of his hand. What is that one? It is great compassion."[329]

And as the *Thorough Exposition of Valid Cognition* explains:

> The proof [of the Buddha's authority] is great compassion.
> From having mastered that....[330]

And as taught in *Entering the Middle Way*:

> The śrāvakas and pratyekabuddhas arose from the Lord of Sages.
> The Buddha arose from the bodhisattvas.
> The causes of bodhisattvas are compassionate mind,
> nondual cognition, and the thought of awakening.[331]

Similarly, all sutras, tantras, and great treatises praise compassion and the thought of awakening.

Furthermore, such scriptures as the *Praise of the Excellence [of the Buddha]* teach at great length the need for discerning wisdom, which is like a bow:

It is said that the angry Mahādeva burned down
[the demigods' city] Tripura with one arrow.
But the one arrow of your gnosis burns
all the afflictions together with their propensities.[332]

And in the *Verse Summary of the Perfection of Wisdom*:

Having understood the nature of all phenomena through discerning wisdom,
he completely transcends the three realms of existence.
After turning the precious wheel, that mightiest of men
will teach the Dharma to living beings, so that suffering may end.[333]

And in the *Guide to the Bodhisattva Way of Life*:

All these branches were taught by the Sage
for the sake of discerning wisdom.
Therefore those who wish to allay sufferings
should generate discerning wisdom.[334]

And as the *Thorough Exposition of Valid Cognition* teaches:

The view of emptiness will free you.
The remaining meditations are for that purpose.[335]

Therefore, just as bow and arrow must go together, so you must join emptiness and compassion. For as the *Compendium of Trainings* teaches:

Because they produce emptiness
whose essence is compassion, their merit becomes pure.[336]

And as Ācārya Saraha said: [325]

Those, dwelling on emptiness, who abandon compassion,
will not find the supreme path.
Those who meditate solely on compassion
will remain in cyclic existence—how could there be liberation?[337]

And as the *Thorough Exposition of Valid Cognition* teaches:

> [The Buddha] taught grace through compassion and truth from
> gnosis together with the means for achieving it.
> He energetically applied himself to teaching that....[338]

The pair, emptiness and compassion, may appear to be incompatible; you need skillful means to be able to practice them without incompatibility. As the *Thorough Exposition of Valid Cognition* explains at great length:

> Having brought to mastery over a long period of time
> many methods in numerous ways,
> all faults and virtues become
> transparent to him.
> Therefore, because his mind, too, is clear,
> he has rid himself of the propensities [to the afflictions], the cause.
>
> The Great Sage applies himself to achieving the welfare of
> others,
> and this is his difference from those such as the rhinoceros-like.
> This is why [Dignāga] held that very person
> who has mastered methods to be the Teacher.[339]

And as the *Enlightenment of Vairocana Tantra* teaches:

> The Great Hero [the Buddha]
> taught a gnosis and a discipline
> unequipped with skillful means
> so that the śrāvakas would enter it.
>
> The buddhas of the three times attained [awakening]
> through the unconditioned, unsurpassed vehicle,
> having trained in practices
> endowed with method and dicerning wisdom.[340]

Hence you will attain buddhahood after completing the preparatory accumulations of merit and gnosis through practicing skillful means and discerning wisdom in conjunction. If you do not bring to completion the preparatory accumulations, you will not be able to correctly recognize and directly realize the nature of mind (*sems ngo 'phrod*). For as the *Verse Summary of the Perfection of Wisdom* teaches:

> As long as the two accumulations are not completed,
> that most excellent emptiness will not be realized.[341]

Therefore, by understanding the surface [level of truth], you become expert in all objects of knowledge and will benefit others completely. If you are not thus expert, you will not understand the norms of ordinary humanity, let alone the Dharma of the āryas, just as in the parable of "the summoning of the well":[342]

> Once upon a time, a king ordered that a well owned by a wealthy brahman be sent on loan to him, but actually he desired to seize the brahman's wealth and was using this [impossible request] as a pretext. The brahman became alarmed and began preparing to pay a ransom. [326]
>
> At that time the wise daughter of the brahman stopped her father and said that she would go and achieve their aim. Thus she went before the king and said to him: "Cattle can be attracted by cattle, and an elephant [can be gained] through another elephant. Just so, Your Highness, please be kind enough to send us a well, and then our well will come to you!"
>
> The king was pleased and gave her a great reward.

Accordingly, even though ignorant people exert themselves strenuously to complete their affairs and those of others, they are unable to accomplish them. But the wise person has the power that is able to accomplish great works for the benefit of self and others.

[Objection]: [The Buddha] teaches such things as:

> Since you are a buddha if you understand mind, you should cultivate a perception of not searching for buddhahood elsewhere.[343]

Hence, what other virtue is necessary for buddhahood?

[Reply:] The above statement has a special intention and was spoken for the sake of the Sāṃkhya of the tīrthikas. The scriptures of the Sāṃkhya say:

> After you have achieved the perfect divine eye,
> you will realize the self of the mind.
> Whatever his or her mode of dress, whoever realizes the "self"
> of the "person" (*puruṣa*) will be liberated.[344]

The Buddha taught the previous [allusion] in order to assist the followers of those doctrines by alluding to buddhahood of the dharmakāya [as being latent in the minds of all sentient beings].[345] The motive of the statement was to lead people such as the followers of the Sāṃkhya, who maintain the innate existence of an omniscient "person" (*puruṣa*) of consciousness in the middle of the heart. As for the criterion that belies the surface meaning of the statement, [this statement taught with a special intention by the Buddha] is shown to be untenable by the reasoning in the verses of the *Guide to the Bodhisattva Way of Life* beginning with:

> If the result existed in the cause,
> then to eat food would be to eat excrement.[346]

And ending with:

> If a worldly person possesses that knowledge,
> why does he not see [the resultant *puruṣa* in the cause]?[347]

Moreover, it is disproved by all the reasoning in the refutation of the Sāṃkhya set forth in such works as *Thorough Exposition of Valid Cognition*.[348] It is also untenable because all the doctrinal formulations in the scriptures, such as those of the "three bodies," would be logically unacceptable were that [sutra's teaching to be accepted literally].

Furthermore, even though we may say, for example, "The lamp flame burns on the cotton wick," in fact without such things as oil and a container, there could be no burning lamp. Or, even though we say, "The arrow kills the foe," without a bow and a person, an arrow would not be able to accomplish its purpose. And though we say, "The crops came forth from seeds," crops cannot grow in the absence of such things as a field, water, fertilizer, and so forth. [327] Or, though we say, "The ears of grain are produced from the field," if ears of grain are produced from plants that have reached full growth, that will be an excellent harvest. But if the ears appear on plants that have not done so, there will be a bad harvest, like that of drought-damaged ears of grain.

Likewise, though it is said that "living beings become buddhas by directly meeting with and recognizing the nature of mind," you will not be able to attain buddhahood if the virtues of merit and gnosis are not fully developed. Moreover, if you base yourself on faith and moral discipline, and exert yourself in practicing the path of the gnosis of emptiness without relying on the skillful means of the perfections or the mantra tradition as your path, you will fall into the cessation of the śrāvaka. Those who have less faith and moral discipline than that but who do not verbally or physically commit great evil deeds and who have to some extent accumulated the virtuous factors will be born as a god of the Sphere of Infinite Space,[349] provided they eliminate the desires of the realm of desire and the discursive thoughts that are attached to matter and confront and recognize the nature of all phenomena as being empty like the sky. Likewise, if you confront and recognize the nature of all phenomena as the mind, you will be born as a god of the Sphere of Infinite Consciousness. If you confront and recognize the nature of all phenomena as nothingness, you will be born in the Sphere of Nothingness. If you confront and recognize the nature of all phenomena as "neither existent nor nonexistent," you will be born as a god of the Sphere of Neither Existence nor Nonexistence. Accordingly, by cultivating and being introduced to that form of emptiness without realizing the selflessness of persons and phenomena, you will be born in the formless realm but will not attain arhatship, let alone buddhahood.

Those who have even less merit—who are unable to sever their attachment to matter; who meditatively cultivate a realization of the inexpressible and unthinkable (*smra bsam brjod med*) and then hold the conceit, "I have realized the teaching"; and who have no firm appreciation of the correct Dharma—will be born in the inopportune circumstances known as the long-lived gods of "the meditative attainment of nonapperception."[350]

Those who are slightly inferior to the above and who, without freeing themselves from the desires of the realm of desire or realizing the two types of selflessness, cultivate a realization of an inexpressible and unthinkable that entails no thinking or cognition at all will be born in the inopportune circumstances of the barbarian or the mute fool. As the *Questions of Sāgaramati Sutra* teaches:

> The bodhisattva who generates and achieves the four meditative concentrations (*dhyāna*) and the four meditative attainments (*samāpatti*) of the formless realm will dwell in those peaceful

> attainments, will disparage the bringing of sentient beings to maturity, will disparage the teaching of the doctrine, will disparage sentient beings and the animate world, will disregard the mental forces of merit, and will experience the unshakable mental forces and delight in solitude. [328] Knowing the realms of desire and form to be faulty, that bodhisattva will experience the taste of the formless realm and by that inferior deed cause his birth in the formless realm. Being born with the same capacities as the long-lived gods, once he is there he will be separated from the sight of buddhas, from learning the teachings, and from the performance of respectful service to the sangha. He will be separated from bringing sentient beings to maturity, from upholding the good doctrine, and from amassing the preparatory accumulation of merit. His moral faculties will become unclear and dull. After his death, wherever he is born he will reap the results of those dull faculties and be listless and sleepy. This is the fifth hook of Māra, that which possesses meditative concentration.
>
> The bodhisattva will become endowed with discerning wisdom but will disparage the mental forces of merit. He will be without skillful means. That is, he will not exert himself in generosity, moral discipline, patience, diligence, or meditative concentration. And thinking that the perfection of wisdom is absolutely supreme while the other perfections are inferior, he will experience the tastes of the absence of discursive elaborations and the absence of notional constructions. To do so is the sixth hook of Māra, that which possesses discerning wisdom.[351]

And as *Achieving Pristine Awareness* teaches:

> He who meditatively cultivates delusion will
> gain delusion through delusion.[352]

Those who are even inferior to the above are those people who have confronted and recognized the nature of mind and who have understood all phenomena as empty but who still neither aspire to the wholesome nor are alarmed by evil deeds; saying, "It makes no difference whether you thrust your hand into a black goat or a white one,"[353] they turn their backs on the meaning of the scriptures and the scriptural divisions, and they scorn the good doctrine and the people who profess it. And if out of ignorance and pride such people commit the ten nonvirtuous deeds in a small way, they will be reborn as animals; if in a middling way, they will be reborn as hungry spirits; and if they commit them in a big way, they will fall into the hells.

Moreover, Ācārya Ārya [Nāgārjuna] has said, for instance:

> Those of small understanding will be ruined
> if they err in viewing emptiness, [329]
> just like wrongly grasping a snake
> or wrongly practicing a magic spell.[354]

And also:

> The conquerors taught emptiness
> to be the deliverance from all views.
> And they taught that nothing can be done
> for those who have a speculative view of emptiness.[355]

And:

> Those who maintain existence go to the fortunate destinies.
> Those who maintain nonexistence go to the lower miserable
> destinies. Through the correct comprehension of reality,
> you will attain the liberation that relies on neither.[356]

And in the *Kāśyapa Chapter Sutra*:

> One who hypostatizes the existence of a substantial self—even be it as huge as the Mount Meru—is not so bad off. But the hypostatizing of emptiness, full of presumption, by some people is something quite different.[357]

And the *King of Meditation Sutra* teaches the example of Udraka:

> Even if worldly people meditate on emptiness,
> they will not turn back the positing of entities.
> They will once again become endowed with their afflictions,
> as when Udraka cultivated this meditative absorption.[358]

Thus at the end of twelve years of concentrated meditating in the meditative absorption of emptiness, Udraka was reborn as a cat. The same sutra teaches:

> Though you reveal to many living beings that the aggregates
> are empty,
> they will not understand how they are without a self.
> And those unknowing people, when challenged,
> will angrily retaliate and will speak harsh words.[359]

Thus this passage indicates that it is mistaken to meditatively cultivate emptiness without understanding the two types of selflessness, and it predicts that if wise people point out their error, those people who cultivate emptiness in meditation will become angry.

[Objection:] Granted that the meditative cultivation of the white panacea has faults. But we, as our preparation, perform the taking of refuge, the generation of the thought of awakening, and the meditation on the tutelary deity and religious master. We perform the placing of the mind in mahāmudrā as the main practice and conclude by means of dedicating the merit. Therefore our practice is superior to the white panacea.[360]

[Reply:] This, too, should be critically examined. If you want to practice this as a meditation of the perfections tradition, you should learn those vast and profound subjects such as the six perfections and the thirty-seven factors conducive to awakening. By learning and reflection you should remove your false imputations about the lack of own-nature of sense objects and the object-apprehending [mind]. You should understand well the selflessness of persons and of phenomena. And you should gird yourself to be able to give away even your head and limbs for a long period of time, such as for three incalculable eons. If you knew how to practice it according to the tradition of such texts as the Five Treatises of Maitreya, it would become a meditation of the perfections tradition. [330] But since the above-mentioned tradition [of mahāmudrā] was not set forth in any sutra or great treatise, it is also not a meditation of the perfections tradition.

[Objection:] This is the mahāmudrā of the mantra tradition.

[Reply:] It is not this, either. If it were of the mantra tradition, it would be the mahāmudrā that is a meditative absorption of the consecrations and of the two stages of the path. But [in the above mahāmudrā] you have not previously received that which matures you for the mantra practices—namely, the consecrations that conform with the tantric scriptures. You do not know how to meditatively cultivate the two stages of the path that are in conformity with the tantras. You have not realized the sense of mahāmudrā that arises from the two stages of tantric practice. You are absolutely ignorant of how to accomplish the [three] stabilizers of that mahāmudrā: the practice possessing conceptual elaborations (**saprapañca*), without conceptual elaborations (*niṣprapañca*), and completely devoid of conceptual elaborations (*suniṣprapañca*). Nor do you know how to proceed through the levels and paths of the inner interdependences. Therefore yours is not the mahāmudrā that was taught in the tantras of the mantra tradition. By means of that meditation alone, you will not be able to prevent the extremes of cyclic existence and nirvana from arising, just as a wall of pebbles cannot repel the current of the River Ganges. But just as a massive rock can repel the current of the Ganges, so the excellent wall of the six perfections or of the two stages of meditation of the mantra tradition can prevent the extremes of cyclic existence and nirvana.

Therefore, no matter how excellent that meditative cultivation may be, because it was taught in neither the perfections nor the mantra tradition, it is a meditation that belongs to neither.[361] It is just as in these examples: however excellent a meditation of the tīrthikas may be, it will not become Buddhist, and however excellent a śrāvaka meditation may be, it will never become the Mahayana.[362]

[Objection:] You will not become a buddha through Dharma that consists of engaging in activities [i.e., religious acts]. The thought "I will meditatively cultivate the lack of conceptualization" is an activity of conceptualizing thought. Therefore, though it is not the actual mahāmudrā, it is a means whereby mahāmudrā can arise.

[Reply:] In that case, your assertion that "you will not become a buddha through a Dharma of engaging in activities" is discarded because the thought "I will meditatively cultivate nonconceptualizing" is an activity of conceptualizing thought. What would you say if I asserted, "It is not feasible for nonconceptualization to arise merely from the thought, 'I will meditatively cultivate nonconceptualizing.' Were that the case, an illness would go away merely by thinking, 'May I be without illness!'"?

[Opponent's response:] The causes of being without illness are to make use of food, medicines, and so forth, but merely the thought "May I be without illness!" is not by itself the cause for being without illness.

[Reply:] By the same token, nonconceptualizing meditative absorption is caused by amassing the accumulations of merit and gnosis, but the thought

"I will meditatively cultivate nonconceptualization" will not by itself cause nonconceptualizing absorption. [331] Therefore, since a result will arise neither from the absence of its cause nor from an incomplete cause, the absence of illness and nonconceptual absorption will arise neither in the absence of their respective causes nor when those causes are incomplete. As the *Verse Summary of the Perfection of Wisdom* teaches:

> As long as the two accumulations are not completed,
> that most excellent emptiness will not be realized.[363]

And in the *Precious Garland*:

> The form body of the buddhas arose
> from the accumulation of merit.
> The dharmakāya, O king, was born
> from the accumulation of gnosis.[364]

To establish somewhat further the sense of the above, [I pose this question:] "In general, when you introduce mind, is that an introduction to the nature of mind alone, or do you also need to introduce the nature of external objects?" The introduction of [the nature of] mind alone is a tīrthika tradition. That is an erroneous path because by means of it you cannot eliminate the dichotomous postulation of apprehending subject and apprehended object. If you also need to introduce the nature of external objects, you must critically examine whether those objects have arisen from a creator god such as Īśvara, as some tīrthikas maintain; from "atoms," as the śrāvakas maintain; from mind, as the adherents of Yogācāra maintain; or from dependent origination, as the Mādhyamikas say.

If these entities are held to be either existent or nonexistent, you must know scripture and reasoning to refute those views because they are nothing more than eternalism or nihilism. Even for maintaining that appearances and mind are dependently originated, you must know the Buddhist scriptures and reasoning. If you do not, you will not properly understand the selflessness of persons and of phenomena. If you have not understood the selflessness of persons, your meditation will be no different from that of the tīrthika. If you have not understood the selflessness of phenomena, your meditation will be no different from that of the śrāvaka. To understand the two types of selflessness, you must first cut off your erroneous imputations by means of the discerning wisdom born from learning and reflection, without which it is impossible to understand selflessness. If you have not understood selflessness, you will not know how to cultivate in meditation [the realization of this] selflessness. If you do not know how to cultivate that in meditation, discerning wisdom born from meditative realization will not arise. If discerning wisdom born from meditative realization does not arise, it is impossible for the path of seeing of the ārya to arise. For as the *King of Meditation Sutra* teaches:

> Though you reveal to many living beings that the aggregates are empty,
> they will not understand how they are without a self.
> And those unknowing people, when challenged,
> will angrily retaliate and will speak harsh words.[365]

And further:

> Even if worldly people meditate on emptiness,
> that will not turn back the positing of entities.[366] [332]

Hence if you did not understand the two types of selflessness, you would not be able to destroy the postulating of entities, and such a [flawed] meditative cultivation of emptiness would be a cause for cyclic existence and lower miserable destinies. Therefore the path of seeing will only arise through discerning wisdom born of the meditative realization that was freed from false imputations by means of fautless learning and reflection. For as the *Thorough Exposition of Valid Cognition* teaches:

> Thus the previously explained knowledge of the yogi
> arises from the meditative realization of those [sixteen aspects] of these [four noble truths].
> [This meditative direct perception], because it has eliminated
> the net of conceptual dichotomization, appears as luminosity.[367]

[Objection:] Everything internal and external is introduced simultaneously as being without own-nature.

[Reply:] Even supposing that, during the actual meditation, emptiness has arisen and has been made the object of meditative cultivation, during the preparation for meditation and in the period after meditation, you will still experience conceptual thoughts and various sensory objects, such as visual forms. At that time, will those various experiences arise from a cause or from no cause? If from a cause, does the result arise from a cause that is identical with itself, different from itself, or both identical and different? If it arises from itself, that is the Sāṃkhya tradition.[368] If it arises from a cause different from itself, that is the system of those who maintain the existence of entities, such as the adherents of Īśvara of the tīrthika traditions or of the śrāvakas. If it arises from a cause that is both identical and different, your position is nothing more than what is included within those two. For them, to arise from no cause is the tradition of the tīrthika nihilists. Hence without scripture and reasoning, those will not be refuted. Without the discerning wisdom born from learning and reflection, it will not be possible to understand scripture and reasoning. Therefore, for the arising of discerning wisdom born of meditative realization, you must first cut off your erroneous imputations by means of the discerning wisdom born from learning. Then you make yourself adept at it by means of the discerning wisdom born from reflection. Then, through discerning wisdom born from meditative realization, that unerring "clear perception" (*gsal snang*) arises.

Therefore, if discerning wisdom born from meditative realization has arisen, mistakes in teaching, composition, and debating will not occur, just as they did not for the tantric adepts of India.[369] In the present day and age, some people claim to possess discerning wisdom born from meditative realization. Yet when they expound, they set forth nothing but contradictions with scripture and reasoning. In their compositions, much language occurs that does not conform with grammar. Regarding their sense, you see many speculations that conflict with scripture and reasoning. Regarding their debating, too, you can see debates that feature some amusing occasions in which they do not discriminate [the proponent's] "initial position" (*pūrvapakṣa*) from [the respondent's] "final position" (*uttarapakṣa*), and in which they do not know what is and is not a defeat situation. To err in such ways is not called "discerning wisdom born from meditative realization." The sutras explain it to be, instead, confused understanding—that is, erroneous conception. [333] Therefore you must remove all false imputations through learning and reflection and meditatively cultivate an object that is free from doubts.

For meditatively cultivating [a realization of] ultimate reality (*gnas lugs kyi don*), many traditions can be seen. The śrāvakas have a meditative cultivation of the four noble truths. The adherents of the Yogācāra, who maintain that the cognitive object does not exist, have a meditation that takes as its object the four yogas taught by Ācārya Śāntipāda: the "one-pointed," the "one taste," the "free from elaboration," and "without meditative cultivation." The Svātantrika Mādhyamikas take as their object the nonsituated integration [of appearance and emptiness]. The Prāsaṅgikas take as their ultimate the nonsituated emptiness.[370]

The followers of the Nyingma ("old") schools of the mantra tradition take the final of the nine vehicles, the *atiyoga*, as their ultimate. The followers of the Sarma ("new") schools take the gnosis of the four consecrations and of the two stages of the path as theirs. For that the intended sense of different tantras is identical, although there are different stages of meditative visualization. Ācārya Saroruhavajra taught a "nonreverting reality." The lord of yogins Virūpa taught an "absolutely immaculate reality." Ācārya Nāgārjuna taught an "integration" (*yuganaddha*) as the final of five stages, and he also took the two stages as the four mudrās: karmamudrā, dharmamudrā, samayamudrā, and mahāmudrā. Though there are many stages such as those, the Buddha and the tantric adepts are of one intent. All these are particular features of the meditative absorptions of the four consecrations and the two stages of the path. But because the profound important points about this are taught within the context of the mantra teachings, I will not explain them here.

In brief, if it is mahāmudrā, it must arise out of the practice of the mantra teachings. For example, though such things as haze may be designated by the term "smoke," since they do not arise from fire they are not smoke as strictly defined. Or even though we say, "The man produces the song of a bird," a real bird's song can issue only from a bird, not from a man. Accordingly, though some may say, "I cultivate mahāmudrā," this is not the real mahāmudrā by which you can become a buddha in this lifetime because it did not arise from the gnosis of the two stages.

Here I have explained just this much of the stages of the tantra because I see that if I do not explain it, some will practice in ignorance due to not understanding the differences among the meditations of the tīrthika, the śrāvaka, the Yogācāra, the Madhyamaka, and the mantra teachings, and thus the mahāmudrā of the mantra tradition will become something like a meditation of the tīrthikas. You should learn about this in more detail from your own religious master. [334]

Achieving unmistaken understanding[371]

This has three parts: the preparation, which is to use theory to cut off conceptual elaborations about ultimate reality; the main practice, which is to use meditation to appropriate the sense [of emptiness] into your experience; and the conclusion, which is use practice to bring that understanding to perfect completion.

The preparation: Using theory to cut off conceptual elaborations about ultimate reality

This first step consists of observing moral discipline and training your mind by means of learning, as explained earlier.[372] Learn the scriptures of the perfections tradition and the reasoning as taught in the Madhyamaka treatises from a teacher who is a learned master—that is, from someone who understands their sense perfectly; thus you should recognize the essential points differentiating the erroneous and nonerroneous doctrines. If you are not able to learn that much, then remove your conceptual elaborations by studying a text that suits your own intellectual level, such as Śāntideva's *Compendium of Trainings* or *Guide to the Bodhisattva Way of Life*.

If you do not understand that much, what you practice could become an erroneous doctrine, like that of the tīrthikas, because you are practicing something that is not the Buddha's teachings while thinking that it is, like the blind being led by the blind. With that in mind, [the Buddha] taught in great detail the disadvantages of not studying and the benefits of learning, such as, "Through learning, you will abandon the useless,"[373] as mentioned above.

Moreover, [the great benefits of teaching the doctrine are] as taught in the *Sutra Teaching the Nonorigination of All Things*:

> Previously, an incalculable eon ago, the tathāgata named Mervabhyudgatarāja appointed a monk named Viśuddhacāritra as the disciple who would maintain his teaching after his nirvana and then passed into nirvana. At that time there also lived a monk named Cāritramati, who possessed a very pure aggregate of moral discipline, had attained the five mundane supranormal insights, possessed many excellent qualities such as being extremely well versed in the Vinaya scriptures, and who devoted himself to meditative concentration and solitude. He built a

monastery and then dwelled there, as did some followers, imitating his training. Then the monk Viśuddhacāritra, together with his followers, went to the monastery where the monk Cāritramati lived and dwelled there. Thereafter, because of his compassion for sentient beings, Viśuddhacāritra went again and again to the town and filled many hundreds and thousands of sentient beings with faith and matured them for awakening. [335]

This caused the monk Cāritramati to lose faith in that bodhisattva. Beating the *gaṇḍi* assembly-plank, he summoned the monastic community and made a regulation. He said, "None from among us is to go into town. You are conducting yourselves there without watchful mindfulness, and you are not observing minimal speech. Therefore what is the use of your going into town? Dwelling in a remote place was allowed and praised by the Blessed One. Hence you should practice dwelling in the bliss of meditative concentration, without going to town."

[The bodhisattva Viśuddhacāritra and his followers] did not obey and again went to town. When they returned, the monk Cāritramati again beat the *gaṇḍi* assembly-plank and summoned the fully ordained monks. He told them, "Henceforth, if you go to town, do not stay in this monastery!"

Then the monk Viśuddhacāritra, to avoid offending the other monk, called together his own followers and told them, "Let none of you go to town." Then all the sentient beings who were being brought to spiritual maturity by those monks at that time became very unhappy because the could not meet those monks, and their roots of virtue diminished. When three months had passed, those monks moved to a different monastery. Then they used to go to such places as towns and cities and among the retinue of the king's palace, and there they taught the Dharma to sentient beings.

The monk Cāritramati saw also that the monk Viśuddhacāritra was going again and again to town. And seeing his disciples as possessing an ordinary conduct, lack of faith arose in his mind. Thus he said to many people, "This monk is corrupt in his moral discipline and lives in society." And thus he turned them away from listening to Dharma teachings.

After the monk Cāritramati died, through the ripening of his deeds he experienced miseries for 99,000 times 10 million eons

> in the Avīci hell. For sixty lifetimes he heard unpleasant words spoken to him. In 32,000 lives he lapsed from the ordained state. [336] For many hundreds and thousands of lifetimes, his moral faculties were dull. O son of good family, at that time I myself was that monk Cāritramati. As for that Viśuddhacāritra, by the root of merit from having taught the doctrine and maintained the doctrine of the Buddha, he attained buddhahood as the Buddha Akṣobhya in the realm of Abhirati in the east.[374]

And also the *Lion's Roar of Queen Śrīmālā Sutra* teaches that all solemn resolutions are included within one resolution. What is that one? It is taught to be: "May I uphold the good Dharma!"[375] Other sutras also state that it is more virtuous to teach one four-part verse to a sentient being than to fill the world with the seven kinds of precious substances and offer it to the Three Jewels. The reason is that the offering of wealth causes the excellent acquisitions of cyclic existence, but the teaching of Dharma causes the qualities of the ārya. Having understood in that way, you should exert yourself in learning and reflection.

If you do not achieve vast learning in that way, you will not understand the two truths. Not understanding those, you will not understand the sense of the profound scriptures, and your mind will not be liberated. But if you understand and gain a mastery of the two truths, you will understand the sense of the scriptures and be liberated. For that reason you must correctly understand the two truths. As Ācārya Ārya [Nāgārjuna] said:

> The teaching of the Dharma by the buddhas
> relies on the two truths:
> the surface truth of the world
> and the truth of ultimate reality.
>
> Whoever does not understand
> the distinction between the two truths
> will not realize the profound reality
> of the Buddha's doctrine.[376]

Therefore, to establish systematically those two, three [topics require explanation]: the definitions of the two truths, analyzing the terms to be defined, and ascertaining the defining marks in their instances.

The definitions of the two truths

Some have said: "The definitions of the two truths are thus: that which can be made an object of mind is the surface truth, while that which is beyond the objects of mind is the ultimate truth."[377] Those people base themselves on the statement in the *Guide to the Bodhisattva Way of Life*:

> Ultimate reality is not within the range of mind.
> Mind is held to be the surface.[378] [337]

Yet these two are the instances of what is being defined and are not the defining marks. Therefore our tradition is as follows: That which is established as an object for a mind that has not conceptually investigated is "the surface level." That which is not established as an object for a conceptually investigating mind is "the ultimately real."[379] The absence of any disproof in relation to each in your own mind is "truth."

Analyzing the terms to be defined

This has four parts: the common characteristic for drawing the distinction, the subjects that are so distinguished, their being a fixed number, and the etymology of their Sanskrit equivalents.

The common characteristic for drawing the distinction. Some say that the two truths have no common characteristic from which a distinction could be drawn because those two have no shared universal. This is unacceptable. Even though no shared universal indeed exists, as the objects of other-exclusion,[380] the two truths on the level of ordinary transactional usage (*vyāvahāra*) cause no incompatibility for merely the mind. As Ācārya Candrakīrti said in the *Commentary on the Sixty Reasonings*,[381] the truths, being established as two, are so in relation to the minds of ordinary people.

The subjects that are so distinguished have three parts: (1) In relation to which kinds of cognition are the two truths divided into surface-level truth and ultimate truth? (2) In relation to whose cognition are the two truths established? (3) Are the two truths identical or different?

In relation to which kinds of cognition are the two truths divided into surface-level truth and ultimate truth?

As *Commentary on the Distinction Between the Two Truths* teaches:

> However things appear, just that is the surface level.
> All else is the other [truth].[382]

Thus all appearances are the surface level. That those are actually unestablished is the ultimately real. The surface level includes two: the correct surface level and the incorrect surface level. The first, the *correct*, is the epistemic or cognitive appearances that arise similarly in the experience of beings of similar past deeds;[383] it is causally effective on the level of conventional pragmatic usage and unestablished upon examination. That is to say, it is everything that appears in unmistaken cognition. The *incorrect* surface level is that which appears as the object of erroneous cognition and is causally inefficient even in transactional usage; this includes all such manifestations as magical illusions or the seeing of two moons or nonexistent hairs through faults of vision.

Concerning this, some assert that the cause of the higher destinies is the correct surface level while the cause of the lower miserable destinies is the erroneous surface level. But since this was not taught in any treatises such as the basic texts of the Madhyamaka or in any sutra, that assertion is meaningless. For as the *Commentary on the Distinction Between the Two Truths* teaches:

> Even though similar in appearance,
> correct and incorrect surface-level truth are differentiated
> because one possesses the power of causal efficiency
> and the other lacks that power.[384]

As for the ultimately real, in this context it is not the causal efficiency that is in accepted usage among the dialecticians; here you should maintain that it is just "freedom from conceptual elaborations" (*niṣprapañca*), the ultimately real that is accepted in the Madhyamaka.[385] [338]

In relation to whose cognition are the two truths established?

In this regard, the śrāvakas say that the minds of ordinary people is the surface level; that the mind of the three classes of āryas in meditative equipoise is the ultimate, but after meditation it is the surface level; and that nirvana is purely the ultimate. This is unacceptable because their tradition holds that nirvana is established as a substance, and thus this is an impossibility.

The adherent of the Yogācāra tradition teaches that "imaginary constructs" (*parikalpita*) are the surface level. Within their "dependent" (*paratantra*), the incorrect dependent is the surface level while the correct dependent is the ultimately real. And the "perfected" (*pariniṣpanna*) is purely the ultimately real. Nevertheless, their nondual cognition is not acceptable as ultimately real, because in the last analysis it amounts to an entity.[386]

The Svātantrika Mādhyamikas teach that each of the two truths exists both with and without conceptualized and verbalized forms (*paryāya*), making a total of four combinations. From among these, phenomena appearing as the objects of the uncritical minds of ordinary people is the surface level that does not involve conceptualized and verbalized forms. [Phenomena appearing] as the object of a critical ordinary mind is the relative (or "surface")[387] that involves conceptualized and verbalized forms. The nonconceptual gnosis of the three classes of ārya is the ultimate,[388] which does not involve conceptualized and verbalized forms. The pure mundane gnosis is the surface level that involves conceptualized and verbalized forms.

For the school that maintains that gnosis exists in the Buddha, the above has no logical fault. However, the gnosis of the Buddha is beyond existence and nonexistence. And the distinction of gnosis into nonconceptual and pure mundane gnosis is made in the thoughts of an ordinary person, whereas on the level of buddhahood they are not two. For as the Madhyamaka school teaches:

> Cyclic existence and nirvana are
> accepted by those who do not see reality.
> Those who see reality do not accept
> either cyclic existence or nirvana.[389]

The Prāsaṅgikas teach that [the object of] the mind of ordinary people is the surface level; that [the object of] the three āryas in meditative equipoise is the ultimate and after meditative equipoise is the surface level; and that nirvana is purely the ultimate reality. That teaching, too, would be acceptable if the Buddha, dwelling in nirvana, had no gnosis. But since this tradition does not maintain a simple nirvana of the Buddha, this is slightly unacceptable because it is incorrect to maintain that gnosis does not exist.

What is the acceptable position? It is: No matter what person they appear in relation to, the appearing aspect of experience is the surface level, the empty aspect is the ultimate, and the indivisible aspect is their integration. For as *Five Stages* teaches: [339]

> Having understood both appearance and emptiness
> in their individual aspects,
> where these are mixed
> is explained as "the integration."[390]

Furthermore, these three principles are the basis for reaching the realization of how entities actually are. To appropriate that into your experience through integrated compassionate means and discerning wisdom is the path to be realized through meditation. Having realized that path, you progress for the time being through the levels and the paths and ultimately to the attainment of the "three bodies" of buddhahood, which is the fruit. This way of exposition does not contradict scripture and reasoning, and it is the intended sense of all the scriptures of definitive meaning.

Are the two truths identical or different?

(1) Are the two truths synonyms that refer to the same thing, like "moon" and "emitter of cool rays"? (2) Or are they different entities, like a pot and a woolen cloth? (3) Or are they identical in nature but with distinct conceptual differentiations, like "fabricated" and "impermanent"? (4) Or are they a thing and its negation, like "entity" and "nonentity"?

(1) They do not have the same nature, for that would involve four logical faults, such as the consequence that the ultimate would become an object of mental objectification just like the surface level.[391]

(2) If their natures were different, this would involve four logical faults, such as the logical consequence that [the two truths would not stand in the

relation of] property-possessor and nature, as explained in the *Sutra Definitely Elucidating the Noble Intention*.[392]

(3) If they were of a single nature, the logical consequence would be that a nature would be established for the ultimate.

(4) If they were a thing and its negation, it is taught that a logical fault would be entailed—namely, that the ultimate would be a nonentity. This teaching would possess that logical fault if you maintained that its nature were established and that the ultimate were something lacking substantial existence [i.e., without causal efficiency]. But it is taught that being without characteristics is a characteristic shared [by all factors of existence].[393] And:

> Śāriputra, in the absence of mind could there exist as a mental object either existence or nonexistence?[394]

And in the *Verse Summary of the Perfection of Wisdom*:

> The two, existence and nonexistence, do not exist as entities.[395]

And as the *Thorough Exposition of Valid Cognition* explains:

> Since things lacking reality have no nature,
> their lacking a nature cannot be examined.
> Words [expressing such unreal entities] are established
> through the expression of [conceptual] differentiation of those two.[396]

Hence there is no fault here if you know how to explain it properly, by way of the "exclusion of other" (*anyāpoha*). But if you do not know how to explain it, you will not be able to avoid the previous faults.

Therefore in our own tradition we present the systems of the ultimate and of conventional usage differently. On the ultimate level they are free from the conceptual elaborations of "identical" and "different." For as the *Sutra Definitely Elucidating the Noble Intention* teaches: [340]

> The domain of the surface level and the reality of the ultimate have a defining mark devoid of both identity and difference. Those people who imagine these to be identical or different adopt inaccurate [opinions].[397]

As for the second system, that of conventional pragmatic usage, we assert purely what has been authoritatively taught: "They have a nondifferentiatable nature with distinct conceptual differentiations, as objects of [conceptualization through] the exclusion of another" or "They are inexpressible as identical or different."

Their being a fixed number. Why are the truth levels determined here as two when other texts also teach four truths, sixteen truths, and so forth?

In general, there are many ways of determining the number of a thing, such as with regard to some necessity or erroneous conception. But here these truth levels are limited to two by the excluding differentiation of the two logical alternatives of a thing and its opposite; thus here erroneous and nonerroneous cognition are the thing and its opposite. And since between them no third category could exist, either of the positive sort—namely, that something is both—or of the negative sort—namely, that something is neither—the truth levels are fixed in number as two.

The etymology of their Sanskrit equivalents. The Sanskrit word for "surface level" is *saṃvṛti*. The *saṃ* stands for *samyak*, "complete" or "correct," while *vṛ* stands for *āvaraṇa*, which means "obscured" or "covered."[398] Thus *saṃvṛti* is "completely obscured" or "thoroughly covered." However, the early Tibetan translators rendered it [not literally but] according to sense as *kun rdzob* ("completely false").

The Sanskrit word for "ultimate reality" is *paramārtha*. The *parama* means "highest" or "superior." The *artha* signifies "meaning," "object," "real thing." Thus they translated it as "superior object" (Tib. *don dam pa*) because it is the object that is found to be without logical fault if examined by superior minds. Therefore the definitions of the two truths and the etymological meanings of their Sanskrit terms are in agreement.

Ascertaining the defining marks in their instances

[Doubt:] The defining mark of the surface level—namely, "that which is established with reference to an uncritical mind"—is established through self-cognizing direct perception as existing in its instance—namely, in "that which is capable of being made an object of mind." But how could the defining mark of the ultimate, "that which is not established with reference to mind when examined critically," be established in its instance, namely, "that which is incapable of being made an object of mind"? For if the instance of the mark were not established with reference to the mind, critical discernment could not be established in relation to it. And if it were established as an instance, that would conflict with its being beyond the range of mind.

[Reply:] In fact there is no incompatibility. For by conceptually differentiating "object of mind" by way of the exclusion of other, "that which is not an object of mind" is established, while by differentiating "nonobject," "object" is established. This is just as, for instance, "that which is not an object of knowledge" is established by conceptually differentiating "object of knowledge," and "object of knowledge" is established by conceptually differentiating "that which is not an object of knowledge." [341] For as the *Thorough Exposition of Valid Cognition* teaches:

> Therefore, for words such as "object of knowledge"
> that are established as conventional usages,
> there exist some conceptual exclusions.[399]

Therefore the ultimate is not an object of knowledge since it is not established with regard to mind if critically examined.[400] And for that reason, because it is beyond the range of mind, it cannot be impaired by any of the faults of mind or conceptual thought, just as when the target does not exist, an arrow cannot strike it. Furthermore, as Ācārya Ārya [Nāgārjuna] taught:

> If I possessed the assertion of any entity,
> I would therefore have that fault.
> Because I have no assertion,
> I am completely free from fault.[401]

[Objection:] Wouldn't this be the same as what the [*Compendium of*] *Higher Knowledge* teaches to be a "speculative theory that admits no assertion" or a "deceitful speculative theory"?[402]

[Reply:] It would not. For example, if a thief does not admit to his theft, it is acceptable to call that "deceitful nonacknowledgment." But someone who has not stolen speaks truthfully when he does not acknowledge theft. How could it be right to call his action "nonadmission [of guilt]" or "deceitful"? Accordingly, it is correct to call "nonadmission" and "deceitful" cases like those of the tīrthikas who, while possessing a thesis, do not admit it through trickery. But how is it correct for anyone to criticize as deceitful our not asserting a thesis because of the freedom from all conceptual elaborations in ultimate reality? Such nonacknowledgment is rightly to be praised as honest speech.[403]

The main practice: Using meditation [to experience emptiness]

This has three parts. The first is *the preparatory ritual*, in which you sit in a comfortable seat in a remote place, assume a cross-legged position, place one hand atop the other in your lap, straighten the spine, gaze past the tip of the nose, and perform the uncommon going for refuge and generation of the thought of awakening.

After that beginning, [*the main practice* is] to meditate in the concentration of the emptiness that possesses the highest of all features—the lack of any substantial self of a person or of phenomena—namely, the perfection of wisdom.

The conclusion is [*the dedication of merit*, in which you] dedicate the root of merit to perfect awakening for the benefit of sentient beings. For one session of daily practice, cultivate nonobjectifying compassion for those sentient beings who have not realized the above, and accomplish all your other activities—such as studying or teaching Dharma—while viewing all appearances as like a dream. Learn the essential points of the meditative absorption of the perfection of wisdom from an expert religious master. [342]

The sense of this is the same as that expressed in the introductory chapter of the *Perfection of Wisdom*, where it says that the Blessed One himself then sat cross-legged on the prepared seat on the lion throne. He straightened his body, "placed his thought before him," and concentrated his mind in the meditative absorption called "the king of meditative absorptions," in which all other meditative absorptions are included and comprehended.[404]

The conclusion: Using practice to bring that understanding to perfect completion

This has two parts: the practice of ordinary people and the practice of āryas.

The practice of ordinary people. If you engage in this practice according to the stages of the five paths, separate modes of practice are taught for the small, middling, and great path of accumulation and for the four [stages of the path of application] that are conducive to penetrations (*nirvedhabhāgīya*). But to make it easier to understand, three modes exist for ordinary people: observing correct conduct, training your discerning wisdom, and achieving meditative absorptions. The first is to *train in moral discipline*. The middle is *to train in discerning wisdom*. And the last is *to train in meditative absorptions*.

Concerning the sequence for practicing those, if you have a pure basis of moral discipline, your discerning wisdom will reach perfection, for by possessing discerning wisdom, your meditative absorptions will be free of delaying diversions. As the *King of Meditation Sutra* teaches:

> The king of meditative absorptions, this meditation on emptiness,
> rests on the head of pure moral discipline.
> Childish people who only meditate on the [empty] nature of
> the factors of existence
> and exert themselves improperly do not understand this.[405]

[Question:] What is that exertion for improper objects?

[Reply:] The intended sense [in that sutra] is that childish people who exert themselves in learning without observing moral discipline and in meditating without having studied thus put their efforts into an improper thing, like a simpleton who begins building a wall without having prepared a foundation. Such people will not understand this king of meditative absorptions.

Likewise, [to explain according to] the stages of the three moral disciplines, first, through *the moral discipline of vows*, you cleanse your body, speech, and mind, just as you would wipe a vessel clean. Next, through *the moral discipline of gathering virtuous factors*, you fill your mind with excellent qualities, just as you would fill a vessel. Then, by *the moral discipline of benefitting sentient beings*, you benefit all sentient beings, just as you would restore sick people to health with an elixir [offered up in the vessel].

Regarding the practices of the above kinds, accomplish all your activities through the method of the perfection of wisdom with the "purity of the three spheres"—the three spheres being the doer of the action, the recipient of the action, and the nature of the action itself, as previously mentioned.[406]

The sutras teach that for quickly attaining perfect and complete buddhahood, the seven-branched worship will bring you to perfect completion. [343] Therefore recite thrice daily and thrice nightly the seven branches of worship taught in scriptures such as in the *Prayer of Excellent Conduct*[407] or the *Prayer of Maitreya*, in treatises such as the *Precious Garland* or *Guide to the Bodhisattva Way of Life*, or in my own *Liturgy of Ten Verses*, in which taking refuge and generating the thought of awakening in its aspiring and engaging aspects have been added.[408] For this [seven-branched worship] is taught to be a special aspect of skillful means.

The practice of āryas is explained below, in the section on the doctrinal system of the levels and paths [in chapter 11].

Correctly accomplishing discerning wisdom

This has two parts: achieving the four excellent qualities and eliminating the seven attachments.

Achieving the four excellent qualities is explained in the lines beginning: "Discerning wisdom: the destruction of the antithesis, and...."[409] Thus these four qualities are: (1) the absence of imperfect discerning wisdom, which is the antithesis of discerning wisdom; (2) realizing the nondiscursive, the absence of a substantial self; (3) fulfilling all the wishes of others, which is to remove the doubts and accomplish the needs of others based on discerning wisdom; and (4) bringing sentient beings to maturity, which means that through discerning wisdom you will establish sentient beings in the three vehicles.

Eliminating the seven attachments is explained in the lines beginning: "The discerning wisdom of the bodhisattva is unattached...."[410] Accordingly, the seven attachments are attachment to: (1) imperfect discerning wisdom, (2) procrastination, (3) premature satisfaction, (4) hopes of getting something in return, (5) the future result of a deed, (6) the antithesis that is the undestroyed latent propensities for it, and (7) distraction, which is twofold, as previously explained [in the chapter on generosity]. Rid yourself of those seven attachments together with the dispositions toward them.

The benefits of producing discerning wisdom

This has two parts: the temporary benefits and the ultimate benefits. There are two classes of *temporary benefits*, those that occur in this life and those occurring in all future lives.

In this life, you will acquire many excellent qualities by thoroughly training yourself in discerning wisdom, such as a wise intelligence about the various objects of knowledge. You will possess a confident presence of mind that is not overawed by anyone. And having received the pure expressions of the religious teachings, your discerning wisdom will be set free, after which your mind becomes at ease, you enter the ranks of those acclaimed as "the learned wise," your fame comes to pervade the whole world of humans and gods, and you become a trusted authority for the whole world. [344]

As to benefits occurring *in all future lives*, wherever you are born in the future, you will have consummate discerning wisdom and sharp moral faculties, be able to retain what you learn, be able to discourse with buddhas and bodhisattvas, cut off your knowledge obscurations, correctly teach the Dharma to others, and so forth. For as the *Verse Summary of the Perfection of Wisdom* teaches:

> Having understood the nature of all phenomena through discerning wisdom, he completely transcends the three realms of existence.[411]

Ultimate benefits. When you become a completely and perfectly awakened buddha, you will comprehend knowable things exactly as they are and in their full variety and extent. You will acquire the confident presence of mind of the four analytical knowledges (*pratisaṃvid*). Through your possession of the four fearlessnesses, you will defeat all evil disputants. For as it is taught:

> Homage to you, excellent teacher,
> because your intelligence is never obstructed with respect to
> the support and the supported—the things to be explained—
> and to speech and knowledge, the means of explaining![412]

This concludes the section on explaining each [perfection] individually.

* * *

Establishing the division of the perfections into six as fixed[413]

This has two parts: the perfections have a fixed number [and they have a fixed sequence]. First, there are many ways a thing can have a *fixed number*, such as the numerical fixity [as two] when differentiating the logical alternatives of a thing and its opposite, and what is entailed with reference to erroneous opinions or special purposes. Here also there are two: the perfections having a fixed number in relation to purpose and their having a fixed number in relation to types of people.

Their having a fixed number in relation to purpose. As the *Ornament of Mahayana Sutras* teaches, [this consists of the following six things]:

> To be perfectly endowed with (1) wealth and (2) body,
> perfect (3) followers and (4) undertakings,
> (5) to not be constantly falling under the power of afflictions,
> and (6) to be unmistaken in your actions.[414]

Thus to accomplish benefits for yourself and others, you need six things, and to achieve those, you need the six perfections. For through generosity you acquire consummate wealth. Likewise, through moral discipline you will acquire a physical existence endowed with worldly well-being. Through patience you will acquire followers. In some sutras it is also taught that a perfectly endowed physical existence is achieved through patience. Through diligence you will undertake activities. Through meditative concentration you will suppress the afflictions, and through discerning wisdom you will be unconfused about all activities. Since for the accomplishment of your own and others' beneficial purposes there is nothing that is not included within those six, no more are necessary. And if any one of those six is omitted, the benefit appropriate to it will not be achieved. [345] Therefore the two possibilities of numbers higher or lower than six are negated.

Their having the fixed number six in relation to types of people. For the benefit of disciples who are householders, there are the two perfections, generosity and patience. For the benefit of ordained people, there is the pair of moral discipline and meditative concentration. For both types of person in common, there is the pair of diligence and discerning wisdom, bringing the total to six. The justification for those groupings is that since householders possess wealth and have more enemies, they must mainly achieve generosity and patience. But since ordained people have minimal wealth and few enemies, they have less need to accomplish both of those as major issues. Moral discipline and meditative concentration are more easily accomplished by ordained people, for they have rid themselves of distractions and dwell in solitude. Another reason is that many householders have broken even the minimal one-day precepts and the vow not to take life. As for meditative concentration, householders find it difficulty with introspection because they are distracted by household work and by caring for children. Diligence and discerning wisdom, which consist respectively of enthusiasm for the wholesome and the understanding of the sense of the

Dharma teachings, should be assiduously developed by both, since they are needed by both.

Their having a fixed sequence. As it is taught:

> These have been explained sequentially
> because the succeeding one arises based on the prior one,
> because they occupy inferior and superior positions,
> and because some are coarse and others are subtle.[415]

Thus the explanation of the sequence of the six perfections has three parts.

First, *the succeeding perfections arise based on the earlier ones.* If you do not have much regard for wealth, you can embark on moral discipline. If you possess the restraint of vows, you can patiently endure being harmed by others. If you possess patient forbearance, you can take up diligence. If you have endeavored diligently, the meditative absorptions will arise. If your mind is meditatively concentrated, you will understand exactly the sense of the Dharma teaching.

Second, *the preceding perfections are relatively inferior and the succeeding ones superior.* Beginning with generosity, which is inferior to moral discipline, [they become progressively higher,] up to discerning wisdom, which is superior to meditative concentration.

Third, *the perfections progress from relative coarseness to subtlety.* Generosity, being easier to take up and practice, is comparatively coarse, while moral discipline, being more difficult to take up and practice, is relatively subtle. Likewise, [such increasing subtlety can be found in each successive pair] up to meditative concentration, which is coarser since it is easier to take up and practice than discerning wisdom, which is subtler since it is harder to take up and practice.

The Sanskrit etymology of the terms for the perfections

The *Ornament of Mahayana Sutras* teaches: [346]

> They are explained as such
> because they are "discarder of poverty," "acquisition of cool,"
> "patient endurance of anger," "highest application,"
> "holding the mind," and "knowledge of the ultimate."[416]

Thus the Sanskrit for "generosity" is *dāna*: [*da* is for] *dāridra*, "poverty," and *na* is *naśa* [i.e., *nāśa*?], "removing" [i.e., "destroying"?], thus "removing poverty." The Sanskrit for "moral discipline" is *śīla*: *śita* ("cool") and *labdha* ("acquired"), and thus "acquiring the cool of nirvana." The Sanskrit for "patience" is *kṣānti*: *kṣa* is *kṣobha* ("agitation"), and *ti* is *śānti* ("pacification"), thus "pacifying the agitated mind." The Sanskrit for "diligence" is *vīrya*: *vi* [i.e., *vīr*?] is *vara* ("the highest") [and *ya* is] *yantra* ("application"); thus it is diligence because it is application to the highest merit. The Sanskrit for "meditative concentration" is *dhyāna*: [*dha* is] *dhara* ("holding") and [*na* is] *mana*[*s*] ("mind"); thus it is meditative concentration because of holding the mind. The Sanskrit for "discerning wisdom" is *prajñā*: [*pra* is] *paramārtha* ("ultimate reality"), and [*jñā* is] *jñāna* ("knowledge"); thus it is "knowledge of ultimate reality."

10. The Four Means of Attraction

HAVING THUS EXPLAINED how to cultivate the six perfections, which brings to perfect completion your own qualities of buddhahood, I will now explain how to cultivate the four means of attraction, which is the point of the words "bringing sentient beings to maturity," the fifth key phrase.[417] This has three parts: their definition, their division, and their having a fixed number.

The definition of the four means of attraction is "the caring for your followers through skillful means in order to bring sentient beings to maturity."

Their division. If you divide up the means of attraction, they are four: generosity, pleasant speech, beneficial conduct, and sameness of purpose.

(1) *Generosity* is to support others materially in order to teach them the Dharma, and for this, you should avoid incorrect generosity and please others through correct generosity, as explained above [in chapter 4].

(2) *Pleasant speech* is to teach the Dharma for the sake of bringing others to maturity after you have gladdened them through generosity. This means to abandon incorrect doctrines and to teach without: conflicting with scripture and reasoning; mixing up provisional meaning and definitive meaning; confusing special intention, hidden intention, and straightforward intention; mixing up the levels of excellent and lesser teachings taught [by the Buddha] for superior and inferior people; treating as incompatible the points of agreement between the śrāvaka and Mahayana; or blending the points that do not agree—such as explaining the sense of the perfections and the mantra teachings as one. [347] In particular, it is to teach those who have committed themselves to the mantra tradition in accordance with the four classes of the tantras. In brief, you should teach through understanding the recipient of the teaching, the differentiations of the doctrine, and the method of teaching. On this the *Ornament of Mahayana Sutras* teaches:

> Thus a bodhisattva who is kind, undiscouraged, compassionate,
> and of good repute and who knows wholesome methods

is an eloquent speaker—by teaching,
he shines beautifully among people like the sun.[418]

As Candrakīrti also said:

The teacher directs disciples
after understanding their mental dispositions.
The wise will attract students,
but the unintelligent will never do this for disciples.[419]

The harmful consequences of erroneous teachings are like those explained in the *Ornament of Mahayana Sutras*:

One who construes the meaning through literal sense of the words
will become vain, and his mind will be destroyed.[420]

And in the *Uttaratantra*:

There is no one in this world wiser than the Conqueror,
and the complete highest reality is understood by the Omniscient One and not by others.
Therefore you should not mix up the sutras promulgated by the Renunciant,
for this destroys the Sage's tradition and will thus also be harmful to the good teaching.[421]

Teaching Dharma in a way that suits the recipient is as stated in the *Guide to the Bodhisattva Way of Life*:

[I should] not [teach] the profound and vast doctrine
to an inferior person nor to a woman unaccompanied by a man.
I should conduct myself with equal reverence
toward both the lesser and superior teachings.

I should not direct someone who is a fit receptacle
for the vast teaching to the lesser teachings.
I should not mislead others using sutras and mantras.
And I should not abandon the conduct [of the bodhisattva].[422]

(3) *Beneficial conduct* consists of benefitting others to induce them to take up the practice of Dharma. After you have materially supported and taught Dharma to someone else, if he or she still does not feel like practicing it as taught, use skillful means to induce him or her to practice it. For example, a person who thinks "Even if I take the aspiring vow to awaken, I will not be able to" should be made to practice by telling him or her, "You need not be frightened. If Māra the evil one, who out of deceit formally accepted the vow from Mañjuśrī and who produced the aspiration to awakening having been threatened by Vajrapāṇi, will attain buddhahood, it goes without saying that you, who produced it out of firm appreciation, will do so."

To someone who thinks "Though I accept it now, I will forget it in future lives," you should offer encouragement to take up the aspiration for awakening by explaining that even though he may forget it, he will not be abandoned by the aspiration to attain awakening. This is because it is taught, for instance, that if you commit a great evil you will not be abandoned by the result-producing force of the deed even if you forget it; you will definitely fall into the miserable destinies. [348] Or if [a person of low position] becomes related by marriage to a person of high position and power, even if the lowly person does not desire [the other's presence], he cannot send him away. As the master Asaṅga said:

> If you are never parted from the aspiring resolve to attain awakening, wherever you are born—whether above, below, or on the same level—you will not forget the thought of awakening.[423]

And in the Jātakas:

> The ripening of the results of actions is impossible to judge. Even the compassionate [bodhisattva] was born as an animal, and there his Dharmic way of perceiving things was not destroyed.[424]

And in the *Four Hundred*:

> By accustoming your mind to reality,
> even though it does not occur in this life,
> it will certainly come about effortlessly in a future existence,
> just like [the results of] past deeds.[425]

Thus, with such words, you should induce others to aspire to awakening by explaining how easy it is to achieve.

For those who think they cannot take up the Mahayana because it is difficult to practice the methods of the six perfections such as are mentioned in the passage, "Renouncing my head, arms, and legs, I have no fearful reservations!"[426] and because of the long periods—such as three incalculable eons—that the perfections require, you should tell them that they ought not be afraid, for beginners should first accustom themselves to small acts of generosity that suit their minds and are within the limits of what they can happily do. But later, when they gain fearless acceptance of birthless factors, their bodies and a cup of cooked vegetables will be seen as alike by them, and they will give away their bodies. In this you should practice following such scriptures as the *Skill in Means Sutra*,[427] which recommends at first giving single cups of water, or as taught in the *Guide to the Bodhisattva Way of Life*:

> The Great Guide at the start encourages
> the giving of [small things] such as cooked vegetables.
> Later, after you have become accustomed to giving those,
> you will gradually [become able to] give even your flesh.
>
> When you are able to produce a perception
> of your own body as being something like cooked vegetables,
> then what will be the difficulty of offering
> your flesh and so forth?[428]

Likewise tell them to observe moral discipline by first successfully accustoming themselves to observing what they are capable of—for instance, the precepts of limited duration or the four basic precepts for one daylight period, a full twenty-four-hour day, a month, or a year. Once it has become impossible for them to commit evil deeds even if incited to do so, then they should commit themselves to the moral discipline of vows and so on.

Similarly, with patience, teach them to begin by cultivating it for a single day at a time, or merely for those people whom they feel close to, and then increasing it more and more.

With diligence, too, have them begin with training themselves in virtue for single daylight periods or single twenty-four-hour periods, and then increasing once they have become thus accustomed.

With meditative concentration, have them train themselves for just single sessions until they attain a concentrated mind. [349]

And you should encourage them to cultivate discerning wisdom, telling them, "Do not be afraid, because having mastered the sense of single verses of scripture through study, you will later correctly understand the sense of the three divisions of the scriptures." In these and other ways, fill them with happy enthusiasm and make them take up the practice of Dharma. For as the *Guide to the Bodhisattva Way of Life* teaches:

> There is nothing that does not become easy
> once you have grown accustomed to it.
> By becoming accustomed to small injuries,
> you come to endure patiently even great injuries.[429]

(4) *Sameness of purpose* is to engage in virtue for the sake of inducing others to take it up. For example, if through laziness or heedlessness people do not apply themselves energetically—even though you have attracted them through generosity, taught them the Dharma, and encouraged them to integrate it into their experience—then to engage them in it, you yourself should also engage in that.

For instance, when you urge someone with the words, "It is greatly virtuous to perform reverent service to the Three Jewels," if that person replies that he or she is unable to do it, then ask that person: "In that case, if I wanted to perform an act of reverent service, would you do it with me?" And if that person replies, "In that case, I would be your partner," he or she will do it. Apply this to all the perfections: in a case where someone says, "I cannot study Dharma," you should reply, "But I am going to study it." Thus the other will reply, "In that case I, too, will study," and will engage in it.

To give an illustration of this method, it is as taught in the following story. Once, when the bodhisattva Sukeśa was entering a city, he saw a woman who was unwilling to let go of her son's corpse. Thereupon he went to a charnel ground, found a corpse similar to that of the dead boy, and followed the woman. Thereupon that woman perceived it as unclean, and after they discussed it together, they both discarded their corpses.

[Doubt:] Is the sense of the four means of attraction not included within the six perfections? [Reply:] Indeed, the sense is so included. But there is no incompatibility because the practice of the six perfections is mainly for perfectly completing your own qualities of buddhahood, whereas the practice of the means of attraction is for bringing other sentient beings to maturity. Therefore the *Ornament of Mahayana Sutras* teaches:

> Generosity is the same [as in the perfections];
> [the others are] pleasant speech, beneficial conduct,
> and sameness of purpose
> because they consist of teaching, inducing others, and practicing
> by example.[430] [350]

Their having a fixed number. Why is their number definitely fixed as four?

Their number is fixed as four because [giving] material things benefits the disciple immediately and the remaining three cause the ultimate benefit: one for the disciple to grasp the words of the six perfections, one for the disciple to engage in the practice of their sense, and one for the disciple to frequently and continually practice that sense in accord [with his or her own practice]. That, too, is taught:

> The means of attraction are explained as four
> because you are a means for benefitting,
> you [make the disciple] take it up, you make him engage in it,
> and you accordingly engage in them yourself.[431]

Furthermore, they are fixed as four because the first is to make the disciple a fit recipient of teachings, the second is for making the disciple full of firm appreciation, the third is for making the disciple accomplish it, and the fourth is for bringing it to perfection. The *Ornament of Mahayana Sutras* teaches:

> The first is an expedient for [making the disciple] into a fit
> recipient.
> Through the second, [the disciple] becomes devotedly
> interested.
> Through the third, [the disciple] is made to achieve it.
> And through the fourth, it is completely mastered.[432]

Therefore, all the means for bringing sentient beings to spiritual maturity that are found within the three times are included here. For as it is taught in the *Ornament of Mahayana Sutras*:

This is a means for bringing sentient beings
to maturity because all that has attracted,
will attract, and is now attracting sentient beings
is thereby like that [set of four means].[433]

11. The Paths and Levels

HAVING EXPLAINED the four means of attraction that bring other sentient beings to maturity, now, to establish the meaning of [the sixth key phrase from the *Ornament of Mahayana Sutras*], "entering into the faultless [levels of an ārya] and the pure fields,"[434] you need to understand the arrangement of the five paths and ten levels, because the words "faultless" and "pure fields" refer to the qualities of an ārya.

The five paths

Two [main subjects require explanation], of which the first is the spiritual paths. This has two parts: general definition of a path and ascertaining the individual natures [of the paths].

General definition of a path. The general definition of spiritual path is "an approach to liberation." Some hold that the conceptual essence of a spiritual path is "that which causes a destination to be reached." But this is untenable, for the path is like an approach that is to be traveled, whereas "that which causes a destination to be reached" is impossible, because that would refer to a person who is the agent of the action of going.[435]

Ascertaining the individual natures of the paths has five parts: the path of accumulation, the path of application, the path of seeing, the path of cultivation, and the path of complete accomplishment. The śrāvaka and Mahayana schools have different traditions for explaining these. [351] Here I will state the Mahayana tradition.[436]

The path of accumulation

This explanation has four parts: [definition, divisions, nature, and Sanskrit etymology.]

The definition of the path of accumulation is "an approach to liberation that is the initial meditative cultivation of nonconceptualizing gnosis by means of universals [or concepts] (*sāmānya*)."

Its divisions. The path of accumulation consist of three levels: small, medium, and great. *The small path of accumulation* is the meditative cultivation of the four foundations of mindfulness. It is uncertain whether [a person on this path] will enter the path of application. *The medium path of accumulation* is the meditative cultivation of the four perfect endeavors.[437] [For a meditator on this path,] the time for entering the path of application is assured. *The great path of accumulation* is the meditative cultivation of the four bases of miraculous powers.[438] For a meditator on this part of the path, the "heat" of the path of application will definitely arise in that very lifetime.

Ascertaining its nature has three parts: [types of person, levels, and objects].

Determining what types of person it arises in. The shared [i.e., śrāvaka] vehicle texts, such as those of the Abhidharma, maintain that the path of accumulation will arise only for males and females of the three continents[439] but will not arise in other beings or in human eunuchs or neuters.[440]

Determining what levels it takes as its basis. The merit of the moral discipline of the ordinary person has its basis in the level of the realm of desire. The merit of occasional exertion in yoga has its basis in the six levels of meditative concentration (*dhyāna*)[441] or in a one-pointed mind of the realm of desire. Other merits that are causes of liberation have their basis in the level of the realm of desire.

Determining what objects it takes as its object. The moral discipline of the ordinary person takes as its object the physical and verbal activities that engage in or desist from something. The occasional exertion in yoga takes as its object the mental objects that help purify conduct,[442] such as repulsiveness, or it takes such things as the body as the objects of the application of mindfulness. The other virtuous factors that are causes of liberation take as their objects the scriptures, as both words and sense.

Some say that on the path of accumulation there is no discerning wisdom born from meditative realization. But this is unacceptable. For as the *Compendium of Higher Knowledge* teaches:

> Practice other virtuous things that are its cause and likewise also discerning among wisdoms born from learning, reflection, and meditative realization. By cultivating these, you will become a fit

> receptacle for the future attainment of direct intuition (*abhisamaya*) and liberation.[443]

The Sanskrit etymology of "path of accumulation." "Accumulation" is called *sambhāra* in Sanskrit. [In that word, *sa* stands for] *santāna* ("continuity"), [*bhā* stands for] *bhāva*[*nā*] ("meditative cultivation"), and [*ra* stands for] *rati* ("repeated"): thus it is "continual, repeated meditative cultivation." "Path" is *mārga*, because it is an approach to be passed through. Therefore it is the "path of accumulation."

Alternatively, "accumulation" refers to the preparatory accumulations of merit and gnosis. [352] Through mastering those, you enter the path that is conducive to liberation, and therefore it is the "path of accumulation." "Liberation" means "extinguishment" (*nirvāṇa*), and because it is mental application that is conducive to that, it is "conducive to liberation."

For the "aggregates of appropriation" [i.e., the personality aggregates as the basis for self-postulation], the followers of the śrāvaka tradition maintain that the antidote that removes them consists of viewing them as a fault-ridden thing, such as a disease or a sore. The followers of the Mahayana maintain that the antidote that overcomes them is the understanding that they are without own-nature.

The path of application

The explanation of this also has four parts.

The definition of the path of application is an approach to liberation in which nonconceptualizing gnosis is meditatively cultivated through conceptual thought and in which the path of accumulation has already been accomplished.

Its divisions consist of three parts: division according to whether [its elements belong to] accumulation or application; division according to its great, medium, or small stages; and division according to how reality is realized.

Division according to whether [its elements belong to] accumulation or application. This has two parts: practices that are both accumulation and application, and practices that are not accumulation but are application. The first exist because there is a continuation [of some practices from the path of accumulation] into the path of application. The second practices are only application, because there is application to the four noble truths or the two types of selflessness [not found in the path of application], and they are "not accumulation" because they are not the actual path of accumulation.

Division according to its great, medium, or small stages has three parts. On the small path of application, there is no certainty of the time when the path of seeing will arise. On the medium path of application, [the time of its arising] is determined. On the great path of application, the path of seeing will definitely arise in this lifetime.

Division according to how reality is realized has four phases: heat, peak, acceptance, and the highest worldly realization.

Heat. This phase occurs as a sign portending the arising of the nonconceptual gnosis on the path of seeing, just as heat occurs as a sign portending the occurrence of fire when wood is rubbed together.

The peak. The Sanskrit for this is *mūrdhan*. This is the peak, or crest, of those whose roots of virtue can be disturbed, and thus it is taught, "One who has attained the peak will not have the root of virtue cut off."[444] It is also called "a point in time or a peak" because it does not last long.

Acceptance is so called because you are not alarmed by emptiness.

The highest worldly realization is so called because it is the highest among the realizations attainable by worldly people. It acts as the predominating condition for attaining the undefiled path of seeing.

Each of these four stages of penetration has four aspects: [object, cognitive mode, nature, and accompanying factors].

The *object* of heat. The *Compendium of Higher Knowledge* teaches: "[What is heat? It is the perception] by a person himself...."[445] Hence the four noble truths are taken as its object, either through a supporting person or by the power of having realized them by yourself, without having been taught by another. [353] Moreover, it takes as its object the four truths individually and not grouped together.

The *cognitive mode* of heat is the attainment of perceptual insight,[446] such as of the understanding of apprehended objects as lacking own-nature or of nonconceptualizing gnosis.

The *nature* of heat is meditative absorption and discerning wisdom. Moreover, to focus one-pointedly on the mental object is done through the faculty of meditative absorption. The clear perceptual insight and the removing of false imputations are achieved through the faculty of discerning wisdom. These two spiritual faculties are specified because they are the main ones, but the three other faculties of faith, diligence, and mindfulness also occur as minor mental factors along with them.

Accompanying factors (*sahāya*) consist of the mind, or mental consciousness, and mental factors that are in association (*saṃprayukta*) with those faculties, such as contact-sensation.

The *object* of the peak is the four noble truths, just as above. The *cognitive mode* of the peak is the intensification of the perceptual insight (*snang ba mched pa*). Its *nature* is meditative absorption and discerning wisdom. Its *accompanying factors* are mind and the mental factors in association with those.[447]

The *object* of acceptance is the same as above. Its *cognitive mode* is penetrating and remaining focused on one aspect [of the truths, namely, that objects lack own-nature]. Its *nature* is meditative absorption and discerning wisdom. The *accompanying factors* are mind and the mental factors in association with those.[448]

The *object* of the highest worldly realization is the same as above. Its *cognitive mode* is the realization of the absence of [a substantial or real] apprehending subject. Its *nature* is meditative absorption and discerning wisdom. The *accompanying factors* are mind and the mental factors that are in association with those.[449]

In this connection, the Vaibhāṣikas and Sautrāntikas do not maintain separate mental objects and cognitive modes in the path of application of the śrāvaka and pratyekabuddha, so the *Compendium of Higher Knowledge*, too, does not explain different objects and cognitive modes.

Some scholars of the Mahayana maintain that the paths of application of all three vehicles are as follows:

1. The heat and peak of the śrāvaka realize that the "apprehended object" consisting of the substantial self of the person is without own-nature, while their acceptance and highest worldly realization realize that the "apprehending subject" consisting of the self of the substantial person is without own-nature.
2. The heat and peak of the pratyekabuddha realize that apprehended objects consisting of a single aspect of the substantiality of both a person and phenomena are without own-nature, while their acceptance and highest worldly realization realize that the apprehending subject consisting of a single aspect of the substantial self of both a person and phenomena is without own-nature.
3. The heat and peak of the bodhisattva realize that the apprehended objects consisting of both the substantiality of people and phenomena are without own-nature, [354] while their acceptance and highest

> worldly realization realize that the apprehending subject consisting of both the substantiality of people and phenomena is without own-nature.

And some maintain another opinion about the intended sense unique to the Mahayana, such as in [Vasubandhu's] commentary on the *Ornament of Mahayana Sutras*, here reflecting the Buddha's intent expressed in the *Sutra of the Salty River*.[450] They maintain that the path of application of the bodhisattva consists of the following: *heat*, which is the meditative absorption in which perceptual insight is attained; *the peak*, which is a meditative absorption in which perceptual insight is intensified; *acceptance*, which is a meditative absorption in which one aspect of actual reality is penetrated; and *the highest worldly realization*, which is the meditative absorption that immediately precedes [direct insight on the path of seeing].

But Ārya Nāgārjuna maintained that the intended sense of the vast, medium, and brief Perfection of Wisdom sutras was that, except for the differences of method and differences of clarity between objects of each of the four stages of "participation in penetration," the paths of application of all three vehicles are not different with respect to their realization of selflessness, and he maintained this in accord with statements such as:

> Even someone who desires to train in the stages of the śrāvaka should train in the perfection of wisdom.[451]

And:

> Whether you intend to become a śrāvaka pupil of the Sugata
> or wish to become a pratyekabuddha or a king of Dharma [i.e.,
> a buddha]
> you will not be able to attain it without recourse to this
> acceptance.[452]

Ascertaining its nature has three parts: [what types of person it arises in, what levels it takes as its basis, and their having a fixed number].

What types of person it arises in. The path of application will arise in males and females born in the three continents and in the six classes of gods in the realm of desire. After the path of accumulation has been produced in their minds in a previous existence, the path of application will arise, no matter which class of god of the realm of desire they are born in. I have also seen some special doctrinal traditions of the Mahayana that explain that the path of application will also arise in certain types of animals, such as nāgas.

What levels it takes as its basis. It takes as its basis the six levels of meditative concentration, that is, the stage of "complete capability" (*mi lcogs pa med pa*), [or irreversibility,] on the preparation [level of the first meditative concentration]; the "actual meditative concentration" (*dngos gzhi* [*tsam po ba*]) and the "special actual meditative concentration" (*dngos gzhi khyad par can*) [of the first meditative concentration]; and also the actual meditative states of the remaining three concentrations. But if the practitioner had not previously become freed of the desires of the realm of desire, his or her attainment will take as its basis the preparation of meditative concentration, whereas if he or she is freed, his or her attainment will be based on the actual meditations themselves.

Pratyekabuddhas who stay in groups practice the path of application based on any of the six levels of meditative concentration. And those who live in complete solitude, like a rhinoceros, will practice it based on the actual practice of the fourth meditative concentration. [355]

As for the path of application of the bodhisattvas, the Vaibhāṣikas maintain that it is based on the fourth meditative concentration because it is taught:

> A Great Teacher [a buddha] and a rhinoceros [a pratyekabuddha]
> have their basis until their awakening in the last of the meditative concentrations.[453]

Also, some adherents of Mahayana schools maintain that the bodhisattvas' practice of the path of application is based on the main meditation of any of the four meditative concentrations.

Their having a fixed number. The Sautrāntikas say that the three—heat, the peak, and acceptance—are the realization that apprehended objects are without own-nature, that the highest worldly realization is the realization that the apprehending subject is without own-nature, and that thereby they total four. Moreover, as to the realization that apprehended objects are without own-nature, the small stage, consisting of the attainment of the preliminary perceptual insight, is heat. The medium stage, consisting of the intensified perceptual insight, is the peak. And the great stage, consisting of firm realization, is acceptance.

In this connection, some scholars from the Mahayana say that heat and the peak realize that apprehended objects are without own-nature, while acceptance and the highest worldly realization realize that the apprehending subject is without own-nature. Moreover, the realization that the apprehended objects belonging to the defiled category lack own-nature is heat. The realization that the apprehended objects belonging to the purified category lack own-nature is the peak. About the realization that the apprehending subject is without own-nature, they also maintain: the realization that an apprehending subject who is based on a supposedly materially existent person is without own-nature is acceptance, while the realization that an apprehending subject based on a person established merely by designation is without own-nature is the highest worldly realization. For as the *Ornament of Clear Realization* teaches:

> By way of [a defiled] thing and its antidote,
> the ideas of apprehended objects are twofold.
> Each has nine subdivisions, on account of specific features,
> such as confusion [and eight others] and the grouping [and
> eight others].
>
> Apprehending the subject is also held to be twofold,
> by way of its being based on matter or nominal designation,
> through [views of?] the natures such as
> being an independent self, and likewise the aggregates, and so on.[454]

On these stages of participation in penetration, both the higher and lower traditions of the Abhidharma [Asaṅga's *Compendium* and Vasubandhu's *Treasury*] agree that except for acceptance, the others are not divided into great, medium, and small. The highest worldly realization is not held to possess any duration, for the *Treasury of Higher Knowledge* states:

> Just as great acceptance is of only a single moment,
> so, too, is highest worldly realization.[455]

Therefore this concentration when you attain the supreme factor is also explained as a "meditative absorption of the same seat."

But some Mahayana adherents maintain that the four stages that participate in penetration are divided into three levels each, thus making up a total of twelve levels. As the *Ornament of Clear Realization* teaches: "Through small, medium, and great...."[456] [356] Therefore the highest worldly realization also possesses a continuous duration.

[Question:] To which class of cognition do those four factors participating in penetration belong?[457] On this, some say that they are yogic direct perception, because a commentary on the *Perfection of Wisdom in Eight Thousand Lines* explains that there is a clear perceptual insight when the factors are participating in penetration.[458] And it is untenable that a clear perceptual insight would exist if it were conceptual cognition.

[Reply:] Let us critically examine this. If that is something you have merely designated as "yogic direct perception," let us not quibble about a mere term. If what you mean is yogic direct perception in the strict sense of the word, that will only occur on the path of seeing.[459]

[Doubt:] The path of seeing is the direct perception of the totality of the omnipresent dharmadhātu, whereas in the path of application it is a direct perception of limited extent.

[Reply:] If you saw reality (*dharmatā*) that was previously unrealized, that seeing would fulfill the definition of the path of seeing, whereas if you posited that [the true yogic direct perception] is the path of seeing because its insight is of great extent, that would entail the absurd consequence that the path of cultivation would also become the path of seeing. Therefore, because the path of seeing is the seeing of reality that has not been seen previously, it is explained as being the path of seeing. There is no explanation of its being the path of seeing by reason of its greater extent. Some people say that āryas are not the only ones in whom the yogic direct perception arises. Such people simply lack familiarity with the scriptures and reasoning.

[Objection:] This contradicts the teaching of a clear perceptual insight [on the path of application].

[Reply:] It does not. The word "clear" (*gsal ba*) refers to great competency (or mastery), as in the commonly recognized expression, "You clearly understood fire" through a spontaneous inference when you saw smoke, or as it is taught in scripture: "That monk, through discerning wisdom born from learning and reflection, has become learned, clear, and wise." But such instances do not signify direct perception. This is also so because in *Clear Differentiation of the Middle and Extremes*, direct perception is explained as being free from conceptual thought and nonerroneous, whereas the factors participating in penetration are explained as involving conceptual thought.[460]

Some hold that [the cognizer of the path of application] is "assumption" that bases itself on scriptures. But this, too, is unacceptable, because we refute assumption.[461] The opinion of some that mental direct perception[462] and memory are subsequent cognitions simply reflects their ignorance of dialectics.[463]

Therefore our own tradition is that self-cognition that has become competent through the three types of discerning wisdom—for example, the self-cognizing perception that has mastered such things as desire—is direct perception.[464]

The Sanskrit etymology of "path of application." The Sanskrit for "path of application" is *prayogamārga*. Its *pra* stands for *paramārtha* ("ultimate reality"), and *yoga* stands for "application." Thus it is the path of application because it applies you to the path of seeing, the direct seeing of the ultimate expanse, or dharmadhātu. [357]

The path of seeing

The explanation has four topics: its definition, its divisions, ascertaining its nature, and its Sanskrit etymology.

The definition of the path of seeing is the first arising of the clear perceptual insight on the approach to liberation.[465]

Its divisions are three: the path of seeing of the śrāvaka, the path of seeing of the pratyekabuddha, and the path of seeing of the bodhisattva.

Ascertaining its nature. This has two parts: how the things to be eliminated by seeing are eliminated, and the doctrinal formulation of how the path of seeing arises.

How the things to be eliminated by seeing are eliminated

This has three parts: [the definition of that which is to be eliminated, their division, and how they are eliminated through an antidote]

The definition of that which is to be eliminated. In general, the definition of mere affliction is "that which makes the continuum of mind untranquil." The definition of that which is to be eliminated by seeing is "that which makes the mind very untranquil through the falsely constructed (*parikalpita*)."

The division of that which is to be eliminated is twofold: the basic afflictions and the secondary afflictions. Because the second class is automatically eliminated through elimination of the first, here I will explain only the first.

The basic afflictions are six: desire, anger, pride, ignorance, doubt, and speculative views. The sixth, speculative views, has five subdivisions: the speculative view of a substantially existent self, the view that maintains an extreme, maintaining an inferior view as the highest view, holding inferior moral discipline and ascetic practice to be supreme, and perverse views.

If you divide those according to the way they are removed, they fall into two classes: those that are to be eliminated by seeing and those to be eliminated by cultivation. Regarding the first, the Vaibhāṣika tradition maintains that they are 88, for as the *Treasury of Higher Knowledge* teaches:

> In the desire realm, these are
> ten, seven, seven, and eight;
> except for the three views [for second and third truths] and two views [for fourth truth];
> seeing suffering and the other [three truths] gradually eliminates [these].[466]

And in Asaṅga's *Establishing Summaries of the Levels of Yogic Practice*, the afflictions to be eliminated are explained as numbering 94,[467] whereas his *Compendium of Higher Knowledge* explains them as numbering 112:[468] in the realm of desire there are the five basic afflictions and the five that are classified as speculative views, thus making ten. These ten apply to all four of the four noble truths, thus yielding 40. In the two higher realms there is no anger, and thus there are only nine [afflictions to be eliminated]. Because these wrongly engage the four noble truths, four times nine equals 36 [in each of the two higher realms; and the entire sum is thus 40 + 36 + 36 = 112].

[Objection:] In the formless realm, no body or speech exists, and therefore it is unacceptable [to assert the existence of] four speculative views [i.e., one to be eliminated with each truth] that maintain superiority of moral discipline and ascetic practices, asserting that certain physical and verbal behaviors can cause the purification of evil deeds or liberation. Therefore the afflictions to be eliminated by seeing should be only 108. [358]

[Reply:] That is not the case, for even though in that circumstance bodily and verbal behavior exists that is held to be a cause for purification or liberation, nevertheless there does exist in a speculative view the maintaining of these as being the cause of purification and liberation. Therefore [such a speculative view] is designated as the view maintaining inferior moral discipline and ascetic practices as supreme.

[Question:] In that case, would that not become here the maintaining [of an inferior view] as supreme? [Reply:] It would not. The mode of apprehending when maintaining an inferior view as supreme is the maintaining of something as supreme, chief, and the like, whereas the mode apprehending when maintaining inferior moral discipline and ascetic practice as supreme is the holding of something to be a cause of purification, liberation, and so forth. Therefore the two modes of apprehending (*'dzin stangs*) differ.

[Objection:] Even though the truths of suffering and its origin are to be included within the three realms, the truths of cessation and the path are undefiled and not to be so included. Hence it is unacceptable to posit "cessations and paths of each of the three realms."

[Reply:] *Establishing Summaries of the Levels of Yogic Practice* teaches: "These are [designated] with respect to the three realms."[469] Since the things to be eliminated—suffering and its cause—are of the realm of desire, a "cessation belonging to the desire realm" is designated regarding the cessation of suffering together with its cause. The method for actually bringing that about is also designated as "the path of the desire realm." The cessation and path of the two higher realms are likewise similar.

[Objection:] The explanation in the *Compendium of Higher Knowledge* of 112 objects to be eliminated by seeing and the explanation of 94[470] in the *Saṃgrahaṇī* are contradictory. [Reply:] Some say that these are, respectively, the traditions of the Yogācāra and Sautrāntika. But this is not the true intended sense. [Question:] What is? [Reply:] These reflect the intention of different sutras of coarser and subtler doctrinal formulations.

How they are eliminated through an antidote. The śrāvakas maintain that they [i.e., the afflictions] are eliminated by a present path that will cease, saying in the *Treasury of Higher Knowledge*:

> By the ceasing [of the present] path,
> its obscurations will be eliminated.[471]

The shared [i.e., śrāvaka] vehicle changes that wording, maintaining that they are eliminated by the antidote that is the future path that is yet to arise, saying: "By the arising path, its obscurations will be eliminated."

The uncommon tradition of the Mahayana accepts neither arising nor cessation because in ultimate reality neither the thing to be eliminated nor its antidote is established. For as it is taught:

> Regarding this, there is nothing to be removed,
> nor is there anything to be posited.
> You should correctly look at reality.
> If you see reality, you are liberated.[472]

And as the *Guide to the Bodhisattva Way of Life* teaches:

> Regarding entities that are thus empty,
> what is there to be gained, and what to be lost?[473] [359]

On the surface level, too, if you critically examine this, it is unacceptable that an affliction to be eliminated is eliminated by an antidote. For if the affliction to be eliminated actually existed, then its antidote would not exist, since there can be no simultaneous contact between such a pair, because when the antidote has arisen, the thing to be eliminated has already ceased. For an uncritical mind, you designate the conventional usage "The thing to be eliminated is eliminated," referring merely to the arising of gnosis. But in fact it is like the simultaneous rising and falling of the two ends of a scale.[474]

The doctrinal formulation of how the path of seeing arises

This has four parts: what types of person it arises in, what levels it takes as its basis, what objects it realizes and the manner of that realization, and whether it arises in one or many moments.

What types of person it arises in. The path of seeing will arise in males and females of the three continents and in the gods of the realm of desire, for those beings have sharp moral faculties, the instructions of the Buddha, and a stronger discontentment [with samsara]. It will not arise in beings born in the miserable destinies, for they are obstructed by the great result of their actions. It will also not arise in gods of the form and formless realms, for as the *Treasury of Higher Knowledge* teaches:

> They are without discontentment, and scripture says,
> "Begin here, end up there."[475]

It will also not arise in those people of the northern continent Uttarakuru, for they are similar to the gods of the two higher realms as they are not discontented.

The special tradition of the Mahayana teaches that it can also arise in other beings, too.

What levels it takes as its basis. This topic has three parts, [śrāvaka, pratyekabuddha, and bodhisattva].

The path of seeing of the śrāvaka takes as its basis any of the six levels of meditative concentration. Moreover, it bases itself on the preparatory stage of the first meditative concentration if the person has not previously become freed from the passion [of the realm of desire]. If the person has previously become freed, then the basis will be the actual practice of the meditative concentration.

The path of seeing is not based on the level of the realm of desire, for the path of seeing possesses tranquility and insight in equal measures, whereas on the level of desire, tranquility is present in smaller measure and distraction exists in great measure. It cannot be based in the formless realm because insight exists in smaller measure there. If you exert yourself, it is possible to produce the path of seeing on such levels as the preparation for the second meditative concentration. Yet since tranquility exists in smaller proportion there, it is difficult to produce.

[Doubt:] In such a case, in the preparatory stage of the first meditative concentration there would also be a similar difficulty.

[Reply:] The arising of the path of seeing should [in the former case?] take as its basis the mind of the actual practice of the meditative concentration, for if you have not attained the actual practice, only the preparation of the first meditative concentration itself is easy. It need not base itself on the preparation of the second because it is enough to base yourself on the actual practice of the first, which is easier. Here I have not written about which levels [the path of seeing of] the stream-winners, once-returners, and nonreturners of the śrāvaka take as their base, for fear that this treatise will grow too long. [360]

The path of seeing of the pratyekabuddha takes as its basis any of the six levels of meditative concentration if the pratyekabuddha is one who lives in groups, or the actual practice of the fourth meditative concentration if he is solitary like a rhinoceros.

[Doubt:] It would be untenable for a rhinoceros-like pratyekabuddha after his death to be born only in the realm of desire, for he has eliminated the afflictions belonging to the third meditative concentration and below.

[Reply:] Even though he would not be born there through his past actions, he would be born there through his resolution.

The path of seeing of the bodhisattva takes as its basis the very pure fourth meditative concentration. It does not base itself on the preparation, for previously, [on the Mahayana path of accumulation,] the bodhisattva has already attained the meditative absorption of the "stream of Dharma."

What objects the path of seeing realizes and the manner of that realization. The shared vehicle maintains that the śrāvaka realizes the selflessness of a person with regard to the four noble truths. Moreover, it takes as its object not the truth that has been divided [into four] but the own-characteristic (*svalakṣana*), "undivided truth." The pratyekabuddha realizes the absence of own-nature of the apprehended objects of the self of both a person and phenomena. The bodhisattva realizes both types of selflessness.

On this, the Abhidharma explains, about each [of the three classes of āryas] individually, the "negation of the sign" regarding sentient beings, the "negation of the sign" regarding phenomena, and the "negation of the sign" of both everywhere.[476] As it is explained in *Establishing Summaries of the Levels of Yogic Practice*:

> After the ultimate root of merit of the stages conducive to penetration, which belongs to the mundane sphere, you focus on the "negation of the sign" of sentient beings, which is taken as the object for each individually. And then there arises the first moment of mind that is freed from small evils belonging to the category of things to be eliminated by seeing. After that, the "negation of the sign" of phenomena is taken as the object for each individually, and there arises the second moment of mind, which is freed from the medium evils belonging to the category of things to be eliminated by seeing. After that, you take as your object the "negation of the sign" of all phenomena, and there arises a third moment of mind, which is freed from the great evils belonging to the category of things to be eliminated by seeing. Thus those are the path of seeing.[477]

These three "negations of the signs" are the tradition of the path of seeing of the shared vehicle, in which the sixteen moments are divided into great, medium, and small. [361]

Some teachers belonging to the unshared Mahayana tradition,[478] such as Ācārya Ārya [Nāgārjuna] and his spiritual son [Āryadeva], do not maintain that the three classes of āryas are different in their realization of selflessness, following such statements as this in the *Perfection of Wisdom*:

> Even someone who desires to train in the stages of the śrāvaka should train just in this perfection of wisdom.[479]

Whether the path of seeing arises in one or many moments. This subject entails two parts: the shared tradition and the unshared tradition. As to *the shared tradition*, the *Treasury of Higher Knowledge* states:

> Fifteen moments are the path of seeing
> because you see what was previously unseen.[480]

With the sixteenth moment comes the "position of fruition" [i.e., the path of cultivation]. Thus the Vaibhāṣikas hold that for all four noble truths there are four stages. [To begin with, for the truth of suffering there are:] (1) receptivity to the knowledge of the factors (*dharmajñāna*) with reference to suffering, (2) the knowledge of the factors with reference to suffering, (3) receptivity to the subsequent knowledge about suffering, and (4) the subsequent knowledge with reference to suffering. And because these are applied in the same way also to the subsequent three truths, the path of seeing is held to arise in sixteen moments. As it is also taught:

> Receptivity and knowledge are, respectively, the uninterrupted path and liberation path.[481]

Hence the receptivities are the immediate path, and the knowledges of the factors are the path of liberation.[482] Moreover, the followers of some schools maintain that the path of seeing arises, for instance, in eight or in four moments, whereas the Sthaviravādins and Mahāsaṃghikas maintain that it arises in one moment. Also some followers of the Mahayana variously hold that it arises in from one to sixteen moments.

The unshared tradition. A sutra teaches: "The bodhisattva attains acceptance of unoriginated factors."[483] Therefore this tradition does not hold that a path of seeing originates in ultimate reality. For as a sutra states:

> Though nonorigination is one truth,
> some say concerning it that four truths exist.
> Abiding in the heart of awakening (*bodhimaṇḍa*), I did not see
> even one truth as established; how could there be four?[484]

And as the *Sixty Reasonings* teaches:

Say there existed distinctions
after the knowledge of the factors:
a person is not wise at all
who imputes origination
to even the most subtle of entities;
such persons do not see conditioned origination.[485] [362]

[Objection:] In that case, this contradicts what sutras teach about the origination of the path of seeing in one moment, in sixteen moments, and so forth.

[Reply:] Those were allusions intended to assist those who maintain the existence of entities.[486] The thing alluded to was dependent origination. The motive was to encourage those who have conceptual attachment to entities to enter [into the higher doctrine]. The disproof of the surface meaning is that it is refuted through the refutation of the four possibilities of production as stated in *Fundamental Verses on the Middle Way*:

There never exists origination for any entity anywhere,
whether from a cause that is the same as itself,
different from itself, both the same and different,
or from the absence of a cause.[487]

Furthermore, if you were to examine how many moments the path of seeing arises in, you would have to examine in how many moments it is also destroyed in, and such a procedure would entail an absurd overextension (*atiprasaṅga*). For as *Fundamental Verses on the Middle Way* teaches:

If you think
"Origination and destruction exist,"
"origination" and "destruction"
are contaminated by confusion.[488]

[Question:] Is not origination that is based on something else true origination?

[Reply:] It is not. As the *Questions of Nāga King Anavatapta Sutra* teaches:

That which has arisen from conditions has not arisen.
It does not possess an own-nature of arising.

> That which is dependent on conditions is emptiness.
> He who understands emptiness is prudent.[489]

And as Ācārya Ārya [Nāgārjuna] also said:

> He did not refute this mundane usage that states
> "Based on this, this originates."
> [But in reality,] that which originates in dependence has no own-nature.
> How could you prove it has?[490]

And it is also explained in great detail with such words as:

> Since no factor of existence exists
> that is not dependently originated,
> no entity whatsoever exists
> that is not emptiness.[491]

Therefore, all factors of existence are not produced.

The Sanskrit etymology of "path of seeing" is *darśanamārga*. It is "seeing" because you see the sphere of reality (*dharmadhātu*) that was not previously seen. It is a "path" because it is an approach (or passage) into liberation. If you trace its etymology back to such words as *nirāsrava*, it is explained as being "undefiled truth" because it is the antidote to the actual defiling passions (*zag pa, āsrava*). It is the "eliminating bliss" because it completely eliminates the afflictions that are to be eliminated by seeing. And it is the first production of a mind that has transcended the mundane sphere because it is the first of the qualities of the ārya. This [concludes the explanation of] the path of seeing.

The path of cultivation

This, too, has three main sections: its definition, its divisions, and its Sanskrit etymology. [363]

The definition of the path of cultivation is "making yourself adept in the approach to liberation through special meditative absorption."[492]

Its divisions are two: the path of cultivation belonging to the mundane sphere and the path of cultivation of the supramundane sphere.

The mundane path of cultivation

The explanation of this has two parts. The *definition of the mundane path of cultivation* is meditative absorption that makes you adept on the approach to the higher realms, taking as its basis the preparation stage of the meditative concentrations. *Ascertaining its nature* has four topics: what types of people it arises in, what levels it takes as its basis, its procedures of reflection, and what function it performs.

What types of person the mundane path of cultivation arises in. This path can arise in males and females of the three continents, in the gods of the realm of desire, and in all but three classes of gods in the two higher realms, for these are meritorious bases for a life. It will not arise in the three lower miserable destinies, in humans from the Uttarakuru continent, in eunuchs or neuters, or in the gods of nonapperception[493] in the form realm, for here the obscurations are present in great measure. It will not arise in the Great Brahma rebirth of the form realm, because this is the life-basis of a perverse view and the main deity is limited to only one. It also will not arise in the "pinnacle of existence" of the formless realm, because that lacks another place in the higher realms that is more tranquil and because there the mind is not clear.

What levels it takes as its basis. It will take as its basis the eight meditative concentrations and meditative attainments of the form and formless realms.

Its procedures of reflection. The explanation of this has three parts: the preparatory stage, the actual practice stage, and their divisions.

The preparatory stage

This consists of seven reflections:[494]

1. *The reflection that perceives the characteristics.* Through knowing—by means of discerning wisdom born from learning and reflection in the realm of desire—that the mind belonging to that realm has many afflictions and, agitated by those, becomes unhappy, resulting in short lifespans, whereas the higher realms are different in that the mind becomes tranquilly pliant, and consequently the meditative

absorption of the first meditative concentration arises. This is the knowledge that the mind of the desire realm is coarse and the mind of the first meditative concentration is tranquil.

2. *The reflection with conviction.* This is the arising of the basic absorption of the first meditative concentration that has transcended learning and reflection through discerning wisdom born from meditative realization as a consequence of having brought your mind to tranquil readiness in the previous reflection. [364]
3. *The reflection of seclusion.* This is the elimination of the manifest afflictions of the realm of desire after the arising of the eliminating antidotes to the [three] great things to be eliminated through meditative cultivation, which occurs as a consequence of having meditated in the previous reflection.
4. *The reflection that imparts joy.* Here you rejoice in eliminating the coarse [sensual pleasure of the lower realm]. Gladdened through the small joy and pleasure that arise from being thus secluded and viewing this seclusion as beneficial, you from time to time spur the mind on to great confidence. That is the antidote that eliminates the medium afflictions.[495]
5. *The reflection that investigates.* As a consequence of your having thus eliminated the majority of afflictions through the antidotes, the thought will occur, "Have I eliminated them all?" This, then, is the reflection that turns the mind to activities conducive to the arising of the afflictions in order to investigate whether or not the afflictions are still arising.
6. *The reflection that attains the culmination of practice.* By investigating in that way, you see that the afflictions are indeed still arising, and by then cultivating as above the aspects of coarseness and calm, the antidote to the weak residual afflictions arises in the mind. This reflection is that practice.
7. *The reflection of the fruit of the culmination of practice.* This is to apply yourself subsequently to appropriating into your experience the fruit of all that has been meditatively cultivated.[496]

As with this first meditative concentration, these same seven reflections then bring about the second meditative concentration continuing on up to the pinnacle of existence.[497]

And, to explain in this connection [the seven reflections as a system of four paths]: the reflection that perceives the characteristics and the reflection with conviction comprise the *path of application*. The reflections of seclusion, imparting joy, and attaining the culmination of practice are the *immediate path*. The reflection that investigates is the *special path*. The reflection of the fruit of the culmination of practice is the *path of liberation*. Within the above immediate path, the small path is the reflection of seclusion, which is the antidote to the strong afflictions. The middle path is the reflection that imparts joy, which is the antidote to the medium afflictions. The great path is the reflection that attains the culmination of practice, which is the antidote to the weak residual afflictions.

The actual practice stage

This stage of meditative concentration has eight parts: the four meditative concentrations of the form realm and the four limits of the stages of meditative attainment of the formless realm. [365]

The four meditative concentrations of the form realm. Regarding these,

1. *The first meditative concentration* has two divisions: ordinary actual practice and special actual practice. *The ordinary actual practice* is taught to possess conceptual thought, to possess investigation, to be endowed with joy and pleasure, and to be born from seclusion. *The special actual practice* is without conceptual thought and is the meditative absorption of mere investigation.
2. *The second meditative concentration* is meditative absorption that possesses joy and pleasure.
3. *The third meditative concentration* is the absorption that lacks mental joy but possesses just physical pleasure.
4. *The fourth meditative concentration* is an absorption of perfect equanimity with neither joy nor pleasure. And since these possess the defiling factors (impurities, *āsrava*), they belong to the mundane sphere.

From among *the four limits of the stages of meditative attainment of the formless realm*, the first is:

1. *The meditative attainment of infinite space.* As for this, when the causal concentration meditatively entered is in the phase of the meditative cultivation of the special path, all factors of existence are mere space, and that is here cultivated as limitless.

2–4. *The meditative attainment of infinite consciousness* and the remaining [two, the formless meditative attainments of *nothingness* and *neither ideation nor nonideation* (the "pinnacle of existence"),] are also similar in their production.

Being based on such things as "thirsting-attachment" (*tṛṣṇā*) and mistaken views, these are defiled meditative concentrations. But if the four correct meditative concentrations and the four formless attainments are freed from the constantly occurring contamination of the impurely enfolding afflictions, they are called "purifying meditative concentration," for they are wholesome. You should learn about these in more detail from other treatises.[498]

Their divisions

The meditative concentrations can be divided by way of nature, by way of what is to be eliminated, and by way of cause and effect.

Division by way of nature. If you divide them by way of their natures, then they are the *four ways of conduciveness*: that which is conducive to decline, that which is conducive to the status quo, that which is conducive to a superior stage, and that which is conducive to penetration. The śrāvakas explain the sense of these by saying that the first conduces to a decrease in level, the second to your own level, the third to a higher level, and the fourth becomes a basis for the path to liberation. Yogācāra adherents teach that the first [concentration] has too great a proportion of the afflictions for there not to be loss of the absorption of meditative concentrations. The second does not possess either declining or improvement. The third acts as a basis for attaining of special excellent qualities such as the superknowledges. The fourth is suitable as a basis for the path of āryas. These should be applied to all four paths, such as the path of application and the immediate path.

Division by way of what is to be eliminated. If divided in this way, they number seventy-two in all because each of the eight levels [i.e., the four meditative concentrations and the four formless attainments]—here the pinnacle of existence is excluded[499]—is divided according to strong, middling, and weak into nine divisions [beginning with the weak-weak, the middle-weak, the strong-weak, and so on; and 8 x 9 = 72]. [366]

Division by way of cause and effect. If you divide them according to cause and result, you get two categories: meditative concentration that meditatively engages in the causes and meditative concentration in which the result arises.

The first of these, *meditative concentration that meditatively engages in the causes*, is continually to cultivate meditatively—on the seven preparatory stages of the first concentration—the application of (1) reverence that is mindful of the virtues [of meditative concentration], and (2) the constant mental engagements. This, too, is divided into three divisions of great, medium, and small. That which possesses neither of the two is the small. That which possesses one or the other of the two is the medium. That which possesses both is the great. Also, during the preparatory stage of each of the remaining three meditative concentrations and the four meditative attainments of the formless realm, these are cultivated in the same way in the three levels of great, medium, and small.

Meditative concentration in which the result arises. The small preparation of the first meditative concentration results in birth as a Brahma's Retinue god. The middle results in birth as one of the foremost of the Brahma's Ministers gods. And the great will result in birth as a Great Brahma god. The same division should be applied to the remaining three meditative concentrations.[500]

Moreover, through meditatively cultivating by turns the defiled and undefiled fourth meditative concentration, you will be born in the five stages of the ārya.[501]

Those deities of the formless realm have no separate [higher or lower classes or] levels because, since they have dispensed with matter, they do not possess palatial dwellings.[502] Nevertheless, by being meditatively cultivated to greater, middling, or lesser degrees, they will be born in the formless states having correspondingly longer or shorter lifespans and more or less power. Their afflictions of desire and the rest will also be either strong, medium, or weak.

Regarding such meditative concentrations, those of the mundane sphere are weak, inferior, and defiled. Those of the śrāvaka and pratyekabuddha are undefiled and vaster than those of the mundane sphere. As for meditative absorptions such as *valiant progress* (*śūraṅgama*) that belong to the buddhas and bodhisattvas dwelling in the perfection of meditative concentration and were taught in the sutras and tantras, even their names are unknown to the śrāvakas and pratyekabuddhas, for the latter do not possess the perfection of meditative concentration.

What function it performs. The function [of the mundane path of cultivation] is to suppress, through practicing the meditative concentrations, the seeds of the things to be eliminated and to act as the basis for excellent qualities, such as the four immeasurable virtues (*apramāna*) and the five superknowledges, and for the path of the ārya.[503]

The supramundane path of cultivation

This entails three topics: its definition, its divisions, and ascertaining its nature.[504] [367]

The definition of the supramundane path of cultivation is that which makes you adept on that very threshold to liberation, the sphere of reality that you saw previously.

Its divisions can be classified in four ways: according to types of people, according to the objects to be eliminated, according to the path, and according to how you become adept.

To divide it *according to person*, there are three: śrāvaka, pratyekabuddha, and bodhisattva.

To divide it *according to the objects to be eliminated*, there are 414 things to be eliminated, and their antidotes number the same.

If you divide it *according to path*, there are four: the path of application, the immediate path, the path of liberation, and the special path.

If you divide it *according to how you become adept*, it is twofold: you are made adept through meditation and through postmeditative activities.

Ascertaining its nature has two parts: how the things to be eliminated through cultivation are eliminated and how the path of cultivation arises.

How the things to be eliminated by cultivation are eliminated has three sections: the definition of the things to be eliminated by cultivation, their divisions, and how they are eliminated through the antidotes.

The definition of the things to be eliminated by cultivation is "the innately arisen afflictions[505] making the mind untranquil."

Their divisions. If you divide [the things to be eliminated through cultivation], there are the six innately arisen afflictions in the realm of desire, and in each of the [two] higher realms there are five each because anger is absent; thus they make up a total of sixteen.

[Objection:] This contradicts the explanation in the *Establishing Summaries of the Levels of Yogic Practice* of there being ten. [Reply:] These are not contradictory; these are the intended senses of different sutras of coarse and subtle doctrinal formulations.

When you divide them each according to strong, middle, and weak into nine subdivisions, such as strong-strong, [middle-strong, weak-strong, etc.], you get a total of 414 [actually the correct number should be: 144—i.e., 9 x 16.].[506]

How they are to be eliminated through the antidotes. You should understand this as explained [above] for the path of seeing.

How the path of cultivation arises involves three topics: what [types of] people it arises in, what levels it takes as its basis, and what objects it takes as its object.

What types of people it arises in. The path of cultivation will arise in males and females of the three continents, in the six divine classes of the realm of desire, in the form realm except that of Great Brahma [of the first concentration] and the meditative attainment of nonapperception [of the fourth concentration], and in the four meditative attainments of the formless realm. The reason it will not arise elsewhere is as explained before.

What levels it takes as its basis entails three topics: [explanations about the śrāvaka, pratyekabuddha, and bodhisattva].

The path of cultivation of the śrāvaka is held to be based on six [levels of the meditative concentrations of the form realm]—the actual practices of the four meditative concentrations, the preparation of the first meditative concentration, and the special main practice [of the first concentration]—and on the first three resultant meditative attainments of the formless realm, making a total of nine bases. [368] The reason it does not base itself on other levels is that the mind of the realm of desire is not serviceable and the mind of the pinnacle of existence is not clear. It also does not base itself on the three preparations of the remaining three meditative concentrations or on the preparations of the three formless-realm meditative attainments because they entail striving for the attainment of superior levels, and therefore produce less calm, so that tranquility and insight are not equally conjoined in them.

[Objection:] The preparation of the first meditative concentration should also be unsuitable as a basis because it has proportionately less tranquility. [Reply:] Though it has less tranquility, it can still be taken as a basis because it is easier than the others.

[Additional objection:] If it will not arise on the basis of a Great Brahma god, it should also not arise in a mind that is the special main practice of the first meditative concentration. [Reply:] Though it would be good in that mind, it is the basis for an existence as a Great Brahma god. The path of cultivation cannot arise in a mind that is connected with Great Brahma because the life-basis of a Great Brahma god, in addition to being only one, is the basis of mentation[507] and perverse views, whereas if it is produced in a mind of similar sort as the basis, the path of cultivation will arise—just as, for example, the seeds kept in a box are not the basis for sprouts whereas seeds of the same sort will produce sprouts if planted in a field.

[Objection:] If it will not arise in the mind of the pinnacle of existence, it should not take as its basis the person at the peak of existence, for if it can be based on the person, what is the incompatibility of its being based on the mind? [Reply:] Even though the person of the pinnacle of existence is excellent, the mind of the ārya will not arise there because in it the movements of mind are unclear. Instead, you must base yourself in the mind of nothingness, [the third formless meditative attainment,] because it is clear. It is just as, for example, you would ask of a minister what the king does not know. This very point is expressed in the *Treasury of Higher Knowledge*:

> The ārya of the pinnacle of existence exhausts
> his impurities if he directly realizes nothingness.[508]

[Objection:] Just as the minds of the three formless attainments are unsuitable as bases for the path of seeing because they are unclear, so these are equally unsuitable as bases for the path of cultivation. [Reply:] Though the śrāvakas have another answer to this, the tenable answer is this: What is the need of throwing away the easy production of the path of seeing based on the six levels of meditative concentration and instead basing yourself on the difficult formless attainments? For the path of cultivation, the āryas born in the formless realm—the nonreturners—must base themselves on the three formless attainments for their realization of arhatship after the elimination of the remainder of things to be eliminated by cultivation, even though that is difficult. This is because they cannot produce it [based on the meditative concentrations] since they have surpassed the upper realm consisting of the minds of the meditative concentrations from the fourth down that possess tranquility and insight in equal conjunction. [369] It is just like making do by energetically using the left hand if you lack a right hand.

Alternatively, you could answer by saying that the path of seeing requires a clear mind because it makes seen the previously unseen reality, whereas for that [path of seeing] it is unsuitable to take the three formless attainments as a basis because they are unclear. But there is no incompatibility in basing the path of cultivation there because the path of cultivation is that which makes you adept in the thing that was seen [on the path of seeing], and it can be mastered even based on an unclear mind.

The path of cultivation of the pratyekabuddha takes as its basis the following levels. The pratyekabuddha who lives in groups takes as his basis for the path of cultivation any of the six levels of meditative concentration. The pratyekabuddha who is solitary like a rhinoceros takes as his basis the main practice of the fourth meditative concentration.

The path of cultivation of the bodhisattva takes as its basis the very pure fourth meditative concentration. Nevertheless, as for the bodhisattva's place of birth, the bodhisattva will be born because of past deeds and resolutions in either the realm of desire or the form realm but not in the formless realm. When they are bringing to mastery their skills in meditative absorption, they enter into the formless attainments and the meditative attainment of cessation (*nirodha samāpatti*) when they meditate in such absorptions as *majestic lion* and *skipping over*.[509]

What objects it takes as its object. The shared vehicle maintains that after the path of seeing, you make yourself adept equally in tranquility and insight, which take as their object the reality of the four noble truths. The special Mahayana tradition is that [the path of cultivation] cultivates a mastery of the gnosis and the reality realized on the path of seeing, in connection with all subjects (*dharmin*).

The Sanskrit etymology of "path of cultivation." The term *bhāvanāmārga* is the "path of cultivation" because it cultivates the thing that has been seen. Because it lacks impurities, it is the "root of merit that has no impurities." And it is known as the "antidote that eliminates" because it is the antidote against those things to be eliminated through cultivation.

The path of [complete] accomplishment

This, too, has four parts: its definition, its divisions, ascertaining its nature, and its Sanskrit etymology.

The definition of the path of complete accomplishment is the meditative cultivation that reaches the end of the approach to the sphere of reality.

Its divisions. If you divide the path of complete accomplishment, there are three: that of the śrāvaka, of the pratyekabuddha, and of the bodhisattva. [370]

Ascertaining its nature involves three topics: what types of people it arises in, what levels it takes as its basis, and what objects it takes as its object.

What types of people it arises in and *what levels it takes as its basis.* The teaching of the śrāvakas resembles their foregoing explanation of the supramundane path of cultivation. The shared vehicle holds that the pratyekabuddha and bodhisattva are born into the physical basis of a human being. In particular, the bodhisattva on this path is born as a brahman or kṣatriya of the central country of this world-continent (Jambudvīpa).[510] And the level he is born from is the vajra-like meditative absorption of the fourth meditative concentration.

The unshared Mahayana tradition holds that the path of complete accomplishment is based on the tenth level (*bhūmi*) and that it arises from the predominating condition of the vajra-like absorption at the end of the extremely pure fourth meditative concentration. Regarding that vajra-like absorption, for the śrāvaka its suppression of the small seeds of the afflictions is the path of application, and its complete uprooting of them is the immediate path. For the bodhisattva its suppression of the small seeds of the affliction and knowable things obscurations is the path of application, and its complete uprooting of them is the immediate path.

What objects it takes as its object. According to the shared tradition, the path of complete accomplishment focuses through the vajra-like absorption on the four noble truths, on the truth of cessation, or on the ten qualities of the level beyond training. Regarding the latter, the ten qualities of the level beyond training are: (1) right view, (2) right thought, (3) right speech, (4) right "ends of action" [i.e., bodily merits], (5) right livelihood, (6) right effort, (7) right mindfulness, (8) right meditative absorption, (9) liberation, and (10) seeing the gnosis of liberation.[511] If you subsume them within the categories of Dharma, right speech, action, and livelihood make up the category of moral discipline. Meditative absorption and mindfulness make up the category of meditative absorption. View, thought, and diligence make up the category of discerning wisdom. "Liberation" makes up the category of liberation. And "seeing the gnosis of liberation" makes up the category of seeing the gnosis of liberation. With regard to the above, the nonconceptualizing [meditation session] is included within supramundane gnosis, and the postmeditative activities are included within the pure mundane gnosis. [371]

According to the unshared Mahayana tradition, the śrāvaka and pratyekabuddha [on the path of complete accomplishment] focus on nirvana as their object. The bodhisattva focuses on nirvana that is not entered into anywhere.

The Sanskrit etymology of "path of complete accomplishment." The Sanskrit *niṣṭhāmārga*[512] is the "path of complete accomplishment" because it brings to completion the elimination of those things to be eliminated and the knowing of those things to be known. Its root of merit is without impurities because it is free of impurities. And it is known as the "distancing antidote" because it prevents the eliminated afflictions from arising again.

Regarding this, the tradition of the shared vehicle is explained in the *Treasury of Higher Knowledge* as:

> For acquiring control over the higher and higher [attainments]
> such as nirvana, there are the faculties of [resolving]
> to come to know perfectly [that which is unknown], of perfect
> knowledge, and of the possession of perfect knowledge.[513]

Thus it is taught that on the path of application there exists the faculty of resolving to know perfectly what is unknown, which brings the path of seeing under your control. On the path of seeing there exists the faculty of perfect knowledge, which brings the path of cultivation under your control. And on the path of cultivation there exists the faculty of being in possession of perfect knowledge, which brings the path of complete accomplishment under control. But the unshared Mahayana tradition does not employ such terminology for these faculties.

The presentation of the ten levels

The explanation of the ordering of the ten levels has three parts: the definition, their divisions, and the formulation of each division.

The definition of the ten levels. The definition of *level* (*bhūmi*) is "that which acts as the basis for special excellent qualities." If you divide the levels, there are two main divisions. The definition of *the levels of practice through conviction* is "that which acts as a basis for the virtues that engage in the qualities of the ārya." The definition of *the supramundane levels* is "that which acts as the basis for the special virtues of the ārya."

Their divisions. If you divide them, you get *the levels of the śrāvaka* and *the levels of the bodhisattva.* As the *Precious Garland* teaches:

> Just as in the Śrāvaka Vehicle
> eight levels of the śrāvaka are taught,
> so in the Mahayana there is taught
> the ten levels of the bodhisattva.[514]

The formulations of each of those divisions. The levels are formulated in two ways, that of the śrāvaka and that of the bodhisattva. [372]

The formulation of the levels of the śrāvaka. These are eight in number: (1) the level of seeing the wholesome, (2) the level of "spiritual lineage," (3) the level of the eighth,[515] (4) the level of thinning, (5) the level that is freed from desire, (6) the level of mastery, (7) the level of the śrāvaka, and (8) the level of the pratyekabuddha.[516] However, since these are not our relevant topic here, I will leave off this subject.

The formulation of the levels of the bodhisattva. The explanation of this has four parts: their divisions, their having a fixed number, their individual excellent qualities, and [the Sanskrit etymology of] the terms.

Their divisions. There are ten: (1) the Joyous, (2) the Stainless, (3) the Shining, (4) the Blazing, (5) Difficult to Master, (6) the Manifested, (7) the Far-Reaching, (8) the Unshakable, (9) the Excellent Intelligence, and (10) the Cloud of Dharma. The first seven are the impure levels, and the last three are the pure levels. Moreover, the level of practice through conviction has much pride. The impure levels have slight pride. And the three pure levels are without pride. For as the *Ornament of Mahayana Sutras* teaches:

> These are held to be prideful,
> with slight pride, and without pride.[517]

Their having a fixed number. The levels are definitely determined as ten because they correspond to the ten perfections. The six perfections correspond to the first six levels, and the four perfections of method, strength, resolution, and gnosis correspond to the remaining four levels.

Their individual excellent qualities have two parts: the qualities of being free from something undesirable and the excellent qualities that consist of a positive attainment.

[Bodhisattvas who have *the qualities of being free from something unde-*

sirable] have crossed over the four great rivers of suffering. For as the *Uttaratantra* teaches:

> The [Mahayana] ārya has completely eliminated
> the sufferings of death, sickness, and old age.
> No birth through the power of past karma and afflictions exists
> for him.
> He does not possess such birth because he lacks those [causes].[518]

Also they are freed from the five fears, for as the *Flower Ornament Sutra* teaches:

> That person who is free of the fears of no livelihood, death, ill repute, the lower miserable destinies, and assemblies possesses no form of timidity.[519]

Such a one is free from the five fears of lack of livelihood, untimely death, disrepute, the lower miserable destinies, and the lack of confident presence of mind amid an assembly. Moreover, he or she is freed from unthinkably many fears [or dangers], just as the *Ten Levels Sutra* teaches.[520] You should also understand by implication that those qualities increase gradually from the first level until the tenth.

Even though they are freed from fears, they show the appearance of experiencing birth, old age, sickness, and death. Regarding this, [bodhisattvas on these levels] are born into cyclic existence according to their own wishes in order to benefit sentient beings. [373] For as the *Uttaratantra* teaches:

> Even though he has transcended birth and the rest,
> because he sees reality exactly as it is,
> the person of compassionate nature shows
> the appearance of birth, death, illness, and aging.[521]

The excellent qualities that consist of a positive attainment. The *Ten Levels Sutra* explains them as twelve sets of a hundred virtues [on the first level] because[522] these virtues arise in a single moment: you attain a hundred meditative absorptions and dwell in them, you see a hundred buddhas, you understand their sustaining powers, one hundred world realms quake, you visit a hundred pure realms, you illuminate a hundred world realms, you bring to spiritual maturity one hundred sentient beings, you dwell for a hundred eons, [your knowledge] penetrates up to the ends of the previous and following hundred eons, you open one hundred "doors of Dharma," you display a hundred bodies, and each of those bodies manifests a retinue of a hundred bodhisattvas.[523]

Those excellent qualities become a thousand [instead of the previous hundred] on the second level. On the third level they become one hundred thousand. On the fourth level, a billion. On the fifth level, ten billion. On the sixth level, a trillion. On the seventh level, a hundred quadrillion. On the eighth level their number is equal to the number of "atoms" in one hundred thousand world realms. On the ninth level they are equal to the "atoms" of a million world realms. On the tenth level you attain a number equal to the "atoms" in inexpressibly many buddhafields, and there also arise other excellent qualities besides. Learn about the excellent qualities of the spiritual levels in more detail from such scriptures as the *Ten Levels Sutra*, the *Sutra Definitely Elucidating the Noble Intention*, and the *Ornament of Mahayana Sutras*.

The Sanskrit etymology of the terms has two parts, [the meaning of the term *bhūmi* and the meanings of the terms for the individual levels].

The meaning of the common term. "Level" in Sanskrit is *bhūmi*. If you trace its etymological derivation, it is said in the *Ornament of Mahayana Sutras*:

> Those are held to be "levels"
> because they remove the fear of infinite beings,
> and because they entail ascending further and further
> upward to those infinite [excellent qualities].[524]

[The *bhū* is for] *bhūta*, "creature"; *mi* is from *amita*, "infinite"; [*bhū* is for] *abhaya*, "fearless"; *mi* is for *amita*, "infinite"; [*bhū* is for] *bhuya*[*s*], "more and more"; *ūrdhvaṃgamana* [*yogita*] is "possessing upward movement."

(2) *The etymological meanings of the individual terms*. This is such as is as stated in the passage beginning:

> The [first] level is taught as Joyous
> because joy will arise for one who sees
> the closeness to awakening and the accomplishment
> of the welfare of sentient beings.[525] [374]

Nowadays here in Tibet, I see some who maintain that buddhahood can be reached without traveling over the paths and levels[526] and who hold that the path of seeing arises without accompanying excellent qualities.[527] But this is not the doctrine of the Buddha because such a teaching is not seen in any sutra, tantra, or great treatise.

Furthermore, regarding those paths and levels, the five paths will be accomplished based on the ultimate thought of awakening, with discerning wisdom (the meditative realization of emptiness as the appropriating cause) and method (the great compassion) as the immediately acting condition. The ten levels are attained based on the relative thought of awakening, with method (the great compassion) as the appropriating cause and discerning wisdom (emptiness) as the immediately acting condition. And when you awaken to buddhahood, the ultimate path is the Dharma body and the ultimate level is the form body.

12. The Ultimate Fruit

HAVING THUS explained the words "entering into the faultless levels and the pure fields," I will now explain the seventh key phrase: "nonsituated nirvana, the highest awakening, and the displaying."[528]

The sense indicated here is the ultimate fruit. Moreover, "nonsituated nirvana" refers to not being situated in cyclic existence because of discerning wisdom, and not being situated in nirvana because of compassion. For as the *Ornament of Clear Realization* teaches:

> Because of understanding, he does not remain in worldly existence. Because of compassion, he does not remain in quiescence.[529]

The "highest awakening" is all the spontaneously achieved shared and unique excellent qualities of buddhahood. "Displaying" is the displaying of the great nirvana. That, too, is not merely the exhaustion of the afflictions or the knowledge that those afflictions will not arise again, in the manner of the nirvana of the śrāvaka. Rather, even though nirvana has been attained, there is the uninterrupted arising of benefits for sentient beings.

The teaching of these points has three parts: the definition of buddhahood, the formulation about the bodies of buddhahood, and the explanation of the excellent qualities of buddhahood.

The definition of buddhahood

The definition of buddhahood is "perfectly complete elimination and gnosis." Here "elimination" means elimination of the affliction and knowledge obscurations together with the propensities toward those obscurations. [375] "Gnosis" is the cognition of objects of knowledge exactly as they are and in their full variety and extent. As Ācārya Maticitra said:

> The Omniscient One possesses all excellent qualities
> and also possesses no defects.
> The Sole Protector does not possess
> the faults or their propensities.[530]

The formulation about the bodies of buddhahood

This has three main parts: the division into three bodies, their inclusion within two bodies, and the investigation of whether or not gnosis exists in those.

The division into three bodies. The "bodies" of buddhahood can be divided into three.

(1) *The body of ultimate nature* (*svabhāvakāya*) possesses the two purities: the natural purity of the "origin" (*dhātu*), and the purity of the freedom from the adventitious stains of the things that are to be eliminated. As the *Ornament of Clear Realization* teaches:

> Those [twenty-one classes of] qualities without impurity
> of the ultimate-nature body of the Sage that have been acquired
> are in every respect pure, and they possess the characteristic
> of being naturally [pure from the beginning].[531]

(2) *The body of enjoyment* (*sambhogakāya*). The dwelling place of this body is in the divine realm of Akaniṣṭha. Its physical body is adorned with the bodily signs and characteristics. Its speech is the continual preaching of the Mahayana teachings. Its mind has the nature of the four gnoses. Its retinue of disciples is made up of bodhisattvas of the tenth level whom [that Buddha] satisfies. As it is taught:

> Because it possesses the thirty-two signs
> and the eighty characteristics and
> partakes of the Mahayana, it is held
> to be the enjoyment body of the Sage.[532]

(3) *The emanation body* (*nirmānakāya*). Its nature is to have arisen through the predominating condition of the enjoyment body. Its place is wherever the beings to be trained dwell, who are as infinite as the bounds of the sky. Its period is unceasing. Its activities are solely the work of benefitting sentient beings. Moreover, if you divide the emanation body, you

get three types: *born emanations*, dwelling in such divine realms as Tuṣita; the *highest emanations*, which are the numerous manifestations of buddhahood such as Śākyamuni; and *fashioned emanations*, which are numerous and include such things as the vina player manifested [by Śākyamuni] for the sake of Supriya, the king of the gandharvas.

Moreover, as it is taught:

> That body that simultaneously accomplishes
> manifold benefits for living beings
> for as long as existence continues
> is the unceasing emanation body of the Sage.[533]

Some sutras and tantras explain the bodies of buddhahood as being four, and according to them, that which is here taught as the ultimate-nature body is designated as the "Dharma body" (*dharmakāya*). And some maintain the special feature consisting of the indivisibility of those three bodies to be the ultimate-nature body. [376] But since this classification is mainly recognized in the tantras of the mantra tradition, I will not explain it here.

Their inclusion within two bodies. If you subsume those three bodies within a briefer classification, they consist of the two: the Dharma body (*dharmakāya*) and material form body (*rūpakāya*). With reference to those, there also exists the explanation of the two as "the body for the benefit of self" and "the body for the benefit of others." Also, the Dharma body is known as the "ultimately real body," and the form body is known as the "surface-level body."

Whether or not gnosis exists in buddhahood entails three parts.

(1) *Refuting the tradition of others.* Some prove the existence of the gnosis of the Buddha and refute the nonexistence of gnosis by means of many scriptural passages and reasonings, such as by saying that a buddha possesses a gnosis that is included within his own mental continuum because he is the Omniscient One, because he is the body that is the fruition of the two preparatory assemblages, because without gnosis the Buddha would become a nonexistent (*abhāva*) or an inanimate thing, because [an absence of gnosis] would entail the consequence that buddhahood would be the same as the cessation (*nirodha*) of the śrāvaka, and because there would be the consequence that [to maintain the contrary] would be equal to the tīrthika nihilist view.

Also, some prove the nonexistence of gnosis in the Buddha's own mental continuum, saying, for instance, that if such gnosis existed, it would possess illusory appearances and a positing of self, and that to say so would be the same as the Yogācāra adherent's theory and would be no different from the tīrthika eternalist view.[534]

Both these opinions are unacceptable, for if, first, gnosis were to exist as something veridically established in a buddha's own mental continuum, there would occur the faults mentioned by the person who maintains the nonexistence of gnosis, such as that this would be equivalent to the tīrthika eternalist's view, that this would be the possession of self-postulation, and that this would be the view of permanence, for this would be equivalent to positing an existent entity. Second, if the gnosis does not exist in the mental continuum of the Buddha himself but is only something appearing in the experiences of others around him, the Buddha would be without excellent qualities.

Furthermore, let us critically examine whether or not "the Buddha" exists. If he does not exist, the cultivation of the path would be pointless, and if he does exist but has no gnosis, he would be an inanimate thing.

[Objection:] Though gnosis does not exist in the Buddha, the benefitting of others is achieved by him through his past aspirations. [Reply:] If an aspiration has here been realized, then why would the aspiration to become a buddha not also be achieved? There is no reason that the aspiration to become a buddha would not be achieved while the aspiration to achieve benefits for others would be achieved. For if the one is achieved, they are equally achievable, and if the one is not achieved, both are equally unachievable. Also the assertion, "The Buddha does not exist, but the aspiration exists," is difficult to establish through reasoning. [377]

(2) *Our own tradition.* In our own tradition there are two levels of truth: the ultimately real, and the surface level.

The ultimately real. The first of these, the ultimate, is free from all extremes of existence and nonexistence, for it is beyond the range of mind. With that sense in mind, the *King of Meditation Sutra* teaches:

> In the factor of existence of nirvana there exists no factor of existence,
> for it is nonexistent and never will exist [independently].
> Those who possess [dualistic] conceptual thought teach existence and nonexistence.
> By conceptualizing in that way, suffering will not be pacified.[535]

And as Ācārya Ārya [Nāgārjuna] said:

> To say "It exists" is the view of eternalism.
> To say "It does not exist" is the view of annihilationism.[536]

And also, for instance:

> How could there exist the four of existence, nonexistence,
> and the others in this quiescence?[537]

In the *Sūtra Requested by Suvikrāntavikrami*, it is also explained that gnosis is free from both existence and nonexistence.[538]

The surface-level truth. On the surface level, too, if you designate mind or the mental factors as gnosis, it does not exist, for this is merely deluded error. But for someone who knows all objects of knowledge without exception, gnosis exists, for he has gained the body of transformation. That transformation, moreover, is explained by Candragomin in his *Buddha Levels*:

> That which is the "store cognition" (*ālayavijñāna*)
> has become the mirror-gnosis, and
> it shines forth as the nature of the sphere of reality (*dharmadhātu*).
> The transformation of defiled mind (*kliṣṭamanas*)
> is held to be the gnosis of equality.
> The transformation of nonsensory cognition (*manovijñāna*)
> is the gnosis possessing discrimination.
> The transformation of the five sensory cognitions
> is the gnosis that accomplishes all aims.[539]

Therefore the surface level of truth is cyclic existence. The ultimately real is nirvana, and the Buddha's nonsituated nirvana is the body of integration. As Ācārya Ārya [Nāgārjuna] said:

> After you have understood in their separate aspects
> cyclic existence and nirvana,
> where these are completely mixed
> is explained as "the integration."[540]

And as it is also said:

> Dwelling in the absorption of the integration,
> he does not train himself anymore in anything.

This is the yogin of the completion stage.
Here the great vajra-holder stage there then occurs
that omniscience possessing the highest of all qualities.[541]

Therefore Ācārya Ārya [Nāgārjuna], too, on the level of theory held the ultimate to be the understanding of reality as devoid of conceptual elaborations. [378] On the level of meditative cultivation, he maintained the ultimate to be the practice of skillful means that does not conflict with ultimate reality. And on the level of the result, he held the ultimate to be the integration of nonsituated nirvana.

(3) *The elimination of objections.* [Doubt:] The previously expressed faults will occur about the existence of gnosis if you maintain that gnosis [is an existent thing that] appears [to its possessor], and the expressed fault about the nonexistence of gnosis will equally occur if it exists merely in the appearances experienced by others. [Reply:] If you hold gnosis to be something manifested to yourself or manifesting to others, that is the apprehended object and apprehending subject. However, through the transformation of subject-object duality, you will achieve the gnosis that is freed from subject and object and that has hence gained designations such as "mirror-like gnosis." Therefore, as the *Ornament of Mahayana Sutras* teaches:

The mirror gnosis is without "mine."
It always possesses nondifferentiation.[542]

And in *Achieving Pristine Awareness*:

The gnosis of all the tathāgatas understands
all entities—yourself and other living beings—
as the same, and thus it is explained
as being the "gnosis of equality."[543]

Because of the transformation of defiled mind (*kliṣṭamanas*) into the gnosis of equality by nature, you have transcended the conventional terminology of your mind and another's mind. As it is also stated in the *Thorough Exposition of Valid Cognition*:

The investigation of visible form and so on
and of mind, whose defining mark is to apprehend thus,

is something that pertains to those of impure minds.
The realized understanding of the Yogin is impossible to
encompass with the mind.[544]

And as taught in *Establishing the Minds of Others*, the gnosis that results from transformation is impossible to encompass with the mind.[545]

The different shared and special properties of the excellent qualities of buddhahood

These are of two sorts: those that are held in common with others and those that are unique [to the Buddha].[546]

Concerning the first, the *qualities of buddhahood held in common with others*, there exist three kinds: those held in common with [meditators of] the worldly sphere, those held in common with the śrāvakas, and those held in common with a bodhisattva who dwells on one of the levels. *Those held in common with [meditators of] the worldly sphere* are the emancipations, the bases of mastery, the bases of totality (*kṛtsna*), and five of the six supernatural perceptions. *Those held in common with the śrāvakas* are such qualities as the sixth supernatural perception, that which knows the exhaustion of the impurities, the lack of afflictions, knowledge from aspiration, and the four analytical knowledges. *Those held in common with a bodhisattva* who dwells on one of the bodhisattva levels include such qualities as the bodily characteristics and marks, the ten controlling powers, and the doors of dhāraṇī. Those *qualities that are unique to a buddha* include the ten powers, the four modes of fearlessness, the eighteen characteristics unique to a buddha, and the thorough destruction of the propensities toward the afflictions.[547]

Here I will praise those shared and exclusive excellent qualities through versified song so that great merit may be acquired in my own mind and in the minds of others. Moreover, I will state their praises first of all as they appear in the *Ornament of Mahayana Sutras* and then add more praises, supplementing what is slightly incomplete there with verses of my own composition.[548]

The four immeasurables

You're compassionate toward sentient beings;
you wish them to meet [with happiness] and part [from
suffering],

and that they be never separated [from happiness]—
I pay homage to you whose wish is to help and benefit.[549]

The four immeasurables can be subsumed within the two: intended benefits and intended happiness. [379] From among them, the intention [that all living beings have] happiness is threefold: *loving kindness*, which is the desire that living beings come into contact with happiness; *compassion*, which is the desire that they be parted from suffering; and *sympathetic joy*, which is the desire that they never be parted from the above two [desirable states, i.e., the possession of happiness and the freedom from suffering]. The intention [that all living beings] benefit is the constant intent that, through *equanimity*, [they may come to view] both the affliction of attachment to happiness and the affliction of aversion to suffering equally.

The emancipations, the bases of mastery, and the bases of totality

O Sage, you are emancipated from all obscurations.
You have mastery over the whole world.
Your knowledge encompasses all objects of knowledge.
Homage to you, whose mind is liberated![550]

Concerning the eight emancipations,[551] such as the first emancipation, in which [the meditator begins still perceiving himself] as possessing physical form while relating to outer forms, here the person of the mundane sphere is not free from either obscuration. The śrāvaka [arhat] and pratyekabuddha have eliminated the affliction obscuration. The Buddha is freed from that, and also from the knowledge obscuration.

Concerning the bases of mastery,[552] a person of the mundane sphere [who reaches this yogic attainment] has dominion merely over his own sphere of experience (*gocara*). The śrāvaka has dominion over world systems numbering one million. The pratyekabuddha has dominion over world systems numbering one billion. And the Buddha has dominion over all world systems.

Concerning the ten bases of totality,[553] a person of the mundane sphere knows to a small extent. The śrāvaka and pratyekabuddha know on a vaster scale. The Buddha sees, encompassing all objects of knowledge with his gnosis.

And [concerning the words "whose mind is liberated"], the person of the world is not liberated [from the afflictions]. The śrāvaka and pratyekabuddha are not liberated from the propensities toward the afflictions and from the knowledge obscurations. But this one, [the Buddha], is liberated. Since by means of these three [attainments, the Buddha] is completely liberated from all factors opposed to the excellent qualities, he is therefore one whose mind is liberated.

The Conqueror's lack of afflictions

> Homage to you who tame absolutely
> the afflictions of all beings without exception,
> to you who destroy [latent] afflictions
> and are compassionate toward the afflicted!

The Buddha tames the afflictions of all sentient beings and applies the antidote to the afflictions and acts kindly toward those people who possess the afflictions. Those like the śrāvakas, thinking of themselves, eliminate merely the arising of their own afflictions but do not remove those of others.[554]

Knowledge from aspiration

> Homage to you [whose knowledge] is spontaneous,
> is not attached, is unhindered,
> is always in the meditative equipoise,
> and can answer all questions![555] [380]

The knowledge from aspiration that is possessed by the śrāvaka [arhat] understands merely an approximation, being based on effort and meditative practice, though it is unable to remove all doubts. But that of a buddha is spontaneously realized, is not attached, is unhindered in knowing all objects of knowledge, is always in the meditative state, and removes the doubts of all questions [posed by others].

The four analytical knowledges

> Homage to you, who are an excellent teacher
> because your intelligence can never be hindered about
> the "support" and the "supported," the things to be explained,
> and about speech and knowledge, the means of explaining![556]

The "support" refers to the Dharma [as verbal expression], which is the exemplification bearing the defining mark. "That which is supported" refers to its sense, which is the defining mark. These first two are the content to be taught. "Speech" refers to etymological explanation, which is the explanation of the meaning of Sanskrit words. "Knowledge" refers to confident presence of mind. These last two are the means of teaching.

The six superknowledges

> Homage to you who go and understand
> the conduct of others, and who, by your speech,
> give excellent instruction about the coming, going,
> and release of sentient beings![557]

Through the bodily miracle,[558] the superknowledge of (1) magical power, he goes to wherever his disciples are staying. By the mental miracle of knowing others' minds,[559] he (2) understands the minds of others. There are four verbal miracles of instruction:[560] The first knows through (3) the divine ear their separate languages. The second through fourth consist of a division of the object of knowledge. The reason for this division is that he gives instructions according to his knowledge of how a being has come into this life from a previous time through (4) remembering past states of existence. He shows beings how they go from this life into future lives through (5) his divine eye that knows deaths and births. And he explains the escape from cyclic existence into liberation through (6) knowing the exhaustion of the impurities. And therefore he has eliminated ignorance about the three times.

The first five superknowledges are impure and are held in common with people of the mundane sphere. The last—that is, the sixth—is free from impurity and not held in common with the trainee.[561]

The bodily characteristics and marks

> When all embodied beings see you,
> they know you to be a great being.
> Homage to you who inspire
> intense faith merely by being seen![562]

Because he is ornamented with the thirty-two bodily characteristics that indicate a great being (*satpuruṣa*) and the eighty excellent marks that beautify him, he inspires faith in all beings by the mere sight of his activities.

The four purities

Homage to you who
have achieved dominion over assuming [of new existence], its
duration and its abandonment,
over emanations and transformation,
and over meditative absorptions and gnosis![563] [381]

The four purities reveal four powers:

1. *The purity of basis* [that is, of the body] has three powers: the power to assume any form desired, the power to live for whatever lifespan is desired, and the power to abandon that existence whenever desired because he has eliminated from the basis absolutely all dispositions toward the afflictions.
2. *The purity of object* is the power that can project emanations of non-existing things and transform existing things.
3. *The purity of mind* is the constant mastery and control of all meditative absorptions since he is free from all evils and has accumulated all merits.
4. *The purity of discerning wisdom* is mastery and control of a gnosis, free from obscurations, that embraces all knowable things because he has brought ignorance to an end.

The ten powers

Homage to you who vanquish evil ones
who lead sentient beings astray
from correct method, refuge, purity,
and the true liberation of the Mahayana![564]

[The ten powers (*bala*) are:]

1. The power consisting of the knowledge of what is possible and impossible.[565]

2. The power of the knowledge of individual heritages of karma [and their results].[566]
3. The power of the knowledge of various dispositions [of disciples].
4. The power of the knowledge of the various spiritual aspirations [of disciples].
5. The power of the knowledge to which degree, higher or lower, the moral faculties [are present in disciples].
6. The power of the knowledge of the paths leading to rebirths everywhere
7. The power of the knowledge of the system of the moral faculties, powers, limbs of awakening, meditative concentrations, emancipations, absorptions, meditative attainments, the defiled, and the purified.
8. The power of the knowledge that remembers former states of existence.
9. The power of the knowledge of future deaths and rebirths through the divine eye.
10. The power of the knowledge of the extinction of the impurities.

Or, in a summarizing verse:

> Knowledge of the possible, of karma, dispositions,
> aspirations, moral faculties, leading everywhere,
> the system, former dwellings, deaths and rebirths,
> and the extinction of impurities—these are the ten powers of
> the Sage.

Here [in the above quote from the *Ornament of Mahayana Sutras*] the function of these powers is explained from one perspective. That is, they are explained as vanquishing the evil ones who deceive sentient beings by leading them away from four things.

(1) *Leading away from correct method.* This is to teach that higher existences and liberation can be attained by such things as sacrificing living animals and committing suicide in water. [382] This deception is averted by the [first power,] knowledge of what is possible and impossible. Through seeing cause and effect correctly, a buddha knows, for example, that through virtuous deeds you go to higher existences but that through evil deeds this would be impossible.

(2) *Leading away from the correct refuge.* This is to assert such things as that even if you commit evil deeds and do not do virtuous deeds, you will

be protected from lower miserable destinies if you propitiate such deities as Īśvara and Viṣṇu. This deception is vanquished by the [second power,] knowledge of the individual heritages of karma [and their results]. You will become happy through deeds of merit such as generosity, but the causes of happiness will not come about through such deities as Īśvara. For as the *Ornament of Mahayana Sutras* teaches:

> Generosity and the others are bases for perfect awakening.
> Īśvara and the rest are not.[567]

(3) *Leading away from real purity.* Some profess that you can become purified through impure actions such as ritual purification and physical mortification. But that is not a correct path. The teaching of such things as meditative concentrations as being the completely correct and sufficient path is averted by [the seventh power,] knowledge of the meditative concentrations, absorptions, and meditative attainments.

(4) *Leading away from salvation, or escape into liberation.* This is to teach a spiritual path that is inappropriate for the person receiving the teachings. That deception is destroyed by the knowledge of higher and lower degrees of the moral faculties and by the remaining six powers. Those seven powers are the following:

(1) [The fifth power,] knowledge of the higher and lower degrees of the moral faculties, is to know whether the five moral faculties such as faith exist to a weaker, middling, or stronger [degree in a disciple], and afterward to teach religion in consonance with that.

(2) [The fourth power,] various spiritual aspirations, is to know to which degree—stronger, middling, or weaker—the desires and thoughts [aspiring to spiritual paths such as that of the śrāvaka are present in] sentient beings.

(3) [The third power,] various dispositions, is the knowledge of whether beings possess the three spiritual lineages[568] or the dispositions of the eighty-four thousand activities of desires and the other afflictions.

(4) [The sixth power,] the paths leading everywhere, is the knowledge of what initial instructions are best for specific disciples, such as the meditation on repulsiveness as the antidote to desire.

(5) [The eighth power,] memory of previous states of existence, recalls the numerous features of previous births: the different names and original designations of the various classes of sentient beings everywhere and the six modes, which are based on the eight foundations. *The eight foundations* are

knowing "This was his name," "This was his lineage," "This was his clan," "This is what he ate," "This was his happiness and suffering," "This was his lifespan," "This was his period," and "He was able to live this long." *The six modes* are the name he was called, his lineage (such as kṣatriya), his parents, his activities such as eating and drinking, his flourishing and decline, and various features of his life. [383] The word "feature"[569] refers to the six modes, while the word "proof"[570] refers to the eight foundations.

(6) [The ninth power,] the divine eye,[571] is the very complete result of the four meditative concentrations in the god realms, and it is "extremely pure" because it is based on completely perfected and pure meditative concentration. The gods of the desire realm possess [an eye] that conforms to the above in name only, whereas since humans lack even that, it is called "superhuman." The objects of that [divine eye] are two: sentient beings who are dying, and those who are being reborn in the intermediate state. [In the latter, some beings have a vision of] "bad color," which is to pass into darkness, like a black blanket or like entering pitch darkness, and "good color," which is to go into light, something like moonlight or Varanasi white cotton cloth. "Bad" and "good" are because those beings go to lower miserable destinies and happy destinies, respectively.

Having committed the evil acts of body, speech, and mind is to have impure moral discipline together with its motivations.[572] Two kinds of perverse views are denying everything and denying āryas. Those whose erroneous attachment to the cause and effect of wrong acts leads them to accumulate wrong deeds bring upon themselves two types of cause and effect in terms of feeling: a pleasant present life but a miserable future one, and miserable experiences in both lives.[573]

Because [perverse views] are the main cause for the lower miserable destinies, it is taught, "By that cause and condition. . . ." The "destruction of body" is the destruction of the mutual connection between the mental aggregates (*nāma*) and the physical aggregate (*rūpa*). The words "after death" (literally, "beneath death") are used because this is the worst of all deaths.

"Lower miserable destiny" (*apāya*) is so called because, having done evil and frightful things, you have gone to an evil place. "Evil state" (*durgati*) is so called because you will experience there much fierce, long-lasting, and uninterrupted suffering. "Fallen state" (*vinipāta*) is so called because it rests below, it has great and terrifying abysses, and because you utter there great pitiful cries. The term "hell existence" (*naraka*) reveals the nature, body, and reality of the hells. Only hell is mentioned because it is the predominate occasion for depression, so it exemplifies all three of the lower miserable destinies.

The virtuous factors are entirely the opposite of the above. "Pleasant states" (*sugati*) are so called because they are preceded by excellent conduct. "Higher destinies" (*svarga*) are so called because they are the highest enjoyment of pleasures.[574]

(7) [The tenth power,] knowledge of the extinction of the impurities, [384] is the elimination of every latent disposition of all the afflictions. The antidotes are the pure mind and discerning wisdom. These are included within the mind that has reached supremacy and surpassing discerning wisdom, that is, the emancipation of the pure mind and the emancipation of discerning wisdom. Moreover, after you have attained this power in that final existence itself based on previous meditative cultivation of the path, you will exactly know, through the sixth superknowledge, "I have won it." And consequently you will reveal it also to others if they desire. Therefore it is explained, "In this life, having made it manifest through superknowledges, it is expressed to others."

The four modes of fearlessness

> Homage to you who teach,
> for the benefit of self and others,
> gnosis, elimination, salvation, its obstacles,
> and who are not overwhelmed by the heterodox tīrthikas![575]

In teaching the four instructions of (1) [gnosis], (2) elimination [of the afflictions], (3) salvation, and (4) that which obstructs it—[the first two] pertaining to his own benefit and [the last two] for the benefit of others—[the Buddha], lacking fear, fright, and timidity amid proud people of the world, overawes those in the assembly: proud individuals such as gods who are puffed up about their place of birth, demons (*māra*) who are conceited about their magical powers, Brahma who is proud of his immeasurable attainments, ascetics who are proud of their excellent qualities, and brahmans who are proud of their lineage.

Religiously principled disputation is to refute truthfully, amid an assembly, another person who possesses faults, with the words: "He possesses such and such faults." But the Buddha does not possess those faults. To refute through falsehood is unprincipled disputation. For even though someone disputes in such a way, that will not be a fault for a noble person because such a procedure is the disputant's own fault but not the fault of the other.[576]

The three absences of guardedness

> Homage to you who,
> without the need for guardedness and because of your
> unforgetfulness,
> speak in a relaxed way in an assembly,
> and because you have eliminated the twin afflictions, attract
> a circle of followers![577]

The Buddha lacks any furtive thoughts, such as "Some may censure me for this," because he is perfectly pure in his bodily, verbal, and mental conduct. Therefore he is unreserved in the midst of assemblies, and he teaches the doctrine in a way that overawes everyone.

[The verse also refers to] three applications of mindfulness. When he gives religious instructions to his disciples, he is free from attachment and aversion toward those of his followers who correctly accomplish it, accomplish it incorrectly, or accomplish it both both ways. Thus he attracts disciples in an excellent way.

The thorough destruction of the propensities toward the afflictions [385]

> Homage to you, Omniscient One, who are truly meaningful
> because you do not possess anything
> but omniscient conduct at all times and
> in [all activities, such as] going and dwelling![578]

Even though for the arhat the afflictions have been extinguished, in such activities as his going, dwelling, and speaking, it is still possible for him to engage in nonomniscient conduct, such as [having accidents through] wrongly handling a mad elephant, a collision with a chariot, and so forth, because he has not eliminated the latent propensities toward the afflictions. But since the Buddha does not possess those latent propensities, his omniscience is truly what it claims to be.

The fact of his unforgetfulness

> In your activities for all beings in the world
> you are never untimely,
> and therefore your deeds are always meaningful.
> Homage to you who are not forgetful![579]

It is possible that śrāvaka [arhats] and pratyekabuddhas may abandon the welfare of sentient beings if they become forgetful. But the Buddha is always timely and never forgetful, when revealing the skillful means for accomplishing that welfare of others, of what place, for what sentient beings, at what time, for what purpose, and in what manner an action is to be done. Therefore his deeds are always fruitful.

Great compassion

> At six times during day and night,
> you gaze over the whole world of living beings.
> Homage to you who possess great compassion
> and are of beneficial intent![580]

The "at six times" mentioned here is merely an illustration. The Buddha at all times has thoughts of beneficial intent, such as "Who among sentient beings are experiencing setbacks?" "Who are flourishing?" and "Who are to be led out from the lower miserable destinies?"

The eighteen characteristics unique to the Buddha

> Homage to you who are superior
> to the śrāvakas and pratyekabuddhas
> by virtue of your conduct, realization,
> gnosis, and activities![581]

The six special characteristics included within "conduct."[582] (1) Physically he is without mistake. For arhats there may occur such things as accidentally colliding with chariots or elephants, falling into a pit of thorny brambles, stepping on a snake, or entering into an occasion for being seduced by a woman. But the Buddha is free from such things.

(2) His speech is free from nonsensical utterances. Arhats may do such things as utter gibberish in a desolate place or inappropriately emit horse laughs. But the Buddha does not possess such verbal behaviors.

(3) His mind never possesses nonmeditative states. The Buddha does not possess behavior such as that of the arhat who engages in nonmeditative activities after arising from meditative states. [386] This is because the Buddha's meditative state and postmeditative activities are integrated.

(4) He never has lapses of memory. While it is possible for an arhat to have memory lapses, the Buddha is not forgetful in his physical acts and speech.

(5) He does not perceive cyclic existence and nirvana as different. The arhat takes cyclic existence to be solely misery and takes nirvana to be bliss. But the Buddha does not have such perceptions, for he has realized that cyclic existence and nirvana are equivalent.

(6) He does not pass over things without individual consideration. It is possible for arhats to abandon the welfare of sentient beings because of not considering each matter, but the Buddha does not possess such conduct, for he passes over a thing only after considering it.

The six special characteristics included within "realization." Because they have not eliminated the knowledge obscurations, it is possible for arhats to experience reverses in the six realizations, beginning with resolve. But for the Buddha this is impossible because his (7) resolve, (8) endeavor, (9) mindfulness, (10) meditative absorption, (11) discerning wisdom, and (12) emancipation do not fail.

The three special characteristics included within "gnosis." The arhat is hindered and impeded in his knowledge of the three times, but the Buddha has acquired gnosis that is without either [hindrance or impediment concerning (13) past, (14) present, or (15) future].

The three special characteristics included within "activities." These are the activities of (16) body, (17) speech, and (18) mind. While it is possible for the activities of the śrāvaka [arhat] on occasion to become neutral deeds even though he applies himself to doing the virtuous, for the Buddha, all activities are preceded by gnosis because their motivating factor is gnosis, and they follow gnosis because they are practiced simultaneously with gnosis.

Therefore, because he is endowed with these eighteen characteristics unique to him, the Buddha becomes the superior even of [other] āryas.

His being omniscient in every respect

Homage to you who
through the three bodies
have acquired the great awakening in every respect
and who resolve the doubts of all sentient beings![583]

The Dharma body (*dharmakāya*) is by nature pure and also free from what is to be removed, the adventitious stains of the afflictions. The enjoyment body (*sambhogakāya*) teaches continually the Mahayana in the Akaniṣṭha pure realm to bodhisattvas on the tenth level. And the emanation body (*nirmāṇakāya*) continually achieves the benefitting of sentient beings through "born" emanations, "highest" emanations, and artificial emanations. Thus the Buddha resolves doubts. By the profundity of the Dharma body and the vastness of the two form bodies, the Buddha understands knowable things exactly as they are and in their full variety and extent. [387] And because the purposes of self and others are achieved, he resolves the doubts of all sentient beings.

The six perfections

Homage to you who are without grasping,
without moral fault, undisturbed,
not [lazily] remaining, unagitated, and
without discursive elaborations about all factors of existence![584]

The Buddha's generosity is without grasping for wealth. His moral discipline has no fault of the moral offences. His patience lacks the disturbance of anger. His diligence is without any dwelling in laziness. His meditative concentration is not agitated by distraction. And his discerning wisdom lacks discursive elaborations about all factors of existence.[585]

His accomplishment of the two purposes

Through your acquisition of all obtainable excellent qualities,
you have accomplished the activities
for benefitting yourself and others.
Homage to you who see all knowable things without exception!

By the Buddha's acquisition of all shared and unique excellent qualities that are to be obtained, he has accomplished absolutely all purposes of self and others and sees all knowable things without exception.

[The thirty-seven factors conducive to awakening]

> Homage to you who have accomplished well
> the ways of mindfulness, the diligences, meditative
> absorptions,
> wonderful moral faculties, powers,
> the limbs of awakening, and the path of the ārya!

[The Buddha is to be praised because he possesses the thirty-seven factors conducive to awakening, which are:][586]

- The four foundations of mindfulness: the knowledge of the body, [feelings, mind, and phenomena] as being like space
- The four perfect endeavors: diligence for eliminating the host of moral faults, diligence to make sure they do not arise again, endeavor to produce the host of excellent qualities that have not arisen, and endeavor to increase those that have arisen
- The four bases of magical powers: the vast meditative absorptions of aspiration, diligence, intention, and analysis
- The five moral faculties, including faith and the others
- The five moral powers, perfectly complete
- The seven limbs of awakening, such as the penetration of Dharma
- The eight branches of the ārya path, such as right view

The minimal accomplishment of these is possessed also by the śrāvaka [arhat] and the [pratyekabuddha], yet only the Buddha possesses its excellent accomplishment.

The nine absorptions

> Homage to you who have brought to perfect completion
> the power that crushes the hard, fallow soil of mind
> through the nine absorptions that have eliminated
> the discursive thinking that belongs to the three cosmic realms! [388]

The nine absorptions are the elimination of the nine relatively coarser and subtler types of conceptual thinking that are included within the three cosmic realms. The elimination of the conceptual thinking of the realm of desire is the first meditative concentration, and likewise it is the absorptions of the second, third, and fourth concentrations. The elimination of the conceptual thinking of the form realm consists of the four meditative attainments: the attainment of infinite space, and likewise that of infinite consciousness, nothingness, and neither existence nor nonexistence. The elimination of all conceptual thought is the meditative attainment of cessation, thus bringing the total number of absorptions to nine. If you engage in meditating on these successively, it is called "the majestic lion." If you engage in them out of their normal sequence, it is called "entering the absorptions by skipping over." With respect to this skipping-over procedure, the *Treasury of Higher Knowledge* teaches the śrāvaka tradition as follows:

> Interspersing the eight levels [of absorptions] in two ways,
> consecutively
> and by jumping over one [level at a time], to advance
> to a third state of a different class
> is to enter the absorptions by skipping over.[587]

But the Mahayana tradition is as taught in the *Ornament of Clear Realization*:

> Having advanced up and returned down in two ways
> through the nine absorptions including cessation,
> to take as an endpoint a nonconcentrated conceptual thought
> of the desire realm and to pass over one,
> two, three, four, five, six, seven, eight levels up to cessation
> differently is to engage in the absorptions through skipping
> over.[588]

The difference between these two does not amount to a contradiction because they are traditions of the śrāvaka and Mahayana, respectively.[589]

Regarding these meditative attainments, the śrāvakas engage in these absorptions of cessation for the sake of making their minds supple and serviceable, and to put an end to their despair at the various appearances [such as feeling and so on of ordinary existence], whereas the bodhisattva practices them for the sake of gaining mastery over meditative absorptions, and the

Buddha spontaneously achieves them precisely through his mastery of meditative absorptions. Moreover, the śrāvaka's engaging in those is dependent on effort. The bodhisattva attains them through small effort. For the Buddha, they are spontaneously achieved without effort, for he has sovereign mastery that crushes [the afflictions:] the "hard, fallow soil" of mind.

The three doors of liberation

> Homage to you who have acquired the highest liberation
> because you are completely devoid of dichotomizing,
> to you who have no wish for appropriating [the defiled
> aggregates],
> to you for whom all phenomenal marks are pacified!

Because he possesses neither apprehended object nor apprehending subject, the Buddha has attained the door of liberation, "emptiness." [389] Because he is free from attachment toward the five impure appropriating aggregates, he has attained "the wishless." And since for him all objectivized phenomenal marks are pacified, he has attained "the markless." While these are also possessed by the śrāvaka [arhat] and pratyekabuddha, nevertheless those two have not eliminated the obscurations of the latent propensities. But since the Buddha has eliminated those, he is supreme.

The destruction of the four māras

> Homage to you who have well subdued
> the harmful hosts of māras
> through having trained your mind
> for many eons in gnosis and compassion!

The root of consummate gnosis is discerning wisdom. And by the realization through that discerning wisdom that the cause of the afflictions—the postulating of a self—is without own-nature, there ensues the spontaneous liberation of its result, the afflictions. And as a consequence the māra of the afflictions is destroyed. The māra of the aggregates is destroyed because on the basis of the above, the aggregates are realized as not established. Since there is no joining [that is, no entering of consciousness into a womb] for one whose aggregates are realized as not established, the māra of death is vanquished.

And the māra of the lesser deities (*devaputra*) is destroyed by the pacification of all harms through the Buddha's viewing all sentient beings as though they were his only son by virtue of the power of his loving kindness, which is the root of his great compassion. Regarding all this, the śrāvakas teach that the Buddha subdued the māra of the afflictions and of the lesser deities in Bodhgaya. At Vaiśālī he subdued the māra of death. And at Kuśīnagarī he subdued the māra of the aggregates. But those of the Mahayana teach:

> First you destroyed the flower victory-banner
> of the māra of the deities.
> Then you destroyed the high mountain of pride
> of the māra of the afflictions.
>
> You conquered the lord of the desire realm
> even without attaining awakening,
> and on the immediate path [of the vajra-like absorption],
> you conquered the lord of the three cosmic realms.[590]

Accordingly, they maintain that the Buddha subdued the māras prior to his attainment of buddhahood.

The ten controlling powers

> Homage to you who accomplish all affairs the world
> through the ten controlling powers
> over inner, outer, both [inner and outer],
> resolution, knowledge, and instruction!

Controlling power over life. This is the ability to live for whatever lifespan is desired, and it is the outcome of having prolonged the lives of sentient beings through generous gifts of wealth.

Controlling power over mind is the serviceability of a buddha's mind for entering into any meditative absorption exactly according to his wishes. It is the outcome of having satisfied the minds of others through generosity.

Controlling power over material goods is receiving material goods exactly according to his wishes, and it is the outcome of having satisfied others with material goods. The above three powers are the results of generosity.

Controlling power over deeds is the ability to achieve deeds of body, speech, and mind just as he wishes. [390] It is the result of having impelled others to faultless deeds of body, speech, and mind by means of his own moral discipline.

Controlling power over rebirth is the ability to achieve whatever forms of existence, body, and so forth that he desires in a new rebirth. His realization of the aspirations that are endowed with moral discipline is their causal condition.

Controlling power over whatever he wishes is such things as transforming even earth into gold. It results from acting in accord with the wishes of sentient beings by means of his patience.

Controlling power over aspirations is the accomplishment of whatever goal he aspires to. It is the result of having accomplished the benefit of sentient beings in exact agreement with their wishes through his diligence.

Controlling power over magical powers is the result of having engaged in meditative absorptions exactly in accord with enlightened intentions through meditative concentration.

Controlling power over gnosis is the result of having applied himself to whatever sentient beings desire through discerning wisdom.

Controlling power over Dharma teachings is the teaching of instructions such as the sutras just as sentient beings desire. It is acquired by the teaching of all Dharma instructions through the perfection of wisdom. These last two controlling powers are the results of discerning wisdom.

Material goods and rebirth are the "outer." Mind is the "inner." Life, deeds, likes, and magical powers are included within "both inner and outer." Aspiration, gnosis, and Dharma teachings are "resolution," "knowledge," and "instruction," respectively. To summarize in a verse:

> Life, mind, and material goods,
> deeds, rebirths, and wishes,
> aspirations, magical powers, gnosis, and Dharma teaching:
> these are the ten controlling powers of the Buddha.

Meditative absorptions

> Homage to you who have attained mastery
> over the meditative absorptions that accomplish and eliminate
> and that are wonderful, spontaneously realized,
> and unhindered about all objects of knowledge!

The meditative absorptions that are superior over others, not dependent on effort, and unimpeded in their activities [include both the "accomplishing" and "eliminating" absorptions]. Absorptions such as *valiant progress* (*śūraṅga*), *jewel seal* (*ratnamudrā*), and *majestic lion* (*siṃha vijṛmbhita*) accomplish something desired, whereas absorptions such as the *vajra-like* and *elimination of all afflictions* eliminate the things that are to be eliminated. You should understand them in more detail as they are explained in the Mother of the Conquerors [i.e., the Perfection of Wisdom sutras].

The doors of dhāraṇī

> Homage to you who open up the treasure deposits
> of Dharma teachings through your dhāraṇīs
> that are the door [granting unimpeded] retention and teaching
> and that with few syllables easily reveal the teachings! [391]

Through the doors of dhāraṇī, such as the inexhaustible Jewel Casket,[591] he opens the door of all Dharmas. Moreover, since he is expert in summarizing inconceivably many syllables into forty-two syllables, and in summarizing those forty-two into one syllable, he is unimpeded in retaining what others say and in his own imparting of teachings. This also is as taught in the Mother [the Perfection of Wisdom sutras] as becoming, through a single syllable, learned in the purified nature and so forth.

Consummate elimination of the afflictions and obscurations

> Homage to you who have completely eliminated the stains
> that are difficult to remove—desire and the other [afflictions]—
> and the basis of conceptual constructions of the spheres of an action,
> together with the propensities toward them, and who are freed from all obscurations!

He is liberated from all the obscurations because he has eliminated both the affliction obscurations, which are desire, anger, and so forth, included within the category of the impurities (*āsrava*), and the knowledge obscuration, which is the conceptual postulation of "self," "place," "wealth," and so forth, included within the category of the "three spheres" [of an action] (*trimaṇḍala*)—together with all propensities toward those obscurations.

Gnosis

> Homage to you who have attained complete buddhahood
> with respect to the gnoses that relate to self and others
> by means of the support and the supported, luminous,
> stainless,
> a treasure lode of excellent qualities, and activities!

The *mirror-like gnosis* is the illumination of the complete mandala of knowable things, like a reflection appearing clearly in a mirror. The *gnosis of equality* is the freedom from the impurities of the postulation of "I" and "mine." The *gnosis of discrimination* is the treasure lode of all excellent qualities such as the powers and the ways of fearlessness. The *gnosis of the accomplishment of works* is the spontaneous realization of all beneficial activities for yourself and others.

Moreover, mirror-like gnosis is the support, while the latter three gnoses are the supported. The former three pertain predominately to the benefits of the Buddha himself, while the latter one[592] relates predominately to the benefitting of others.

Excellent qualities of speech

> Homage to you who excellently sound forth
> to the whole world of men and gods your speech,
> which is a fearless lion's roar
> possessing sixty aspects!

The sixty aspects of [a buddha's] speech are those such as softness, sweetness, and audibility over long distances. For a more detailed description, they are as explained in the *Inconceivable Secret Sutra*.[593]

Transformation [392]

> You have changed that which is the defiled stream
> of ordinary existence through realizing the truth of the path.

> Homage to you who know as gnosis
> the [impurities] that operate in all living beings!

The body of gnosis that possesses no impurities is achieved from the transformation of the aggregates, elements, and sensory bases that possess impurities. The occurrence of the inconceivably great gnosis that is the transformation of all the karma and afflictions of living beings is as taught in the *Ornament of Mahayana Sutras* and the *Compendium of the Mahayana*.

The distinction of his endowments

> Homage to you who are consummately endowed
> through your having attained control of such endowments as
> those of the worldly, the śrāvakas, the rhinoceroses, and the sons
> and the supreme endowments of the Great Teacher!

All the endowments of such gods of the mundane sphere as Śakra and Brahma are eclipsed by those of the śrāvaka—that is, the arhat. That one is eclipsed by the rhinoceros—that is, the pratyekabuddha. That one is eclipsed by the [Conqueror's] son—that is, the bodhisattva. And that one is eclipsed by the Great Teacher, that is, the Buddha. As the *Ornament of Mahayana Sutras* teaches:

> The endowments of the person of the mundane sphere
> are eclipsed by those of the śrāvakas.
> Those of the śrāvakas
> are eclipsed by those of the pratyekabuddha.
>
> Those cannot measure up to even
> a fraction of those of the bodhisattva.
> And those cannot measure up to even
> a fraction of the endowments of the perfect Buddha.[594]

For example, when Ārya Upagupta was sitting engaged in meditative concentration, Māra the evil one placed over his head a garland of flowers in order to mock him. At that the ārya placed around the evil one's neck the putrid, worm-infested corpse of a dog.

Also, for example, when infinitely many world systems were being successively destroyed by fire, Mañjuśrī said: "O Śāriputra, shall we go there by means of your magical powers or shall we go by means of mine?"

Śāriputra thought, If we go by means of my magic powers, it will take a long time. Let's see how strong Mañjuśrī's magical powers are. "Let's go by means of yours."

"In that case, close your eyes for just a bit." When Śāriputra was just beginning to close his eyes, [Mañjuśrī said:] "Now open them!"

When Śāriputra opened them, they had already arrived. Śāriputra said, "Your magical power is inconceivable!"

"Just so," Mañjuśrī said. "My liberated conduct is not within the domain of those of inferior aspiration, including śrāvakas such as yourself."

His status as the supreme refuge [393]

> Homage to you who are the refuge
> of all living beings in the world
> because of your acquisition of the shared and preeminent
> qualities
> that are powerful and extremely wondrous!

From among those [qualities of the Buddha explained above,] the infinite states, emancipations, bases of mastery, bases of totality, and five of the superknowledges are qualities shared with some beings of the mundane sphere. His superknowledge of the extinction of impurities, his absence of afflictions, knowledge from aspiration, analytical knowledges, factors conducive to awakening, nine absorptions, three doors of liberation, and so forth are shared with the śrāvaka [arhat]. The remaining magical powers and some meditative absorptions and transformations are shared with bodhisattvas of the seven impure levels. Some qualities, such as the transformation of defiled mind and the physical characteristics are shared with the bodhisattva of the eighth level. The door of dhāraṇī and the great analytical knowledges are shared with the ninth level. Some attainments, such as certain meditative absorptions and the ten powers, are held in common with the tenth level. Since the śrāvakas do not maintain the ten levels of the bodhisattva, these qualities are called "held in common with the sons."

The others, such as the eighteen unique qualities of the Buddha, the four ways of fearlessness, and the three types of unguardedness, are specific qualities of the Buddha alone. Because he has acquired such excellent qualities, he is the supreme refuge of the entire animate world, including the gods.

Dedicating the merit of the praises

Having thus completed the section consisting of praises, I dedicate the merit thereby achieved:

> By illuminating the precious jewel-doctrine of the Buddha
> whose possessions have thus been praised,
> may all living beings perfectly see
> the ultimate reality of knowable things![595]

The Great Teacher who has the "possessions" of such excellent qualities is the Lord Buddha alone. And his doctrine is like a treasure cache of jewels since it grants all that you need or want. By this merit resulting from having opened up and illuminated that treasure, may all living beings clearly see all knowable things exactly as they are and in their full variety and extent! [394]

The Conclusion of the Treatise

With the idea of benefitting living beings,
I have illuminated the Sage's intent exactly as it is
according to the teachings of Maitreya, the son of the Conqueror,
who correctly perceives the sense of the profound and vast sutras.

Clearly establishing as noncontradictory through reason
the vast conduct of the "extremely vast" sutras
and the ultimate reality of the theory of the Perfection of Wisdom [sutras],
I have expounded this treatise of mine according to the teaching of my master.

Nowadays the doctrine of the Śākya Sage has become weak,
like a fire whose fuel is exhausted,
so those intelligent people who desire to realize buddhahood
should ponder well and uphold it according to the teachings of the Sage.

The ultimate reality of phenomena is completely hidden
and ordinary persons' engagement[596] with it erroneous.
So whatever excellence of this work is due to the grace of my masters;
what faults there may be are solely of my own mind.

The Buddha, the lamp of the world, has vanished,
and most learned people have already passed away.
So unintelligent, uneducated people propounding spurious opinions
are nowadays mixing up the Sugata's doctrine here in Tibet.

If you teach this Dharma wrongly, it would be a great moral fault.
If you teach it well, most people become angry.

Though teaching Dharma in the degenerate age is indeed difficult,
I have composed this with the thought of benefitting living beings.

Having mentally gathered together all the merit
of this [composition] and all other roots of virtue,
may I attain the station of omniscient king,
so that I may achieve the welfare of sentient beings reaching to
the limits of the sky!

The stages for entering into the path of the bodhisattva called *Clarifying the Sage's Intent* was composed by the illustrious Sakya Paṇḍita, an upholder of the Buddhist scriptures.

Here
it is
completed.

* * *

Since I have taught this assembly discourse to all in Ü, Tsang, and Kham provinces, all my disciples have received its textual transmission. Therefore may you refer to this text and teach it! And may you practice according to it!

Appendix 1.
Table of Tibetan Transliteration

Phonetic spelling	Wylie transliteration
Akhu Chin Sherap Gyatso	A khu chin Shes rab rgya mtsho
Akya Yongzin Yangchen Gawai Lodrö	A kya Yongs 'dzin Dbyangs can dga' ba'i blo gros
Ami Thargyal	A mi thar rgyal
Batsaludor	Rba tsa klu rdor
Bodong É	Bo dong e
Bodong Paṇchen Choklé Namgyal	Bo dong Paṇ chen Phyogs las rnam rgyal
Bonpo	Bon po
Chakhar	Phya mkhar
Chakri Gongkhawa	Lcags ri Gong kha pa
Changtön	Lcang ston
Chapa Chökyi Sengé	Phywa pa Chos kyi seng ge
Chegom Sherap Dorjé	Lce sgom Shes rab rdo rje
Chengawa Tsultrim Bar	Spyan snga ba Tshul khrims 'bar
Chim Jampaiyang	Mchims 'Jam pa'i dbyangs
Chim Namkha Drak	Mchims Nam mkha' grags
Cho Mama	Gco Rma rma
Chökyap Sangpo	Chos skyab bzang po
Chö (lineage)	Gcod
Dakla Gampo (monastery)	Dwags la sgam po
Dakpo Kagyü	Dwags po bka' brgyud
Dakpo Lhajé (= Gampopa)	Dwags po lha rje
Dakpo Rinpoché (= Gampopa)	Dwags po rin po che
Darma Kyap	Dar ma skyabs
Darma Rinchen	Dar ma rin chen
Dergé	Sde dge

Dingboché	Lding po che
Dodé Pal (=Shang Dodé Pal)	Mdo sde dpal
Dokham	Mdo khams
Döl	Dol
Dölpa Marshurwa (=Dölpa Sherap Gyatso)	Dol pa Dmar zhur ba
Dölpa Rinpoché (=Dölpa Sherap Gyatso)	Dol pa rin po che
Dölpa Sherap Gyatso	Dol pa Shes rab rgya mtsho
Domé	Mdo smad
Döndrup Gyaltsen	Don grub rgyal mtshan
Dotön Sherap Drak of Narthang	Snar thang pa Rdo ston Shes rab grags
Drakgyap	Brag rgyab
Drak	Sbrags
Drakarwa	Brag dkar ba
Drakpa Gyaltsen	Grags pa rgyal mtshan
Drapa	Grab pa
Drapa Phodrang Dingpa	Grab pa Pho brang sdings pa
Drepung Losal Ling	'Bras spungs blo gsal gling
Drigang	'Bri sgang
Drigung	'Bri gung
Drigung Chöjé Jikten Gönpo Rinchen Pal	'Bri gung chos rje 'Jig rten mgon po Rin chen dpal
Drinpa Sumpa	Mgrin pa gsum pa
Dro	'Bro
Drokmi Lotsāwa	'Brog mi lo tsā ba
Drolungpa Lodrö Jungné	Gro lung pa Blo gros 'byung gnas
Dromchu	Grom chu
Dromtön Gyalwai Jungné	'Brom ston Rgyal ba'i 'byung gnas
Dromtönpa	'Brom ston pa
Drotön Dutsi Drak	Gro ston Bdud rtsi grags
Drukpa Kagyü	'Brug pa bka' brgyud
Dza Paltrul	Rdza Dpal sprul
Dzokchen Nyingthik	Rdzogs chen nying thig
Dungkar Losang Trinlé	Dung dkar Blo bzang 'phrin las
Entsa Trawo	Dben tsha khra bo
Gampopa Sönam Rinchen	Sgam po pa Bsod nams rin chen

Gang Gyamo	Gangs rgya mo
Ganggya	Gangs rgya
Geluk	Dge lugs
Geshé Dölpa (= Dölpa Sherap Gyatso)	Dge bshes Dol pa
Geshé Drakgyal	Dge bshes Grags rgyal
Geshé Tönpa (= Dromtönpa)	Dge bshes Ston pa
Geshé Yagepa	Dge bshes Ya gad pa
Gö	'Gos
Gö Lotsāwa Shönu Pal	'Gos lo tsā ba Gzhon nu dpal
Gomchö = Gompa Chökyi Sherap	Sgom pa Chos kyi shes rab
Gomön = Gompa Gyamön	Sgom pa Rgya mon
Gompa Rinchen Lama	Sgom pa Rin chen bla ma
Gompa Sherap Rinchen	Sgom pa Shes rab rin chen
Gorampa Sönam Sengé	Go rams pa Bsod nams seng ge
Gönpawa	Dgon pa ba
Gugé	Gu ge
Gya Yöndak	Rgya yon bdag
Gyajin Mikdzé	Brgya byin mig bzad
Gyal	Rgyal
Gyalsé Thokmé Sangpo	Rgyal sras Thogs med bzang po
Gyangro	Rgyang ro
Gyaphu	Rgya phu
Gyegom Shönu Drak	Dgyer sgom Gzhon nu grags
Gyiltön (= Tsangpa Gyiltön)	Gyil ston
Ja Chekhawa (Yeshé Dorjé)	Bya 'Chad kha ba (Ye shes rdo rje)
Ja Duldzinpa	Bya 'Dul ba 'dzin pa
Jamgön Kongtrul Lodrö Tayé	'Jam mgon kong sprul Blo gros mtha' yas
Jang	Byang
Jangchup	Byang chub
Jangchup Ö	Byang chub 'od
Jayulpa (Jayulwa) Shönu Ö	Bya yul pa (ba) Gzhon nu 'od
Jé Drigungpa	Rje 'Bri gung pa
Jé Phakmodrupa	Rje Phag mo gru pa
Jé Shardong Rinpoché	Rje Shar gdong rin po che
Jetsun Drakpa Gyaltsen	Rje btsun Grags pa rgyal mtshan
Jetsun Milarepa (= Mila)	Rje btsun Mi la ras pa
Jolek	Jo legs

Jotsun Yönten Rinchen	Jo btsun Yon tan Rin chen
Kadampa	Bka' gdams pa
Kagyü	Bka' brgyud
Kamapa Sherap Ö	Ka ma pa Shes rab 'od
Karma Trinlepa	Karma 'phrin las pa
Khache Paṇchen	Kha che paṇ chen
Kham	Khams
Khartok	Mkhar thog
Khedrup	Mkhas grub
Khenchen Chökyap Sangpo	Mkhan chen Chos skyabs bzang po
Khenchen Kashipa Drakpa Shönu	Mkhan chen Bka' bzhi pa Grags pa gzhon nu
Khenchen Namkha Gyaltsen	Mkhan chen Nam mkha' rgyal mtshan
Khenchen Sönam Drakpa	Mkhan chen Bsod nams grags pa
Khenchen Sulphuwa Könchok Palsangpo	Mkhan chen Zul phu ba Dkon mchog dpal bzang po
Khenchen Thrangu Rinpoché	Mkhan chen Khra 'gu rin po che
Khenpo Appey	Mkhan po A pad
Khenpo Tsultrim Gyamtso Rinpoché	Mkhan po Tshul khrims rgya mtsho rin po che
Khetsun Sangpo	Mkhas btsun bzang po
Khön Könchok Gyalpo	'Khon Dkon mchog rgyal po
Khyung Rinchen Drak	Khyung Rin chen grags
Könchok Lhundrup	Dkon mchog lhun grub
Könchok Tenpé Drönmé	Dkon mchog bstan pa'i sgron me
Könchok Tsultrim	Dkon mchog tshul khrims
Kyapjé Kalu Rinpoché	Skyabs rje Ka lu rin po che
Kyichu	Skyid chu
Kyirong	Skyid rong
Laksorwa	Lag sor ba
Lama Serlingpa	Bla ma Gser gling pa
Lamdré	lam 'bras
lamrim	lam rim
Lari Tönpa Sangyé Bar	Sla ri ston pa Sangs rgyas 'bar
Lekpai Sherap (= Ngok Lekpai Sherap)	Legs pa'i shes rab
Lha Chenpo	Lha chen po
Lha Drigangpa	Lha 'Bri sgang pa

Lha Drogön	Lha 'Gro mgon
Lha Drowai Gönpo	Lha 'Gro ba'i mgon po
Lha Trangpowa	Lha 'Phrang po ba
Lhodrak Drupchen Namkha Gyaltsen	Lho brag grub chen Nam mkha' rgyal mtshan
Ligom Shönu Drak	Li sgom Gzhon nu grags
Loteng	Lo steng
Lotsul Darma	Lo tshul Dar ma
Lochen Jangchup Tsemo	Lo chen Byang chub rtse mo
lojong	blo sbyong
Lopa Sangyé Gompa	Lo pa Sangs rgyas sgom pa
Lopön Gawa Sangpo	Slob dpon Dga' ba bzang po
Losang Shedrup Gyatso	Blo bzang bshad sgrub rgya mtsho
Lotsāwa Chenpo (=Ngok Loden Sherap)	Lo tsā ba chen po
Lowo Khenchen Sönam Lhundrup	Glo bo mkhan chen Bsod nams lhun grub
Ma Gewai Lodrö	Rma Dge ba'i blo gros
Malgyo Lotsāwa	Mal gyo lo tsā ba
Mangyul Gungthang	Mang yul gung thang
Marpa Lotsāwa	Mar pa lo tsā ba
Maryul Loden	Mar yul Blo ldan
Milarepa	Mi la ras pa
Mönlam Drakpa	Smon lam grags pa
Möndrapa Tsultrim Tashi	Mon grab pa Tshul khrims bkra shis
Müchen Sempa Chenpo Könchok Gyaltsen	Mus chen Sems dpa' chen po Dkon mchog rgyal mtshan
Muken	Mu khen
Naktso Lotsāwa Tsultrim Gyalwa	Nag tsho lo tsā ba Tshul khrims rgyal ba
Naljorpa Amé Jangchup Rinchen	Rnal 'byor pa A mes Byang chub rin chen
Naljorpa Chenpo	Rnal 'byor pa chen po
Namkha Gyalpo	Nam mkha' rgyal po
Namkhaupa	Nam kha'u pa
Nampa	Rnam pa
Namparwa	Rnam par ba
Namseng	Nam seng

Narthang	Snar thang
Neusurpa	Sne'u zur ba
Ngawang Chödrak	Ngag dbang chos grags
Ngari	Mnga' ris
Ngari Gezé Jangchup	Mnga' ris Dge mdzes byang chub
Ngok Lekpai Sherap	Rngog Legs pa'i shes rab
Ngok Loden Sherap	Rngog Blo ldan shes rab
Ngok Lotsāwa (= Ngok Loden Sherap)	Rngog Blo tsā ba chen po
Ngok Sherap Ö	Rngog Shes rab 'od
Ngokpa	Rngog pa
Ngorpa	Ngor pa
Ngulchu Thokmé Sanpo	Dngul chu Thogs med bzang po
Nyang	Myang
Nyawön	Nya dbon
Nyenpo	Nyan po
Nyethang	Snye thang
Nyingma	Rnying ma
Nyukrumpa	Snyug rum pa
Ön	'On
Palpung	Dpal spungs
Paṇchen Drakpa Gyaltsen	Paṇ chen Grags pa rgyal mtshan
Pang	Dpang
Pang Lotsāwa Lodrö Tenpa	Dpang lo tsā ba Blo gros brtan pa
Phakmodrupa Dorjé Gyalpo	Phag mo gru pa Rdo rje rgyal po
Phenpo	'Phan po
Phenyul	'Phan yul
Phodrang Dingpa	Pho brang sdings pa
Phuchungwa	Phu chung ba
Phuchungwa Shönu Gyaltsen	Phu chung ba Gzhon nu rgyal mtshan
Pö	Bod
Potowa Rinchen Sal	Po to ba Rin chen gsal
Purang	Pu hrangs (place name)
Radreng (also known as Reting)	Rwa sgreng (monastery)
Rampa Lhading	Ram pa lha lding
Rendawa Shönu Lodrö	Red mda'ba Gzhon nu blo gros
Rimo	Ri mo

Rinchen Drak (= Khyung Rinchen Drak)	Rin chen grags
Rinchen Gangpa	Rin chen sgang pa
Rinchen Lama	Rin chen bla ma
Rinchen Sangpo (Ratnabhadra)	Rin chen bzang po
Rok Marshurwa	Rog Dmar zhur ba
Rok Sherap Gyatso	Rog Shes rab rgya mtsho
Rok Takjenpa	Rog Stag can pa
Rongpa Chaksorwa	Rong pa Phyag sor pa
Rongtön Sheja Kunrik	Rong ston She bya kun rig
Rongzom Paṇḍita	Rong zom Paṇḍita
Sasang Mati	Sa bzang Mati
Sachen Kunga Nyingpo	Sa chen Kun dga' snying po
Sakya Drakpa Gyaltsen	Sa skya Grag pa rgyal mtshan
Sakya Khön	Sa skya 'Khon
Sakya Paṇḍita Kunga Gyaltsen (= Sapaṇ)	Sa skya Paṇḍita Kun dga' rgyal mtshan
Salo Jampai Dorjé Jamyang Kunga Sönam	Sa lo 'Jam pa'i rdorje 'Jam dbyangs kun dga' bsod nams
Salu	Sa lu
Sangphu	Gsang phu
Sangphu Neuthok	Gsang phu Ne'u thog
Sangphuwa	Gsang phu ba
Sangwai Jin	Gsang ba'i byin
Sangyé Tenzin, [Sakya] Khenpo	Sangs rgyas bstan 'dzin, [Sa skya] Mkhan po
Sapaṇ (= Sakya Paṇḍita)	Sa paṇ
Sarmapa	Gsar ma pa
Saten Tönpa	Za stan ston pa
Sé Chilbuwa (Chökyi Gyaltsen)	Se Spyil bu ba (Chos kyi rgyal mtshan)
Semodru	Se mo gru
Sempa Chenpo Kyapchok Palsangpo	Sems dpa' chen po Skyabs mchog dpal bzang po
Sengé Sangpo	Seng ge bzang po
Serlingpa	Gser gling pa
Setsun	Se btsun
Shākya Chokden, Serdok Paṇchen	Shākya mchog ldan, Gser mdog paṇ chen

Shalu	Zhwa lu
Shamar Karmapa	Zhwa dmar Kar ma pa
Shang Dodé Pal	Zhang Mdo sde dpal
Shang Tsalpa Tsöndrü Drak	Zhang Tshal pa Brtson 'grus grags
Shangchenwa Darma Sönam	Zhangs chen ba Dar ma bsod nams
Shangshung	Zhang zhung
Shangtön Chöbar	Zhang ston Chos 'bar
Sharawa	Sha ra ba
Shenga Shenphen Chökyi Ngangwa, Khenpo	Gzhan dga' Gzhan phan chos kyi snang ba, Mkhan po
Sherap Dorjé	Shes rab rdo rje
Sherap Gyatso (= Geshé Dölpa)	Shes rab rgya mtsho
Sherap Kyap	Shes rab skyabs
Sherap Yungdrung	Shes rab g.yung drung
Shijé	Zhi byed
Shinjé Shekyi Naljorpa	Gshin rje bshed kyi rnal 'byor pa
Sho (place name)	Gzho
Shöl	Zhol
Shönu Öser	Gzhon nu 'od zer
Shukhen	Gzhu mkhan
Shungkhen	Gzhung mkhan (a variant of Gzhu mkhan)
Sönam Drakpa	Bsod nams grags pa
Sönam Rinchen	Bsod nams rin chen
Sönam Tsemo	Bsod nams rtse mo
Taklung	Stag lung
Tashi Lhunpo	Bkra shis lhun po
Tashi Namgyal	Bkra shis rnam rgyal
Teu Nagong	Ste'u sna gong
tenrim	bstan rim
Tera	Te ra
Thakma Kachen	Thag ma dka' chen
Tholing	Tho ling
Thoyön Yeshé Döndrup	Tho yon Ye shes don grub
Thrangu Rinpoché	Khra' gu Rin po che
Thugar	Thu gar
Thuken Chökyi Nyima	Thu'u bkwan Chos kyi nyi ma
Thupten Namgyal	Thub bstan rnam rgyal

Tobchupal Shenyen	Stobs bcu dpal bshes gnyen
Tölung	Stod lung
Tölungpa	Stod lung pa
Tönpa Mikzé	Ston pa Mig mdzes
Trak	Sprags
Trisong Detsen	Khri srong lde btsan
Trophu Lotsāwa	Khro phu lo tsā ba
Tsalpa Kunga Dorjé	Tshal pa Kun dga' rdo rje
Tsang	Gtsang (place name)
Tsangna Shukdenpa	Gtsang na Zhug ldan pa
Tsangnyön Heruka	Gtsang smyon He ru ka
Tsangpa Gyiltön	Gtsang pa Gyil ston
tsen tsen	btsan tsen
Tsendu Hangdu	Tsan du hang du
Tsipri	Rtsib ri
Tsonawa Sherap Sangpo	Mtsho sna ba Shes rab bzang po
Tsultrim Sangpo	Tshul khrims bzang po
Tsongkhapa Losang Drakpa	Tsong kha pa Blo bzang grags pa
Ü	Dbus
Üpa Losal	Dbus pa Blo gsal
Ushangdo	'U shang rdo
Wa Yeshé Wangpo	Dba' Ye shes dbang po
Yagepa	Ya gad pa
Yangchen Gawai Lodrö	Dbyangs can Dga' ba'i blo gros
Yangang	Yang gang
Yarlung Jowo Shākya Rinchen Dé	Yar lung Jo bo Shākya rin chen sde
Yeshé Bar	Ye shes 'bar
yetak	yas stags
Yönten Rinchen	Yon tan rin chen
Yungchung	G.yung chung

Appendix 2. Outline of *Clarifying the Sage's Intent*

Spiritual Potential (Chapter 1)

Taking Refuge (Chapter 2)

Generating the Resolve to Attain Awakening (Chapter 3)

The Perfection of Generosity (Chapter 4)

[Here the overarching Tibetan topical outline is interrupted by independent outlines for each of the six perfections:]

[Topic 1: The Pefection of Generosity]

[Topic 2:] The Perfection of Moral Discipline (Chapter 5)

[Topic 3:] The Perfection of Patience (Chapter 6)

[Topic 4:] The Perfection of Diligence (Chapter 7)

[Topic 5:] The Perfection of Meditative Concentration (Chapter 8)

[Topic 6:] The Perfection of Wisdom (Chapter 9)

[Resumption of interrupted overarching Tibetan topical outline:]

[II.] The Four Means of Attraction (Chapter 10)

The Paths and Levels (Chapter 11)

The Ultimate Fruit (Chapter 12)

Notes

Notes to the Introduction

1. This introduction was written by David Jackson with contributions from Ulrike Roesler and Ken Holmes and edited by Thupten Jinpa.
2. Mind training (*blo sbyong*) is another genre that descends from the Kadam school. Its distinctive modality is the transformation of one's own suffering into a means to overcome self-cherishing and advance along the path. For examples of mind training teachings, see Thupten Jinpa, *Mind Training* (volume 1 of the Library of Tibetan Classics).
3. On the distinction between *lamrim* and *tenrim*, see also Thupten Jinpa, *Book of Kadam* (Library of Tibetan Classics 2), 4.
4. See the discussion of Tsongkhapa's lamrims at the end of this introduction. Tucci 1949 and others have asserted that Tsongkhapa's *Great Treatise on the Stages of the Path to Enlightenment* follows the graded-path system of the *Abhisamayālaṃkāra*, no doubt on the basis of Tsongkhapa's statement at the beginning of his treatise: "These instructions, in general, are those of the *Ornament for Clear Knowledge*, composed by the venerable Maitreya" (Tsongkhapa, *Great Treatise on the Stages of the Path*, 35). More recently, Bhikkhu Pāsādika has argued for the important influence of Nāgārjuna's *Compendium of Sutra Quotations* (*Mahāsūtrasamuccaya*) on Atiśa and on the formation of the subsequent lamrim genre (see Pāsādika, "The Indian Origins of the Lam-rim"). The arguments are not completely convincing, though the *Compendium* is prominently mentioned among similar Indian texts. See Seyfort Ruegg, "Introduction," in Tsongkhapa, *Great Treatise*, 25, and note 8 below.
5. On Atiśa's *Sādhana for Practicing the Mahayana Path*, see note 8 below.
6. See Thupten Jinpa, "Introduction," in ITC, xiv.
7. On Atiśa's modest immediate impact, see Davidson, *Tibetan Renaissance*, 110, and idem, "Atiśa's A Lamp for the Path to Awakening."
8. Composed at the Tholing temple of Shangshung (i.e., Gugé in Ngari Province), the text of Atiśa's *Lamp* was translated from Sanskrit into Tibetan by the author with the Tibetan translator Ma Gewai Lodrö. The work appears in the Tibetan Tengyur, the collection of canonical commentarial literature. In addition to his *Lamp for the Path to Awakening*, Atiśa composed other brief summaries of Mahayana practice that appear in the Tengyur but have been largely overlooked. Two noteworthy examples are his *Sādhana for Practicing the Mahayana Path* and the even shorter *Very Brief Sādhana for Practicing the Mahayana Path*. As *sādhanas* these are formally

liturgies to be used in practice; however, they cover the full range of topics of a tenrim and reflect Atiśa's way of teaching the graded path to his Tibetan audience. See Roesler, *Frühe Quellen*, 44–46. Elsewhere in Atiśa's Mahayana writings, a similar set of graded doctrinal stages can be found in his analysis of the *Compendium of Sutra Quotations* (*Mahāsūtrasamuccaya*), an anthology of Mahayana scriptural quotations that the Tibetan canon attributes to Nāgārjuna. See Pāsādika, "The Indian Origins of the Lam-rim," 6–7.

9. Atiśa, *Bodhipathapradīpapañjikā*, Toh 3948 Tengyur, dbu ma, *khi*. This commentary was translated by Atiśa himself with Naktso Lotsāwa Tsultrim Gyalwa (b. 1011), who, incidentally, wrote a tenrim of his own, the so-called *Tenrim of Naktso*. Though this work survived and was taught at least as late as the fourteenth century (it was studied, for instance, by Khenchen Sönam Drakpa, 1273–1345), its contents and structure are unknown (Khetsun Sangpo, *Biographical Dictionary of Tibet*, vol. 5, 459). In the colophon to Atiśa's text, Naktso mentions that he alone among Tibetans had been favored by Atiśa with the highest tantric teachings.
10. This small work lends itself to many other ways and levels of analysis. Sherburne (*A Lamp for the Path*, 1) provides a detailed topical outline of Atiśa's *Lamp*.
11. Quite a few lamrims by early Kadampa masters are listed among the bibliographical rarities of Akhu Chin Sherap Gyatso (Akhu Chin, *Materials for a History of Tibetan Literature, Part 3*; hereafter abbreviated MHTL). These include the lamrim of Neusurpa (MHTL 11115); that of Chayulwa (MHTL 11116); the lamrim consisting of the notes of Möndrapa based on Tsonawa's teachings (MHTL 11119); that consisting of notes by Gompa Sherap Rinchen on the teachings of Gyegom Shönu Drak (MHTL 11127); that consisting of the teachings of Lha Trangpowa as set down by one of his students (MHTL 11128); the great lamrim of Rinchen Gangpa (MHTL 11129); the lamrim consisting of Mönlam Drakpa's record of the teachings of Neusurpa's disciple Ngari Gezé Jangchup (MHTL 11130); the great lamrim by Kor (MHTL 11131), who was another student of Ngari Gezé Jangchup; that of Geshé Yagepa (MHTL 11132); that of Kamapa Sherap Ö (MHTL 11133); and that of Ngok Sherap Ö (MHTL 11134), which might be a mistake for the previous one. In addition, numerous commentaries and subcommentaries on the *Lamp for the Path to Awakening* existed. Akhu Chin lists quite a few (MHTL 11099–11106), including those of Sé Chilbuwa and Dotön Sherap Drak.
12. As far as we can tell, the *Blue Compendium* by Dölpa *is* the earliest Tibetan lamrim work that has been preserved. The initial version of *Dharma Exemplified*, described below, was composed slightly earlier, but it was later replaced by the version of Chegom Sherap Dorjé (1124/25–1204/5), which was the only one to survive. The Sangphu Kadampa teachers Drolungpa and Gampopa were of course very early, too, but they wrote tenrim works. To our knowledge, the works from Naktso Lotsāwa's Kadam lineage are not extant, although we do have quotations from them.
13. Phakmodrupa had several teachers in the Kadam school. His own tenrim text is discussed below.
14. This is how Per Sørensen has explained the translation of the title as "Blue Udder"; see Sørensen, "The Prolific Ascetic lCe-sgom śes-rab rdo-rje," note 25.
15. On the designation *be('u) bum*, see also Stein, *Tibetan Civilization*, 267; Roesler, *Frühe Quellen*, 155.
16. See Stearns, *Luminous Lives*, 32–33, 36, and 38.

17. See Thuken Chökyi Nyima, *Crystal Mirror of Philosophical Systems*, 111: "Evidently, there were many texts on the stages of the path written by Kadampas; the two most famous are the *Blue Udder* and *Dharma Examples*."
18. Jé Shardong Rinpoché, *Pure Crystal Mirror: An Explanation on the Root Text and Commentary of the Blue Compendium*, part 4 of his collected works (hereafter abbreviated Shardong), 2: "The *Blue Compendium* is a lamrim containing the meaning, and the *Dharma Exemplified: A Heap of Jewels* is a lamrim in examples. These two complement each other and are like the right and the left hand."
19. Here "core texts" (*gzhung*) means the canonical scriptures in general, and in particular the texts that are of special importance in this tradition: two works by Śāntideva (*Guide to the Bodhisattva Way of Life* and *Compendium of Trainings*), two works by Asaṅga (*Bodhisattva Levels* and via Maitreya, *Ornament of Mahayana Sutras*), the *Collection of Aphorisms*, and Āryaśūra's *Jātakamālā*.
20. The *Book of Kadam* (*Bka' gdams glegs bam*) is a diverse collection with two main parts. The first part, the "Father Teachings," contains Atiśa's famous *Necklace of the Bodhisattva* (*Bodhisattvamaṇyāvali*), several biographical works, and a long dialogue, sometimes with rapid exchanges, between Atiśa and Dromtönpa that ranges widely over Buddhist topics, both general and esoteric. The second part, the "Son Teachings," consists mostly of stories of Dromtönpa's previous existences and seems to have been intended to elevate the status of Drom as a high-level bodhisattva. For a translation of the core texts in this collection, see Thupten Jinpa, *Book of Kadam*.
21. These are Chegom Sherap Dorjé's dates according to van der Kuijp, "On the Fifteenth Century *Lho rong chos 'byung*."
22. See, e.g., Akya Yongzin's word commentary on *Dharma Exemplified*, namely, his *Explanation of Difficult Words in the Dharma Exemplified*, p. 519.
23. Similar passages are found in the *Book of Kadam* (see note 20 above).
24. *Be'u bum sngon po'i 'grel pa*. Lha Drigangpa was named after Drigang in the Ön Valley and was a disciple of Neusurpa as well. Eimer (*Berichte über das Leben des Atiśa*, 164–65) assumes that he was born before 1118 and died after 1192; van der Kuijp ("Tibetan Historiography," 52n25) tentatively identifies him with the second abbot of Drikung Monastery who lived 1154–1221, but this would contradict the fact that he was a personal disciple of Dölpa Rinpoché (who died in 1131). Moreover, we know that Lha Drowai Gönpo (1186–1239) was a nephew of Lha Drigangpa. See Yarlung Jowo Shākya Rinchen Dé, *Yar lung jo bo'i chos 'byung*, 108.
25. Roesler, *Frühe Quellen*.
26. On the life, works, and dates of Ngok Loden Sherap, see Ralf Kramer, *The Great Tibetan Translator: Life and Works of rNgog Blo ldan shes rab (1059–1109)*.
27. Drolungpa, *Great Tenrim* (*Bstan rim chen mo,* short for *Great Treatise on the Stages of the Doctrine*). Döndrup Gyaltsen, *Treasury of Gems*, 8, mentions what would also appear to be a very brief version of this great work: *The Basic Verses of Drolungpa's Tenrim*. This may be the *Bstan rim bsdus pa'i lam rim* ascribed to Drolungpa, whose publication along with the *Great Tenrim* in Tibet, in a volume of rare early Kadam writings, was announced in recent years.
28. Thuken, *Crystal Mirror*, 105.
29. See also Dungkar Losang Trinlé, *Great Tibetan Dictionary*, who in his annotations to Tsalpa Kunga Dorjé's *Red Annals* (374n338) mentions Tsongkhapa's respect for the *Great Tenrim*. His high estimation probably influenced several Geluk teachers

of the late nineteenth or early twentieth century to have it carved onto blocks at the Shöl printery near Lhasa. Although those printing blocks were destroyed in the 1960s during the Cultural Revolution, at least two prints survived outside Tibet: one in a Mongolian temple and one at the Bihar Research Society in Patna, India (Jackson, *The "Miscellaneous Series" of Tibetan Texts in the Bihar Research Society*, 164–65, cat. no. 1289.) On the basis of the Mongolian exemplar, the work was input in South India and published as an ACIP (Asian Classics Input Project) digital text, and thus made widely available.

30. Points 2 through 5 are thus the four thoughts that turn the mind.
31. See note 548 of the translation in this volume of Sapaṇ's *Clarifying the Sage's Intent* for the spot at which Sapaṇ begins to quote Drolungpa's *Great Tenrim* word for word.
32. The length of Drolungpa's *Great Tenrim* may be why it is not included in this volume. Readers of Tibetan should refer to Thupten Jinpa's intriguing discussion of this work (ITC, xix–xxv). In addition to the surviving tenrim treatises briefly described above, several other tenrims are mentioned in bibliographical sources but are thought to be no longer extant. One such case is the tenrim composed by Atiśa's translator Naktso Lotsāwa. The *Red Annals* of Tsalpa Kunga Dorjé (composed 1346) states that Naktso's disciple Rongpa Chaksorwa (fl. mid-eleventh century) stayed his whole life in meditative retreat, only coming out to mediate a violent dispute. At that time he was invited to Ushangdo, where he gave a religious discourse to some five hundred monks. Among those present, four assistant teachers each took notes of his sermons, and from them, four tenrims came into being, those by the so-called four sons of Rongpa: Ja Dulzinpa, Rok Takjenpa, Tsangna Shukdenpa, and Namparwa. The tradition of these masters was the Instruction Lineage of Rongpa (*rong pa'i bka' brgyud*). (See Tsalpa Kunga Dorjé, *Red Annals*, 65–66.) Another unavailable but possibly related treatise was the so-called *Highest Path* of Narthang abbot Drotön Dutsi Drak (fl. early thirteen century), which is listed by Akhu Chin Sherap Gyatso among the lamrim works proper (MHTL 11117). He also lists its commentary by Chim Namkha Drak (1210–85), which became known to the later tradition as "the tenrim of Chim Namkha Drak" (MHTL 11118). Several related works are also mentioned by Döndrup Gyaltsen (*Treasury of Gems*, pp. 9 and 11): the tenrim of Neusurpa with Abhidharmic explanations (*mngon pa'i gsung gros*); the examples and tenrim (*dpe bstan rim*, the word *dpe* referring here to the *Dpe chos, Dharma Exemplified*) of Jayulpa; the tenrim of Lopa Sangyé Gompa; and the tenrim of Lotsul Darma. Dr. Dan Martin kindly pointed out this last source.
33. See Guenther, *The Jewel Ornament of Liberation*; Gampopa's *Ornament* was also translated by Khenpo Konchog Gyaltsen in 1998 (Gyaltsen, *The Jewel Ornament of Liberation*).
34. The following brief sketch of Gampopa's life is based mainly on Gö Lotsāwa, *Blue Annals*, *nya*, 21b–26a; Roerich, *The Blue Annals*, 451–62. See also Guenther, *The Jewel Ornament of Liberation*, xi–xii.
35. This common spelling in English, Milarepa, runs together the two distinct elements of his name, Mila and Repa.
36. For Peter Alan Roberts's overview of the development of the Kagyü school in Tibet and the doctrinal threads that underpin it, see his introduction to volume 5 in the

Library of Tibetan Classics, *Mahāmudrā and Related Instructions* (Boston: Wisdom, 2011).

37. Gö Lotsāwa, *Blue Annals*, *nya*, 25b.
38. Drolungpa, *Great Tenrim*, 39b and 370b–371a.
39. *Ornament of Precious Liberation* was apparently not the only such work that Gampopa wrote. Akhu Chin Sherap Gyatso, in his compilation of bibliographical rarities, after listing this work together with other "*lam rim*" (MHTL 11120), mentions two related works by Gampopa: the *Lam mchog rin chen 'phreng ba* (MHTL 11121) and the *Bstan bcos lung gi nyi 'od* (MHTL 11122).
40. Thuken, *Crystal Mirror*, 103: "Phakmodrupa received the Kadam teaching from Geshé Dölpa and also wrote a treatise on the stages of the teaching." A fifty-two-folio copy of Phakmodrupa's rare work turned up in India in the 1970s and was reproduced from a manuscript copy of an original xylograph edition in 1977.
41. This subject (and the teaching of the importance of faith as a key prerequisite) occurs also in the Sakya Lamdré introductory instructions, in the first section known as the Three Appearances (*snang ba gsum*).
42. Phakmodrupa, *How to Enter into the Buddha's Doctrine by Stages*, 46b.
43. For a detailed study on the existence of gnosis on the level of buddhahood, see Almogi, *Rong-zom-pa's Discourses on Buddhology*.
44. *Clarifying the Sage's Intent* has inspired an abridgement and modern adaptation by Geshe Wangyal and Brian Cutillo (see Sakya Pandita, *Illuminations*). Mr. Hidetoshi Fushimi submitted and defended in 2000 at Hamburg University a dissertation entitled "The Perfection of Discriminative Understanding Chapter from the *Elucidation of the Sage's Intention*," a work that when published will list other contributions to the secondary literature.
45. These were but the latest of a long series of destroyed temples, from the ninth to early thirteenth centuries, as many sites of Buddhist culture in Asia stood defenseless against the militant expansion of Arab-led Islam or the pillaging by Islamic Turkic rulers who raided from Afghanistan deeper and deeper into northern India.
46. Rongzom Paṇḍita of the late tenth century was an even earlier example of broad scholarship.
47. Sapaṇ's teacher Śākyaśrībhadra wrote a brief but noteworthy summary of the bodhisattva's path. We might be tempted to classify this little-known work as an Indian Buddhist lamrim, since the phrase "stages of the path" is prominently featured in its title, *The Abbreviated Stages of the Path of the Bodhisattva*. Śākyaśrībhadra composed it at the earnest request of the translator Trophu Lotsāwa (1173–1250), the main host who had invited him and his party to Tibet. He must have written it during the nine-year period (1204–13) when he taught and traveled in Tibet, before he returned westward to his native home of Kashmir. The two translated it together while staying at the temple of Salu at Gyangro, the place near Shalu in the lower Nyang Valley where Sapaṇ received monastic ordination in 1208. It is the last among the later Indian treatises of this sort.

    Śākyaśrībhadra's work lacks a summarizing outline and is too short to need chapter divisions: it is only about thirty verses long. Like a similar treatise of Buddhaśrījñāna, it does not utilize the division into the three spiritual orientations, despite being called a lamrim. Some topics are mentioned more than once, and the versified translation of the probably versified original makes it difficult to follow in places. Nevertheless, these following main and subsidiary topics can be extracted:

1. How to attend upon the teacher, and a brief summary of the treatise
2. The difficulty of obtaining a free and well-endowed human existence
3. The quick destruction of one's freedom; impermanence
4. The moral cause and effect of virtuous and evil deeds
5. The suffering of cyclic existence
6. Producing the thought of awakening
7. The cultivation of emptiness and compassion
8. The thirty-seven factors conducive to awakening
9. The five paths
10. Reasoning through which one can understand insubstantiality
11. The three bodies of buddhahood

This work, like the other writings of Śākyaśrībhadra, was probably studied and absorbed by Sakya Paṇḍita at some point during their association.

48. Tibetan tradition says that Asaṅga received the "five texts of Maitreya"—the *Ornament of Mahayana Sutras* (*Mahāyānasūtrālaṃkāra*), *Madhyāntavibhāga*, *Abhisamayālaṃkāra*, *Uttaratantra*, and *Dharmadharmatāvibhaṅga*—from Maitreya himself while on a visit to Tuṣita Heaven and came back and wrote them down; in the Tengyur they are accordingly attributed to Maitreya. Some scholars assume that the texts go back to an Indian master named Maitreya(nātha) who may have been Asaṅga's teacher.
49. The chapter enumeration for the *Ornament of Mahayana Sutras* in this volume follows the Tibetan translations of the work in construing the first six verses as a distinct chapter. Thus, elsewhere, these two verses may be found in what is labeled chapter 19.
50. Sönam Tsemo, *The General System of Tantras*, 13a–b.
51. Chim Jampaiyang (*Detailed Abhidharma Commentary*, 120) defines "appreciating" (*mos pa*, *adhimokṣa*) as "to desire or to hold an object as possessing valuable qualities" (*'dod pa'am dmigs pa la yon tan can du 'dzin pa*).
52. There is reason to doubt the correctness of the ordering of these topics and the corresponding chapter divisions in the standard Dergé edition of Sapaṇ's *Clarifying the Sage's Intent.* This formal problem of chapter division was pointed out in one of the minor commentatorial works by Lowo Khenchen, but it is too complicated to go into here.
53. Not all these topics are clearly indicated in the initial printing of the new Tibetan edition from the Institute of Tibetan Classics, which overlooks spiritual lineage as the subject of chapter 1 and calls the perfection of wisdom chapter "The Conduct of the Āryas."
54. Thupten Jinpa, "Introduction," in Institute of Tibetan Classics, *Bstan pa la'jug pa'i rim pa ston pa'i gzhung gces btus*, xvii and xviii.
55. Drolungpa, *Great Tenrim*, 521b–527a.
56. Gorampa notes this in one of his minor works, in a 1481 reply to Tsultrim Sangpo, a disciple of their mutual teacher Müchen Sempa Chenpo Könchok Gyaltsen (1388–1469). Tsultrim Sangpo mentions having heard that the system of Perfection Vehicle stages of the path taught in Sönam Tsemo's *General System of the Tantras* did not come down from Sachen Kunga Nyingpo through the lineage of

the Indian siddha Virūpa but rather was the system of the stages of the path based on the *Ornament of Mahayana Sutras* as transmitted through the lineage of Ngok Lotsāwa Loden Sherap and Chapa Chökyi Sengé. Gorampa, *Dris lan pad mo bzhad pa*, 326. Compare to van der Kuijp, *Contributions to the Development of Tibetan Buddhist Epistemology*, 268n69.

57. A few more hints about Drolungpa's shorter tenrim can be gleaned from the writings of a second great Sakya scholar of the fifteenth century, Shākya Chokden. This master, who was well schooled in the traditions of Ngok and Sangphu, asserts in his biography of Rongtön Sheja Kunrik (1367–1449) that Rongtön received the "teachings belonging to the doctrinal realm of the [bodhisattva's] conduct, including the *Entry for the Conqueror's Sons* that had been transmitted through the lineage from Ngok Lotsāwa." Shākya Chokden, *Rje btsun thams cad*, 307.
58. Thuken, *Crystal Mirror*, 105.
59. Still other puzzling references to this or a similar work exist: it is recorded, for instance, that Khenchen Sönam Drakpa (1273–1345) had studied a text entitled the *Rgyal sras lam 'jug* from Khenchen Kashipa Drakpa Shönnu (see Khetsun Sangpo, *Biographical Dictionary of Tibet*, vol. 5, 457). Could this be a misspelling or an alternative title of the same *Entry for the Conqueror's Sons* (*Rgyal sras 'jug ngogs*) of Ngok Loden Sherap or Drolungpa? Or is it a similar mistaking of the popular alternative title of *Clarifying the Sage's Intent*, namely, the *Rgyal sras lam bzang*? Or is it yet another independent work?
60. Tsongkhapa, *Great Treatise*; Sopa et al., *Steps on the Path to Enlightenment*.
61. On the crucial role that Rendawa played in Tsongkhapa's spiritual development, see Roloff, *Red mda' ba, Buddhist Yogi-Scholar*.
62. See Seyfort Ruegg, "Introduction," in Tsongkhapa, *Great Treatise*, 23.
63. Tsongkhapa, *Great Treatise*.
64. Tsongkhapa, *Record of Teachings Received* (*Gsan yig*), 25a: (1) Atiśa, (2) Gönpawa [is Dromtön missing?], (3) Neusurpa, (4) Thakma Kachen, (5) Namseng, (6) Namkha Gyalpo, (7) Sengé Sangpo, (8) Khenchen Namkha Gyaltsen, and (9) Tsongkhapa.
65. Ibid., 25b–26a: (1) Atiśa, (2) Dromtön, (3) Potowa, (4) Sharawa, (5) Ja Chekhawa (Yeshé Dorjé), (6) Sé Chilbuwa (Chökyi Gyaltsen), (7) Lha Chenpo, (8) Lha Drogön, (9) Shangchenwa Darma Sönam, (10) Tsonawa Sherap Sangpo, (11) Lopön Gawa Sangpo, (12) Khenchen Chökyap Sangpo, and (13) Tsongkhapa.
66. Ibid., 26a. Tsongkhapa adds here that this is also his lineage for the bodhisattva vows in the Yogācāra tradition: (1) Buddha, (2) Maitreya, (3) Asaṅga, (4) Vasubandhu, (5) Sthiramati, (6 and 7) Kusalī the elder and younger, (8) Suvarṇadvīpa; after guru number (9) Atiśa, the lineage continues the same, down to (18) Tsonawa, who transmitted it to (19) Möndrapa Tsultrim Tashi, (20) Khenchen Chökyap Sangpo, and (21) Tsongkhapa.
67. See Bodong Paṇchen, *A Detailed Exposition of the Stages of the Path of the Three Personality Types Arranged as Practical Instructions*, and also Jackson, "The *bsTan rim* (Stages of the Doctrine) and Similar Graded Expositions of the *Bodhisattva*'s Path," 122. When reprinted in 1977, the publisher mistakenly identified its author as "the early Kadampa Sangwai Jin," for that name does appear in the author's colophon. But that was one of several pen names that Bodong Paṇchen used, this one having been received by him in a vision.

Notes to The Blue Compendium

1. The subdivisions into seven chapters as well as the numbered headings are not part of the Tibetan text of *The Blue Compendium.* The numbered headings, which also appear in the Institute of Tibetan Classics' Tibetan edition, come from the 1991 Beijing edition of Lha Drigangpa's *Commentary on the Blue Compendium* (hereafter abbreviated Lha Drigangpa). *The Blue Compendium* was composed in a free sequence of verses in an eight-syllable meter. It is not subdivided into stanzas of four lines each, and sometimes a new sentence or a new thought even begins in the middle of a line. Therefore this translation is subdivided into lines but does not give stanza numbers. The paragraphs correspond to the portions commented on in Lha Drigangpa's commentary.
2. See chapter 2 of Śāntideva's *Śikṣāsamuccaya*.
3. Tib. *de bas chos 'brel ma brtags mang min*. I follow the interpretation in Lha Drigangpa, p. 63: "Therefore, in the beginning, before one has thoroughly examined whether the teacher is capable, one does not [need to] heed everything."
4. According to Lha Drigangpa, p. 64, this refers to an instruction that Potowa gave at Shukhen when Tsangpa Gyiltön, a disciple of Chengawa, had decided to stay with Geshé Yagepa and asked about the right way of relying on the lama.
5. Lha Drigangpa, p. 65, refers to a statement by the Nepalese teacher Tsendu Hangdu: "When I teach the Dharma according to the perfections, people in Tibet do not cherish it; when I teach according to the secret mantra, they hold it in high esteem. [However,] there is no difference between the two."
6. Aśvaghoṣa, *Gurupañcāśikā*, Toh 3721 Tengyur, rgyud, *tshu*, 10a3.
7. According to Lha Drigangpa, p. 69, this refers to the way of judging the qualities of the teacher, like some people say that aged cheese is good, others say it's bad.
8. Tib. *chos mchog*. This is the last stage of the path of application, the second of the five paths of Mahayana Buddhism.
9. In sum, you should please the teacher through (a) making material and mental offerings of respect and (b) practicing according to his instructions.
10. The present-tense *gsung* "he says", which is used here, typically refers to the words of the person the author has received the teaching from—in this work usually Dölpa Rinpoché's teacher Potowa.
11. Tib. *spobs pa*, Skt. *pratibhāna*. Lha Drigangpa, (p. 76) quotes a passage from the *Sutra Encouraging Nobler Intention* (*Adhyāśayasaṃcodanasūtra*), where the four kinds of "confidence" or "readiness in speech" relate to the knowledge that the words of the buddha are (a) endowed with meaning and (b) with Dharma, (c) they show the benefit of reaching nirvana, and (d) they show the defects of samsara. Someone whose speech has these qualities should be regarded as a buddha, and we should listen to his instructions. The same quotation is found in chapter 1 of Śāntideva's *Compendium of Trainings*.
12. Lha Drigangpa, p. 77, explains that Lari Tönpa Sangyé Bar (Skt. Buddhajvāla) once asked Potowa about this, and Potowa said: "To obtain the blessing, your own faith and respect and the lama's being pleased need to come together. If someone is full of faith and respect but the lama is not pleased, the blessing will not arise in this lifetime, though it will be the cause of meeting him again in the future."
13. Lha Drigangpa, p. 78, relates how Rinchen Sangpo (Skt. Ratnabhadra) was asked

by one of his disciples for a sādhana. After some time the disciple complained that despite practicing he had still not attained the respective siddhis and asked if the instructions had perhaps been incomplete. Rinchen Sangpo told him to take ablutions when practicing. The disciple followed his advice and obtained the desired result. This shows how crucial the teacher's guidance is.

14. This refers to a quotation from the *Sarvadharmavaipulyasaṃgrahasūtra* in chapter 4 of Śāntideva's *Śikṣāsamuccaya*, Toh 3940 Tengyur, dbu ma, *khi*, 58a2.
15. The *Letter to a Friend* (*Suhṛllekha*) is a letter of Buddhist advice by the philosopher Nāgārjuna (second century C.E.) to a king of the Sātavāhana dynasty. The first three stanzas explain why the king should listen to these instructions.
16. Lha Drigangpa (p. 83) gives a brief summary of the legend, as found in *Great Passing into Nirvana Sutra* (Toh 119 Kangyur, mdo sde, *ta*, 183b3). Sunakṣatra was a monk in the order of Buddha Śākyamuni for twenty years, but he had no faith and held wrong views. He held a non-Buddhist ascetic to be an arhat, though the Buddha predicted that in seven days this ascetic would die and be reborn as a hungry ghost. Even when this came true, Sunakṣatra still had no faith, so the Buddha predicted that his good karma would be cut off and he would be reborn in hell for a long time. The legend is also contained in the Pali canon; see Eimer, "Die Sunakṣatra-Episode im Kommentar zum Be'u bum sṅon po."
17. This refers to the introductory statement of Atiśa's *Lamp for the Path to Awakening*, in which Atiśa declares that he is going to explain the path to awakening at the request of his disciple Jangchup Ö, the king of Western Tibet.
18. Jambudvīpa (Tib. *'dzam bu gling*; "black plum island") is the continent in Indian Buddhist cosmology that contains our human world.
19. One of Lha Drigangpa's (p. 86) explanations is that he was named Three-Necked One (Drinpa Sumpa) after the meditation deity of the Guhyasamāja tantra, who has three heads. Another explanation is that this name refers to his three tantric transmission lineages.
20. Lha Drigangpa (p. 87, see also Shardong, pp. 167–68) tells the story of how Yamāriyogin was meditating at the base of a tree when someone came to cut it down. Unable to dissuade the woodcutter, Yamāriyogin became angry, asking, "Don't you know who I am?" Then five people came from the city; he stabbed each of them with a knife. Realizing that he was a great tantric master, the people asked him to have mercy on those he had killed. He told them to wash his feet and pour the water on their wounds, whereupon the dead people were revived and stood up. He announced that due to this brief moment of anger he had not mastered the siddhi of mahāmudrā in this lifetime but he would do so in the future.
21. Lha Drigangpa (pp. 88–89) explains that "the Lama of Blessing" refers to Atiśa's teacher Ḍombhipa, who had received the blessing coming down from Vajrapāṇi and transmitted to a ḍākinī, then to Tilopa, and then to Nāropa. When Atiśa and Ḍombhipa were traveling together, Atiśa asked him for his blessing. One night Atiśa dreamed about a monk eating the flesh of a human arm. Puzzled, Atiśa asked the monk what he was doing, and the monk replied that he was just eating a demon's arm that had been given to him. Through this dream Atiśa mastered a special state of contemplation. This episode is also mentioned in Atiśa's biography; see Eimer, *Rnam thar rgyas pa: Materialien zu einer Biographie des Atiśa*, I: 163 and II: 25–26.

22. The five major "fields of knowledge" are Buddhist philosophy, logic, grammar, crafts, and arts. The *locus classicus* for these five disciplines is the commentary on stanza 11:60 of the *Ornament of Mahayana Sutras* by Maitreya/Asaṅga (see note 120 below). Biographical records about Atiśa do not fail to mention that he was proficient in the five fields of knowledge; see the comparison of different lists in Eimer, *Berichte über das Leben des Atiśa*, 208–9.
23. According to Lha Drigangpa (p. 92), this refers to the beginning of Atiśa's *Lamp for the Path to Awakening*: "I shall explain the correct methods as taught by the teachers".
24. According to Lha Drigangpa, this is a reference to the chapter on moral discipline from Asaṅga's *Bodhisattva Levels* (Toh 4037 Tengyur, sems tsam, *wi*, 39a4), where it is stated that part of the qualification of the teacher in whose presence one generates the thought of awakening is that he be free of those qualities that are contrary to the six perfections.
25. *Subāhuparipṛcchātantra*, Toh 805 Kangyur, rgyud 'bum, *wa*, 119b3.
26. According to Indian theory, the world goes through a repeated series of world ages, beginning with a "golden age" and ending with a dark age or age of discord (*kaliyuga*), before the cosmos is destroyed and then recreated again. We live in the dark age in which living conditions deteriorate, virtues decrease and vices increase, and the Dharma gradually disappears. Lha Drigangpa (p. 94) quotes a passage from the *Questions of Subāhu Tantra* that explains that a teacher of tantric practice should be endowed with sixteen qualities but that, since such a person is hard to find in our dark age, it is also sufficient if the teacher has half of these qualities, or even just four or two of them.
27. Lha Drigangpa (p. 96) tells the story of how a nobleman from Purang in western Tibet asked Atiśa's disciple Rinchen Lama for personal instruction. Rinchen Lama was not pleased with this because it seemed that the nobleman did not cherish Atiśa's teaching appropriately. One time, when Rinchen Lama was called to perform a healing ritual for a servant of the nobleman, he told him never to disparage Atiśa's teaching.
28. Lha Drigangpa (p. 99) quotes the *Ornament of Mahayana Sutras* 19:31 (Toh 4020 Tengyur, sems tsam, *phi*, 29b3) by Maitreya/Asaṅga in this context. On the four reliances, see glossary.
29. Yogācāra-Madhyamaka refers to a combination of the two main traditions of Mahayana philosophy, which Atiśa studied with his teacher Avadhūtipa. See also the passage on Serlingpa and Atiśa in section 20 below ("How to meditate combining method and wisdom").
30. According to the commentaries, *'gul ba* ("to move," "to be in motion"), is similar in meaning to the expression "having been born as a human being" (see Lha Drigangpa, p. 102) or designates a "capable or diligent person" (*mi 'jon thang can nam rus pa can zhig*; see Shardong, p. 209).
31. Lha Drigangpa (p. 116) tells the story of a man who was caught by a group of bandits. When they were about to kill him, he said, "Let me make my last will." They said that he had nobody to give his last will to. He answered that he would give it to the wind, and if anyone heard it, that person should take revenge for him. The bandits killed him but were so amazed at his words that they told the story to

their wives, the rumor spread, and finally it reached the victim's relatives, who took revenge on the bandits. The moral is that even when a teaching does not have an immediate effect, it may bring the desired consequences in the future. Lha Drigangpa ascribes the story to Dromtönpa. It is also contained in Potowa's *Dharma Exemplified*.

32. Lha Drigangpa (p. 117) tells the following story: In Gang Gyamo, in the region of Gyal (in Phenpo, north of Lhasa), Geshé Drakgyal asked to be instructed in Atiśa's *Lamp for the Path to Awakening*. When he received this teaching, Geshé Drakgyal was told the following story: An old nobleman named Batsaludor had been ordained and received the ordination name Yönten Rinchen. When he was listening to the lamrim teaching of Geshé Potowa, he suddenly said: "Dear Geshé! This gradual training is a teaching for young people who have plenty of time! I am old and have no time. Pray, give me a teaching for the aged!" Geshé Potowa answered with a simile, saying: "A smith from lower Dokham made needles with long and uneven eyes, explaining that 'I make them long, as I was taught by my father, who never told me whether or not it was good.' In a similar way, when my disciple Jotsun Yönten Rinchen says, 'I am old and don't have much time; give me a teaching for the aged!' my answer is, 'When you were young, you had a family and took care of the immediate needs of your children without thinking of the teaching. Now you are old, have turned toward the teaching, and are in need of a teaching for the aged. I possess only the teaching of the old lay Buddhist Dromtönpa, which is this very graded path. I do not have different teachings for the old and the young.'"
33. The Buddhist tradition enumerates six recollections (mentioned, for instance, in stanza 4 of Nāgārjuna's *Letter to a Friend*): recollection of the Buddha, the Dharma, the Sangha, generosity, renunciation, and the gods.
34. Lha Drigangpa (p. 127) quotes the following stanza from the *King of Meditation Sutra* (Toh Kangyur, mdo sde, *da*, 13b7):

    You must be instructed and comprehend [the good qualities] thoroughly.
    If you have examined in many ways what they are like,
    this examination that is focused on them
    will make you completely understand their nature.

35. In general, recollection of deities is meant to improve your own qualities and behavior by thinking of the good qualities of the gods. Shardong (pp. 280–81) explains in this context that the recollection of the gods is contained in the recollection of the Sangha.
36. Lha Drigangpa (pp. 132–33) relates how Potowa was staying in the temple of Lo (in a side valley of the Kyichu) and met an aged gentleman from the region, who asked him how one could possibly know that the Buddha had really existed. Potowa asked him how he could know that his ancestor Teu Nagong had existed. The gentleman replied that he knew it because of his various well-known deeds and because the whole lineage stemming from him down to his own person was known by name. Potowa explained that the same applied to the Buddha and the lineage of teachers stemming from him, and so the gentleman finally gained faith in the Buddha. The story is also contained in Potowa's *Dharma Exemplified*.
37. The seven jewels mentioned in stanza 32 of Nāgārjuna's *Letter to a Friend* (*Suhṛllekha*, Toh 4182 Tengyur, spring yig, *nge*, 40b7) are (1) faith (in the Three Jewels),

(2) moral discipline, (3) generosity, (4) listening (to the Dharma), (5) scrupulousness, (6) shame (which makes one avoid bad deeds), and (7) wisdom. In the *Precious Garland* (*Ratnāvalī*) 1:5, Nāgārjuna states that "wisdom is chief and faith its prerequisite." See also Lha Drigangpa, p. 135.

38. "Leisure" (*dal ba*) is a technical term for the eight freedoms that enable a human being to practice the Dharma (see glossary). Together with the term "endowment" (*'byor ba*), it forms the compound *dal 'byor* (translated here as "precious human body"), which describes rebirth as a human being who is equipped with everything necessary to seek and obtain liberation.
39. Two people made pastry shells (*skyu*) filled with melted butter, but one of them was not careful enough with forming the dough, and the shell broke before he could get it into his mouth. The other one told him that he had to be more careful. The story is found in Lha Drigangpa (p. 140) and also in Potowa's *Dharma Exemplified*.
40. This refers to the very first stanza of Nāgārjuna's *Letter to a Friend* (*Suhṛllekha*).
41. The three trainings (*bslab pa gsum*) are the trainings in moral discipline, meditation, and wisdom. See also note 71 below.
42. Lha Drigangpa (pp. 143–44) relates the story in more detail. It is also contained in Potowa's *Dharma Exemplified*.
43. This refers to Nāgārjuna's *Ratnāvalī* stanza 4:3 (Toh 4158 Tengyur, spring yig, *ge*, 118a7), where Nāgārjuna tells the king that he is going to instruct him in his royal duties out of compassion, even if what he has to say is not always agreeable.
44. *Śīlasaṃyuktasūtra*, Toh 303 Kangyur, mdo sde, *sa*, 40b6.
45. Lha Drigangpa (p. 147) relates the following story: In Potowa's home region there was a drought and therefore a famine. When a family had a meal, the little child hid his portion behind his back and ate from the food of his father and big brother, but suddenly his food was snatched away by a dog and so he lost his share. The story is also contained in Potowa's *Dharma Exemplified*.
46. My translation is strongly based on the commentaries. Lha Drigangpa (p. 149) renders the following conversation: Potowa said that if, out of the thousand monks who had assembled at Trak and Khartok, only one hundred would take the teaching about the precious human body seriously and act accordingly, then the teaching of the Buddha that was on the verge of disappearing would remain a little longer. Phuchungwa replied that even ten would be sufficient. Potowa said that even a single one would do. See also Shardong, pp. 322–23.
47. According to Lha Drigangpa (p. 149), people hold on to good persons just as roasted grain sticks to grease (literally, "snot" (*snabs*); in this context the word seems to signify something sticky, like grease in a frying pan). Also, earth and gravel cling to large stones when they are carried in a strong current. Therefore even a few good people are enough to help many others stay on the right track.
48. Lha Drigangpa (p. 149) explains this as a reference to Potowa's statement that he taught people both secretly (this way) and in public (the other way).
49. See Nāgārjuna's *Ratnāvalī* 4:6.
50. *Mthong sa* ("field of vision," "the state of seeing"). The commentary reads *mtho sa* ("a high position," "a high state") instead; see Lha Drigangpa, p. 158.
51. I have translated the verse as I understand the root text. The commentary, however, takes this as something negative: "If we have turned all these teachings into an instruction for simpletons by using them like a tool for obtaining food, and we

then sever [these instructions] in our mind by reaching a high state like meditation on emptiness, it is as if we have been put in an iron fortress without doors." Lha Drigangpa, pp. 157–58.

52. Śāntideva, *Guide to the Bodhisattva Way of Life* (*Bodhisattvacaryāvatāra*) 4:15. Toh 3871 Tengyur, dbu ma, *la,* 8b5.
53. Lha Drigangpa (p. 158) relates a story told by Potowa: The fortress of Chakhar in Phenpo had been conquered by enemies and held by them for a long time. One day an old man heard people say that the fortress had been won back, and he said: "That Chakhar has been won isn't just a dream, is it?" The meaning in this context is something like: "This [precious human body] isn't just a dream, is it? Since I have obtained it, I must practice diligently!"
54. It is a widespread Buddhist belief that the inner attitude at the moment of death is decisive for the kind of rebirth a person is going to take. See the discussion in Schmithausen, "Zur Frage, ob ein Bodhisattva unter bestimmten Voraussetzungen in einer neutralen Geisteshaltung (*avyākṛta-citta*) töten darf."
55. See the *Verses Addressed to Prasenajit* (*Prasenajidgāthā*) in the Kangyur (Toh 322 Kangyur, mdo sde, *sa,* 201b1) and Nāgārjuna's *Letter to a Friend* (*Suhṛllekha*), stanza 19 (Toh 4182 Tengyur, spring yig, *nge,* 41b3).
56. Lha Drigangpa (p. 164) quotes the first line of this *Aspiration Prayer of Nāgārjuna* (*Āryanāgārjunapraṇidhāna*).
57. As Lha Drigangpa (pp. 164–65) explains, this means that you should not rely on half-hearted teachers who make a lot of promises but don't keep them. The commentary relates how Potowa was staying at Radeng and saw a woman who was pursuing an escaped *dri* (female yak) but was unable to follow it across the river. When an old yak entered the river, the woman held on to it and thought it would lead her to the other side, but the yak stopped in the middle and did not move any farther. Potowa reflects that some teachers are just like the old yak: They make their students enter the Buddhist path, but then they stop and don't lead them to the end.
58. This refers to Nāgārjuna's *Precious Garland* 4:13.
59. According to Lha Drigangpa (p. 186) this refers to the tenets of the Vaibhāṣika school. The argument is that in the three lower forms of rebirth and in the two higher realms (the form realm and the formless realm), there can be no ripening of former deeds, because otherwise one would constantly be reborn in the same place.
60. The northern continent of Uttarakuru is omitted here because the beings there live a life in bliss and peace and do not accumulate any negative karma.
61. Lha Drigangpa (p. 187) quotes a statement by Dromtönpa that the law of karma (cause and effect) is secret, but that because he is getting old and the Buddhist teaching has decayed, he has had to teach it openly.
62. See, for example, the *Enlightenment of Vairocana, Vairocanābhisaṃbodhi,* Toh 494 Kangyur, rgyud, *tha,* 152a6.
63. Lha Drigangpa (p. 189) relates that Potowa gave these explanations with reference to Nāgārjuna's *Letter to a Friend* when he was staying at Saten Tönpa's place in Dingboche in upper Gyal.
64. When the people from Gyal and Tölung were at war, people did not cross the pass between the two regions from fear that they might be seized and killed by the enemies; in the same way, we should avoid bad deeds out of caution, even if we do not firmly believe in the law of cause and effect. In Tera there was a drought, but

nevertheless people sowed seeds, hoping that they would bear fruit; in the same way, we should do good deeds hoping for good results even if we have doubts about the law of cause and effect. See Lha Drigangpa, p. 190, and Shardong, pp. 418–19.

65. Lha Drigangpa (pp. 190–91) relates the following episodes: (1) in Drakgyap (where Potowa lived as a novice) the crows and owls carried away each other's young and killed them; (2) a snake used to eat the young of the lizard, but one day the lizard caught the snake by its neck and killed it; (3) a snake lived in the nests of the swallows, and although the birds came in great numbers, the snake wouldn't come out. One day two birds stayed on a rock near the nest and called; when the snake stuck its head out, one of the birds seized it by the neck and dropped it on the other side of the river.
66. Lha Drigangpa (p. 192) quotes Śāntideva's *Guide to the Bodhisattva Way of Life* 7:40 (Toh 3871 Tengyur, dbu ma, *la,* 21b5) in this context.
67. This is a reference to Śāntideva's *Guide to the Bodhisattva Way of Life* 4:25: "For a long time will my body burn in the unbearable fires of hell, and for a long time will my untrained mind burn in the fires of repentance."
68. Lha Drigangpa (pp. 195–96) tells the story of a monk from Vikramaśīla Monastery who stole monastic property. Because of this he was reborn as a hungry ghost with a twisted leg who lived in a cave. When some children from the city of Muken threw stones at the cave, he caught one of the children and entered the child's body. This tale is used to show that a hungry ghost, although he knows that he should not harm a child, cannot control his actions and therefore commits further harmful deeds.
69. Lha Drigangpa (p. 203) explains that according to Asaṅga the right view is gained on the level of forbearance (*bzod pa*), the fourth level of the path of application, which is the second of the five paths of Mahayana Buddhism. According to some teachers of the Kadam school, right view can already be attained during the first of the five paths, the path of accumulation.
70. Lha Drigangpa (pp. 206–7) explains these examples with reference to the *Lotus Sutra.*
71. As already noted in note 41, the three trainings (*bslab pa gsum*) are the training in wisdom, meditation, and moral discipline. Wisdom removes ignorance and therefore is the antidote that averts the original cause of the chain of dependent origination. Wisdom requires meditation, and meditation requires moral discipline.
72. Lha Drigangpa (p. 212) describes a dream of Potowa about a house with many doors; this is interpreted as a metaphor for the many possible ways to liberation.
73. Lha Drigangpa (pp. 216–17) tells how Potowa fell ill and stayed in his home region with an old friend, a spiritual teacher called Changtön, who told Potowa that despite his efforts he had had no success in his religious practice, and he asked for advice and blessing. Potowa's explanation for the lack of success was that all of us, even the buddhas, have been in the cycle of rebirth for innumerable eons. Remaining lazy is the wrong attitude, and we must make a serious effort now, in this very lifetime.
74. The four immeasurables are love, compassion, equanimity, and joy.

75. According to Lha Drigangpa (p. 229) this refers to a stanza from the first chapter of Śāntideva's *Compendium of Trainings*.
76. The Vaibhāṣika ("adherents of the [*Mahā-*]*Vibhāṣa*"), a school of the Hinayana, is a philosophical school within the Sarvāstivāda tradition that—as the name indicates—bases its views mainly on an important commentary on the Abhidharma.
77. See Lha Drigangpa pp. 229f. This work attributed to Aśvaghoṣa should not be confused with the well-known Mahayana work by the same name attributed to Maitreya. On problems related to the identification of the work attributed to Aśvaghoṣa, see Thupten Jinpa, *Mind Training*, p. 589n160 and Hanisch, "New Evidence of Aśvaghoṣa's *Sūtrālaṃkāra*."
78. The *Nāgarājabherīgāthā* is a versified *jātaka* tale in which the Buddha speaks about his and his disciples' former lives as *nāgas*, or snake-like beings.
79. According to Lha Drigangpa (p. 231) this refers to the saying: "When you give water to a friend, even the enemy will be happy; if you strike the enemy with your sword, even the friend will be afraid."
80. *Stages of Meditation I* (*Bhāvanākrama*), Toh 3915, dbu ma, *ki*, 23b5.
81. According to Lha Drigangpa (p. 232) Potowa made this statement about the yogi Sherap Dorjé.
82. As Lha Drigangpa (p. 232) explains, those practitioners whose "mind is powerful" can begin by reflecting on emptiness. They recognize that all phenomena are empty, and therefore that sentient beings suffer needlessly when they believe in the true existence of phenomena. From this thought arises compassion, and out of this develops loving kindness. See also the more elaborate explication in Shardong, pp. 533–35.
83. This idea stems from Indian animal lore: a snake poisons birds with its breath so that the birds drop into its mouth with no chance for escape. In the same way, a bodhisattva should care for all sentient beings without being able to turn away.
84. Lha Drigangpa (p. 238) gives the example of a servant who asked his master whether he wanted a hot or a cold meal. He ended up trying to provide both at the same time, and the food was merely tepid.
85. According to Lha Drigangpa (p. 239) this refers to chapter 54 of the *Marvelous Array Sutra* (*Gaṇḍavyūhasūtra*, Toh 44 Kangyur, phal chen, *a*, 309b1), where Maitreya instructs Sudhana.
86. Lha Drigangpa (pp. 240ff.) provides several stories about Atiśa and his contemporaries in which various deities confirm that the thought of awakening is the only avenue for those who want to obtain buddhahood quickly.
87. Lha Drigangpa (p. 246) tells the story of Atiśa's teacher Dharmarakṣita, who held the views of the Vaibhāṣikas and did not worship the bodhisattvas but was very compassionate. When someone was sick and needed human flesh in order to recover, he cut flesh from his thigh and gave it to him. He did feel pain because he had not attained the abilities of a bodhisattva, but in a dream Avalokiteśvara appeared to him and praised his deed. This episode is also mentioned in Eimer, *Rnam thar rgyas pa: Materialien zu einer Biographie des Atiśa*, I: 201 and II: 114.
88. In this context, "faith" refers specifically to the belief in the karmic law of cause and effect. See also Lha Drigangpa, p. 248.
89. The three spheres of activity (*'khor gsum*) are the agent, the act, and the object of

the action. To purify them means to give up the notion these are three discrete entities and to understand them as being empty.

90. This means that even if we are not fully able to live like a bodhisattva in this life, taking the bodhisattva vow is like sowing a seed that will ripen in our future lives and make us able to follow the bodhisattva practices. Lha Drigangpa (p. 252) states that, according to Atiśa, the "great seal" (*mahāmudrā*) corresponds to reaching the path of seeing (*mthong lam*).
91. The sixfold armor into six refers to a subdivision into six different aspects of the six perfections as presented in Maitreya's *Ornament of Clear Realization* (*Abhisamayālaṃkāra*), while the fourfold framework of discarding, guarding, purifying and increasing is contained in Śāntideva's *Compendium of Trainings* (*Śikṣāsamuccaya*), which is structured according to these four activities. See also Shardong, p. 603.
92. Maitreya, *Mahāyānasūtrālaṃkāra* 17:72, Toh 4020 Tengyur, sem tsam, *phi,* 26b6.
93. According to Lha Drigangpa (p. 257) this passage refers to the view of Hashang Mahayana, the Chinese teacher who, in the famous Samyé debate, maintained that awakening can be obtained in a single moment through wisdom alone and that the step-by-step practice of the other perfections is not necessary.
94. The exegetical tradition distinguishes between sutras that should not be taken literally but require interpretation (*neyārtha*), and sutras that contain the definitive meaning (*nītārtha*).
95. The seven unwholesome actions are the three unwholesome actions of the body (killing, stealing, and sexual misconduct) and four unwholesome actions of speech (lying, slander, harsh speech, and idle gossip).
96. The four instructions in the *Sutra Encouraging Nobler Intention* (*Adhyāśayasaṃcodanasūtra*) are: (1) to not gather pupils before we are mature enough, (2) to stay away from people who are not educated, (3) to reside in a remote place, and (4) to make efforts to tame our minds. Toh 69 Kangyur, dkon brtsegs, *ca*, 135a4.
97. Lha Drigangpa (p. 263) explains that just as a horse with a sore back can only carry a load when the back has been healed, people who have not yet gained mastery over themselves must first train the mind to be able to help others.
98. This refers to Ratnadāsa's *Guṇāparyantastotra.*
99. The commentary contains a longer discussion of the problem of moral transgressions that are committed out of compassion by a bodhisattva. In sum, the evaluation and the karmic effect of an action depend on the motivation (Lha Drigangpa, p. 262).
100. Here Lha Drigangpa (p. 266) repeats the story of how Atiśa's teacher Dharmarakṣita gave flesh from his thigh to a sick person.
101. Mahayana ethics are subdivided into three kinds of moral discipline: (1) the morality of abstention from misbehavior, (2) the morality of gathering virtues, and (3) the morality of acting for the welfare of other sentient beings. See, for example, the chapter on moral discipline from Asaṅga's *Bodhisattva Levels.*
102. Lha Drigangpa (p. 269) quotes stanzas 6:1 and 6:7 of Śāntideva's *Guide to the Bodhisattva Way of Life* (Toh 3871 Tengyur, dbu ma, *la*, 14b3) in this context.
103. The thought that we will have to leave all our possessions and every pleasure behind when we die will make us indifferent toward all wordly advantages. Therefore we

will be equally content with the pleasant and the unpleasant states among the eight wordly concerns. See Lha Drigangpa, pp. 270–71.

104. According to Lha Drigangpa (p. 271), this refers to stanza 29 from Nāgārjuna's *Letter to a Friend.*
105. See Lha Drigangpa, pp. 269–70.
106. The analogy is the following: Just as a treasure well hidden does not attract thieves, so the spiritual treasure of striving for liberation will not be taken away or be corrupted by others as long as the practitioner gains no fame and receives no honor or service from others; see Lha Drigangpa, p. 273.
107. A man from Domé was carrying a cup of honey mixed with butter. A bee appeared and drank to its heart's content, and when it had left, many other bees appeared and drank until the cup was empty; see Lha Drigangpa, p. 274.
108. As Lha Drigangpa (pp. 275–76) explains, the examples describe different attitudes. The first example refers to a Buddhist of the Hinayana who seeks his own liberation, the example of the mother whose son is in prison illustrates a bodhisattva who wants to save others, and the example of the burning house refers to a person who wants to escape from the cycle of rebirth, but not without saving the other sentient beings, too.
109. Lha Drigangpa (p. 278) illustrates the disadvantages of acting too hastily with a story of robbers who appeared in Semodru in Upper Gyal. One man wanted to help stop them, but when he grabbed his bow and arrow and rushed out of the house, he banged against the door frame and broke the bow. His son likewise took his own bow and ran, but he too broke his bow. The robbers escaped unharmed.
110. Lha Drigangpa (p. 278) describes how merchants from Kham prepare for a journey in such a leisurely way as though they did not want to leave at all. But when the time to depart comes, nothing can stop them, not even snowfall or enemies.
111. "The one who died at Sangphu" refers to the yogi Sherap Dorjé (see note 81).
112. Maitreya, *Mahāyānasūtrālaṃkāra* 16:3, Toh 4020 Tengyur, sem tsam, *phi*, 21a2.
113. Lha Drigangpa (p. 282) relates an episode in which Ligom Shönu Drak, an uncle of Chengawa, asked Potowa if there were another way to attain liberation than the one given here. Potowa confirmed that this is the only way.
114. This refers to stanza 61 from Nāgārjuna's *Letter to a Friend* (Toh 4182 Tengyur, spring yig, *nge*, 43b2). On the "four wheels," four circumstances conducive to Dharma practice, see the glossary.
115. The woman is asked how she is doing, and answers with a song that refers metaphorically to her happy family life, being surrounded by her son, her daughter-in-law, and her grandchild (Lha Drigangpa, p. 286). In a similar way, a person who is endowed with the four wheels has everything needed for a good spiritual life.
116. Lha Drigangpa (p. 286) quotes Potowa as saying that the four wheels (see glossary) are hard to find in Tibet. However, the commentary goes on, although geographically the "middle country" where the Buddhadharma flourishes is in India, it can also be found in Tibet, because it is located wherever people practice the Mahayana. Therefore the first of the four wheels—the appropriate place—can also be found in Tibet.
117. Lha Drigangpa (p. 288) comments that in India all activities are subject to the secular law and to the caste system, while in Tibet people have more individual autonomy, which is an advantage when practicing the Mahayana.

118. This means that the second of the four wheels—the good teacher, or noble spiritual mentor—can be encountered in Tibet in the form of the Kadam teachings.
119. Nāgārjuna, *Ratnāvalī* 2:26, Toh 4158 Tengyur, spring yig, *ge*, 111b3.
120. Maitreya, *Mahāyānasūtrālaṃkāra* 11:60, Toh 4020 Tengyur, sems tsam, *phi*, 15b4.
121. By doing this, the third of the four wheels—an aspiration prayer for the future—can be accomplished.
122. Lha Drigangpa (p. 293) quotes a stanza by Asaṅga: "Sentient beings wander in the cycle of rebirth because they are obscured and without the [necessary] causes, and so even all the victorious ones are unable [to change this]."
123. This explains how the fourth of the four wheels—accumulation of merit—can also be accomplished.
124. Śantideva, *Bodhicāryāvatāra* 7:1, 3871 Toh Tengyur, dbu ma, *la*, 230b7.
125. *Clear Differentiation of the Middle and Extremes* (*Madhāntavibhāga*) 4:17, Toh 4021 Tengyur, sem tsam, *phi*, 43b4. The five fruits, or types of results, according to Lha Drigangpa (pp. 295f.), are: (1) the ripening (of good karma), (2) power (i.e., that one is physically and mentally capable), (3) the concordant cause, (4) enhancement (of meditative concentration), and (5) the cessational results (i.e., becoming free of the five mental poisons).
126. Lha Drigangpa (p. 298) gives a much more elaborate characterization of the two kinds of meditation: (1) tranquility (*śamatha*) leads to one-pointedness and makes the meditator reach the first stage of meditative concentration; (2) insight (*vipaśyanā*), in contrast, makes the meditator reach the path of seeing, which is more difficult and can only be attained after accumulating merit in many lifetimes. Tranquility requires moral discipline, whereas insight requires erudition, because wisdom is based on knowledge. The analysis involved in insight meditation concerns topics like suffering, compassion, and emptiness.
127. Lha Drigangpa (pp. 299–300) adds several examples of the feats of accomplished meditation masters of Potowa's times.
128. This translation is based on the commentaries. According to Lha Drigangpa (p. 299), Potowa related that a man from Kham called Yeshé Bar was thought well of by everyone, but later he returned to Kham, where he practiced sorcery and thereby harmed others (see also Shardong, p. 716). Potowa commented that this man had obviously not been able to abandon his old behavior: he had had success in cultivating meditative stability, but he was not able to conquer his former afflictions. The point is that meditative stabilization alone does not free you from suffering. You must have insight as well.
129. At the end of the first chapter of Śāntideva's *Compendium of Trainings*.
130. This rendering is based on the commentary. Lha Drigangpa (pp. 301–2) relates the three stories alluded to here: (1) Someone had meditated a lot and was born as the son of a government minister. When he had grown up and become a minister himself, a yogi reminded him of his former meditation, and contemplation was born in him and he became a yogi. (2) Atiśa's teacher Ḍombhipa obtained supernatural knowledge through his encounter with Nāropa. (3) A novice had studied well with his teacher; while he was tying up his sash, a yogi appeared and reminded him of meditation, and through this he obtained supernatural faculties. The peculiar vocabulary used in the description of this scene is explained in the commentary by

Akya Yongdzin Yangchen Gawai Lodrö, *Explanation of Some Difficult Words in the Blue Compendium: The Dispeller of Darkness*, p. 480.

131. This reference is not altogether clear. The stanza here speaks of *nags sbyin*, which means "giving of a forest". Lha Drigangpa (p. 303) glosses this with *nags chags*, which looks like a variant spelling for *nag chags* ("cattle"?). Then the commentary speaks of *nags chags bud me* ("*nags chags* [and / to wit] women") and quotes Nāgārjuna's *Precious Garland* (*Ratnāvalī*) 3:59 (Toh 4158 Tengyur, spring yig, *ge*, 116b5). Here the king is told that there are various kinds of gifts, depending on the needs of the recipients—for instance, the gift of beautiful girls to those seeking a wife. (Canonical parallels of the *Precious Garland* stanza are discussed in Eda, "Freigebigkeit in Bezug auf Frauen?!") If the stanza from *The Blue Compendium* is indeed intended to refer to this stanza from the *Precious Garland*, we should read *nag sbyin* and take *nag* as a short form of *nag mo* ("woman"), as I have done here. In the present context, the quote then underpins that various means may be appropriate, depending on the practitioner.

132. Lha Drigangpa (p. 305) describes how the bird teases the dog by always flying a little farther away and in the end disappears, leaving the frustrated dog behind. The example is also found in Potowa's *Dharma Exemplified*.

133. In the technical sense, the "summit of existence" is the fourth of the four formless attainments (*snyoms 'jug*, Skt. *samāpatti*), where the meditator abides with a one-pointed mind, neither with nor without conceptions (see Shardong, p. 728).

134. Someone who does not accept that phenomena are empty will take them as independently existing entities, whereas someone who falls into the other extreme will believe that things like the law of karma and compassion toward all sentient beings are nonexistent, and thus that it does not matter how we act or whether we are compassionate. If a practitioner first gets used to all the preliminary steps of the Buddhist path, these two errors will not occur. The aspect of method here consists of all the preliminary steps of the path and the first five of the six perfections of a bodhisattva.

135. Lha Drigangpa (pp. 314–15) tells the following stories: (1) A king had a beautiful wife. While he was away fighting a war against a neighboring kingdom, his wife died. The clever ministers found a way to break the sad news to the king without disturbing him too much: They sent a messenger to tell the king that the queen had got an abscess on her eyebrow. A little later, another messenger told him that the abscess had become much bigger, and so on. When the king was told that the whole head of his wife had become one big sore, he wished that she might die. When he was finally told that the queen had died, he was not distressed about this news. (2) When cattle or horses are trained to carry a load, this is done gradually by giving them progressively more to carry. (3) The third example is a well-known story from the *Lotus Sutra* where a father is separated from his son. The father becomes a wealthy man. The son, poor and destitute, happens to come to the city where the father lives. The father realizes that his son would be scared should he reveal to him that he is his father. Therefore he hires him to do some menial work for him, and gradually the son takes over more and more responsibilities. Only after preparing him in this way does the father finally disclose his identity and tell the son that he is his proper heir. (4) Someone who is afraid of entering the sea is introduced to it

gradually by going deeper and deeper into the water, until he can enter it without being afraid.

136. Lha Drigangpa (p. 316) quotes a similar statement from Nāgārjuna's *Precious Garland* 2:1–2 and 3:76.

137. Chapter 14 of Śāntideva's *Compendium of Trainings* (*Śikṣāsamuccaya*) quotes a long passage from the *Pitāputrasamāgamasūtra*, Toh 60 Kangyur, dkon brtsegs, *nga*, 127b4. Here, different kinds of phenomena are analyzed to show that everything is ultimately empty.

138. Lha Drigangpa (pp. 317–18) describes how three people from the eastern province of Kham found their way to the central province of Ü even though they had never traveled there before. They knew that they had to travel west, so each evening at sunset they placed their staff on the ground, pointing to the west, and in the morning they went where the staff pointed. In this way they finally reached Ü.

139. This refers to the following parable: A king had a bad minister. When they were staying on the rooftop of a fortress, a magician created an illusory lake with a boat and a ferryman. Thinking he was embarking on the boat, the minister instead fell from the rooftop. The lake corresponds to samsara, the one embarking on the boat to the Buddhist practitioner, the boat to the Buddhist practices, the ferryman to the teacher, and reaching the other shore to nirvana. On the ultimate level of truth, however, none of these is real (Lha Drigangpa p. 321, see also Potowa's *Dharma Exemplified*).

140. As Lha Drigangpa (p. 321) explains, we say that the sky has a form, like being round or having four directions. But when we examine it properly, the sky has no shape at all.

141. Nāgārjuna, *Ratnāvalī* 2:5, Toh 4158 Tengyur, spring yig, *ge*, 110b7. In commenting on this stanza, Lha Drigangpa (p. 328) explains that we first examine whether phenomena do exist; when we find nothing, then we also cannot meaningfully claim that there is something nonexistent.

142. A woman in Radeng said while meditating on herself in the form of Avalokiteśvara: "My head is adorned by the Lord of the Victorious Ones, and my body is as white as the snow mountains." Her husband replied: "What about this mole? Your body is not really white." Like the husband, we may see ourselves as imperfect while following the steps of the Buddhist path, but once we have completed the path, we will realize that the true nature of all beings and all phenomena is the same and does not have different characteristics (Lha Drigangpa, p. 329).

143. As in the examples of the magician and the minister mentioned above (see note 139) and of a person with an eye disease, wrong views are not dispelled as long as we regard things from the level of relative truth. When we regard things from the level of ultimate truth, the wrong views are gone, so there is nothing that needs removing.

144. Once when a man wanted to cross a river, the water appeared to him to be flowing uphill. A person on the opposite shore called out, "It does not really do so." Believing that, the man thought, "I must be deluded by some poisonous vapor from the water. Water can't flow uphill." Thus he safely crossed the river. Here the man is like the beginning practitioner; his heeding the advice of the person on the other shore is like relying on the scriptures; and the thought that water cannot run uphill is relying on reasoning (Lha Drigangpa, pp. 334–35).

145. This translation follows the Beijing 1991 edition, which reads *rang la rang gnas*, "we rest in ourselves." The commentary by Lha Drigangpa (p. 335), however, suggests the reading *rang la rang gnod*, "we have harmed ourselves," explaining that when we reach the path of seeing, we will feel ashamed of our former behavior and understand that we have harmed ourselves before. Thupten Jinpa's Tibetan edition emends the line to *rang la rang gnong*, "we feel ashamed."
146. This refers to the philosophical school that maintains that awakening can be attained in a single instant. The question of sudden or gradual enlightenment was discussed in a debate at Samyé Monastery at the end of the eighth century between the Chinese teacher Hashang Mahayana, who argued for sudden awakening, and the Indian scholar Kamalaśīla, who argued for a gradual approach. According to Tibetan tradition, the Tibetan judges, headed by King Trisong Detsen himself, declared Kamalaśīla the winner of the debate. Lha Drigangpa (pp. 336ff.) gives an interesting description of this famous debate. See also Eimer, "Eine frühe Quelle zur literarischen Tradition über die 'Debatte von Bsam yas.'"
147. Setsun was a teacher Dromtönpa studied with in Kham before going to western Tibet and meeting Atiśa.
148. This is a reference to the nirvana of the arhats, which according to the Mahayana is not full awakening. A śrāvaka or pratyekabuddha arhat must re-enter the cycle of rebirths and follow the bodhisattva path in order to attain full awakening, and thus the state of cessation of the afflictions is characterized here as a fetter that holds us back from buddhahood.
149. As it says in the *Questions of Ratnacūḍa Sutra*, just as a painter who paints a universal monarch (*cakravartin*) must pay attention to every detail in order to make the painting complete, so the Buddhist practitioner must take care to combine all the necessary components. See Lha Drigangpa, p. 339.
150. The characteristics of samsaric existence are that it is impermanent, that it entails suffering, and that it is without a self.
151. As Lha Drigangpa (pp. 340–41) explains, the result of the path are the two bodies: a buddha's Dharma body (*dharmakāya*), which is not bound to samsara, and a buddha's form body (*rūpakāya*), which is not bound to nirvana. This state is called "non-abiding" or "nonsituated nirvana" (*apratiṣṭhita-nirvāṇa*).
152. These three examples from the scriptures show that a bodhisattva does not abandon the beings still suffering in samsara. When a father reaches the city after a dangerous journey, he will remember his son who is still in the wilderness and retrieve him. Someone who has escaped a burning house will return to save his children. When a mother sees that her son has fallen into a cesspit, she will jump into it to rescue him.
153. Lha Drigangpa (p. 346) gives some examples for the various names of this state, like "being endowed with the essence of emptiness and compassion," "loving kindness without conceptions," "identity of appearences and emptiness," "method and wisdom combined," and so on.
154. *Entering the Middle Way* (*Madhyamakāvatāra*) 1:8, Toh 3861 Tengyur, dbu ma, *'a*, 202a1, and its autocommentary *Madhyamakāvatārabhāṣya*, Toh 3862 Tengyur, dbu ma, *'a*, 224b3.
155. As Lha Drigangpa (pp. 346–47) states, it has been claimed that the śrāvakas only realize that the person does not possess a self, whereas the adherents of Mahayana realize that both person and phenomena are without a self. However, in reality the

śrāvakas do know about both aspects of selflessness. On the first six of the bodhisattva levels, there is still the risk of falling into the attitude of a śrāvaka or pratyekabuddha. From the seventh level on, a bodhisattva is no longer subject to this risk.

156. The following passage is an exegesis of Atiśa's *Penetrating the Two Truths* (*Satyadvayāvatāra*), Toh 3902 Tengyur, dbu ma, *a*, 72a3.
157. Lha Drigangpa (p. 350) mentions in this context that Atiśa studied with the Cittamātra, or Yogācāra, teacher Serlingpa (who belonged to the true-aspectarian [*rnam bden*] school of Cittamātra), the tantra teacher Śāntipa (who belonged to the false-aspectarian [*rnam rdzun*] school of Cittamātra), and the Madhyamaka teachers Kusali and Avadhūtipa. The Kadampas as well as their Gelukpa successors philosophically favor the Madhyamaka theory of the two levels of truth but combine it with a Yogācāra approach to practice.
158. This is, as Lha Driganpa points out, a reference to Ratnākaraśānti's *Instructions on Contemplating the Perfection of Wisdom* (*Prajñāpāramitābhāvanopadeśa*), where he refutes Haribhadra's Madhyamaka interpretation of the *Perfection of Wisdom in Eight Thousand Lines*.
159. According to the Svātantrika view of the three paṇdits from eastern India (Jñānagarbha, Śāntarakṣita, and Kamalaśīla), there is a "nominal ultimate," with an object and a perceiver, and an "actual ultimate," where both the object and the perceiver are understood to be empty.
160. See stanza 2 of Atiśa's *Penetrating the Two Truths*. The moon in the water is one of several philosophical similes illustrating the illusory nature of the perception of a self: When the moon is reflected in water it looks real, but it will disappear if the water is stirred. Likewise, the notion of a self will disappear when examined with discriminating insight.
161. Ibid., stanza 3.
162. Ibid., stanza 19.
163. These two lines are quoted from Śāntideva's *Guide to the Bodhisattva Way of Life* 9:15 (Toh 3871 Tengyur, dbu ma, *la*, 31b1) and are therefore in a seven-syllable meter, not in the usual eight-syllable meter of Dölpa Rinpoché's verses. Śāntideva's opponents have argued that if there are two levels of truth, then it would follow that the Buddha has entered nirvana according to the ultimate truth, but on the level of relative truth he would still be in samsara, and therefore there would be no benefit in achieving enlightenment. Śāntideva answers that when the causes and conditions for existence have ceased, the Buddha will not be part of samsara any more. The whole following passage of Dölpa Rinpoché's versification of Potowa's teachings is closely related to chapter 9 of Śāntideva's work.
164. The view of the śrāvakas is that existence ceases in nirvana, like an oil lamp that is extinguished when the oil has been consumed. Someone who reaches this state of *parinirvāṇa*, or complete liberation, ceases to act in the world.
165. According to Lha Drigangpa (p. 358), this refers to Śāntideva's *Guide to the Bodhisattva Way of Life* 9:34, which Lha Drigangpa suggests can be read as stating that even the continuity of wisdom ceases at the time of buddhahood. The issue of whether or not there is a continuity of wisdom once one has attained buddhahood appears to have been an important question for Tibetan thinkers of this period.
166. This is a reference to Śāntideva's *Guide to the Bodhisattva Way of Life* 9:37–38: If a

healer has erected a pole, empowering it with a Garuḍa charm against venom, and the healer then dies, the pole will still heal afflicted beings after his death.

167. According to Lha Drigangpa (p. 361) *phag mgo* ("pig's head") is a medical treatment, and *byi tshe* is probably identical to the medical plant *byi tsher*, which could be translated literally as "mouse thorn." Eimer's edition of a parallel passage in Atiśa's biography (see next note) has two different readings: *byi tshe* (as in our text) and *rtsi rtsi* (= *tsi tsi*, "mouse").
168. Lha Drigangpa (p. 361) describes how Naljorpa lit Atiśa's lamp when it had been extinguished and mended the roof when it was leaking. Atiśa asked him how this was done and wondered, "How come that the master did not do that!" This episode has an interesting parallel in Atiśa's biography, where it is Dromtönpa who lights Atiśa's lamp; see Eimer, *Rnam thar rgyas pa*, paragraph 087 (vol. I, pp. 178–79, and vol. II, p. 62).
169. This heading has been added for the sake of clarity; none is given in the editions of Lha Drigangpa's commentary.
170. "Never present your neck to anyone" means that you should not be too close with others; otherwise you will be at their mercy, like a dog that is grabbed by the throat (see Lha Drigangpa, p. 365).
171. According to traditional belief, leprosy is caused by evil spirits who could do harm to the practitioner. It is also sometimes considered a consequence of bad karma or immoral behavior and thus an indicator of a bad character.
172. Lha Drigangpa's commentary (p. 368) reads *ran tshod 'phral gzung* ("you must leave at the right time") instead of *rang tshod 'phral gzung* ("you should immediately understand your situation") in Dölpa's root verses. Both expressions make sense, but I prefer the reading of the commentary.
173. According to Lha Drigangpa (p. 368) this means that the donor and the monk will have the same feelings, and therefore there will be no spiritual progress for the renunciate.
174. As Lha Drigangpa (p. 370) explains, the suffering of the Buddhist path is small compared to the endless and needless suffering of the beings who wander in samsara. With respect to hardships, we should avoid the extremes; as beginners, we need not perform dramatic feats like sacrificing our lives. It is enough to begin with the minor hardships of an ascetic lifestyle.
175. Generosity is mentioned here as an example of the perfections in general.
176. The text reads *khad nas tshod blangs* ("having taken measure by degrees"), whereas Lha Drigangpa (p. 374) reads *khong nas tshod blangs* ("having measured [our abilities] within").
177. Lha Drigangpa (pp. 376–77) relates a story about a father who gave his wealth to his eldest son, while to his youngest he gave the instruction to ask old people for advice when necessary. By doing so, the younger son overcame many obstacles during his adventures and finally wed the queen of the country.
178. A king had an eye disease, and his physician told him that he could only be cured by the milk of a woman who had never slept with any man but her husband. The king offered a reward if such a woman would turn up. A woman said to her husband: "I'm like that, so I'll get the reward!" The husband asked his friend what to do, and the friend advised him to tell the wife exactly the opposite. So the man told his wife: "You won't get the reward because it requires a woman who has slept

with a hundred men." She said: "I've done that—I'll get it!" But when she counted, she only came up with ninety-nine. Because the husband had asked his friend, the woman did not go to the king and so did not get punished by the king for telling lies (Lha Drigangpa, pp. 377–78).

179. For the four wheels, see the glossary.
180. In identifying these qualities of a noble person (ārya), Lha Driganpa (p.333) cites Maitreya's *Ornament of Mahayana Sutras* 13:8, where, in fact, five but not six such qualities are listed: (1) possessing vast learning, (2) seeing the truth, (3) being skilled in speech, (4) being compassionate, and (5) having self-confidence. Lha Drigangpa adds being worthy of honor by others as the seventh (actually the sixth) quality. Of these, he states, having a decisive view of emptiness that perceives the truth of all phenomena and being compassionate are the two principal ones.
181. The four means of attraction are (1) giving what others need, (2) speaking pleasantly, (3) working for the benefit of others, and (4) acting according to one's words. See glossary.
182. The four powers are (1) *the power of remorse*, to feel remorse for the harmful deed, (2) *the power of renouncing the deed*, to promise not to do the harmful deed again, (3) *the power of the basis*, to take refuge in an object of refuge and generate the thought of awakening, and (4) *the power of the antidote*, to counteract the harmful deeds through our beneficial actions. Some authors list the four powers in a different order.
183. The four root transgressions for a monk are taking life, taking what is not given, sexual misconduct, and making false claims about one's spiritual attainments.
184. Lha Drigangpa (p. 409) specifies that there are five kinds of people who possess this strength: those who (1) practice tantra, (2) have accomplished the generation stage (in meditation), (3) have become firm in perceiving phenomena as empty, (4) are endowed with love and compassion and the thought of awakening, and (5) are filled with respect for their lama. The commentary continues with a number of stories about early Kadampa masters who subdued evil spirits when they were staying in solitary places such as mountain caves.
185. This heading has been added for the sake of clarity.
186. This image is taken from Śāntideva's *Guide to the Bodhisattva Way of Life* 5:48ff.
187. This refers to a quotation from the *Candraprabha Sutra*, more commonly known as the *King of Meditation Sutra* (*Samādhirājasūtra*, Toh 127 Kangyur, mdo sde, *da*, 85b3), in chapter 5 of Śāntideva's *Compendium of Trainings*.
188. This refers to stanza 20 of Nāgārjuna's *Letter to a Friend*, Toh 4182 Tengyur, spring yig, *nge*, 41b4.
189. Lha Drigangpa (p. 421) tells the story of a man who said, "Even if I am reborn as a camel, won't this have an end at some point?" In the same way, people think, "Even if I am reborn in hell, won't this be over at some point?"
190. Lha Drigangpa (p. 422) elaborates that it is particularly important to never have a harmful or disrespectful attitude toward a bodhisattva, and since we cannot know in which form a bodhisattva may appear, we must generally be full of respect toward all living beings and regard them as teachers.
191. Ami Thargyal said: "What are the borders of Tibet?" Dromtönpa said: "Thargyal should forget about the borders of Tibet and examine his own boundaries!" (Lha Drigangpa, p. 423).

192. This heading has been added for the sake of clarity.
193. This refers to a passage from chapter 4 of Śāntideva's *Compendium of Training* (*Śikṣāsamuccaya*) Toh 3940 Tengyur, dbu ma, *khi*, 58a2. The *Extensive Compendium of All Dharma* and *Lotus Sutra* are quoted to the effect that in reality all the different vehicles are one and the same and have the same purpose (the *ekayāna* or "one-vehicle" point of view).
194. The seven transgressions are those committed with body and speech (see note 95 above); the ten transgressions include the three committed with the mind.
195. This and the following verses refer to a passage from the *Sutra on Going to Laṅka* (*Laṅkāvatārasūtra*); see Lha Drigangpa, pp. 426–27.
196. In chapter 8 of Śāntideva's *Compendium of Trainings* (*Śikṣāsamuccaya*), Toh 3940 Tengyur, dbu ma, *khi*, 53a4.
197. According to Lha Drigangpa (pp. 431–32) this is what Atiśa said to Dromtönpa, who therefore founded the monastery of Radeng.
198. For the four instructions in the *Adhyāśayasaṃcodanasūtra*, see note 96 above.
199. Śāntideva, *Śikṣāsamuccaya*, chapter 4; Toh 3940 Tengyur, dbu ma, *khi*, 11a7.
200. When Potowa was teaching in Trak and Khartok, there were beggars sitting around the assembled Sangha who defended the hut against dogs, brought wood and leaves to feed the fire, and so on (Lha Drigangpa, pp. 433–34).
201. Śāntideva, *Compendium of Trainings* (*Śikṣāsamuccaya*), chapter 4, Toh Toh 3940 Tengyur, dbu ma, *khi*, 34a6.
202. Maitreya, *Ornament of Mahayana Sutras* 12:15, Toh 4020 Tengyur, sems tsam, *phi*, 13b6.
203. Śāntideva's *Guide to the Bodhisattva Way of Life* 5:8.
204. The word *bgegs* used here signifies both an obstruction and an evil spirit that causes obstacles. The following passage deals with both.
205. The teacher Sherap Yungdrung was a coward. One evening the light of a butter lamp in the temple fell on a broom. Sherap Yungdrung thought that it was a ghost and screamed. Some other monks came to his assistance and discovered what the "ghost" really was (Lha Drigangpa, p. 438). The next two anecdotes run along similar lines.
206. This refers to the hope of having good meditation experiences, such as seeing one's meditation deity, and to the fear that demons and evil spirits might appear.
207. According to Lha Drigangpa (pp. 439–40), this refers to a passage from the *Questions of Gaganagañja Sutra* (*Gaganagañjaparipṛcchāsūtra*).
208. An old monk from Shangshung came to Radeng Monastery and asked, "Whom must I greet respectfully in this monastery?" He was sent from one monk to the other and saluted everyone, and finally he was even sent to greet the dogs.
209. This refers to a quotation from the *Questions of the Layman Ugra Sutra* (*Gṛhapatyugraparipṛcchāsūtra*) in chapter 11 of Śāntideva's *Compendium of Trainings*.
210. The ten religious actions are: (1) writing Buddhist texts, (2) religious worship, (3) generosity, (4) listening to the Dharma, (5) memorizing it, (6) reading it, (7) preaching, (8) recitation, (9) thinking about the Dharma, and (10) meditating on it.
211. Maitreya, *Mahāyānasūtrālaṃkāra* 11:6, Toh 4020 Tengyur, sems tsam, *phi*, 12b4.
212. The king of Brisha had a non-Buddhist teacher who taught that if he killed human beings he would gain subjects, and if he killed cattle he would gain wealth. The king

had done many meritorious deeds and through this merit was able to recognize this view to be wrong (Lha Drigangpa, p. 450).

213. Literally "one who has adopted Avalokiteśara's habit." Lha Drigangpa (pp. 450–51) explains that this person was a non-Buddhist who had taken an oath to wear long hair. When he became a Buddhist, he saw that Avalokiteśvara was wearing long hair, so he decided not to cut his hair either.
214. These stories can be found in the Mūlasarvāstivāda Vinaya and in the *Divyāvadāna* anthology; see Andy Rotman's translation in *Divine Stories: Divyāvadāna* (Boston: Wisdom Publications). The well-known story of Cūḍapantha, who overcomes his slow intellect, is in volume 2 (forthcoming), and the tale of Svāgata, who overcomes his ill-fatedness, is in volume 1 (2008: 289–323).
215. This is what the root text seems to say. The respective passage in the commentary, however, says that if not all the monks can come, they can also appoint a single monk who receives the offerings (see Lha Drigangpa, p. 545).
216. This heading has been added for the sake of clarity.
217. Lha Drigangpa (p. 458) explains that this has been said with respect to persons with particularly sharp mental faculties, who are able to use the tantric practices as a fast method for reaching liberation.
218. The word "league" (*yojana*, a distance of several miles) has been added from the commentary (Lha Drigangpa, p. 459), where it is mentioned that he travels the distance of five hundred *yojana* to the east in order to meet his teacher.
219. This passage alludes to the legend of Sadāprarudita contained in the *Perfection of Wisdom in Eight Thousand Lines* (*Aṣṭasāhasrikāprajñāpāramitā*) and partly quoted in chapter 2 of Śāntideva's *Compendium of Trainings*. A voice from the sky told him that he must learn the perfection of wisdom from the bodhisattva Dharmodgata who would be his spiritual mentor. Sadāprarudita sacrificed his own flesh to be able to receive Dharmodgata's instructions and was later miraculously restored to wholeness.

Notes to Ornament of Precious Liberation

1. Youthful Mañjuśrī—Mañjuśrī Kumārabhuta—is one of the names of the great bodhisattva Mañjuśrī. It signifies his status as a tenth-level bodhisattva: one of those who remain ever young, not "aging" into full buddhahood.
2. The Palpung edition has, "When will delusion be fully clarified? It will be clarified when highest enlightenment is reached."
3. These boldface synopses are an important part of the text. They are memorized by students as a way of recollecting its subject matter. Each of the six headings in this opening synopsis constitutes a chapter of the book, with the exception of the fourth, which is spread over sixteen chapters.
4. The text says "lesser beings," but since that is comparing them with exalted beings, such as buddhas and realized bodhisattvas, the meaning is that they are regular, worldly beings.
5. *Samādhirājasūtra*, Toh 127 Kangyur, mdo sde, *da*, 32a7.
6. *Mahāparinirvāṇasūtra* (shorter version), Toh 120 Kangyur, mdo sde, *tha*, 112a4.
7. *Mahāparinirvāṇasūtra* (longer version), Toh 119 Kangyur, mdo sde, *tha*, 111b1.
8. Maitreya, *Mahāyānasūtrālaṃkāra* 10:37, Toh 4020 Tengyur, sems tsam, *phi*, 10a5.

9. Maitreya, *Uttaratantra* 1:27, Toh 4024 Tengyur, sems tsam, *phi*, 56a2.
10. Asaṅga's discussion of the six shortcomings and how the convergence of them deprives one of the spiritual potential is found in his *Śrāvaka Levels* (*Śrāvakabhūmi*), Toh 4036. Tengyur, sem stam, *dzi*, 7b5. It is difficult to determine whether Gampopa is here citing from another source or versifying this same citation.
11. Maitreya, *Mahāyānasūtrālaṃkāra* 4:11, Toh 4020 Tengyur, sems tsam, *phi*, 4a6.
12. *Mahākaruṇāpuṇḍarīkasūtra*, Toh 111 Kangyur, mdo sde, *cha*, 87a7.
13. The source of this quote has not been identified.
14. The source of this quote has not been identified.
15. Jambudvīpa in this context refers principally to India.
16. *Saddharmapuṇḍarīkasūtra*, Toh 113 Kangyur, mdo sde, *ja*, 54b1.
17. Ibid., 75a3.
18. The term *bodhicitta*, or "thought of awakening," can be used to describe the aspiration of the Hinayana paths. When such is the case, the more familiar bodhicitta of the bodhisattva is known as *great bodhicitta*.
19. *Saddharmapuṇḍarīkasūtra*, Toh 113 Kangyur, mdo sde, *ja*, 40b1.
20. These synonyms are very helpful in understanding the connotations of *rigs*, the Tibetan translation of the Sanskrit term *gotra*. It is a *potential* one is born with, if that term is seen through its meaning of "family," remembering that caste and profession were so closely linked to birth family. It is like a *seed*, containing from the outset the genetic information of its fruit; it is like the one prime *element* permeating all existence; and it is the *essential nature* of all things, once the veil of illusions has fallen.
21. This is the first mention of the two obscurations (*avaraṇa*) in this text, the afflictions obscuration (*kleśāvaraṇa*) and the knowledge obscuration (*jñeyāvaraṇa*).
22. The Palpung edition has "a lack of care."
23. *Daśadharmakasūtra*, Toh 53 Kangyur, dkon brtsegs, *kha*, 167b7.
24. Ibid., 168a1.
25. Maitreya, *Mahāyānasūtrālaṃkāra*, Toh 4020 Tengyur, sems tsam, *phi*, 4a3.
26. Prajñākaramati, *Commentary on the Guide to the Bodhisattva Way of Life* (*Bodhicaryāvatārapañjikā*), Toh 3872 Tengyur, mdo 'grel, *la*, 45b5.
27. The Tibetan *ngo tsha* signifies a personal sense of dignity that makes you ashamed of yourself for committing unworthy actions, whereas a respect for others (*khrel*) signifies being concerned about what others will think or say.
28. The Palpung and Beijing editions say, "This makes them unsuited for a vigorous quest for virtue."
29. Śāntideva, *Bodhicaryāvatāra* 6:21, Toh 3871 Tengyur, dbu ma, *la*, 14a7.
30. Asaṅga, *Śrāvaka Levels* (*Śrāvakabhūmi*), Toh 4036 Tengyur, sems tsam, *dzi*, 3b4.
31. The "actions of immediate consequence" are so called because they cause you to be reborn immediately in the lower realms after death, without passing through the intermediate state (*bardo*) as most people do.
32. "Others" here implies benefactors who help create appropriate material circumstances.
33. *Bodhisattvapiṭaka*, Toh 56 Kangyur, dkon brtsegs, *ga*, 67b5.
34. *Mahākaruṇāpuṇḍarīkasūtra*, Toh 111 Kangyur, mdo sde, *cha*, 69a2.
35. *Gaṇḍavyūhasūtra*, Toh 44 Kangyur, phal chen, *ga*, 381a7.
36. Śāntideva, *Bodhicaryāvatāra* 1:4a, Toh 3871 Tengyur, dbu ma, *la*, 1a5.

37. Ibid. 4:20, 8b6.
38. *Host of Flowers Sutra* (*Kusumasaṃcayasūtra*), Toh 266 Kangyur, mdo sde, *'a*, 302a7.
39. Śāntideva, *Bodhicaryāvatāra* 1:4b, Toh 3871 Tengyur, dbu ma, *la*, 1a5.
40. The term *puruṣa* had great significance in the other religions of India and was therefore a loaded term. This is the Buddhist way of appropriating it.
41. Atiśa, *Bodhipathapradīpa* verse 2ab, Toh 3947 Tengyur, dbu ma, *khi*, 238b1.
42. Ibid. verse 3, 238b1.
43. Ibid. verse 4, 238b1.
44. Ibid. verse 5, 238b2.
45. Candragomin, *Letter to a Student* (*Śiṣyalekha*) verse 64, Toh 4183 Tengyur, spring yig, *nge*, 50a2. *Nāgas* are generally of serpentine form but possess powers that ordinary snakes do not. *Kiṃnaras* are half-human, half-horse beings. *Uragas*—literally, those that "slide on their bellies"—are one of the eight classes of spirits.
46. Śāntideva, *Bodhicaryāvatāra* 2:58, Toh 3871 Tengyur, dbu ma, *la*, 6a6.
47. Ibid. 7:14, 20b4.
48. The source of this quote has not been identified.
49. Śāntideva, *Guide to the Bodhisattva Way of Life* (*Bodhicaryāvatāra*) 5:66, Toh 3871 Tengyur, dbu ma, *la*, 12b6.
50. *Daśadharmakasūtra*, Toh 53 Kangyur, dkon brtsegs, *kha*, 166a3.
51. *Avataṃsakasūtra*, Toh 44 Kangyur, phal chen, *ka*, 90b5.
52. *Lalitavistarasūtra*, Toh 95 Kangyur, mdo sde, *kha*, 49b5.
53. The desire realm (Skt. *kamadhātu*, Tib. *'dod khams*) is one of the three realms of existence (see glossary). It is often translated literally as "desire realm," on account of the Tibetan *'dod*, and it can be explained in that way—as a domain where beings have much desire. However, there is another explanation in which *'dod* is short for *'dod pa'i yon tan* ("fields of the senses"), since its beings' experiences are principally those of the five sense consciousnesses. Another translation would therefore be "sensorial realms."
54. The Tibetan term translated here as "admiration" is *dang ba*. The term literally connotes "clarity" but can also mean "joy," because a person has joyful confidence in the Three Jewels and so forth. When used in a more Vajrayana context of faith due to clear realization that confirms the value of the Three Jewels, the term can also mean "lucidity."
55. Vasubandhu, *Abhidharmakośabhāṣyam*, Toh 4090 Tengyur, mngon pa, *ku*, 64a1.
56. Nāgārjuna, *Ratnāvalī* 1:6, Toh 4158 Tengyur, spring yig, *ge*, 107a5.
57. *Ratnolkānāmadhāraṇīsūtra*, Toh 145 Kangyur, mdo sde, *pa*, 63b5.
58. *Bodhisattvapiṭaka*, Toh 56 Kangyur, dkon brtsegs, *ga*, 186a1.
59. *Ratnaguṇasaṃcayagāthā*, Toh 13 Kangyur, sher phyin, *ka*, 9a6.
60. *Aṣṭasāhasrikāprajñāpāramitā*, Toh 12 Kangyur, sher phyin, *ka*, 216b1.
61. The *Instructions for Liberation of Śrī Saṃbhava* is found in the *Flower Ornament Sutra* (*Avataṃsakasūtra*), Toh 44 Kangyur, phal chen, ā, 286a5.
62. Śāntideva, *Guide to the Bodhisattva Way of Life* (*Bodhicaryāvatāra*) 5:28, Toh 3871 Tengyur, dbu ma, *la*, 11a6.
63. *Flower Ornament Sutra* (*Avataṃsakasūtra*), Toh 44 Kangyur, phal chen, ā, 284b3.

64. The *Instructions for Liberation of Upāsikā Acalā* is found in the *Flower Ornament Sutra* (*Avataṃsakasūtra*), Toh 44 Kangyur, phal chen, ā, 36b3.
65. Indrabhūti, *Achieving Pristine Awareness* (*Jñānasiddhisādhanopāyikā*), Toh 2219 Tengyur, rgyud 'grel, *wi*, 51a2.
66. *Gaṇḍavyūhasūtra*, Toh 44 Kangyur, phal chen, *a*, 286a7.
67. Asaṅga, *Bodhisattvabhūmi*, Toh 4037 Tengyur, sems tsam, *wi*, 127a3.
68. Maitreya, *Mahāyānasūtrālaṃkāra* 15:5, Toh 4020 Tengyur, sems tsam, *phi*, 16b6.
69. Śāntideva, *Bodhicaryāvatāra* 5:102, Toh 3871 Tengyur, dbu ma, *la*, 14a5.
70. *Gaṇḍavyūhasūtra*, Toh 44 Kangyur, phal chen, *a*, 305a3.
71. Ibid., 343a2.
72. *Perfection of Wisdom in Eight Thousand Lines* (*Aṣṭasāhasrikāprajñāpāramitā*), Toh 12 Kangyur, sher phyin, *ka*, 261a3.
73. The bodhisattva Sudhana was sent to King Anala to learn compassion, but when he arrived, he saw what seemed to be the king judging and punishing evildoers mercilessly. Thus he initially doubted the king's bodhisattva qualities. However, he listened to his inner voice and went to the king, who then took him to wonderful paradises and explained that he could manifest visions of the worst punishments or the greatest rewards in order to instill confidence in moral discipline in his subjects.
74. Maitreya, *Mahāyānasūtrālaṃkāra*, Toh 4020 Tengyur, sems tsam, *phi*, 25b4.
75. *Flower Ornament Sutra* (*Avataṃsakasūtra*), Toh 44 Kangyur, phal chen, ā, 288b1.
76. These three "faults of the container" refer respectively to being unreceptive, nonretentive, or soiled by the afflictions.
77. *Flower Ornament Sutra* (*Avataṃsakasūtra*), Toh 44 Kangyur, phal chen, ā, 285a2.
78. *Aṣṭasāhasrikāprajñāpāramitā*, Toh 12 Kangyur, sher phyin, *ka*, 267b3.
79. This is the general synopsis for part IV of the text, and it covers the sixteen chapters to come, each of which has its own synopsis and sometimes consists of internal subchapters, each having its own synopsis. The first teaching mentioned here (on impermanence) is addressed below in the present chapter, the second teaching (on suffering and karma) is covered in chapters 5 and 6, the third teaching (on love and compassion) in chapter 7, and the fourth teaching (on the bodhisattva path) in chapters 8–19.
80. The four remedies that follow are repeated as subheadings for individual sections below.
81. *Gaṇḍavyūhasūtra* (chapter 45 in the *Flower Ornament Sutra*), Toh 44 Kangyur, phal chen, ā, 284b2.
82. *White Lotus of Great Compassion Sutra* (*Mahākaruṇāpuṇḍarīkasūtra*), Toh 111 Kangyur, mdo sde, *cha*, 75a6.
83. *Udānavarga* 1:22, Toh 326 Kangyur, *sa*, 209b6.
84. Vasubandhu, *Abhidharmakośa* 3:102, Toh 4089 Tengyur, mngon pa, *ku*, 10b6.
85. Ibid. 3:101, 10b4.
86. *Vīradattagṛhapatiparipṛcchāsūtra*, Toh 72 Kangyur, dkon brtsegs, *ca*, 201b2.
87. *Lalitavistarasūtra*, Toh 95 Kangyur, mdo sde, *kha*, 88a2.
88. Śāntideva, *Bodhicaryāvatāra* 2:39, Toh 3871 Tengyur, dbu ma, *la*, 5b2.
89. Ibid. 2:35, 5a6.
90. *Eliminating Suffering* (*Śokavinodana*), Toh 4177 Tengyur, spring yig, *nge*, 33a6.
91. "Seers of truth" (Skt. *ṛṣi*, Tib. *drang srong*) were highly accomplished meditators of

India, renowned for their supernatural abilities. In early times, the rishis and rishikas (female rishis) were poet-seers; in later times, their name came to mean those who spoke only the truth. Straightforwardness and truthfulness are conveyed by the Tibetan translation.

92. Aśvaghoṣa, *Eliminating Suffering* (*Śokavinodana*), Toh 4177 Tengyur, spring yig, *nge*, 33a6.
93. *Udānavarga* 1:25, Toh 326 Kangyur, mdo sde, *sa*, 210a1.
94. Aśvaghoṣa, *Eliminating Suffering* (*Śokavinodana*), Toh 4177 Tengyur, spring yig, *nge*, 33b3. The plantain has no heartwood. Sentient beings have no single enduring, central component guaranteeing life.
95. *Udānavarga* 1:3; Toh 326 Kangyur, mdo sde, *sa*, 209a2.
96. *Crown Jewel Dhāraṇī Sutra* (*Ratnaketudhāraṇīsūtra*), Toh 138 Kangyur, mdo sde, *na*, 211b3.
97. *Ratnaketudhāraṇīsūtra*, Toh 138 Kangyur, mdo sde, *na*, 211b3.
98. *Udānavarga* 1:14, Toh 326 Kangyur, mdo sde, *sa*, 210a6.
99. The source of this citation has not been located.
100. *Udānavarga* 1:14, Toh 326 Kangyur, mdo sde, *sa*, 209b1.
101. Vasubandhu, *Abhidharmakośa* 3:78, Toh 4089 Tengyur, mngon pa, *ku*, 9b7. The "end" and "beginning" are the low points and high points of lifespan in our world system over a cosmic eon.
102. *Udānavarga* 1:9–10, Toh 326 Kangyur, mdo sde, *sa*, 209a5.
103. Śāntideva, *Bodhicaryāvatāra* 5:62–63, Toh 3871 Tengyur, dbu ma, *la*, 12b5.
104. Nāgārjuna, *Suhṛllekha* verse 55, Toh 4182 Tengyur, spring yig, *nge*, 43a6.
105. Śāntideva, *Bodhicaryāvatāra* 6:59, Toh 3871 Tengyur, dbu ma, *la*, 16b7.
106. This is a misattribution in the original. The citation is actually found in the *Collection of Aphorisms*. See *Udānavarga* 1:42, Toh 326 Kangyur, mdo sde, *sa*, 210b:3.
107. This is a reference to the various ways of disposing of a corpse according to the four elements and astrology. Although Gampopa attributes this quotation to Śāntideva, it is not found in the *Bodhicaryāvatara.*
108. The source of this quote has not been located.
109. Yaśomitra, *Abhidharmakośaṭīkā*, Toh 4092 Tengyur, mngon pa, *gu*, 3b3.
110. *Karuṇāpuṇḍarīkasūtra*, Toh 112 Kangyur, mdo sde, *cha*, 157b6.
111. Nāgārjuna, *Suhṛllekha* verse 69cd, Toh 4182 Tengyur, spring yig, *nge*, 44a1.
112. Ibid. verse 69ab, 43b7.
113. Ibid. verse 74b–d, 44a4.
114. Vasubandhu, *Abhidharmakośa* 3:58 Toh 4089 Tengyur, mngon pa, *ku*, 9a4.
115. Nāgārjuna, *Letter to a Friend* (*Suhṛllekha*) verse 78cd, Toh 4182 Tengyur, spring yig, *nge*, 44a6.
116. Candragomin, Śiṣyalekha verse 45, Toh 4183 Tengyur, spring yig, *nge*, 49a1.
117. Nāgārjuna, *Letter to a Friend* (*Suhṛllekha*) verse 78ab, Toh 4182 Tengyur, spring yig, *nge*, 44a6.
118. Ibid. verse 79, 44a7.
119. Ibid. verse 82cd, 44b2.
120. Vasubandhu, *Treasury of Higher Knowledge* (*Abhidharmakośa*) 3:82, Toh 4089 Tengyur, mngon pa, *ku*, 10a2.
121. The Beijing edition has 12,960 billion instead of 12,990 billion.

122. The Beijing edition has 103,680 billion instead of 100,680 billion.
123. The Beijing edition has 829,040 billion; Palpung has 825,400 billion.
124. The Beijing edition has 53,840,160 billion; Palpung has 51,840,160 billion.
125. From Vasubandhu, *Treasury of Higher Knowledge* (*Abhidharmakośa*) 3:83, Toh 4089 Tengyur, mngon pa, *ku*, 10a2.
126. Ibid. 3:59, 9a4.
127. Śāntideva, *Bodhicaryāvatāra* 5:7–8ab, Toh 3871 Tengyur, *la*, 10b1.
128. Vasubandhu, *Treasury of Higher Knowledge* (*Abhidharmakośa*) 3:59, Toh 4089 Tengyur, mngon pa, *ku*, 9a4.
129. In the *Lifespan Sutra* (*Āyuṣparyantasūtra*), Toh 307 Kangyur, mdo sde, *sa*, 143b2.
130. *Treasury of Abhidharma* (*Abhidharmakośa*) 3:84, Toh 4089 Tengyur, mngon pa, *ku*, 10a3.
131. *Vinayavastu*, Toh 1, Kangyur, 'dul ba, *ka*, 100b:3.
132. In Nāgārjuna's *Letter to a Friend* (*Suhṛllekha*), Toh 4182 Tengyur, spring yig, *nge*, 45a1.
133. Koṭikarṇa ("Ten Million in the Ear") was so called because he was born with a divine jewel worth ten million ounces of gold set in his ear. He set out as a merchant, to please his father, but was abandoned by his servants and then lost in a desert, where he spent twelve years with various types of hungry spirits. They were lucid about the past actions that had caused their plight and gave him messages for the human realm, to which he returned. He became a monk under Mahākatyāyana, gaining deep realization. *Basis of Vinaya* (*Vinayavastu*), Toh 1 Kangyur, 'dul ba, *ka*, 251b3. A translation of this story appears in Rotman, *Divine Stories*, 39–70.
134. Vasubandu, *Treasury of Higher Knowledge* (*Abhidharmakośa*) 3:83, Toh 4089 Tengyur, mngon pa, *ku*, 10a3.
135. Nāgārjuna's *Letter to a Friend* (*Suhṛllekha*) verse 90cd, Toh 4182 Tengyur, spring yig, *nge*, 44b7.
136. Ibid. verse 90ab, 44b7.
137. The source of this quote has not been identified.
138. Vasubandhu, *Treasury of Higher Knowledge* (*Abhidharmakośa*) 3:83, Toh 4089 Tengyur, mngon pa, *ku*, 10a3.
139. *Nandagarbhāvakrāntinirdeśa*, Toh 57 Kangyur, dkon brtsegs, *ga*, 223b7.
140. The four modes of birth are: spontaneous, from a womb, from an egg, or from heat and moisture.
141. It is not that the sperm and ovum are particularly impure compared to other bodily substances, but that they form part of the thirty-six impure physical substances of which a human body is composed.
142. *Nanda's Abiding in the Womb* (*Nandagarbhāvakrāntinirdeśa*), Toh 57 Kangyur, dkon brtsegs, *ga*, 238a1.
143. *One Hundred Stories* (*Avadānaśataka*), Toh 343 Kangyur, mdo sde, ām, 254a6.
144. *Nandagarbhāvakrāntinirdeśa*, Toh 57 Kangyur, dkon brtsegs, *ga*, 231b2.
145. Candragomin, *Śiṣyalekha* verse 19, Toh 4183 Tengyur, spring yig, *nge*, 47b3.
146. *Lalitavistarasūtra*, Toh 95 Kangyur, mdo sde, *kha*, 88b4.
147. Ibid., 88b5.
148. *Rājāvavādakasūtra*, Toh 221 Kangyur, mdo sde, *dza*, 10b5.

149. In Nāgārjuna's *Letter to a Friend* (*Suhṛllekha*) verse 102ab, Toh 4182 Tengyur, spring yig, 45b1.
150. In the longer *Great Passing into Nirvana Sutra* (*Mahāparinirvāṇasūtra*), Toh 119 Kangyur, mdo sde, *nya*, 302a3.
151. *Nandagarbhāvakrāntinirdeśa*, Toh 57 Kangyur, dkon brtsegs, *ga*, 228a5.
152. Although the text attributes this quotation to the *Meeting of Father and Son Sutra* (*Pitāputrasamāgamasūtra*), it is actually found in the *Questions of Pūrṇa Sutra* (*Pūrṇaparipṛcchāsūtra*), Toh 61 Kangyur, dkon brtsegs, *nga*, 171a5.
153. Nāgārjuna, *Letter to a Friend* (*Suhṛllekha*) verse 103, Toh 4182 Tengyur, spring yig, *nge*, 45b1.
154. *Karmaśataka*, Toh 340 Kangyur, mdo sde, *ha*, 106a7.
155. *Mahākaruṇāpuṇḍarīkasūtra*, Toh 111 Kangyur, mdo sde, *cha*, 62b3.
156. Vasubandhu, *Abhidharmakośa* 4:1a, Toh 4089 Tengyur, mngon pa, *ku*, 10b7.
157. Asaṅga, *Abhidharmasamuccaya*, Toh 4049 Tengyur, sems tsam, *ri*, 85a8.
158. Vasubandhu, *Abhidharmakośa* 4:1b, Toh 4089 Tengyur, mngon pa, *ku*, 10b7.
159. Nāgārjuna, *Mūlamadhyamakakārikā* 17:2, Toh 3824 Tengyur, dbu ma, *tsa*, 9b2.
160. Vasubandu, *Abhidharmakośa* 4:1cd, Toh 4089 Tengyur, mngon pa, *ku*, 10b7.
161. The traditional way of describing karma—as "action, cause and effect"—shows an assumption that the consequences of an action are actually part and parcel of that action rather than something else that happens later due to the action.
162. The five actions that have immediate result at death (i.e., no intermediate state but immediate rebirth in the worst realms) are parricide, matricide, killing an arhat, creating divisions in the Sangha, and injuring a buddha.
163. The truths of cessation and of the path are the third and fourth of the so-called noble truths, which are more accurately rendered the *four truths of the noble ones*.
164. The thorn-like view is a view that denies the long-term consequences of actions (karma) on their doer and only acknowledges their immediate consequences.
165. Nāgārjuna, *Ratnāvalī* 3:29, Toh 4158 Tengyur, spring yig, *ge*, 115b3.
166. Ibid. 1:20ab and 21ab, 107b5.
167. Ibid. 1:20cd and 21cd, 107b5.
168. Ibid. 1:24, 107b7.
169. Asaṅga, *Abhidharmasamuccaya*, Toh 4049 Tengyur, sems tsam, *ri*, 89b6.
170. *Basis of Vinaya* (*Vinayavastu*), Toh 1 Kangyur, 'dul ba, *ka*, 41a1.
171. Asaṅga, *Abhidharmasamuccaya*, Toh 4049 Tengyur, sems tsam, *ri*, 89b6.
172. This quotation is actually from the longer *Great Passing into Nirvana Sutra* (*Mahāparinirvāṇasūtra*), Toh 119 Kangyur, mdo sde, *nya*, 354a5.
173. *Surataparipṛcchāsūtra*, Toh 71 Kangyur, dkon brtsegs, *ca*, 181b7.
174. Śāntideva, *Bodhicaryāvatāra* 1:34, Toh 3871 Tengyur, dbu ma, *la*, 3b2.
175. *Udānavarga* 28:25, Toh 326 Kangyur, mdo sde, *sa*, 273a3.
176. Ibid. 28:26, 273a3.
177. In Atiśa, *Lamp for the Path to Awakening* (*Bodhipathapradīpa*) verse 4, Toh 3947 Tengyur, dbu ma, *khi*, 238b1.
178. King Kṛkin had seven daughters with powerful karma due to their Dharma practice in former lives. This gave them radical feelings of renunciation. They refused all the royal benefits offered them by their father and eventually obtained his permission to leave palace life to practice Dharma. They later also refused the gifts of the god

Indra, who offered them divine substances when he saw them dressed in rags and meditating assiduously in a charnel ground.

179. *Karmaśataka*, Toh 340 Kangyur, mdo sde, *ha*, 16a3.
180. This quote actually comes from the longer *Great Passing into Nirvana Sutra* (*Mahāparinirvāṇasūtra*), Toh 119 Kangyur, *ka*, 354a5.
181. The source of this quote has not been identified.
182. *Extensive Explantion of Root Vajrayana Downfalls* (*Vajrayānamūlāpattiṭīkā*), Toh 2488 Tengyur, rgyud 'grel, *thi*, 16a5.
183. Mañjuśrīkīrti, *Extensive Explantion of Root Vajrayana Downfalls* (*Vajrayānamūlāpattiṭīkā*), Toh 2488 Tengyur, rgyud 'grel, *thi*, 10b2.
184. *Akṣayamatinirdeśasūtra*, Toh 175 Kangyur, mdo sde, *ma*, 132a3. "The patience accepting unborn phenomena" (*mi skye ba'i chos la bzod pa*), translated elsewhere also as "acceptance of unoriginated factors," is a bodhisattva's stable realization of emptiness.
185. *Aṣṭasāhasrikāprajñāpāramitā*, Toh 12 Kangyur, sher phyin, *ka*, 139b4.
186. This cannonical text, *Beginningless Time Sutra*, does not appear to exist in the Tibetan canon. However, the "Questions" chapter of the longer *Great Passing into Nirvana Sutra* does contain a version extremely similar to this quotation: *Mahāparinirvāṇasūtra*, Toh 119 Kangyur, mdo sde, *ta*, 11b4.
187. Nāgārjuna, *Suhṛllekha* 68cd, Toh 4182 Tengyur, spring yig, *nge*, 43b7.
188. The *Prayer of Excellent Conduct* (*Bhadracaryāpraṇidhāna*) is part of the *Flower Ornament Sutra* (*Avataṃsakasūtra*), Toh 44 Kangyur, phal chen, ā, 361a6.
189. Maitreya, *Mahāyānasūtrālaṃkāra* 14:20, Toh 4020 Tengyur, sems tsam, *phi*, 18b1.
190. *Candraprabha Sutra* is one of several names for the *King of Meditation Sutra* (*Samādhirājasūtra*), Toh 127 Kangyur, mdo sde, 115b6. Gampopa himself is considered an incarnation of the Buddha's interlocutor in this sutra, Candraprabhakumāra.
191. Nāgārjuna, *Ratnāvalī* 3:83, Toh 4158 Tengyur, spring yig, *ge*, 117b3.
192. In the ITC critical edition as well as the Tsipri edition, it reads "you will derive/ hundredfold benefits from loving kindness." Here we have chosen to follow the reading of the Beijing and Palpung editions instead.
193. Nāgārjuna, *Ratnāvalī* 3:84–85, Toh 4158 Tengyur, spring yig, *ge*, 117b4.
194. A former incarnation of Buddha Śākyamuni, the brahman Mahādatta was a wealthy prince whose heart was saddened by the poverty he saw in his land and by knowing the harmful thoughts and actions to which poverty gives rise. He set out on an epic and arduous journey to collect wish-fulfilling gems powerful enough to dispel all the poverty in his world. His long quest bore fruit, and he was able to help innumerable beings due to his loving concern for their happiness. This story is found in chapter 3 of the *Sage and Fool Sutra*, Toh 341 Kangyur, mdo sde, *a*, 223a3.
195. King Bāla Maitreya was another former incarnation of Buddha Śākyamuni. His loving mind and prayers were so strong that it protected his subjects from flesh-eating demons. Five such rakṣas, very hungry because of this, came to him to plead their case. He gave them his own flesh and blood. The strong karmic connection created by this selfless act led them eventually to meet him again and again, finally becoming Kauṇḍinya and the four other ascetics who were Śākyamuni's meditation companions before his enlightenment and subsequently among the first to receive

his teachings. *Sage and Fool Sutra* (*Damamūkanāmasūtra*), chapter 12, Toh 341 Kangyur, mdo sde, *a*, 155b4.

196. The source of this quotation has not been identified.
197. *Perfectly Gathering the Qualities* [*of Avalokiteśvara*] *Sutra* (*Dharmasaṃgītisūtra*), Toh 238 Kangyur, mdo sde, *zha*, 84a6.
198. Ibid., 84a7.
199. The *Sutra of the Tathāgata's Secrets* has not been found. However, this quotation was found in the *Enlightenment of Vairocana* (*Vairocanābhisaṃbodhi*), Toh 494 Kangyur, rgyud, *tha*, 143a5.
200. In Atiśa, *Lamp for the Path to Awakening* (*Bodhipathapradīpa*) verse 5, Toh 3947 Tengyur, dbu ma, *kha*, 238b2.
201. The Beijing and Palpung texts add "for there to be practice [bodhicitta]."
202. This fuller explanation is found in chapter 1, on the essence of buddhahood.
203. *Great Sutra of the Supreme Victory* (*Dhvajāgranāmamahāsūtra*), Toh 293 Kangyur, mdo sde, *sha*, 267a3.
204. *Mañjuśrīvikrīḍitasūtra*, Toh 96 Kangyur, mdo sde, *kha*, 237a1.
205. *Sutra of the Play of Manjuśrī* (*Mañjuśrīvikrīḍitasūtra*), Toh 96 Kangyur, mdo sde, *kha*, 237a2.
206. *Mahāparinirvāṇasūtra* (longer version), Toh 119 Kangyur, mdo sde, *nya*, 120a7.
207. The "four stages of result" are stream-enterer, once-returner, nonreturner, and arhat.
208. Maitreya, *Uttaratantra* 1:21, Toh 4024 Tengyur, sems tsam, *phi*, 55b6.
209. Ibid.
210. Ibid. 1:20, 55b6.
211. Ibid.
212. *Detailed Explanation of the Uttaratantra* (*Mahāyānottaratantraśāstravyākhyā*), Toh 4025 Tengyur, sems tsam, *phi*, 84b7.
213. *Mahāmokṣasūtra*, Toh 264 Kangyur, mdo sde, *'a*, 229a3.
214. Maitreya, *Uttaratantra* 1:19, Toh 4024 Tengyur, sems tsam, *phi*, 55b5.
215. See glossary. The idea here is that these actions are performed without perceiving any of the elements involved—object, agent, or act—to possess self-existence.
216. This is a gloss of the word *buddha*.
217. Tib. *chos kyi dbyings kyi rjes su song ba*, conveys the idea of sharing the nature of the dharmadhātu.
218. *Anavataptanāgarājaparipṛcchāsūtra*, Toh 156 Kangyur, mdo sde, *pha*, 250a7.
219. The view of the "perishable collection" (*'jig tshogs*; *satkāya*) is the misconception that self as an individual truly exists. The term refers to mistaken views of one's own existence and identity as real conceived on the basis of the perishable aggregates (*skandha*), one's body and mind.
220. Maitreya, *Mahāyānasūtrālaṃkāra* 10:7, Toh 4020 Tengyur, sems tsam, *phi*, 9a1.
221. *Mahāparinirvāṇasūtra* (longer version), Toh 119 Kangyur, mdo sde, *nya*, 120a5.
222. Ibid.
223. I have translated the Tibetan *mu stega pa* as "the misguided," following the Kagyü-lineage explanation for this term, which is far from the oft-used "heretic," as they are truly devoted to a spiritual path that has many beneficial elements. In Buddhist scriptures, the term refers to the proponents of the non-Buddhist philosophical schools.

224. *Mahāparinirvāṇasūtra*, Toh 119 Kangyur, mdo sde, *nya*, 120a6.
225. In itself, and as the basis for all the other precepts, taking refuge is a cause of great merit, since the karmic power of a vow such as refuge acts continuously, even in sleep.
226. The temporary lay precepts (*bsnyen gnas*, *upavāsatha*) are eight precepts observed for twenty-four-hour periods on special occasions: not to kill, steal, lie, have sex, take intoxicants, eat after the appointed time (usually noon), wear adornments, sing or dance, or use high seats or beds.
227. The names of these seven levels in Sanskrit are respectively *bhikṣu*, *bhikṣuṇī*, *śrāmaṇera*, *śikṣamāṇā*, *śrāmaṇerikā*, *upāsaka*, and *upāsikā*.
228. Asaṅga, *Bodhisattvabhūmi*, Toh 4037 Tengyur, sems tsam, *wi*, 74b7.
229. Maitreya, *Mahāyānasūtrālaṃkāra* 5:4, Toh 4020 Tengyur, sems tsam, *phi*, 4b4.
230. Atiśa, *Bodhipathapradīpa* verse 20, Toh 3947 Tengyur, dbu ma, *khi*, 239a4.
231. Sthiramati, *Detailed Exposition of the Ornament of Mahayana Sutras* (*Sūtrālaṃkāravṛttibhāṣya*), Toh 4034 Tengyur, sems tsam, *mi*, 53b1.
232. Ibid. The "meditative concentration vow" (*dhyānasaṃvara*) is the conceptual and artificial dedication of the mind needed to develop profound absorption. It requires discipline. When it bears fruit, the "untainted vow" (*anāsravasaṃvara*), natural to the state of meditative concentration itself, supplants the artifice, which need no longer be maintained.
233. Maitreya, *Abhisamayālaṃkāra* 1:18ab, Toh 3786 Tengyur, shes phyin, *ka*, 2b5.
234. The text here lists this twentieth bodhicitta as resembling an "echo" (*sgra brnyan*), but in Gampopa's explanation below, it is given as "melodious sound" (*sgra snyan*). The spellings in Tibetan are very close. As the Sanskrit here is ānandokti, *sgra snyan* is the better choice.
235. Maitreya, *Abhisamayālaṃkāra* 1:19–20, Toh 3786 Tengyur, shes phyin, *ka*, 2b5.
236. The paths of seeing and cultivation are defined differently by Gampopa here than in the later chapters dedicated to the phases of the path (chapter 18) and the bodhisattva levels (chapter 19). The more usual allocation of the path of seeing to the first bodhisattva level alone is here extended up to the seventh level, while the path of cultivation is confined to the nondual eighth through tenth levels.
237. *Dhāraṇī* (Tib. *gzungs*) here refers to the ability to associate many things to a key trigger, such as a syllable, and the way this leads to retention of knowledge and experience. In higher phases of the path, simply uttering, and remaining within, the key trigger can spontaneously activate one's accumulated knowledge and experience.
238. Maitreya, *Mahāyānasūtrālaṃkāra* 5:2, Toh 4020 Tengyur, sems tsam, *phi*, 4b2.
239. *Saṃdhinirmocanasūtra*, Toh 106 Kangyur, mdo sde, *ca*, 34b7.
240. Ibid.
241. Ibid.
242. Maitreya, *Mahāyānasūtrālaṃkāra*, Toh 4020 Tengyur, sems tsam, *phi*, 4b6.
243. Sthiramati, *Sūtrālaṃkāravṛttibhāṣya*, Toh 1034 Tengyur, sems tsam, *mi*, 54a7.
244. Śāntideva, *Bodhicaryāvatāra* 1:15, Toh 3871 Tengyur, dbu ma, *la*, 2b4.
245. Ibid. 1:16, 2b5.
246. Asaṅga, *Abhidharmasamuccaya*, Toh 4049 Tengyur, sems tsam, *ri*, 95b4.
247. Asaṅga, *Bodhisattvabhūmi*, Toh 4037 Tengyur, sems tsam, *wi*, 7b3.
248. Maitreya, *Mahāyānasūtrālaṃkāra*, Toh 4020 Tengyur, sems tsam, *phi*, 4b3.

249. In the *Marvelous Array Sutra* (*Gaṇḍavyūhasūtra*), in the *Flower Ornament Sutra*, Toh 44 Kangyur, phal chen, *a*, 361a6.
250. *Daśadharmakasūtra*, Toh 53 Kangyur, dkon brtsegs, *kha*, 168a1.
251. Asaṅga, *Bodhisattvabhūmi*, Toh 4037 Tengyur, sems tsam, *wi*, 9a3.
252. Maitreya, *Mahāyānasūtrālaṃkāra* 5:7, Toh 4020 Tengyur, sems tsam, *phi*, 4b5.
253. Ibid. 5:8, 4b6.
254. Atiśa, *Bodhipathapradīpa* verses 22cd–23, Toh 3947 Tengyur, dbu ma, *khi*, 239a5.
255. Asaṅga, *Bodhisattvabhūmi*, Toh 4037 Tengyur, sems tsam, *wi*, 82a7.
256. Ibid., 83b2.
257. Śāntideva, *Śikṣāsamuccaya*, Toh 3940 Tengyur, dbu ma, *khi*, 9b1.
258. Maitreya, *Mahāyānasūtrālaṃkāra* 18:1, Toh 4020 Tengyur, sems tsam, *phi*, 25a4.
259. Mahāmudrā (Tib. *phyag rgya chen po*), the central teaching and practice of the Kagyü tradition, is both meditation on and realization of the empty nature of the mind. The meditation can be done with tantric visualization practice, which is what "medition on the deities' forms" refers to in this sentence.
260. The source of this quote has not been identified.
261. *Susthitamatidevaputraparipṛcchāsūtra*, Toh 80 Kangyur, dkon brtsegs, *ca* 300a3.
262. *Siṃhanādasūtra*, Toh 67 Kangyur, dkon brtsegs, *ca*, 103b6.
263. Nāgārjuna, *Ratnāvalī* 4:73, Toh 4158 Tengyur, spring yig, *ge*, 121a1.
264. Ibid. 1:20ab and 21ab, 107b5.
265. Śāntideva, *Bodhicaryāvatāra* 2:63, Toh 3871 Tengyur, dbu ma, *la*, 6b1.
266. *Mahāparinirvāṇasūtra* (longer version), Toh 119 Kangyur, mdo sde, *nya*, 305b1.
267. Ibid., 305b2.
268. *Caturdharmanirdeśasūtra*, Toh 249 Kangyur, mdo sde, *za*, 59b1.
269. *Vīradattagṛhapatiparipṛcchāsūtra*, Toh 72 Kangyur, dkon brstegs, *ca*, 201b6.
270. Ibid., 201b7.
271. Śāntideva, *Bodhicaryāvatāra* 2:34–35, Toh 3871 Tengyur, dbu ma *la*, 5a6.
272. Ibid. 2:40, 5b2.
273. Ibid. 2:41, 5b3.
274. Candragomin, *Śiṣyalekha* verse 34, Toh 4183 Tengyur, spring yig, *nge*, 48a7.
275. Śāntideva, *Guide to the Bodhisattva Way of Life* (*Bodhicaryāvatāra*) 2:44–45, Toh 3871 Tengyur, dbu ma, *la*, 5b4.
276. Nāgārjuna, *Letter to a Friend* (*Suhṛllekha*) verse 84, Toh 4182 Tengyur, spring yig, *nge*, 44b3.
277. Śāntideva, *Guide to the Bodhisattva Way of Life* (*Bodhicaryāvatāra*) 2:32, Toh 3871 Tengyur, dbu ma, *la*, 5a5.
278. Ibid. 2:33, 5a5.
279. In the *Sage and Fool Sutra* (*Damamūkanāmasūtra*), Toh 341 Kangyur, mdo sde, *a*, 253 b4.
280. There are several versions of this well-known story. For a fuller account, see Gombrich's "Who Was Aṅgulimāla?" in his *How Buddhism Began* (New Delhi: Munishiram Manoharlal, 2002), pp. 135ff.
281. Nāgārjuna, *Letter to a Friend* (*Suhṛllekha*) verse 14, Toh 4182 Tengyur, spring yig, *nge*, 41a7. For more on Udayana, Nanda, and Ajātaśatru, see notes 293, 297, and 303 below.
282. Asaṅga, *Abhidharmasamuccaya* chap. 1, Toh 4049 Tengyur, sems tsam, *ri*, 19b4.
283. A *Treasury of the Tathāgatas* is not to be found in the Tibetan canon, but this

quote appears in Śāntideva, *Compendium of Trainings* (*Śikṣāsamuccaya*), Toh 3940 Tengyur, dbu ma, *khi*, 96a7.

284. Kamalaśīla, *Diamond Cutter Sutra Commentary*, (*Vajracchedikāṭīkā*), Toh 3817 Kangyur, mdo 'grel, *ma*, 226b7.
285. *Subāhuparipṛcchātantra*, Toh 805 Kangyur, rgyud 'bum, *wa*, 126b6.
286. *Puṣpakūṭadhāraṇī*, Toh 886 Kangyur, gzungs 'dus, *e*, 160b2.
287. The chapter mentioned has not been identified, but this statement is found in Śāntideva's *Śikṣāsamuccaya*, Toh 3940 Tengyur, dbu ma, *khi*, 97a7.
288. *Vinayavastu*, Toh 1 Kangyur, 'dul ba, *ka*, 125a2.
289. *Mahāparinirvāṇasūtra* (longer version), Toh 119 Kangyur, mdo sde, *nya*, 304b5.
290. Ibid., 305b5.
291. Toh 555 Kangyur, rgyud, *pa*, 44b4.
292. *Sutra of Golden Light*, Toh 555 Kangyur, rgyud, *pa*, 44b4.
293. Story from *Basis of Vinaya* (*Vinayavastu*) verse 14, Toh 1 Kangyur, 'dul ba, *ka*, 120b1. Udayana's mother brought him up alone. To prevent his having an illicit liaison with a neighbor, she locked him in his room. Overcome by rage, he killed his mother. His overwhelming remorse eventually led him to become a Buddhist monk, though he was later expelled from the Sangha. By that time he had become very devout and learned. As a layman, he built and sponsored retreats for monks. At death he was reborn immediately in hell, but through his good deeds he swiftly migrated to the god realms, where he practiced well and progressed.
294. Nāgārjuna, *Letter to a Friend* (*Suhṛllekha*), Toh 4182 Tengyur, spring yig, *nge*, 41a7.
295. Śāntideva, *Guide to the Bodhisattva Way of Life* (*Bodhicaryāvatāra*) 2:65, Toh 3871 Tengyur, dbu ma, *la*, 6b3.
296. *Nanda's Abiding in the Womb* (*Nandagarbhāvakrāntinirdeśa*), Toh 57 Kangyur, dkon brtsegs, *ga*, 205b2.
297. Nanda was the Buddha's nephew and heir to a throne. He was enthralled with his wife's beauty and talents and, more generally, was an extreme romantic. Even when he became a monk, his mind was constantly distracted by romantic thoughts and attachment. The Buddha took him to both heaven and hell, to show the future rebirths he would gain if he continued to think and act through passion and self-centeredness. Terrified by the prospect of his future, he deeply resolved to forsake his mind's clinging. He eventually became an arhat. His story comprises one of the most celebrated works of Sanskrit literature: Aśvaghoṣa's *Saundarananda*. See Linda Covill's translation in *Handsome Nanda* (New York: New York University Press, 2007).
298. Nāgārjuna, *Letter to a Friend* (*Suhṛllekha*) verse 14, Toh 4182 Tengyur, spring yig, *nge*, 41a7.
299. *Sūkarikāvadāna*, Toh 345 Kangyur, mdo sde, *aṃ*, 290b6. In this story, a god who is nearing the end of his life is in agony, for he sees he is about to be reborn in the womb of a pig in the city of Rājagṛha. Śakra, king of the gods, comes upon him and encourages him to take refuge in Buddha, Dharma, and Sangha. The god does so and is instead reborn in Tuṣita Paradise. See Rotman, *Divine Stories*, 325–28.
300. *Mahāparinirvāṇasūtra* (longer version), Toh 119 Kangyur, mdo sde, *nya*, 120a6.
301. *Gaṇḍavyūhasūtra*, Toh 44 Kangyur, phal chen, *a*, 310a4 and 310a7.
302. Śāntideva, *Bodhicaryāvatāra* 1:13, Toh 3871 Tengyur, dbu ma, *la*, 2b3.
303. Ajātaśatru was monarch of a kingdom in central India. His father, Bimbisāra, was a patron of the Buddha and also a highly advanced Buddhist who had attained

the state of stream-enterer. Ajātaśatru was drawn into several harmful actions by Devadatta, the Buddha's jealous cousin. One of them was an assassination attempt on the Buddha. Another was the killing of Bimbisāra. Having committed two of the five "evils of no reprieve," Ajātaśatru became covered with foul-smelling boils and was destined to go straight to hell at death. He sought refuge in the Buddha and managed to purify his misdeeds, mainly through the power of practicing bodhicitta. His story is in the longer *Great Passing into Nirvana Sutra* (*Mahāparinirvāṇasūtra*), Toh 119 Kangyur, mdo sde, *ta*, 199b4.

304. Nāgārjuna, *Letter to a Friend* (*Suhṛllekha*) verse 14, Toh 4182 Tengyur, spring yig, *nge*, 41a7.
305. Cited in Śāntideva, *Śikṣāsamuccaya*, Toh 3940, Tengyur, dbu ma *khi*, 97a4.
306. Śāntideva, *Bodhicaryāvatāra* 3:3, Toh 3871 Tengyur, dbu ma, *la*, 6b6.
307. Ibid. 3:5, 6b6.
308. Ibid. 3:6, 6b6.
309. Ibid. 3:7, 6b7.
310. From the *Sutra Describing the Qualities of the Buddhafield of Mañjuśrī* (*Mañjuśrībuddhakṣetraguṇavyūhasūtra*), Toh 59 Kangyur, dkon brtsegs, *ga*, 279a7.
311. Śāntideva, *Bodhicaryāvatāra* 3:23–24, Toh 3871 Tengyur, dbu ma, *la*, 7b2.
312. Ibid. 3:24, 7b3. The last line here varies in some canonical editions.
313. The following readings of the *Bhadrakalpikasūtra* owe a particular debt to Peter Skilling for his careful analysis and suggestions.
314. *Bhadrakalpikasūtra*, Toh 94 Kangyur, mdo sde, *ka*, 316b5.
315. Ibid., 289a4.
316. Ibid., 296a6. The Sanskrit Vijṛmbhitagāmī for *bsgyings ldan bzhud* is speculative.
317. This entire passage of the actual ceremony of conferring the bodhisattva vows is from the moral discipline chapter of Asaṅga's *Bodhisattva Levels* (*Bodhisattvabhūmi*, Toh 4037 Tengyur, sems tsam, *wi*, 83a4). For an alternative translation, see Mark Tatz, *Asaṅga's Chapter on Ethics*, 61.
318. Asaṅga, *Bodhisattvabhūmi*, Toh 4037 Tengyur, sems tsam, *wi*, 7b6.
319. Ibid., 8a3.
320. Śāntideva, *Bodhicaryāvatāra* 1:14ab, Toh 3871 Tengyur, dbu ma, *la*, 2b4. Some Buddhist texts describe the end of our universe through destruction by various waves of elements, including seven successive burnings. This is the disintegration of the fire element, i.e., the release of its remaining latent energy.
321. Asaṅga, *Bodhisattvabhūmi*, Toh 4037 Tengyur, sems tsam, *wi*, 8a1.
322. *Vīradattagṛhapatiparipṛcchāsūtra*, Toh 72 Kangyur, dkon brtsegs, *ca*, 202b6.
323. Ibid.
324. *Gaṇḍavyūhasūtra*, Toh 44 Kangyur, phal chen, *a*, 309b6.
325. Asaṅga, *Bodhisattvabhūmi*, Toh 4037 Tengyur, sems tsam, *wi*, 7b7. The "two extremes" here are the extremes of samsara and nirvana—being imprisoned within samsaric existence controlled by karma and affliction or falling into the meditative absorption of a solitary peace of personal nirvana.
326. Śāntideva, *Bodhicaryāvatāra* 1:19, Toh 3871 Tengyur, dbu ma, *la*, 2b7.
327. Ibid. 1:29–30, 3a6.
328. Ibid. 4:4, 8a4.
329. Ibid. 4:9, 8a7.
330. Ibid. 4:11, 8b1.

331. Asaṅga, *Bodhisattvabhūmi*, Toh 4037 Tengyur, sems tsam, *wi*, 97b4. A *defeat* (*pham pa*, *pārājika*) is a complete breakage by a monk or nun of one of the four root prātimokṣa precepts (no killing, lying, stealing, or sexual intercourse). *Great involvement* is committing any of the four offenses analogous to the grounds of defeat wherein (a) the bodhisattva makes a regular practice of it, (b) generates not the slightest sense of shame and embarassment, (c) is pleased with and glad of it, and (d) has a view for its good qualities. If one or more of these are missing, then the degree of involvement is characterized as being lesser or medium. For Asaṅga's discussion of these points, see Tatz, *Asanga's Chapter on Ethics*, pp. 64–65.
332. Asaṅga, *Yogācārabhūmiviniścayasaṃgrahaṇī*, Toh 4038 Tengyur, sems tsam, *zhi*, 38b6.
333. Śāntideva, *Śikṣāsamuccaya*, Toh 3940 Tengyur, dbu ma, *khi*, 99a7.
334. See note 331 above for these offenses and involvements.
335. Candragomin, *Twenty Verses on the Bodhisattva Vow* (*Bodhisattvasaṃvaraviṃśaka*) verse 8, Toh 4081 Tengyur, sems tsam, *hi*, 166b5. This verse lists four different ways of dealing with infraction of the bodhisattva vow. If the vow has been broken due to either the loss of the aspiration bodhicitta or through the commitment of any of the four offences with great involvement, one then needs to retake the vow afresh. If the infraction consists of committing any of the four offences with a medium involvement, one then needs to declare it and purify it in the presence of at least three people. For the rest, by which the author means the commitment of any of the four offences with a lesser involvement, one then needs to rectify this by purifying it in the presence of a single person. Finally, if the infraction consists of violating any of the secondary precepts with or without manifest afflictions present in one's mind, one can then purify it within one's own mind, as if taking one's own mind as the witness.
336. *Anavataptanāgarājaparipṛcchāsūtra*, Toh 156 Kangyur, mdo sde, *pha*, 208b4.
337. This seemingly shocking statement probably refers to śrāvakas and pratyekabuddhas who are deeply absorbed in the bliss of meditative concentrations, where the sense gates are oblivious to input and the mind is so absorbed in its own peace that it is oblivious to everything else.
338. The source for this quote has not been identified.
339. Atiśa, *Bodhipathapradīpa* verse 12, Toh 3947 Tengyur, dbu ma, *khi*, 238b6.
340. *Marvelous Array Sutra* (*Gaṇḍavyūhasūtra*), in *Flower Ornament Sutra* (*Avataṃsakasūtra*), Toh 44 Kangyur, phal chen, *a*, 309b1.
341. Ibid., 311b2.
342. Ibid., 310b4–5.
343. Ibid., 310b2.
344. Atiśa, *Bodhipathapradīpa* verse 34, Toh 3947 Tengyur, dbu ma, *khi*, 239b5.
345. The four means of gathering beings are four ways a Dharma master gathers a following: through generosity (especially of Dharma), pleasing speech, appropriate conduct, and actions consistent with the teachings.
346. Vasubhandhu, *Sambhāraparikathā*, Toh 4166 Tengyur, spring yig, *ge*, 173b2.
347. Atiśa, *Bodhipathapradīpa* verse 18ab, Toh 3947 Tengyur, dbu ma, *khi*, 239a2.
348. Atiśa, *Ritual Order for Bodhicitta and Vows* (*Cittotpādasaṃvaravidhikrama*), Toh 3969 Tengyur, dbu ma, *gi*, 246a3. Many contemporary masters attribute these words to Buddha Śākyamuni three cosmic eons ago, when he first gave rise to bodhicitta.
349. Atiśa, *Bodhipathapradīpa* verse 18cd, Toh 3947 Tengyur, dbu ma, *khi*, 239a3.

350. *Kāśyapaparivartasūtra*, Toh 87 Kangyur, dkon brtseg, *cha*, 120a6.
351. Ibid., 120b3.
352. This means telling lies for self-interest. Lies that may save others from harm, and lies in other altruistic instances, may be the most appropriate thing a bodhisattva could do (Khenchen Thrangu Rinpoché).
353. In the Tibetan original, there is a parenthetical sentence immediately following this sentence that reads: "Chengawa and Jayulwa speak of Mahayana virtuous actions, while Gya Yöndak says that it is the same for any virtuous action, be it that of the Mahayana or the Hinayana. In the case of engaging in giving, for example, the act as well as the agent becomes good if one has been engaged in a giving..." It is unclear whether this annotation is part of the original or was added on by a subsequent editor.
354. Atiśa, *Bodhipathapradīpa* verse 32a–c, Toh 3947 Tengyur, dbu ma, *khi*, 239b3.
355. Maitreya, *Mahāyānasūtrālaṃkāra* 16:7, Toh 4020 Tengyur, sems tsam, *phi*, 21b2.
356. *Subāhuparipṛcchāsūtra*, Toh 70 Kangyur, dkon brtsegs, *ca* 154a6.
357. "Environment" is to be taken here in the widest sense of people, life circumstances, and places.
358. Maitreya, *Mahāyānasūtrālaṃkāra* 17:2, Toh 4020 Tengyur, sems tsam, *phi*, 21a6.
359. Ibid. 17:14, 21b7.
360. Ibid. 17:8, 21b3.
361. This, and the following etymologies, are those of the Sanskrit terms for the perfections. *Dāna*, the Sanskrit for generosity, comes from a root meaning "to sweep away," the implication being that it sweeps away greed and clinging. Coolness was a sought-after quality in hot India, and the relief of *śīla* (moral discipline) is compared to the shade of a cool tree in contrast to the searing summer heat of the passions. There is not a precise match in English for the broad uses of the word *kṣānti* (patience) as understood in Buddhism. *Patience* here is not a static waiting but refers to an ability to dynamically cope with situations that may otherwise trigger anger. Similarly, no single English term seems to translate the various implications of the Sanskrit *vīrya*, which means "energetic," "efficient," or "courageous"—all relevant meanings (see chapter 15 on diligence below). The Tibetan *brtson 'grus* means "industrious diligence." The etymology of "diligence" takes us to the Latin *diligere*, denoting a sense of joy (the same root as "delight"), and to find joy in Dharma lies at the heart of this perfection and leads automatically to industrious perseverance.
362. Maitreya, *Mahāyānasūtrālaṃkāra* 17:15, Toh 4020 Tengyur, sems tsam, *phi*, 21b7.
363. Maitreya, *Abhisamayālaṃkāra* 1:43, Toh 3786 Tengyur, shes phyin, *ka*, 3b4.
364. Maitreya, *Mahāyānasūtrālaṃkāra* 19:39, Toh 4020 Tengyur, sems tsam, *phi*, 30a1.
365. *Ratnaguṇasaṃcayagāthā*, Toh 13 Kangyur, sher phyin, *ka*, 19a1.
366. *Vinayavastu*, Toh 1 Kangyur, 'dul ba, *ka*, 256a6. See the summary of Śroṇa Koṭikarṇa's story in note 133 above.
367. Ibid., 256b7.
368. *Ratnaguṇasaṃcayagāthā*, Toh 13 Kangyur, sher phyin, *ka*, 19b1.
369. Nāgārjuna, *Suhṛllekha* verse 6cd, Toh 4182 Tengyur, spring yig, *nge*, 41a2.
370. Candrakīrti, *Madhyamakāvatāra* 1:10, Toh 3861 Tengyur, dbu ma, *'a*, 202a2.
371. *Ratnaguṇasaṃcayagāthā*, Toh 13 Kangyur, sher spyin, *ka*, 19b1.
372. *Bodhisattvapiṭaka*, Toh 56 Kangyur, dkon brtsegs, *ga*, 61a3.
373. *Ratnameghasūtra*, Toh 231 Kangyur, mdo sde, *wa*, 12a7.

374. *Gṛhapatyugraparipṛcchāsūtra*, Toh 63 Kangyur, dkon brtsegs, *nga*, 264b5.
375. Asaṅga, *Bodhisattvabhūmi*, Toh 4037 Tengyur, sems tsam, *wi*, 61b4.
376. Ibid., 63b5.
377. Ibid., 73a6.
378. Ibid., 65b3.
379. Ibid., 66a1.
380. There is the following in parenthetical passage in the Tibetan original, perhaps added by a later editor: "The *Precious Garland* says: 'Should poison benefit someone,/ then poison should be given./ If it is not beneficial to the person,/ even the best food should not be given. // It is said that chopping off a finger/ bitten by a poisonous snake is beneficial;/ the Buddha taught that even unpleasant things/ should be done if they benefit others.'" Nāgārjuna, *Ratnāvalī* 3:63–64, Toh 4158 Tengyur, spring yig, *ge*, 116b7.
381. The *Questions of Nārāyaṇa Sutra* is another title for the *Sutra of the Absorption that Gathers All Merit* (*Sarvapuṇyasamuccayasamādhisūtra*), Toh 134 Kangyur, mdo sde, *na*, 85a5.
382. Śāntideva, *Bodhicaryāvatāra* 3:87, Toh 3871 Tengyur, dbu ma, *la*, 13b4.
383. A.k.a. *Sutra of the Absorption that Gathers All Merit* (*Sarvapuṇyasamuccayasamādhisūtra*), Toh 134 Kangyur, mdo sde, *na*, 83b7.
384. Maitreya, *Mahāyānasūtrālaṃkāra* 9:16, Toh 4020 Tengyur, sems tsam, *phi*, 8a5.
385. Śāntideva, *Bodhicaryāvatāra* 5:85d, Toh 3871 Tengyur, dbu ma, *la*, 13b3.
386. Ibid. 5:81cd, 13b1.
387. Asaṅga, *Bodhisattvabhūmi*, Toh 4037 Tengyur, sems tsam, *wi*, 71b7.
388. Asaṅga, *Abhidharmasamuccaya*, Toh 4049 Tengyur, sems tsam, *ri*, 16a1.
389. Asaṅga, *Bodhisattvabhūmi*, Toh 4037 Tengyur, sems tsam, *wi*, 72a7.
390. *Ratnaguṇasaṃcayagāthā*, Toh 13 Kangyur, sher phyin, *ka*, 10a5.
391. *Kāśyapaparivartasūtra*, Toh 87 Kangyur, dkon brtsegs, *cha*, 125b4.
392. *Ratnaguṇasaṃcayagāthā*, Toh 13 Kangyur, sher phyin, *ka*, 15a5.
393. Asaṅga, *Bodhisattvabhūmi*, Toh 4037 Tengyur, sems tsam, *wi*, 72b1.
394. A.k.a. *King of Meditation Sutra* (*Samādhirājasūtra*), Toh 127 Kangyur, mdo sde, *da*, 85b7.
395. *Saddharmapuṇḍarīkasūtra*, Toh 113 Kangyur, mdo sde, *ja*, 106a3.
396. *King of Meditation Sutra* (*Samādhirājasūtra*), Toh 127 Kangyur, mdo sde, *da*, 106a4.
397. *Sāgaramatiparipṛcchāsūtra*, Toh 152 Kangyur, mdo sde, *pha*, 110b7.
398. Ibid., 111b1.
399. *Bodhisattvapiṭaka*, Toh 56 Kangyur, dkon brtsegs, *ga*, 60b6.
400. *Ratnaguṇasaṃcayagāthā*, Toh 13 Kangyur, sher phyin, *ka*, 39a3.
401. Asaṅga, *Bodhisattvabhūmi*, Toh 4037 Tengyur, sems tsam, *wi*, 65b1.
402. *Akṣayamatinirdeśasūtra*, Toh 175 Kangyur, mdo sde, *ma*, 107a1.
403. Śāntideva, *Śikṣāsamuccaya*, Toh 3939 Tengyur, dbu ma, *khi*, 2b6.
404. *Ratnacūḍaparipṛcchāsūtra*, Toh 91 Kangyur, dkon brtsegs, *cha*, 215b2.
405. Asaṅga, *Bodhisattvabhūmi*, Toh 4037 Tengyur, sems tsam, *wi*, 73b6.
406. *Ratnaguṇasaṃcayagāthā*, Toh 13 Kangyur, sher phyin, *ka*, 19b1.
407. Asaṅga, *Bodhisattvabhūmi*, Toh 4037 Tengyur, sems tsam, *wi*, 65b2.
408. Nāgārjuna, *Ratnāvalī* 3:91, Toh 4158 Tengyur, spring yig, *ge*, 118a1.
409. Nāgārjuna, *Ratnāvalī* 3:89, Toh 4158 Tengyur, spring yig, *ge*, 117b6.

410. Candrakīrti, *Madhyamakāvatāra* 2:4ab, Toh 3861 Tengyur, dbu ma, *'a*, 202b3.
411. *Śīlasaṃyuktasūtra*, Toh 303 Kangyur, mdo sde, *sa*, 127b2.
412. Ibid.
413. *Ratnaguṇasaṃcayagāthā*, Toh 13 Kangyur, sher phyin, *ka*, 19b2.
414. Nāgārjuna, *Suhṛllekha* 7, Toh 4182 Tengyur, spring yig, *nge*, 41a2.
415. Candrakīrti, *Madhyamakāvatāra* 2:6, Toh 3861 Tengyur, dbu ma, *'a*, 202b5.
416. A.k.a. *King of Meditation Sutra* (*Samādhirājasūtra*), Toh 127 Kangyur, mdo sde, *da*, 89a5.
417. This quotation does not seem to be from the *Meeting of Father and Son Sutra* but from the sutra that immediately follows it in the Kangyur, i.e., the *Questions of Pūrṇa Sutra* (*Pūrṇaparipṛcchāsūtra*), Toh 61 Kangyur, dkon brtsegs, *nga*, 187b4.
418. *Questions of Pūrṇa Sutra* (*Pūrṇaparipṛcchāsūtra*), Toh 61 Kangyur, dkon brtsegs, *nga*, 187b4.
419. *Śīlasaṃyuktasūtra*, Toh 303 Kangyur, mdo sde, *sa*, 127a7.
420. Asaṅga, *Bodhisattvabhūmi*, Toh 4037 Tengyur, sems tsam, *wi*, 74a3.
421. Ibid., 74b7.
422. A.k.a. *Sutra of the Absorption that Gathers All Merit* (*Sarvapuṇyasamuccayasamādhisūtra*), Toh 134 Kangyur, mdo sde, *na*, 87b6.
423. Of the above, 1 through 5 are root downfalls associated with a monarch, and 1 through 4, along with 6, are those associated with a minister.
424. Śāntideva, *Śikṣāsamuccaya*, Toh 3940 Tengyur, dbu ma, *khi*, 43a5. Numbering here has been added for clarity.
425. Candragomin, *Saṃvaraviṃśaka* verses 6–7, Toh 4081 Tengyur, sems tsam, *hi*, 166b4.
426. Ibid. verse 9, 166b46.
427. Asaṅga, *Bodhisattvabhūmi*, Toh 4037 Tengyur, sems tsam, *wi*, 75a1.
428. Ibid., 79a3.
429. Śāntideva, *Guide to the Bodhisattva Way of Life* (*Bodhicaryāvatāra*) 5:71, Toh 3871 Tengyur, dbu ma, *la*, 13a2.
430. Ibid. 5:80, 13b2.
431. Ibid. 5:92cd, 13b6.
432. Ibid. 5:92ab, 13b6.
433. Ibid. 5:72, 13a2.
434. Ibid. 5:96, 14a1.
435. This quotation was not found in the *Clouds of Jewels Sutra*, but it occurs in the *Sutra Encouraging Nobler Intention* (*Adhyāśayasaṃcodanasūtra*), Toh 69 Kangyur, dkon brtsegs, *ca*, 145b1.
436. A.k.a. *King of Meditation Sutra* (*Samādhirājasūtra*), Toh 127 Kangyur, mdo sde, *da*, 85b4.
437. *Sarvadharmāpravṛttinirdeśasūtra*, Toh 180 Kangyur, mdo sde, *ma*, 274b4.
438. Śāntideva, *Guide to the Bodhisattva Way of Life* (*Bodhicaryāvatāra*) 5:79, Toh 3871 Tengyur, dbu ma, *la*, 13a6.
439. *Adhyāśayasaṃcodanasūtra*, Toh 69 Kangyur, dkon brtsegs, *ca*, 142a5.
440. *Pitāputrasamāgamasūtra*, Toh 60 Kangyur, dkon brtsegs, *nga*, 162a5.
441. *Adhyāśayasaṃcodanasūtra*, Toh 69 Kangyur, dkon brtsegs, *ca*, 147a4. Quoted also in Śāntideva, *Śikṣāsamuccaya*, Toh 3940 Tengyur, dbu ma, *khi*, 65a2.

442. *Adhyāśayasaṃcodanasūtra*, Toh 69 Kangyur, dkon brtsegs, *ca*, 147a5. Quoted also in Śāntideva, *Śikṣāsamuccaya*, Toh 3940 Tengyur, dbu ma, *khi*, 65a2.
443. The cross-reference is to the section on enhancing generosity in the preceding chapter (see p. 261–62).
444. Asaṅga, *Bodhisattvabhūmi*, Toh 4037 Tengyur, sems tsam, *wi*, 101a4.
445. *Bodhisattvapiṭaka*, Toh 56 Kangyur, dkon brtsegs, *ga*, 84a4.
446. A.k.a. the *Sutra of the Absorption that Gathers All Merit* (*Sarvapuṇyasamuccayasamādhisūtra*), Toh 134 Kangyur, mdo sde, *na*, 88b5.
447. Ibid., 89a3.
448. *Bodhisattvapiṭaka*, Toh 56 Kangyur, dkon brtsegs, *ga*, 98b2.
449. Śāntideva, *Bodhicaryāvatāra* 6:1, Toh 3871 Tengyur, dbu ma, *la*, 14b3.
450. Ibid. 6:3, 14b4.
451. Ibid. 6:5cd, 14b5.
452. Ibid. 6:5ab, 14b5.
453. *Bodhisattvapiṭaka*, Toh 56 Kangyur, dkon brtsegs, *ga*, 98b3.
454. *Ratnaguṇasaṃcayagāthā* 24:4, Toh 13 Kangyur, sher phyin, *ka*, 14b4.
455. Śāntideva, *Guide to the Bodhisattva Way of Life* (*Bodhicaryāvatāra*) 6:2, Toh 3871 Tengyur, dbu ma, *la*, 14b4.
456. Ibid. 6:6cd, 14b6.
457. Although our author attributes this quotation to the *Meeting of Father and Son Sutra* it is actually from the sutra that immediately follows it in the Dergé Kangyur, i.e., the *Questions of Pūrṇa Sutra* (*Pūrṇaparipṛcchāsūtra*), Toh 61 Kangyur, dkon brtsegs, *nga*, 170b5.
458. Were one less literal, this definition of patience provided here could be translated as "to be able to cope with anything."
459. Asaṅga, *Bodhisattvabhūmi*, Toh 4037 Tengyur, sems tsam, *wi*, 101b7.
460. Śāntideva, *Guide to the Bodhisattva Way of Life* (*Bodhicaryāvatāra*) 6:31, Toh 3871 Tengyur, dbu ma, *la*, 15b6.
461. Ibid. 6:42, 16a5.
462. Ibid. 6:43, 16a6.
463. Ibid. 6:44, 16a6.
464. Ibid. 6:67, 17a5.
465. Ibid. 6:48, 16b1.
466. Ibid. 6:107cd–108, 18b7.
467. Ibid. 6:119, 19a6.
468. Ibid. 6:112cd, 19a2.
469. Asaṅga, *Bodhisattvabhūmi*, Toh 4037 Tengyur, sems tsam, *wi*, 102b2.
470. Ibid., 103b7.
471. Śāntideva, *Bodhicaryāvatāra* 7:22, Toh 3871 Tengyur, dbu ma, *la*, 21a1.
472. Ibid. 6:20, 15a7.
473. Asaṅga, *Bodhisattvabhūmi*, Toh 4037 Tengyur, sems tsam, *wi*, 105a5.
474. Ibid., 107a3.
475. Śāntideva, *Bodhicaryāvatāra* 6:134, Toh 3871 Tengyur, dbu ma, *la*, 20a3.
476. *Sāgaramatiparipṛcchāsūtra*, Toh 152 Kangyur, mdo sde, *pha*, 40a5.
477. *Ratnaguṇasaṃcayagāthā*, Toh 13 Kangyur, sher phyin, *ka*, 19b2.
478. The Sanskrit *satkāya* was freely rendered into Tibetan as *'jig tshogs*, which refers to

the five aggregates and their nature as being both perishable (*'jig*) and composite (*tshogs*). Each aggregate can each be mistaken for a lasting and/or unitary self, as "me" or "mine." And with four types of mistaken approaches to any of these five, one ends up with the twenty major aberrant views of personhood (*satkāyadṛṣṭi*), or as sometime rendered from the Tibetan, "view of the transitory collection."

479. Maitreya, *Mahāyānasūtrālaṃkāra*, Toh 4020 Tengyur, sems tsam, *phi*, 24b2.
480. Maitreya, *Mahāyānasūtrālaṃkāravṛtti*, Toh 4021 Tengyur, sems tsam, *phi*, 201b5.
481. *Sāgaramatiparipṛcchāsūtra*, Toh 152 Kangyur, mdo sde, *pha*, 40a7.
482. *Pūrṇaparipṛcchāsūtra*, Toh 61 Kangyur, dkon brtsegs, *nga*, 187b5.
483. This is not verbatim, but the meaning is that found in Asaṅga's *Abhidharmasamuccaya*, Toh 4049 Tengyur, sems tsam, *ri*, 49a1.
484. Vasubandhu, *Sūtrālaṁkārabhāṣya*, Toh 4026 Tengyur, sems tsam, *phi*, 201b5.
485. *Sutra on Moral Discipline* (*Śīlasaṃyuktasūtra*), Toh 303 Kangyur, mdo sde, *sa*, 127a4.
486. Śāntideva, *Bodhicaryāvatāra* 7:7ab, Toh 3871 Tengyur, dbu ma, *la*, 20a7.
487. Ibid. 7:7cd, 20a7.
488. Ibid. 2:33, 5a5.
489. Ibid. 7:72, 23a4.
490. Nāgārjuna, *Suhṛllekha* verse 104, Toh 4182 Tengyur, spring yig, *nge*, 45b3.
491. Śāntideva, *Guide to the Bodhisattva Way of Life* (*Bodhicaryāvatāra*) 7:18–19, Toh 3871 Tengyur, dbu ma, *la*, 20b6.
492. *Bodhisattvapiṭaka*, Toh 56 Kangyur, dkon brtsegs, *ga*, 116a7.
493. *Varmavyūhanirdeśasūtra*, Toh 51 Kengyur, dkon brtsegs, *kha*, vol. 1, 76a6.
494. *Akṣayamatinirdeśasūtra*, Toh 175 Kangyur, mdo sde, *ma*, 105b7.
495. Asaṅga, *Bodhisattvabhūmi*, Toh 4037 Tengyur, sems tsam, *wi*, 107b3.
496. Śāntideva, *Bodhicaryāvatāra* 7:60, Toh 3871 Tengyur, dbu ma, *la*, 23a3.
497. Ibid. 7:71, 23a3.
498. *Ratnameghasūtra*, Toh 231 Kangyur, mdo sde, *wa*, 20b2.
499. Śāntideva, *Guide to the Bodhisattva Way of Life* (*Bodhicaryāvatāra*) 7:66, Toh 3871 Tengyur, dbu ma, *la*, 22b7.
500. *Vajraketusūtra*. Toh 30 Kangyur, shes rab sna tshogs, *ka*.
501. Śāntideva, *Guide to the Bodhisattva Way of Life* (*Bodhicaryāvatāra*) 7:65, Toh 3871 Tengyur, dbu ma, *la*, 22b6.
502. Asaṅga, *Bodhisattvabhūmi*, Toh 4037 Tengyur, sems tsam, *wi*, 110b6.
503. Maitreya, *Mahāyānasūtrālaṃkāra*, Toh 4020 Tengyur, sems tsam, *phi*, 24b1.
504. Śāntideva, *Bodhicaryāvatāra* 8:1, Toh 3871 Tengyur, dbu ma, *la*, 23a7.
505. Atiśa, *Bodhipathapradīpa* verse 38, Toh 3947 Tengyur, dbu ma, *khi*, 239b7.
506. Ibid. verse 35, 239b5.
507. Nāgārjuna, *Suhṛllekha*, Toh 4182 Tengyur, spring yig, *nge*, 45b4.
508. *Ratnaguṇasaṃcayagāthā*, Toh 13 Kangyur, sher phyin, *ka*, 19b3.
509. Śāntideva, *Bodhicaryāvatāra* 8:4, Toh 3871 Tengyur, dbu ma, *la*, 23b1.
510. *Dharmasaṃgītisūtra*, Toh 238 Kangyur, mdo sde, *zha*, 42a6.
511. Maitreya, *Mahāyānasūtrālaṃkāra*, Toh 4020 Tengyur, sems tsam, *phi*, 23a4. The three types of enlightenment refer to the arhat states of śrāvakas and prateyakabuddhas and to buddhahood.
512. Asaṅga, *Bodhisattvabhūmi*, Toh 4037 Tengyur, sems tsam, *wi*, 111a2.
513. Śāntideva, *Bodhicaryāvatāra* 8:2ab, Toh 3871 Tengyur, dbu ma, *la*, 23a7.

514. Ibid. 8:3ab, 23b1.
515. *Adhyāśayasaṃcodanasūtra*, Toh 69 Kangyur, dkon brtsegs, *ca*, 143b2.
516. A.k.a. *King of Meditation Sutra* (*Samādhirājasūtra*), Toh 127 Kangyur, mdo sde, *da*, 16a2.
517. Śāntideva, *Bodhicaryāvatāra* 8:8ab, Toh 3871 Tengyur, dbu ma, *la*, 23b3.
518. Ibid. 8:14cd–15a, 24a1.
519. *King of Meditation Sutra* (*Samādhirājasūtra*), Toh 127 Kangyur, mdo sde, *da*, 16a3.
520. Śāntideva, *Bodhicaryāvatāra* 8:20cd, Toh 3871 Tengyur, dbu ma, *la*, 24a4.
521. Ibid. 8:18cd, 24a3.
522. Vasubhandu, *Abhidharmakośa*, Toh 4089 Tengyur, mngon pa, *ku*, 10a4.
523. *King of Meditation Sutra* (*Samādhirājasūtra*), Toh 127 Kangyur, mdo sde, *da*, 16a5.
524. Ibid., 93b7.
525. Ibid., 98a3.
526. *Gṛhapatyugraparipṛcchāsūtra*, Toh 63 Kangyur, dkon brtsegs, *nga*, 279b2.
527. Whatever the original Indian sutra alluded to, with these two references to bears, the terms were translated into Tibetan as the generic bear (*dom*), famous for its savagery, and the bear of the north (*dred*), famous for its stupidity.
528. This is a reference to (1) loving kindness focused on sentient beings, (2) loving kindness focused on the nature of things, and (3) loving kindness with no objective reference. See page 189.
529. *Śālistambasūtra*, Toh 210 Kangyur, mdo sde, *tsha*, 116a4.
530. The dependent origination of external phenomena and the environment is not discussed here in this text.
531. "Formations" (Skt. *saṃskāra*, Tib. *'du byed*). This term is often translated as "compositional factors," "compounded phenomena," or "mental formations." Since neither the Sanskrit nor the Tibetan contains a reference to mind, and since mentioning mind creates certain problems, I have omitted "mental." The second link of dependent origination can also be explained in several ways. Sometimes it refers to the immediate coming into being of the notion of self, then other, and so on. At other times it refers to the whole backlog of conditioning that one has at any given moment: a person's karmic formations from past conditioning.
532. *Rice Shoot Sutra* (*Śālistambasūtra*), Toh 210 Kangyur, mdo sde, *tsha*, 116a7.
533. There are four modes of birth: from an egg, from a womb, spontaneous, and from ambient conditions.
534. Nāgārjuna, *Pratītyasamutpādahṛdayakārikā*, Toh 3836 Tengyur, dbu ma, *tsa*, 46b2.
535. "Tainted" in the context of karma means tainted by dualistic concepts, be it virtuous or nonvirtuous karma.
536. The *Ten Levels Sutra* (*Daśabhūmikasūtra*) is the popular name given to chapter 31 of the *Flower Ornament Sutra* (*Avataṃsakasūtra*), Toh 44 Kangyur, phal chen, *kha*, 222b2.
537. *Rice Shoot Sutra* (*Śālistambasūtra*), Toh 210 Kangyur, mdo sde, *tsha*, 116b4.
538. Śāntideva, *Bodhicaryāvatāra* 8:90, Toh 3871 Tengyur, dbu ma, *la*, 27a2.
539. Ibid. 8:130b–d, 28b3.
540. Ibid. 8:113, 28a1.
541. Vasubandhu, *Commentary on the Treasury of Higher Knowledge* (*Abhidharmakośabhāṣya*), Toh 4090 Tengyur, mngon pa, *khu*, 11b1.
542. At the heart of the Kagyü lineage lie two major streams of transmission. The first, referred to here, is that of the Mahāmudrā meditations of Saraha, passed down via

a lineage including Maitripa and Marpa and here referred to under one of its other names, Innate Union (*lhan cig skyes sbyor*; *sahajayoga*). The other stream of transmission is that of the Six Dharmas of Nāropa, which conveys the quintessence of the father, mother, and nondual tantras.

543. This entire paragraph is absent in the Tshurphu edition of the text. It seems that, unless we treat this paragraph as part of the parenthetical annotation, its inclusion interrupts the flow of the text.
544. Asaṅga, *Bodhisattvabhūmi*, Toh 4037 Tengyur, sems tsam, *wi*, 111a5.
545. Maitreya, *Mahāyānasūtrālaṃkāra*, Toh 4020 Tengyur, sems tsam, *phi*, 31a2.
546. Asaṅga, *Bodhisattvabhūmi*, Toh 4037 Tengyur, sems tsam, *wi*, 113a4.
547. Nāgārjuna, *Letter to a Friend* (*Suhṛllekha*), Toh 4182 Tengyur, spring yig, *nga*, 42b4.
548. *Ratnaguṇasaṃcayagāthā*, Toh 13 Kangyur, sher phyin, *ka*, 6a5.
549. Candrakīrti, *Madhyamakāvatāra* 6:2, Toh 3861 Tengyur, dbu ma, *'a*, 204a1.
550. *Ratnaguṇasaṃcayagāthā*, Toh 13 Kangyur, sher phyin, *ka*, 19b3.
551. Atiśa, *Bodhipathapradīpa* verse 43, Toh 3947 Tengyur, dbu ma, *khi*, 240a2.
552. *Akṣayamatinirdeśasūtra*, Toh 175 Kangyur, mdo sde, *ma*, 170a7.
553. *Vimalakīrtinirdeśasūtra*, Toh 176 Kangyur, mdo sde, *ma*, 201b1.
554. *Anavataptanāgarājaparipṛcchāsūtra*, Toh 156 Kangyur, mdo sde, *pha*, 228b3.
555. *Gayāśīrṣasūtra*, Toh 109 Kangyur, mdo sde, *ca*, 290a1.
556. Śāntideva, *Bodhicaryāvatāra* 9:1ab, Toh 3871 Tengyur, dbu ma, *la*, 30b7.
557. Asaṅga, *Abhidharmasamuccaya*, Toh 4049 Tengyur, sems tsam, *ri*, 48b3.
558. "Creative skill" is used here for the Tibetan *bzo ba rig pa*. This is often translated as "arts and crafts," yet covers the much wider scope of all knowledge of how things come into being. The field so often translated as "medicine" also has a broader sense: It is the knowledge of how to act on the causal processes to prevent or reduce the harm they would normally cause.
559. *Saptaśatikāprajñāpāramitā*, Toh 90 Kangyur, dkon brtsegs, *cha*, 197b6.
560. *Ratnaguṇasaṃcayagāthā*, Toh 13 Kangyur, sher phyin, *ka*, 3b1.
561. Atiśa, *Bodhipathapradīpa* verse 47, Toh 3947 Tengyur, dbu ma, *khi*, 240a5.
562. Ibid. verse 48, 240a5.
563. In the critical Tibetan edition, the Beijing edition, as well as the Tsipri edition, there is the following reading: "What then are the two kinds of self or mind?... What is the self or mind of persons?" In these editions, in these two instances *self* (*bdag*) is equated with *mind* (*sems*), thus giving rise to a somewhat awkward reading of the text. Here, we have chosen to follow the reading of the Palpung edition.
564. Dharmakīrti, *Pramāṇavārttika*, "Pramāṇasidhi" chapter, verse 221, Toh 4210 Tengyur, tshad ma, *che*, 116a1.
565. This is reference to the etymology of *dharma*, the root *dhṛ* of which gives a sense of "holding," "possessing." Thus each distinct phenomenon known by the mind has its own characteristics.
566. Nāgārjuna, *Ratnāvalī* 1:28ab, Toh 4158 Tengyur, spring yig, *ge*, 108a2.
567. Ibid. 1:28cd, 108a2.
568. This passage is a summary of well-rehearsed arguments found in the Perfection of Wisdom literature. It consists of a minute examination of the successive moments of time of a supposed creation and an exploration of the very notion of "cause": one thing disappearing and another occurring.

569. Nāgārjuna, *Ratnāvalī* 1:37a–c, Toh 4158 Tengyur, spring yig, *ge*, 108a6.
570. Vasubandhu, *Viṃśatikā*, Toh 4056 Tengyur, sems tsam, *shi*, 3b3.
571. *Avataṃsakasūtra*, Toh 44 Kangyur, phal chen, *kha*, 220b4.
572. *Laṅkāvatārasūtra*, Toh 107 Kangyur, mdo sde, *ca*, 165a6.
573. Ibid., 165a5.
574. This parenthetical sentence appears as an annotation, written in a small font, embedded in the original Tibetan text.
575. Literally, "Does it have the three times?"
576. Nāgārjuna, *Ratnāvalī* 1:69, Toh 4158 Tengyur, spring yig, *ge*, 109a1.
577. *Kāśyapaparivartasūtra*, Toh 87 Kangyur, dkon brtseg, *cha*, 139a2.
578. *Dam pa'i chos yongs su 'dzin pa'i mdo*. The source of this quotation has not been identified.
579. *Dharmatāsvabhāvaśūnyatācalapratisarvālokasūtra*, Toh 128 Kangyur, mdo sde, *da*, 172b3.
580. Śāntideva, *Bodhicaryāvatāra* 9:22, Toh 3871 Tengyur, dbu ma, *la*, 31b5.
581. This is not verbatim but based on Tilopa's *Treasury of Dohas* (*Dohakoṣa*), Toh 2281 Tengyur, rgyud 'grel, *zhi*, 136b2. Tilopa is found in the Tengyur and other sources under the similar-sounding names of Tillipa, Tailikapada, Talika, and Tilopada.
582. *Dharmadhātuprakṛtyasambhedanirdeśasūtra*, Toh 52 Kangyur, dkon brtsegs, *kha*, 143a3.
583. Śāntideva, *Bodhicaryāvatāra* 9:60cd, Toh 3871 Tengyur, dbu ma, *la*, 33a4.
584. Ibid. 9:61cd, Toh 3871 Tengyur, dbu ma, *la*, 33a5.
585. *Song of an Inexhaustible Treasure of Instruction* (*Dohakoṣopadeśagīti*), Toh 2264 Tengyur, rgyud 'grel, *zhi*, 29a4.
586. *Laṅkāvatārasūtra*, Toh 107 Kangyur, mdo sde, *ca*, 180b3.
587. Nāgārjuna, *Ratnāvalī* 1:98cd, Toh 4158 Tengyur, spring yig, *ga*, 10b2.
588. *Song of an Inexhaustible Treasure of Instruction* (*Dohakoṣopadeśagīti*), Toh 2264 Tengyur, rgyud 'grel, *zhi*, 29a4.
589. *Kāśyapaparivartasūtra*, Toh 87 Kangyur, dkon brtsegs, *cha*, 132b1.
590. Nāgārjuna, *Mūlamadhyamakakārikā* 13:8cd, Toh 3824 Tengyur, dbu ma, *tsa*, 8a6.
591. Nāgārjuna, *Ratnāvalī* 1:57ab, Toh 4158 Tengyur, spring yig, *ge*, 109a2
592. Nāgārjuna, *Mūlamadhyamakakārikā* 15:10ab, Toh 3824 Tengur, dbu ma, *tsa*, 9a2.
593. Nāgārjuna, *Ratnāvalī* 1:56, Toh 4158 Tengyur, spring yig, *ge*, 109a2.
594. Ibid. 1:57cd, 109a3. The text in parentheses corresponds to the smaller letters within the quoted text in the Tibetan edition.
595. Nāgārjuna, Mūlamadhyamakakārikā 15:10cd, Toh 3824 Tengur, dbu ma, *tsa*, 9a2.
596. *Trisaṃvaranirdeśaparivarta*, Toh 45 Kangyur, dkon brtsegs, *ka*, 130b1.
597. *Guide to the Bodhisattva Way of Life* (*Bodhicaryāvatāra*) 9:102cd and 103b–d, Toh 3871 Tengyur, dbu ma, *la*, 34b7.
598. *Instructions on Madhyamaka* (*Madhyamakopadeśa*), Toh 3929 Tengyur, dbu ma, *ki*, 95b5. This entire quotation from Atiśa is missing in the Palpung edition of the text.
599. Maitreya, *Abhisamayālaṃkāra* 3:1, Toh 3786 Tengyur, shes phyin, *ka*, 6b4.
600. Nāgārjuna, *Ratnāvalī* 1:42ab, Toh 4158 Tengyur, sprin yig, *ge*, 108b2.
601. Nāgārjuna, *Mūlamadhyamakakārikā* 25:5ab, Toh 3824 Tengur, dbu ma, *tsa*, 16a7.
602. Ibid. 25:7d, 16b2.
603. Nāgārjuna, *Ratnāvalī* 42cd, Toh 4158 Tengyur, spring yig, *ge*, 108b2.

604. Śāntideva, *Bodhicaryāvatāra* 9:34, Toh 3871 Tengyur, dbu ma, *la*, 32a4.
605. *Brahmaviśeṣacintiparipṛcchāsūtra*, Toh 160 Kangyur, mdo sde, *ba*, 33b3.
606. Nāgārjuna, *Mūlamadhyamakakārikā* 25:3, Toh 3824 Tengyur, dbu ma, *tsa*, 16a6.
607. The *Precious Space Jewel Sutra* (*Nam mkha' rin po che'i mdo*) source of this famous quotation has not been identified. But the verse appears, among other places, in Maitreya's *Ornament of Clear Realization* (*Abhisamayālaṃkāra*) 5:21, Toh 3786 Tengyur, shes phyin, *ka*, 10a3 and in his *Uttaratantra* 1:154, Toh 4024 D, sems tsam *phi*, 61b5.
608. *Suvikrāntavikramiparipṛcchāsūtra*, Toh 14 Kangyur, shes rab sna tshogs, *ka*, 23a5.
609. *Sgra can 'dzin gyis yum la bstod pa*. Although this verse homage to the *Perfection of Wisdom* attributed to the Buddha's son Rāhula is well known, its exact source in the canonical texts remains unidentified.
610. The Tibetan for what is translated here as "natural settled state" is archaic: *rnal du dbab pa*. The meaning of this was defined by later Tibetan translators as "abiding within its own natural dominion, untroubled by harm from what is other."
611. *Saptaśatikānāmaprajñāpāramitā*, Toh 90 Kangyur, dkon brtsegs, *cha*, 204a5.
612. The Palpung edition of the text does not have this sentence.
613. This translation of this famous six-point instruction from Tilopa follows the traditional meaning more than a strictly literal interpretation. The traditional explanation sets them into a time context as follows: "Not dwelling on [the past], not intending [about the future], not analyzing [the present, in terms of 'being' in the present]."
614. A scriptural source of this and the previous quote from Tilopa has not been identified. Some pith advice belongs to the intimate instructions handed down orally (*man ngag*) and was only committed to writing generations after its originator.
615. Although our author ascribes this quote to Nāgārjuna, most probably the verse is from Saraha's *Treasury of Spiritual Songs* (*Dohakoṣagīti*), Toh 2224 Tengyur, rgyud 'grel, *wi*, 74b3.
616. The source of this quote ascribed to Nāgārjuna has not been identified.
617. The source of this quote from Śavaripa has not been identified.
618. The source of this quote has not been identified.
619. *Treasury of Spiritual Songs* (*Dohakoṣagīti*) verse 16, Toh 2224 Tengyur, rgyud, *wi*, 71b2.
620. *Song of Seeing Dharmadhātu* (*Dharmadhātudarśanagīti*), verses 2–3, Toh 2314 Tengyur, rgyud 'grel, *shi*, 255a1.
621. Source unidentified.
622. *Saptaśatikānāmaprajñāpāramitā*, Toh 90 Kangyur, dkon brtsegs, *cha*, 186a3.
623. *Aṣṭasāhasrikāprajñāpāramitā*, Toh 12 Kangyur, sher phyin, *ka*, 167b5.
624. Ibid., 111b2.
625. *Ratnaguṇasaṃcayagāthā*, Toh 13 Kangyur, sher phyin, *ka*, 3a7.
626. *Advice on Cheating Death* (*Mṛtyuvañcanopadeśa*), Toh 1748 Tengyur, rgyud 'grel, *sha*, 133b1.
627. *Dharmasaṃgītisūtra*, Toh 238 Kangyur, mdo sde, *zha*, 68b5.
628. Atiśa, *Penetrating the Two Truths* (*Satyadvayāvatāra*), Toh 3902 Tengyur, dbu ma, *a*, 72a6. Gampopa refers to *Satyadvayāvatāra* as the *Shorter Text on Middle Way Two Truths*.

629. *Ratnaguṇasaṃcayagāthā*, Toh 13 Kangyur, sher phyin, *ka*, 8b3.
630. Ibid., 2b4.
631. *Samādhirājasūtra*, Toh 127 Kangyur, mdo sde, *da*, 26b2.
632. *Spyod pa'i de kho na nyid*, **Caryātattva*. The source of this quote has not been identified.
633. *Verse Summary of the Perfection of Wisdom* (*Ratnaguṇasaṃcayagāthā*), Toh 13 Kangyur, sher phyin, *ka*, 2b2.
634. *De kho na nyid bstan pa'i mdo*. The sutra that is the source of this quote has not been found.
635. *Mahāsamayavaipulyasūtra*, Toh 265 Kangyur, mdo sde, *'a*, 287b5. Intriguingly, a large part of the text, starting from this point up to the section relating to the signs of having cultivated wisdom (p. 337), is missing in the Palpung edition. This variance represents a significant difference between the texts, especially since the section missing in the Palpung edition deals specifically with an important standpoint of the simultaneist (*gcig bcar ba*) approach to the path—that all key elements of the path to buddhahood are embodied within the single practice of understanding the nature of your mind.
636. *Gtsug tor chen po'i mdo*. The source of this quote has not been identified.
637. Approximation of *Mahāyānaprasādaprabhāvanasūtra*, Toh 144 Kangyur, mdo sde, *pa*, 32b6.
638. *Sarvadharmāpravṛttinirdeśasūtra*, Toh 180 Kangyur, mdo sde, *ma*, 294a5.
639. *Daśacakrakṣitigarbhasūtra*, Toh 239 Kangyur, mdo sde, *zha*, 138b2.
640. Ibid., 139b5.
641. *Anavataptanāgarājaparipṛcchāsūtra*, Toh 156 Kangyur, mdo sde, *pha*, 250a6.
642. *Sems bskyed chen po mdo*. This sutra has not been identified.
643. *Hevajratantra*, Toh 417 Kangyur, rgyud, *nga*, 6a7.
644. *Sarvabuddhasamayoga*, Toh 366 Kangyur, rgyud, *ka*, 152a6. The term *yoga* means "fusion" or "union." In the lines cited here, the term refers to a union with the deity during the completion stage of tantra, while "the yogi" here is the tantric meditator.
645. *Vajraśekharatantra*, Toh 480 Kangyur, rgyud, *nya*, 155b1.
646. *Amṛtaguhyatantrarāja*, Toh 401 Kangyur, rgyud, *ga*, 234b6.
647. *Vajrasamādhidharmākṣara*, Toh 135 Kangyur, mdo sde, *na*, 125b7, but not identical to Gampopa's quote.
648. *Brahmaviśeṣacintiparipṛcchāsūtra*, Toh 160 Kangyur, mdo sde, *ba*, 58a2.
649. *Daśacakrakṣitigarbhasūtra*, Toh 239 Kangyur, mdo sde, *zha*, 224a6.
650. Ibid., 225b2.
651. Ibid., 226b2.
652. Ibid., 227b4.
653. A *Precious Space Sutra* has not been identified, but this quote is found in Nāgārjuna's *Five Stages* (*Pañcakrama*), Toh 1802 Tengyur, rgyud 'grel, *ngi*.
654. *Pitāputrasamāgamasūtra*, Toh 60 Kangyur, dkon brtsegs, *nga*, 99b3.
655. *Amṛtaguhyatantrarāja*, Toh 401 Kangyur, rgyud, *ga*, 234b7.
656. *Las rnam par dag pa'i mdo*. This quotation is given by Vimalamitra as coming from the *Great Liberation Sutra*, in his *Meditating on Nonthought, Penetrating Simultaneity* (*Sakṛtprāveśikanirvikalpabhāvanārtha*), Toh 3910 Tengyur, dbu ma, *ki*, 13b1.
657. *Susthitamatidevaputraparipṛcchāsūtra*, Toh 80 Kangyur, dkon brtsegs, *cha*, 12b1.

658. *Daśacakrakṣitigarbhasūtra*, Toh 239 Kangyur, mdo sde, *zha*, 120b3.
659. *Rab tu mi gnas pa'i rgyud.* This sutra has not been identified.
660. *Treasury of Spiritual Songs* (*Dohakoṣagīti*), Toh 2224 Tengyur, rgyud 'grel, *wi*, 71b.
661. *Amṛtaguhyatantrarāja*, Toh 401 Kangyur, rgyud, *ga*, 234b2.
662. *Jñānālokālaṃkāra*; *Ye shes snang ba rgyan gyi mdo.* This quotation does not appear in present versions of this sutra.
663. *Śrīmahāsaṃbhārodayatantra*, Toh 373 Kangyur, rgyud, *kha*, 309b3.
664. The source of this quote has not been established.
665. Atiśa, *Lamp for the Summary of Conduct* (*Caryāsaṃgrahapradīpa*), Toh 3960 Tengyur, dbu ma, *khi*, 313a5.
666. Nāgārjuna, *Ratnāvalī* 3:88, Toh 4158 Tengyur, spring yig, *ge*, 117b6.
667. *Saptaśatikānāmaprajñāpāramitā*, Toh 90 Kangyur, dkon brtsegs, *cha*, 203b7.
668. *Ratnaguṇasaṃcayagāthā*, Toh 13 Kangyur, sher phyin, *ka*, 16a7.
669. Atiśa, *Bodhipathapradīpa* verse 59b, Toh 3947 Tengyur, dbu ma, *khi*, 240b4. As is explained below in the text, the "heat" here is metaphorical and has nothing to do with an experience of heat during meditation. The metaphor is one of approaching a blaze, such as a bonfire, and reaching that initial point where the heat can be felt. The "blaze" referred to is that of pristine awareness.
670. Ibid. verse 59c, 240b5.
671. Literally, "qualities without needing to train" or "qualities of the phase of no-more learning." These spontaneous qualities are contrasted to the previous four phases of the path, where effort and training are needed for qualities to arise.
672. Atiśa, *Bodhipathapradīpa* verse 59c, Toh 3947 Tengyur, dbu ma, *khi*, 240b5.
673. *Ten Levels Sutra* (*Daśabhūmikasūtra*), Toh 44 Kangyur, phal chen, *kha*, 120a2.
674. Maitreya, *Mahāyānasūtrālaṃkāra* 21:32, Toh 4020 Tengyur, sems tsam, *phi*, 37b3.
675. The list of various trainings needed for mastery of this and the following nine bodhisattva levels are to be found in Maitreya's *Ornament of Clear Realization* and its commentaries.
676. Maitreya, *Abhisamayālaṃkāra* 1:49, Toh 3786 Tengyur, shes phyin, *ka*, 3b7.
677. *Ten Levels Sutra* (*Daśabhūmikasūtra*), Toh 44 Kangyur, phal chen, *kha*, 182b5.
678. Ibid., 182a5.
679. These three factors are important in their own right and often cited as the activities of great bodhisattvas. Reference will be made back to this list of three in the following nine levels.
680. *Ten Levels Sutra* (*Daśabhūmikasūtra*), Toh 44 Kangyur, phal chen, *kha*, 183a2.
681. Maitreya, *Madhyāntavibhāga* 2:16a, Toh 4021 Tengyur, sems tsam, *phi*, 42a1.
682. The usual number is eighty-eight, based on Maitreya's *Ornament of Clear Realization*. Eighty-two could have been an early slip, by Gampopa himself or by a copyist or woodblock carver, that has been reproduced ever since.
683. *Ten Levels Sutra* (*Daśabhūmikasūtra*), Toh 44 Kangyur, phal chen, *kha*, 126a5.
684. Nāgārjuna, *Ratnāvalī* 5:42, Toh 4158 Tengyur, spring yig, *ge*, 123b4.
685. *Ten Levels Sutra* (*Daśabhūmikasūtra*), Toh 44 Kangyur, phal chen, *kha*, 125a6.
686. Maitreya, *Ornament of Mahayana Sutras* (*Mahāyānasūtrālaṃkāra*) 21:33, Toh 4020 Tengyur, sems tsam, *phi*, 37b4.
687. Maitreya, *Ornament of Clear Realization* (*Abhisamayālaṃkāra*) 1:52, Toh 3786 Tengyur, shes phyin, *ka*, 4a2.
688. *Ten Levels Sutra* (*Daśabhūmikasūtra*), Toh 44 Kangyur, phal chen, *kha*, 193a4.

689. Maitreya, *Clear Differentiation of the Middle and Extremes* (*Madhyāntavibhāga*) 2:16a, Toh 4021 Tengyur, sems tsam, *phi*, 42a7.
690. Nāgārjuna, *Ratnāvalī* 5:44, Toh 4158 Tengyur, spring yig, *ge*, 133b5.
691. "And so forth" refers back to the list of twelve specific abilities mentioned for the first bodhisattva level, the only difference being in their numbers. For instance, on the first level, it was hundred, on the second level thousand, on the third ten thousand, and so on.
692. Maitreya, *Ornament of Mahayana Sutras* (*Mahāyānasūtrālaṃkāra*) 20:33, Toh 4020 Tengyur, sems tsam, *phi*, 37b4.
693. Maitreya, *Ornament of Clear Realization* (*Abhisamayālaṃkāra*) 1:53, Toh 3786 Tengyur, shes phyin, *ka*, 4a3.
694. *Ten Levels Sutra* (*Daśabhūmikasūtra*), Toh 44 Kangyur, phal chen, *kha*, 201a7.
695. Maitreya, *Clear Differentiation of the Middle and Extremes* (*Madhyāntavibhāga*) 2:16b, Toh 4021 Tengyur, sems tsam, *phi*, 42a7.
696. Nāgārjuna, *Precious Garland* (*Ratnāvalī*) 5:46cd, Toh 4158 Tengyur, sprin yig, *ge*, 123b6.
697. Maitreya, *Ornament of Mahayana Sutras* (*Mahāyānasūtrālaṃkāra*) 20:34, Toh 4020 Tengyur, sems tsam, *phi*, 37b4.
698. Maitreya, *Ornament of Clear Realization* (*Abhisamayālaṃkāra*) 1:53, Toh 3786 Tengyur, shes phyin, *ka*, 4a3.
699. *Ten Levels Sutra* (*Daśabhūmikasūtra*), Toh 44 Kangyur, phal chen, *kha*, 208b7.
700. Maitreya, *Clear Differentiation of the Middle and Extremes* (*Madhyāntavibhāga*) 2:16c, Toh 4021 Tengyur, sems tsam, *phi*, 42a7.
701. Nāgārjuna, *Precious Garland* (*Ratnāvalī*) 5:48, Toh 4158 Tengyur, spring yig, *ge*, 123b7.
702. Maitreya, *Ornament of Mahayana Sutras* (*Mahāyānasūtrālaṃkāra*) 21:35, Toh 4020 Tengyur, sems tsam, *phi*, 32b5.
703. Maitreya, *Ornament of Clear Realization* (*Abhisamayālaṃkāra*) 1:56, Toh 3786 Tengyur, shes phyin, *ka*, 4a4.
704. *Ten Levels Sutra* (*Daśabhūmikasūtra*), Toh 44 Kangyur, phal chen, *kha*, 215b6.
705. Maitreya, *Clear Differentiation of the Middle and Extremes* (*Madhyāntavibhāga*) 2:16d, Toh 4021 Tengyur, sems tsam, *phi*, 42a7. "Ten sorts of sameness" refers to a list found in the *Ten Levels Sutra* where, in presenting the emptiness of all phenomena, the sutra identifies two basic kinds of sameness—the sameness of all phenomena with respect to their absence of inherent existence and the sameness of all phenomena with respect to their absence of signs. These two are then explained further in terms of eight kinds of sameness.
706. Nāgārjuna, *Precious Garland* (*Ratnāvalī*) 5:50, Toh 4158 Tengyur, spring yig, 124a1.
707. As long as samsara or nirvana seem real, separate from and different from each other, the mind falls into the general "impurity" of being sway to concepts. The profound wisdom of this sixth level reveals mind's innate and pristine purity, and this automatically dispels such dualistic elaborations.
708. Maitreya, *Ornament of Mahayana Sutras* (*Mahāyānasūtrālaṃkāra*) 21:36, Toh 4020 Tengyur, sems tsam, *phi*, 32b5.
709. Maitreya, *Ornament of Clear Realization* (*Abhisamayālaṃkāra*) 1:57, Toh 3786 Tengyur, shes phyin, *ka*, 4a5.
710. *Ten Levels Sutra* (*Daśabhūmikasūtra*), Toh 44 Kangyur, phal chen, *kha*, 215a5.

711. Maitreya, *Clear Differentiation of the Middle and Extremes* (*Madhyāntavibhāga*) 2:17a, Toh 4021 Tengyur, sems tsam, *phi*, 42a1.
712. Nāgārjuna, *Precious Garland* (*Ratnāvalī*) 5:52, Toh 4158 Tengyur, spring yig, *ge*, 224a3.
713. Maitreya, *Ornament of Mahayana Sutras* (*Mahāyānasūtrālaṃkāra*), Toh 4020 Tengyur, sems tsam, *phi*, 37b6.
714. Maitreya, *Ornament of Clear Realization* (*Abhisamayālaṃkāra*) 1:59a, Toh 3786 Tengyur, sher chen, *ka*, 4a6.
715. Ibid. 1:62a, 4a7.
716. *Ten Levels Sutra* (*Daśabhūmikasūtra*), Toh 44 Kangyur, phal chen, *kha*, 236a2.
717. Maitreya, *Clear Differentiation of the Middle and Extremes* (*Madhyāntavibhāga*) 2:17b, Toh 4021 Tengyur, sems tsam, *phi*, 42a1.
718. Tib. *dbang sgyur* or *gzhan 'phrul dbang byed*, Skt. *paranirmitavaśavartin*. These gods are the highest within the desire realm and exercise dominion over others' manifestations for their own enjoyment.
719. Nāgārjuna, *Precious Garland* (*Ratnāvalī*) 5:54, Toh 4158 Tengyur, spring yig, *ge*, 224a4.
720. Maitreya, *Ornament of Mahayana Sutras* (*Mahāyānasūtrālaṃkāra*) 21:37, Toh 4020 Tengyur, sems tsam, *phi*, 32b6.
721. Maitreya, *Ornament of Clear Realization* (*Abhisamayālaṃkāra*) 1:66ab, Toh 3786 Tengyur, sher chen, *ka*, 4b3.
722. *Ten Levels Sutra* (*Daśabhūmikasūtra*), Toh 44 Kangyur, phal chen, *kha*, 247b3.
723. Maitreya, *Clear Differentiation of the Middle and Extremes* (*Madhyāntavibhāga*) 2:17c, Toh 4021 Tengyur, sems tsam, *phi*, 42a1.
724. Ibid. 2:17d, 42a2.
725. Nāgārjuna, *Precious Garland* (*Ratnāvalī*) 5:56, Toh 4158 Tengyur, spring yig, *ge*, 224a5.
726. Maitreya, *Ornament of Mahayana Sutras* (*Mahāyānasūtrālaṃkāra*) 21:38, Toh 4020 Tengyur, sems tsam, *phi*, 37b7.
727. Maitreya, *Ornament of Clear Realization* (*Abhisamayālaṃkāra*) 1:68ab, Toh 3786 Tengyur, shes phyin, *ka*, 4b4. The twelve factors as listed in the *Ornament of Clear Realizations* are, in addition to the two listed in the text, (3) possessing a steafast confidence, (4) being conceived in an excellent womb, (5) being of excellent caste, (6) being of excellent family lineage, (7) having excellent parents, (8) having excellent retinue, (9) possessing excellent birth, (10) attaining excellent renunciation, (11) being endowed with an excellent site, such as with the presence of bodhi tree, and (12) bearing excellent higher qualities.
728. The *Ten Levels Sutra* (*Daśabhūmikasūtra*), Toh 44 Kangyur, phal chen, *kha*, 257b6.
729. Ibid., 254b1.
730. Nāgārjuna, *Precious Garland* (*Ratnāvalī*) 5:56, Toh 4158 Tengyur, spring yig, *ge*, 224a6.
731. "Countless" is the last of the series of names that ancient India had for each multiple of ten, from 100 up to 10^{51}. This extraordinary range of names was needed for comparing differences in lifespan and so forth in the various levels of the cosmos.
732. Maitreya, *Ornament of Mahayana Sutras* (*Mahāyānasūtrālaṃkāra*) 21:38, Toh 4020 Tengyur, sems tsam, *phi*, 37b7.

733. *Ten Levels Sutra* (*Daśabhūmikasūtra*), Toh 44, phal chen *kha*, 261b2.
734. Nāgārjuna, *Ratnāvalī* 5:59, Toh 4158 Tengyur, spring yig, *ga*, 224a6.
735. This passage is in reduced print in the Tsipri xylograph, which is the basis of the critical Tibetan edition produced for *The Library of Tibetan Classics* series. To indicate this, we have presented it within parenthesis. This entire parenthetical paragraph is not found in the Palpung edition, which suggests the possibility that it could be a later addition by an editor.
736. *Ten Levels Sutra* (*Daśabhūmikasūtra*), Toh 44 Kangyur, phal chen, *kha*, 274b1.
737. Ibid., 273b6.
738. The higher five of the seventeen form-realm paradises are known as the "pure realms," not to be confused with pure lands of buddhas. The highest of those heavens is Akaniṣṭha, or Supreme.
739. Nāgārjuna, *Precious Garland* (*Ratnāvalī*) 5:60, Toh 4158 Tengyur, spring yig, *ge*, 224a7.
740. Candrakīrti, *Madhyamakāvatāra* 11:9, Toh 3861 Tengyur, dbu ma, *'a*, 216a3.
741. "Core" is used here in contrast to the skin and flesh of the fruit, which are used as examples in lower levels.
742. Asaṅga, *Bodhisattvabhūmi*, Toh 4037 Tengyur, sems tsam, *wi*, 184b3.
743. This is the fifth line of the six-line topical summary presented by the author in the opening section of the text on page 122.
744. Atiśa, *Bodhipathapradīpa* verse 59d, Toh 3947 Tengyur, dbu ma, *khi*, 240b5.
745. The Tibetan *spangs pa* literally means "abandon," "renunciation," or "shedding." However, to translate this important point as such would be misleading, suggesting deliberate actions of renunciation, of letting go. Such imagery is too gross for what happens here. In this section, we are looking at the end result of a very fine and thorough process of *purification* that has been going on throughout the bodhisattva levels, using the most refined meditation.
746. *Ratnaguṇasaṃcayagāthā*, Toh 13 Kangyur, sher phyin, *ka*, 6b2.
747. *Śatasāhasrikāprajñāpāramitā*, Toh 8 Kangyur, sher phyin, *'a*, 343b3. This is also in the *Perfection of Wisdom in Twenty-Five Thousand Lines* that immediately follows the *Perfection of Wisdom in Eight Thousand Lines* version in the Dergé Kangyur, Toh 9, sher phyin, *'a*, 314b7.
748. *Śatasāhasrikāprajñāpāramitā*, Toh 8 Kangyur, sher phyin, *'a*, 333a7.
749. Maitreya, *Mahāyānasūtrālaṃkāra* 10:31, Toh 4020 Tengyur, sems tsam, *phi*, 10a1.
750. Ibid. 9:67, 11b4.
751. Although Gampopa does not name the source of this quote, these lines can be found in the famed translator Ngok Loden Sherap's *A Letter Entitled "Droplets of Nectar,"* p. 709, line 6.
752. *Verse Summary of the Perfection of Wisdom* (*Ratnaguṇasaṃcayagāthā*), Toh 13 Kangyur, sher phyin, *ka*, 8b3.
753. Vasubandhu, *Commentary on the Treasury of Higher Knowledge* (*Abhidharmakośabhāṣyam*) 1:92, Toh 4090 Tengyur, mngon pa, *ku*, 92b4.
754. Maitreya, *Uttaratantra* 2:53, Toh 4024 Tengyur, sems tsam, *phi*, 64b2.
755. *Dharmasaṃgītisūtra*, Toh 238 Kangyur, mdo sde, *zha*, 43b4.
756. *Pitāputrasamāgamasūtra*, Toh 60 Kangyur, dkon brtsegs, *nga*, 111a3.
757. *Lalitavistarasūtra*, Toh 95 Kangyur, mdo sde, *kha*. This sentence is in small font in

the Tibetan original, indicating it to be an embedded annotation; it is missing in the Palpung edition.

758. The source of this quote has not been identified.
759. Ngok Loden Sherap, *Letter Entitled "Droplets of Nectar,"* p. 709, line 7.
760. *Anantamukhapariśodhananirdeśaparivartasūtra*, Toh 46 Kangyur, dkon brtsegs, *ka*, 49b7.
761. Udbhaṭasiddhasvāmin, *Praise of the Excellence [of the Buddha]* (*Viśeṣastava*), Toh 1109 Tengyur, bstod tshogs, *ka*, 3b6.
762. Although it is clear by the usage of the term *geshé* that it is referring to a Kadampa master, who that specific master is remained undetermined.
763. Most probably the author is here citing his teacher Milarepa's oral teaching, not a specific text.
764. Maitreya, *Mahāyānasūtrālaṃkāra*, Toh 4020 Tengyur, sems tsam, *phi*, 6b1.
765. Maitreya, *Uttaratantra* 2:4, Toh 4024 Tengyur, sems tsam, *phi*, 62b2.
766. Maitreya, *Mahāyānasūtrālaṃkāra* 10:12, Toh 4020 Tengyur, sems tsam, *phi*, 9a4.
767. Candrakīrti, *Seventy Stanzas on Going for Refuge* (*Triśaraṇasaptatī*), Toh 3971 Tengyur, dbu ma, *gi*, 251a2.
768. *Suvarṇaprabhāsottamasūtra*, Toh 556 Kangyur, rgyud, *pa*, 164b1.
769. Maitreya, *Mahāyānasūtrālaṃkāra*, Toh 4020 Tengyur, sems tsam, *phi*, 11b3.
770. *Aṣṭasāhasrikāprajñāpāramitā*, Toh 12 Kangyur, sher phyin, *ka*, 277b3.
771. *Samādhirājasūtra*, Toh 127 Kangyur, mdo sde, *da*, 62a7.
772. The final stage of the path of preparation, just prior to transition into the ārya state.
773. Maitreya, *Uttaratantra* 2:38, Toh 4024 Tengyur, sems tsam, *phi*, 63b7.
774. Maitreya, *Mahāyānasūtrālaṃkāra* 10:62, Toh 4020 Tengyur, sems tsam, *phi*, 11b1.
775. Ibid. 10:61, 11a7.
776. Maitreya, *Abhisamayālaṃkāra* 8:12, Toh 3786 Tengyur, shes phyin, *ka*, 11b7.
777. Maitreya, *Mahāyānasūtrālaṃkāra* 9:64, Toh 4020 Tengyur, sems tsam, *phi*, 11b2.
778. Maitreya, *Uttaratantra* 2:53, Toh 4024 Tengyur, sems tsam, *phi*, 64b3.
779. Ibid. 2:41, 64a3.
780. Maitreya, *Abhisamayālaṃkāra* 8:33, Toh 3786 Tengyur, shes phyin, *ka*, 12b6.
781. Maitreya, *Mahāyānasūtrālaṃkāra* 10:66ab, Toh 4020 Tengyur, sems tsam, *phi*, 11b3.
782. Ibid. 10:66cd, 11b4.
783. This is the final line of the six-line topical summary presented by the author in the opening section of the text on page 122.
784. Maitreya, *Uttaratantra* 4:13, Toh 4024 Tengyur, sems tsam, *phi*, 67b7.
785. *Vaidūrya* has been translated as "lapis lazuli" and as "beryl." Khenchen Thrangu Rinpoché explains that it is in fact a gem found only in the god realms.
786. Maitreya, *Uttaratantra* 4:14, Toh 4024 Tengyur, sems tsam, *phi*, 67b2.
787. Ibid. 4:31–32, 67b4. In the Tibetan original, embedded in the above quotation in verse is the following parenthetical sentence in smaller type: (That is, with the four seals that are the sign of the buddhas' teachings: "All conditioned things are impermanent," "All phenomena are devoid of self-entity," "All tainted phenomena are in the nature of suffering," and "Nirvana is peace.") Incidently, this parenthetical sentence is not found in the Palpung edition.
788. Ibid. 4:33, 67b5.
789. Ibid. 4:44, 69a5.

790. Ibid. 4:45, 69a6.
791. Ibid. 4:56–57, 69b7.
792. Ibid. 4:62–63, 69b7.
793. Ibid. 4:65, 70a6.
794. Ibid. 4:70–71, 70b3.

Notes to Clarifying the Sage's Intent

1. I completed my translation of this treatise before the Institute of Tibetan Classics (ITC) Tibetan edition was published, and thus I did not have access to the 427 endnotes of that edition (pp. 453–72). The references to passages or works in the Dergé edition of Kangyur and Tengur canons that were traced by the ITC editors were kindly added to my endnotes by Lea Groth-Wilson and thus can now be consulted. In my original notes I had gathered a number of my own source identifications, mainly to the Peking (P) editon of the canon.
2. Cf. Candrakīrti's *Entering the Middle Way* (*Madhyamakāvatāra*) 1:1, Toh 3861 Tengyur, dbu ma *'a*, 202a2, quoted by Sapaṇ at the end of his text. See page 498.
3. Chim Jampaiyang (*Detailed Abhidharma Commentary*, 74a) defines "appreciating" (*mos pa*) as "to desire or to hold an object as possessing valuable qualities" (*'dod pa'am dmigs pa la yon tan can du 'dzin pa*).
4. Maitreya, *Mahāyānasūtrālaṃkāra* 20:61–62, Toh 4020 Tengyur, sems tsam, *phi*, 35a4; P 5521, sems tsam, *phi*. Numbering for themes in this citation have been added in accord with Sapaṇ's presentation to assist the reader. These lines are supposed to be at least a little cryptic, a terse list of themes requiring a whole book to explain. Later Sakya scholars discuss this ordering and whether it accords exactly with Sapaṇ's topics. The verse is quoted by Vasubandhu, *Commentary on the Ornament of Mahayana Sutras* (*Sūtrālaṃkārabhāṣya*); Toh 4026 Tengyur, sems tsam, *phi*; P 5527 Tengyur, sems tsam, *phi*. In the TG version of these verses, the fifth topic, "bringing sentient beings to maturity" (*sems can rnams yongs smin byed dang*), has been moved up to fourth in the list, with "entering into the faultless [levels of an ārya]" turned into the fifth. This change in ordering is discussed in the introduction to this volume.
5. Maitreya, *Mahāyānasūtrālaṃkāra* 4:4; Toh 4020 Tengyur, sems tsam, *phi*, 4a2.
6. On the developed spiritual potential (*rgyas pa'i rigs*), see also Ngawang Chödrak, *Setting Exquisite Gems*, 30.6, where he gives Gorampa's interpretation in the context of *Abhisamayālaṃkāra* exegesis—that is, Perfection of Wisdom scholastics.
7. Sthiramati similarly explains the etymology of the Sanskrit term *gotra* in his *Detailed Exposition of the Ornament of Mahayana Sutras* (*Sūtrālaṃkāravṛttibhāṣya*), P 5531, sems tsam, *mi*, 48a.
8. *Nges par bshad*: *nirūpyate* (*ni-rūp*), "ascertained, determined," or even "defined"?
9. Maitreya, *Mahāyānasūtrālaṃkāra* 4:5, Toh 4020 Tengyur, sems tsam, *phi*, 4a3. As quoted by Vasubandhu, *Sūtrālaṃkārabhāṣya*, P 5527, sems tsam, *phi*, 146a: *sbyor ba'i sngon du snying rje dang// mos pa dang ni bzod pa dang// dge ba yang dag spyod pa ni// rigs kyi rtags su shes par bya//*. Cf. Guenther, *Jewel Ornament*, 7.
10. Maitreya, *Mahāyānasūtrālaṃkāra* 4:6, Toh 4020 Tengyur, sems tsam, *phi*, 4a4. Quoted also in Vasubandhu, *Sūtrālaṃkārabhāṣya*, P 5527, sems tsam, *phi*, 144b.
11. *Nītiśāstra*, chap. 8, Toh 4334 Tengyur, *ngo*, 136a3. This is the Tibetan version of

the *Treatise on Political Morals* by Cāṇakya, a minister of Candragupta, sometimes called the Machiavelli of India. Mr. Hidetoshi Fushimi found a similar verse, but about the lifelong dependency of women, in the Tibetan translation of the *Nītiśāstra*, P 5826, *go*, 184a1–2.

12. On severed spiritual potential, see Sthiramati, *Detailed Exposition of the Ornament of Mahayana Sutras* (*Sūtrālaṃkāravṛttibhāṣya*), Toh 4034 Tengyur, sems tsam *mi*, 48a3–49b1; P 5531, sems tsam, *mi*, 52b and 53b. This spiritual status is called *rigs med pa* (*agotra*) in the *Mahāyānasūtrālaṃkāra*. The Tibetan term *rigs chad rigs* was used by Gampopa in his *Ornament of Liberation* (*Thar rgyan*), on which see Guenther, *Jewel Ornament*, 12n21.
13. That is, to liberation. In Sthiramati's *Sūtrālaṃkāravṛttibhāṣya*, Toh 4034 Tengyur, sems tsam *mi*, 48a5; P 5531, sems tsam, *mi*, 52b and 53b, the line reads: *la la thar phyogs dge ba med*, and in Sanskrit for *thar* one finds *mokṣa*.
14. Maitreya, *Mahāyānasūtrālaṃkāra* 4:11, Toh 4020 Tengyur, sems tsam, *phi*, 4a6. As quoted by Vasubandhu, *Sūtrālaṃkārabhāṣya*, P 5527, sems tsam, *phi*, 146b: *la la gcig tu nyes par spyod nges yod// la la dkar po'i chos rnams kun tu bcom// la la thar pa'i cha mthun dge ba med//*. Note not only the different ordering of the lines but also slight differences in terminology in the TG version: *la la dkar po'i cha mthun dge ba med// la la gcig tu nyes par spyod rjes 'brang// la la dkar po'i chos kun rnam par 'jom// dkar po dman pa yod pa rgyu dang bral* Cf. Guenther, *Jewel Ornament*, 3–4, who translates the verse as alluding to four, not five, points.
15. Cf. Seyfort Ruegg, *La Théorie du Tathāgatagarbha et du Gotra*, 80.
16. Correct *bya ba* (in ITC and other versions) to read *bya pa*, "bird hunter," as is clear from Shang Dodé Pal, a disciple of Sapaṇ, in his *sgrung 'grel* "story commentary" on the present work.
17. The story of the bird hunters of King Prasenajit is told by Shang Dodé Pal, *Commentary*, 3a4–6b1. The story actually begins with the long tale of the frightful serial murderer Aṅgulimāla and how he was tamed and ordained as a monk by Buddha Śākyamuni, which greatly impressed King Prasenajit. Then the Buddha has the five hundred bird hunters who were then hunting on that king's lands summoned. Prasenajit ordered them to stop hunting at once, promising them other good livelihoods and threatening to execute them if they did not stop. The hunters were not deterred. They handed their nets and other implements to their sons and nephews, urging them to go on with their old life of hunting, stubbornly accepting execution themselves. Finally the Buddha converted them by magically manifesting as an expert old bird hunter who could shoot a divine garuḍa with a single arrow, impressing them with his own incomparable hunting skills. More about Prasenajit (Pāli: Pasenadi), king of Kośala and pious supporter of the Buddha, is told by Malalasekera, *Dictionary of Pāli Proper Names*.
18. The story of the stubbornly impious Chinese child is told by Shang Dodé Pal, *Commentary*, 6b1. Once a Chinese boy was brought by his parents to a Buddhist temple and introduced to its sacred contents, but he did not even want to look. Then his parents put a sacred image of Avalokiteśvara in a pot and told him, "Your deity is in that pot. Fetch it!" Covering his eyes and nose with his clothing, the boy took the deity outside in the pot, putting it down with the words, "*Your* sacred image is in there!" thus showing a lack of spiritual potential.

19. This is a reference to the second key topic from the *Ornament of Mahāyāna Sūtras* (*Mahāyānasūtrālaṃkāra* 20:61) quoted above on page 385.
20. Maitreya, *Mahāyānasūtrālaṃkāra* 10:8, Toh 4020 Tengyur, sems tsam, *phi*, 9a1.
21. *Great Sutra of the Supreme Victory* (*Dhvajāgramahāsūtra*), Toh 293 Kangyur, mdo sde, *sha*, 267a3. Compare Guenther, *Jewel Ornament*, 100n9, and page 200 above.
22. Thus the Buddha embodies both Dharma and Sangha. Maitreya, *Uttaratantra* 1:20–21, Toh 4024 Tengyur, sems tsam, *phi*, 55b5; P 5525, sems tsam, *phi*, 55b8–56a2. For a slightly different rendering of these lines in English, see Ken Holmes' translation on page 202 of this volume.
23. Sapaṇ here refers to a traditional enumeration of eight types of āryas accepted by the śrāvakas as together forming their ārya sangha. See, for instance, Sakaki, *Mahāvyutpatti*, nos. 5131–38. Later Tibetan scholiasts refer to these eight spiritual fruits as the *zhugs gnas brgyad*—the (four) enterings (*zhugs pa*) and (four) persistings (*gnas pa*), for eight in all.
24. This teaching is attributed to the Drigungpa. Cf. Sapaṇ, *Clear Differentiation of the Three Codes* 1:7; Rhoton, *A Clear Differentiation of the Three Codes*, 42; and Gorampa, *Detailed Commentary on Differentiation of the Three Vows*, 25b, and *Dispelling Errors about the Three Vows*, 5. See also Sangyé Tenzin, *A Gloss Commentary on Sa skya Paṇḍita Kun dga' rgyal mtshan's sDom gsum rab dbye*, 4a6.
25. *Mahāyānasūtrālaṃkāra* 3:1, Toh 4020 Tengyur, sems tsam, *phi*, 3a3. The four special characteristics of Mahayana refuge-taking are omnipresence, commitment, realization, and outshining.
26. Maitreya, *Uttaratantra* 1:19, Toh 4024 Tengyur, sems tsam, *phi*, 55b5; P 5525, sems tsam, *phi*, 55b8: *ston pa'i* (TG *pa*) *bstan pa slob don* (TG *dpon*) *gyis// theg pa gsum dang byed gsum la// mos pa rnams kyi dbang byas nas// skyabs gsum rnam par bzhag* (TG *gzhag*) *pa yin//*.
27. Sapaṇ explains the desirable qualities of a good religious teacher in his *Entrance Gate for the Wise*, chapter 2.
28. I was told that the "three bodhisattva tantric commentators" (known also by its abbreviated name *sems 'grel skor gsum*) are a Kālacakra commentary by Sucandra, a Hevajra commentary by Vajragarbha (*Hevajrapiṇḍārthaṭīkā*, Toh 1180 Tengyur), and a Cakrasaṃvara commentary by Vajrapāṇi (b. 1017).
29. The Seven Works on Accomplishment (*grub pa sde bdun*) is a corpus of seven tantric works preserved in the Peking Tengyur: Padmavajra, *Guhyasiddhi*, 2217 Tengyur P, rgyud 'grel, *wi*, and so on (2221 P, 2222 P, 2223 P, 2228 P, 2229 P, and 2230 P), or in the Dergé Tengyur, Toh 3061 and so on.
30. See Advayavajra (alias Maitripāda), *Removing Bad Views* (*Kudṛṣṭinirghāta*), Toh 2229 Tengyur, rgyud 'grel, *wi*; P 3073, rgyud 'grel, *mi*. See also Sapaṇ, *Clear Differentiation* 3:218–19; Rhoton, *A Clear Differentiation*, 189n48. Gorampa, *Detailed Commentary on Differentiation of the Three Vows*, 117b, refers to these works and also to the present passage in the TG for instructions on this point.
31. One would expect the "great master of Sakya" to be Drakpa Gyaltsen, but a relevant passage could only be found in a work by his brother Sönam Tsemo: no. 11 in the Dergé edition of Sönam Tsemo's collected works titled *Practice for Beginners and How to Tread on the Stages of the Path* (*Dang po'i las can gyi bya ba'i rim pa dang lam rim bgrod tshul*). Food offerings are discussed on page 145.1.6. When commenting on a parallel discussion in Sapaṇ's *Clear Differentiation of the Three*

Codes 3:218 in his own *Detailed Commentary on Differentiation of the Three Vows*, 117b (p. 177.2.6), Gorampa refers to the present passage of the TG and to works by Jetsun Drakpa Gyaltsen and Advayavajra. Gorampa, *Dispelling Errors*, 263.4.6, replies to the question of Shākya Chokden relating to the finding of this work in Drakpa Gyaltsen's writings. Cf. Sapaṇ, *Clear Differentiation* 3:219; Rhoton, *A Clear Differentiation*, 189n48.

32. Source not located.
33. Gorampa, *Detailed Commentary*, 117b, describes this teaching as having originated in a dream of the Kadampa geshé Chengawa.
34. This unlocated passage from the *Sutra of Hārītī* is also cited in Sapaṇ, *Clear Differentiation* 3:219. The story of the demoness Hārītī and her five hundred sons, and the Buddha's promise that his followers would offer lumps of food to her and her offspring, is told in Vinaya sources. Monks still make these offerings.
35. This passage from the *Vajra Peak Tantra* (*Vajraśekharatantra*) Toh 480 Kangyur, rgyud, *nya*, 162b1, is also cited in Sapaṇ, *Clear Differentiation* 3:218.
36. Steven Weinberger located relevant passages in two Kālacakra tantras: Toh 362 Kangyur, rgyud, *ka*, 101a3–5, and Toh 363 Kangyur, rgyud, *ka*, 139a7–b2.
37. The same point is made by Sapaṇ in his *Clear Differentiation* 3:220. Gorampa, *Detailed Commentary*, 118a, explains that swollen-chested sacrificial cakes were offered by the Kadampas (of Narthang Monastery) and three-sided ones by Drigungpa masters.
38. Śāntideva, *Bodhisattvacaryāvatāra* 5:96, Toh 3871 Tengyur, dbu ma, *la*, 14a1.
39. Cf. the brief sleeping yoga by Sapaṇ entitled *Points of Contemplation on the Infinite Secrets*. In the sutra (nontantric) tradition, only a prayer is practiced, not visualization.
40. *Gocarapariśuddhisūtra* (*Spyod yul yongs su dag pa'i mdo*), chapter 16 of the *Flower Ornament Sutra*. See also note 201 below about a summary of the text in the Tengyur.
41. *Basis of Vinaya* (*Vinayavastu*), Toh 1 Kangyur, 'dul ba, *ka*, 278a4. The medicine section (*sman gyi gzhi*) is one of seventeen sections (*gzhi*).
42. *Great Passing into Nirvana Sutra* (*Mahāparinirvāṇasūtra*), Toh 119 Kangyur, mdo sde, *tha*, 120a5. The same quote is found in the Tengyur work attributed to Karo, *Conpendium of the Stages of Meditation Sutra* (**Bhāvanākramasūtrasamuccaya*), Toh 3933 Tengyur, dbu ma, *ki*, 137b. Cf. Guenther, *Jewel Ornament*, 105, who identifies it as such.
43. Cf. Drigung Chöjé Jikten Gönpo, *Collected Writings* 4:420, who recommends not paying respect through prostration to worldly deities after going for refuge in the Buddha.
44. See, for example, Lowo Khenchen, *Sutra Exposition*, 5a2–14a1.
45. The third key topic quoted from the *Ornament of Mahayana Sutras* at the outset of this text.
46. On the teachers and texts of the Vijñānavāda and Madhyamaka traditions, see also Sapaṇ's *Ritual for Generating the Thought of Awakening*, his *Scriptural Sources for Generating the Thought of Awakening*, and his *Reply to the Questions of the Translator from Chak*, question 9, which appears in Rhoton, *A Clear Differentiation*, 216–18. See also Gorampa, *Detailed Commentary*, 153.3.5–154.1.2. Drolungpa's *Great Tenrim* (206a–b) similarly explains the existence of two different rituals for gener-

ating bodhicitta and the vows of the bodhisattva—the Madhyamaka and Yogācāra traditions.

47. On the ritual production of ultimate bodhicitta, see also Lowo Khenchen, *Ornament to the Intended Meaning of Dispelling Errors*, 288 (39b). Here he quotes the *Reply to Gurtön's Questions* (*Gur ston dris lan*). See Jackson, "Several Works of Unusual Provenance Ascribed to Sa skya Paṇḍita," 250.
48. *Enlightenment of Vairocana* (*Vairocanābhisambodhi*), Toh 494 Kangyur, rgyud, *tha*, 242a1–3. Thanks to Steven Weinberger for this reference. In Stephen Hodge's English translation, see pages 417–18.
49. See also the related discussions in Sapaṇ's *Clear Differentiation* 2:20–29, and in his *Reply to the Questions of the Translator of Lowo*, 414.3.2, translated in Rhoton, *A Clear Differentiation*, 226.
50. In general, there are two ways to answer an objection: (1) directly, through an actual reply (*lan rnal ma*), and (2) indirectly, by analogy, called in Tibetan "balancing" or a parity of reasoning (*mgo snyoms* or *mgo bsgre*). Some special ways of reasoning through analogy are used in Madhyamaka. See Sapaṇ, *Entrance Gate for the Wise* 3:51, autocommentary, and Jackson, *The Entrance Gate for the Wise*, 434n157.
51. Maitreya, *Mahāyānasūtrālaṃkāra* 7:5, Toh 4020 Tengyur, sems tsam, *phi*, 6b3. These two lines as quoted here differ slightly from the available canonical version in parentheses: *gang zhig (phyir) yod pa mi mthong med mthong ba// de 'dra'i mun nag rnam pa 'di ci (de gang) zhig.*
52. The power of the cause here is one's spiritual inclination; the power of the roots is the virtuous acts one has performed. Ibid. 5:7a, 4b5.
53. Ibid. 5:7d, 4b5.
54. Ibid. 5:8, 4b6.
55. "Highest worldly realization" is the fourth and final stage on the path of application prior to the path of seeing.
56. Maitreya, *Mahāyānasūtrālaṃkāra* 11:11ab, Toh 4020 Tengyur, sems tsam, *phi*, 13a2.
57. Śāntideva, *Bodhisattvacaryāvatāra* 7:18–19, Toh 3871 Tengyur, dbu ma, *la*, 20b6.
58. This tale is found in Gopadatta, *Stories of Seven Young Women* (*Saptakumārarikāvadāna*), Toh 4147, Tengyur, 'dul ba, *su*, 244b3.
59. I can only interpret the Tibetan term *kham can* here to mean "greedy," and suggest the emendation *ham can*. In Rotman, *Divine Stories*, 140, the parallel passage reads: "Gautama, you abandoned a wheel-turner's kingdom and went forth as a renunciant. How is it that now you knowingly tell lies for the sake of some alms of barley-meal? Who will believe you that this is the fruit of such a small seed?"
60. *Bhadrakalpikasūtra*, Toh 94 Kangyur, mdo sde, *ka*, on 289a4 (grass lights); P 762, mdo sna tshogs, *i*, 319b6 (grass lights), 347a6 (dung cakes), and 348a5 (arura fruit). Gampopa cites the same sutra more extensively on this topic on pages 233–34 above.
61. *Bhadrakalpikasūtra*, Toh 94 Kangyur, mdo sde, *ka*, 289a4; P 762, mdo sna tshogs, *i*, 372b1.
62. Steven Weinberger suggested that *thun* possibly refers to *thun gtor*, or "session tormas," ritual cakes presented at the end of certain activities.
63. Śāntideva, *Bodhisattvacaryāvatāra* 7:30, Toh 3871 Tengyur, dbu ma, *la*, 21a6.
64. *Sarvadurgatipariśodhanatantra*. Passage not located.

65. I read here *ne'u 'don pa*, archaic for "to set free or pardon the guilty."
66. Vasubandhu, *Abhidharmakośa* 4:55, Toh 4089 Tengyur, mngon pa, *ku*, 21a6. In the Dergé Tengyur edition, the order of the two lines is reversed.
67. Shang Dodé Pal's commentary does not relate the story of King Bhīmasena.
68. An eon and an instant are the same in both being empty from the absolute viewpoint. On "understanding the three times as equal," see Asaṅga, *Compendium of the Mahayana* (*Mahāyānasaṃgraha*) 2:33a, Toh 4048 Tengyur, sems tsam, *ri*.
69. Shang Dodé Pal, *Commentary*, 9b2–12a5, tells the story of how Dignāga became distraught by the vexations of his opponents and wanted to attain his own liberation. He threw his writing slate into the air and said, "As long as this remains in the air, I will adhere to the Mahayana, but as soon as it touches the earth, I will adopt the śrāvaka tradition." When the object did not fall to earth, Dignāga looked up to see Mañjuśrī holding it in the air.
70. Maitreya, *Mahāyānasūtrālaṃkāra* 18:39, Toh 4020 Tengyur, sems tsam, *phi*, 26b7; P 5521, sems tsam, *phi*, 30a5.
71. This refers to one-sided methods for gaining liberation, such as the white panacea (*dkar po chig thub*) that Sapaṇ discusses below on page 489.
72. As cited in Śāntideva, *Compendium of Trainings* (*Śikṣāsamuccaya*), Toh 3940 Tengyur, dbu ma, *khi*, 7b7. The same passage is quoted by Drolungpa, *Great Tenrim*, 193b. The citation in Sapan's text appears to be an abbreviation. It is quoted at greater length in Kamalaśīla's *Stages of Meditation* (*Bhāvanākrama*), Toh 3915, Tengyur, dbu ma, *ki*, 24b1.
73. *Kāśyapa Chapter Sutra* (*Kāśyapaparivartasūtra*), Toh 87 Kangyur, dkon brtsegs, *cha*, 120a6. As I was informed by Jonathan Silk, the same passage is quoted in Śāntideva's *Compendium of Trainings* and in Atiśa's *Instructions on Madhyamaka* (*Madhyamakopadeśa*), Toh 3930 Tengyur, dbu ma, *ki*, 139a5; P 5325, dbu ma, *a*, 115a3. The above passages are also quoted by Gampopa, *Ornament of Precious Liberation*; see page 247 in the present volume.
74. *Kāśyapa Chapter Sutra* (*Kāśyapaparivartasūtra*), Toh 87 Kangyur, dkon brtsegs, *cha*, 120b3. The wording in the actual sutra in the Dergé Kangyur is slightly different from how Sapaṇ quotes it here in the text.
75. *Bhadracaryāpraṇidhāna*, Toh 1095 Kangyur, gzungs 'dus, *waṃ*. See also Tatz, "Translation of the *Bhadracarīpraṇidhāna*."
76. *Confession of Infractions for the Bodhisattva* may refer to works such as Toh 3973 Tengyur, dbu ma, *gi* (P 5368, dbu ma, *khi*), and Toh 3974 Tengyur, dbu ma, *gi* (P 5369, dbu ma, *khi*), both of which are called simply "rituals for the confession of infractions" (*Ltung ba bshags pa'i cho ga*).
77. *Maitreyapraṇidhāna*, Toh 1096 Kangyur, gzugs, *waṃ*.
78. Nāgārjuna's *Precious Garland* (*Ratnāvalī*), 5:66–85. These twenty verses of prayers also constitute a separate work in the Tengyur (Toh 4388 Tengyur, sna tshogs, *nyo*; P 5928, ngo mtshar bstan bcos, *mo*).
79. *Saptāṅgasaddharmacaryāvatāra*, Toh 3980 Tengyur, dbu ma, *gi*; P 5371, mdo 'grel, *khi*.
80. Sapaṇ's *Liturgy of Ten Verses* (*Chos spyod bcu pa*) is not included in the Dergé edition of his Collected Works, but it survives in manuscripts. See Jackson, "Fragments of a Golden Manuscript of Sa-skya Paṇḍita's Works," p. 24, no. 23.

81. Shang Dodé Pal does not name any specific stories here.
82. *Ākāśagarbhasūtra*, Toh 260 Kangyur, mngo sde, *za*, 276a7. Fourteen "root transgressions" are mentioned here. This source is also recommended in Sapaṇ, *Clear Differentiation* 2:10. See also the lists in Tatz, *Asanga's Chapter on Ethics*, appendix B. Here Tatz translates P 926, 287a4–287b6. Śāntideva in his *Compendium of Trainings* lists eighteen root transgressions, including the fourteen from the *Sky Essence Sutra* and one from the *Skill in Means Sutra* (*Upāyakauśalyasūtra*).
83. The Heap of Jewels (Ratnakūṭa) collection of sutras is also recommended in the same context in Sapaṇ, *Clear Differentiation* 2:10. See also Kapstein and Dorje, *The Nyingma School of Tibetan Buddhism*, 235. According to Tatz, in his *Asanga's Chapter on Ethics*, the Yogāgāra has only four root transgressions, following the *Twenty Verses* (*Saṃvaraviṃśaka*) of Candragomin. Tatz, *Asanga's Chapter on Ethics*, note 21, mentions Gorampa, *Detailed Commentary*, 67b6–68a6, and also Gorampa, *Dispelling Errors*, on question no. 47 of Shākya Chokden, relating to the transgressions explained in Śāntideva's *Compendium of Trainings* (*Śikṣāsamuccaya*) and Asaṅga's *Bodhisattva Levels* (*Bodhisattvabhūmi*) and their relation to the sutra accounts.
84. This refers to confession and purification through a recitation ritual such as Śāntideva's *Ritual for Reciting the Hundred-Syllable Mantra and for Confessing Faults* (*Tathāgatahṛdayapāpadeśanāvidhi*), Toh 3941 Tengyur; P 5337 and 5438. For related rituals of confession, see the works in the Tengyur, Toh 3973 and 3974, respectively P 5368 and 5369.
85. This is a reference to the fourth key topic from the *Ornament of Mahayana Sutras* passage cited in the opening of the text.
86. "Clear analysis" or "detailed differentiation" (*rab tu dbye ba*). As this subsection is extensive, the Sanskrit etymology heading does not appear until the end of chapter 9.
87. At this point the overarching Tibetan topical outline is interrupted for presentations of each of the six perfections, which have their own internal outlines; the heading "establishing that division as fixed" resumes at the end of chapter 9.
88. *Precious Garland* (*Ratnāvalī*) 4:15, Toh 4158 Tengyur, spring yig, *ge*, 18b6.
89. Sapaṇ, *Jewel Treasure of Aphorisms* 74 = 3:16. This work in nine chapters is translated in Bosson, *A Treasury of Aphoristic Jewels*, and in Davenport, *Ordinary Wisdom*. The two numbering schemes depend on whether verses are numbered consecutively within chapters or across the entire composition.
90. Sapaṇ, *Jewel Treasure of Aphorisms* 402 = 9:4. See also the commentary of Sangyé Tenzin (p. 332), who quotes Candrakīrti, *Madhyamakāvatāra* 1:10; translated in Davenport, *Ordinary Wisdom*, 257. Cf. Guenther, *Jewel Ornament*, 153.
91. *Ratnaguṇasaṃcayagāthā* 31:11b, Toh 13 Kangyur, shes phyin, *ka*, 19a1. Quoted also in Gampopa's *Ornament* in chapter 12 on page 253 of this volume.
92. Taught in the *Questions of Ṛṣi Vyāsa Sutra* (*Ṛṣivyāsaparipṛcchāsūtra*), Toh 489 Kangyur, dkon brtsegs, *cha*, 563.
93. Śāntideva, *Bodhisattvacaryāvatāra* 8:79, Toh 3871 Tengyur, dbu ma, *la*, 26b2.
94. Tibetan scholars such as Sapan discriminated between "intermediary" and summarizing verses as the two main types of verses in commentaries or doctrinal writings. The verse here is Sapaṇ's own composition.
95. On the story of King Anantayaśa or Amitayaśa (Grags pa mtha' yas) from the *Meeting of Father and Son Sutra* (*Pitāputrasamagamasūtra*), see Shang Dodé Pal's commentary, 12a5. For the story of King Māndhātā (Nga las nu) from the *Basis of Vinaya*

(*Vinayavastu*), see fol. 13a4, and for the story from the *Pitāputrasamagamasūtra*, see fol. 18a4. This part of the Māndhātā story in question—his ascendency and fall—is told in the *Bhaiṣajyavastu* section of the *Basis of Vinaya* (*Vinayavastu*), Toh 1 Kangyur, 'dul ba, *kha* 169b6ff. For a translation of the story as it appears in the *Divyāvadāna*, see Rotman, *Divine Stories*, 364.

96. *Upālipariprcchāsūtra*, Toh 68 Kangyur, dkon brtsegs, *ca*, 119a5.
97. Śāntideva, *Bodhisattvacaryāvatāra* 7:25–26, Toh 3871 Tengyur, dbu ma, *la*, 21a3.
98. *Upāyakauśalyasūtra*. The exact quote has not been located in the Dergé Kangyur edition of the sutra. ITC gives: Toh 353 Kangyur, mdo sde, *ah*, 153b1, which is an error.
99. *Ṛṣivyāsaparipṛcchāsūtra*, Toh 93 Kangyur, dkon brtsegs, *cha*, 281a1.
100. Here two lines are missing from all known versions of the Tibetan text, probably by haplography. See *Ṛṣivyāsaparipṛcchāsūtra*, Toh 93 Kangyur, dkon brtsegs, *cha*, 281a, P 760, dkon brtsegs, *'i*, 289b4: *gang yang sbyin pa....* The venerable Khenpo Appey composed two lines to fill this gap: *rnam smin the tshom byin rjes 'gyod// 'di yis phyi mar bdag la byin.*
101. *Good Eon Sutra* (*Bhadrakalpikasūtra*), Toh 94 Kangyur, mdo sde, *ka*, 336b5. This sentence occurs in Chim Jampaiyang, 386a, where it is identified as from a Vinaya scripture.
102. Maitreya, *Mahāyānasūtrālaṃkāra* 17:42, Toh 4020 Tengyur, sems tsam, *phi*, 23a6.
103. Source of this citation has not been located.
104. For a similar statement in a sutra, see the *Puṇṇovādasutta*, M 3:145, in Ñāṇamoli and Bodhi, *Middle Length Discourses*, 1118–19.
105. Paraphrased from an unspecified sutra. Similar lists of great donations occur in many sutras, but usually including "drink" (*skom/ btung ba*) as the second item. But for a description of a great donation that starts similarly, see the *Vast Manifestation Sutra* (*Lalitavistarasūtra*), Toh 95 Kangyur, mdo sde, *kha*, 54a.
106. Although in Sapan's text the final line reads "will not be quickly fulfilled" (*bsam pa myur du rdzogs mi 'gyur*), the canonical version of Śantideva's text does not contain the negative "not" (*mi*). So no negative has been translated.
107. Śāntideva, *Bodhisattvacaryāvatāra* 5:86–87, Toh 3871 Tengyur, dbu ma, *la*, 13b3.
108. On renunciation, renunciation to a high degree, and great renunciation, see Lowo Khenchen, *Sutra Exposition*, 134.2, quoting from the "Establishing the Rules of Discipline" (*'Dul ba rnam par gtan la dbab pa*) section in the *Questions of Upāli Sutra.*
109. *Perfection of Wisdom in Twenty-Five Thousand Lines* (*Pañcaviṃśatisāhasrikāprajñāpāramitā*), Toh 9 Kangyur, sher phyin, *a*, 95b3. Note that the phrase *thabs la mkhas pas* is not part of the quote.
110. Ibid. Cf. *Verse Summary of the Perfection of Wisdom* 31:10.
111. Once the future Buddha was Viśvāntara, a crown prince of Śibi with a passion for charity. He shocked and annoyed his subjects by giving away the best elephant in the kingdom, which led to his banishment in the forest with just his wife and two children. There he selflessly gave away his son and daughter to a brahman and ultimately even his wife (to the god Śakra disguised as a begging brahman). These extreme human gifts were, however, later restored to him. For his story see *Jātakamālā* (Toh 4150 Tengyur, skyes rabs, *hu*) of Āryaśūra, no. 9 (Khoroche, *Once*

the Buddha Was a Monkey, 58–73); and Kṣemendra, *Bodhisattvāvadānakalpalatā* (Toh 4155 Tengyur, skyes rabs, *ke*), no. 24. The story is also abridged from different scriptural sources by Shang Dodé Pal in his commentary, 20a5.

112. Once the future Buddha was born as a certain Śivi king who was extremely generous. Eventually the king of the gods, Śakra, disguised as an blind old brahman, came to test him, begging for the gift of his eyes. Out of pure generosity the king gave them, and he was reduced to miserable blindness, though in the end Śakra revealed himself and restored the lost eyes. For his story see Āryaśūra, *Jātakamālā*, no. 2 (Khoroche, *Once the Buddha Was a Monkey*, 10–17); and Kṣemendra, *Bodhisattvāvadānakalpalatā*, no. 91. Shang Dodé Pal does not repeat it.

113. Once the future Buddha was born as an excellent noble-minded hare (śaśa = ri bong) who lived in a beautiful forest glade with three close animal companions: an otter, a jackal, and a monkey. Being intelligent, religious minded, and extremely generous, the hare once conceived the thought of giving his own body away to feed others, for want of anything else. The next day the king of the gods, Śakra, to test him, appeared nearby as a starving brahman who was lost in the forest. Though his animal friends each found something to offer their hungry guest, the hare, who only had his flesh to give, jumped into a bed of flaming coals, willingly sacrificing himself. Then Śakra revealed himself, honoring the hare in many ways for his great generosity. See Shang Dodé Pal, *Commentary*, 35b5. See Āryaśūra, *Jātakamālā*, no. 6 (Khoroche, *Once the Buddha Was a Monkay*, 32–38); Haribhaṭa, *Jātakamālā*, no. 4; and Kṣemendra, *Bodhisattvāvadānakalpalatā*, no. 104.

114. Once the future Buddha was King Candraprabha, who lived many eons ago in this world as a fabulously powerful and wealthy universal emperor. He was extremely generous, supporting the poor and hungry. He aroused the obsessive jealousy of Bhimasena, king of a bordering country, who decided to kill him, offering half his kingdom as reward to anyone who could bring Candraprabha's decapitated head to him. A greedy and wicked local brahman took him up and tried to enter Candraprabha's empire to carry out the deed, though he was stopped at the gate by a protective deity. When the brahman finally got inside and made his request, the king agreed to give his head after seven days. Though his loyal ministers tried various means to stop the king, such as substituting several heads made of gold and precious jewels, he finally went through with the act, severing his head in a garden grove of campaka trees, using a tree leaf as a blade. When doing so he uttered a fervent prayer that a miraculous stupa would one day appear on that site and that by the merit of his deed all beings would be freed from samsara. For the complete story of King Candraprabha, a *jātaka* (also a separate work: *Candraprabhāvadāna*), see the *Sage and Fool Sutra,* Toh 341 Kangyur, mdo sde, *a*, 197a4. See also Shang Dodé Pal, *Commentary*, 39a6; *Divyāvadāna*, no. 22; Haribhaṭa, *Jātakamālā*, no. 5; and Kṣemendra, *Bodhisattvāvadānakalpalatā*, no. 5.

115. King Kanakavarṇa (Gser mdog) was an extremely wise and generous king of the city of Kanaka who lived long ago. Though he ruled in harmony with the Dharma, once a great drought afflicted his land. He emptied his treasuries to help his afflicted subjects, but finally not a single morsel of food was left, even for the king. When a pratyekabuddha appeared in the sky and gave him food, the king insisted on using it all to sustain the starving poor. Afterward rain and food miraculously showered

from the skies. On the tale of King Kanakavarṇa, see the *Past Life of Kanakavarṇa* (*Kanakavarṇapūrvayoga*), Toh 350 Kangyur, mdo sde, *aḥ*, 51b1; *Divyāvadāna*, no. 20, and Kṣemendra, *Bodhisattvāvadānakalpalatā*, no. 43.

116. Shang Dodé Pal, *Commentary*, 42b6, tells the story of King Śrīsena, the incredibly wealthy and powerful ruler of all Jambudvipa in the distant past who gave away half his body. He was religious minded and encited his subjects to live in accord with Dharma, with the result that many were reborn after death as gods. This aroused the notice of Śakra, who predicted that the king was generous enough to give away half his body and tested him to see whether he would actually do it.
117. Maitreya, *Mahāyānasūtrālaṃkāra* 17:8, Toh 4020 Tengyur, sems tsam, *phi*, 21b3.
118. No such earlier reference could be located.
119. Maitreya, *Mahāyānasūtrālaṃkāra* 17:30, Toh 4020 Tengyur, sems tsam, *phi*, 22b2.
120. Śāntideva, *Bodhisattvacaryāvatāra* 6:133, Toh 3871 Tengyur, dbu ma, *la*, 20a2.
121. Maitreya, *Mahāyānasūtrālaṃkāra* 17:55a, Toh 4020 Tengyur, sems tsam, *phi*, 27b4.
122. *Ratnaguṇasaṃcayagāthā* 32:1a–c, Toh 13 Kangyur, sher phyin, *ka*, 19b1.
123. "Sky treasury" (*gaganaganja*) refers to gaining access in the future as a buddha to a fabulous magical inexhaustible source of wealth.
124. *Samādhirājasūtra* 9:34cd; Toh 127 Kangyur, mdo sde, *da*, 27a6. See Cüppers, *The IXth Chapter of the Samādhirājasūtra*.
125. Nāgārjuna, *Precious Garland* (*Ratnāvalī*) 1:14acd, 15a, 16ab, 18cd; Toh 4158 Tengyur, spring yig, *ge*, 107b2.
126. Shang Dodé Pal explains at this point the sufferings of cyclic existence experienced after you commit evil deeds (52a); the arrangement of cyclic existence; the physical layout; its inhabitants in the hells (62a), hungry spirits (87a), animals (93a3), humans (95b), and gods (97b); this includes the long story of Rāhu and the fights between the gods and demigods, (98b).
127. *Short Vinaya* (*Vinayakṣudrakavastu*), Toh 6 Kangyur, 'dul ba, *tha*, 280a7. For the *jātaka* of the nāga king Elapatra, see Shang Dodé Pal, *Commentary*, 112b2–115b. Elapatra, in disguise, went to hear the Buddha teach in Rājagṛha. The Buddha, seeing through his disguise, tells him that since his nāga form was a consequence of a breaking a precept by cutting down an *elapatra* tree in anger while a monk during the time of Buddha Kāśyapa, he must assume his natural form if he is to receive the Buddha's instruction. Next day, there appeared at the gathering a giant serpent whose tail stretched all the way to Taxila and on whose head grew a giant *elapatra* tree.
128. *Subāhuparipṛcchātantra*, Toh 805 Kangyur, rgyud 'bum, *wa*, 122a1; P 428, rgyud, *tsha*, 183b5. The verse is also quoted in the autocommentary to Sapaṇ's *Entrance Gate for the Wise* 3:20. Cf. page 465 below, where Vasubandu, *Treasury of Higher Knowledge* 6:9, is quoted to the same effect. Cf. also *Collection of Aphorisms* 3:1.
129. Dharmakīrti, *Pramāṇavārttika* 2:255, Toh 4210 Tengyur, tshad ma, *ce*, 117a6.
130. Nāgārjuna, *Fundamental Verses on the Middle Way* (*Mūlamadhyamakakārikā*) 26:11bc–12ab, Toh 3824 Tengyur, dbu ma, *tsa*, 17b4.
131. The ITC source, *Great Passing into Nirvana Sutra* (longer version) (*Mahāparinirvāṇasūtra*), Toh 119 Kangyur, mdo sde, *nya*, 6a2, is obviously an error. This citation is in *Seal Enhancing the Force of Faith Sutra* (*Śraddhābalādhānāvatāra-*

mudrāsūtra), Toh 201 Kangyur, mdo sde, *tsha,* 58a3. In the sūtra itself, the phrase reads differently.

132. Sunayaśrī, *Upāsakasamvarāṣṭaka*, Toh 4141 Tengyur, 'dul ba, *su*, 156b7.
133. *Collection of Aphorisms* (*Udānavarga*) 33:1, Toh 326 Kangyur, mdo sde, *sa*, 248b1. In the Dergé edition of the sutra, the third line reads differently.
134. Candragomin is considered a typical example of the lay cleric, or *gomin*, ordination.
135. The specific quotation was not located in this collection.
136. Anonymous, *Treasury of Nouns* (*Subantaratnākara*), Toh 4430 Tengyur, sna tshogs, *no*, 130b7. The Sanskrit dictionary of Monier-Williams 1899 lists eight of the nine meanings: (1) voice (from *gai*), (2) sky (here Tib. *phyogs*), (3) earth, (4) rays of light, (5) ox, (6) eye, (7) vajra/thunderbolt, (8) a region of the sky (= heaven?), and (9) water. On the third meaning, cf. Sapaṇ, *Clear Differentiation* 3:561, where the etymology for *gopā* is "earth-nurturer" (*sa 'tsho*).
137. Monier-Williams, *A Sanskrit-English Dictionary*, p. 364, defines *gomin* as "owner of many cattle" and "a layman adhering to Buddha's faith." He defines the name Gautama as a patronymic from the name *Gotama* ("largest ox").
138. *Susiddhikaratantra*, Toh 807 Kangyur, rgyud, *wa*, 175b6.
139. Unspecified sutra. Not located.
140. This story is found in the *Basis of Vinaya* (*Vinayavastu*), Toh 1 Kangyur, 'dul ba, *ka*, 122b1.
141. Once the future Buddha lived as an expert and highly successful sea captain named Supāraga, who even in old age kindly agreed to accompany a long and dangerous trading voyage from India to Suvarṇadvīpa. The ship became greatly imperiled and was only saved by the power of the prayer of its wise captain. For that *jātaka* see Shang Dodé Pal's commentary, 115b1. See also Āryaśūra, *Jātakamālā*, no. 14 (Khoroche, *Once the Buddha Was a Monkey*, 303–16).
142. At this point (folio 130a) Shang Dodé Pal tells the *jātaka* story of the brahman boy Kumāramegha (*gzhon nu sprin*), who after his death became a deity who tried to help the sick when the human world was filled with a horrible plague. He emanated himself as an animal whose curative and inexhaustible flesh he ordered the sick to eat. On folio 133a1, Shang Dodé Pal explains the comparison with cattle in the slaughter pen, with a final quote from the *Collection of Aphorisms* 22:2: "An infantile fool acts like he is immortal. A wise person applies himself to the holy Dharma like a sick man in the night."
143. Sapaṇ, *Jewel Treasure of Aphorisms* 449 = 9:51.
144. Defeats (*pārājika*) are those most serious offenses against the monastic rule that entail expulsion from the Sangha: sex, theft, murder, and false claims of spiritual attainment.
145. Many eons ago the future Buddha lived as a handsome brahman youth Jyotis, who practiced meditating celibately in a remote place. Impelled by a girl who violently fell in live with him and was about to kill herself when he rejected her advances, he gave up his strict solitary practice to save her life. He decided to live with her as husband for twelve years but then to resume his yogic practice, which he did. See Shang Dodé Pal, *Commentary*, 120a.
146. See note 141 above on the sea captain Supāraga.

147. For the story of the bodhisattva Supuṣpacandra, see Shang Dodé Pal, *Commentary*, 121a2.
148. This is the story mentioned above in note 142, where Indra is incarnated as an animal whose inexhaustible flesh cures an epidemic.
149. Maitreya, *Ornament of Mahayana Sutras* (*Mahāyānasūtrālaṃkāra*) 17:9, Toh 4020 Tengyur, sems tsam, *phi*, 21b3.
150. Ibid. 17:31ab, 22b3.
151. These are the distraction of attention and the distraction of conceptual thinking discussed in the chapter on generosity, page 424.
152. *Samādhirājasūtra* 6:7, Toh 127 Kangyur, mdo sde, *da*, 13b1. This is also quoted and explained by Sapaṇ below, page 523.
153. *Prātimokṣasūtra*, Toh 2 Kangyur, 'dul ba, *ca*, 2b1.
154. Nāgārjuna, *Ratnāvalī* 3:87ab, Toh 4158 Tengyur, spring yig, *ge*, 117b5.
155. Vasubandhu, *Saptaguṇaparivarṇananākathā*, Toh 4163 Tengyur, 4163, spring yig, *ge*, 168a7.
156. *Ratnaguṇasaṃcayagāthā* 32:2ab, Toh 13 Kangyur, sher phyin, *ka*, 19b2.
157. Maitreya, *Mahāyānasūtrālaṃkāra* 21:53, Toh 4020 Tengyur, sems tsam, *phi*, 38b2. The twin afflictions here are desire and hatred. Also quoted and explained below.
158. Śāntideva, *Bodhisattvacaryāvatāra* 6:3, Toh 3871 Tengyur, dbu ma, *la*, 14b4.
159. I read "censure" (*dpya' ba*) instead of "cherish" (*bca' ba*).
160. Śāntideva, *Bodhisattvacaryāvatāra* 6:4, Toh 3871 Tengyur, dbu ma, *la*, 14b5.
161. Ibid. 6:5ab, 14b5.
162. Ibid. 6:5cd, 14b5.
163. *Bodhisattva Collection* (*Bodhisattvapiṭaka*), Toh 56 Kangyur, dkon brtsegs, *ga*, 98b2.
164. Śāntideva, *Bodhisattvacaryāvatāra* 6:1, Toh 3871 Tengyur, dbu ma, *la*, 14b3.
165. Nāgārjuna, *Ratnāvalī* 3:29, Toh 4158 Tengyur, spring yig, *ge*, 115b3.
166. Śāntideva, *Bodhisattvacaryāvatāra* 6:7, Toh 3871 Tengyur, dbu ma, *la*, 14b7.
167. Ibid. 6:10, 15a1.
168. Ibid. 6:6cd, 14b6.
169. According to the Prajñākaramati's *Bodhicaryāvatārapañjikā*, Toh 3872 Tengyur, this threefold practice of patience was taught based on the *Perfectly Gathering the Qualities [of Avalokiteśvara] Sutra* (*Dharmasaṃgītisūtra*).
170. Unspecified sutra. Not located.
171. Śāntideva, *Bodhisattvacaryāvatāra* 6:39d, Toh 3871 Tengyur, dbu ma, *la*, 16a4.
172. Ibid. 5:12, 10b4.
173. Ibid. 6:40d, 16a4.
174. Vasubandhu, *Abhidharmakośa* 3:37ab, Toh 4089 Tengyur, mngon pa, *ku*, 8a6. See also Chim Jampaiyang, *Small Treasury* (*Mdzod chung*), 128a (p. 255). Karma is likened to a rice seed with its husk that has the potential to sprout; it is like medicine for, once its effect has been made felt, it will not do so again; and just as the flower is a direct contributing factor for the arising of a fruit, karma is also an immediate cause of its result.
175. Śāntideva, *Bodhisattvacaryāvatāra* 6:42, Toh 3871 Tengyur, dbu ma, *la*, 16a5.
176. Ibid. 6:43, 16a6.
177. Ibid. 6:68, 17a5.
178. Ibid. 6:47, 16a1.

179. Ibid. 9:151–154ab, 36b5.
180. See, for example, Guṇaprabha, *Vinaya Sutra* (*Vinayasūtra*), Toh 4117 Tengyur, 'dul ba, *wu*, 29a4.
181. Nāgārjuna, *Letter to a Friend* (*Suhṛllekha*) 68cd, Toh 4182 Tengyur, spring yig, *nge*, 43b7.
182. *Vajraśekharatantra*, Toh 480 Kangyur, rgyud, *nya*, 149a4; P 0113, rgyud, *nya*, 162b2.
183. Śāntideva, *Bodhisattvacaryāvatāra* 6:104, Toh 3871 Tengyur, dbu ma, *la*, 18b5.
184. Ibid. 6:111, 19a2.
185. Ibid. 6:107, 18b6.
186. Ibid. 6:72, 17b1.
187. Maitreya, *Mahāyānasūtrālaṃkāra* 17:10, Toh 4020 Tengyur, sems tsam, *phi*, 21b4.
188. Ibid. 17:32, 22b3.
189. Śāntideva, *Bodhisattvacaryāvatāra* 6:134, Toh 3871 Tengyur, dbu ma, *la*, 20a3.
190. *Ratnaguṇasaṃcayagāthā* 32:2cd, Toh 13 Kangyur, sher phyin, *ka*, 19b2.
191. Nāgārjuna, *Suhṛllekha* 15cd, Toh 4182 Tengyur, spring yig, *nge*, 41b1.
192. Maitreya, *Mahāyānasūtrālaṃkāra* 21:50, Toh 4020 Tengyur, sems tsam, *phi*, 38a7. Also quoted and explained below.
193. Śāntideva, *Bodhisattvacaryāvatāra* 7:2a, Toh 3871 Tengyur, dbu ma, *la*, 20a4.
194. Ibid. 7:53, 22a6.
195. I found no elaboration of this in Shang Dodé Pal's commentary.
196. The ITC source, *Perfection of Wisdom in Eight Thousand Lines* (*Aṣṭasāhasrikāprajñāpāramitā*) Toh 12 Kangyur, sher phyin, *ka*, 225a3, is erroneous. A more likely source is the *Perfection of Wisdom in a Hundred Thousand Lines* (*Śatasāhasrikāprajñāpāramitā*), Toh 8 Kangyur, sher phyin, *a*, 313b3, where it reads: *le los ni rang gi don yang bya bar mi nus na/ gzhan gyi don lta ci smros ...*
197. Śāntideva, *Bodhisattvacaryāvatāra* 7:11, Toh 3871 Tengyur, dbu ma, *la*, 20b2.
198. Ibid. 7:2–3, 20a4.
199. Ibid. 7:4–8, 20a5–20a7.
200. *Avataṃsakasūtra*, Toh 44 Kangyur, phal chen, *ka*, 212a5.
201. No such work of Jñānagarbha is contained in Tengyur, but a similar title is attributed to Rāhulabhadra: *Summary of the Bodhisattva's Completely Pure Conduct Sutra* (*Bodhisattvagocarapariśuddhisūtrārthasaṃgraha*), Toh 3965 Tengyur, dbu ma, *gi*.
202. These seven riches are, as listed in Atiśa's *Bodhisattva's Jewel Garland*, those of faith, moral discipline, giving, learning, conscience, shame, and insight. See Jinpa, *Book of Kadam*, 64.
203. Chapter 16 of the *Flower Ornament Sutra* (*Avataṃsakasūtra*). Passage not located. Quoted in a similar context by Drolungpa, *Great Tenrim*, 292b.
204. ITC does not provide source for this quotation, but it is found in the *Verse Summary of the Perfection of Wisdom* (*Ratnaguṇasaṃcayagāthā*), Toh 13 Kangyur, sher phyin, *ka* 10a5.
205. Śāntideva, *Bodhisattvacaryāvatāra* 5:101, Toh 3871 Tengyur, dbu ma, *la*, 14a4.
206. *Four Hundred* (*Catuḥśataka*) 5:5, Toh 3846 Tengyur, dbu ma, *tsha*, 6a5.
207. Asaṅga, *Compendium of the Mahayana* (*Mahāyānasaṃgraha*) 10:28, Toh 4048 Tengyur, sems tsam, *ri*, 40b1.
208. "A learned wise one" (*mkhas pa mkhas pa*). See also Sapaṇ's Collected Works, SKB,

vol. 5, 337.1.6: *mkhas pa mkhas pa'i grangs su bgrang ba la//* and 337.4.4: *mkhas pa mkhas pa'i tshogs kyis yongs bskor ba//.*

209. Maitreya, *Mahāyānasūtrālaṃkāra* 17:11, Toh 4020 Tengyur, sems tsam, *phi*, 21b5.
210. Ibid. 17:33, 22b4.
211. *Ratnaguṇasaṃcayagāthā* 32:3ab, Toh 13 Kangyur, sher phyin, *ka*, 19b2.
212. Maitreya, *Mahāyānasūtrālaṃkāra* 10:27, Toh 4020 Tengyur, sems tsam, *phi*, 9b6.
213. Ibid. 21:55, 38b4. ITC gives Asaṅga, *Hymn of Praise to the Good Qualities of the Dharmakāya* (**Dharmakāyāśrayāsāmānyaguṇastotra*), Toh 1115 Tengyur, bstod tshogs, *ka*, 62a6.
214. Śāntideva, *Bodhisattvacaryāvatāra* 8:1cd, Toh 3871 Tengyur, dbu ma, *la*, 23a7.
215. Ibid. 9:160, 32a1.
216. *Samādhirājasūtra* 9:36, Toh 127 Kangyur, mdo sde, *da*, 27a7. Also quoted below, page 505.
217. Dharmakīrti, *Pramāṇavārttika*, 2:212cd, Toh 4210 Tengyur, tshad ma, *ce*, 115b4.
218. *Vairocanābhisambodhi*, Toh 494 Kangyur, rgyud, *tha*, 152b1; P 126, rgyud, *tha*, 185b7. Also quoted below, page 500, and in Sapaṇ, *Clear Differentiation* 3:358–59.
219. Śāntideva, *Bodhisattvacaryāvatāra* 8:7–8, Toh 3871 Tengyur, dbu ma, *la*, 23a7.
220. Ibid. 8:10, 23b5.
221. Ibid. 8:12, 13ab, 14cd, and 15a, 23b6.
222. Ibid. 8:16–19b, 24a2.
223. Ibid. 8:22–24, 24a5.
224. See, for example, *Basis of Vinaya* (*Vinayavastu*), Toh 1 Kangyur, 'dul ba, *ka*, 293b1.
225. For more on the name Sunakṣatra and the evolution of the use of his story in Tibet, see Eimer and Tsering, "Legs-skar/Skar-bzang/Sunakṣatra." See also Rhoton, *A Clear Differentiation*, 255.
226. Korakkhattiya was a naked ascetic in Uttarakā who bellowed like a dog and licked up food on all fours. He was later born among fearsome demigods who experience extreme thirst.
227. Unspecified work of Maitripāda, alias Advayavajra. The phrase "the absence of material things" (*zang zing med pa*) can also mean "without sensual desire."
228. Śāntideva, *Bodhisattvacaryāvatāra* 8:79a, Toh 3871 Tengyur, dbu ma, *la*, 26b2.
229. Ibid. 8:80, 26b3.
230. Ibid. 8:25–29, 24a7.
231. Ibid. 8:34–36, 24b5.
232. A white utpala, *Nymphoea lotus*.
233. Āryaśūra, *Garland of Jātaka Tales* (*Jātakamāla*) 32, Toh 4150 Tengyur, skyes rabs, *hu*, 128b2. In Koroche, *Once the Buddha Was a Monkey*, 239, working from the Sanskrit, this passage is rendered: "How pathetic is our earthly state,' he thought to himself. 'It's horribly transitory. This magnificient Kaumudī festival will soon be just a memory.'"
234. See below, chapter 11, where the practices of "meditative concentration shared by the mundane and supramundane spheres" are explained in connection with the teachings on the path of cultivation (*bhāvanāmārga*).
235. Vasubandhu, *Abhidharmakośa* 6:9, Toh 4089 Tengyur, mngon pa, *ku*, 19a2.
236. Maitreya, *Mahāyānasūtrālaṃkāra* 21:43, Toh 4020 Tengyur, sems tsam, *phi*, 38a3. Also quoted and explained below.
237. Ibid. 18:39, 26b7. Quoted above by Sapan on page 410.
238. The *Vajraśekharatantra* passage not located.

239. *King of Meditation Sutra* (*Samādhirājasūtra*), Toh 127 Kangyur, mdo sde, *da*, 115b6.
240. Nāgārjuna, *Ratnāvalī* 3:83, Toh 4158 Tengyur, spring yig, *ge*, 117b3.
241. Āryaśūra, *Garland of Jātaka Tales* (*Jātakamāla*), no. 8 (Khoroche, *Once the Buddha Was a Monkey*, 47–57). Once the future Buddha lived as the kind and generous King Matrībala. On one occasion his kingdom was visited by four flesh-eating ogres, who could not, for some reason, afflict his subjects by attacking and eating them. Learning that the country was protected by a powerful talisman—its noble-minded king—they decided to visit him, disguising themselves as brahmans. Refusing other normal human food, they requested instead to drink his blood and eat his flesh, revealing their true terrifying forms as demons. The king granted their wish, as a supreme act of generosity, but finally was restored to health by medicines applied by the god Śakra. See also Shang Dodé Pal's commentary, 133a5.
242. A son and mother were crossing at the confluence of the Ganges and Jamunā, and both drowned, each trying to save the other. Through that merit, both were reborn as gods. A Hindu seer with supernatural powers living nearby is said to have witnessed their excellent rebirth and thought it was caused by the holiness of that place. See Shang Dodé Pal's commentary, 137b6.
243. Maitreya, *Mahāyānasūtrālaṃkāra* 18:29–30, Toh 4020 Tengyur, sems tsam, *phi*, 26b1.
244. Ibid. 18:62, 28a2.
245. Ibid. 9:13, 9a5.
246. See the examples taught by Shang Dodé Pal, *Commentary*, 52a. After giving an elaborate account of the physical universe, following the Abhidharma, and other topics, from 62b he gives details of the various sufferings of samsara's inhabitants.
247. Maitreya, *Mahāyānasūtrālaṃkāra* 18:63, Toh 4020 Tengyur, sems tsam, *phi*, 28a3.
248. Sutra not located.
249. Maitreya, *Mahāyānasūtrālaṃkāra* 18:46, Toh 4020 Tengyur, sems tsam, *phi*, 27a5.
250. Read *reg*?
251. *Dharmasaṃgītisūtra*, Toh 238 Kangyur, mngo sde, *zha*, 84a5. The citation here appears to be an abridgement of the passage in the Kangyur.
252. Śāntideva, *Bodhisattvacaryāvatāra* 8:90, Toh 3871 Tengyur, dbu ma, *lam*, 27a2.
253. *Letter to a Friend* (*Suhṛllekha*) 68cd, Toh 4182 Tengyur, spring yig, *nge*, 43b7. Sapaṇ quotes same verse above at page 443. Cf. page 192 in Gampopa's *Ornament* above, where he cites a related sutra passage.
254. Śāntideva, *Bodhisattvacaryāvatāra* 8:97cd, Toh 3871 Tengyur, dbu ma, *la*, 27a6.
255. Ibid. 8:98, 27a6.
256. Ibid. 8:99cd, 27a7. See also Deshung, *Three Levels*, 297.
257. Śāntideva, *Bodhisattvacaryāvatāra* 8:131, Toh 3871 Tengyur, dbu ma, *la*, 28b4.
258. Ibid. 8:140, 28b2.
259. Nāgārjuna, *Ratnāvalī* 5:84c–87b, Toh 4158 Tengyur, spring yig, *ge*, 125a6.
260. Śāntideva, *Bodhisattvacaryāvatāra* 10:56, Toh 3871 Tengyur, dbu ma, *la*, 40a3.
261. Shākya Chokden, *Golden Scalpel of Elegant Discourse*, 6:640.1, identifies the proponent as Jé Drigungpa, quoting him as asserting that you should not practice this exchange until you have reached the eighth bodhisattva level. On the next page Shākya Chokden quotes Jé Phakmodrupa.
262. For the story of Captain Maitrakanyakā (Kṣemendra, *Bodhisattvāvadānakalpalatā*, no. 92), whose head was crushed in hell by a great wheel as retribution for kicking

his mother's head but who was reborn in Tuṣita upon wishing his own suffering would serve to remove the suffering of all who faced a similar fate, see the references in Rhoton, *A Clear Differentiation*, 93n10. This story is told in Deshung, *Three Levels*, 287–88. For the story of the boat captain's son "Byams pa mchod sbyin," illustrating how you should never disrespect your parents, see Shang Dodé Pal, *Commentary*, 138a4.

263. *Skill in Means Sutra* (*Upāyakauśalyasūtra*), Toh 353 Kangyur, mdo sde, *aḥ*, 117a2. For showing pity for the sufferings of his hell-realm companion, the future Buddha is beaten to death by the slave driver and is immediately reborn among the gods. This story is retold in Deshung Rinpoche, *Three Levels*, 309.
264. Cf. Sapaṇ, *Clear Differentiation* 2:36; Rhoton, *A Clear Differentiation*, 93n9; and Gorampa, *Detailed Commentary*, 72b.
265. Śāntideva, *Bodhisattvacaryāvatāra* 8:131, Toh 3871 Tengyur, dbu ma, *la*, 28b4.
266. Ibid. 8:168, 30a3.
267. Ibid. 8:169–70ab, 30a4.
268. Ibid. 8:170cd–171, 30a4.
269. Ibid. 8:172, 30a5.
270. Ibid. 8:155, 29b3.
271. Ibid. 8:159, 29b4.
272. Ibid. 8:160, 29b6.
273. Ibid. 8:161ab, 29b6.
274. Ibid. 8:161cd–162, 29b7.
275. Ibid. 8:163, 29b7.
276. Ibid. 8:164ab, 30a1.
277. Ibid. 8:164cd–166, 30a1.
278. Ibid. 8:156, 29b4.
279. Ibid. 8:157, 29b4.
280. Nāgārjuna, *Fundamental Verses on the Middle Way* (*Mūlamadhyamakakārikā*) 24:11, Toh 3824 Tengyur, dbu ma, *tsa*, 14a2.
281. Nāgārjuna, *Commentary on the Thought of Awakening* (*Bodhicittavivaraṅa*) verse 49, Toh 1800 Tengyur, rgyud, *ngi*, 40a5. In the Dergé Tengyur edition, the last line of the stanza reads "That is not true meditation" (*de de sgom par byed ma min*). For an English translation of this verse text, see http://tibetanclassics.org/en/media-resources/text.
282. Maitreya, *Mahāyānasūtrālaṃkāra* 17:12, Toh 4020 Tengyur, sems tsam, *phi*, 21b5.
283. Ibid. 17:34, 22b4.
284. *Ratnaguṇasaṃcayagāthā* 32:3cd, Toh 13 Kangyur, sher phyin, *ka*, 19b3.
285. Maitreya, *Mahāyānasūtrālaṃkāra* 21:51, Toh 4020 Tengyur, sems tsam, *phi*, 18a7. Also quoted and explained below on page 581.
286. Sapaṇ's definition makes clear that what he is talking about is not far from "wisdom" in one of the usual senses of the English word—namely, the power of discerning and judging properly what is true or right. "Discerning insight" would be a good direct translation for *shes rab* here (*prajñā* in Sanskrit), as he defines it, and I have decided in this translation to render the word in most cases as "discerning wisdom." The main exception is when it forms part of the established term *perfection of wisdom*, in which case I follow established tradition and render it as just

"wisdom." Depending on context, the term can also be translated as "acumen" or "intelligence."

287. See, for example, Guṇaprabha, *Detailed Autocommentary on the Vinaya Sutra* (*Vinayasūtravṛttyabhidhānasvavyākhyāna*), Toh 4119 Tengyur, 'dul ba, *zhu*, 32b3.
288. Cāṇakya, *Nītiśāstra*, Toh 4334 Tengyur, thun mong ba lugs kyi bstan bcos, *ngo*, 136a7.
289. Ibid., 137b5.
290. Sapaṇ, *Jewel Treasure of Aphorisms* 69 = 3:11.
291. Śāntideva, *Bodhisattvacaryāvatāra* 5:24, Toh 3871 Tengyur, dbu ma, *la*, 11a4.
292. Vasubhandu, *Abhidharmakośa* 1:3, Toh 4089 Tengyur, mngon pa, *ku*, 1a4.
293. Dharmakīrti, *Pramāṇavārttika* 2:213ab, Toh 4210 Tengyur, tshad ma, *ce*, 114b5. "View of self on a transitory collection," *'jig tshogs la lta ba* (Skt. *satkāyadṛṣṭi*), is a technical term refering to the false view that a substantial person—a true referent of the first person pronoun "I"—exists on the basis of the physical and mental aggregates, either as separate from them or identical to them. The "transitory collection" is these physical and mental aggregates that consitute a person's existence.
294. Ibid. 1:239cd, 103b5.
295. Not located.
296. *Collection of Aphorisms* (*Udānavarga*) 22:6, Toh 326 Kangyur, mdo sde, *sa*, 228b2.
297. Not located.
298. Like a deceitful butcher who sells donkey or horse meat after showing a deer tail to the gullible customer, falsely claiming the meat is venison. Found in Sapaṇ, *Clear Differentiation* 3:472. See also Sapaṇ, *Jewel Treasure of Aphorisms* 153 = 5:9.
299. In other words, a deceitful teacher may present himself as completely harmless, like a crafty hunter who, disguided as a harmless ascetic, lures unsuspecting wild animals too close. Cf. Edgerton, *Pañcatantra*, 119–20, as suggested by Mr. Hidetoshi Fushimi.
300. I am baffled by this metaphor. Correct to read *rlubs 'dzugs pa* ("put in a hole")? Cf. Edgerton, *Pañcatantra*, 148–49, as suggested by Mr. Hidetoshi Fushimi.
301. Cf. Sapaṇ's *Entrance Gate for the Wise*, 3:43–45, and his autocommentary on the *Treasure of Reasoning*, *da*, 30b2.
302. Cf. Sapaṇ, *Entrance Gate for the Wise* 3:44.
303. See Sapaṇ's autocommentary on the *Treasure of Reasoning*, *da* 30b1–36a2. Sapaṇ's *Treasure of Reasoning* itself refutes mainly the two lower schools, though he does take the Madhyamaka into consideration in one passage. When he reaches the highest level of Dharmakīrti's thought there (169.3.5), it is not the Madhyamaka. But in the *Entrance Gate for the Wise* 3:48, at the end of the autocommentary, Sapaṇ carries the critique one level higher. See also Jackson, *Entrance Gate*, 424n144.
304. Sapaṇ's *Analysis of Established Tenets* is now lost. See Jackson, "Two Grub mtha' Treatises of Sa-skya Paṇḍita."
305. Translated in Jackson, *Enlightenment by a Single Means*, 177–80. Cf. the parallel passage in Sapaṇ, *Clear Differentiation* 3:167–73.
306. *Dkar po chig thub*, the "white singly efficacious" remedy. The Dharma of conventional usage is that which can be conveyed through words, including conventional Buddhist practices.
307. The *lon* which I translated "dam" may mean "reply." The titles of the five works are roughly rendered from the Tibetan: *Bsam gtan nyal ba'i 'khor lo*, *Bsam gtan gyi lon*,

[Bsam gtan gyi] yang lon, *Lta ba'i rgyab sha*, and *Mdo sde brgyad cu['i] khungs*. The original Chinese titles of Mohoyen's works were no doubt quite different.

308. Nagao, "The Silence of the Buddha," 147, refers to similar statements or analogies in *Awakening of Faith*, Taishō 32, 576a, and in Nāgārjuna's *Refutation of Arguments*, verses 3 and 25.
309. On the motif of the shoe or boot left behind, see Seyfort Ruegg, *Buddha-Nature, Mind and the Problem of Gradualism*, 13n16.
310. Sapaṇ gives these as *Rgyal bzhed*, *Dba' bzhed*, and *'Ba' bzhed*. On the "Testament of Ba" (*Sba bzhed* or *'Ba' bzhed*) and the other two early Tibetan histories, see Seyfort Ruegg, *Buddha-nature*, 67ff. and note 136. Sapaṇ's mention of these sources was noted by A. Vostrikov already in the 1930s. See also the references in Jackson, *Entrance Gate*, 403n104.
311. Translated in Jackson, *Enlightenment by a Single Means*, 180–81. Cf. the similar criticisms in Sapaṇ, *Clear Differentiation* 3:174–75; Rhoton, *A Clear Differentiation*, 118–19; and Sapaṇ, *Letter to the Buddhas and Bodhisattvas*, 6b3f.
312. For a similar passage, *Establishing the Four Mudrās* (*Caturmudrāniścaya*), Toh 2225 Tengyur, rgyud, *wi*, 77b7; P 3069, rgyud 'grel, *mi*, 82b: *Chos kyi phyag rgya ma shes pas las kyi phyag rgya bcos ma 'ba' zhig las lhan cig skyes pa'i rang bzhin bcos ma ma yin pa ji ltar 'byung zhing skye bar 'gyur*. For more details on this source and its attributions, see Rhoton, *A Clear Differentiation*, 187n36. Cf. Tashi Namgyal, *Detailed Explanation of Mahāmudrā*, 88b–89b; Lhalungpa, *Mahāmudrā*, 99–100. Cf. Gorampa, *Detailed Commentary*, 111b, and *Dispelling Errors*, 45b.
313. Indrabhūti, *Achieving Pristine Awareness* (*Jñānasiddhisādhanopāyikā*) 5:2cd, Toh 2219 Tengyur, rgyud, *wi*, 45a2; P 3063, 49a. In the Dergé edition of Indrabhūti's text, the two lines read: *smongs pa bsgom pas rmongs pa ni/ tshul ngan rnams kyis thob par 'gyur/*. This verse is quoted again below (see note 352).
314. Not located.
315. *Mañjuśrīnāmasaṃgīti*, Toh 360 Kangyur, rgyud, *ka*, 10a5.
316. *Perfection of Wisdom in Twenty-Five Thousand Lines* (*Pañcaviṃśatisāhasrikāprajñāpāramitā*), Toh 9 Kangyur, sher phyin, *a*, 130b3.
317. *Ratnaguṇasaṃcayagāthā* 31:5, Toh 13 Kangyur, sher phyin, *ka*, 18b3.
318. *Questions of Susthitamati Devaputra Sutra* (*Susthitamatidevaputraparipṛcchāsūtra*), Toh 80 Kangyur, dkon brtsegs, *cha*, 16a1. P 760, zi, 344a7. What is presented in Sapan's text appears to be an abbreviation from this sutra.
319. Maitreya, *Mahāyānasūtrālaṃkāra* 12:59, Toh 4020 Tengyur, sems tsam, *phi*, 15b3. The two śrāvaka āryas referred to in this passage are those who are free from the desires of the realm of desire and those who not yet free from such desires.
320. *Sems tsam rgyan*. This is another name for Ratnākaraśānti's commentary on Śāntarakṣita's *Ornament of the Middle Way*.
321. *Man ngag*, his commentary on the Perfection of Wisdom (*Prajñāpāramitopadeśa*), Toh 4079, P 5579.
322. Cf. Sapaṇ, *Clear Differentiation* 3:396; Rhoton, *A Clear Differentiation*, 148. See also Gorampa, *Detailed Commentary*, 190.1.
323. Shang Tsalpa, *Ultimate Supreme Path*, 71. Translated by Peter Alan Roberts in *Mahāmudrā and Related Instructions* (Boston: Wisdom Publications, 2011), 122.
324. *Śatasāhasrikāprajñāpāramitā*, Toh 8 Kangyur, sher phyin, *ta*, 325b2.

325. Not yet located in a canonical source. But Mr. Hidetoshi Fushimi located the quote in an early Tibetan *cig car ba* manual recovered from Dunhuang: Pelliot Tibetan 116, *Dmigs su med pa'i tshul gcig pa'i gzhung*, 133.4f. It is also quoted by Sapaṇ in his *Bka' gdams nam mkha' 'bum*, *na* 243b5. Absence of mindfulness and mental activities are criticized by Kamalaśīla in his third *Stages of Meditation* (*Bhāvaṇākrama*), Toh 3917 Tengyur, dbu ma, *ki*, 62a.
326. *Perfection of Wisdom in Eight Thousand Lines* (*Aṣṭasāhasrikāprajñāpāramitā*), Toh 12 Kangyur, shes phyin, *ka*, 3a3; P 734, sher phyin, *mi*, 3a7. Cf. Lhalungpa, *Mahāmudrā*, 219 (Tashi Namgyal, 205a); and Shenga, *Gloss Commentary on the Abhidharmasamuccaya*, 17b1.
327. Vasubandhu, *Treasury of Higher Knowledge* (*Abhidharmakośa*) 6:5ab, Toh 4089 Tengyur, mngon pa, *ku*, 18b7.
328. This unspecified work of Candragomin was not located.
329. *Dharmasaṃgītisūtra*, Toh 238 Kangyur, mdo sde, *zha* 84b5; P 904, mdo sna tshogs, *vu* 91a3.
330. Dharmakīrti, *Pramāṇavārttika* 2:34a, Toh 4210 Tengyur, tshad ma, *ce*, 108b7.
331. Candrakīrti, *Madhyamakāvatāra* 1:1, Toh 3861 Tengyur, dbu ma, *'a*, 201a1.
332. Udbhaṭasiddhasvāmin, *Viśeṣaṣṭava*, Toh 1109 Tengyur, bstod tshogs, *ka*, 1a4; P 2001, bstod tshogs, *ka*, 2a3.
333. *Ratnaguṇasaṃcayagāthā* 32:4, Toh 13 Kangyur, sher phyin, *ka*, 19b3.
334. Śāntideva, *Bodhisattvacaryāvatāra* 9:1, Toh 3871 Tengyur, dbu ma, *la*, 30b7.
335. Dharmakīrti, *Pramāṇavārttika* 2:255, Toh 4210 Tengyur, tshad ma, *ce*, 117a6.
336. Śāntideva, *Śikṣāsamuccaya* 21cd, Toh 3939 Tengyur, dbu ma, *khi*, 2b5.
337. Saraha, *Dohakoṣagīti*, Toh 2224 Tengyur, rgyud, *zhi*, 71b1; P 3068, rgyud 'grel, *mi*, 75b2.
338. Dharmakīrti, *Pramāṇavārttika* 282c–283a, Toh 4210 Tengyur, tshad ma, *ce*, 118a7.
339. Ibid. 136c–138d, 112b5. The "rhinoceros-like" (*bse ru*) are the prateyakabuddhas, who like rhinos (or like the horn of a rhino) are typically solitary.
340. *Vairocanābhisambodhi*, Toh 494 Kangyur, rgyud, *tha*, 152b1; P 126, rgyud, *tha*, 185b7. This passage is also quoted above, on page 459 Sapaṇ also quotes it in his *Clear Differentiation* 3:357–60, and his *Letter to the Noble-Minded* (Rhoton, *A Clear Differentiation*, 234).
341. *Ratnaguṇasaṃcayagāthā* 20:10cd, Toh 13 Kangyur, sher phyin, *ka*.
342. A similar legend is explained in Martön Chökyi Gyalpo's commentary on Sapaṇ's *Jewel Treasure of Aphorisms*, 114.
343. This passage is found in *Discourse on the Gnosis of Passing* (*Ātyayajnānasūtra*), Toh 122 Kangyur, mdo sde, *tha*, 153a5; P 790, mdo sna tshogs, *tu*, 159a6.
344. This statement from a Sāṃkhya text not located.
345. On the fourfold analysis of allusive statements used here and below, page 533, see Jackson, *Entrance Gate*, 393n83. See also Sapaṇ, *Clear Differentiation* 1:139–40; Rhoton, *A Clear Differentiation*, 58.
346. Śāntideva, *Bodhisattvacaryāvatāra* 9:135, Toh 3871 Tengyur, dbu ma, *la*, 36a4.
347. Ibid. 9:137, 36a5.
348. Dharmakīrti, *Pramāṇavārttika* 2:165f, Toh 4210 Tengyur, tshad ma, *ce*.
349. Ākāśānantyāyatana, the lowest of the four abodes of the formless realm (*arūpadhātu*). The passage continues by ascending through the remaining abodes.

350. *'Du shes med par skyes pa*, *asaṃjñisattva*. These gods in one part of the Bṛhatphala heaven abide in a kind of faux nirvana, fascination for which obstructs them from seeking true liberation.
351. *Sāgaramatiparipṛcchāsūtra*, Toh 152 Kangyur, mdo sde, *pha*, 96a4; P 819, mdo sna tshogs, *pu*, 107b3.
352. Indrabhūti, *Jñānasiddhisādhanopāyikā*, 5:2cd, Toh 2219 Tengyur, rgyud, *wi*, 15a2; P 3063, rgyud 'grel, *mi*, 49a. Quoted above on page 494.
353. This analogy possibly means that it makes no difference whether a goat is white or black when you have killed it and are removing its entrails.
354. Nāgārjuna, *Fundamental Verses on the Middle Way* (*Mūlamadhyamakakārikā*) 24:11, Toh 3824 Tengyur, dbu ma, *tsa*, 14a2.
355. Ibid. 13:8, 8a6.
356. Nāgārjuna, *Precious Garland* (*Ratnāvalī*) 1:57, Toh 4158 Tengyur, spring yig, *ge*, 109a2.
357. *Kāśyapaparivartasūtra*, Toh 87 Kangyur, dkon brtsegs, *cha*, 132b1; Staël-Holstein, *The Kāçyapaparivarta*, 96.
358. *Samādhirājasūtra* 9:36, Toh 127 Kangyur, mdo sde, *da*, 27a7. Also quoted above and below.
359. Ibid. 9:42, Toh 127 Kangyur, mdo sde, *da*, 27b4. Also quoted above.
360. Cf. Sapaṇ, *Clear Differentiation* 3:348f.
361. In his *Clear Differentiation*, chapter 3, Sapaṇ also criticizes teachings (mainly Shijé or Chö?) for being neither the perfections nor mantra tradition. See also Karma Trinlepa, *The Songs of Esoteric Practice* (*mgur*) *and Replies to Doctrinal Questions* (*dris lan*), p. 187 (*ca* 51a3), for his reply on this point.
362. Cf. Sapaṇ, *Clear Differentiation* 3:449.
363. *Ratnaguṇasaṃcayagāthā* 20:10cd, Toh 13 Kangyur, sher phyin, *ka*, 12a2. Also quoted above.
364. Nāgārjuna, *Ratnāvalī* 3:12, Toh 4158 Tengyur, spring yig, *ge*, 115a1.
365. *Samādhirājasūtra* 9:42, Toh 127 Kangyur, mdo sde, *da*, 27b4. Also quoted above.
366. Ibid. 9:36ab, 27a7. Also quoted above twice.
367. Dharmakīrti, *Pramāṇavārttika* 281, Toh 4210 Tengyur, tshad ma, *ce*, 129a4.
368. Cf. Sapaṇ, *Entrance Gate for the Wise* 3:64.
369. These three activities of a scholar are the subject of Sapaṇ's *Entrance Gate for the Wise*. See Jackson, *Entrance Gate*, 191ff.
370. Shākya Chokden, *Collected Works* 17:473, answers questions of the Fourth Shamarpa about this classification of Madhyamaka.
371. This heading was introduced on page 488.
372. See above, page 497.
373. *Collection of Aphorisms* (*Udānavarga*) 22:6, Toh 326 Kangyur, mdo sde, *sa*, 228b2.
374. *Sarvadharmāpravṛttinirdeśasūtra*, Toh 180 D, mdo sde, *ma*, 273b2. Here Sapaṇ summarizes the passage P 847, mdo sna tshogs, *bu*, 285b7ff.
375. Śrīmālādevīsiṃhanādasūtra, Toh 92 Kangyur, dkon brtsegs, *cha*, 258b6. This is a paraphrase of a passage.
376. *Fundamental Verses on the Middle Way* (*Mūlamadhyamakakārikā*) 24:8–9, Toh 3824 Tengyur, dbu ma, *tsa*, 14b7.
377. This is the position of the Kadampas of Sangphu Monastery Ngok Loden Sherap, Drolungpa, and Khyung Rinchen Drak.
378. Śāntideva, *Bodhisattvacaryāvatāra* 9:2cd, Toh 3871 Tengyur, dbu ma, *la*, 31a1.

379. Cf. the very similar definition of ultimate truth by Üpa Losal, as recorded in Mimaki, *Blo gsal grub mtha'*, 148–49: *de nyid dpyad na blo ma 'khrul pa la cir yang ma grub pa.*
380. *Gzhan sel.* That is, as objects of language and conceptual thought, which operate through excluding opposites.
381. Candrakīrti, *Yuktiṣaṣṭikāvṛtti*, P 5265 and Toh 3864 Tengyur, dbu ma, *sa*, 8a2.
382. Jñānagarbha, *Satyadvayavibhaṅgakārikā* verse 3cd, Toh 3881 Tengyur, dbu ma, *sa*, 1a4. See also Eckel, *Jñānagarbha's Commentary*, 71.
383. This refers to such shared experiences as, in this world, experiencing fire as hot and ice as cold.
384. Jñānagarbha, *Satyadvayavibhaṅgakārikā*, verse 12, Toh 3881 Tengyur, dbu ma *sa*, 2a4.
385. See also below, page 573, and Jackson, *Entrance Gate*, 188n55 and 396n95.
386. For Yogācāras nondual cognition is neither subjective nor objective and is classed as the correct dependent. See also Jackson, *Entrance Gate*, 186n42 and 418–19n131.
387. My translation corrects the Dergé edition (and other versions of the text) to read *kun rdzob* ("relative" or "surface level") here.
388. My translation corrects the Tibetan text to read *don dam* ("ultimate") here.
389. Nāgārjuna, *Yuktiṣaṣṭikā* verse 5, Toh 3825 Tengyur, dbu ma, *tsa*, 20a4.
390. Nāgārjuna, *Pañcakrama,* Toh 1802 Tengyur, rgyud, *ngi*, 56a2. P 2667, rgyud 'grel, *gi*, 62b6. The quote appears later in the text with a slightly different wording on page 575.
391. These four faults are enumerated by Sönam Tsemo in his *Bodhisattvacaryāvatāra* commentary, *ca*, 288b. See also Drolungpa, *Great Tenrim*, 357b.
392. *Saṃdhinirmocanasūtra* 3:3–5, Toh 106 Kangyur, mdo sde, *ca*, 7a7. The opening section of chapter 3 of this sutra presents four logical faults for each of the two prongs of the identity relation between the two truths—namely, they are identical or they are different.
393. A passage saying as much can be found in the *Perfection of Wisdom in Eight Thousand Lines* (*Aṣṭasāhasrikāprajñāpāramitā*), P 734, sher phyin, *mi*, 116a4.
394. Ibid., 3a8. This sutra is also quoted in the autocommentary to Sapaṇ's *Entrance Gate for the Wise* 3:51.
395. *Ratnaguṇasaṃcayagāthā* 1:13c, Toh 13 Kangyur, sher phyin, *ka*, 2b4.
396. Dharmakīrti, *Pramāṇavārttika* 1:185, Toh 4210 Tengyur, tshad ma, *ce*, 101b4.
397. *Saṃdhinirmocanasūtra* 3:7, Toh 106 Kangyur, mdo sde, *ca*, 9b1.
398. *Samyak*, "complete" or "correct," is Tibetan *yang dag pa*; *vṛ* for āvaraṇa, which means "obscured" (*sgrib pa*) or "covered" (*'gebs pa*).
399. Dharmakīrti, *Pramāṇavārttika* 1:123b–d, Toh 4210 Tengyur, tshad ma, *ce*, 96a7. Cf. the similar argumentation in Sapaṇ's autocommentary on the *Treasure of Reasoning*, 63b. Here the readings *dpyad* should be emended to *bcad.*
400. Ngok Loden Sherap and Drolungpa similarly held the ultimate not to be the object of ordinary mind.
401. *Refutation of Objections* (*Vigrahavyāvartanī*) verse 29, Toh 3828 Tengyur, dbu ma, *tsa*, 128b2.
402. Asaṅga, *Abhidharmasamuccaya*, Toh 4049 Tengyur, sems tsam, *ri*, 104b7; P P5550, sems tsam, *li*, 104b6. Cf. Sapaṇ, *Entrance Gate for the Wise* 3:37, autocommentary, and Jackson, *Entrance Gate*, 341 and 395n90. The "deceitful speculative theory" (*ngan g.yo'i lta ba, kusrtidṛṣṭi*) is listed among twenty-eight evil speculative views

(*lta ba ngan pa, asaddṛṣṭi*) near the end of the "Ascertaining the Dharma" (*Dharmaviniścaya*) section of the *Abhidharmasamuccaya*. See Rahula, *Le Compendium*, 140, and Tatia, *Abhidharmasamuccaya-bhāṣyam*, 113. See also Shenga, *Gloss Commentary on the Abhidharmasamuccaya*, 297.5 (149a5).

403. See the similar explanation in Sapaṇ, *Entrance Gate for the Wise* 3:37, second half of the autocommentary; Jackson, *Entrance Gate*, 342.
404. *Perfection of Wisdom in a Hundred Thousand Lines* (*Śatasāhasrikāprajñāpāramitā*), Toh 8 Kangyur, sher phyin, *ka*, 3b6; P 730, sher phyin, *ra*, 4a1.
405. *Samādhirājasūtra* 6:7, Toh 127 Kangyur, mdo sde, *da*, 13b1. Also quoted above.
406. *Trimaṇḍalaviśuddhi*. These three were alluded to above on page 424.
407. This is the well-known aspiration prayer titled *Bhadracaryāpraṇidhāna*, which is also part 4 of the *Flower Ornament Sutra* (*Avataṃsakasūtra*), Toh 44 Kangyur, phal chen, *a*, 352b7.
408. These prayers and liturgies were recommended above, page 413, as regular practices for increasing bodhicitta.
409. Maitreya, *Mahāyānasūtrālaṃkāra* 17:13, Toh 4020 Tengyur, sems tsam, *phi*, 21b6.
410. Ibid. 17:35, Toh 4020 Tengyur, sems tsam, *phi*, 22b5.
411. *Ratnaguṇasaṃcayagāthā* 32:4ab, Toh 13 Kangyur, sher phyin, *ka*, 19b3. The entire verse is quoted above on page 499.
412. Maitreya, *Ornament of Mahayana Sutras* (*Mahāyānasūtrālaṃkāra*) 21:47, Toh 4020 Tengyur, sems tsam, *phi*, 38a5. Also quoted and explained below.
413. This section was introduced on the opening page of chapter 4.
414. Maitreya, *Mahāyānasūtrālaṃkāra* 17:47; Toh 4020 Tengyur, sems tsam, *phi*, 38a5.
415. Maitreya, *Ornament of Mahayana Sutras* (*Mahāyānasūtrālaṃkāra*) 17:14, Toh 4020 Tengyur, sems tsam, *phi*, 21b7.
416. Maitreya, *Mahāyānasūtrālaṃkāra* 17:15, Toh 4020 Tengyur, sems tsam, *phi*, 21b7.
417. Maitreya, *Ornament of Mahayana Sutras* (*Mahāyānasūtrālaṃkāra*) 19:58, Toh 4020 Tengyur, sems tsam, *phi*, 30a6.
418. Ibid. 13:23, Toh 4020 Tengyur, sems tsam, *phi*, 12b3.
419. *Commentary on the Four Hundred* (*Catuḥśatakaṭīkā*), Toh 3865 Tengyur, bdu ma, *ya*, 110a7. In the Dergé Tengyur edition of Candrakīrti's work, the stanza reads quite differently: "A teacher who can transform his students/ on the basis of understanding their minds/ should look after students;/ it's inappropriate for the unintelligent to do so."
420. Maitreya, *Mahāyānasūtrālaṃkāra* 2:14, Toh 4020 Tengyur, sems tsam, *phi*, 3a1.
421. Maitreya, *Uttaratantra* 5:20, Toh 4024 Tengyur, sems tsam, *phi*, 72b6.
422. Śāntideva, *Bodhisattvacaryāvatāra* 5:89–90, Toh 3871 Tengyur, dbu ma, *la*, 39b5.
423. *Bodhisattva Levels* (*Bodhisattvabhūmi*), Toh 4037 Tengyur, sems tsam, *wi*, 86a5.
424. Āryaśūra, *Garland of Jātaka Tales* (*Jātakamāla*), Toh 4150 Tengyur, skye rabs, *hu*, 131a7. Khoroche (*Once the Buddha Was a Monkey*, 245) renders this passage as "...the lord spoke of it being impossible to judge the rightness or the rewards of one's actions, since he who was the soul of pity was nevetheless born as an animal and in that state could still recognize what was right."
425. Āryadeva, *Catuḥśataka* 8:22, Toh 3846 Tengyur, dbu ma, *tsha*, 10a2.
426. *Verse Summary of the Perfection of Wisdom* (*Ratnaguṇasaṃcayagāthā*) 31:9, Toh 13 Kangyur, sher phyin, *ka*; Conze, *Pefection of Wisdom*, p. 69.
427. *Upāyakauśalyasūtra*. Also cited above on the same point; see note 98.

428. Śāntideva, *Bodhisattvacaryāvatāra* 7:25–26, Toh 3871 Tengyur, dbu ma, *la*, 21a3. Also quoted in chapter on generosity.
429. Śāntideva, *Bodhisattvacaryāvatāra* 6:14, Toh 3871 Tengyur, dbu ma, *la*, 15a3.
430. Maitreya, *Mahāyānasūtrālaṃkāra* 17:73, Toh 4020 Tengyur, sems tsam, *phi*, 24b6.
431. Ibid. 17:74, 24b7.
432. Ibid. 17:75, 24b7.
433. Ibid 17:79, 25a2.
434. Maitreya, *Mahāyānasūtrālaṃkāra* 20:63, Toh 4020 Tengyur, sems tsam, *phi*, 35a4, cited in the opening of the text on page 386.
435. A similar definition of the path, including the rejection of this alternative definition proposed by others, is found also in Chim Jampaiyang, *Detailed Abhidharma Commentary*, 512.
436. Sapaṇ here follows primarily on the system of Asaṅga's *Compendium of Higher Knowledge* (*Abhidharmasamuccaya*), Toh 4049 Tengyur, sems tsam, *ri*, 92b3. See Boin-Webb, *Abhidharmasamuccaya*, pp. 140ff.
437. For these four, see below on page 590. Gampopa addresses them in his text on page 340.
438. See page 590 below for these four also.
439. This refers to the four continents of Abhidharma cosmology less the northern continent of Uttarakuru. As Sapaṇ explains below, certain other high meditative attainments (such as the path of seeing) will also not arise in the people of the northern continent Uttarakuru (among many other types of beings), for they possess obscurations in great measure or because they resemble the gods of the two higher realms in lacking discontent.
440. Similar points are discussed by Chim Jampaiyang in his *Detailed Abhidharma Commentary* in his explanation of the path of accumulation (*tshogs lam*).
441. The six levels of meditative concentrations (*bsam gtan sa drug*) are: the access phase of the first level of concentration, the ordinary and extraordinary levels of the first concentration, followed by the second to the fourth levels of meditative concentration.
442. This is one of the four types of meditation objects mentioned in, for example, chapter 3 of Asaṅga's *Compendium of Higher Knowledge*. The four are: (1) pervasive object (*khyab pa'i dmigs pa*), (2) object purifying conduct, (*spyod pa rnam sbyong*), (3) object purifying afflictions (*nyon mongs rnam sbyong*), and (4) object of a learned (*mkhas pa'i dmigs pa*).
443. Asaṅga, *Abhidharmasamuccaya* 2:4.1; Boin-Webb, *Abhidharmasamuccaya*, p. 141, Toh 4049 Tengyur, sems tsam, *ri*, 92b3.
444. Vasubandhu, *Treasury of Higher Knowledge* (*Abhidharmakośa*) 6:23, Toh 4089 Tengyur, mngon pa, *ku*, 19b3.
445. See Asaṅga, *Abhidharmasamuccaya*, Toh 4049 Tengyur, sems tsam, *ri*, 92b5: *dro bar gyur pa gang zhe na/ so so rang gis bden pa rnams la snang ba thob pa'i ting nge 'dzin dang/ shes rab mtshungs par ldan pa dang bcas pa'o//*.
446. Perceptual insight (*snang ba*) is literally "clarity." See the discussion of *āloka labdha* (*snang ba thob pa*) in the *Mahāyānasūtrālaṃkāra*.
447. Asaṅga, *Abhidharmasamuccaya*, Toh 4049 Tengyur, sems tsam, *ri*, 92b6: *rtse mo gang zhe na/ so so rang gis bden pa rnams la snang ba mched pa'i ting nge 'dzin dang/ shes rab mtshungs par ldan pa dang bcas pa'o//*.
448. Ibid.: *bzod pa gang zhe na/ so so rang gis bden pa rnams kyi phyogs gcig la zhugs pa*

dang rjes su song ba'i ting nge 'dzin dang shes rab mtshungs par ldan pa dang bcas pa'o//.

449. Ibid.: *'jig rten pa'i chos kyi mchog gang zhe na/ so so rang gis bden pa rnams la de ma thag pa'i sems kyi ting nge 'dzin dang shes rab mtshungs par ldan pa dang bcas pa'o//.*

450. *Sutra of the Salty River* (*Kṣāranadīsūtra, Chu bo tsha sgo can gyi mdo*); not extant. Cf. the parallel quotes or references in Vasubandhu, *Sūtrālaṃkārabhāṣya*, P 5527, *phi*, 192a5; Asvabhāva, *Sūtrālaṃkāraṭīkā*, P 5530, *bi*, 114a; and Sthiramati, *Sūtrālaṃkāravṛttibhāṣya*, P 5531, *mi*, 271a. This sutra is quoted on another point once in a commentary by Ratnākaraśānti on the *Compendium of Sutras* (*Sūtrasamuccayabhāṣyaratnālokālaṃkāra*), Toh 3935 Tengyur, dbu ma, *ki*.

451. This is the version of a passage from the *Perfection of Wisdom in Twenty-Five Thousand Lines* that Candrakīrti quotes in his *Clear Words* (*Prasannapadā*), Toh 1785 Tengyur, dbu ma *'a*, 114b3. It is close to the wording of the *Perfection of Wisdom in Twenty-Five Thousand Lines*, Toh 9 Kangyur, sher phyin, *ka*, 125b3.

452. *Verse Summary of the Perfection of Wisdom* (*Ratnaguṇasaṃcayagāthā*), Toh 13 Kangyur, sher phyin, *ka*, 3b5 that Candrakīrti quotes in his commentary *Prasannapadā* (*Tshig gsal*, P 5260). See Toh 1785 Tengyur, dbu ma, *'a*, 114b4.

453. Vasubandhu, *Treasury of Higher Knowledge* (*Abhidharmakośa*) 6:24, Toh 4089 Tengyur, mngon pa, *ku*, 19b3.

454. Maitreya, *Abhisamayālaṃkāra* 1:34–35, Toh 3786 Tengyur, shes phyin, *ka*, 3a6.

455. Vasubandhu, *Abhidharmakośa* 6:19, Toh 4089 Tengyur, mngon pa, *ku*, 19b1; P 5590, *gu*, 20b4. In Vasubhandu's text, the lines read *de ni skad cig gcig de bzhin// chos mchog*.... Sapaṇ's wording matches Haribhadra's commentary on the *Perfection of Wisdom in Eight Thousand Lines*, Toh 3791 Tengyur, shes phyin, *cha*, 246b7.

456. Maitreya, *Abhisamayālaṃkāra* 2:18b, Toh 3786 Tengyur, shes phyin, *ka*, 5b3. The stanza reads *rnam rtog bzhi po rten brten pa/ chung dang 'bring dang chen po rnams// nyan thos bse ru lta bu dang// bcas pa dag las khyad par 'phags//.*

457. A synopsis of Sapaṇ's presentation here is found in Chim Jampaiyang, *Detailed Abhidharma Commentary*, 525: *'o na sbyor lam gyi mnyam gzhag gi blo de chos kyi dbyings la blo'i rigs ci yin zhe na/*....

458. *Aṣṭasāhasrikā Prajñāpāramitā*, Toh 3791 Tengyur, shes phyin, *cha*, 23a7.

459. Sapaṇ holds that there are four kinds of direct perception (*mngon sum*): (1) sensory, (2) mental (*yid kyi*), (3) reflexive (mind perceiving itself, *rang rig*), and (4) yogic direct perception (*rnal 'byor*), the last of which only occurs on the path of seeing and higher.

460. Maitreya, *Madhyāntavibhāga*, 4:12a, Toh 4021 Tengyur, sems tsam, *phi*, 43a6: *rjes su mthun la phyin ci log*. Chim (p. 526) also adds the quotation from Maitreya's *Uttaratantra*: *rgyud bla ma las/ so so'i skye bo phyin ci log/ bden pa mthong ba bzlog pa ste//.*

461. Sapaṇ refers to his own refutation of assumption (*yid dpyod*) as an independent epistemological category in chapter 2 of his *Treasury of Reasoning*. Sapaṇ's criticisms of this type are often motivated by the desire for maximum conceptual simplicity and economy of description. He says in the autocommentary to his *Treasury of Reasoning* (pp. 71–72) that there are only three faulty logical marks (*rtags skyon can*), and similarly only three kinds of invalid, unreliable cognition (*tshad ma ma yin pa'i blo*), though those three can be divided into two classes: mistaken cognition

(*log rtog*) and doubt (*the tshom*), and further into the single class of non-knowing (*ma rtogs pa*). Hence all wrong knowing can be reduced to one category. This is in harmony with Dharmakīrti's teaching that by their nature the two valid cognitions can be reduced to reflexive direct perception (*rang rig mngon sum*) and that the two classes of objects of cognition can likewise be reduced to just own characteristic (*rang mtshan*). Sapaṇ regrets that Tibetan epistemologists from Chapa Chökyi Sengé onward abandoned that single overarching category of not knowing, the chief of invalid cognitions, in favor of what seemed a pointless division into five invalid cognitions.

462. Here the fact that mental perception is held to occur as a second moment after the contact of sense object with sense organ may have led to this apparently Tibetan theory that such perception (together with memory, *dran pa*) should be classified as subsequent knowing (*bcad shes*).

463. Correct to *bcad pa'i yul can* (that is, *bcad shes*), instead of Dergé's *dpyad pa'i yul can*. See the quotation of this position and its criticism by Chim Jampaiyang, *Detailed Abhidharma Commentary*, 526: *kha cig gis bcad shes dang/ ....* . Note that subsequent knowing is, like assumption, one of the seven categories of knowing minds in the dialectic system of Chapa Chökyi Sengé and his followers. Sapaṇ rejected them as epistemological categories in their own right. Neither is a reliable source of knowledge, but both can be correct.

464. Sapaṇ's position that the knower is reflexive direct perception (*rang rig mngon sum*) is unusual and requires explanation. Most later scholars accepted that a memory or recollective subsequent knower would function here. Chim Jampaiyang summarizes this view (in his *Detailed Abhidharma Commentary*, 526), stating that the knower on the path of accumulation is discriminating knowledge that arose through the two (not three) activities of learning and reflection: "This [knower of the path of application] is just the correct memory of the matter concerning the dharmadhātu that was previously understood through discriminating knowledge that arose through learning and reflection. But to the extent that this knower falsely imputes that universal (or 'object of conceptual thought') to be an external thing, it is simply a mistaken cognition."

465. Khenpo Appey suggests that, as with the previous two paths, the word *rnam grol gyi 'jug ngogs*, "the approach to liberation," is to be expected as part of the definition, and the reading of the Dergé edition of Sapaṇ's text here as *chos kyi dbyings gyi 'jug ngogs*, "the approach to the sphere of reality (*dharmadhātu*)," is probably corrupt. This same problem occurs in the two later definitions of paths, where *rnam grol* would again be expected instead of *chos kyi dbyings*.

466. Vasubandhu, *Abhidharmakośa* 5:4, Toh 4089 Tengyur, mngon pa, *ku*, 16a2. Thus the afflictions to be eliminated in the desire realm are 10 + 7 + 7 + 8 = 32. In the two higher spheres, anger does not arise as an object in the seeing of all four noble truths, so four factors must be subtracted from each, bringing the total to 28 in each of these two spheres.

467. The number 94 is reached by excluding three sets of 6, or 18 in all, from the total of 112 (Sapaṇ explains how 112 is reached in the text that follows). *Yogācārabhūmiviniscayasamgrahanī*, Toh 4038 Tengyur, sems tsam, *zhi*, 95b4: *du zhig mthong bas*

spang bar bya ba dag yin la don kyang mthong bas spang bar bya ba dag yin zhe na/ smras pa. . . .

468. *Abhidharmasamuccaya*, chapter 2, Toh 4049 Tengyur, sems tsam, *ri*, 84b4: *'dod pa'i khams na mthong bas spang par bya ba ni bcu'o// . . . de dg mdor bsdus na nyon mongs pa brgya bcu rtsa gnyis ni . . . .*
469. Exact quote and source not located.
470. Here the Dergé edition's reading "ninety-nine" is obviously wrong.
471. Vasubandhu, *Abhidharmakośa* 6:77, Toh 4089 Tengyur, mngon pa, *ku*, 22b3.
472. *Ornament of Clear Realization* (*Abhisamayālaṃkāra*) 5:21, Toh 3786 Tengyur, shes phyin *ka*, 10a3. The exact stanza appears also as *Uttaratantra* 1:154.
473. Śāntideva, *Bodhisattvacaryāvatāra* 9:151, Toh 3871 Tengyur, dbu ma, *la*, 36a6.
474. Read *srang mda'i mthon dman*. This is a simile commonly found, for instance, in Madhyamaka treatises.
475. Vasubandhu, *Abhidharmakośa* 6:55, Toh 4089 Tengyur, mngon pa, *ku*, 20b6. In other words, nonreturners have to generate discontentment in the desire realm before shifting to a higher realm, for formless minds cannot do that. See Chim, *Detailed Abhidharma Commentary*, 560–61, who says the scripture in question is called the *Ten Times Ten Sutra* (*Bcu tshan bcu pa'i mdo*).
476. This reference to "the Abhidharma" as the source of these statements about the "negation of the sign" (*brda bsal ba*)—that is, a self—regarding sentient beings, phenomena, and both sentient beings and phenomena everywhere may refer to the *Abhidharmasamuccaya*. Ven. Khenpo Appey referred me to the commentary of Sasang Mati Paṇchen, 254, who glosses *brda* as *'du shes* and explains these three in connection with one individual person, not as here, in relation to the three classes of āryas.
477. Asaṅga, *Yogācārabhūmiviniscayasamgrahanī*, Toh 4038 Tengyur, sems tsam, *zhi*, 69a5.
478. The "shared" (that is, śrāvaka) tradition simply means "held in common," whereas "unshared" means unique to the Mahayana.
479. *Prajñāpāramitāsūtra*, Toh 12 Kangyur, sher phyin, *ka*, 3b2. See references to same quote in its occurrence above on page 542.
480. Vasubandhu, *Treasury of Higher Knowledge*, *Abhidharmakośa* 6:28cd, Toh 4089 Tengyur, mngon pa, *ku*, 19b6.
481. Ibid. 6:28ab, 19b6.
482. See Sapaṇ's description below on page 556 of the seven reflections as a system of four paths.
483. Although ITC gives *Questions of Susthitamati Devaputra Sutra* (*Susthitamatideva-putraparipṛcchāsūtra*), Toh 80 Kangyur, dkon brtsegs, *ca*, 3b3, a better source could be 5a2. There we find the phrase *byang chub sems dpa' mi skye ba la bzod pa*, albeit without the genitive cited by Sapaṇ—that is, *byang chub sems dpa'* instead of *byang chub sems pa'i*.
484. Unspecified sutra. Not located.
485. Nāgārjuna, *Yuktiṣaṣṭikā* 11c–12, Toh 3825 Tengyur, mdo 'grel, *tsa*, 20a7; P 5225, dbu ma, *tsa*, 12. Lowo Khenchen in his *Entrance Gate for the Wise* commentary interprets the "unwise person" of the verse to be one who maintains the existence of a momentary nondual gnosis, the very tradition of the Mind Only.
486. On the fourfold analysis of allusive statements used here and above on page 502, see Jackson, *Entrance Gate*, 393n83.

487. Nāgārjuna, *Mūlamadhyamakakārikā* 1:1, Toh 3824 Tengyur, dbu ma, *tsa*, 1a3.
488. Ibid. 21:11, 12b4.
489. *Anavataptanāgarājaparipṛcchāsūtra*, Toh 156 Kangyur, mdo sde, *pha*, 230b2–3; and P [33] 823, mdo sna tshogs, *pu*, 238a6: *rkyen las skyes pa gang yin de ma skyes// de la skye ba ngo bo nyid kyis med// rkyen la rag las gang yin stong par gsungs// stong nyid gang shes de ni bag yod pa'o//*. Line 1 of P reads *te* instead of *de*. See Mimaki, *Blo gsal grub mtha'*, 225n572. Also quoted in Sapaṇ, *Entrance Gate for the Wise* autocommentary 3:48 (Jackson, *Entrance Gate*, 423n143). The version found in *Blo gsal grub mtha'*, 108b5–6, is the same as in *Entrance Gate* except that it reads *stong par bshad* in line 3 where *Entrance Gate* reads *stong pa nyid*.
490. *Seventy Verses on Emptiness* (*Śūnyatāsaptatikārikā*) 71, Toh 3826 Tengyur, dbu ma, *tsa*, 26b6.
491. Nāgārjuna, *Fundamental Vereses on the Middle Way* (*Mūlamadhyamakakārikā*) 24:19, Toh 3824, Tengyur, dbu ma, *tsa*, 15a6.
492. I have emended to read: *ting nge 'dzin khyad par can gyis rnam grol gyi 'jug ngogs la goms par byed pa'o/*. The words *gyis rnam grol* are missing in D.
493. See note 350 above.
494. On the seven reflections, see also Asaṅga, *Śrāvakabhūmi*, P 5537, sems tsam, *wi*, 3.28. Florin Deleanu 2006 investigated as his main subject the chapter on the Mundane Path (*Laukikamārga*) in the *Śrāvakabhūmi*, one of the earliest strata in the important early Yogācāra doctrinal compilation *Yogācārabhūmi* of Indian Mahayana Buddhism. Cf. Wayman, *Analysis of the Śrāvakabhūmi Manuscript*, 126; and idem, *Calming the Mind and Discerning the Real*, 67. Khenpo Appey explained *yid la byed pa* here not in the common technical sense of "attention" but simply as "to meditate" (*sgom pa*) or "to think" (*bsam pa*), and I have accordingly used "reflection."
495. D's *dad pa* should possibly be emended to read *dga' ba*.
496. The fruit is attaining the first meditative concentration. This is the main practice (*dngos gzhi*) of the first meditative concentration in other accounts, including in Asaṅga's Śrāvaka Level (*śrāvakabhūmi*).
497. The sentence "Moreover, through meditatively cultivating by turns the defiled and undefiled fourth meditative concentration, you will be born in the five stages of the ārya" has been removed from here and inserted into its correct context on page 259 below. The corruption, which appears in the Tibetan text on ITC page 364, appears likewise in all known Tibetan editions.
498. Could Sapaṇ be referring to "other treatises" such as Vasubandhu's *Abhidharmakośa* and Asaṅga's *Abhidharmasamuccaya*? Sapaṇ's account of these classic śrāvaka methods of meditation based on the *Śrāvaka Levels* is a rarity in Tibetan doctrinal writings.
499. It is unclear why Sapaṇ excludes the pinnacle of existence since the eighth attainment *is* the pinnacle of existence.
500. See also Asaṅga, *Śrāvakabhūmi*, Toh 4036 Tengyur, sems tsam, *dzi*, 176b7 [P 5537, 3.28.6.1].
501. See note 497 above.
502. See also Asaṅga, *Śrāvakabhūmi*, Toh 4036 Tengyur, sems tsam, *dzi*, 177a6 [3.28.6.5].
503. See also Asaṅga, *Śrāvakabhūmi*, Toh 4036 Tengyur, sems tsam, *dzi*, 104b7 [P 3.14]. Here four aspects of the functioning of yoga practice (*rnal 'byor du bya ba*) are discussed.

504. The Dergé edition gives a fourth subtopic, the etymological explanation of the Sanskrit term. This is redundant, since that final heading was already enumerated above on page 554.
505. *Nyon mongs pa dag*. The Dergé edition reads *bdag*. If "inborn self" (*lhan cig skyes pa'i bdag*) is correct, which seems unlikely, then it could perhaps be glossed as "the erroneous conception of an inborn self." Reading "the afflictions" (*nyon mongs pa*) here instead would better fit the following commentary.
506. Here I have corrected the number here between brackets from 414 to 144, and give the math to support it. The occurence of the similar number 414 above it was probably what threw off some careless scribe.
507. Or, instead of "mentation" (*x*) read "thirsting attachment" (*sred*)?
508. Vasubandhu, *Abhidharmakośa* 8:20, Toh 4089 Tengyur, mngon pa, *ku*, 24b1.
509. "Majestic lion" (*seng ge rnam par brgyings pa, siṃha vijṛmbhita*) and "skipping over" (*thod rgal*) are explained in Maitreya's *Ornament of Clear Realization* 5:23. Sapaṇ also discusses these below on page 591.
510. The shared tradition here is that of such treatises as Asaṅga's *Compendium of Higher Knowledge*. The "central country" (*madhyadeśa*), classically conceived, is the Magadha region of the Ganges plain.
511. The ninth quality, "liberation," is in the sense of firm appreciation. And the final quality, "seeing the gnosis of liberation," is the gnosis of the ārya on the path beyond training (*vimuktijñānadarśana*).
512. This path is also commonly known as the path of no more training (*aśaikṣamārga*).
513. Vasubandhu, *Abhidharmakośa* 2:4, Toh 4089 Tengyur, mngon pa, *ku*, 1a3. According to Khenpo Appey, Sapaṇ's interpretation differs here from the usual exegesis of this verse.
514. Nāgārjuna, *Ratnāvalī* 5:40, Toh 4158 Tengyur, spring yig, *ge*, 123b3.
515. "Eighth" here refers to the stream-enterer trainee, who is the lowest in the list of eight realized beings enumerated in the non-Mahayana sources, the remaining ones being: (2) the one abiding in the fruit of stream entry and the trainees and the ones abiding in the fruits of (3–4) a once-returner, (5–6) a nonreturner, and (7–8) an arhat.
516. The list diverges in some respects from its usual explanation in the *Abhisamayālaṃkāra* commentaries. Cf. R. Sakaki, *Mahāvyutpatti*, nos. 1141–46. Khenpo Appey referred me also to Nyawön's *Dispelling Mental Darkness*, vol. 1: 608; and Ngulchu Thokmé Sangpo's *Precious Garland*, 497 (fol. 249).
517. Maitreya, *Mahāyānasūtrālaṃkāra* 12:75, Toh 4020 Tengyur, sems tsam, *phi*, 16b5.
518. Maitreya, *Uttaratantra* 1:67, Toh 4024 Tengyur, sems tsam, *phi*, 57b3.
519. *Avataṃsakasūtra*, Toh 44 Kangyur, phal chen, *kha*, 186b5.
520. *Daśabhūmikasūtra*, Toh 44 Kangyur, phal chen, *kha*, 200a4.
521. Maitreya, *Uttaratantra* 1:68, Toh 4024 Tengyur, sems tsam, *phi*, 4b4.
522. Omit *phyir*?
523. *Daśabhūmikasūtra,* Toh 44 Kangyur, phal chen, *kha*, 185a7.
524. Maitreya, *Mahāyānasūtrālaṃkāra* 21:40, Toh 4020 Tengyur, sems tsam, *phi*, 38a1. See also Ngulchu Thokmé Sangpo, *Precious Garland*, 519 (fol. 269).
525. Maitreya, *Ornament of Mahayana Sutras* (*Mahāyānasūtrālaṃkāra*) 21:32, Toh 4020 Tengyur, sems tsam, *phi*, 37b3. The remaining levels are glossed in verses 33–38.
526. This was a special mahāmudrā teaching of Shang Tsalpa. See also Sapaṇ, *Clear Dif-*

ferentiation 3:376; Rhoton, *A Clear Differentiation*, 193n81, and Gorampa, *Detailed Commentary*, 140b.

527. Sapaṇ, *Clear Differentiation* 3:190–92; Rhoton, *A Clear Differentiation*, 187n41. See also Jackson, "Birds in the Egg and Newborn Lion Cubs," and Gorampa's *Detailed Commentary*, 113a, and *Dispelling Errors*, 46.
528. This is a reference to the seventh key theme listed in the lines quoted from *Ornament of Mahayana Sutras* 20:61–62 in the opening section of the text.
529. Maitreya, *Abhisamayālaṃkāra* 1:10, Toh 3786 Tengyur, shes phyin, *ka*, 2b7.
530. Aśvaghoṣa, *Praise in Hundred and Fifty Stanzas* (*Śatapañcāśatakastotra*), Toh 1147 Tengyur, bstod tshogs, *ka*, 110a4.
531. Maitreya, *Abhisamayālaṃkāra* 8:1, Toh 3786 Tengyur, shes phyin, *ka*, 11a7.
532. Ibid. 8:12, 11b7.
533. Ibid. 8:33, 12b6.
534. See the detailed study on the existence of gnosis on the level of buddhahood in Almogi, *Rong-zom-pa's Discourses on Buddhology*.
535. *Samādhirājasūtra* 9:26, Toh 127 Kangyur, mdo sde, *da*, 26b7.
536. *Fundamental Verses on the Middle Way* (*Mūlamadhyamakakārikā*) 15:10ab, Toh 3824 Tengyur, dbu ma, *tsa*, 9a2.
537. Ibid. 22:12ab, 13b2. In the Dergé edition of the *Fundamental Verses,* the two lines read: "How could the four—eternal, noneternal, and so on—exist in that which is free of intrinsic nature?"
538. *Suvikrāntavikramiparipṛcchāsūtra*, Toh 14 Kangyur, shes rab sna tshogs, *ka*, 23b5.
539. Candragomin, *Buddhabhūmi* (*Sangs rgyas kyi sa*). Not located.
540. Nāgārjuna, *Pañcakrama*, Toh 1802 Tengyur, rgyud, *ngi*, 56a2; P 2667, rgyud 'grel, *gi*, 62b6. The quote appears above on page 518 with a slightly different wording.
541. Ibid., 14b1.
542. Maitreya, *Mahāyānasūtrālaṃkāra* 10:68a, Toh 4020 Tengyur, sems tsam, *phi*, 11b4.
543. Indrabhūti, *Jñānasiddhisādhanopāyikā*, Toh 2219 Tengyur, rgyud, *wi*, 38b7.
544. Dharmakīrti, *Pramāṇavārttika* 3:532, Toh 4210 Tengyur, tshad ma, *ce*, 138b6.
545. Dharmakīrti, *Saṃtānāntarasiddhi*, Toh 4219 Tengyur, tshad ma, *che*, 359a6.
546. I have added the following introductory paragraph that was missing from the Dergé edition on the basis of the Shalu and Luphu manuscripts, as noted in ITC, 470n395. The existence of this passage in both independent manuscripts is proof that it was probably omitted in the main manuscript upon which Dergé was based. I could not yet check this in the Sakya xylograph or other sources. Proof that the Shalu manuscript belongs to an independent textual tradition is also given by the following and final notes (nn. 396 and 427).
547. This classification into shared and special qualities is treated by Sapaṇ on page 577 below. The principal Indian sources for the list of these qualities of a buddha include Maitreya's *Ornament of Clear Realizations* (chapter 4), Asaṅga's *Compendium of Higher Knowledge* (chapter 4), Vasubhandu's *Treasury of Higher Knowledge* (chapter 7), and Candrakīrti's *Entering the Middle Way* (chapter 10).
548. Beginning here, for several folios Sapaṇ follows word for word Drolungpa's *Great Tenrim*, which likewise includes the same praises of the Buddha from chapter 21 of the *Mahāyānasūtrālaṃkāra* (as was first pointed out to me by Mr. Kazuo Kano when we read this passage together in Hamburg). After seventeen such verses, Sapaṇ begins the praises of his own composition.

549. Maitreya, *Mahāyānasūtrālaṃkāra* 21:43, Toh 4020 Tengyur, sems tsam, *phi*, 38a3. This verse is also quoted and explained above on page 466. The four immeasurables are wholesome attitudes cultivated toward all beings: (1) benevolence or loving kindness (*byams pa*), (2) compassion (*snying rje*), (3) sympathetic joy (*dga' ba*), and (4) equanimity (*btang snyom*). In Maitreya's *Mahāyānasūtrālaṃkāra* and Asaṅga's *Abhidharmasamuccaya*, equanimity has a special Mahayana sense of wishing benefit; see also Boin-Webb, *Abhidharmasamuccaya*, 223.
550. Maitreya, *Mahāyānasūtrālaṃkāra* 21:44, Toh 4020 Tengyur, sems tsam, *phi*, 38a4.
551. On the emancipations (*rnam par thar*) of yogic concentration practice, see also Vasubandhu, *Abhidharmakośa* 8:32, and Boin-Webb, *Abhidharmasamuccaya*, 223, "deliverances." In his commentary Sapaṇ does not explain what these three special yogic practices or attainments are, but he establishes the Buddha's qualities as superior to those of the others who might possess them.
552. On the eight bases of mastery (*zil gyis gnon pa skye mched brgyad*), see also Vasubandhu, *Abhidharmakośa* 8:35, and Boin-Webb, *Abhidharmasamuccaya*, 224, "spheres of mastery."
553. The ten bases of totality (*zad par gyi skye mched*, *kṛtsnāyatana*, Pali *kaṣina*) are explained by Nārada in *A Manual of Abhidhamma*, 117n7, as a series of concentration exercises in which you concentrate in sequence on ten different circular objects: (1) the elements earth, (2) water, (3) fire, and (4) air; the colors (5) blue, (6) yellow, (7) red, and (8) white; and (9) light and (10) space. The outer physical object of concentration is first concentrated on long enough to be able to visualize it with closed eyes. This inner visualization is then focused on until it develops into a purified, abstract concept. Concentrating on this final abstracted image eventually results in proximate and ecstatic concentrations (*samādhi*). See also Vasubandhu, *Abhidharmakośa* 8:36, and Boin-Webb, *Abhidharmasamuccaya*, 225, and note 105, "spheres of totalization."
554. Maitreya, *Mahāyānasūtrālaṃkāra* 21:45, Toh 4020 Tengyur, sems tsam, *phi*, 38a4. On "lack of afflictions" (*nyon mongs med*, *araṇā*), see also Vasubandhu, *Abhidharmakośa* 7:35, and Boin-Webb, *Abhidharmasamuccaya*, 226, "non-contention."
555. Maitreya, *Mahāyānasūtrālaṃkāra* 21:46, Toh 4020 Tengyur, sems tsam, *phi*, 38a5. On "knowledge from aspiration" (*smon nas shes pa*, *praṇidhijñāna*), see also Vasubandhu, *Abhidharmakośa* 7:35, 8:37ab, and Boin-Webb, *Abhidharmasamuccaya*, 226, "knowledge of the aspiration (resolution)."
556. Maitreya, *Mahāyānasūtrālaṃkāra* 21:47, Toh 4020 Tengyur, sems tsam, *phi*, 38a5.
557. Ibid. 21:48, 38a6. On the superknowledges (*mngon par shes pa*, *mngon shes rnam drug*), see also Vasubandhu, *Abhidharmakośa* 7:42.
558. Sapaṇ here classifies the six superknowledges as types of the *three miracles* (*cho 'phrul*), of the Buddha—the bodily miracle (magical power), the mental miracle of knowing others' minds (clairvoyance), and the verbal miracle of instruction (the last four superknowledges).
559. Zhang et al., *Extensive Tibetan-Tibetan-Chinese Dictionary*, classifies this not as pertaining to the mind (*thugs*) but as the all-expressing miracle of speech (*gsung kun tu brjod pa'i cho 'phrul*), defining it: *gzhan gyi sems shes pa'i sgo nas nyes dmigs dang legs pa'i yon tan gang yin pa de dag gzhan gyi sems dang mthun par ston pa/.*
560. Zhang et al., *Extensive Tibetan-Tibetan-Chinese Dictionary*, calls this not speech

(*gsung*) but mind (*thugs*) and defines it: *rjes su bstan pa'i cho 'phrul, sems kyi rgyud la nyon mongs pa'i shas gang che ba brtags nas gnyen po de dang de ston pa.*

561. *Śaikṣa.* In other words, one who is on the lower seven śrāvaka levels before reaching the eighth, that of the arhat.
562. Maitreya, *Mahāyānasūtrālaṃkāra* 21:49, Toh 4020 Tengyur, sems tsam, *phi*, 38a7: bodily characteristics and marks (*mtshan dang dpe byed*). This verse is also quoted above at the end of chapter 6.
563. Ibid. 21:50, 38a7: the four purities (*yongs su dag pa bzhi, pariśuddha/pariśuddhi*). This verse is also quoted above at the end of chapter 8.
564. Ibid. 21:51, 38b1.
565. Chim Jampaiyang, *Detailed Abhidharma Commentary*, 617, explains *gnas dang gnas min pa* in this context as "possible and impossible" (*srid pa dang mi srid pa*).
566. Chim Jampaiyang, *Detailed Abhidharma Commentary*, 617, calls this power *zag bcas gyi las dang 'bras bu rnam par smin pa sna tshogs mkhyen pa'i stobs*, and Zhang et al., *Extensive Tibetan-Tibetan-Chinese Dictionary*, gives simply *las kyi rnam smin mkhyen pa'i stobs*. Sapaṇ here calls it *las kyi bdag gir bya ba mkhyen pa'i stobs*, as in Asvabhāva's *Detailed Commentary on the Ornament of Mahayana Sutras* (*Sūtrālaṃkāraṭīkā*), Toh 4029 Tengyur, sems tsam, *bi*, 171b6.
567. Maitreya, *Mahāyānasūtrālaṃkāra* 12:66, Toh 4020 Tengyur, sems tsam, *phi*, 15b7.
568. That is, the dispotions toward the śrāvaka, pratyekabuddha, and Mahayana paths. Chim Jampaiyang, *Detailed Abhidharma Commentary*, 618, explains *khams* here as a spiritual disposition or ingrained tendency of mind.
569. *Rnam pa.* The reference to "features" here is to sutra passages in which the Buddha relates his memories of previous states of existences.
570. Dergé's *don rtags* is emended here to *dan rtags* ("proof"). Drolungpa, *Great Tenrim*, uses exactly the same rare expression, and indeed Sapaṇ quotes from him here.
571. Divine eye is knowing the future deaths and rebirths of yourself and others. Chim Jampaiyang, *Detailed Abhidharma Commentary*, (618): "The knowledge of death, transference, and intermediate state refers to knowing the future existence of oneself and others" (*'chi ba dang 'pho ba bar do dang skye ba mkhyen pa ni rang gzhan gyi ma 'ongs pa'i srid pa mkhyen pa ste*).
572. I read here *ldan pa* (emendation), or *ldan pa ni* (Drolungpa, *Great Tenrim*), instead of *ldan pa'i* (Dergé).
573. "Four causes and results in terms of feeling" (*catvāridharmasamādānāni*) are listed in the *Great Sanskrit and Tibetan Glossary* (*Mahāvyutpatti*), P 5832: see Sakaki, *Mahāvyutpatti*, no. 1560. The remaining two are presumably a miserable present life but a pleasant future one, and pleasant experiences in both lives.
574. See also Jackson, *Entrance Gate*, 382n40, on the term *mtho ris* (*svarga*). For the Buddhist, *svarga* includes the three higher realms of existence—not only the heavens of the gods and the demigods but also the realm of humans. Hence, my translations "higher destinies" or "fortunate realms of existence." It is often opposed to *ngan song*.
575. Maitreya, *Mahāyānasūtrālaṃkāra* 21:52, Toh 4020 Tengyur, sems tsam, *phi*, 38b1. On the "four modes of fearlessness" (*mi 'jigs pa bzhi, vaiśāradya*), see Vasubandhu, *Abhidharmakośa* 7:32, Toh 4089 Tengyur, mngon pa, *ku*, 22b7.
576. See also Sapaṇ, *Entrance Gate for the Wise* 3:13; Jackson, *Entrance Gate*, 378n26.
577. Maitreya, *Mahāyānasūtrālaṃkāra* 21:53, Toh 4020 Tengyur, sems tsam, *phi*, 38b2.

This verse is also quoted above, page 436; "absence of guardedness" (*bsrung ba med pa gsum*).

578. Ibid. 21:54, Toh 4020 38b3.
579. Ibid. 21:55, 38b3; *dran pa nye bar gzhag pa*, *smṛtyupasthāna/-upasthiti*, Vasubandhu, *Abhidharmakośa* 7:16, 7:44, Toh 4089 Tengyur, mngon pa, *ku*, 22a6. This verse is also quoted above at the end of chapter 7.
580. Maitreya, *Mahāyānasūtrālaṃkāra* 21:56, Toh 4020 Tengyur, sems tsam, *phi*, 38b4; *thugs rje chen po*, *mahākṛpā*, Vasubandhu, *Abhidharmakośa* 7:33, Toh 4089 Tengyur, mngon pa, *ku*, 22b7.
581. Maitreya, *Mahāyānasūtrālaṃkāra* 21:57, Toh 4020 Tengyur, sems tsam, *phi*, 38b4.
582. The division of the enlightened qualities into shared and special is also treated by Chim Jampaiyang in his *Detailed Abhidharma Commentary*, 616, and lists the eighteen special qualities of a buddha as the ten powers of the buddha, the four modes of fearlessness, plus three foundations of mindfulness, and great compassion. Chim specifies that this list, according to *Abhidharmakośa*, is *not* the same as the fourfold Mahayana classification of eighteen special buddha-qualities taught in the *Mahāyānasūtrālaṃkāra*. He then quotes the same *Mahāyānasūtrālaṃkāra* verse 21:57 as a representative of this alternative Mahayana list.
583. Maitreya, *Mahāyānasūtrālaṃkāra* 21:58, Toh 4020 Tengyur, sems tsam, *phi*, 38b4.
584. Ibid. 21:59, 38b6.
585. Here begins Sapaṇ's addenda to the verses of praise from the *Ornament of Mahayana Sutras*. The final three verses of the *Mahāyānasūtrālaṃkāra* (20:60–62) were not included or commented on.
586. Sapaṇ explains these thirty-seven factors according to the Mahayana system not Vasubandhu's *Abhidharmakośa*.
587. Vasubandhu, *Abhidharmakośa* 8:18c–19b, Toh 4089 Tengyur, mngon pa, *ku*, 24a7.
588. Maitreya, *Abhisamayālaṃkāra* 5:24–25, Toh 3786 Tengyur, shes phyin, *ka*, 8a5.
589. See Lamotte, *Le Traite*, 1048.
590. Unnamed Mahayana source. Not located.
591. *Za ma tog bkod pa*, Skt. *karaṇḍavyūha*. This does not refer to the sutra of the same name but to a long dhāraṇī, a.k.a. the *zad mi shes pa'i za ma tog*, in the *Sutra of Golden Light* (*Suvarṇaprabhāsottamasūtra*), Toh 556 Kangyur, rgyud, *pa*, 197b.
592. The Dergé edition, 97a, reads *gnyis*; correct to *gcig*.
593. *Tathāgatācintyaguhyanirdeśasūtra*, Toh 47 Kangyur, dkon brtsegs, *ka*. Quote not located.
594. Maitreya, *Mahāyānasūtrālaṃkāra* 10:38–39, Toh 4020 Tengyur, sems tsam, *phi*, 10a6.
595. The Dergé edition, 98b, reads: *yis* ("by"), but I emend to *yi* ("of").
596. Possibly correct *spyod* to *dpyod*, "discernment"?

Glossary

Abhidharma (*chos mngon pa*). *See* Three Baskets.

absorptions. *See* eight absorptions *and* nine absorptions.

afflictions (*nyon mongs, kleśa*). Dissonant mental states, both thoughts and emotions, that have their root in ignorance and that disturb the person from deep within. The classical Abhidharma texts list six root afflictions—attachment, aversion, pride, afflicted doubt, ignorance, and afflicted views—and twenty afflictions that are derivative of these root afflictions.

aggregates (*phung po, skandha*). *See* five aggregates.

analytical knowledge (*so so yang dag par rig pa*). *See* four analytical knowledges.

antidote (*gnyen po, pratipakṣa*). Just as specific medicines are seen as antidotes for specific illnesses, so specific mental states such as courage and compassion are identified as antidotes to specific mental ills. The Tibetan term *gnyen po* is sometimes translated "aid" or "remedy" as well.

arhat (*dgra bcom pa*). In Sanskrit, a term of respect (literally, "worthy," "venerable," "respectable," etc.), in Tibetan it was rendered with a different etymology as "foe destroyer." An arhat has eliminated all the afflictions and has thus attained nirvana.

ārya (*'phags pa*). *See* noble one.

aspiration bodhicitta or **aspiring thought of awakening** (*smon pa'i sems bskyed, praṇdihicitta*). *See* bodhicitta.

aspiration prayer (*smon lam, praṇidhāna*). A solemn oath or vow, such as that of a bodhisattva, that creates a karmic seed for future attainment.

bases of mastery (*zil gyis gnon pa skye mched, abhibhāyatana*). Typically eight, these are graduated levels of withdrawal from the senses that lead to deeper states of meditative concentration (*dhyāna*).

bases of totality (*zad par gyi skye mched, kṛtsnāyatana*). A series of meditative exercises in which you concentrate in sequence on ten different circular objects: the elements (1) earth, (2) water, (3) fire, and (4) air; the colors (5) blue, (6) yellow, (7) red, and (8) white; and finally (9) light and (10) space.

Blessed One (*bcom ldan 'das, bhagavān*). Traditional epithet of the Buddha. An ancient Indian term of high respect used for spiritual masters.

bodhicitta (*byang chub kyi sems*, and *sems bskyed, cittotpāda*, "producing the intention"). The "thought of awakening," an altruistic resolve to attain buddhahood for the benefit of all beings. Bodhicitta is characterized by an *objective*, the full awakening of buddhahood, and a *purpose*, the fulfillment of others' welfare. *Relative bodhicitta* refers to this altruistic resolve, whereas *ultimate bodhicitta* refers to a direct realization of the emptiness of the fully awakened mind. *Aspiring bodhicitta* is the wish to attain the genuine thought of awakening, whereas *engaging bodhicitta* is the actual training in the thought of awakening by way of the six perfections.

bodhisattva (*byang chub sems dpa'*). A person who has cultivated bodhicitta and is on the Mahayana path to buddhahood.

bodies of buddhahood (*sku, kāya*). The five bodies of buddhahood are: (1) The emanation body (*sprul sku, nirmāṇakāya*), (2) the enjoyment body (*longs sku, saṃbhogakāya*) (3) the Dharma body (*chos sku, dharmakāya*), and (4–5) the ultimate-nature body, (*ngo bo nyid kyi sku, svabhāvakāya*), which consists of two facets of the Dharma body: a buddha's mind purified of all defilements and the natural purity of that mind that is its emptiness.

buddhafield (*sangs rgyas kyi zhing, buddhakṣetra*). The expanse of specific, enlightened experience proper to a particular buddha, just like the kingdom of a monarch.

Cittamātra (*sems tsam*). The philosophical "mind only" school, also known as Yogācāra ("school of yoga practice") or Vijñānavāda ("doctrine of consciousness"). As the name indicates, the school maintains that external phenomena are a function of the mind, and its adherents advocate a meditative union (*yoga*) with the essential nature of the mind. The school was founded by Asaṅga (fourth century C.E.), who received these doctrines from Maitreya. The Cittamātra is one of two main streams of Mahayana Buddhism along with Madhyamaka.

compassion (*snying rje, karuṇā*). A mental state that wishes for others to be free from suffering. In its highest form, *compassion* is a synonym for great compassion (*snying rje chen po*)—a universal, nondiscriminatory compassion that wishes all beings to be free of suffering.

conqueror (*rgyal ba, jina*). Traditional epithet of a fully awakened buddha.

Conqueror's son (*rgyal ba'i sras po, jinaputra*). Traditional epithet of a bodhisattva.

cosmic sphere (*khams, dhātu*). *See* three realms of existence.

cyclic existence (*'khor ba, saṃsāra*). *See* samsara.

deep insight (*lhag mthong, vipaśyanā*). *See* insight.

defiling aggregates of personality. *See* five aggregates.

desire realm or **sphere** (*'dod khams, kāmadhātu*). One of the three realms of existence. Its beings' experiences are principally those of the five sense consciousnesses, whether the lower rebirths of hell beings, hungry ghosts, and animals, or the higher rebriths of humans and gods. This is contrasted with the mental consciousness, which produces the meditative experiences of the form and formless realms. *See also* three realms.

developed spiritual potential (*rgyas pa'i rigs*). In Yogācāra Buddhism this is understood to refer to the potential possessed by those who have produced *bodhicitta*.

dhāraṇī (*gzungs*). A verbal device, similar to a mantra, that encapsulates the meaning of longer Dharma texts, aiding in retention and integration. Can be longer or as short as a single syllable.

dharmadhātu (*chos kyi dbyings*). The ultimate expanse, sphere of reality, or mode of being, of things. A synonym for *ultimate nature*.

dharmakāya (*chos sku*). One of the embodiments of buddhahood (see *bodies of buddhahood*). Dharmakāya (literally, "truth body" or "buddha body of reality") refers to the ultimate reality of a buddha's enlightened mind—unborn, free of the limits of conceptual elaborations, empty of intrinsic existence, naturally radiant, beyond duality, and spacious like the sky. The other two buddha bodies, the enjoyment body (*longs sku,* *saṃbhogakāya*) and the emanation body (*sprul sku, nirmāṇakāya*), are progressively grosser bodies that arise from the basic dharmakāya nature. Thus the two latter embodiments are referred to collectively as a buddha's "form body" (*gzugs sku, rūpakāya*).

dharmatā (*chos nyid*). Translated as "reality," "the nature of things," or "universal essence," the Sanskrit term and its Tibetan equivalent refer to the ultimate mode of being of things. As such, the term is often used as a synonym for *emptiness* and *suchness*.

discerning wisdom (*shes rab, prajñā*). *See* wisdom.

discursive thought (*rtog pa'i spros pa, kalpanāprapañca*). Conceptual elaborations. The opposite of *nondiscursive awareness*.

eight absorptions. The four meditative concentrations (*dhyāna*) and the four meditative attainments (*samāpatti*). *See also* nine absorptions.

eight kinds of freedom (*dal ba, kṣaṇa*). These eight "leisures" enable a human being to practice the Buddhist doctrine: (1) not holding wrong views, (2) not being born in a barbaric land, (3) not being born in a region where no buddha has appeared, (4) not being born as an idiot or mute, and not having become (5) a hell being, (6) a hungry ghost, (7) an animal, or (8) a god.

eight worldly concerns (*'jig rten chos brgyad, aṣṭalokadharma*). Gain and loss, pleasure and pain, praise and blame, and fame and infamy.

eightfold path of the noble ones (*'phags pa'i lam yan lag brgyad pa, āryāṣṭāṅgamārga*) (1) right view (2) right thought, (3) right speech, (4) right action, (5) right livelihood, (6) right effort, (7) right mindfulness, and (8) right meditation.

emanation body (*sprul sku, nirmāṇakāya*). One of three (or five) bodies of buddhahood. *See* bodies of buddhahood; dhamakāya; form body.

emancipations (*rnam par thar pa, vimokṣa*). The eight emancipations are levels of liberation associated with the cultivation of meditative absorption.

emptiness (*stong pa nyid, śūnyatā*). According to the Perfection of Wisdom sutras, all things and events, including our own existence, are devoid of any independent, substantial, and intrinsic reality. This emptiness of intrinsic existence is phenomena's ultimate mode of being—the way phenomena actually are. The second-century master Nāgārjuna was the earliest systematic proponent of the theory of emptiness, and his writings provide the philosophical foundation of the Madhymaka school of the Mahayana tradition. Seeing emptiness, the ultimate nature of all things, is the indispensable gateway to liberation and enlightenment.

engaging thought of awakening / engaged bodhicitta (*'jug pa'i sems bskyed, prasthāna-citta*). *See* bodhicitta.

enjoyment body (*longs spyod rdzogs pa'i sku, saṃbhogakāya*). *See* bodies of buddhahood; dharmakāya; form body.

false imputations (*sgro 'dogs*). Projections of nonexistent entities onto reality. Removing false imputations is an essential part of perceiving or understanding reality correctly.

five aggregates (*phung po lnga, skandha*). Form, feeling, discernment, formations, and consciousness, which together are our basis for erroneously imputing the existence of a self.

five fields of knowledge (*rig gnas lnga, pañcavidyāsthāna*). (1) Sanskrit grammar, (2) logic and epistemology, (3) arts and crafts, (4) medicine, and (5) inner science (Dharma teachings). These five fields of classical knowledge according to Indian Buddhism were adopted as a formal division of knowledge disciplines in the Tibetan tradition.

five gnoses (*ye shes lnga, pañcajñāna*). The five aspects or types of pristine awareness or exalted wisdom: (1) mirror-like (*me long lta bu, ādarśa*), (2) equality (*mnyam nyid, samatā*), (3) individually discerning (*sor rtogs, pratyavekṣaṇa*), (4) action-achieving (*bya grub, kṛtyānuṣṭhāna*), and (5) dharmadhātu (*chos dbyings*). *See also* gnosis.

five paths (*lam lnga, pañcamarga*). The paths of (1) accumulation, (2) application, (3) seeing, (4) cultivation, and (5) complete accomplishment.

form body (*gzugs sku, rūpakāya*). A collective term for two of the bodies of buddhahood—the enjoyment body (*longs sku, saṃbhogakāya*) and the emanation body (*sprul sku, nirmāṇakāya*). *See also* bodies of buddhahood; dharmakāya.

formless realm (*gzugs med kyi khams, arūpadhātu*). *See* three realms of existence.

four analytical knowledges (*so so yang dag par rig pa bzhi, pratisaṃvid*). The four unlimited forms of wisdom attained by a fully awakened buddha: (1) analytical knowledge of the Dharma [as verbal expression] (*chos*), (2) analytical knowledge of the sense (*don*), (3) analytical knowledge of etymological explanation [of the meaning of Sanskrit words] (*nges pa'i tshig*), and (4) analytical knowledge of confident presence of mind (*spobs pa*).

four bases of magical powers (*caturṛddhipāda, rdzu 'phrul gyi rkang pa bzhi*). These four elements of the thirty-seven factors conducive to awakening are prerequisites to acquiring magical power and spiritual success. These are the meditative absorptions of aspiration (*chanda*), diligence (*vīrya*), intention (*citta*), and analysis (*mīmāṃsā*).

four foundations of mindfulness (*dran pa nyer bzhag bzhi, catuḥ-smṛtyupasthāna*). A series of meditations consisting in mindfulness, or recollection, of four different objects: (1) the body, (2) feelings, (3) mind, and (4) phenomena.

four fearlessnesses (*mi 'jigs pa bzhi, caturvaiśāradya*). Fearlessness with respect to (1) the perfect fulfillment of the powers, (2) the perfect fulfillment of the abandonments, (3) revealing the obstacles, and (4) revealing the path to definite freedom. These are qualities of an enlightened buddha.

four formless attainments (*snyoms 'jug bzhi*). *See* four meditative attainments.

four gnoses (*ye shes bzhi*). The first four of the *five gnoses*. These mental qualities are possessed only by buddhas. *See also* gnosis.

four immeasurables (*tshad med bzhi, caturapramāṇa*). (1) Immeasurable compassion, (2) immeasurable loving kindness, (3) immeasurable sympathetic joy, and (4) immeasurable equanimity.

four impediments. *See* four remedies.

four means of attraction (*bsdus ba'i dngos po bzhi, saṃgrahavastu*). (1) Giving what is immediately needed (such as material goods), (2) using pleasant speech, (3) giving sound spiritual advice, and (4) living in accord with what you teach. These four factors are the primary means by which a bodhisattva attracts others and enhances their minds (whereas the six perfections are the primary factors for developing and enhancing the bodhisattva's own mind).

four meditative attainments (*snyoms 'jug bzhi, samāpatti*). The four meditative absorptions of the formless realm (or sphere): (1) infinite space, (2) infinite consciousness, (3) nothingness, and (4) neither ideation nor nonideation (i.e., the *pinnacle of existence*).

four meditative concentrations (*bsam gtan bzhi, dhyāna*). The four meditative absorptions of the form realm. These so-called first, second, third, and fourth concentrations are deepening levels of concentration and precede the four meditative attainments.

four perfect endeavors (*yang dag par spong ba bzhi, catvāri samyakprahāṇāni*). Literally, four "restraints" (*prahāṇāni*), these four elements of the thirty-seven factors conducive to awaking are understood as endeavors (*pradhānāni*) by the commentarial tradition. They are reliquishing nonvirtues, avoiding new nonvirtues, generating virtues, and further developing virtues.

four powers (*stobs bzhi, caturbala*). The four key elements necessary for successful purification of harmful deeds through confession: (1) the power of the support, which refers to the objects of refuge, such as the Three Jewels; (2) the power of remorse; (3) the power of the applying the remedy, the actual purification rite; and (4) the power of the resolve to not commit the harmful act again.

four purities (*yongs su dag pa bzhi, catvāri pariśuddha*). The purity of the basis (the body), of the object (external appearances), of mind (meditative states), and of discerning wisdom.

four reliances (*rton pa bzhi, catvāri pratisaraṇāni*). (1) Relying on the teaching and not on a person, (2) relying on the meaning and not on the words, (3) relying on wisdom and not on ordinary knowing, and (4) relying on the definitive meaning (*nges don*) and not on the interpretable meaning (*drang don*).

four remedies (*gnyen po bzhi, pratipakṣa*). These four remedy the four impediments: (1) meditation on impermanence, which remedies attachment to the experiences of this life; (2) meditation on the defects of samsara and on actions and their consequences, which remedies attachment to worldly well-being in general; (3) meditation on love and compassion, which remedies attachment to the well-being of meditative peace; and (4) the teachings concerning the cultivation of bodhicitta, which remedies ignorance of how to attain buddhahood.

four root transgressions (*pham pa bzhi, pārājika*). The are transgressions of the four root precepts of a monastic: taking life, stealing, sexual misconduct, and falsely representing one's own spiritual attainments.

four wheels (*'khor lo bzhi, catvāri cakrāṇi*). (1) Living in a favorable environment, (2) relying on a good teacher, (3) making the right aspirational prayer for the future, and (4) accumulating merit.

free (or devoid) of all conceptual elaborations (*spros bral, niṣprapañca*). An important quality of ultimate reality in the Madhyamaka school.

gandharva (*dri za*). A class of beings, a kind of lesser god, that often appear as celestial musicians in classical Indian literature and may dwell in forests. The Tibetan word literally means "smell eater."

gnosis (*ye shes, jñāna*). Often contrasted with ordinary consciousness (*rnam shes, vijñāna*), *gnosis* refers to a buddha's fully awakened wisdom and also the uncontaminated gnosis of the noble ones that is characterized by the direct realization of emptiness. Also translated in this volume as *pristine awareness*.

great seal (*phyag rgya chen po*). *See* mahāmudrā.

Hinayana (*theg dman, hīnayāna*). From the perspective of Mahayana, the "lesser vehicle" teachings and practices expounded by the Buddha in his initial turning of the Dharma wheel. It sets as its ideal the nirvana of an arhat. Philosophically, it is prone to realism, as expressed in two major schools, Vaibhāṣika and Sautrāntika. From the Tibetan point of view, Hinayana is foundational but is superseded by the Buddha's later Mahayana and Secret Mantra Vehicle teachings.

hungry spirit (*yi dwags, preta*). Beings whose karma is too good for rebirth in the hells but too bad for rebirth as a demigod. They are subject to various torments of extreme deprivation and craving, suffering in particular from hunger and thirst because their bellies are huge but their throats are as thin as the eye of a needle. It is said that rebirth as a hungry spirit can be caused by emotions such as stinginess or envy.

insight (*lhag mthong, vipaśyanā*). An advanced meditative state in which the meditator has successfully attained physical and mental pliancy as a result of having applied analytic meditation on a basis of *tranquility* (*śamatha*). Sometimes the term is also used to embrace all analytic (as opposed to absorptive) meditation practices.

loving kindness (*byams pa, maitrī*). A mental factor wishing others to achieve happiness.

Madhyamaka (*dbu ma*). A school of Mahayana Buddhism founded on the teachings of Nāgārjuna (second century C.E.). This school is named after its philosophical "middle way" between absolute assertion or negation of the existence of phenonema. It is called "middle" because it distances itself from any "extreme" notions, Buddhist or non-Buddhist. Phenonema exist only in a conditioned way and do not have an inherent nature of their own; in that sense, they are described as being "empty" or "void" (*śūnya*) from the perspective of *ultimate truth*.

mahāmudrā (*phyag rgya chen po*). Literally, "great seal," this is meditation practice aimed at direct realization of emptiness by way of looking at the nature of one's own mind. The name is applied both to the result and to the techniques of meditation that lead to that result. The mahāmudrā lineage originated in India with Saraha and continued in Tibet predominantly in the Kagyü school.

mandala (*dkyil 'khor, maṇḍala*). In any tantric system, the abode of a buddha deity, which represents an enlightened transformation of our ordinary environment.

mantra (*gsang sngags*). A ritual incantation of Sanskrit syllables connected to a particular deity or text. "Mantra" is also a synonym for tantra, especially in the usage "secret mantra."

māra (*bdud*). A term for various evils that afflict beings, namely, the four māras of the aggregates (*skandha*), afflictions (*kleśa*), death (*mṛtyu*), and involvement with sense pleasure (*devaputra*). Māra is also frequently personified as a devil-like tempter.

meditation (*sgom, bhāvanā*). Both the Sanskrit and the Tibetan terms for meditation connote the notion of cultivation, such as the cultivation of certain mental habits or states. The Tibetan term carries a strong sense of cultivating familiarity, be it with a chosen object, topic, or a particular way of thinking or being.

meditative absorption (*ting nge 'dzin, samādhi*). Single-pointed absorption or focus of the mind on a chosen object. In the Abhidharma taxonomy of mental factors, the term refers to a mental factor whose primary function is to ensure the stability of the mind. This mental factor is part of a group of mental factors present in all unmistaken cognition. *Meditative absorption* can also refer to a specific advanced meditative state, such as the direct single-pointed realization of emptiness. *See also* eight *and* nine absorptions.

meditative attainments (*snyoms 'jug, samāpatti*). *See* four meditative attainments.

meditative attainment of cessation (*'gog pa'i snyoms 'jug, nirodha samāpatti*). The highest of the *nine absorptions*.

meditative concentration (*bsam gtan, dhyāna*). The subject of the fifth of the six perfections. *See also* four meditative concentrations.

moral discipline (*tshul khrims, śīla*). Adherence to ethical codes.

nāga (*klu*). *Nāga* is a name given to a wide-ranging class of beings, generally of serpentine form but possessing powers that ordinary snakes do not have. The range goes from the animal realm through to the divine realms, with the more elevated types living in palaces and guarding fortunes, much like dragons. They tend to be associated with the water element.

natural spiritual potential (*rang bzhin gyi rigs*). This is a Yogācāra concept of a spiritual potential present in all living beings (*compare to* developed spiritual potential).

nature of things (*chos nyid*). One possible translation for *dharmatā*, reality, which in other contexts is translated as "true nature" or "universal essence."

nine absorptions (*snyoms par 'jug pa dgu*). These are the eight absorptions plus the final one, the meditative attainment of cessation.

nirvana (*mya ngan las 'das pa, nirvāṇa*). Liberation from *samsara*, and hence the extinction of suffering.

noble one (*'phags pa, ārya*). A being on the path who has gained direct realization of the truth of emptiness on the path of seeing. Noble ones are contrasted with ordinary beings, whose understanding of the truth remains bound by language and concepts.

nonobjectifying compassion (*dmigs pa med pa'i snying rje, anālambanā-karuṇā*). Wishing that sentient beings be free from suffering while seeing that beings as well as suffering and its causes are all illusory appearances, without own-nature.

nonsituated nirvana (*mi gnas pa'i mya ngan las 'das pa, apratiṣṭhita-nirvāṇa*). The nirvana of a buddha that does not situate itself in the extremes of samsara or the extinction of ordinary nirvana. Not to be confused with "nirvana without remainder" (*lhag pa med pa'i mya ngan las 'das pa*), a state of cessation that it hopes to avoid.

obscurations (*sgrib pa, āvaraṇa*). *See* two obcurations.

ordinary people or beings (*so so'i skye bo, pṛthagjana*). Those who have not yet attained the state of an ārya, or noble one (*'phags pa*), such as those on the first two of the *five paths*.

own-nature (*rang bzhin, svabhāva*). The qualities specific to an entity or state, such as the heat of fire or the wetness of water. In deeper contexts, this term occurs as part of a pair, along with *ngo bo*, used also by Tibetans to translate *svabhāva*, in which case *ngo bo* refers to a more inner nature (such as the mind's emptiness) and *rang bzhin* indicates a more tangible property (such as the mind's clarity). *Ngo bo* and *rang bzhin* could in that case be respectively translated as *essence* and *own-nature*. Also sometimes translated "inherent existence."

path of accumulation (*tshogs lam, saṃbhāramārga*). The first of the *five paths*, an overarching scheme mapping the full path to englightenment. For the Mahayana practitioner, this path begins with the generation of bodhicitta, and what is accumulated is the merit, knowledge, and meditative stability necessary to pursue the higher attainments.

path of application (*sbyor lam, prayogamārga*). The second in the five-path scheme, it consists of four progressively more refined realizations about the nature of reality, preparing one for the direct realization on the path of seeing. The four levels are called heat, the peak, fearless acceptance, and highest worldly realization.

path of complete accomplishment (*mthar phyin pa'i lam, niṣṭhāmārga*). The fifth and final path in the five-path scheme, sometimes called the *path of no more training* (*mi slob lam, aśaikṣamārga*) in contrast to the lower "training" paths, where further development is still required.

path of cultivation (*sgom lam, bhāvanāmārga*). The fourth path in the five-path scheme, where the afflictions are eradicated through a process of purification, and where the Mahayana practitioner eradicates the two obscurations by traversing the ten bodhisattva stages.

path of seeing (*mthong lam, darśanamārga*). The third path in the five-path scheme, where the ordinary being becomes an ārya through seeing ultimate reality directly in meditative equipoise (*samāhita*) and has a direct realization of the four truths of an ārya, the so-called four noble truths.

perfection of diligence (*brtson 'grus kyi pha rol tu phyin pa, vīryapāramitā*). The fourth of the six perfections.

perfection of generosity (*sbyin pa'i pha rol tu phyin pa, dānapāramitā*). The first of the six perfections of the bodhisattva.

perfection of meditative concentration (*bsam gtan gyi pha rol tu phyin pa, dhyānapāramitā*). The fifth of the six perfections of the bodhisattva.

perfection of moral discipline (*tshul khrims kyi pha rol tu phyin pa, śīlapāramitā*). The second of the six perfections.

perfection of patience (*bzod pa'i pha rol tu phyin pa, kṣāntipāramitā*). The third of the six perfections.

perfection of wisdom (*shes rab kyi pha rol tu phyin pa, prajñāpāramitā*). The sixth of the perfections that lie at the heart of the practice of the bodhisattva. The term refers also to a class of Mahayana scriptures that outlines the essential aspects of meditation on emptiness and their associated parths and resultant states.

pinnacle of existence (*srid rtse, bhavāgra*). The fourth meditative attainment of the formless realm (or immaterial sphere)—in other words, the fourth formless meditative stage of neither ideation nor nonideation. *See also* four meditative attainments.

prātimokṣa vows (*so sor thar pa,*). The precepts of "individual liberation" are one of the three sets of vows (the others being bodhisattva vows and tantric vows), those concerned primarily with restraining outward activity. Described typically in seven categories for seven different types of practitioners, they include the levels of monastic discipline and the vows for lay Buddhists.

pratyekabuddha (*rang sangs rgyas*). Literally, a "solitary realizer" or "self-enlightened one," a pratyekabuddha is an adept who seeks liberation on the basis of autonomous practice. *See also* śrāvaka.

precious human body (*dal 'byor, kṣaṇasampad*). Rebirth under favorable conditions, possessing the *eight kinds of freedom* and the ten endowments (*'byor ba*) for practicing the Dharma.

pristine awareness. An alternate rendering of *gnosis* (*ye shes, jñāna*).

relative bodhicitta (*kun rdzob sems bskyed*). *See* bodhicitta.

relative truth (*kun rdzob bden pa, saṃvṛtisatya*). *See* two truths.

samsara (*'khor ba, saṃsāra*). The perpetual cycle of birth, death, and rebirth caused by karma and the emotional afflictions. Freedom from samsara, or cyclic existence, is characterized as *nirvana* (the extinction of suffering). But in the Mahayana, both are considered extremes to be avoided.

Sautrantika. A Hinayana school whose name means "Followers of the Sutras." They emerged as a reaction to the Vaibhāṣika, preferring the original discourses to the Abhidharma *Mahāvibhāṣa*.

self-cognition (*rang rig, svasaṃvitti* or *svasaṃvedana*). This refers to a special self-referential perception that Sakya Paṇḍita maintains is the cognizer on the path of application, the second of five paths.

self-entity (*bdag* or *bdag nyid*, *ātman*). This refers to the illusions that minds can create about two main areas of "things" (*dharma*), believing them to have ultimate existence in their own right. Were such to be possible, a thing would not depend on other things for its existence but would exist innately. The two main areas of such projected belief are (1) that perceiving persons exist ultimately (individual self-entity), and (2) that perceived phenomena exist ultimately (phenomenal self-entity). A more detailed presentation of how the various Buddhist traditions treat the relative and ultimate existence of things is found in their treatises on emptiness.

self-postulation (*bdag tu 'dzin pa* or *bdag 'dzin*, *ahaṃkāra* or *ātmagraha*). The habitual positing or postulating of the existence of a self.

selflessness of persons (*gang zag gi bdag med*, *pudgalanairātmya*). A person's lack of a substantial self-entity distinct from the five aggregates. This type of selflessness is affirmed by all Buddhist schools.

selflessness of phenomena (*chos kyi bdag med*, *dharmanairātmya*). An extension of the selflessness of persons to reflect the pervasive lack of a self-entity that characterizes all phenomena. The assertion of the two types of selflessness is characteristic of the Mahayana Buddhist schools.

six perfections (*phar phyin drug*, *ṣaḍpāramitā*). These are: (1) generosity, (2) moral discipline, (3) patience or forbearance, (4) diligence, (5) meditative concentration, and (6) wisdom.

spiritual potential (*rigs*, *gotra*) Literally, "[spiritual] lineage," a Yogācāra concept referring to a living being's potential to develop into a buddha. *See also* natural spiritual potential *and* developed spiritual potential.

śrāvaka (*nyan thos*). An ordained follower of the Buddha whose primary spiritual objective is to attain liberation from samsara. The Sanskrit term and its Tibetan equivalent are sometimes translated as "hearer" (which stays close to the literal meaning) or "disciple." śrāvakas, who seek liberation through listening to others' instruction, are often paired with pratyekabuddhas, who seek liberation on the basis of autonomous practice.

suchness (*de bzhin nyid*, *tathatā*). The reality of things as they are; often used as a synonym for *emptiness*.

superknowledges (*mngon shes*, *abhijñā*). Supernatural powers attained by adepts (*siddha*) or other accomplished meditators, including clairvoyance.

supramundane (*'jig rten las 'das pa*, *lokottara*). A spiritual category that relates to the transcendental, that is, to life or people freed from the faults of samsara. The opposite of worldly or mundane.

tantra (*rgyud*). A highly advanced system of thought and meditative practice wherein the very aspects of the resultant states of buddhahood are brought into the path right from the start. Unlike the practices of general Mahayana, engagement in the meditative practices of tantra requires prior initiation into the teachings. The term *tantra* can also refer to the literature or tantric texts that expound these systems of thought and practice. Often the term is used as a shorthand for Tantrayana or Vajrayana, where it is contrasted with the Sutra Vehicle or Perfection Vehicle.

ten directions (*phyogs bcu*). The four cardinal directions, their intermediaries, plus up and down.

ten nonvirtues (*mi dge ba bcu, daśa-akuśala*). Killing, stealing, sexual misconduct, lying, slander, prattle, harsh speech, covetous thoughts, harmful thoughts, and wrong views.

ten powers (*stobs bcu, daśabala*). Ten powers that are possessed by buddhas, namely, the powers of knowing (1) what is lawfully appropriate or inappropriate, (2) the fruitional effects of karma, (3) the diverse aspirations of sentient beings, (4) the diverse mental dispositions, (5) the level of mental faculties of sentient beings, (6) the paths that lead to all destinations, (7) the concentrations, liberating paths, meditative stabilizations, and absorptive states, (8) the states of sentient beings' past lives, (9) the future deaths and rebirths of sentient beings, and (10) the cessation of all contaminants.

ten virtues (*dge ba bcu, daśa-kuśala*). Abstaining from the ten nonvirtues.

thought of awakening. *See* bodhicitta.

Three Baskets (*sde snod gsum, tripiṭaka*). The threefold classification of the teachings attributed to the Buddha—Vinaya (discipline), Sūtra (discourses), and Abhidharma (higher knowledge). This categorizaion does not encompass the tantras.

three bodies of buddhahood (*sku gsum, trikāya*). (1) The emanation body (*nirmāṇakāya, sprul sku*), (2) the enjoyment body (*saṃbhogakāya, longs sku*), and (3) the Dharma body (*dharmakāya, chos sku*). *See also* bodies of buddhahood.

three realms (or spheres) of existence (*khams gsum, tridhātu*). The three realms are those of (1) the desire realm (*kāmadhātu*), which includes the six types of rebirth from the hell beings up to the devas, (2) the form realm (*rūpadhātu*), which is characterized by states of meditative concentration, and (3) the formless realm (*arūpadhātu*), where beings with no physical form abide in highly refined meditative states for tens of thousands of eons.

three spheres of activity (*'khor gsum, trimaṇḍala*). The three key elements of an action—namely, the object of the action, the agent of the act, and the act itself—that together form the basis of grasping at the substantial reality of actions and events.

three trainings (*bslab pa gsum, triśikṣā*). The trainings in moral discipline, meditation, and wisdom.

tīrthika (*mu stegs pa*). A propent of one of the non-Buddhist Indian philosophies.

tranquility (*zhi gnas, śamatha*). Literally, "calm abiding," a meditative state in which the meditator has attained a physical and mental pliancy derived from focusing the mind. It is characterized by stable single-pointed attention on a chosen object with all mental distractions calmed. Tranquility is an essential basis for cultivating *insight* (*vipaśyanā*). Sometimes the term is applied to the actual meditative practice that leads to the state of tranquility.

two accumulations (*tshogs gnyis, saṃbhāradvaya*). The prepatory amassing of meritorious acts (*punya*) and of sound knowledge (*jñāna*), without whose completion buddhahood is impossible.

two obscurations (*sgrib pa gnyis, āvaraṇa*). The afflictions obscuration and the knowledge obscuration. The knowledge obscuration (*jñeyāvaraṇa, shes bya'i sgrib pa*) consists of the subtle residue of dualistic thinking and obstructs perfect wisdom and omniscience; it is only abandoned by buddhas. It is much finer than the afflictions obscuration (*kleśāvaraṇa, nyon mongs pa'i sgrib pa*), which consists of the mental poisons, such as anger, desire, confusion, pride, and jealousy, along with their innate tendencies, which are abandoned by arhats upon attaining nirvana. *See also* afflictions

two truths (*bden pa gnyis, satyadvaya*). Relative (or conventional) truth (*kun rdzob bden pa, saṃvṛtisatya*) and ultimate (or absolute) truth (*don dam bden pa, paramārthasatya*). According to the Madhyamaka school, ultimate truth refers to emptiness—the absence of intrinsic existence of all phenomena. In contrast, relative truth refers to the empirical aspect of reality as experienced through perception, thought, and language.

ultimate (*don dam, paramārtha*). The opposite of relative or conventional (*kun rdzob*).

ultimate bodhicitta (*don dam sems bskyed*). *See* bodhicitta.

ultimate expanse (*chos kyi dbyings*). *See* dharmadhātu.

ultimate nature (*gnas lugs*). Refers to the ultimate mode of being of things, which for a Mahayana Buddhist is *emptiness*.

ultimate-nature body (*ngo bo nyid kyi sku shin tu rnam par dag pa, svabhāvakāya*). An englightened form sometimes equivalent to the Dharma body and sometimes treated separately. *See* bodies of buddhahood.

ultimate truth (*don dam bden pa, paramārthasatya*). *See* two truths.

universal essence (*chos nyid*). *See* dharmatā.

universal monarch (*'khor los sgyur ba'i rgyal po, cakravartin*). Literally, "wheel turner." One of the best worldly incarnations possible, these soveriegns have seven exceptional attributes (such as a perfect queen, minister, and so on), including a wheel that, somewhat like a flying saucer, is their means of transport across the world systems they govern. There are four types of universal monarchs, denoted by their iron, copper, silver, or golden wheels.

Uṣṇīṣavijayā (*rnam rgyal ma*). An eight-armed white goddess propitiated to enhance longevity.

Vaibhāṣika (*bye brag smar ba*). "Particularists" is one possible transation for this Hinayana school. They hold the external universe to be composed of indivisible particles and the mind to be a series of indivisible instants of awareness. Their name means "Followers of the *Great Treatise* (*Mahāvibhāṣa*)."

vajra (*rdo rje*). The vajra is the ultimate weapon wielded by the god Indra. It can destroy anything, yet nothing can destroy it. This is a famous metaphor for the eternal buddha mind.

Vinaya (*'dul ba*). One of the three baskets of scripture. *See* Three Baskets.

Vijñānavāda. *See* Cittamātra.

wisdom (*shes rab, prajñā*). The Sanskrit term and its Tibetan equivalent can also be translated as "discerning wisdom" (or "insight") or as "intelligence," depending on context. In the Abhidharma taxonomy of mental factors, *prajñā* refers to a specific mental factor that helps evaluate the properties or qualities of an object. The term can refer simply to intelligence or mental aptitude. In the context of the Mahayana path, *prajñā* refers to the wisdom aspect of the path, consisting primarily of deep insight into the emptiness of all phenomena. It is also the name of the sixth perfection.

yakṣa (*gnod sbyin*). A broad range of beings, mainly spirits, some belonging to the hungry spirits realm and others, more elevated, to the god realms. Their Tibetan name literally means "harm doers," and this is often the case. However, it is also applied to the gods of wealth and to some of the four guardians of the Heaven of the Four Great Kings.

Yogācāra. *See* Cittamātra.

Bibliography

Works Cited by the Authors

Kangyur (Canonical Scriptures)

Advice to a King Sutra. Rājāvavādakasūtra. Rgyal po la gdams pa'i mdo. Toh 221, mdo sde, *dza* 78a1–84b4.

Akṣayamati Sutra. Akṣayamatinirdeśasūtra. Blo gros mi zad pas bstan pa'i mdo. Toh 175, mdo sde, *ma* 79a1–174b7.

Attention to Mindfulness Sutra. Smṛtyupasthānasūtra. Dam pa'i chos dran pa nye bar gzhag pa'i mdo. Toh 287, mdo sde, *ya* 82a1–*sha* 229b7.

Basis of Vinaya. Vinayavastu. 'Dul ba gzhi. Toh 1, 'dul ba, *ka* 1b1–*nga* 302a5. P 1030 'dul ba, *khe* 1b1–*ce* 277a5.

Bodhisattva Collection. Bodhisattvapiṭaka. Byang chub sems dpa'i sde snod. Toh 56, dkon brtsegs, *kha* 255b1–*ga* 205a7.

Bodhisattva's Completely Pure Conduct Sutra. Bodhisattvagocarapariśuddhisūtra. Chapter 16 of the *Flower Ornament Sutra.*

Candraprabha Sutra. See *King of Meditation Sutra.*

Clouds of Jewels Sutra. Ratnameghasūtra. Dkon mchog sprin gyi mdo. Toh 231, mdo sde, *wa* 1b1–112b7.

Collection of Aphorisms. Udānavarga. Ched du brjod pa'i tshoms. Toh 326, mdo sde, *sa* 209a1–253a7. P 992, mdo sna tshogs, *shu* 218b1–261b8.

Compendium of Principles. Tattvasaṃgraha. De bzhin gshegs pa thams cad kyi de kho na nyid bsdus pa'i mdo. Toh 479 Kangyur, rgyud, *nya* 1b1–142a7.

Crown Jewel Dhāraṇī Sutra. Ratnaketudhāraṇīsūtra. 'Dus pa chen po rin po che tog gi gzungs gyi mdo. Toh 138, mdo sde, *na* 187b3–277b7.

Dhāraṇī of the 108 Names of Ākāśagarbha. Ākāśagarbhāṣṭottaraśatakadhāraṇī. Nam mkha'i snying po'i mtshan brgya rtsa brgyad pa gzungs sngags dang bcas pa. Toh 636, rgyud, *ba* 109a5–112a4, and Toh 876, gzungs 'dus, *'e* 104b6–107b3.

Diamond Cutter Sutra. Vajracchedikāsūtra. Shes rab kyi pha rol tu phyin pa rdo rje gcod pa'i mdo. Toh 16, sher phyin, *ka* 121a1–132b7.

Diamond Meditative Absorption Scripture. Vajrasamādhidharmākṣara. Rdo rje'i ting nge 'dzin gyi chos kyi yi ge. Toh 135, mdo sde, *na* 122a1–144b2.

Discourse on the Gnosis of Passing. Ātyayajñānasūtra, 'Da' ka ye shes kyi mdo. Toh 122, mdo sde, *tha* 153a1–153b1; P 790, mdo sna tshogs, *tu* 159a1–159b2.

Enlightenment of Vairocana. Vairocanābhisambodhi. Rnam snang mngon byang. Toh 494, rgyud, *tha* 151b2–260a7; P 126, rgyud, *tha* 115b2–225b2.

Excellent Accomplishment Tantra. Susiddhikaratantra. Legs par grub par byed pa'i rgyud. Toh 807, rgyud, *wa* 168a1–222b7.

Extensive Compendium of All Dharma. Sarvadharmavaidalyasaṃgraha. Rnam par 'thag pa thams cad bsdus pa. Toh 227, mdo sde, *dza* 177a3–188b7.

Flower Ornament Sutra. Avataṃsakasūtra. Phal po che (*Sangs rgyas phal po che'i mdo*). Toh 44, phal chen, *ka–a.* P 761, phal chen, *yi–hi.*

Gayāśīrṣa Hill Sutra. Gayāśīrṣasūtra. Ga ya mgo'i ri kyi mdo. Toh 109, mdo sde, *ca* 285a1–292a7.

Good Eon Sutra. Bhadrakalpikasūtra. Bskal pa bzang po'i mdo. Toh 94, mdo sde, *ka* 1b1–340a5. P 762, mdo sna tshogs, *i* 1b1–376a5.

Great Liberation Sutra. Mahāmokṣasūtra. Thar pa chen po'i mdo. Toh 264, mdo sde, *'a* 210a1–264a1.

Great Passing into Nirvana Sutra (longer version). *Mahāparinirvāṇasūtra. Mya ngan las 'das pa'i mdo.* Toh 119, mdo sde, *nya* 1b1–ta 339a7.

Great Passing into Nirvana Sutra (shorter version). *Mahāparinirvāṇasūtra. Mya ngan las 'das pa'i mdo.* Toh 120, mdo sde, *tha* 1b1–151a4.

Great Sutra of the Supreme Victory. Dhvajāgramahāsūtra. Mdo chen po rgyal mtshan dam pa. Toh 293 Kangyur, mdo sde, *sha* 265b4–267a7.

Heap of Flowers Dhāraṇī. Puṣpakūṭadhāraṇī. Me tog brtsegs pa'i gzungs. Toh 886, gzungs 'dus, *e* 159b1–161b3.

Heap of Jewels collection of sutras. Ratnakūṭa. The Dkon brtsegs section of the Kangyur consisting of six volumes and forty-nine distinct works, from Toh 45 through to Toh 93. Tibetan authors often cite the collection rather than the constituent texts.

Heart Sutra. Prajñāpāramitāhṛdayasūtra. Shes rab kyi pha rol tu phyin pa'i snying po'i mdo. Toh 21, shes phyin, *ka* 144b6–146a3, and Toh 531, rgyud, *na* 94b1–95b3.

Hevajra Tantra. Kye'i rdo rje'i rgyud. Toh 417, rgyud, *nga* 1b1–30a3.

Host of Flowers Sutra. Kusumasaṃcayasūtra. Me tog gi tshogs gyi mdo. Toh 266, mdo sde, *'a* 288a1–319a6.

Inconceivable Secret Sutra. Tathāgatācintyaguhyanirdeśasūtra. De bzhin gshegs pa'i gsang ba bsam gyis mi khyab pa bstan pa'i mdo. Toh 47, dkon brtsegs, *ka* 100a1–203a7.

Infinite Means of Purification Sutra. Anantamukhapariśodhananirdeśaparivartasūtra. Sgo mtha' yas pa rnam par sbyong ba bstan pa'i le'u kyi mdo. Toh 46, dkon brtsegs, *ka* 45b1–99b7.

Instructions for Liberation of Śrī Saṃbhava. A biography found in the *Flower Ornament Sutra.*

Instructions for Liberation of Upāsika Acalā. A biography found in the *Flower Ornament Sutra.*

Jewel Lamp Dhāraṇī Sutra. Ratnolkānāmadhāraṇīsūtra. Dkon mchog ta la la'i gzungs zhes bya ba'i mdo. Toh 145, mdo sde, *pa* 34a4–82a3, and Toh 847, gzungs, *'e* 3b6–54b7.

Kālacakra Tantra. Paramādibuddhoddhrita-kālacakratantra. Mchog gi dang po sangs rgyas las phyung ba rgyud kyi rgyal po dpal dus kyi 'khor lo. Toh 362, rgyud, *ka* 22a1–128b7.

Kālacakra Tantra. Kālacakratantra-uttaratantrahṛdaya. Dus kyi 'khor lo'i rgyud phyi ma rgyud kyi snying po. Toh 363, rgyud, *ka* 129a1–144a7.

Kāśyapa Chapter Sutra. Kāśyapaparivartasūtra. 'Od srungs kyis zhus pa'i mdo. Toh 87, dkon brtsegs, *cha* 119b1–151b7.

King of Meditation Sutra. Samādhirājasūtra. Ting nge 'dzin rgyal po'i mdo. Toh 127, mdo sde, *da* 1b1–170b7. P 795, mdo sna tshogs, *thu* 1b1–185a8. Also known as the *Candraprabhasūtra.*

King of Secret Nectar Tantra. Amṛtaguhyatantrarāja. Gsang ba 'dud rtsi'i rgyud kyi rgyal po. Toh 401, rgyud, *ga* 233a5–235a5.

Lifespan Sutra. Āyuṣparyantasūtra. Tshe'i mtha'i mdo. Toh 307, mdo sde, *sa* 139a4–145b3.

Lion's Roar of Queen Śrīmālā Sutra. Śrīmālādevīsiṃhanādasūtra. Dpal phreng seng ge sgra'i mdo. Toh 92, dkon brtsegs, *cha* 255a1–277b7.

Lion's Roar Sutra. Siṃhanādasūtra. Byams pa'i seng ge'i sgra chen po'i mdo. Toh 67, dkon brtsegs, *ca* 68a1–114b7. P 760, part 23, dkon brtsegs, *zi* 58b6–111a2.

Lotus Sutra. Saddharmapuṇḍarīkasūtra. Dam pa'i chos padma dkar po zhes bya ba theg pa chen po'i mdo. Toh 113, mdo sde, *ja* 1b1–180b7.

Marvelous Array Sutra. Gaṇḍavyūhasūtra. Sdong po bkod pa'i mdo. Chapter 45 of the *Flower Ornament Sutra.*

Meeting of Father and Son Sutra. Pitāputrasamāgamasūtra. Yab dang sras mjal ba'i mdo. Toh 60, dkon brtsegs, *nga* 1b1–168a7.

Nanda's Abiding in the Womb. Nandagarbhāvakrāntinirdeśa. Dga' bo mngal du 'jug pa bstan pa'i mdo. Toh 57, dkon brtsegs, *ga* 205a7–236b7.

One Hundred Stories (of Great Deeds). Avadānaśataka (short for Pūrṇapramukhāvadānaśataka). Gang po la sogs pa'i rtogs pa brjod pa brgya pa. Toh 343, mdo sde, *ām* 1b1–286b7.

One Hundred [Stories] about Karma. Karmaśataka. Las brgya tham pa. Toh 340, mdo sde, *ha* 1b1–*a* 128b7.

Past Life of Kanakavarṇa. Kanakavarṇapūrvayoga. Gser mdog gi sngon gyi sbyor ba. Toh 350, mdo sde, *aḥ* 50a5–55b7.

Perfection of Wisdom in Eight Thousand Lines. Aṣṭasāhasrikāprajñāpāramitā. Shes rab kyi pha rol tu phyin pa brgyad stong pa. Toh 12, sher phyin, *ka* 1b1–286a6. P 734, sher phyin, *mi* 1b1–312a8.

Perfection of Wisdom in a Hundred Thousand Lines. Śatasāhasrikāprajñāpāramitā. Shes rab kyi pha rol tu phyin pa stong phrag brgya pa. Toh 8, sher phyin *ka–'a.* P 730, sher phyin *ra–ji.*

Perfection of Wisdom in Seven Hundred Lines. Saptaśatikāprajñāpāramitā. Shes rab kyi pha rol tu phyin pa bdun brgya pa. Toh 24, sher phyin, *ka* 148a1–174a2, and Toh 90, dkon brtsegs, *cha* 182b6–209b7.

Perfection of Wisdom in Twenty-Five Thousand Lines. Pañcaviṃśatisāhasrikāprajñāpāramitā. Shes rab kyi pha rol tu phyin pa stong phrag nyi shu lnga pa. Toh 9, sher phyin, *ka* 1b1–*ga* 381a5.

Perfectly Gathering the Qualities [of Avalokiteśvara] Sutra. Dharmasaṃgītisūtra. Chos yang dag par sdud pa'i mdo. Toh 238, mdo sde, *zha* 1b1–99b7. P 904, mdo sna tshogs, *wu* 1b1–107b5.

Prātimokṣasūtra. So sor thar pa'i mdo. Toh 2, 'dul ba, *ca* 1b1–20b7.

Prayer of Excellent Conduct. Bhadracaryāpraṇidhāna. Bzang po spyod pa'i smon lam gyi rgyal po. Toh 1095, gzungs 'dus, *waṃ* 262b5–266a3. P 716, rgyud, *ya* 268a2–271b4. P 1038, 'dul ba, *phe* 296b1–299a7, and P 5924, ngo mtshar bstan bcos, *mo* 288b6–292a7. Also part 4 of the *Flower Ornament Sutra.*

Prayer of Maitreya. Maitreyapraṇidhāna. Byams pa'i smon lam. Toh 1096, gzugs, *waṃ* 266a4–267a5. P 7 17, rgyud, *ya* 271b4–272b6, and P 1039 'dul ba, *phe* 299a7–300a6.

Questions of Brahma Viśeṣacinti Sutra. Brahmaviśeṣacintiparipṛcchāsūtra. Tshangs pa khyad pa rsems kyi zhus pa. Toh 160, mdo sde, *ba* 23a1–100b7.

Questions of Gaganagañja Sutra. Gaganagañjaparipṛcchāsūtra. Nam mka' mdzod kyi mdo. Toh 148, mdo sde, *pa* 243a1–330a7.

Questions of the Layman Ugra Sutra. Gṛhapatyugraparipṛcchāsūtra. Khyim bdag drag shul can gyis zhus pa'i mdo. Toh 63, dkon brtsegs, *nga* 257a7–288a4.

Questions of the Layman Vīradatta Sutra. Vīradattagṛhapatiparipṛcchāsūtra. Khyim bdag dpas byin gyis zhus pa'i mdo. Toh 72, dkon brtsegs, *ca* 194a1–240b1.

Questions of Nāga King Anavatapta Sutra. Anavataptanāgarājaparipṛcchāsūtra. Klu'i rgyal po ma dros pas zhus pa'i mdo. Toh 156, mdo sde, *pha* 206a1–253b7. P 823, mdo sna tshogs, *pu* 213b7–260b7.

Questions of Nārāyaṇa Sutra. See *Sutra of the Absorption that Gathers All Merit.*

Questions of Pūrṇa Sutra. Pūrṇaparipṛcchāsūtra. Gang pos zhus pa'i mdo. Toh 61, dkon brtsegs, *nga* 168b1–227a6.

Questions of Ratnacūḍa Sutra. Ratnacūḍaparipṛcchāsūtra. Gtsug na rin po ches zhus pa'i mdo. Toh 91, dkon brtsegs, *cha* 210a1–254b7.

Questions of Ṛṣi Vyāsa Sutra. Ṛṣivyāsaparipṛcchāsūtra. Drang srong rgyas pas zhus pa'i mdo. Toh 93, dkon brtsegs, *cha* 278a1–299a7. P 760, dkon brtsegs, *'i* 285a8–311a6.

Questions of Sāgaramati Sutra. Sāgaramatiparipṛcchāsūtra. Blo gros rgya mtsho zhus pa'i mdo. Toh 152, mdo sde, *pha* 1b1–115b7. P 819, mdo sna tshogs, *pu* 1b1–124a5.

Questions of Subāhu Sutra. Subāhuparipṛcchāsūtra. Lag bzangs kyis zhus pa'i mdo. Toh 70, dkon brtsegs, *ca* 154a1–180b7.

Questions of Subāhu Tantra. Subāhuparipṛcchātantra. Dpung bzang gis zhus pa'i rgyud. Toh 805, rgyud 'bum *wa*, 118a1–140b7. P 428, rgyud *tsha*, 179b6–202a4 .

Questions of Surata Sutra. Surataparipṛcchāsūtra. Nges pas zhus pa'i mdo. Toh 71, dkon brtsegs, *ca* 181a1–193b7.

Questions of the Devaputra Susthitamati Sutra. Susthitamatidevaputraparipṛcchāsūtra. Lha'i bu blo gros rab gnas kyis zhus pa'i mdo. Toh 80, dkon brtsegs, *ca* 285a1–*cha* 27a4.

Questions of Upāli Sutra. (Vinayaviniścaya-)Upāliparipṛcchāsūtra. ('Dul ba rnam par gtan la dbab pa) nye bar 'khor gyis zhus pa'i mdo. Toh 68, dkon brtsegs, *ca* 115a1–131a7; dkon brtsegs, *zi* 111a3–129a8.

Recitation of Mañjuśrī's Names. Mañjuśrīnāmasaṃgīti. 'Jam dpal ye shes sems dpa'i don dam pa'i mtshan yang dag par brjod pa. Toh 360, rgyud, *ka* 1b1–13b7.

Rice Shoot Sutra. Śālistambasūtra. Sa lu'i ljang ba'i mdo. Toh 210, mdo sde, *tsha* 116b2–123b1.

Sage and Fool Sutra. Damamūkanāmasūtra. 'Dzangs blun zhes bya ba'i mdo. Toh 341, mdo sde, *a* 129a1–298a7.

Section Discussing the Realization of the Lord of the World. In the *Perfectly Gathering the Qualities Sutra* (see above).

Seal Enhancing the Force of Faith Sūtra. Śraddhābalādhānāvatāramudrāsūtra. Dad pa'i stobs bskyed pa la 'jug pa'i phyag rgya'i mdo. Toh 201, mdo sde, *tsha* 1b1–63a5.

Short Vinaya. Vinayakṣudrakavastu. 'Dul ba phran tshegs kyi gzhi. Toh 6, 'dul ba, *tha–da.*

Skill in Means Sutra. Upāyakauśalyasūtra. Gsang chen thabs la mkhas pa'i mdo. Toh 353, mdo sde, *a* 86a2–198b7. P 1022 mdo sna tshogs, *ke* 89a1–204b1 (see above). *Thabs mkhas chen po sangs rgyas drin lan bsab pa'i mdo,* translated from Chinese.

Sky Essence Sutra. Ākāśagarbhasūtra. Nam mkha'i snying po'i mdo. Toh 260, mngo sde, *za* 264a4–283b2. P 926, mdo sna tshogs, *zhu* 278b4–298b2.

Story of the Sow. Sūkarikāvadāna. Phag mo'i rtogs brjod. Toh 345, mdo sde, *am* 289b2–291a7.

Sutra of the Absorption that Gathers All Merit. Sarvapuṇyasamuccayasamādhisūtra. Bsod nams thams cad bsdus pa'i ting nge 'dzin gyi mdo. Toh 134, mdo sde, *na* 70b2–121b7.

Sutra Adorning the Brilliance of Pristine Awareness. Jñānālokālaṃkārasūtra. Ye shes snang ba'i rgyan rgyi mdo. Toh 100, mdo sde, *ga* 276a1–305a7.

Sutra Definitely Elucidating the Noble Intention. Saṃdhinirmocanasūtra. Dgongs pa nges par 'grel pa'i mdo. Toh 106, mdo sde, *ca* 1b1–55b7. P 774, mdo sna tshogs, *ngu 1b1–60b7.*

Sutra Describing the Qualities of the Buddhafield of Mañjuśrī. Mañjuśrībuddhakṣetraguṇavyūhasūtra. 'Jam dpal gyi sangs rgyas kyi zhing gi yon tan bkod pa'i mdo. Toh 59, dkon brtsegs, *ga* 248b1–297a3.

Sutra Encouraging Nobler Intention. Adhyāśayasaṃcodanasūtra. Lhag pa'i bsam pa bskul ba'i mdo. Toh 69, dkon brtsegs, *ca* 131a7–153b7.

Sutra on Excellently Nurturing Faith in the Mahayana. Mahāyānaprasādaprabhāvanasūtra. Theg pa chen po la dad pa rab tu sgom pa'i mdo. Toh 144, mdo sde, *pa* 6b6–34a3.

Sutra on the Full Development of Great Realization. Mahāsamayavaipulyasūtra. Rtogs pa chen po yongs su rgyas pa'i mdo. Toh 265, mdo sde, *'a* 264a1–287b7.

Sutra on Going to Laṅka. Laṅkāvatārasūtra. Lang kar gshegs pa'i mdo. Toh 107, mdo sde, *cha* 56a1–191b7.

Sutra of Golden Light. Translated from Chinese. *Gser 'od dam pa mchog tu rnam par rgyal ba'i mdo.* Toh 555, rgyud, *pa* 19a1–151a7. Also *Suvarṇaprabhāsottamasūtrendrarājasūtra. Gser 'od dam pa mdo sde'i dbang po'i rgyal po.* Toh 556, rgyud, *pa* 151b1–273a7.

Sutra on the Indivisibility of the Dharmadhātu. Dharmadhātuprakṛtyasambhedanirdeśasūtra. Chos kyi dbyings kyi rang bzhin dbyer med pa bstan pa'i mdo. Toh 52, dkon brtsegs, *kha* 140b1–164a5.

Sutra of the Play of Manjuśrī. Mañjuśrīvikrīḍitasūtra. 'Jam dpal rnam par rol pa'i mdo. Toh 96, mdo sde, *kha* 217a1–241b7.

Sutra Requested by Suvikrāntavikrami. Suvikrāntavikramiparipṛcchāsūtra. Rab kyi rtsal gyis rnam par gnon pas zhus pa'i mdo. Toh 14, shes rab sna tshogs, *ka* 20a1–103b7; P 736 sher phyin, *tsi* 22b1–113b8.

Sutra on Moral Discipline. Śīlasaṃyuktasūtra. Tshul khrims yang dag par ldan pa'i mdo. Toh 303, mdo sde, *sa* 127a2–127b7.

Sutra Teaching the Four Qualities. Caturdharmanirdeśasūtra. Chos bzhi bstan pa'i mdo. Toh 249, mdo sde, *za* 55a5–59b7.

Sutra Teaching the Nonorigination of All Things. Sarvadharmāpravṛttinirdeśasūtra. Chos thams cad 'byung ba med par bstan pa'i mdo. Toh 180, mdo sde, *ma* 267a1–296a6. P 847, mdo sna tshogs, *bu* 279a6–311a4.

Sutra Teaching the Wearing of Armor. Varmavyūhanirdeśasūtra. Go cha'i bkod pa bstan pa'i mdo. Toh 51, dkon brtsegs, *kha* 70b1–140a7.

Tantra of the Arising of the Supremely Blissful. Mahāsaṃvārodayatantra. Dpal bde mchog 'byung ba'i rgyud. Toh 373, rgyud, *kha* 265a1–311a6.

Teachings of Vimalakīrti Sutra. Vimalakīrtinirdeśasūtra. Dri ma med par grags pas bstan pa'i mdo. Toh 176, mdo sde, *ma*, 175a1–239b7.

Ten Dharmas Sutra. Daśadharmakasūtra. Chos bcu pa'i mdo. Toh 53, dkon brtsegs, *kha* 164a6–184b6.

Ten Levels Sutra. Daśabhūmikasūtra. Sa bcu pa'i mdo. Chapter 31 of the *Flower Ornament Sutra.*

Ten Wheels of Kṣitigarbha Sutra. Daśacakrakṣitigarbhasūtra. 'Dus pa chen po las sa'i snying po'i 'khor lo bcu pa'i mdo. Toh 239, mdo sde, *zha* 100a1–241b4.

Three Vows Chapter. Trisaṃvaranirdeśaparivarta. Sdom pa gsum bstan pa'i le'u kyi mdo. Toh 45, dkon brtsegs, *ka* 1b1–45a7.

Union with All the Buddhas. Sarvabuddhasamayoga. Sangs rgyas thams cad dang mnyam par sbyor ba mkha' 'gro ma sgyu ma bde ba'i mchog. Toh 366, rgyud, *ka* 151b1–193a6.

Unwavering Suchness Sutra. Dharmatāsvabhāvaśūnyatācalapratisarvālokasūtra. Chos nyid rang gi ngo bo stong pa nyid las mi g.yo bar tha dad par thams cad la snang ba'i mdo. Toh 128, mdo sde, *da* 171a1–174b4.

Vajra Peak Tantra. Vajraśekharatantra. Rdo rje rtse mo'i rgyud. Toh 480, rgyud, *nya 142b1–274a5*. P 113, rgyud, *nya* 162b2–301b8.

Vajra Victory Banner Sutra. Vajraketusūtra. Rdo rje rgyal mtshan gyi mdo. Toh 30 Kangyur, shes rab sna tshogs, *ka* 178b6–179a7.

Vast Manifestation Sutra. Lalitavistarasūtra. Rgya cher rol pa'i mdo. Toh 95, mdo sde, *kha* 1b1–216b7. P 763, mdo sna tshogs, *ku* 1a1–246a5.

Verse Summary of the Perfection of Wisdom. (*Prajñāpāramitā-*) *Ratnaguṇasaṃcayagāthā. Shes rab kyi pha rol tu phyin pa sdud pa tshigs su bcad pa.* Toh 13, sher phyin, *ka* 1b1–19b7. P 735, sher phyin, *tsi* 1b1–22a8.

Verses Addressed to Prasenajit. Prasenajidgāthā. Gsal rgyal gyi tshigs su bcad pa. Toh 322, mdo sde, *sa* 201a6–204a4.

Verses about Bherī, the King of the Snake Spirits. Nāgarājabherīgāthā. Klu'i rgyal po rnga sgra'i tshigs su bcad pa. Toh 325, mdo sde, *sa* 204b3–208b7.

White Lotus of Compassion Sutra. Karuṇāpuṇḍarīkasūtra. Snying rje pad ma dkar po'i mdo. Toh 112, mdo sde, *cha* 129a1–297a7.

White Lotus of Great Compassion Sutra. Mahākaruṇāpuṇḍarīkasūtra. Snying rje chen po'i pad ma dkar po'i mdo. Toh 111, mdo sde, *cha* 56a1–128b7.

Tengyur (Canonical Treatises)

Advayavajra (Gnyis su med pa'i rdo rje; alias Maitripāda). *Removing Bad Views. Kudṛṣṭinirghāta. Lta ba ngan pa sel ba.* Toh 2229, rgyud 'grel, *wi 104b7–110a2*. P 3073, rgyud 'grel, *mi* 113a7–119a8.

Anonymous. *Treasury of Nouns. Subantaratnākara. Su pa'i mtha' rin chen 'byung gnas.* Toh 4430, sna tshogs, *no* 122b3–134a6.

Āryadeva. *Four Hundred. Catuḥśataka. Bzhi brgya pa.* Toh 3846, dbu ma, *tsha* 1a1–18a7.

Āryaśūra. *Garland of Jātaka Tales. Jātakamāla. Skyes rabs gi rgyud.* Toh 4150, skye rabs, *hu* 1b1–135a7.

Asaṅga. *See also* Maitreya for texts (such as the *Mahāyānasūtrālaṃkāra*) that Tibetan tradition says Asaṅga received from Maitreya and that are therefore attributed to Maitreya in the Tengyur.

———. *Bodhisattva Levels, from the Yogic Conduct Levels. Bodhisattvabhūmi* (short for *Yogācārabhūmau Bodhisattvabhūmi*). *Byang chub sems dpa'i sa* (short for *Rnal 'byor spyod pa'i sa las byang chub sems dpa'i sa*). Toh 4037, sems tsam, *wi* 1b1–213a7. P 5538, sems tsam, *zhi* 1–247a8.

———. *Commentary on the Ornament of Mahayana Sutras. Sūtrālaṃkāravyākhyā. Mdo sde'i rgyan gyi rnam par bshad pa.* Toh 4026, sems tsam, *phi* 129b1–260a7. P 5527, sems tsam, *phi* 135b7–287a8.

———. *Compendium of Higher Knowledge. Abhidharmasamuccaya. Chos mngon pa kun las btus pa.* Toh 4049, sems tsam, *ri* 44b1–120a7. P 5550, sems tsam, *li* 51a2–141b2.

———. *Compendium of the Mahayana. Mahāyānasaṃgraha. Theg pa chen po bsdus pa.* Toh 4048, sems tsam, *ri* 1a1–43a7; P 5549, sems tsam, *li* 1–51a2.

———. *Detailed Explanation of the Uttaratantra. Mahāyānottaratantraśāstravyākhyā. Theg pa chen po'i rgyud bla ma'i bstan bcos kyi rnam par bshad pa.* Toh 4025, sems tsam, *phi* 74b1–129a7.

———. *Establishing Summaries of the Levels of Yogic Practice. Yogācārabhūmiviniścayasaṃgrahaṇī. Rnal 'byor spyod pa'i sa rnam par gtan la dbab pa bsdu ba.* Toh 4038, sems tsam, *zhi* 1a1–127a4. P 5539, sems tsam, *zi* 1–'*i* 142b8.

———. *Hymn of Praise to the Good Qualities of the Dharmakāya. *Dharmakāyāśrayāsāmānyaguṇastotra. Chos kyi sku la gnas pa'i yon tan la bstod pa.* Toh 1115, bstod tshegs, *ka* 61b6–62b3.

———. *Śrāvaka Levels, from the Yogic Conduct Levels. Śrāvakabhūmi (short for Yogācārabhūmau Śrāvakabhūmi). Nyan thos kyi sa* (short for *Rnal 'byor spyod pa'i sa las nyan thos kyi sa*). Toh 4036, sems tsam, *dzi 1a1–195a7*. P 5537, sems tsam, *wi* 1a–236a.

Asvabhāva (Ngo bo nyid med pa). *Detailed Commentary on the Ornament of Mahayana Sutras. Sūtrālaṃkāraṭīkā. Theg pa chen po'i mdo sde'i rgyan gyi rgya cher bshad pa.* Toh 4029, sems tsam, *bi* 38b6–174a7. P 5530, sems tsam, *bi* 45a5–196a7.

Aśvaghoṣa (a.k.a. Mātṛceṭa). *Eliminating Suffering. Śokavinodana. Mya ngan bsal ba.* Toh 4177, spring yig, *nge* 33a2–34a3.

———. *Fifty Verses about the Guru. Gurupañcāśikā. Bla ma lnga bcu pa.* Toh 3721, rgyud, *tshu* 10a2–12a2.

———. *Praise in Hundred and Fifty Stanzas. Śatapañcāśatakastotra.* Brgya lnga bcu pa zhes bya ba'i bstod pa. Toh 1147, bstod tshogs, *ka* 110a3–116a5.

Atiśa (Dīpaṃkaraśrījñāna). *Commentary on the Difficult Points in the Lamp for the Path to Awakening. Bodhipathapradīpapañjikā. Byang chub lam gyi sgron ma'i dka' 'grel.* Toh 3948, dbu ma, *khi* 241a4–293a4. P 5344, dbu ma, *ki* 277b6–339b2.

———. *Instructions on Madhyamaka. Madhyamakopadeśa. Dbu ma'i man ngag.* Toh 3929, dbu ma, *ki* 95b1–96a7.

———. *Instructions on Madhyamaka. Ratnakaraṇḍodghāṭanāmamadhyamakopadeśa. Dbu ma'i man ngag rin po che'i za ma tog kha phye ba zhes bya ba.* Toh 3930, dbu ma, *ki* 96b1–116b7.

———. *Lamp for the Path to Awakening. Bodhipathapradīpa. Byang chub lam gyi sgron ma.* Toh 3947, dbu ma, *khi* 238a6–241a4, and Toh 4465, jo bo'i chos chung, *gi* 1b1–4b4. P 5343, dbu ma, *ki* 274b1–277b6, and P 5378, dbu ma, *gi* 1–5b5.

———. *Lamp for the Summary of Conduct. Caryāsaṃgrahapradīpa. Spyod pa bsdus pa'i sgron ma.* Toh 3960, dbu ma, *khi* 312b3–313a7.

———. *Penetrating the Two Truths. Satyadvayāvatāra. Bden pa gnyis la 'jug pa.* Toh 3902, dbu ma, *a* 72a3–73a7, and Toh 4467, jo bo'i chos chung, *pho* 5b3–6b5.

———. *Ritual Order for Bodhicitta and Vows. Cittotpādasaṃvaravidhikrama. Sems bskyed pa dang sdom pa'i cho ga'i rim pa.* Toh 3969, dbu ma, *gi* 245a2–248b2.

———. *Sādhana for Practicing the Mahayana Path. Theg pa chen po'i lam gyi sgrub thabs yi ger bsdus pa.* Toh 3954, dbu ma, *khi* 299a5–302b6, and Toh 4479, jo bo'i chos chung, *gi* 24a3–27b4. P 5351, dbu ma, *ki* 348a6–352a8, and P 5392 dbu ma, *gi* 30b3–35a1.

———. *Song of Seeing Dharmadhātu. Dharmadhātudarśanagīti. Chos kyi dbyings lta ba'i glu.* Toh 2314, rgyud, *shi* 254b7–260b5.

———. *Very Brief Sādhana for Practicing the Mahayana Path. Theg pa chen po'i lam gyi sgrub thabs shin tu bsdus pa.* Toh 3955, dbu ma, *khi* 302b6–303a6, and Toh 4480, jo bo'i chos chung *gi,* 27b4–28a4. P 5352, dbu ma *ki,* 352a8–353a1, and P 5393 dbu ma *gi,* 35a2–35b2.

Cāṇakya. *Treatise on Political Morals. Nītiśāstra. Tsa na ka'i lugs kyi bstan bcos.* Toh 4334, thun mong ba, *ngo* 127b6–137b6. P 5826, thun mong ba lugs kyi bstan bcos, *go* 174a5–185b7.

Candragomin. *Letter to a Student. Śiṣyalekha. Slob ma la springs pa'i spring yig.* Toh 4183, spring yig, *nge* 46b3–53a6.

———. *Twenty Verses on the Bodhisattva Vow. Bodhisattvasaṃvaraviṃśaka. Byang chub sems dpa'i sdom pa nyi shu pa.* Toh 4081, sems tsam, *hi* 166b1–167a5.

Candrakīrti. *Clear Words. Prasannapadā. Dbu ma rtsa ba'i 'grel pa tshigs gsal ba.* Toh 3860, mdo 'grel, *'a* 1a1–200a7. P 5260, dbu ma, *'a* 1a1–224a3.

———. *Commentary on [Āryadeva's] Four Hundred. Catuḥśatakaṭīkā. Bzhi brgya pa'i rgya cher 'grel pa.* Toh 3865, dbu ma, *ya* 30b6–239a7.

———. *Commentary on the Sixty Reasonings. Yuktiṣaṣṭikāvṛtti. Rigs pa drug bcu pa'i 'grel pa.* Toh 3864, mdo 'grel, *ya* 1a1–30b6. P 5265, dbu ma, *ya* 1a1–33b3.

———. *Entering the Middle Way. Madhyamakāvatāra. Dbu ma la 'jug pa'i tshig le'ur byas pa.* Toh 3861, dbu ma, *'a* 201b1–219a7. P 5262, dbu ma, *'a* 245a2–260b5.

———. *Seventy Stanzas on Going for Refuge. Triśaraṇasaptatī. Gsum la skyabs su 'gro ba bdun cu pa.* Toh 3971, dbu ma, *gi* 251a1–253b2.

Dharmakīrti. *Establishing the Mind of Others. Saṃtānāntarasiddhi. Rgyud gzhan grub pa zhes bya ba'i rab tu byed pa.* Toh 4219, tshad ma, *che* 355b5–359a7. P 5716, tshad ma, *ce* 400a7–404b3.

———. *Thorough Exposition of Valid Cognition. Pramāṇavārttika. Tshad ma rnam 'grel gyi tshig le'ur byas pa.* Toh 4210, tshad ma, *che* 94b1–151a7.

Gopadatta. *Stories of Seven Young Women. Saptakumārarikāvadāna. Gzhon nu ma bdun gyi rtogs pa brjod pa.* Toh 4147, 'dul ba, *su* 244b1–252b6.

Great Sanskrit and Tibetan Glossary. Mahāvyutpatti. Bye brag tu rtogs par byed pa chen po. Toh 4346, sna tshogs *co, 1b1–131a4;* P 5832, ngo mtshar bstan bcos, *go* 204b7–310a8. A Sanskrit-Tibetan-Chinese edition is found in Sakaki, *Mahāvyutpatti.*

Guṇaprabha. *Vinaya Sutra. Vinayasūtra. 'Dul ba'i mdo.* Toh 4117, 'dul ba, *wu* 1b1–100a7. P 5619, 'dul ba'i 'grel pa, *zu* 1–109b8.

———. *Detailed Autocommentary on the Vinaya Sutra. Vinayasūtravṛttyabhidhāna-svavyākhyāna. 'Dul ba'i mdo'i 'grel pa mngon par brjod pa rang gi rnam bshad.* Toh 4119, 'dul ba, *zhu–zu.* P 5621, 'dul ba'i 'grel pa, *'u–yu.*

Haribhadra. Great Commentary on the Perfection of Wisdom Sutra in Eight Thousand Verses. Aṣṭasāhasrikāprajñāpāramitāvyākhyānābhisamayālaṃkārāloka. Shes rab kyi pha rol tu phyin pa brgyad stong pa'i bshad pa mngon par rtogs pa'i rgyan gyi snang ba. Toh 3791, shes phyin, cha 1b1–*341a7.*

Karo. *Conpendium of the Stages of Meditation Sutra. *Bhāvanākramasūtrasamuccaya. Sgom pa'i rim pa mdo kun las bdus pa.* Toh 3933, dbu ma, *ki* 125b1–148a7.

Indrabhūti. *Achieving Pristine Awareness. Jñānasiddhisādhanopāyikā. Ye shes grub pa zhes bya ba'i sgrub thabs.* Toh 2219, rgyud, *wi* 36b7–60b6. P 3063, rgyud 'grel, *mi* 39b5–64a8.

Jñānagarbha. *Commentary on the Distinction Between the Two Truths. Satyadvayavibhaṅgakārikā. Bden gnyis rnam 'byed.* Toh 3881, dbu ma, *sa* 1b1–3b3.

Kamalaśīla. *Diamond Cutter Sutra Commentary. Vajracchedikāṭīkā. 'Phags pa shes rab kyi pha rol tu phyin pa rdo rje gcod pa'i rgya cher 'grel pa.* Toh 3817, mdo 'grel, *ma* 204a1–267a7.

———. *Stages of Meditation. Bhāvanākrama. Sgom pa'i rim pa.* Toh 3915–17, dbu ma, *ki* 22a1–68b7.

Kṣemendra. *Bodhisattvāvadānakalpalatā. Byang chub sems dpa'i rtogs pa brjod pa dpag bsam gyi 'khri shing.* Toh 4155, skyes rab, *ke–khe.*

Maitreya (or Asaṅga). *Clear Differentiation of the Middle and Extremes. Madhyāntavibhāga. Dbus dang mtha' rnam par 'byed pa.* Toh 4021, sems tsam, *phi* 40b1–45a6.

———. *Ornament of Clear Realization. Abhisamayālaṃkāra. Mngon rtogs rgyan.* Toh 3786, shes phyin, *ka* 1b1–13a7. P 5184, sher phyin, *ka* 1a1–15b3.

———. *Ornament of Mahayana Sutras. Mahāyānasūtrālaṃkāra. Theg pa chen po mdo sde'i rgyan.* Toh 4020, sems tsam, *phi* 1a1–39a4. P 5521, sems tsam, *phi* 1–43b3.

———. *Uttaratantra* (*Mahāyānottaratantraśāstra*, or *Ratnagotravibhāga*). *Rgyud bla ma* (*Theg pa chen po rgyud bla ma'i bstan bcos*). Toh 4024, sems tsam, *phi* 54b1–73a7. P 5525, sems tsam, *phi* 54b7–74b6.

Mañjuśrīkīrti. Extensive Explantion of Root Vajrayana Downfalls. Vajrayānamūlāpattiṭīkā. Rdo rje theg pa'i rtsa ba'i ltung ba'i rgya cher bshad pa. Toh 2488, rgyud 'grel, *thi* 197b7–231b7.

Nāgārjuna. *Aspiration Prayer of Nāgārjuna. Āryanāgārjunapraṇidhāna. Klu sgrub kyi smon lam.* Toh 4387, sna tshogs, *nyo* 317b4–318a4. (Traditionally ascribed to Nāgārjuna.)

———. *Commentary on the Thought of Awakening. Bodhicittavivaraṇa. Byang chub sems kyi 'grel pa.* Toh 1800, rgyud, *ngi* 38a5–42b5. P2665, rgyud 'grel, *gi* 42b7–48a2.

———. *Compendium of Sūtra Quotations. Mahāsūtrasamuccaya. Mdo kun las btus pa chen po.* Toh 3961, dbu ma, *gi* 1a1–198a7. P 5358, dbu ma, *khi* 1–231a. (Attributed by the Tibetan canon to Nāgārjuna.)

———. *Five Stages. Pañcakrama. Rim pa lnga pa.* Toh 1802, rgyud, *ngi* 45a5–57a1. P 2667, rgyud 'grel, *gi* 50b7–64a1.

———. *Fundamental Verses on the Middle Way. Mūlamadhyamakakārikā. Dbu ma rtsa ba'i tshig le'ur byas pa shes rab.* Toh 3824, dbu ma, *tsa* 1a1–19a6. P 5224, dbu ma, *tsa* 1a1–22a4.

———. *Letter to a Friend. Suhṛllekha. Bshes pa'i spring yig. Toh 4182, spring yig, nge* 40b4–46b3. P 5682, sprin yig, *nge 282b8–290a4.*
———. *Precious Garland. Ratnāvalī. Dbu ma rin chen phreng ba. Toh 4158,* spring yig, *ge* 107a1–126a4. P 5658, sprin yig, *nge* 129a5–152b4.
———. *Refutation of Arguments. Vigrahavyāvartanī. Rtsod pa bzlog pa'i tshig le'ur byas pa.* Toh 3828, dbu ma, *tsa* 27a1–29a7.
———. *Seventy Verses on Emptiness. Śūnyatāsaptatikārikā. Stong pa nyid bdun cu pa'i tshig le'ur byas pa.* Toh 3826, dbu ma, *tsa* 24a6–27a1.
———. *Shoots of Wisdom: Treatise on Ethics. Nītiśāstraprajñādaṇḍa. Lugs kyi bstan bcos shes rab sdong po.* Toh 4329, thun mong ba lugs jtu bstan bcos, *ngo* 103a7–113a4. P 5821, thun mong ba lugs kyi bstan bcos, *go* 145a4–156b7.
———. *Sixty Reasonings. Yuktiṣaṣṭikā. Rigs pa drug cu pa'i thig le'ur byas pa.* Toh 3825, mdo 'grel, *tsa* 20b1–22b6. P 5225, dbu ma, *tsa* 22b2–25a7.
———. *Verses on the Essence of Dependent Origination. Pratītyasamutpādahṛdayakārikā. Rten cing 'grel par 'byung ba'i snying po'i tshig le'ur byas pa.* Toh 3836, mdo 'grel, *tsa* 146b2–146b7.
Padmavajra. *Guhyasiddhi. 'Gsang ba grub pa'.* Toh 2217, rgyud 'grel, *wi 1a1–28b4. P* 3061, rgyud 'grel, *mi 1a1–31a6.*
Prajñākaramati. *Commentary on the Guide to the Bodhisattva Way of Life. Bodhicaryāvatārapañjikā. Byang chub kyi spyod pa la 'jug pa'i dka' 'grel.* Toh 3872, mdo 'grel, *la* 41b1–288a7.
Rāhulabhadra. *Summary of the Bodhisattva's Completely Pure Conduct Sutra. Bodhisattvagocarapariśuddhisūtrārthasaṃgraha. Byang chub sems dpa'i spyod yul yongs su dag pa'i mdo.* Toh 3965, dbu ma, *gi* 235b1–237a3. P 5360, dbu ma, *khi* 272a6–274a8.
Ratnadāsa (Dkon mchog 'bangs). *Praise of the Virtues without End. Guṇāparyantastotra. Yon tan mtha' yas bstod pa.* Toh 1155, bstod tshogs, *ka* 196a6–200b1.
Ratnākaraśānti. *Commentary on Ornament of the Middle Way. Madhyamālaṃkāropadeśa. Dbu ma rgyan gyi man ngag.* Toh 4085, sems tsam, *hi* 223b2–231a7.
———. *Jewel Radiance Ornamenting of the Compendium of Sutras. Sūtrasamuccayabhāṣyaratnālokālaṃkāra. Mdo kun las btus pa'i bshad pa rin po che snang ba'i rgyan.* Toh 3935, dbu ma, *ki* 215a5–334a3.
Śākyaśrībhadra. *The Abbreviated Stages of the Path of the Bodhisattva. Bodhisattvamārgakramasaṃgraha. Byang chub sems dpa'i lam gyi rim pa mdor bsdus pa.* Toh 3962, dbu ma, *gi* 198b1–199b5. P 5372, mdo 'grel, *khi* 299b–301b.
———. *Seven Branches of Worship. Saptāṅgasaddharmacaryāvatāra. Dam pa'i chos spyod pa la 'jug pa'i yan lag bdun pa.* Toh 3980, dbu ma, *gi* 258b5–259a7. P 5371, mdo 'grel, *khi* 298b3–299b2.
Śāntarakṣita. *Commentary to the Twenty Verses on the Vows. Saṃvaraviṃśakavṛtti. Sdom pa nyi shu pa'i 'grel pa.* Toh 4082, sems tsam, *hi* 167a6–184b3.
Śāntideva. *Compendium of Trainings. Śikṣāsamuccaya. Bslab pa kun las btus pa.* Toh 3940, dbu ma, *khi* 3a2–194b5. P 5536, dbu ma, *ki,* 3a8–225b3.
———. *Compendium of Trainings in Stanzas. Śikṣāsamuccayakārikā. Bslab pa kun las btus pa'i tshig le'ur byas pa.* Toh 3939, dbu ma, *khi* 1a1–3a2.
———. *Guide to the Bodhisattva Way of Life. Bodhisattvacaryāvatāra. Byang chub sems dpa'i spyod pa la 'jug pa.* Toh 3871, dub ma, *la* 1b1–40a7. P 5272, dbu ma, *la* 1a1–42b.
———. *Ritual for Reciting the Hundred-Syllable Mantra and for Confessing Faults. Tathāgatahṛdayapāpadeśanāvidhi. De bzhin gshegs pa'i snying po'i yi ge brgya pa'i*

srung ba dang sdig pa bshag pa'i cho ga. Toh 3941, dbu ma, *khi 194b5–195b2,* and Toh 4525, jo bo'i chos chung *gi*, 135b3–136a7. P 5337, dbu ma, *ki* 225b3–226b1, and P 5438, dbu ma, *gi* 162a7–163a4.

Saraha. *Song of an Inexhaustible Treasure of Instruction. Dohakoṣopadeśagīti. Mi zad pa'i gter mdzod man ngag gi glu zhes bya ba.* Toh 2264, rgyud, *zhi* 28b6–33b4. P 3111, rgyud 'grel, tsi 34a2–39b5.

———. *Treasury of Spiritual Songs. Dohakoṣagīti. Do ha mdzod kyi glu.* Toh 2224, rgyud, *wi* 70b5–77a3. P 3068, rgyud 'grel, *mi* 74b6–81b8.

Sthiramati. *Detailed Exposition of the Ornament of Mahayana Sutras. Sūtrālaṃkāra-vṛttibhāṣya. Mdo sde'i rgyan gyi 'grel bshad.* Toh 4034, sems tsam, *mi* 1a1–*tsi* 266a7. P 5531 sems tsam, *mi* 1a1–*tsi* 308a8.

Sunayaśrī. *Eight Verses on the Vows of Lay Ordination. Upāsakasamvarāṣṭaka. Dge bsnyen gyi sdom pa brgyad pa.* Toh 4141, 'dul ba, *su* 156b5–157a3. P 5642, 'dul ba'i 'grel pa, *u* 190b4–191a5.

Tillipa (i.e., Tilopa). *Treasury of Dohas. Dohakoṣa. Do ha mdzod.* Toh 2281, rgyud, *zhi* 136a4–137b6.

Udbhaṭasiddhasvāmin. *Praise of the Excellence* [*of the Buddha*]. *Viśeṣastava. Khyad par du 'phags pa'i bstod pa.* Toh 1109, bstod tshogs, *ka* 1a1–4b7. P 2001, bstod tshogs, *ka* 1b1–5b3.

Vāgīśvarakīrti. *Advice on Cheating Death. Mṛtyuvañcanopadeśa. 'Chi ba bslu ba'i man ngag.* Toh 1748, rgyud, *sha* 118b7–133b3.

Vasubandhu. *Commentary on the Ornament of Mahayana Sutras. Sūtrālaṃkārabhāṣya. Mdo sde'i rgyan gyi bshad pa.* Toh 4026, sems tsam, *phi* 129b1–260a7. P 5527 sems tsam, *phi* 135b7–287a8.

———. *Commentary on the Treasury of Higher Knowledge. Abhidharmakośabhāṣya. Chos mngon pa'i mdzod kyi bshad pa.* Toh 4090, mngon pa, *ku* 26b1–*khu* 95a7. P 5591, mngon pa'i bstan bcos, *gu* 27b6–*ngu* 109a8.

———. *Discourse Explaining Seven Qualities. Saptaguṇaparivarṇanakathā. Yon tan bdun yongs su brjod pa'i gtam.* Toh 4163, 4163, spring yig, *ge* 168a4–169a1. P 5663, sprin yig, *nge* 202a6–203a5.

———. *A Discussion of Accumulation. Sambhāraparikathā. Tshogs kyi gtam.* Toh 4166, spring yig, *ge* 173b1–175a4.

———. *Treasury of Higher Knowledge. Abhidharmakośa. Chos mngon pa'i mdzod kyi tshig le'ur byas pa.* Toh 4089, mngon pa, *ku* 1a1–25a7. P 5590, mngon pa'i bstan bcos, *gu 1–27b6.*

———. *Twenty Stanzas. Viṃśatikākārikā. Nyi shu pa'i tshig le'ur byas pa.* Toh 4056, sems tsam, *shi* 3a4–4a2.

Vimalamitra. *Meditating on Nonthought, Penetrating Simultaneity. Sakṛtprāveśika-nirvikalpabhāvanārtha. Cig car 'jug pa rnam par mi rtog pa'i bsgom don.* Toh 3910, dbu ma, *ki* 6b1–13b4.

Yaśomitra. *Commentary on the Treasury of Higher Knowledge. Abhidharmakośaṭīkā. Chos mngon pa'i mdzod kyi 'grel bshad.* Toh 4092, mngon pa, *gu* 1b1–*ngu* 333a7.

Tibetan Works

Akya Yongzin Yangchen Gawai Lodrö (A kya Yongs 'dzin Dbyangs can dga' ba'i blo gros, 1740–1827). *Explanation of Some Difficult Words in the Blue Compendium: The Dispeller of Darkness. Be'u bum sngon po'i ming brda go dka' ba 'ga' zhig bshad pa som nyi'i mun sel.* Contained in *Gangs can rig brgya'i sgo 'byed lde mig (deb bcu drug pa): Bka' gdams be'u bum sngon po'i rtsa 'grel*, 464–86. Beijing: Mi rigs dpe skrun khang, 1991.

———. *Explanation of Difficult Words in the Dharma Exemplified: A Heap of Jewels: A Feast for the Mind. Dpe chos rin chen spungs pa'i brda bkrol don gnyer yid kyi dga' ston.* Contained in *Gangs can rig brgya'i sgo 'byed lde mig (deb bcu drug pa): Bka' gdams be'u bum sngon po'i rtsa 'grel*, 502–20. Beijing: Mi rigs dpe skrun khang, 1991.

Chegom Sherap Dorjé (Lce sgom Shes rab rdo rje, 1124/25–1204/05). *Extensive Commentary on the Dharma Exemplified: A Heap of Jewels. Dpe chos rin chen spungs pa'i 'bum 'grel.* At least four blockprint editions and two manuscripts of this work are extant. It is available in the following modern editions: (1) the 'Bras spungs edition initiated by the Seventh Dalai Lama, reproduced in (a) *Gangs can rig brgya'i sgo 'byed lde mig (deb bcu bdun pa): Dpe chos dang dpe chos rin chen spungs pa* (Beijing: Mi rigs dpe skrun khang, 1991), and (b) *Dpe chos rin chen spungs pa*, ed. Mongolian Lama Guru Deva (Sarnath, Varanasi: Pleasure of Elegant Sayings Press, 1965); (2) *Dpe chos rin chen spungs pa'i 'bum 'grel: Detailed Explanation of the Examples Used in Po-to-ba Rin-chen-gsal's Dpe chos rtsa ba and Dge-bśes Wa-brag-dkar-ba's Dpe chos rin chen spuṅs pa—Popular Presentation of the Principles of the Bka'-gdams-pa Approach to Lamaist Practice by Lce Sgom-pa śes-rab-rdo-rje*, reproduced from a rare manuscript from Zanskar in Ladakh (Jammu & Kashmir) by Topden Tshering (Delhi, 1975); and (3) *Dpe chos rin chen spungs pa'i 'bum 'grel: Detailed Explanation of the Examples (dpe) Used in Po to ba Rin chen gsal's Dpe chos rtsa ba and Dge-bshes Wa brag dkar ba's Dpe chos rin chen spungs pa—Popular Presentation of the Principles of the Bka' gdams pa Approach to Lamaist Practice*, by Lce Sgom pa shes rab rdo rje, reproduced from a manuscript from Limi Watse Rinchenling (Bir, H.P.: D. Tsondu Senghe, 1985).

Dölpa Sherap Gyatso (Dol pa Shes rab rgya mtsho, 1059–1131). *The Blue Compendium. Be'u bum sngon po.* The root verses of are available in the following editions: (1) the root verses of the *Be'u bum sngon po* from the Dga' ldan chos 'khor gling woodblocks, reprinted in *Gangs can rig brgya'i sgo 'byed lde mig (deb bcu drug pa): Bka' gdams kyi man ngag be'u bum sngon po'i rtsa 'grel* (Beijing: Mi rigs dpe skrun khang, 1991), pp. 1–46; (2) the root verses with the commentary by Lha Drigangpa, reproduced in *Bka' gdams kyi man ngag be'u bum sngon po'i 'grel pa: A Commentary on Dge-bshes Dol-pa Shes-rab-rgya-mtsho's Be'u bum sngon po by Lha 'Bri sgang pa*, from a print from the Tashi Lhunpo blocks from the library of the Kusho of Gangon by D. Tsondu Senghe (Bir, H.P., 1976), 241 folios; and (3) the ITC critical edition based on the two editions mentioned above.

Gampopa Sönam Rinchen (Sgam po pa Bsod nams rin chen, a.k.a. Dakpo Lhajé, Dwags po Lha rje, 1079–1153). *Ornament of Precious Liberation. Dam chos yid bzhin nor bu thar pa rin po che'i rgyan.* Rumtek xylographic edition, established by H. H. the Sixteenth Gyalwang Karmapa after the Dergé edition.

Lha Drigangpa (Lha 'Bri sgang pa, fl. twelfth century). *Be'u bum sngon po'i 'grel pa.* This commentary is available in (1) a 1976 edition, *Bka' gdams kyi man ṅag be'u bum sṅon po'i 'grel pa. A Commentary on Dge-bśes Dol-pa Śes-rab-rgya-mtsho's Be'u bum sṅon po by Lha 'Bri-sgaṅ-pa*, reproduced from a print from the Tashi Lhunpo blocks from the library of the Kusho of Gangon by D. Tsondu Senghe (Bir, H.P., 1976); and (2) a 1991 modern edition, cited most frequently in Ulrike Roesler's translation here of *The Blue Compendium*: the Drepung edition initiated by the Seventh Dalai Lama, modern typeset edition in *Gangs can rig brgya'i sgo 'byed lde mig (deb bcu drug pa):*

Bka' gdams be'u bum sngon po'i rtsa 'grel (Beijing: Mi rigs dpe skrun khang, 1991), pp. 47–463. (Abbreviated Lha Drigangpa.)

Ngok Loden Sherap (Rngog Blo ldan shes rab, 1059–1109). *A Letter Entitled "Droplets of Nectar." Spring yig bdud rtsi'i thigs pa.* In *Bka' gdams gsung 'bum phyogs bsgrigs*, vol. 1. Chengdu: Sichuan Publishing House, 2006.

Potowa Rinchen Sal (Po to ba Rin chen gsal, 1027/31–1105). *Dharma Exemplified. Dpe chos.* See Chegom Sherap Dorjé.

Sapaṇ (short for Sakya Paṇḍita Kunga Gyaltsen, Sa skya Paṇḍita Kun dga' rgyal mtshan, 1182–1251). *Analysis of Established Tenets. Grub pa'i mtha'i dbye ba.* Not extant.

———. *Ḷiturgy of Ten Verses. Chos spyod bcu pa.* Not included in the Dergé edition of Sa paṇ's Collected Works, but it survives. See D. Jackson, "Fragments of a Golden Manuscript of Sa-skya Paṇḍita's Works," p. 24, no. 23.

———. *Ritual for Generating the Thought of Awakening. Dbu ma lugs kyi sems bskyed kyi cho ga.* Collected Works, no. 21. SKB, vol. 5, 264.3.1–273.2.6 (*da* 221a–239a).

———. *Treasure of Reasoning. Rigs pa'i gter* (short for *Tshad ma rigs pa'i gter*). SKB, vol. 5, 155.1.1–167.1.6 (*da* 1a–25a.6).

Shang Tsalpa Tsöndrü Drak (Zhang Tshal pa Brtson 'grus grags). *The Ultimate Supreme Path. Lam zab mthar thug.* In *Mnyam med bka' brgyud lugs kyi phyag rgya chen po dang 'brel ba'i chos skor. Bod kyi gtsug lag gces btus 5.* New Delhi: Institute of Tibetan Classics, 2008.

Shardong Rinpoché, Jé (Rje Shar gdong Rin po che, 1922–2001). *Pure Crystal Mirror: An Explanation on the Root Text and Commentary of the Blue Compendium. Be'u bum sngon po'i rtsa 'grel gyi bshad pa dwangs shel me long. Rje shar gdong blo bzang bshad sgrub rgya mtsho'i gsung 'bum*, part 4. Xining: Mtsho sngon mi rigs dpe skrun khang, 1999. (Abbreviated Shardong.)

Sönam Tsemo (Bsod nams rtse mo, 1142–82). *The Practice for Beginners. Las dang po pa'i bya ba.* In idem, *Dang po'i las can gyi bya ba'i rim pa dang lam rim bgrod tshul.* SKB, vol. 2, 143.2.1–147.2.1 (*ga* 288a–296a).

Works Consulted by the Translators

Akhu Chin Sherap Gyatso (A khu chin Shes rab rgya mtsho, 1803–75). *Materials for a History of Tibetan Literature, Part 3. Dpe rgyun dkon pa 'ga' zhig gi tho yig.* Śata-Piṭaka Series, vol. 30, 503–601. New Delhi: International Academy of Indian Culture, 1963. Reprinted Kyoto: Rinsen, 1981. (Abbreviated MHTL.)

Almogi, Olga. *Rong-zom-pa's Discourses on Buddhology: A Study of Various Conceptions of Buddhahood with Special Reference to the Controversy Surrounding the Existence of Gnosis (jnana: ye shes) as Presented by the Eleventh-Century Tibetan Scholar Rong-zom Chos-kyi-bzang-po.* Tokyo: The International Institute for Buddhist Studies, 2009.

Bodong Paṇchen Choklé Namgyal, alias Sangwé Jin (Bo dong Paṇ chen Phyogs las rnam rgyal, alias Gsang ba'i byin, 1375–1451). *A Detailed Exposition of the Stages of the Path of the Three Personality Types Arranged as Practical Instructions. Skyes bu gsum gyi lam rim rgyas pa khrid du sbyar ba.* New Delhi: Ngawang Topgyal, 1977.

Boin-Webb, Sara, trans. *Abhidharmasamuccaya: The Compendium of the Higher Teaching (Philosophy) by Asaṅga.* English translation from Walpola Rahula's 1971 French translation. Fremont, CA: Asian Humanities Press, 2001.

Bosson, James E., ed. and trans. *A Treasury of Aphoristic Jewels: The Subhāṣitaratnanidhi of Sa Skya Paṇḍita in Tibetan and Mongolian.* Indiana University Publications, Uralic and Altaic Series 92. Bloomington: Indiana University Press, 1969.

Chang, Garma C. C. *The Hundred Thousand Songs of Milarepa.* Boston: Shambhala, 1999.

Chim Jampaiyang (Mchims 'Jam pa'i dbyangs, 14th century). *Detailed Abhidharma Commentary. Mdzod 'grel mngon pa'i rgyan (Chos mngon pa'i mdzod kyi tshig le'ur byas pa'i 'grel pa mngon pa'i rgyan).* Bod kyi gtsug lag gces btus 23. New Delhi: Institute of Tibetan Classics, 2009.

———. *Small Treasury. Mdzod chung* (cover title, short for *A Concise Exposition of the Abhidharmakosha of Ācārya Vasubandhu, Chos mngon pa gsal byed legs par bshad pa'i rgya mtsho*). Sarnath, U.P.: Sakya Students' Union, 1978. "Reproduced from a set of prints from the 19th century xylographic redaction prepared at the behest of 'Jam dbyangs Mkhyen brtse'i dbang po."

Cleary, Thomas. *Flower Ornament Scripture: A Translation of the Avatamsaka Sutra.* Boston: Shambhala Publications, 1993.

Conze, Edward, trans. *The Perfection of Wisdom in Eight Thousand Lines and Its Verse Summary.* Bolinas, Calif.: Four Seasons Foundation, 1975.

Covill, Linda, trans. *Handsome Nanda by Ashvaghosha.* New York: New York University Press, 2007.

Cüppers, Christoph, ed. *The IXth Chapter of the Samādhirājasūtra: A Text-Critical Contribution to the Study of the Mahāyāna Sūtras.* Alt- und Neu-Indische Studien 41. Wiesbaden: Franz Steiner Verlag, 1990.

Davenport, John T., trans. *Ordinary Wisdom: Sakya Pandita's Treasury of Good Advice.* Boston: Wisdom Publications, 2000.

Davidson, Ronald M. "Atiśa's A Lamp for the Path to Awakening." In *Buddhism in Practice*, edited by Donald S. Lopez, Jr., 290–301. Princeton, NJ: Princeton University Press, 1995.

———. *Tibetan Renaissance: Tantric Buddhism in the Rebirth of Tibetan Culture.* New York: Columbia University Press, 2005.

Deleanu, Florin. *The Chapter on the Mundane Path (Laukikamārga) in the Śrāvakabhūmi, a Trilingual Edition (Sanskrit, Tibetan, Chinese), Annotated Translation, and Introductory Study.* Tokyo: The International Institute for Buddhist Studies, 2006.

Deshung Rinpoche, Kunga Tenpai Nyima. *The Three Levels of Spiritual Perception: An Oral Commentary on the Three Visions (Snang gsum) of Ngorchen Konchog Lhundrub.* Translated by Jared Rhoton. Boston: Wisdom, 2nd ed., 2003.

Döndrup Gyaltsen (Don grub rgyal mtshan), ed. *Treasury of Gems: Selected Anthology of the Well-Uttered Insights of the Teachings of the Precious Kadam Tradition. Legs par bshad pa bka' gdams rin po che'i gsung gi gces btus nor bu'i bang mdzod.* Bir, India: D. Tsondu Senghe, 1985.

Drigung Chöjé Jikten Gönpo Rinchen Pal ('Bri gung Chos rje 'Jig rten mgon po Rin chen dpal). *Collected Writings.* 5 vols. New Delhi: Khangsar Tulku, 1969–70.

Drolungpa Lodrö Jungné (Gro lung pa Blo gros 'byung gnas, fl. late eleventh to early twelfth century). *Great Tenrim. Bstan rim chen mo* (short for *Great Treatise on the*

Stages of the Doctrine. Bde bar gshegs pa'i bstan pa rin po che la 'jug pa'i lam gyi rim pa rnam par bshad pa). Xylograph, Bihar Research Society, Patna.

Dungkar Losang Trinlé (Dung dkar Blo bzang 'phrin las). *Great Tibetan Dictionary. Dung dkar tshig mdzod chen mo. Mkhas dbang dung dkar blo bzang 'prin las mchig gis mdzad pa'i bod rig pa'i tshig mdzod chen mo*. Xining: Grung go'i bod rig pa dpe skrun khang, 2002.

Eckel, Malcom David. *Jñānagarbha's Commentary on the Distinction Between the Two Truths*. Albany: State University of New York Press, 1987.

Eda, Akimichi. "Freigebigkeit in Bezug auf Frauen?!" In *Indica et Tibetica: Festschrift für Michael Hahn, Zum 65. Geburtstag von Freunden und Schülern überreicht*, edited by Konrad Klaus and Jens-Uwe Hartmann, 139–44. Wiener Studien zur Tibetologie und Buddhismuskunde 66. Vienna: Arbeitskreis für tibetische und buddhistische Studien, 2007.

Edgerton, Franklin, trans. *Pañcatantra*. London: George Allen and Unwin, 1965.

Eimer, Helmut. *Berichte über das Leben des Atiśa (Dīpaṃkaraśrījñāna): Eine Untersuchung der Quellen*. Wiesbaden: Harrassowitz, 1977.

———. "Der Untergang der Stadt Roruka: Eine Episode des Udrāyaṇāvadāna in der Fassung des Be'u bum sṅon po'i 'grel pa." In *Bauddhavidyāsudhākaraḥ: Studies in Honour of Heinz Bechert on the Occasion of His 65th Birthday*, edited by Petra Kieffer-Pülz and Jens-Uwe Hartmann, 71–80. Indica et Tibetica 30. Swisttal-Odendorf, 1997.

———. "Die Sunakṣatra-Episode im Kommentar zum Be'u bum sṅon po." In *Hinduismus und Buddhismus*, edited by Harry Falk, 101–11. Festschrift für Ulrich Schneider. Freiburg, 1987.

———. "Eine frühe Quelle zur literarischen Tradition über die 'Debatte von Bsam yas.'" In *Tibetan History and Language: Studies Dedicated to Uray Géza on His Seventieth Birthday*, edited by Ernst Steinkellner, 163–72. Wiener Studien zur Tibetologie und Buddhismuskunde 26. Vienna: Arbeitskreis für tibetische und buddhistische Studien, 1991.

———. *Rnam thar rgyas pa. Materialien zu einer Biographie des Atiśa (Dīpaṃkaraśrījñāna)*, 2 vols. Asiatische Forschungen 67. Wiesbaden: Otto Harrassowitz, 1979.

Eimer, Helmut, and Pema Tsering. "Legs-skar/Skar-bzang/Sunakṣatra." In *The Buddhist Forum III*, edited by Tadeusz Skorupski and Ulrich Pagel, 1–10. London: SOAS, University of London, 1994.

Fushimi, Hidetoshi. "The Perfection of Discriminative Understanding Chapter from the 'Elucidation of the Sage's Intention': Sa-skya Paṇḍita on the Theory and Practice of the Bodhisattva's Path." Unpublished PhD dissertation, University of Hamburg, 2000.

Gampopa Sönam Rinchen (Sgam po pa Bsod nams rin chen, 1079–1153). *Ornament of Liberation. Thar rgyan* (short for *Dam chos yid bzhin gyi nor bu thar pa rin po che'i rgyan zhes bya ba theg pa chen po'i lam gyi bshad pa*). Thimphu, 1985.

Gö Lotsāwa Shönu Pal ('Gos Lo tsā ba Gzhon nu dpal, 1392–1481). *The Blue Annals. Deb ther sngon po*. Śata-Piṭaka Series 212. New Delhi: International Academy of Indian Culture, 1974. For an English translation, see Roerich, *The Blue Annals*.

Gombrich, Richard F. *How Buddhism Began: The Conditioned Genesis of the Early Teachings*. New Delhi: Munishiram Manoharlal Publishers, 2002.

Gorampa Sönam Sengé (Go rams pa Bsod nams seng ge, 1429–89). *A Blossoming Lotus: Replies to Questions. Dris lan pad mo bzhad pa.* SKB, vol. 14, 321.2–334.2 (*tha* 28a–72a). Tokyo: Tōyō Bunko, 1969.

———. *Detailed Commentary on Differentiation of the Three Vows. Sdom gsum rnam bshad.* (*Clarifying the Intended Meaning of the Victor's Scriptures: A Detailed Commentary on Clear Differentiation of the Three Systems of Vows. Sdom pa gsum gyi rab tu dbye ba'i rnam bshad rgyal ba'i gsung rab kyi dgongs pa gsal ba*). SKB, vol. 14, 119.1.1–199.3.6 (*ta* 1a–161a).

———. *Dispelling Errors about the Three Vows. Sdom gsum 'khrul spong.* (*Dispelling Errors about the Three Vows: A Reply to the Questions and Controversy Surrounding [Sapaṇ's] Treatise on the Three Systems of Vows. Sdom pa gsum gyi bstan bcos la dris shing rtsod pa'i lan sdom gsum 'phrul spong.*). SKB, vol. 14, 240.4.1–273.2.6 (*ta* 246a–311a).

Guenther, Herbert V., trans. *The Jewel Ornament of Liberation* by Gampopa. London: Rider, 1959. Reprinted Boulder: Shambhala, 1971.

Gyaltsen, Khenpo Konchog, trans. *The Jewel Ornament of Liberation: The Wish-Fulfilling Gem of the Noble Teachings by Gampopa.* Edited by Ani K. Trinlay Chödron. Ithaca: Snow Lion, 1998.

Hahn, Michael, ed. *Nāgārjuna's Ratnāvalī, vol. 1: The Basic Texts (Sanskrit, Tibetan, Chinese).* Indica et Tibetica 1. Bonn: Indica et Tibetica Verlag, 1982.

Hodge, Stephen, trans. *The Mahā-Vairocana-Abhisaṃbodhi Tantra with Buddhaguhya's Commentary.* London: RoutledgeCurzon, 2003.

Holmes, Ken. *Maitreya on Buddha Nature.* A translation from Tibetan of Maitreyanath's *Mahāyānottaratantra śāstra* with edited version of contemporary commentary by Khenchen Thrangu Rinpoche. Forres, Scotland: Altea Publishing, 1999.

Holmes, Ken, and Katia Holmes. *Gems of Dharma, Jewels of Freedom.* A translation of Gampopa's *Ornament of Precious Liberation.* Forres, Scotland: Altea Publishing, 1995.

Hopkins, Jeffrey, trans. *The Precious Garland and The Song of the Four Mindfulnesses* by Nāgārjuna and the Seventh Dalai Lama. Delhi: Vikas Publishing House, 1975.

Jackson, David P. "Birds in the Egg and Newborn Lion Cubs: Metaphors for the Potentialities and Limitations of 'All-at-once' Enlightenment." In *Tibetan Studies, Proceedings of the Fifth Seminar of the International Association of Tibetan Studies, Narita,* vol. 1, 95–114. Narita: Naritasan Shinshoji, 1992.

———. "The *bsTan rim* (Stages of the Doctrine) and Similar Graded Expositions of the Bodhisattva's Path." In *Tibetan Literature: Studies in Genre,* edited by José Cabezón and Roger R. Jackson, 229–43. Ithaca, NY: Snow Lion, 1996.

———. *Enlightenment by a Single Means: Tibetan Controversies on the "Self-Sufficient White Remedy" (Dkar po chig thub).* Beiträge zur Kultur- und Geistesgeschichte Asiens 12. Vienna: Verlag der Österreichischen Akademie der Wissenschaften, 1994.

———. *The Entrance Gate for the Wise (Section III): Sa-skya Paṇḍita on Indian and Tibetan Traditions of Pramāṇa and Philosophical Debate.* Wiener Studien zur Tibetologie und Buddhismuskunde 17, 2 parts. Vienna: Arbeitskreis für Tibetische und Buddhistische Studien, Universität Wien, 1987.

———. "Fragments of a Golden Manuscript of Sa-skya Paṇḍita's Works." In Shakapba Memorial Issue of *The Tibet Journal,* edited by Hugh E. Richardson 16.1 (1991): 3–33.

———. *The "Miscellaneous Series" of Tibetan Texts in the Bihar Research Society, Patna: A Handlist*. Tibetan and Indo-Tibetan Studies 2. Stuttgart: Franz Steiner Verlag, 1989.

———. "Sa-skya Paṇḍita the 'Polemicist': Ancient Debates and Modern Interpretations." *Journal of the International Association of Buddhist Studies* 13.2 (1990): 17–116.

———. "Several Works of Unusual Provenance Ascribed to Sa skya Paṇḍita." In *Tibetan History and Language: Studies Dedicated to Uray Geza on His Seventieth Birthday*, edited by Ernst Steinkellner. Wiener Studien zur Tibetologie und Buddhismuskunde 26, 233–54. Vienna: Arbeitskreis für Tibetische und Buddhistische Studien, Universität Wien, 1991.

———. "Two Grub mtha' Treatises of Sa-skya Paṇḍita: One Lost and One Forged." *The Tibet Journal* 10.1 (1985): 3–13.

Jamgön Kongtrul Lodrö Tayé. *Buddhist Ethics*, translated by International Translation Committee of V. V. Kalu Rinpoché. A translation of the fifth part of Jamgön Kongtrul's *Treasury of Knowledge* (*Shes bya mdzod*). Ithaca, NY: Snow Lion, 1998.

———. *Treasury of Knowledge: Myriad Worlds*, translated by International Translation Committee of V. V. Kalu Rinpoché. A translation of the first part of Jamgön Kongtrul's *Treasury of Knowledge* (*Shes bya mdzod*). Ithaca, NY: Snow Lion, 2003.

Jinpa, Thupten. "Introduction" (in Tibetan). In *Bstan pa la'jug pa'i rim pa ston pa'i gzhung gces btus*, by Dge bshes Dol pa, Sgam po pa bsod nams rin chen, and Sa pan kun dga' rgyal mtsan. Bod kyi gtsug lag gces btus 10. Sarnath: Institute of Tibetan Classics, 2009. (Volume abbreviated ITC.)

———, trans. and ed. *The Book of Kadam: The Core Texts*. Attributed to Atiśa and Dromtönpa. The Library of Tibetan Classics 2. Boston: Wisdom, 2008.

———, trans. and ed. *Mind Training: The Great Collection*. Compiled by Shönu Gyalchok and Könchok Gyaltsen. The Library of Tibetan Classics 1. Boston: Wisdom, 2006.

Kapstein, Matthew, and Gyurme Dorje, trans. *The Nyingma School of Tibetan Buddhism: Its Fundamentals and History* by Dudjom Rinpoche Jikdrel Yeshe Dorje. 2 vols. Boston: Wisdom Publications, 1991.

Karma Trinlepa (Karma phrin las pa). *The Songs of Esoteric Practice (mgur) and Replies to Doctrinal Questions (dris lan)*. New Delhi: Ngawang Tobgay, 1975.

Khetsun Sangpo (Mkhas btsun bzang po). *Biographical Dictionary of Tibet and Tibetan Buddhism*. 12 vols. Dharamsala: Library of Tibetan Works and Archives, 1973–79.

Khoroche, Peter. *Once the Buddha Was a Monkey: Ārya Śūra's Jātakamāla*. Chicago: University of Chicago Press, 1989.

Könchok Lhundrup, Ngorchen (Dkon mchog lhun grub, Ngor chen, 1447–1557). *Beautiful Ornament of the Three Visions. Snang gsum mdzes rgyan. (An Ornament Beautifying the Three Visions: A Discourse on the Path's Preliminary Practices that Extensively Explains the Path with the Result Teachings According to Their Main Source Text. Lam 'bras bu dang bcas pa'i gdams ngag gi gzhung shing rgyas pa gzhung ji lta ba bzhin bkri ba'i lam gyi sngon 'gro'i khrid yig snang gsum mdzes par byed pa'i rgyan). Lam 'bras tshogs bshad by Dkon-mchog-lhun-grub*, vol. 4, 75–270. Dehra Dun (U.P.): Sakya Centre, 1985 (Sde dge blocks). *Sa skya Lam 'bras Literature Series* 24 (= Tshogs bshad skor, vol. 4), 75–269. Digital scans exist: TBRC W28765.

Kramer, Jowita. *Kategorien der Wirklichkeit im frühen Yogācāra: Der Fünf-vastu-Abschnitt in der Viniścayasaṃgrahaṇī der Yogācārabhūmi.* Contributions to Tibetan Studies 4. Wiesbaden: Dr. Ludwig Reichert Verlag, 2005.

———. *A Noble Monk from Mustang: Life and Works of Glo-bo mKhan-chen (1456–1532).* Vienna: Arbeitskreis für tibetische und buddhistische Studien, Universität Wien, 2008.

Kramer, Ralf. *The Great Tibetan Translator: Life and Works of rNgog Blo ldan shes rab (1059–1109).* Munich: Indus Verlag, 2007.

Lamotte, E. *Le Traite de la Grande Vertu de Sagesse de Nāgārjuna (Mahāprajñāpāramitāśāstra).* Five volumes (1 and 2 [1949], 3 [1970], 4 [1976], and 5 [1980]). Louvain: Institut Orientaliste, 1949–80.

———. *Saṃdhinirmocana Sūtra.* Louvain-Paris, 1935.

Lévi, S., ed. *Asaṅga, Mahāyāna-Sūtrālaṃkāra, expose de la doctrine du Grand Vehicule selon le systeme Yogācāra. Tome I: texte.* Paris: Chamion, 1907.

———, trans. *Asaṅga, Mahāyāna-Sūtrālaṃkāra, expose de la doctrine du Grand Vehicule selon le systeme Yogācāra. Tome II: traduction, introduction, index.* Paris: Chamion, 1911.

Lhalungpa, Lobsang P., trans. *Mahāmudrā—The Moonlight: Quintessence of Mind and Meditation* by Dakpo Tashi Namgyal. Boston: Wisdom, 2006.

Lindtner, C. *Nagarjuniana: Studies in the Writings and Philosophy of Nāgārjuna.* Indiske Studier 4. Copenhagen: Akademisk Forlag, 1982.

Lowo Khenchen Sönam Lhundrup (Glo bo Mkhan chen Bsod nams lhun grub, 1456–1532). *Beautiful Ornament of the Excellent Path: A Teaching Manual for the Primer Clarifying the Sage's Intent. Thub pa'i dgongs pa gsal ba zhes bya ba'i gzhung gi bshad thabs lam bzang mdzes rgyan.* In idem, *Exegesis of the Thub pa'i dgongs pa rab gsal and Tshad ma rigs gter.* Manduwala, India: Pal Ewam Chodan Ngorpa Centre, 1985, vol. 1, 67–77.1 (1a–6a.1). The first of two similar brief works described together by J. Kramer, *A Noble Monk from Mustang,* p. 254, as no. 314.

———. *Biography of Kun dga' dbang phyug. Bla ma'i rnam thar rin chen 'phreng ba.* See J. Kramer, *A Noble Monk from Mustang,* p. 177, no. 88.

———. *Exegesis of the Thub pa'i dgongs pa rab gsal and Tshad ma rigs gter: Two Works by Sa skya Paṇḍi ta Kun dga' rgyal mtshan on the Fundamentals of Buddhist Practice and Logic.* Selected writings of Glo bo mkhan chen Bsod nams lhun grub, vols. 1–2. Manduwala, India: Pal Ewam Chodan Ngorpa Centre, 1985.

———. *Four Works Elucidating the Proper Interpretation of the Sa skya pa Approach to Buddhist Tantra. Rgyud sde spyi yi rnam par bzhag pa'i gsal byed nyi ma'i 'od zer, Mngon par rtogs pa rin po che ljon shing gi gsal byed rin chen sgron me, Spyi rnam brgal lan 'og min gsal byed gong ma'i dgongs rgyan, Sdom pa gsum gyi rab tu dbye ba'i dris lan lung gi tshad ma 'khrul spongs dgongs rgyan.* Selected writings of Glo bo mkhan chen Bsod nams lhun grub, vol. 4. Manduwala, India: Pal Ewam Chodan Ngorpa Centre, 1985.

———. *Ornament to the Intended Meaning of Dispelling Errors: A Reply to the Questions and Controversy Surrounding [Sapaṇ's] Treatise on the Three Systems of Vows, A Scriptural Witness. Sdom pa gsum gyi rab tu dbye ba'i dris lan lung gi tshad ma 'khrul spong dgongs rgyan.* Rgyud sde spyi rnam gsal byed sogs. Manduwala, India: Pal Ewam Chodan Ngorpa Centre, 1985, 209–321 (1a–57a).

———. *Ornament of Mañjuśrī's Intended Meaning: A Teaching Manual for Clarifying the Sage's Intent. Thub pa'i dgongs gsal gyi 'chad thabs 'jam dbyangs dgongs rgyan.* In idem, *Exegesis of the Thub pa'i dgongs pa rab gsal and Tshad ma rigs gter.* Manduwala, India: Pal Ewam Chodan Ngorpa Centre, 1985, vol. 1, 77.1–95 (fols. 6a–15a). The second of two similar brief works described together by J. Kramer, *A Noble Monk from Mustang*, p. 254, as no. 314.

———. *Sutra Exposition. Mdo'i rnam bshad. (Precious Treasury: An Exposition of the Sutra Quotations Relevant to Clarifying the Sage's Intent. Thub pa'i dgongs pa gsal ba'i bstan bcos kyi mdo rnam par bshad pa rin po che'i gter).* In idem, *Exegesis of the Thub pa'i dgongs pa rab gsal and Tshad ma rigs gter.* Manduwala, India: Pal Ewam Chodan Ngorpa Centre, 1985, vol. 1, 97–251 (1a–78a). *See* also J. Kramer, *A Noble Monk from Mustang, p.* 256, no. 315.

Malalasekera, G. P. *Dictionary of Pāli Proper Names.* London: Luzac and Co., 1960.

Martön Chökyi Gyalpo (Dmar ston Chos kyi rgyal po). *Commentary on [Sapaṇ's] "Jewel Treasure of Aphorisms." Legs par bshad pa rin po che'i gter zhes bya ba'i 'grel pa.* Dharamsala: Tibetan Cultural Printing Press, 1982.

Mimaki, K., trans. *Blo gsal grub mtha': Chapitres IX (Vaibhāṣika) et XI (Yogācāra) édité, et Chapitre XII (Mādhyamika) édité et traduit.* Kyoto: Zinbun Kagaku Kenkyusyo, Université de Kyoto, 1982. (An edition and translation of three chapters of Üpa Losal's treatise on philosophical tenets.)

Monier-Williams, Monier, et al. *A Sanskrit-English Dictionary.* Oxford: Clarendon Press, 1899. Reprinted Oxford, 1976.

Nagao, G. M. "The Silence of the Buddha and Its Madhyamic Interpretation." *Studies in Indology and Buddhology.* Kyoto: Hozokan, 1955.

Ñāṇamoli, Bhikkhu, and Bhikkhu Bodhi, trans. *The Middle Length Discourses of the Buddha: A New Translation of the Majjhima Nikāya.* Boston: Wisdom, 1995.

Nārada Thera. 1970. *A Manual of Abhidhamma: Abhidhammattha Sangaha.* Colombo, 1956. Reprinted Rangoon: Buddha Sāsana Council, 1970.

Ngawang Chödrak (Ngag dbang chos grags). *Setting Exquisite Gems in the Jewelry of Judicious Scholars: A Detailed Discussion Differentiating the Tenets of Earlier and Later Scholars of Tibet, Together with Exhaustive Doctrinal Considerations. Bod kyi mkhas pa snga phyi dag gi grub mtha'i shan 'byed mtha' dpyod dang bcas pa'i 'bel ba'i gtam skyes dpyod ldan mkhas pa'i lus rgyan rin chen mdzes pa'i phra tshom bkod pa.* Thimphu: Kunsang Topgyal and Mani Dorje, 1979.

Ngulchu Thokmé Sangpo (Dngul chu Thogs med bzang po). *Precious Garland: A Detailed Commentary on the Mahāyānasūtrālaṃkāra. Theg pa chen po mdo sde'i rgyan gyi 'grel pa rin po che'i phreng ba.* Gangtok: Gonpo Tsetan, 1979.

Nyawön Kunga Pal (Nya dbon Kun dga' dpal, 1285–1379). *Dispelling Mental Darkness: An Abhisamayālaṃkāra Commentary. Mngon rtogs rgyan gyi bshad sbyar yid kyi mun sel*, 2 vols. Labrang: Bla brang bkra shis 'khyil, 2000. TBRC W14076.

Pāsādika, Bhikkhu. "The Indian Origins of the Lam-rim of Central Asia." *The Tibet Journal* 13.1 (1988): 3–11.

Patrul Rinpoche (1808–87). *The Words of My Perfect Teacher.* Translated by the Padmakara Translation Group. The Sacred Literature Series. Boston: Shambhala, 2nd rev. ed, 1998.

——— [Pal-trül O-gyen Jig-me Ch'ö-kyi Wang-po Rin-po-ch'e]. *Kun-zang La-may Zhal-lung: The Oral Instruction of Kun-zang La-ma on the Preliminary Practices of Dzog-ch'en Long-ch'en Nying-tig.* Translated and edited by Sonam T. Kazi. Upper Montclair, NJ: Diamond-Lotus Publishing, 2 vols., 1989, 1993.

Phakmodrupa Dorjé Gyalpo (Phag mo gru pa Rdo rje rgyal po, 1110–70). *How to Enter into the Buddha's Doctrine by Stages. Sangs rgyas kyi bstan pa la rim gyis 'jug pa'i tshul.* Bir: Zogyam and Pema Lodoe, 1977.

Rahula, Walpola, trans. *Le Compendium de la super-doctrine (philosophie) (Abhidharma-samuccaya) d'Asaṅga.* Publications de l'École Française d'Extrème-Orient 78. Paris: École Française d'Extrème-Orient, 1971. For an English translation of Rahula's French translation, see Boin-Webb, *Abhidharmasamuccaya.*

Rhoton, Jared Douglas. "A Study of the Sdom gsum of Sa-paṇ." Ph.D. dissertation, Columbia University, New York, 1985.

———, trans. *A Clear Differentiation of the Three Codes by Sakya Pandita Kunga Gyal-tshen.* Albany: State University of New York Press, 2002.

Rigzin, Tsepak. *Tibetan-English Dictionary of Buddhist Terminology.* Revised and enlarged edition. Dharamsala: Library of Tibetan Works and Archives, 1993.

Roerich, George N. *The Blue Annals.* Dehli: Motilal Banarsidass, 1976.

Roesler, Ulrike. *Frühe Quellen zum buddhistischen Stufenweg in Tibet: Indische und tibetische Traditionen im dPe chos des Po-to-ba Rin-chen-gsal.* Wiesbaden: Reichert Verlag, 2011.

Roloff, Carola. *Red mda' ba, Buddhist Yogi-Scholar of the Fourteenth Century: The Forgotten Reviver of Madhyamaka Philosophy in Tibet.* Wiesbaden: Dr. Ludwig Reichert Verlag, 2009.

Rotman, Andy, trans. *Divine Stories: Divyāvadāna*, vol. 1. Boston: Wisdom Publications, 2008.

Sakaki, R., ed. *Mahāvyutpatti.* Kyoto: Shingonshu Kyoto Daigaku, 1916. Reprinted Tokyo: Suzuki Research Foundation, 1962. (Sanskrit-Tibetan-Chinese edition.)

Sakya Pandita. *Illuminations: A Guide to Essential Buddhist Practices.* Translated by Geshe Wangyal and Cutillo. Novata, CA: Lotsawa, 1988. (An abridgement and modern adaptation of Sapaṇ's *Clarifying the Sage's Intent.*)

Sakya Paṇḍita Kunga Gyaltsen. *See* Sapaṇ.

Sangyé Tenzin, [Sakya] Khenpo (Sangs rgyas bstan 'dzin, [Sa skya] Mkhan po). *A Gloss Commentary of Sa skya Paṇḍita Kun dga' rgyal mtshan's sDom gsum rab dbye. Sdom pa gsum gyi rab tu dbye ba'i mchan 'grel.* New Delhi: T. G. Dhongthog, 1979. "Reproduced from a xyolographic [sic] print from Shar khum bu, Nepal."

———. *A Treasury Yielding Whatever Excellent Sayings Are Desired. Legs bshad 'dod dgu 'byung ba'i gter mdzod.* Kalimpong: Sakya Khenpo Sangey Tenzin, 1974. (Commentary on Sa paṇ's *Sa skya legs bshad.*) Translated in Davenport, *Ordinary Wisdom.*

Sapaṇ (short for Sakya Paṇḍita Kunga Gyaltsen, Sa skya Paṇḍita Kun dga' rgyal mtshan, 1182–1251). *Autocommentary on the Treasure of Reasoning. Rigs gter rang 'grel* (short for *Tshad ma rigs pa'i gter gyi rang 'grel*). SKB, vol. 5, 167.2.1–264.2.6 (*da* 26a1–220a6).

———. *Clarifying the Sage's Intent. Thub pa'i dgongs gsal* (short for *Thub pa'i dgongs pa rab tu gsal ba,* Skt. title *Munimataprakāśanāmaśāstra*). SKB, vol. 5, 1.1–50.1 (*tha* 1a–99a). (Abbreviated TG.)

———. *Clear Differentiation of the Three Codes. Sdom gsum rab dbye* (short for *Sdom pa gsum gyi rab tu dbye ba*). SKB., vol. 5, 297.1.1–320.4.5 (*na* 1a–48b.5). English translation in Rhoton, *A Clear Differentiation of the Three Codes.*

———. *Entrance Gate for the Wise. Mkhas 'jug* (short for *Mkhas pa rnams 'jug pa'i sgo;).* SKB, vol. 5, 81.1.1–111.3.6 (*tha* 163a–224a).

———. *Jewel Treasure of Aphorisms. Sa skya legs bshad* (short for *Legs par bshad pa rin po che'i gter*). SKB, vol. 5, 50.2.1–61.2.6 (*tha 100a–122b).* Tibetan and Mongolian texts with English translations are given in Bosson, *A Treasury of Aphoristic Jewels.* A translation of the text along with the contemporary commentary by Sangyé Tenzin appears in Davenport, *Ordinary Wisdom.*

———. *A Letter to the Buddhas and Bodhisattvas of the Ten Directions. Phyogs bcu'i sangs rgyas dang byang chub sems pa rnams la zhu ba'i 'phrin yig.* SKB, vol. 5, 323.3–330.3 (*na* 55a–69a). English translation in Rhoton, *A Clear Differentiation of the Three Codes.*

———. *Points of Contemplation on the Infinte Secrets. Snang ba mtha' yas kyi sgom don.* In SKB, vol. 5 (no. 87 in his Collected Works).

———. *Reply to the Questions of the Translator from Chak. Chag lo tsā ba'i zhus lan.* SKB, vol. 5, 409.1.1–414.2.1 (*na* 229b.1–240a.1). English translation in Rhoton, *A Clear Differentiation of the Three Codes.*

———. *Reply to the Questions of the Translator of Lowo. Glo bo lo tsā ba'i zhus lan.* SKB, vol. 5, 414.2.2–415.2.3 (*na* 240a–242a). English translation in Rhoton, *A Clear Differentiation of the Three Codes.*

———. *Ritual for Generating the Thought of Awakening. Dbu ma lugs kyi sems bskyed kyi cho ga.* Collected Works, no. 21. SKB, vol. 5, 264.3.1–273.2.6 (*da* 221a–239a).

———. *Scriptural Sources for Generating the Thought of Awakening. Sems bskyed lung sbyor* (short for *Byang chub kyi mchog tu sems skyed pa'i cho ga'i lung sbyor*). Collected Works, no. 22. SKB, vol. 5, 273.2.6ff. (*da* 239a–).

———. *Treasure of Reasoning. Rigs pa'i gter* (short for *Tshad ma rigs pa'i gter).* SKB, vol. 5, 155.1.1–167.1.6 (*da* 1a–25a.6).

Sasang Mati Paṇchen Lodrö Gyaltsen (Sa bzang Ma ti paṇ chen Blo gros rgyal mtshan, 1294–1376). *Commentary on the Abhidharmasamuccaya. Dam pa'i chos mngon pa kun las btus pa'i 'grel ba shes bya rab gsal snang ba.* 2 vols. Gangtok: Gonpo Tsheten, 1977.

Schmidt, Erik Pema Kunzang, Richard Barron, Jeffrey Hopkins, James Valby, and Ives Waldo. 2003. *Rangjung Yeshe Tibetan-English Dictionary. Kathmandu: Rangjung Yeshe Publications, 2003.*

Schmithausen, Lambert. "Zur Frage, ob ein Bodhisattva unter bestimmten Voraussetzungen in einer neutralen Geisteshaltung (*avyākṛta-citta*) töten darf." In *Indica et Tibetica: Festschrift für Michael Hahn*, edited by Konrad Klaus and Jens-Uwe Hartmann, 423–40. Wiener Studien zur Tibetologie und Buddhismuskunde 66. Vienna, Arbeitskreis für Tibetische und Buddhistische Studien, Universität Wien, 2007.

Seyfort Ruegg, David. *Buddha-nature, Mind and the Problem of Gradualism in a Comparative Perspective. Jordan Lectures, 1987.* London: School of Oriental and African Studies, University of London, 1989.

———. *"Introduction." In* Lamrim Chenmo Translation Committee, *The Great Treatise on the Stages of the Path to Enlightenment.* Vol. 1. Ithaca, NY: Snow Lion, 2000.

———. *La théorie du Tathagatagarbha et du Gotra: Études sur la soteriologie et la gnoseologie du Boudhisme.* Publications de l'École Française d'Extrème-Orient 70. Paris: École Française d'Extrème-Orient, 1969.

———. *The Literature of the Madhyamaka School of Philosophy in India.* A History of Indian Literature, vol. 7, fasc. 1. Wiesbaden: Otto Harrassowitz, 1981.

Shākya Chokden, Serdok Paṇchen (Shākya mchog ldan, Gser mdog Paṇ chen, 1428–1507). *Collected Works (Gsung 'bum) of Gser-mdog Paṇ-chen Shākya-mchog-ldan.* 24 vols. Thimphu: Kunsang Topgyay, 1975.

———. *Golden Scalpel of Elegant Discourse: Bringing Certainty to the Discussions of the Treatise Clear Differentiation of the Three Codes. Sdom pa gsum gyi rab tu dbye ba'i bstan bcos [las brtsam pa'i] 'bel gtam rnam par nges pa legs bshad gser gyi thur ma. Collected Works, vol. 6, 439–648, and vol. 7, 1–229.* Thimphu: Kunsang Topgyay, 1975.

———. *Pleasant Sea of Wondrous Faith: The Saintly Life of the Omniscient Master, Spiritual Teacher [Rongtön] Shākya Gyaltsen. Rje btsun thams cad mkhyen pa bshes gnyen shākya rgyal mtshan gyi rnam thar ngo mtshar dad pa'i rol mtsho.* Collected Works, vol. 16, 299–377. Thimphu: Kunsang Topgyay, 1975.

Shang Dodé Pal (Zhang Mdo sde dpal, fl. thirteenth century). *Commentary on the Stories in Clarifying the Sage's Intent. Thub pa'i dgongs gsal gyi sgrung 'grel. (Moonlight: A Commentary on the Stories in Clarifying the Sage's Intent, the Path of the Ārya Bodhisattvas. Thub pa'i dgongs gsal rgyal sras 'phags pa'i lam gyi sgrung 'grel zla ba'i 'od zer).* Published in Glo bo Mkhan chen Bsod nams lhun grub, *Exegesis of the Thub pa'i dgongs pa rab gsal and Tshad ma rigs gter.* Manduwala, India: Pal Ewam Chodan Ngorpa Centre, 1985, vol. 1 (1a–144a).

Shenga Shenphen Chökyi Ngangwa, Khenpo (Gzhan dga' Gzhan phan chos kyi snang ba, Mkhan po). *Gloss Commentary on the Abhidharmasamuccaya. Chos mngon pa* (short for *Chos mngon pa kun las btus pa zhes bya ba'i mchan 'grel*). New Delhi: 'Dan ma sprul sku, 1976.

Sherburne, Richard, S. J., trans. *A Lamp for the Path and Commentary of Atiśa.* London: George Allen & Unwin, 1983.

———. *The Complete Works of Atiśa, Śrī Dīpaṃkara Jñāna, Jo-bo-rje: The "Lamp for the Path," the "Commentary," together with the newly translated "Twenty-five Key Texts" (Tibetan and English).* New Delhi: Aditya Prakashan, 2000.

Sobisch, Jan-Ulrich. *The Vow Theories in Tibetan Buddhism: A Comparative Study of Major Traditions from the Twelfth Through Nineteenth Centuries.* Wiesbaden: Dr. Ludwig Reichert Verlag, 2002.

Sönam Tsemo, Lobpön (Bsod nams rtse mo, Slob dpon, 1142–82). *Commentary on the Guide to the Bodhisattva Way of Life. Byang chub sems dpa'i spyod pa la 'jug pa'i 'grel pa..* SKB, vol. 2, 457.4.1–515.2.6 (*ca* 220a–335a). (Commentary on Śāntideva's *Bodhisattvacaryāvatāra.*)

———. *The General System of Tantras. Rgyud sde spyi'i rnam gzhag.* SKB, vol. 2, 1.1–36.3 (*ga* 1a–74a). Tokyo: Tōyō Bunko, 1968.

———. *The Sequence of the Beginner's Practice and How to Traverse the Stages of the Path. Dang po'i las can gyi bya ba'i rim pa dang lam rim bgrod tshul.* Collected Works, no. 11. SKB, vol. 2, 143.2.1–147.2.1 (*ga* 288a–296a).

Sopa, Geshe Lhundub, et al. *Steps on the Path to Enlightenment: A Commentary on Tsongkhapa's Lamrim Chenmo.* 5 vols. Boston: Wisdom, 2004–.

Sørensen, Per K. "The Prolific Ascetic lCe-sgom śes-rab rdo-rje *alias* lCe-sgom zhig-po: Allusive, but Elusive." *Journal of the Nepal Research Centre* 11 (1999): 175–200.

Staël-Holstein, Alexander von, ed. *The Kāçyapaparivarta: A Mahāyānasūtra of the Ratnakūṭa Class*, edited in the original Sanskrit, in Tibetan and in Chinese. Shanghai: Shangwu Yinshuguan, 1926.

Stearns, Cyrus. *Luminous Lives: The Story of the Early Masters of the Lam 'bras Tradition in Tibet.* Studies in Indian and Tibetan Buddhism. Boston: Wisdom, 2001.

———, trans. and ed. *Taking the Result as the Path: Core Teachings of the Sakya Lamdré Tradition.* The Library of Tibetan Classics 4. Boston: Wisdom, 2006.

Stein, R. A. *Tibetan Civilization.* Translated by J. E. Stapleton Driver. Stanford, CA: Stanford University Press, 1972.

Tai Situ Rinpoche. *Relative World, Ultimate Mind.* New Delhi, India: Penguin Books India, 1999.

Tashi Namgyal, Gampo Chenga (Bkra shis rnam rgyal, Sgam po spyan snga). *Detailed Explanation of Mahāmudrā. Phyag chen rnam bshad. (Moonlight: An Elegant Discourse Clarifying the Stages of Meditation of Mahāmudrā, the Ultimate Meaning. Nges don phyag rgya chen po'i sgom rim gsal bar byed pa'i legs bshad zla ba'i 'od zer).* Rtsib ri spar ma. Vol. 3, 1–759 (*ga* 1a–380a). Darjeeling: Kagyud Sungrab Nyamso Khang, 1984. For an English translation, see Lhalungpa, *Mahāmudrā.*

Tatia, Nathmal. 1976. *Abhidharmasamuccaya-bhāṣyam.* Tibetan Sanskrit Works Series 17. Patna: K. P. Jayaswal Research Institute, 1976.

Tatz, Mark, trans. *Asanga's Chapter on Ethics with the Commentary of Tsong-kha-pa, The Basic Path to Awakening.* Studies in Asian Thought and Religion 4. Lewiston and Queenston, NY: Edwin Mellen Press, 1986.

———. "Translation of the *Bhadracarīpraṇidhāna* (*bZang spyod smon lam*)." In *Studies in Indo-Asian Art and Culture*, edited by Lokesh Chandra, vol. 5, 153–76. New Delhi: International Academy of Indian Culture, 1977.

Thrangu Rinpoche, Khenchen. *Life and Teachings of Gampopa.* Aukland: Zhyisil Chokyi Ghatsal Trust, 2004.

Thuken Losang Chökyi Nyima (Thu'u bkwan Blo bzang chos kyi nyi ma, 1737–1802). *The Crystal Mirror of Philosophical Systems: A Tibetan Study of Asian Religious Thought.* Trans. Lhundub Sopa et al. The Library of Tibetan Classics 25. Boston: Wisdom, 2009.

———. *Crystal Mirror of Philosophical Systems. Grub mtha' thams cad kyi khungs dang 'dod tshul ston pa legs bshad shel gyi me long.* Collected Works, vol. 2, 5–519. New Delhi, 1969.

Thurman, Robert, ed. *Life and Teachings of Tsong Khapa.* Dharamsala: Library of Tibetan Works and Archives, 1981.

Thurman, Robert, et al., trans. *Maitreyanātha's Ornament for the Scriptures of the Universal Vehicle, recorded by Āryāsaṅga, explained by Vasubandhu.* New York: American Institute of Buddhist Studies, 1979.

Tsalpa Kunga Dorjé (Tshal pa Kun dga' rdo rje, 14th century). *The Red Annals. Deb ther dmar po rnams kyi dang po lu lan deb ther.* Dung dkar Blo bzang 'phrin las, editor and annotator. Beijing: Mi rigs dpe skrun khang, 1981.

Tsongkhapa Losang Drakpa (Tsong kha pa Blo bzang grags pa, 1357–1419). *Great Lamrim. Lam rim chen mo* (short for *The Stages of the Path of Awakening: A Treatise that Expounds Exhaustively All Stages of Practice of the Three Spiritual Types, Skyes bu gsum gyi nyams su blang ba'i rim pa thams cad tshang bar ston pa'i byang chub lam gyi rim pa).*

——— *[Tsong Kha Pa]. The Great Treatise on the Stages of the Path to Enlightenment.* 3 vols. Translated by the Lamrim Chenmo Translation Committee. Ithaca, NY: Snow Lion, 2000, 2004.

———. *Outline of the Great Stages of the Path to Awakening. Byang chub lam rim chen mo'i sa bcad.* Xylograph, 16 fols. Lhasa: Zhol spar khang.

———. *Record of Teachings Received. Gsan yig* (short for *Rje rin po che blo bzang grags pa'i dpal gyi gsan yig*). Asian Classics Input Project (ACIP) text no. S5267M.ACT (2002 release).

Tucci, Guiseppe. *Tibetan Painted Scrolls.* Rome: La Libreria dello Stato, 3 vols, 1949. Reprinted Kyoto: Rinsen Book Co., 2 vols., 1980.

Üpa Losal (Dbus pa Blo gsal). Üpa Losal's Treatise on Philosophical Tenets. *Blo gsal grub mtha'. See* Mimaki, trans., *Blo gsal grub mtha'.*

van der Kuijp, Leonard. *Contributions to the Development of Tibetan Buddhist Epistemology from the Eleventh to the Thirteenth Century.* Alt- und Neu-Indische Studien 26. Wiesbaden: Franz Steiner Verlag, 1983.

———. "On the Fifteenth Century *Lho rong chos 'byung* by Rta tshag Tshe dbang rgyal and Its Importance for Tibetan Political and Religious History." *Aspects of Tibetan History, Lungta* 14 (2001): 57–76.

———. "Tibetan Historiography." In *Tibetan Literature: Studies in Genre,* edited by José I. Cabezón and Roger R. Jackson, 39–56. Ithaca: Snow Lion Press, 1996.

Wayman, Alex. *Analysis of the Śrāvakabhūmi Manuscript.* University of California Publications in Classical Philology 17. Berkeley, 1961.

———. *Calming the Mind and Discerning the Real: Buddhist Meditation and the Middle View, from the Lam rim chen mo of Tson kha pa.* New York. Reprinted Delhi: Motilal Banarsidass, 1978.

Yarlung Jowo Shakya Rinchen De (Yar lung Jo bo Shākya Rin chen sde). [*Yarlung Jowo's Buddhist History*]. *Yar lung jo bo'i chos 'byung.* Chengdu: Si khron mi rigs dpe skrun khang, 1987.

Yuyama Akira, ed. *Prajñā-pāramitā-ratna-guṇa-saṃcaya-gāthā (Sanskrit Recension A).* Cambridge and New York: Cambridge University Press, 1976.

Zhang Yisun et al., eds. [*Extensive Tibetan-Tibetan-Chinese Dictionary*]. *Bod rgya tshig mdzod chen mo.* Beijing: Mi rigs dpe skrun khang. Published in 3 vols. in 1985; 2 vols. in 1993.

Index

D

F

M

T

About the Contributors

KEN HOLMES studied in Dharamsala before joining Samye Ling in Scotland, the first Tibetan monastery in the West, in 1970. There, he and his wife Katia have devoted the past forty years to researching, translating, publishing, and teaching the practice and study texts of Tibetan Buddhism. As the center's Director of Studies, Ken spends much of the year teaching at Samye Ling's branches in Europe and Africa. Previous publications include *Maitreya on Buddha Nature*; an earlier translation (with Katia) of the *Ornament of Precious Liberation* found in this volume; *Karmapa*; and a novel, *Tibet or Not Tibet* (in French).

DAVID P. JACKSON has studied the writings of Sakya Paṇḍita for some years, publishing in 1987 the third chapter of another of Sapaṇ's major works, the *Entrance Gate for the Wise*. He also investigated the recent history of the Sakya school, publishing a biography of the twentieth-century Sakyapa mystic Dezhung Rinpoche (1906–87) entitled *A Saint in Seattle* (Boston: Wisdom, 2003). His research on the history of Tibetan painting resulted in several catalogs including *Patron and Painter: Situ Panchen and the Revival of the Encampment Style* (New York: Rubin Museum of Art, 2009).

ULRIKE ROESLER received her PhD in Indian Studies from the University of Münster (Germany) with a thesis on the notion of "light" in the Vedas. For more than a decade she has been teaching Indian and Tibetan Studies as well as Buddhist Studies at the universities of Marburg, Freiburg, and Oxford. Her research interests include Indo-Tibetan Buddhism, the history of the Tibetan Kadam school, and Tibetan biographical and narrative literature. Her German translation and study of Potowa Rinchen Sal's *Dharma Exemplified* (*Dpe chos*) was published by Reichert Verlag (Weisbaden) in 2011. With Linda Covill and Sarah Shaw, she coedited *Lives Lived, Lives Imagined: Biography in the Buddhist Traditions* (Boston: Wisdom Publications, 2010).

The Institute of Tibetan Classics

The Institute of Tibetan Classics is a nonprofit, charitable educational organization based in Montreal, Canada. It is dedicated to two primary objectives: (1) to preserve and promote the study and deep appreciation of Tibet's rich intellectual, spiritual, and artistic heritage, especially among the Tibetan-speaking communities worldwide; and (2) to make the classical Tibetan knowledge and literature a truly global heritage, its spiritual and intellectual resources open to all.

To learn more about the Institute of Tibetan Classics and its various projects, please visit www.tibetanclassics.org or write to this address:

Institute of Tibetan Classics
304 Aberdare Road
Montreal (Quebec) H3P 3K3
Canada

The Library of Tibetan Classics

"This new series edited by Thupten Jinpa and published by Wisdom Publications is a landmark in the study of Tibetan culture in general and Tibetan Buddhism in particular. Each volume contains a lucid introduction and outstanding translations that, while aimed at the general public, will benefit those in the field of Tibetan Studies immensely as well."

—Leonard van der Kuijp, Harvard University

"This is an invaluable set of translations by highly competent scholar-practitioners. The series spans the breadth of the history of Tibetan religion, providing entry to a vast culture of spiritual cultivation."

—Jeffrey Hopkins, University of Virginia

"Erudite in all respects, this series is at the same time accessible and engagingly translated. As such, it belongs in all college and university libraries as well as in good public libraries. *The Library of Tibetan Classics* is on its way to becoming a truly extraordinary spiritual and literary accomplishment."

—Janice D. Willis, Wesleyan University

Following is a list of the thirty-two proposed volumes in *The Library of Tibetan Classics*. Some volumes are translations of single texts, while others are compilations of multiple texts, and each volume will be roughly the same length. Except for those volumes already published, the renderings of titles below are tentative and liable to change. The Institute of Tibetan Classics has contracted numerous established translators in its efforts, and work is progressing on all the volumes concurrently.

1. *Mind Training: The Great Collection*, compiled by Shönu Gyalchok and Könchok Gyaltsen (fifteenth century). NOW AVAILABLE
2. *The Book of Kadam: The Core Texts*, attributed to Atiśa and Dromtönpa (eleventh century). NOW AVAILABLE
3. *The Great Chariot: A Treatise on the Great Perfection*, Longchen Rapjampa (1308–63)
4. *Taking the Result As the Path: Core Teachings of the Sakya Lamdré Tradition*, Jamyang Khyentsé Wangchuk (1524–68) et al. NOW AVAILABLE
5. *Mahāmudrā and Related Instructions: Core Teachings of the Kagyü School*. NOW AVAILABLE
6. *Stages of the Path and the Ear-Whispered Instructions: Core Teachings of the Geluk School*
7. *Ocean of Definitive Meaning: A Teaching for the Mountain Hermit*, Dölpopa Sherap Gyaltsen (1292–1361)
8. *Miscellaneous Tibetan Buddhist Lineages: The Core Teachings*, Jamgön Kongtrül (1813–90)
9. *Sutra, Tantra, and the Mind Cycle: Core Teachings of the Bön School*
10. *Stages of the Buddha's Teachings: Three Key Texts*. NOW AVAILABLE
11. *The Bodhisattva's Altruistic Ideal: Selected Key Texts*
12. *The Ethics of the Three Codes*
13. *Sādhanas: Vajrayana Buddhist Meditation Manuals*
14. *Ornament of Stainless Light: An Exposition of the Kālacakra Tantra*, Khedrup Norsang Gyatso (1423–1513). NOW AVAILABLE
15. *A Lamp to Illuminate the Five Stages*, Tsongkhapa (1357–1419). NOW AVAILABLE
16. *Studies in the Perfection of Wisdom*
17. *Treatises on Buddha Nature*
18. *Differentiations of the Profound View: Interpretations of Emptiness in Tibet*
19. *Elucidation of the Intent: A Thorough Exposition of "Entering the Middle Way,"* Tsongkhapa (1357–1419)
20. *Tibetan Buddhist Epistemology I: The Sakya School*
21. *Tibetan Buddhist Epistemology II: The Geluk School*
22. *Tibetan Buddhist Psychology and Phenomenology: Selected Texts*
23. *Ornament of Abhidharma: A Commentary on the "Abhidharmakośa,"* Chim Jampalyang (thirteenth century)
24. *A Beautiful Adornment of Mount Meru: Presentation of Classical Indian Philosophies*, Changkya Rölpai Dorjé (1717–86)

25. *The Crystal Mirror of Philosophical Systems: A Tibetan Study of Asian Religious Thought*, Thuken Losang Chökyi Nyima (1737–1802). NOW AVAILABLE
26. *Gateway for Being Learned and Realized: Selected Texts*
27. *The Well-Uttered Insights: Advice on Everyday Wisdom, Civility, and Basic Human Values*
28. *Mirror of Beryl: A Historical Introduction to Tibetan Medicine*, Desi Sangyé Gyatso (1653–1705). NOW AVAILABLE
29. *Selected Texts on Tibetan Astronomy and Astrology*
30. *Art and Literature: An Anthology*
31. *Tales from the Tibetan Operas*
32. *Selected Historical Works*

To receive a brochure describing all the volumes or to stay informed about *The Library of Tibetan Classics*, please write to:

info@wisdompubs.org

or send a request by post to:

Wisdom Publications
Attn: Library of Tibetan Classics
199 Elm Street
Somerville, MA 02144 USA

The complete catalog containing descriptions of each volume can also be found online at wisdompubs.org.

Become a Benefactor of the Library of Tibetan Classics

The Library of Tibetan Classics' scope, importance, and commitment to the finest quality make it a tremendous financial undertaking. We invite you to become a benefactor, joining us in creating this profoundly important human resource. Contributors of two thousand dollars or more will receive a copy of each future volume as it becomes available, and will have their names listed in all subsequent volumes. Larger donations will go even further in supporting *The Library of Tibetan Classics*, preserving the creativity, wisdom, and scholarship of centuries past, so that it may help illuminate the world for future generations.

To contribute, please either visit our website at wisdompubs.org, call us at (617) 776-7416, or send a check made out to Wisdom Publications or credit card information to the address below.

Library of Tibetan Classics Fund
Wisdom Publications
199 Elm Street
Somerville, MA 02144
USA

Please note that contributions of lesser amounts are also welcome and are invaluable to the development of the series. Wisdom is a 501(c)3 nonprofit corporation, and all contributions are tax-deductible to the extent allowed by law.

If you have any questions, please do not hesitate to call us or email us at advancement@wisdompubs.org.

To keep up to date on the status of *The Library of Tibetan Classics*, visit the series page on our website, and subscribe to our newsletter while you are there.

Wisdom

About Wisdom Publications

Wisdom Publications is the leading publisher of classic and contemporary Buddhist books and practical works on mindfulness. To learn more about us or to explore our other books, please visit our website at wisdompubs.org or contact us as the address below.

Wisdom Publications
199 Elm Street
Somerville, MA 02144 USA

We are a 501(c)(3) organization, and donations in support of our mission are tax deductible.